BIBLIOTHECA EPHEMERIDUM THEOLOGICARUM LOVANIENSIUM

CXXXV

LIBERATION THEOLOGIES ON SHIFTING GROUNDS

A CLASH OF SOCIO-ECONOMIC AND CULTURAL PARADIGMS

EDITED BY

G. DE SCHRIJVER

LEUVEN
UNIVERSITY PRESS

UITGEVERIJ PEETERS
LEUVEN

1998

CIP KONINKLIJKE BIBLIOTHEEK ALBERT I, BRUSSEL

ISBN 90 6186 883 1 (Leuven University Press)
D/1998/1869/24
ISBN 90 429 0302 3 (Uitgeverij Peeters)
D/1998/0602/254

Leuven University Press / Presses Universitaires de Louvain
Universitaire Pers Leuven
Blijde Inkomststraat 5, B-3000 Leuven-Louvain (Belgium)

© 1998, Uitgeverij Peeters, Bondgenotenlaan 153, B-3000 Leuven (Belgium)

PREFACE

After some twenty-five years of employing socio-economic analysis as their fundamental methodology, theologies of liberation have recently come to also include cultural perspectives. This shift in attention reflects the awareness that issues of liberation, even on a socio-economic level, cannot be treated properly without paying attention to the cultural contexts. Since 1994 the Center for Liberation Theology (Faculty of Theology, KULeuven) has been engaged in a research project entitled: Paradigm-shift in Third World Theologies of Liberation: From Socio-economic Analysis to Cultural Analysis: Assessment and Status of the Question. In 1995 this project received a research grant from the Fund for Scientific Research (F.W.O).

This theme became the central focus of an international Symposium (November 21-23, 1996), in which the Center's Coordinator conducted an analysis of the current situation, assessing it in the light of the transition from modernity to postmodernity, and of globalization. His discussion paper constitutes the first part of this volume. It reviews the intra-ecclesial shift from economic to cultural concerns, examines the relationship between classical liberation theology and modernity, and touches upon the challenge posed by the fall of the Berlin Wall (which reflects the globalization of the neo-liberal market economy, no longer restrained by national borders). After the exploration of this panorama a three-fold reading of the globalization process is given: the world-wide spread of a commodified culture; culture politics in the context of the global world system (including mechanisms of exclusion); and globalization in the domain of electronic means of communication. This three-fold reading has been undertaken in order not only to grasp the complexity of the 'new world order', but also to trace in it possible germs of liberative actions. Some of these are examined more carefully, such as the emergence of the 'new movements', the re-affirmation of peoples' cultural identities, the strengthening of bonds of solidarity, and the new opportunities for becoming more reflexive and cautious against productivism.

Seven Third-World theologians from three continents in the South were invited to the Symposium as key-respondents to the discussion paper: They had been asked to assess the paradigm-shift hypothesis as to its scientific validity, and its applicability to theology in the light of their own contexts, or to propose alternative ideas. Their texts make up the second part of this volume.

Besides the seven key-respondents, a select group of other theologians and social scientists, from both the South and the North, was invited to take part in the discussions. To that effect discussion groups were formed which deliberated on whether or not a paradigm shift has really taken place, and on whether certain shifts in emphasis can be said to relate to the phenomenon of globalization. The results were reported in plenary sessions. An evocation of the inner dynamic of this part can be found in the first section of part three: "Assessments of the Symposium". Participants who read a short paper were given the opportunity to elaborate on their text. These and other articles have been collected under the headings: "Postmodernity and Globalization" and "'Paradigm shift' from Various Perspectives".

Having outlined the basic structure of this book, which reflects the dynamism of the symposium itself, I take the opportunity to sincerely thank all the estimated scholars who have been so generous as to contribute. The result of their efforts is interdisciplinary, but never fails to reflect the particular contexts out of which each of the participants developed his or her approach.

Finally, I want to express my gratitude to all those who have been, and still are, active in the research programs of the Center for Liberation Theology, J. Haers, s.j., L. Boeve, E. Guzman, and D. Gonzalez. To the first two I owe special thanks for the energy they spent in the preparation and steering of the Symposium. Special thanks, as well, to the last two, because they offered a lot of help in the research and writing process of the Discussion Paper, and, last but not least, in the editing of this book, a process to which also A. Pragasam, and J. Castillo-Coronado joined the best of their efforts. Lastly I want to thank the staff of the Faculty of Theology for the support they gave to the symposium, and Professor F. Neirynck for his keen interest in the production of this volume.

Georges DE SCHRIJVER s.j.

LIBERATION THEOLOGIES
ON SHIFTING GROUNDS

CONTENTS

II. Postmodernity and Globalization

III. "Paradigm Shift" from Various Perspectives

INDEXES

PART ONE

DISCUSSION PAPER

1

PARADIGM SHIFT IN THIRD-WORLD THEOLOGIES OF LIBERATION FROM SOCIO-ECONOMIC ANALYSIS TO CULTURAL ANALYSIS?

I. INTRA-ECCLESIAL DEVELOPMENTS

The fact of a paradigm shift in Third-World theologies of liberation from socio-economic analysis to cultural analysis can be gleaned from their different publications where socio-economic and cultural analyses stand in tension with each other. In EATWOT conferences since the 1980s, for instance, it has already been made known to the Latin-American liberation theologians that they concern themselves too much with 'economism', i.e., the linking of the praxis of the faith to the struggle against economic oppression. African and especially Asian liberation theologians want to see this method complemented with a revaluation of the local culture. In short, as Latin-American liberation theologians struggle against injustice that oppresses the poor in a capitalistic market-economy, then the theologians of the other 'southern' continents also set out to struggle against injustice that oppresses local cultures by the imposition of uniform rational modern culture. In addition, this shift of attention from the economically oppressed to the culturally oppressed is also seen quite clearly on the level of church pronouncements, in particular, the Latin-American bishops' conferences from 1968 to 1992. Let us take a brief review of the fact of that shift in the documents of Medellin, Puebla and Santo Domingo.

The second General Conference of Latin-American Bishops at Medellin in 1968 courageously took to heart Vatican II's break-through of the false opposition between the spiritual and the temporal realms. With this foundation and likewise encouraged by Paul VI's *Populorum progressio*, Medellin spoke up for the poor, the victims of injustice, and called for "the better ordering of human society [as a] vital concern to the Kingdom of God" (Med 1, no. 5).

It is within the whole tone of the Medellin document that we can glean the Latin-American bishops' radical position of a preferential option for poor. The radicalness of their option lies in their expressed commitment to integral liberation of the poor where these poor masses themselves become the very authors of their human development. To this end, in synchrony with the Gospel's depiction of the Lord's mandate to preach the good news to the poor, the Latin-American bishops set the ecclesiastical institutions at the service of the poor sector's emancipation. They pleaded for the establishment of intermediate structures in society that would allow real participation, especially by the poor peasants and workers, in the construction of a new and just society. In short, the church communities in Latin America were to be engaged in the conscientization of the poor towards social transformation. In the economic sphere, Medellin had latched on to the former framework of the dependency of Third World countries on the economic strength of the First World nations in a sort of neo-colonial condition. Included in the bishops' plea for surmounting this economic dependency is their criticism of the wealthy classes' complicity with foreign investors in accumulating profit at the expense of keeping the vast majority of the Latin-American population in the fetters of poverty.

In sum, two keywords can be taken as embodying the main thrust of Medellin: development and social change. Medellin wagered on social transformation by critically pointing to class division as an obstacle. It denounced the dramatic antagonism between the rich and the poor in Latin-American countries which gives rise to a kind of "superimposition of cultures" (Med 1, no. 2), i.e., the dominance of the few elite who tend to embrace a westernized mentality and lifestyle, over the majority poor in rural and even urban settings who continue within a particular sub-culture that is not always given expression in the public scene.

From that point, Medellin's assessment of popular religiosity and culture in Latin America becomes interesting. While the bishops endorsed a concept of religion that allowed for the investment of religious potential in the promotion of human development, they were aware that popular masses among whom this process was expected to take place possessed a diversity of religious expressions. All these manifestations of popular religiosity were seen as standing in need of the church's assistance in order that they may be raised to higher levels of worship that did away with forms of fatalism and enhanced human awareness of being "co-creator with God and master of [one's] own destiny" (Med 6, no. 12). However, this assessment of popular religion was to take the context of the sub-cultures of the poor themselves as its frame of reference, not any westernized cultural interpretation of the middle and upper classes. Furthermore, respect for these religious expressions was deemed appropriate for they nevertheless contained the 'seeds of the Word' which could constitute an 'evangelical preparation' (Med 6, no. 5) that would entail their purification and incorporation into the faith of the church.

This theme on the church's relationship towards local culture and popular religiosity takes center stage in the subsequent Latin-American bishops' conference in Puebla.

On the level of organization and procedure, we are all aware of the marked difference of the Puebla conference in 1979 from its predecessor, Medellin; and this difference was not necessarily for the better. From the nomination of the then new chairman of the CELAM to the meticulous selection of the participants and the exclusion of others (liberation theologians), the whole procedure of Puebla reeked of a discipline imposed by the Vatican that set to "rescue 'the spiritual dimension, as distinguished from the socio-economic and political preoccupations of the liberation movement'" that came more to the fore in Medellin.

Puebla focused on the evangelization of culture, a new topic in comparison with the main focus of Medellin. Where Medellin was inspired by *Gaudium et spes* and *Populorum progressio*, this time, Puebla found its inspiration in Paul VI's *Evangelii nuntiandi* (1975) which links the Church's abiding concern for the social question process with the evangelization of cultures. To be sure, Puebla does not fail to reiterate Medellin's basic position: "With renewed hope in the vivifying power of the Spirit, we are going to take up once again the position of the Latin-American episcopate in Medellin, which adopted a clear and prophetic option expressing preference for, and solidarity with the poor. We do this despite the distortions and interpretations of some, who vitiate the spirit of Medellin, and despite the disregard, and even hostility of others" (Puebla, no. 1134). Neither did Puebla condemn liberation theology, although it did not actually confirm it either. The bishops at Puebla apparently intended to treat the lacunae inherent in a social-justice approach, namely, the absence of a consideration of cultural development considered to be essential to 'integral development'. Only uplifting the socio-economic conditions of the poor, it seemed, will not lead to the emergence of a new culture. A primary role is attributed to culture as the mediating element between the socio-economic reality and religious consciousness. As CELAM later on made clear, "if Medellin has offered a primarily socio-economic analysis, Puebla completes this analysis presently with socio-economic data in an anthropological and historico-cultural, and thus more global perspective"[2]. What is actually behind this shift from social analysis to culture in the understanding of the Latin-American bishops at Puebla?

1. M. SANDOVAL, *Report from the Conference*, in J. EAGLESON & PH. SCHARPER, *Puebla and Beyond: Documentation and Commentary*, Maryknoll, NY, Orbis, 1979, p. 34.
2. CELAM, *Réflexions sur Puebla*, Bogotá, CELAM, 1981, p. 45.

For the bishops at Puebla, culture is defined, firstly, in its connection with religion, the heart and well-spring of cultural values; secondly, it is seen as embodied in a particular people (or ethnic group); and thirdly, it is conceived of as an expression of the concrete ways in which (ethnic) communities of people relate to nature, to each other, and to God. In this more ethnological rather than sociological definition, a longing for the revitalization of the power of past cultural expressions as a means to curb the spreading negative influences of modernity is revealed. While modernity may be praised in that it offers effective instruments for human development, it also needs to be criticized, according to Puebla, for its furtherance of secularism, consumerism, hedonism and atheism. The bishops at Puebla were confident that 'Latin-American culture[s]' with its deep-seated religiosity will enable the faithful to "incorporate the values of the new urban-industrial civilization into a new vital synthesis, which will continue to be grounded on faith in God rather than on atheism that is the logical consequence of the movement towards secularism" (Puebla, no. 436).

Thus, the bishops at Puebla stressed an evangelization of cultures that firstly, makes use of the good elements in local cultures to incarnate the spirit of the gospel and secondly, denounces and corrects whatever is sinful in cultures in order to purify them[3]. Evangelization in Latin America will therefore have to include the preservation of the contemplative and festive character of the people as well as the fostering of its religiosity of 'nearness to the earth' as happy exemplifications of the way the gospel message can be "translated into the anthropological idiom and symbols of the culture in which it immerses itself" (Puebla, no. 404). Evangelization will also have to deal with the age-old inconsistency of the impoverished condition of the Latin-American people forced to live in injustice by making the faith stronger so that it may affect "the criteria and the decisions of those responsible for the ideological leadership and the organization of our people's socio-economic life together" (Puebla, no. 437) in a positive way. Puebla thus denounces the sinfulness of the local elite in their departure from and betrayal of the catholic ethos of the people (in contrast to Medellin which, in terms of social analysis, blamed the elite for collaborating with an economic world order turned oppressive). The revival of cultural roots is presented as the actual incentive to liberation. The religiosity of the Latin-American people often is turned into a cry for true liberation. In short, Puebla propounds a cultural approach to the people's resistance, a strategy meant to

---

3. See *Puebla*, nos. 401 and 405.

replace the Marxist socio-economic analysis and its distrust of religion and popular culture.

When it comes to popular religiosity and native Latin-American cultures in particular, however, Puebla eventually found itself trapped into a serious inconsistency. With its program of the 'liberation of culture,' Puebla wanted to achieve the Christianization of the industrial and urban areas of the continent. To do this, the bishops deemed it imperative to honor the *religiosidad popular* that would protect the Christian Latino values of old from erosion in the confrontation with modernity. However, when confronted themselves with that aspect of popular religiosity that belonged to the many indigenous peoples in Latin America, the bishops remained rather undecided about what to do with their "ancestral type" of religious practices. On the one hand, they are aware that the church had to do something to alleviate the plight of indigenous peoples. On the other hand, they were not all that willing to encourage the indigenous peoples to go back to their cultural roots so as to generate a liberative potential of their own. Only those elements in their culture that are consonant with Christian faith seem to get the encouragement for revitalization. Here lies Puebla's inconsistency since it tends to deprive the indigenous cultures of their basic religious expressions, which manifestly conflicts with [Puebla's] general concept of culture according to which a particular religion constitutes the heart of a particular culture. Puebla honors the values of particular cultures, not however the fact that they also have their proper religion. This non-recognition of indigenous religions will become the Santo Domingo conference's legacy.

Again, like the Puebla conference, the latest Latin-American bishops' conference at Santo Domingo in 1992 left much to be desired in terms of its organization and its procedure due to the inroad manoeuvres orchestrated by the Vatican. Obviously wanting to avoid an overall negative assessment of the discovery of the Americas, the Vatican ensured that the Santo Domingo conference would take place as a real celebration of the quincentennial anniversary of Christian faith on the continent in spite of Christianity's arrival having been accompanied by crimes perpetrated by the conquerors. In this regard, the bishop-participants in Santo Domingo centered their discussions on Pope John Paul II's *Opening Address to the Fourth General Conference of the Latin-American Episcopate* which was divided into three parts: new evangelization, human development, and Christian culture. What is striking in the final Santo Domingo document is that this new, perfected evangelization – aimed at the ever-present antagonism between *mestizaje* religiosity and culture on the one hand, and the history of suffering inflicted on the poor masses on the other – is addressed to all the Christian milieus: including the middle-class, and those influential in the world of economics and the mass media. It no longer primarily wagers, as in the heydays of Medellin on the 'evangelizing potential of the poor' themselves.

A certain unevenness in Santo Domingo's concepts of evangelization and inculturation of the gospel can be evidenced in a careful analysis of the different layers of the final document. On the one hand, reflecting the Vatican officials' influence behind the document, the new evangelization means an integration of the existent cultures and sub-cultures into the one old Catholic substratum, emphasizing the importance of doctrinal purity in matters of faith and mores. At the moment when all-encompassing ideologies in society have collapsed, part of Santo Domingo presents the reliance on Catholic culture as a recognizable 'way of life' as filling up this vacuum and cementing a bond of unity among the Latin-American nations. On the other hand, this time reflecting the voice of some progressive Latin-American bishops, evangelization via a more pluralistic inculturation is seen as a revitalization of Christian life via a cross-fertilization by a range of values highlighted in the new social movements. While continuing to be in line with Medellin's program of social justice, these values are now complemented with commitments to new burning issues, partially related to the question of cultural identity: indigenous movements, women's movements, neighborhood and youngster movements, the ecological movement, and human rights activists, all of which have arisen mostly outside the church and under the leadership of lay people. Inculturation of the faith means, thus, to enrich the living faith with action programs emerging from outside the confines of the church, and to which also non-confessional humanists are committed in their concern about the well-being of humanity.

Could it be that this clearer approach to the 'other' – the recognition of women, indigenous peoples and blacks – is Santo Domingo's greatest theoretical contribution in comparison with earlier church documents[4] which does not discount the fact, however, that much remains to be done on the level of practice? Santo Domingo has been the most critical Latin-American ecclesiastical document of modern culture to date, and has thus hailed, unsurprisingly, the advent of postmodernity, calling it "the product of the failure of the reductionist pretensions of modern reason" (Santo Domingo, no. 252). Moreover, the present-day collapse

---

4. See J. SOBRINO, *The Winds in Santo Domingo and the Evangelization of Culture*, in A. HENNELEY (ed.), *Santo Domingo and Beyond*, Maryknoll, NY, Orbis, 1993, p. 26.

of the grand stories has been Santo Domingo's cue to present the catholic church as the despised 'other' worthy of respect and fellowship for her human wisdom, moral integrity and custody of divine revelation. In short, the grand narrative of reason will rightly be replaced with the grand narrative of the church's witness to her divine mission. One suspects here that the church's claim to sapiential 'otherness' as being a genuine antidote to modernity's uniform rationality is contaminated by her own thinking in hegemonic terms in turn. Thus on the whole, Santo Domingo shuns away from recognizing a legitimate pluralism in catholic theology, pays lip-service to an inculturation "from within cultures," and prefers instead, under the influence of the Vatican, a (self-) glorification of a restorationist type of catholicism.

In the course of the Church's dialogue with (post)modern culture, she has shown a growing tendency to take a position of self-defence, losing the courage she once showed during Vatican II and Medellin. In the Latin-American church in particular, this tendency has become apparent in the *intra-ecclesial* shift from socio-economic analysis to (Christian) culture in what is supposed to be a liberating praxis of the poor. In what follows, we submit as a framework for evaluating this shift the transition from modernity to postmodernity in our contemporary society. The same framework will be used to assess, more in particular, the "classical" enterprise of Liberation Theology, as well as the new agenda for doing Liberation Theology which has been recently proposed by some authors favorable to the movement. An analysis of Liberation Theology will be given further on in this article.

II. MODERNITY

1. *The Five Pillars of Modernity*

Stated in a succinct way, one can propound that the five pillars of modernity are the following: confidence in science-based technology, the sovereignty of the nation-states, bureaucratic rationality, profit maximization, and the belief in steady progress. All the five pillars rest on a methodology that aims at rationally comprehending things in terms of their standardized universal order. In this definition of rationality, one recognizes the achievements of the scientific and philosophical methods used respectively by Galileo, Kepler, and Newton (physics), and Descartes, Locke, and Leibniz (philosophy). Or as Stephen Toulmin says: "Modern science and technology can thus be seen, as a source either of blessings, or of problems, or both. In either case, their intellectual origin makes the 1630s the most plausible starting date for (scientific) Modernity. Then, it seems scientific inquiries became 'rational' – thanks to Galileo in astronomy and mechanics, and to Descartes in logic and epistemology. Thirty years later this commitment to 'rationality' was extended into the practical realm, when the political and diplomatic system of the European states was reorganized on the basis of *nations*. From then on, at least in theory, the warrant for a sovereign monarch's exercise of power lay less in the fact of an inherited feudal title than in the will of the people who consented to this rule: once this became the recognized basis of state authority, politics could also be analysed in the new 'rational' terms"[5]. In this quote, the first three pillars have been touched upon.

It will amaze some to hear that scientific modernity can be traced back to Galileo. But this is not that strange if one knows that Galileo, with the help of a spy-glass, had observed facts that entailed the collapse of the pre-copernican cosmology. Furthermore, his experiments in the realm of the fall-movement had paved the way for Newton's mechanical laws, more specifically for the universal law of gravitation, which applied to the movements of stars as well as to free-fall motions on earth. This led to the sobering view that the sacred canopy of the starry sky, which till then had functioned as a quintessential realm of perfect motions, was a sheer illusion. The celestial explanation of order in nature and in human society was groundless, and had to be substituted with a new scientific approach, based on mathematically-constructed laws in physics and technology, and on the rational ordering subject (Descartes, Kant) in the domain of human society.

2. *Nation-State and the Modern Concept of Culture*

A bit later, rational planning also permeated the organization of the nation-state. One found it unreasonable that small feudal units, each with their own local customs, filled the space of linguistically kindred territories. The nation-state began to be born, with its centralized and uniform organizational patterns in matters of jurisprudence, taxation, police, army, education, means of transportation and communication, language, culture policies, and after a while, geometrical city planning. Also, the word culture or civilization acquired a new connotation: rationally

5. S. TOULMIN, *Cosmopolis. The Hidden Agenda of Modernity*, New York, Free Press, 1990, p. 9. Toulmin also recognizes the existence (and emergence) of a "humanistic" modernity starting from the Renaissance.

accountable behavior passes for what is civilized, whereas regional habits are stigmatized as vulgar. As Foucault has pointed out in his studies on modernization, even the penitentiary system took on a modern form: they were meant to re-educate all those who refused to adapt their life-styles to the rationally planned nation-state. This state also increased its potential of bureaucrats and planners (cf. Max Weber's study about rationalization in western civilization).

In the 18th century, there arose also this phenomenon: a series of enlightened philosophers, who believed in the birth of rational society, began to put their intellectual acuity in the service of the new civilization. Technically, they can be called 'organic intellectuals,' i.e., intellectuals who give a legitimation to the newly-planned rational forms of society. Zygmunt Bauman gives a fine description of the agenda of these intellectuals. More in particular, he underlines that, from now onward, the population is seen as 'manageable': "The aspects of human life now picked up for conscious regulation came to be known as culture... The immediate interest that led to the coining of the idea of 'culture' as such aspects of human life which can be consciously regulated and given deliberately selective choice (unlike the other aspects that human powers were still unable or unwilling to reach) was one in the practice of changing the ways of life viewed as a symptom, and a source, of the morbid resilience of local autonomy pitted against the universalistic ambitions of the modern state. Culture, civilizing, refining were so many names given to the crusade proclaimed against the 'vulgar', 'beastly', 'superstitious' habits and customs of the forces allegedly presiding over their perpetuation". With missionary zeal, the enlightened philosophers combated the backward mentality not only of agrarian, feudal society but also of the clergy, who were deemed responsible for the perpetuation of this backwardness: "Les philosophes named the clergy, old wives, and folk proverbs as the teachers responsible for the lamentable state of popular habits... The choice was not any more between a guided and regimented education and the autonomous self-constitution of a form of life – but between good and bad education. Not only was knowledge power, all power was knowledge. And efficient power had to rely on good knowledge for its efficiency"[6].

True, a certain alliance between culture and power has always existed. In ancient Athens, too, the intellectuals had set out to impose their patterns of civilization on other peoples, which they called barbarians.

---

6. Z. BAUMAN, *Intimations of Postmodernity*, London - New York, Routledge, 1992, pp. 8-9.

But what happened in early modernity was something unique, for the simple reason that both the culture policy and the nation-state, which backed this enterprise, could rely on the efficiency of the newly discovered scientific rationality. The state became the embodiment of rational order, as the indisputable legislator[7]. The organic intellectuals, who supported the new society's rational order, did not shun away from adopting the same legislative style: they made use of the categorical imperative, which says what individuals and groups ought to do, on penalty of being regarded as irrational.

3. *Capitalism and the Belief in Steady Progress*

In order to understand the next two pillars of modernity – profit maximization and the belief in steady progress – one ought also to recognize that the modern nation-state, endowed with a bureaucratic apparatus of its own, created at the same time a free space for the citizens to take economically remunerating initiatives. This free space is technically called the 'civil society' (see Hegel). In the civil society, especially after the French revolution, the bourgeoisie were given the right to organize democratic decision-making processes and to set up voluntary associations and businesses, while protection of private property was regulated by law. It was in civil society, often in concurrence with the state administration, that industries, factories, commerce, and business could flourish, which eventually led to the industrial revolution of the 18th and 19th centuries. The steam engine (1750) and, later, electricity made the creation of heavy industries – coal and steel production – possible. Railway-nets, ports, and canals for ships formed the infrastructure for national and international trade overseas. The belief in progress was born. New technologies superseded old ones and became more and more refined; patents protected the technological inventions, which now could also be exported.

---

7. See *ibid.*, p. 10: "(All this) entailed a wholly new concept of government, its scope and responsibilities. The government was now seen as the force that – knowingly or by default – shapes the external framework of human life; the idea that society is 'man-made' represented the unprecedented ambition of the modern state to actually *make* the society; and an unheard-of mobilization of resources that rendered such making a viable proposition. The concept of state-laws was also new; the idea of their postulated 'rationality' represented a new intention to use legislation for moulding social life according to the precepts of reason. All in all, rational government meant the newly perceived malleability of social life, its needs to be shaped, its amenability to being remade according to designs embodied in the action of external agencies – power being tantamount to the effectiveness of such action".

The most salient feature in this respect is the capitalist organization of production processes and of the world economy as a whole. Capitalism as a system is based on the sheer endless accumulation of capital, whereby "an agency is capitalist in virtue of the fact that its money is endowed with the 'power to breeding' (Marx's expression) systematically and persistently, regardless of the nature of the particular commodities and activities that are incidentally the medium at any given time"[8]. Specialists in this matter point to four systemic cycles that can be identified in the accumulation of capital: (i) a Genoese cycle (15th – early 17th centuries), a Dutch cycle (late 16th – 18th centuries), (iii) a British cycle (18th – early 20th centuries), and (iv) a US cycle (late 19th century onward). Within these cycles, one has to place the discovery and colonization of the Americas, the workings of the Dutch East Indian company, the consolidation of the British commonwealth, and the rise of the US as a world power. The existence of these systemic circles make it clear that the world-wide expansion of capitalism is based on agreements made within interstate systems, and that these agreements lead to a division of labor. The economies of some countries score low for the world market, whereas other score high. Wallerstein calls this "the establishment of one single 'division of labor'"[9], in which means of violence are used to reduce certain countries to a situation of dependence. For the system must see to it that, for the appropriation of surplus value to maximally increase, somewhere on the globe manpower can be found that is willing to work more and to be paid less.

4. Abstract Thinking as the Motor for Change

The above description makes it clear that modernity is a multilayered phenomenon. Authors who set out to look for a common denominator underneath the listed changes, currently point to the rise of scientific thinking and its capacity for elaborating abstract laws and systems. Newton's mathematical formula of the law of gravitation, e.g., abstracts from the particular features of the concrete thing in order to focus only on the physical qualities that obey the general, universally applicable regularity of the mechanical system. This way, 'abstract' science gets a grasp or control over the workings of the empirical data, and succeeds in predicting what is going to happen in the subsequent stages of these workings.

8. G. ARRIGHI, *The Long Twentieth Century*, London-New York, Verso, 1994, p. 8.
9. I. WALLERSTEIN, *Culture as the Ideological Battleground of the Modern World-System*, in *TCS* 7 (1990) 31-55, p. 35.

This trend comes to bear also on the social moulding of the modern nation-state, as well as on the economic planning of enterprises in civil society. The planning comes to the fore in these two domains, and takes on the form of binding directives meant to shape the concrete behavior of people in a way that no exceptions can be allowed to the general rule.

To get an idea of how modern 'abstraction' works, one would do well to let oneself be impressed by modernity's new understanding of space and time, for here one sees most perfectly what modernity's innovations are all about. In modernity, the rhythm of time becomes disembedded from local places to an extent that this dislodgement opens up the avenue for a new concept of space. The clock, a modern invention, regulates the time-schedule of the working day, while the space-span resulting from the measured time disconnects itself from the bonds space once had with local place. The spatial reality within which modern people conduct their planning suddenly crosses the borders of traditional localities. Abstract generalities hold sway over the concrete particular things, putting the latter into the service of all-encompassing efficiency.

Anthony Giddens puts this as follows: "To understand the intimate connections between modernity and the transformation of time and space, we have to start by drawing some contrasts with time-space relations in the pre-modern world: (i) All pre-modern cultures possessed modes of the calculation of time. The calendar, for example, was as distinctive a feature of agrarian states as the invention of writing. But the time reckoning, which formed the basis of day-to-day life, certainly for the majority of the people, always linked time with [local] space – and was usually imprecise and variable. No one could tell the time of the day, without reference to other socio-spatial markers: 'when' was almost universally either connected with 'where' or identified by regular natural occurrences". In other words, if one wanted to tell the time of the day, one had to make sure where the sun stood at that moment, looked at from one's own location. (ii) This changes with modern times: "The invention of the mechanical clock and its diffusion to virtually all members of the population (a phenomenon which dates at its earliest from the late eighteenth century) were of key significance in the separation of time from space. The clock expressed a uniform dimension of 'empty' time, quantified in such a way as to permit the precise designation of 'zones' of the day (e.g. the 'working day')"[10]. From this, it follows that whoever in modern societies ventures to live without a watch, will soon

---

10. A. GIDDENS, *The Consequences of Modernity*, Cambridge, Polity Press, 1990, p. 17.

for human dignity as the *locus theologicus* from which new forms of 'doing' theology can arise. The aim and purpose of interpreting the scriptures afresh, in function of the needs of the poor, is to inspire them to work for a revolutionary change toward a more just and equitable society by means of popular struggles and organizations[23].

The practice of engaging in new interpretations and re-readings of scripture is, as such, nothing exceptional. This would have to occur if the faith were to be handed down from generation to generation. The motivating force of faith ought to be assimilated again and again, throughout the ages, and in accordance with the existential needs the believers of a particular time are experiencing. Faith that does not undergo re-interpretations can hardly be called a living faith. The exceptional and, for some, shocking thing, however, is the fact that liberation theologians have ventured to re-interpret the faith within a cognitive framework – Marxist social analysis – which more often than not has been associated with atheism[24]. As to be expected, this led to a special symbiosis between 'modern' thought-forms and traditional belief (understood, to be sure, as *fides quaerens intellectum*). Although this symbiosis points to a two-way process of mutual fertilization, for the purpose of my analysis, I am going to focus on the 'modern' input into this 'merger', an input that – as empirical studies show – makes the believers more responsible and confident in their understanding of religion and the world[25]. Two

---

23. J.B. Libânio has pointed out the importance of what he calls the "social imaginary": (in the case of Liberation Theology) "el imaginario social se configura a partir de una realidad alternativa, utópica, de cuño participativo, que se realizará fundamentalmente a través de la toma de consciencia, la organización y la lucha popular, y no a través de reformas instucionales". J.B. LIBANIO, *Reflexiones a partir de la teología de la liberación. La implicación mutua de la doctrina social de la Iglesia y la teología de la liberación*, in P. HÜNERMANN & J.C. SCANNONE (eds.), *América Latina y la doctrina social de la Iglesia. Diálogo latinoamericano-alemán, 1: Reflexiones metodológicas*, Buenos Aires, Ediciones Paulinas, 1992, p. 177.

24. The main reason why this step could be taken lies in the fact that *Gaudium et spes* initiated a nuanced discussion about the origin and humanistic nature of certain forms of atheism, and also discussed the modalities under which the 'autonomy of the created realm' could be acknowledged and made fruitful among believers.

25. See in this respect, D.H. LEVINE, *Popular Groups, Popular Culture, and Popular Religion*, in ID. (ed.), *Constructing Culture and Power in Latin America*, Ann Arbor, University of Michigan Press, 1993, pp. 171-225. Having examined the changing attitudes to religion in some basic communities Levine comes to the conclusion that "experience with participatory and egalitarian group life is particularly important. By working together to understand religion and the world and acting together in ways that bridge the two, members assert themselves as capable, articulate, and confident people. Whatever the topic is Bible study, cooperatives, or prayer, we come back to how people see themselves as autonomous and capable actors and acquire confidence in the values of their own critical reason" (p. 213).

feel lost; he/she is going to miss the trains that depart at fixed hours and minutes. Trains run according to a coordination across time.

Thus, time becomes disconnected from locally experienced occurrences, and only continues to exist in the mode of a formal scheme of mathematized time units. A similar dislocation takes place in the way modernity conceives of a vacant space that is independent of locale, and which is able to stretch across various, even non-adjacent, places. "The 'emptying of time' is in large part the precondition for the 'emptying' of space"[11].

In 19th-century colonial Africa, the rhythm of the working day, as well as the choice to set up local industries, was decided from planning offices in London, Paris, Brussels or Berlin. This management across the borders of continents has of course its own history. It rests on the basis of two major achievements: (i) "the 'discovery' of 'remote' regions of the world by western travelers and explorers"; and "the progressive charting of the globe that led to the creation of universal maps, in which perspective played little part in the representation of geographical position and form", and which "established space as 'independent' of any particular place or region"[12]. As a consequence, planners could start marking off regions that were deemed to be economically more attractive or, possibly, equivalent virtually in terms of profit-calculation. "Modern organizations are able to connect to the local and the global in ways which would have been unthinkable in traditional societies and in so doing routinely affect the lives of many millions of people"[13].

5. Disruption of Local Cultures

All this has far-reaching consequences. Because traditional life-forms are linked to a particular region or locality, modernity's supra-local spatiality is bound to undermine traditional concepts and habits. The variety of traditional ways of conduct is going to be superseded by just one universally binding 'rational' rule of behavior. A good example is Immanuel Kant's formulation of the categorical imperative, which is void in content (i.e., not filled in with local norms or habits) but absolutely binding in its formal character of universally binding obligation (the obligation to act rationally in all circumstances). Couched in the language of classical philosophy, this means that abstract and formal unity and uniformity get

11. *Ibid.*, p. 18.
12. *Ibid.*, p. 19.
13. *Ibid.*, p. 20.

precedence over the disparity of the manifold. The one, encompassing schema of the 'moral law', with its universal claim to rational conduct, is so compelling that it forces the varied forms of behavior to adopt the one mandatory pattern. Apparently, the centralizing pull emanating from the one organizational center is so vehement that the basic characteristic of modernity can rightly be called logocentrism.

At this juncture, one cannot omit to mention the dialectical character of modernity, for besides the trend to uniformity, modernity also possesses and promotes a dynamic thrust towards change, precisely because of the propagation and universalization of abstract thinking. Indeed, one would be mistaken to think that modern 'abstraction' and 'mathematization' must necessarily lead to the creation of static life-forms. On the contrary, the capacity for abstract thinking makes it precisely possible for powerful changes to be ushered in. Mathematical time and space constitute, so to speak, the coordinates within which traditional, local, and time-bound social relations and practices can be broken down and rebuilt in a revolutionary way. Traditional societies owe their static character to their tendency to reproduce local habits and organizational patterns from generation to generation in the same way. Identical re-enactment of the age-old, unchangeable customs was, in pre-modern times, the rule of thumb. Modernity, on the contrary, has developed the tools that enable people to break away from the selfsame reproduction of social life. For with the help of abstract time- and space-concepts, it now becomes possible to dissolve the constraints of the traditional network of social relations, and to drastically reshape social reality in the direction of 'progress' and of a 'march towards a better future': "The 'disembedding' or 'lifting out' of social relations from local contexts of interaction (leads to) their restructuring across indefinite spans of time-space"[14]. Also, Giddens points out that the modern 'differentiation of functions', which some sociologists (e.g., Niklas Luhmann) regard as typical of modernity, in fact depends on the latter's capacity for unpacking and recombining particular constellations and patterns in the social fabric, a capacity that in turn is based on the abstract use of time and space. Differentiation of functions goes hand in hand with the innovation techniques of modern planning. These techniques enable people to replace dominant, but still relatively unsophisticated, constellations with new, diversified ones according to a rhythm of innovations without limits.

14. *Ibid.*, p. 21.

III. CLASSIC LIBERATION THEOLOGY AND ITS RELATION
TO MODERNITY

1. *Dependency Theory*

Without doubt, one of the offsprings of modernity is capitalism, whose contradictions and discrimination mechanisms have been denounced by Karl Marx and his admirers. The question can be raised, therefore, whether or not Marx and the anti-capitalist liberation theologians are to be regarded as either 'anti-modern' or 'pre-modern'? Apparently not, if one takes modernity to be a form of life in which universal rationality prevails[15].

In the case of Marx, he regarded his analysis of capital accumulation and its alienating effects on the working class as 'scientific'[16]. He systematically sought to uncover the hidden mechanisms that accounted for the accretion of surplus value at the expense of the 19th-century industrial workers. But he also sought to reconstruct the dialectics of history, according to which a classless society would become the heir of the capitalist production system once the latter's contradictions initiated a world-wide revolution. Although Marx did not shy away from doing an amount of detailed historical research on various fronts, the scientific ideal he nurtured was such that he wanted to place the results thereof in a universally applicable scheme of interpretation, if not of practical strategy. This is that much obvious that an author like Lyotard, a renegade of Marxism, repeatedly amuses himself by quoting historical slaughters perpetrated by communist ideologues in the name of their knowledge of the logic of history. He sees in these slaughters grounds for his claim that the great stories of modernity have lost their credibility[17].

Coming closer to the background from which Liberation Theology arose – the theory of dependency – pretty much the same can be observed.

---

15. F. HINKELAMMERT, *Taking Stock of Latin-American Liberation Theology Today*, in *CQ* 76 (1995-96) 18-29, p. 29. This author takes a somewhat different view, when he says: "Thus, Liberation Theology arrives as a critique of modernity, and not only of capitalism. It ends up stating a crisis of western society itself. However, Liberation Theology is not postmodern". Other authors prefer to speak of a 'dialectical surmounting' of modernity, reached at by positioning oneself at the underside of history, and by doing so, reformulating the process of emancipation. See J. TAMAYO, *Presente y futuro de la teología de la liberación*, Madrid, San Pablo, 1994, p. 42.

16. I. WALLERSTEIN, *Culture as the Ideological Battleground* (n. 9), p. 52: "The fetishism of science by the antisystemic movements – for example, Marx's designation of his ideas as 'scientific socialism' –was a natural expression of the post-1789 triumph of Enlightenment ideas in the world-system".

17. J.-F. LYOTARD, *The Postmodern Explained*, Minneapolis, University of Minnesota Press, 1992, pp. 28-29.

This theory too is critical of patterns of hegemony inherent in world capitalism, but it does not envision an abandonment of modernity's critical approach. A close look at some passages from Gustavo Gutiérrez's *A Theology of Liberation* will make this clear. These passages deal with the difference between development and dependency, as worked out by Cardoso and Faletto, though at a first glance, the passages might suggest that the authors flatly distance themselves from modernity and westernization.

Referring to Cardoso and Faletto, Gutiérrez typifies the development programs set up by international organizations as "an ideology of modernization which explained the transition of Latin-American societies from traditionalism to modernism, from underdevelopment to development". Development takes as its ideal "the modern society" or "industrial society", and supposes that, provided enough funds are going to be invested, those Latin-American countries willing to make serious efforts, will be able to gradually catch up with the high standard of living in the West. "In achieving, however, these goals, social, political, and cultural obstacles originating from the archaic political structures proper to the underdeveloped countries – also referred to as 'traditional societies' or 'transitional societies' – had to be overcome"[18].

Gutiérrez gives little comment on the disruption of 'traditional societies', including their cultural habits, under the pressure of modernization. What matters to him is the fact that the development programs, in spite of their promises, did not work. Hence, he deems that a more detailed analysis is required which, besides the economic aspect, would also probe into the geopolitical situation of the Latin-American countries. Linear programs of development are fallacious because they omit to pay sufficient attention to what Wallerstein calls the 'international division of labor' within capitalism. Gutiérrez's critique reads as follows: "It has become ever clearer that underdevelopment is the end result of a process. Therefore it must be studied from a historical perspective, that is, in relationship to the development and expansion of the great capitalist countries. The underdevelopment of the poor countries, as an overall social fact, appears in its true light: as the historical by-product of the development of other countries. The dynamics of the capitalist economy lead to the establishment of a center and a periphery, simultaneously generating progress and growing wealth for the few, and social imbalances, political tensions, and poverty for the many"[19].

18. G. GUTIÉRREZ, *A Theology of Liberation*, Maryknoll, NY, Orbis, [15]1988, p. 50.
19. *Ibid.*, p. 51.

From this insertion of peripheral into hegemonic capitalism, Gutiérrez draws some far-reaching conclusions, which for the purpose of our study, merit to be listed.

a) The actual economic situation is such that, on a world-wide scale, the gap between the poor and the rich continues to grow. Of course, the colonial experience of the Latin-American countries offer them some lessons on the facts of economic dependence. Yet what they are beholding now − a massive intrusion of domineering multinational corporations − is a phenomenon that exceeds all past episodes.

b) The accretion of dependence by the peripheral countries requires an analysis that delves below the confrontations between states and interstate-alliances; we need to put this confrontation "within the framework of the world wide class struggle"[20].

c) The solution lies in an option for socialism and a rupture from the capitalist world-system: "autonomous Latin-American development is not viable within the framework of the international capitalist system"[21].

d) Opting out of the capitalist camp (Cuba is quoted as the example) does not mean, however, that the Latin-American countries will have to copy some western type of socialism (read: communism). In this respect, Gutiérrez refers to what José Carlos Mariátegui had stood for in the 1920s: the creation of an Indo-American socialism that follows its own pace of development and organization and which takes into account the indigenous sensitivities, including the remembrance of the people's agelong suffering under foreign domination.

e) What matters above all is to keep alive the utopia of building up a "different society in which [humanity] will be free from all servitude, in which it will be the artisan of its own destiny"[22].

2. *Theology's Contribution to Liberation from Dependence*

Like his fellow liberation theologians, Gutiérrez seems to have realized that the best way for him to contribute to the process of socioeconomic liberation is to take up the task of an 'organic intellectual'. For a theologian, this entails participation in the actualization of God's preference for the downtrodden, as testified in the scriptures. The organic theologian will deem the indigence of the poor masses and their struggle

20. *Ibid.*, p. 54.
21. *Ibid.*, p. 54.
22. *Ibid.*, p. 56.

aspects, taken from Gutiérrez's theology, will be highlighted: (i) the 'self-generation' of the human species through the medium of labor, and (ii) conscientization in the context of the pedagogy of the oppressed.

(i) In a central passage of *A Theology of Liberation*, while commenting on the exodus event, Gutiérrez points out that what happened here – the amazing passage from bondage to the people's march towards the promised land – is closely connected in Second Isaiah to God's orderly creation of the universe out of chaos. God's action upon the world becomes palpable whenever chaotic existence gives way to a creative impulse toward an unexpected and new fulfilment. Linking this idea with a Teilhardian perspective, which sees the whole of creation evolving toward a christic point Omega, Gutiérrez goes on to develop the vision of humankind's historical contribution to the growth of the richness of both humanity and the rest of creation. In line with other theologies (e.g. process theology), he affirms that the members of the human community are called to be co-creators with God. But at the same time, he does not lose sight of his starting-point, Israel's release from captivity, from a situation of oppression. To become a co-creator with God presupposes that one will do away with the hindrances that impede this co-creatorship. Creation, as a dynamic biblical reality, prospers when JHWH inspires the oppressed to break out of servitude. At this juncture, one can see that modern thought ('emancipation') and biblical thought ('empowered by God to be co-creators') enter into a particular symbiosis. Gutiérrez writes: "By working, transforming the world, breaking out of servitude, building a just society, and assuming its destiny in history, *humankind forges itself*". In contrast, "in Egypt, work is alienated and, far from building a just society, contributes rather to increasing injustice and to widening the gap between exploiters and exploited"[26]. To make the transition from 'work which is alienated' to 'working for' the building of a just society, is to entrust oneself to God's creative impulse.

The programmatic statement that humankind is called to forge itself by transforming the world is not only 'modern' but also, and more importantly, reminiscent of Marx[27]. But Gutiérrez also fills it with a Christian content by linking transformation with salvation. Salvation consists in the sense of wholeness human beings experience while engaging in the building up, without distortion, of their human communities. This sense of wholeness is both the result of their commitment

26. G. GUTIÉRREZ (n. 18), p. 90.
27. Cf. K. MARX, *Nationalökonomie und Philosophie*, MEGA, I,3, D 111-116, Frankfurt, 1929.

and the inner inspiration prompting them to embark further on the realization of this program: "Salvation – totally and freely given by God, the communion of human beings with God and among themselves – is the inner force and fullness of this movement of *human self-generation* initiated by God's work of creation. Consequently, when we assert that humanity fulfills itself by continuing the work of creation *by means of its labor*, we are saying that it places itself by this very fact, within an all-embracing salvific process. To work, *to transform the world*, *is to become… [a more developed human being] and to build the human community*; it is also to save. Likewise the struggle against misery and exploitation and to build a just society is already part of a saving action, which is moving towards its complete fulfillment"[28].

The descriptive content of personal and social wholeness, which includes the conditions that must be fulfilled (just reward for one's work, putting an end to exploitation) to make this wholeness flourish, is taken from Marx's humanistic writings. This does not imply, however, that the breakthrough of wholeness is seen as alien to God's grace. Gutiérrez and his fellow liberation theologians regularly fall back on basic attitudes of traditional Christianity such as the habit of referring back to God, the giver of all things, our dearest achievements and longings in spite of deficiencies. It would be unfair to treat Gutiérrez as if he were oblivious of transcendent reality[29]. The symbiosis with Marxist themes has mainly the effect of 'deprivatizing' religion (to use Metz's terminology); it puts religion at the service of the humanization of people, especially of those groups of the human family who find themselves at the underside of history.

(ii) This brings us to the question of 'conscientization'. The fact that human beings, especially the downtrodden, should be raised to the awareness that they have to put efforts in making themselves the authors of their own history, is for Gutiérrez something self-evident in a scientific

28. G. GUTIÉRREZ (n. 18), p. 91. Italics mine, to put in relief the 'Marxian' input.

29. John Milbank blames liberation theology for not being able to pass a theological judgement on reality; instead of criticizing society in theological terms, liberation theologians content themselves with criticizing it in sociological terms (an enterprise, which, then, in a second step, is presented as justified by introducing the reference to God). See J. MILBANK, *Theology and Social Theory: Beyond Secular Reason*, Oxford, Blackwell, [1990], 1995, pp. 245-249. Milbank, on the contrary, proposes to take seriously the meta-narrative of theology proper, as distinct from any secular narrative. He hereby opts for a 'postmodern' way of theologizing, when asserting that "Christianity starts to appear – even 'objectively' – as not just different, but as the difference from all other cultural systems, which it exposes as threatened by incipient nihilism" (*ibid.*, p. 381). The question to be asked, however, is whether such a claim to 'preferential difference' can still be maintained within a postmodern context.

age. He hereby refers to the scientific achievements of the 15th and 16th centuries which have led to the Copernican revolution, and he observes that, as a consequence, "humankind abandoned its former image of the world and itself... 'It is because of its physics that metaphysics grows old' [Gilson]"[30]. Indeed, it is only by unearthing the real causes of things that we come to understand better the workings of the natural world and of humankind's role and dealings with it. Nature need no longer be feared as a destructive God. One of the paradoxes of our mastery of nature, however, is that certain mystifications that used to beset the mythical understanding of the world make their reapparance, in an altered form, in the social fabric. Socio-economic determinisms, or perhaps deterministic ideologies, have come to replace physical determinisms. Paraphrasing Marx: man's consciousness is conditioned by social forms of life, instead of consciousness being able to control them. This social conditioning may take on the form of apparently cogent sets of ideas such as the following: "the economic development autonomously proceeds under the direction of an invisible hand", or "the social process of production has mastery over man, instead of the opposite", or "it is 'natural' for a society to be organized for the benefit of a minority class of individuals who pursue their own self-interest"[31]. Hence, Gutiérrez insists, there is the need, especially in the social sciences, to get at the true causes, i.e., the "socioeconomic determinants of (humanity's) ideological creations" in order to enable the masses to become "freer and more lucid in relation to them", so that they may "have greater control and rational grasp of historical initiatives"[32].

In this context, Gutiérrez refers to Paulo Freire's 'pedagogy of the oppressed' whose aim is to free people from attitudes of blind submission to fate, be it fate imposed by nature or by social structures. The

---

30. G. GUTIÉRREZ (n. 18), p. 18.
31. I take the examples from R. PEET, *World Capitalism and the Destruction of Regional Cultures*, in R.J. JOHNSTON & P.J. TAYLOR (eds.), *A World in Crisis? Geographical Perspectives* Oxford, Blackwell, 1989, p. 188.
32. *Ibid.*, pp. 19-20. J. MILBANK (n. 29), p. 244, refers to this passage in Gutiérrez and blames it for overoptimistically wagering on freedom: "The release of freedom alone is supposed to make socialism possible, but what is forgotten here... is the priority of *justice* as far as socialism is concerned, and the continued need, even in a socialist society, 'to make equal – the unequal', according to agreed-upon measures in all processes of exchange". Milbank's emphasis on 'agreements' in order to establish a just society, seems to loose sight of Gutiérrez's point that especially the downtrodden need to have a grasp of social mechanisms, in order to 'free themselves from blindly falling prey to hidden determinants which they do not understand' or, to use Milbank's own categories: 'in order to enable them to act as mature partners in the discussions about policy-making').

important point for Freire is that the poor come to realize that, in order to rid themselves of a passive attitude to life, they must try to overcome their naive and often magical understanding of reality and to develop an increasingly critical understanding[33]. Naive consciousness "does not deal with problems, gives too much value to the past, tends to mythical explanations, and tends towards (fruitless) debate", whereas critical consciousness "delves into problems, is open to new ideas, replaces magical explanations with real causes, and tends to (critical) dialogue". The conscious act of passing from naive to critical consciousness is technically called 'conscientization'. "In this process the oppressed reject the oppressive consciousness which dwells in them, become aware of their situation, and find their own language. They become, by themselves, less dependent and freer, as they commit themselves to the transformation and building up of society"[34]. Gutiérrez calls this espousal of critical insight the starting-point for a permanent cultural revolution.

3. *Marxist Thought on Culture as an Ideological Apparatus: The Question of Theory and Praxis*

In his discussion of Paulo Freire, Gutiérrez deals only indirectly with the Marxist critique of religion. An assessment of Marx's position, however, is explicitly undertaken by T. Kudo and C. Tovar in a study that makes use of Gutiérrez' unedited course notes on 'Marxism and Christian faith' (1975)[35]. The study is illuminative in many respects; it not only tackles the question about liberation theology's 'subversive character' (subversive of the status quo and the dominant ideologies) but also tries to explain how a liberation ideology is necessarily born from praxis.

As is well known, Marx contended that religion would disappear once human consciousness had discarded its alienating, ideological thought-patterns. According to the aforementioned authors, however, this pronouncement ought to be qualified for two reasons: (i) In his later writings[36], Marx subsumed religion under the umbrella of ideological forms that are generated within the superstructure in view of lending a justification to the development and organization of material life in society. (ii) From this, it follows that religion must be assessed on the same footing as other

---

33. P. FREIRE, *Education for Critical Consciousness*, London, Sheed & Ward, 1973, p. 46.

34. G. GUTIÉRREZ (n. 18), p. 57.

35. T. KUDO & C. TOVAR, *La crítica de la religión: Ensayo sobre la consciencia social en Marx*, Lima, CEP, (1977), ³1982.

36. See K. MARX, *Zur Kritik der politischen Ökonomie*, MEW, 8-9, G. 425-427.

ideological forms. Just as art, politics, law, and philosophy can either justify reality in a distorted way or, when linked to an authentic praxis of social change, display a correct explanation of reality, religion too can either serve to legitimize the status quo or act as a factor for social change. Religion can either endorse an ideology that calls for a peaceful coexistence of the classes, or enter the conflict-ridden areas of society and put its inspiring potential at the service of the subordinated groups, whose radical praxes defy the appeasing ideology of the prevailing culture.

Ideology, thus, takes on a double meaning: a pejorative one in the case of the procedures that deceptively universalize the self-serving interests of the ruling class, and a positive one that expresses the authentic insights of the non-ruling classes as well as the correctness of their cause. To make this difference clear, one needs to distinguish between the truth of the situation and the way this truth is presented differently by the dominating and the dominated social strata.

The members of the dominant class do have some grasp of the fact that their power rests upon an unequal division of labor. Because they want to perpetuate their favourable situation, they make things appear as if no socio-structural changes are needed at all. They set out to downplay the seriousness of class antagonisms, and they try to convince themselves and the rest of society about the higher good, the abstract idea that, for human society, nothing is more noble and beautiful than inner harmony. Although they know about the restless state of affairs in society[37], they try to foreclose public discussion especially as regards issues related to the economic rights of the poor. They clothe their manipulative decisions in the mystifying language of noble ideals, which are meant to throw dust into the eyes of the exploited.

The revolutionary class, however, is in the truth because of its insightful praxis of vindication. It has shaken off the distorted consciousness impressed upon it through deception; it sees through the manipulations of the exploiters[38]. Marxist analysis wagers on the power of the exploited class to debunk the mystifications of those ideologies that call for conformity. It accounts for this stand by pointing to the emergence of

37. "Ideology in a pejorative sense is recognition of the existing state of affairs, but at the same time a denial of the real situation and thus deceptive abuse of the exploited by the exploiter". See T. KUDO & C. TOVAR (n. 35), p. 100.

38. "The consciousness of the exploited class is real consciousness, in so far as it is indeed revolutionary consciousness, i.e. their state of consciousness corresponds with reality and accordingly expresses in a real manner the truth of the actual social relations; instead of regarding the latter as unchangeable, it wagers on the transformative power of a historical praxis in order to overthrow the seemingly unchangeable state of affairs". See *ibid.*, p. 103.

the people's "praxis as a rebellious class" and the "sweeping vigor of their praxis-oriented ideology", which defies the ideology of prevailing culture. "The Marxist analysis of the ideology of the ruling class has methodologically its focus on the real resistance of the oppressed class, much more than on the brute fact of their being oppressed and ruled"[39]. If one recalls that this resistance is frequently born of collective memories of suffering, it is not hard to understand why Christian believers have not hesitated to add the sweeping vigor of their 'ideology' (in this case, the prophetic tradition of denunciation) to the praxis of the defiant poor.

Although Gutiérrez seems to eschew an explicit treatment of the ideology debate[40], he does not hide his awareness of it. The issue shows up in his discussion of the two-planes theology: "Is the church fulfilling a purely religious role when by its silence or friendly relationships it lends legitimacy to a dictatorial and oppressive government? We discover, then, that the policy of non-intervention in political affairs holds for certain actions which involve ecclesiastical authorities, but not for others. In other words, the principle is not applied when it is a question of maintaining the status quo, but it is wielded when, for example, a lay apostolic movement or a group of priests holds an attitude considered subversive to the established order. Concretely, in Latin America the distinction of planes model has the effect of concealing the real political option of a large sector of the Church – that is, support of the established order... The dominant groups, who have always used the Church to defend their interests and maintain their privileged position, today – as they see 'subversive' tendencies gaining ground in the heart of Christian community – call for a return to the purely religious and spiritual function of the Church"[41].

IV. THE SOBERING DIVIDE: THE FALL OF THE BERLIN WALL

In his attempt at evaluating the future of liberation theology, Jürgen Moltmann welcomes the fact that the monumental work *Mysterium Liberationis* (1990) has broken new ground in exploring topics like a theology of life and Christian spirituality, but he also points out that (with the

---

39. *Ibid.*, p. 116.
40. The ideology-debate is explicitly treated by J.L. SEGUNDO, *Teología de la liberación: Respuesta al Cardenal Ratzinger*, Madrid, Cristiandad, 1985, pp. 138-174. Liberación y hermenéutica: de la lucha de clases a la violencia.
41. G. GUTIÉRREZ (n. 18), pp. 40-41.

exception of Dussel's contribution) these developments have relegated to the background the earlier confrontation with Marxism. Most remarkably, he observes, no mention at all is made of the changes in the East bloc, which when the book came out, had already led to the fall of the Berlin wall, the implosion of state socialism, and the dismantling of the Soviet Union[42]. Yet whoever takes to heart the cause of the poor masses in the Third World will have to admit that this collapse marks a turning point in history, if not a point of no return. Till now, there had existed something like a viable alternative to capitalism – an egalitarian society with state-owned industries and a welfare system to meet the basic needs of all – but suddenly this dream was gone. Fukuyama's programmatic work *The End of History*[43] has made it provocatively clear: the triumph of the neoliberal free market is the final accomplishment of history, after which no alternative solution can claim to be valid. World-wide left experiments are out. Nicaragua and Cuba turned out to be failures. Communist China and Vietnam have already ushered in market-oriented economies, whereas for brisk capitalistic development, the tone is set by the new tigers of East Asia. The old utopia of liberation – from capitalism – has lost its mystique and quasi-religious appeal; its militants are filled with despair, powerlessness, and disillusionment. Especially in Latin America, the crisis of the left is palpable everywhere. Right-wing presidents got elected in El Salvador, Mexico, and Brazil (F.H. Cardoso, once the architect of the dependency theory, won over the populist Lula). Trade unions have lost their clout, and the general feeling is that insertion in the global free market is inevitable.

The new state of affairs presents a world order with no alternatives, while feelings of solidarity are crumbling. In this light, it is instructive to see how the old tenets of liberation theology are assessed now, especially by authors who have sympathized with its objectives and its option for the poor. In what follows, I limit my review to the two main topics examined above: the theory of dependency, and the unity of praxis and conscientization.

(a) In his article *Theology of liberation and the collapse of existing socialism*, Gerhard Kruip lists the positive marks liberation theology should continue to uphold. These are the option for the poor, the dialectical relationship between theology and praxis, the necessity of changing structures and minds simultaneously, and its theological critique of the

---

42. J. MOLTMANN, *Die Zukunft der Befreiungstheologie*, in *Or* 59 (1995) 207-210. The reference is to I. ELLACURIA & J. SOBRINO (eds.), *Mysterium Liberationis: Conceptos fundamentales de la teología de la liberación*, Madrid, Trotta, 1992.

43. F. FUKUYAMA, *The End of History and the Last Man*, New York, Free Press, 1992.

Marxist theory of religion. "These are theological understandings which retain their validity even if the situation in which they were first achieved has changed". But he is quick to add that what liberation theology should revise is "its judgement about market economies. The market can no longer be treated as 'intrinsice malum' by theological thinking that only sees the fetishism of consumerism and has no regard for the higher output and better regulation efforts of market economies"[44]. In line with this, he points out that dependency theory, ever since the 1980s, has lost its credibility for the following reasons: (i) it is empirically questionable that the poor get poorer just because the rich get richer; inferior conditions in the Third World are also partially due to the higher birth rates in these countries; (ii) in spite of external dependence, many countries have succeeded in improving their GDP (Chile e.g. with 3 percent per capita in the 1980s) because of their dynamic insertion in the world market; (iii) The East Asian 'tigers' deliver the proof that external factors do not necessarily lead to underdevelopment. And finally, there is the remarkable fact that even Gustavo Gutiérrez, in the new foreword to the 15th anniversary edition of *A Theology of Liberation* (1988), has distanced himself from a theory he once helped to promote[45].

If the market is not intrinsically unethical, this does not mean that market operations do not stand in need of being tempered with social regulations that have been decided upon by the political community. Kruip wagers on the type of 'social-democratic market' which has been and still is workable in Germany. There, social security regulations coexist with the competitive dealings of companies on the free market. He recommends this model as a blueprint for other nations, acknowledging that it will be up to each country to look for the appropriate means to make it work. For Third World countries, this would imply that they should put efforts in augmenting that space in civil society which serves as the arena for public discussion and democratic consensus-formation. He invites the liberation theologians to give a place, in their 'social imagery', to the urgent need of building a social-democracy in

---

44. G. KRUIP, *Die Theologie der Befreiung und der Zusammenbruch des realen Sozialismuseine unbewältigte Herausforderung*, in ZMR 80 (1996) 3-25, p. 25.

45. G. GUTIÉRREZ, *Introduction to the revised edition*, in *A Theology of Liberation*, p. xxiv: "It is clear, for example, that the theory of dependence, which was so extensively used in the early years of our encounter with the Latin-American world, is now an inadequate tool, because it does not take sufficient account of the internal dynamics of each country or of the vast dimensions of the world of the poor. In addition, Latin-American scientists are increasingly alert to factors of which they were not conscious earlier and which show that the world economy has evolved".

view of alleviating the needs of the weakest in a society with a free market system[46].

To drive home his point, Kruip engages in a critical discussion with Hinkelammert's presentation of the fetishism of capital. According to Hinkelammert, capitalism acts as a deadly Moloch, who in order to augment the volume of circulating money, needs bloody sacrifices (e.g., drastic cuts in social services and health care are required to enable the government to pay back its foreign debts). This view contains, in Kruip's opinion, many overstatements; more in particular, it overlooks the fact that fetishism is not just typical of a regime in which the means of production are privately owned. Fetishism is, in the first instance, a 'thingification' that is unavoidable in as much as it naturally flows from the increasing refinement of production and market operations. The fact that products begin to lead a life of their own, above the heads of producers and consumers, goes hand in hand with the differentiation of specialized functions as is typical of complex societies. Not even the East bloc, where private property was abolished, had been able to stop this process, which on the contrary, made its reappearance at the level of anonymous state administration. This leads Kruip to conclude that Marx's analysis of fetishism displays a nostalgia for face-to-face relations, which were current in pre-industrial times. There is a "grief over the loss of traditional forms of life which were more 'humane'"[47]. To counter this loss of 'face-to-face communication' in the production and market processes, he proposes, in line with Habermas, to take advantage of the communicative language we have at our disposal in civil society. Citizens of democratic societies have plenty of opportunities to engage in communicative discourse and to discuss the ways in which they would want to socially coordinate the exchange game of the market. This socio-political meta-discourse (meta-game) is what should matter to praxis-oriented theologians, for it allows them to denounce options that grant unrestricted freedom to the game of the market which in that case subdue human beings to an empire of 'things.' Such theologians should encourage societies in which the game of the market is coordinated in view of meeting the common needs of the people: "It is imperative for liberation theology to espouse a social-democratic version of its initial enterprise; only then will it be able to keep pace with modern theory-formation in the social sciences, and to gain relevance for the

---

46. See also J.C. SCANNONE, *Doctrina social de la iglesia y teología de la liberación*, in *Med* 80 (1994) 546-565, p. 561.

47. G. KRUIP (n. 44), p. 20.

political action of Christians in the context of complex modern societies"[48].

(b) Kruip also suggests a revision of the praxis commitment (conscientization) to the extent that closer attention will have to be paid to the
diverse cultural roots of the poor masses. This readjustment program
was occasioned by the liberation theologians' perception of the lacunas
in their own system – lacunas that in the meantime have been filled in
by a range of 'new movements' committed to such causes as indigenous
revival, feminist emancipation, and the conservation of nature[49]. Some
of the lacunas were already touched upon in the *Essays in Honor of
Gustavo Gutiérrez* (1989)[50]; they also regularly show up in interviews
delivered by liberation theologians in reaction to the events in Eastern
Europe.

For example, when asked about their reactions as regards the implosion of East Germany, Leonardo Boff and Frei Betto came up with the
following observations, which partly deal with an assessment of the past,
and partly – as in points (iv) and (v) – try to lay down a blueprint for
the future[51]: (i) Liberation Theology has never identified itself with the
bureaucratic and totalitarian system of Soviet Socialism, but has, on the
contrary, pursued a Latin-American reading of Marx adapted to the cultural setting of the sub-continent. (ii) Liberation theology was born from
the religious experience of a suffering people and from their Christian
socio-political praxis; it has never been a direct offspring of Marxism.
To opt for the poor is not the same as opting for a particular social system; as soon as the system proves to be deficient, it must be replaced
with something better. (iii) In focusing on the structural causes of massive poverty, liberation theology is particularly critical of the capitalist
system. In the face of the disintegration of socialism, the search for other
alternatives cannot be abandoned; some liberation theologians have
even sharpened their critique of capitalism by pointing a finger of scorn
to the mechanisms of 'exclusion' which have gradually come to replace
those of 'exploitation'. (iv) The new situation brings to the fore the importance of 'personal' elements such as ethical reflection, spirituality, and
questions of individual and collective meaning. To probe into these dimensions and to make them fruitful, a new acquaintance with indigenous

---

48. *Ibid.*, pp. 21-22.
49. These themes also figured on the agenda of the Santo Domingo Conference.
50. See M. ELLIS & O. MADURO (eds.), *The Future of Liberation Theology: Essays in
Honor of Gustavo Gutiérrez*, Maryknoll, NY, Orbis, 1989.
51. F. BETTO, *El fracaso del socialismo alemán y los desafios a la izquierda latinoamericana*, in *Pg* 29 (1990) 1-7. See also G. KRUIP (n. 44), pp. 9-11.

popular wisdom and popular religiosity is required as a proper means to bring about a genuine 'revolution in everyday life'. (v) Liberation theology has to acknowledge that the life-world of the poor is more complex than had been thought before; this life-world is rather heterogeneous and beset by clashing interests. The poor are not just the ones who are exploited in the labor situation; they also and more specifically comprise indios, peasant workers, jobless slum-dwellers, women, sick people, and youth with bleak prospects for the future. Each of them has specific problems. And then comes the conclusion with respect to the change or complementarity in method: "the tools of analysis are departing from the standard model of Marx-inspired economy and sociology to also include analyses made with the help of cultural sciences"[52].

It is worthwhile to pause and ponder on the change in method which is alluded to at the end of the foregoing considerations, and which logically flows from the proposed new agenda for action. The probing into indigenous wisdom, as well as the special attention paid to questions of gender, race, and culture – youth culture, peasants' culture, urban culture, and counterculture – presupposes an approach that departs from the classical (classist) socio-economic analysis, which till then served as the basic mediation for 'doing' liberation theology. I will try then to depict the core elements the new program has given up or bracketed – to the discontent, without doubt, of those who set great store by the distinctive characteristics of a Marxist-inspired analysis and the social consciousness-raising that is part of it.

What is mainly striking is not only the fragmented panorama of the fields of action but also the determination to uncouple those fields from any unifying center that might command the march for revolutionary change. This dispersal sharply contrasts with the Marxist revolutionary consciousness, whose force is based on the exploited people's collective will "to overthrow the seemingly unchangeable state of affairs"[53]. This collective will is essential in the formation of a unified class consciousness, yet it is obviously this core element which, in the new approach, has been relegated to the background. This is something that one not only has to recognize; it asks also for a proper explanation, to which I am going to proceed in the next pages. But before going any further, let us see in more detail what Marxist revolutionary consciousness is about.

First of all, Marxist revolutionary consciousness does not exist apart from the people's commonly-shared political will to establish the society

---

52. G. KRUIP (n. 44), p. 11.
53. T. KUDO & C. TOVAR (n. 35), p. 103.

of the future, in which the contradictions and mystifications that are still virulent in capitalism will have been overcome[54]. This social consciousness carries the Marxist teleological view of history; scientific socialism knows for certain that, by a compelling teleology of events, it is going to replace capitalism. Socialism, in this view, is not just one among other alternatives to the capitalist world order; its inner impulse flows from the conviction that socialism alone – on the shoulders of the new, rising 'universal class', the proletariat – will solve the 'riddle of history'. This implies that the conscientized masses see before their eyes something of the imminent breakthrough of the new civilization[55]. Tentative steps, procrastinations of the dream, or eschatological provisos are not part of the program, for they reveal hesitancies a militant should not have. Whoever gives in to such temptations is a 'revisionist' or 'reformist,' somebody whose consciousness has not yet been cleansed fully of alienations. The grand story of 'the forward march of socialism' requires a total act of faith in the higher synthesis that is to come; this faith must be kept alive by the militancy of the unified proletariat, whose historical destiny makes them close ranks beyond the differences of race, gender, and cultural habits. The undivided bloc of the protagonists of history only thinks in universal categories, and is wary of the particular.

When one reads this account of a monolithic militancy – I take my information from sociological studies and not from *Libertatis Nuntius* – one cannot help but think of the missionary zeal with which the grandfather of Marxism, modernity, has propagated the necessity and the obligation of the standardized rational conduct, which allegedly assures its adherents steady progress. On the whole, I believe that Zygmunt Bauman is correct when he observes that those who celebrate the collapse of communism also celebrate the end of modernity, for communism desperately attempted to make modernity work[56]. We are then confronted

54. Cf. A. GIDDENS, *Beyond Left and Right: The Future of Radical Politics*, Cambridge, Polity Press, (1994), 1995, pp. 51-56.

55. See also *ibid.*, p. 249: "Socialist thought, particularly in Marx's version, diagnosed the irrationalities of history, but showed that history provided its own means of overcoming them. If Marx's idea of the coming classless society was never particularly coherent, his account of the revolutionary role of the proletariat was compelling: the 'riddle of history' was resolved by the actions of the oppressed class. Particularly in its Marxist form, socialism invoked a providentialism having deep roots in European culture. History poses problems for us, expressed as social contradictions; but those very contradictions promise a higher synthesis, driving us onward. Today we must break with providentialism, in whatever guise it might present itself".

56. Z. BAUMAN (n. 6), p. 222: "I think that people who celebrate the collapse of communism, as I do, celebrate more than that without always knowing it. They celebrate the end of modernity actually, because what collapsed was the most decisive attempt to make modernity work; and it failed. It failed as blatantly as the attempt was blatant".

with this question: how could we or should we imagine the workings of a 'socialism' within the postmodern setting or within complex societies?

V. POSTMODERNITY AND GLOBALIZATION

1. *How Does Postmodernity Relate to Modernity?*

'Postmodernity' is a recent phenomenon in the field of cultural studies; nonetheless, its emergence was well under way in the First World from the beginning of this century, and it reached its full unfolding in the affluent post-1945 decades. Far from being just a by-product of modernity, postmodernity must be seen as modernity having reached the stage where it became conscious "of its true nature – *modernity for itself*"[57]. It is reflexive modernization in contrast with simple modernization[58]. While simple modernization rested on the rigid application of scientific methods under the aegis of clarity, homogeneity, and universality, the very result of this enterprise was an accelerated production of new commodities. Postmodernity thus is the 'consequence' of modernity, which was basically attuned to the formal rhythm of increasing novelty. The distinguishing feature, however, is the phenomenon that postmodern people realize from within what the acceleration process of modernization is all about. They are, so to speak, used to sitting comfortably in the high-speed train of modernity, and to take in the shifting panorama of the unstoppable innovations and changing perspectives[59].

The new cultural reflexivity comes to the fore in the way time is experienced as fragmentized. To find satisfaction in the ever-new 'now moment' has become the ideal to live by. Postmoderns expect the now-experience of tomorrow to be qualitatively different from the now-experience of today. They are used to celebrating the fleeting qualities of life and to enjoy the surface of existence in terms of pure instantaneity[60]. Fragmentation and instantaneity also produce an a-historical leveling

---

57. Z. BAUMAN (n. 6), p. 187.
58. A. GIDDENS (n. 54), p. 42.
59. For this reason, they are able to banter their situation, e.g., by marketing architectural constructions in which old style elements are shockingly mixed into brand new wholes.
60. Cf. D. HARVEY, *The Condition of Postmodernity: An Inquiry into the Origin of Cultural Change*, Oxford, Blackwell, (1990), 1993, p. 59: "The collapse of time horizons and the preoccupation with instantaneity have in part arisen through the contemporary emphasis in cultural production on events, spectacles, and media images. Cultural producers have learnt to explore and use new technologies, the media, and ultimately multimedia possibilities. The effect, however, has been to re-emphasize the fleeting qualities of modern life and even to celebrate them".

down of all viewed time-images, and a deletion of the boundaries between reality and fiction. Television, as the typical postmodern medium of communication, succeeds in mixing up historical accounts of the past with advertisements of the present, and this collage makes it difficult to differentiate entertainment from serious information[61].

2. *Breakdown of 'Classical' Unifying Centers*

This sketch of the postmodern life-style is situated mainly at the personal level of experience. But there are also 'objective' grounds that account for a free-wheeling decenteredness. They relate to various domains such as (i) the new notion of science, (ii) multiple choice in getting information, and (iii) the decline of Euro-centrism.

(i) As far as science is concerned, its modern, denotative function has been replaced with performative language. In modernity, the aim of knowledge was to shed a light on the phenomena; the cognitive apparatus had the pretension to 'represent' the truth extracted from the subject-matter under investigation. In each field of knowledge, something had to be objectively valid or not. And this commonly shared scientific outlook was able to create a bond of unity among the members of the various communities of research, even when they specialized in their own domains. In postmodernity, this universalist type of science has expired; one is left with 'an indefinite number of meaning-generating agencies', each of which is pragmatic and self-referential. Meaning is produced locally and in accordance with the adjustable and fragmentary rules of a specific field – thus an encompassing legitimation framework of scientificity exists no longer[62]. For postmodern pragmatism, 'truth' boils down to efficiency and competitiveness in the market. What counts is the answer to the following questions: What is the new language-game good for? What are its unprecedented effects? Accordingly, 'grounding' questions can only take the form of a tautology: What is the use of this

---

61. "Television is, as B. Taylor points out, 'the first cultural medium in the whole history to present the artistic achievements of the past as a stitched-together collage of equi-important and simultaneously existing phenomena, largely divorced from geography and material history and transported to the living rooms and studios of the West in a more or less uninterrupted flow'. It posits a viewer, furthermore, 'who shares the medium's own perception of history as an endless reserve of equal events'". See D. HARVEY (n. 60), p. 61. Also in B. TAYLOR, *Modernism, Post-modernism, Realism: A Critical Perspective for Art*, Winchester, Winchester School of Art Press, 1987, pp. 103-105.

62. Cf. Z. BAUMAN (n. 6), p. 37: "'The grand narrative has lost its credibility'. Having lost its discursive unity, science ceased to be such a grand narrative. It has been dethroned and demoted to a collection of language games none of which enjoys a privileged status or wields power to adjudicate in other games".

particular research program set up to produce utility[63]? The alliance between scientific research and the free market leads to an unending multiplication of disparate language-games designed to promote ever-new marketable products. Also, the procedural practice of providing proofs to theories is closely linked to performativity, i.e., to the profit calculation of input/output[64].

(ii) The proliferation of specialized branches of knowledge, especially when combined with the spreading effects of mass media, leads to a consumer market in which a plurality of world views are both available and competing with each other. It is up to the consumers to make their choice or choices and to make out which messages sound the most convincing, at least for the moment. Mass media play a decisive role in the birth of a postmodern society, but instead of making this postmodern society more 'transparent,' they render it more complex, even chaotic[65]. Nonetheless, this relative 'chaos' paves the way for a 'reflexive' personality. The postmodern person is forced to ponder on the provisional options one has to make, and realizes that these too lay open to further revisions. At any rate, to commit oneself, once and for all, to a singular and exclusive truth no longer chimes with the postmodern person, whose life strategy consists in the avoidance of being fixed. Any life-style pattern, no mater how appealing, "is only one among other forms of life"[66].

---

63. "The question (overt or implied) now asked by professionalist students, the State, or institutions of higher education is no longer: 'Is it true?' but 'What use is it?' In the context of the mercantilization of knowledge, more often than not this question is equivalent to: 'Is it salable?' And in the context of power-growth: 'Is it efficient?'" See J.-F. LYOTARD, *The Postmodern Condition: A Report on Knowledge*, Minneapolis, University of Minnesota Press, 1984 [French original, 1979]), p. 51.

64. This leads to cynical situations For example, laboratories specialized in providing proofs are expensive. This means pragmatically: "No money – no proof – and that means no verification of statements and no truth. The games of scientific language become the games of the rich, in which whoever is wealthier has the best chance of being right. An equation between wealth, efficiency, and truth is thus established". J.-F. LYOTARD (n. 63), p. 45.

65. G. VATTIMO, *The Transparent Society*, Cambridge, Polity Press, 1992, p. 7. "Newspapers, radio, television, what is now called telematics... have been decisive in bringing about the dissolution of centralized perspectives... What actually happened, in spite of the efforts of the monopolies and major centres of capital, is that radio, television and newspapers became elements in a general explosion and proliferation of *Weltanschauungen*, of world views... The freedom given to so many cultures and *Weltanschauungen* has belied the very ideal of a transparent society".

66. See Z. BAUMAN, *Life in Fragments. Essays in Postmodern Morality*, Oxford, Blackwell, 1995, p. 89: "The hub of postmodern life strategy is not identity building but the avoidance of being fixed"; A. GIDDENS, (n. 96): "Established ways of doing things – in matters of medicine, political allegiance, diet, sexuality, and many others – may in various contexts be persisted with. Yet it is difficult not to be conscious that any lifestyle pattern – no matter how traditional – is only one among other possible forms of life" (p. 96).

Vattimo puts it as follows: "The increase in possible information of the myriad forms of reality makes it increasingly difficult to conceive of a single reality. It may be that in the world of mass media a 'prophecy' of Nietzsche's is fulfilled: in the end the true world becomes a fable"[67].

(iii) Another fact that also accounts for the decentering attitude of postmodernity (or reflexive modernity[68]) is the crisis in European colonialism after the 1939-45 world war. Asian and African colonized countries shook off the yoke of foreign dominance; this enfranchisement dealt a serious blow to the European self-image. The Europeans were used to thinking of themselves as the champions who had brought 'higher' civilization to other parts of the world. But in the course of the revolts of the colonies, it dawned on many of them that their civilizing mission had only been successful through the use of force and coercion[69]. The recognition of the otherness of the 'other' – other nations and peoples with their own traditions and ways of life – posed a challenge to many intellectuals. At any rate, the new situation put an end to the unquestioned western dream of moulding the whole world into a pattern with just one center of universal significance[70].

3. *The End of the Grand Stories: Two Versions*

a) Jean-François Lyotard

The phrase 'the end of the grand stories' was coined by Jean-François Lyotard. By this, he means that we are witnessing the dissolution of those universal principles that the organic intellectuals of modernity had advanced as authoritative rules for insuring the rational improvement of social organization and individual conduct under the leadership of the modern, centralized state. Without the firm will to promote these principles, no

---

67. G. VATTIMO (n. 65), p. 7.

68. A. Giddens prefers this term.

69. "The so-called 'primitive' peoples colonized by Europe in the good and rightful name of 'superior' and more evolved civilization have rebelled, making a unilinear and centralized history *de facto* problematic. The European modern) ideal of humanity has been revealed as one ideal amongst others, not necessarily worse, but unable, without, violence, to obtain as the true essence of all men". See G. VATTIMO (n. 65), p. 5. See also A. GIDDENS (n. 10), pp. 52-53.

70. See also Z. BAUMAN, (n. 6), pp. 35-36: "As the postmodern perspective, like its predecessors, has been developed within the western world, acceptance of plurality of sovereignties means first and foremost the surrender of the (diachronically and synchronically) dominant position of the west. What has been assumed to be the most accomplished ... (indeed, the only formation of universal significance) throughout the modern era – has been reduced now to the status of a mere one among the many".

modern government could be given legitimacy or credit for its practice of nation-building and the administration of colonies. The grand story of state-steered advance had been introduced to mobilize the social forces around the implementation of this program. Lyotard finds the ideologically backed imposition of a standard model of social engineering defective and dated mainly for two reasons. First, it leads to the rise of totalitarian states, and second, its own logic is bound to eventually block the steady progress it promises, since real progress in knowledge rests on the release of research programs from centralized authorities.

At this juncture, I would like to point to a certain unevenness in Lyotard's search for an alternative to the grand narratives. Then, I shall proceed to examine the extent to which this unevenness has been overcome by sociologists like Giddens and Bauman in their explanations of the same state of affairs. But first, a few words about the unevenness.

In his book *La condition postmoderne* (1979), Lyotard takes it for granted that, because of their pragmatism and focus on performative practice, postmodern scientists feel no longer the need to look for a speculative legitimation of what they are doing. The foreseeable development of knowledge is such that telematics, computers, and electronic networks are increasingly going to push the many heterogeneous fields of research to develop their own specialized courses and language games. This development would make encompassing knowledge and expertise – as modern organic intellectuals still claimed to possess – neither possible nor desirable anymore. The release of specialties from monolithic centers of overall control acts as the new 'law' of history. This move coincides with the fall of metaphysics and the crisis of the university institution, which in the past relied on metaphysical thinking[71]. Enterprises grow more diversified, and along with them, the web of social organization is drawn into processes of complexification. Instead of believing in the unidirectional mobilizing power of a "grand narrative, such as the dialectics of Spirit, the hermeneutics of meaning, the emancipation of the rational or working subject, or of the creation of wealth"[72], postmoderns find themselves living in an ever-changing social whole, which as soon as it found its self-regulative equilibrium, would be thrown off balance again because of some unexpected performative move in one of the subsystems. In line with other postmodern philosophers, Lyotard

---

71. J.-F. LYOTARD (n. 63), p. xxiv: "Simplifying to the extreme, I define *postmodern* as incredulity toward metanarratives... To the obsolescence of the metanarrative apparatus of legitimation corresponds, most notably, the crisis of metaphysical philosophy and of the university institution which in the past relied on it".

72. *Ibid.*

proclaims, on the one hand, the death of the human agent, in order to give prevalence to a systems theory in which the interacting potential of the various subsystems are expected to keep the entire system in balance. On the other hand, he refuses to explain the transformations of the system in cybernetic terms, for to accept some encompassing steering mechanism would mitigate against the heterogeneous developments of the subsystems. This very heterogeneity accounts for both deregulative effects and non-unidirectional creations of novelty.

These considerations, however, exhibit only one side of the coin, notably the description of the postmodern persons' incredulity towards metanarratives, whose disintegration they precipitate through the diversity and heterogeneity of the postmodern performances. The other side of the coin is given in Lyotard's considerations about the non-presentable character of the idea of the 'sublime'[73], whose absolute but vacant sanctuary should be shielded against profanation. As will be depicted in greater detail below, the 'unpresentable' issues a warning against the rise of new totalizing practices, though one is prone to think that such practices can never occur again after the evaporation of the grand stories. And this points to an unevenness in Lyotard's analysis of the postmodern condition.

For Lyotard, the sublime is a noumenal idea with regulative content, but it can never be rendered present in empirical representations. The experience of the sublime, in terms of the majestic void, throws one off balance because of its entirely unpresentable character; it forbids any attempt at establishing a totalizing discourse, one disrespectful of alterity. Lyotard's insistence on "saving the honor of the name" is well-known[74]. What may cause some surprise, however, is his persistence in inculcating this message repeatedly into his contemporary readers. It would seem then that, in his estimation, even the postmodern persons, who presumably have already lost the memory of the grand stories, continue

73. Lyotard borrrows this notion from Kant, but fills it with connotations taken from our contemporary situation.

74. J.-F. LYOTARD (n. 17), pp. 15-16: "It should be made clear that it is not up to us to *provide reality*, but to invent allusions to what is conceivable but not representable. And this task should not lead us to expect the slightest reconciliation between 'language games'. Kant, in naming them the faculties, knew that they are separated by an abyss and that only a transcendental illusion (Hegel's) can hope to totalize them into a real unity. But he knew that the price of this illusion is terror. The nineteenth and twentieth centuries have given us our fill of terror. We have paid dearly for our nostalgia for the all and the one, for a reconciliation of the concept and the sensible, for a transparent and communicable experience. Beneath the general demand for relaxation and appeasement, we hear murmurings of desire to reinstitute terror and fulfill the phantasm of taking possession of reality. The answer is this: war on totality. Let us attest to the unpresentable; let us activate the 'differends' and save the honor of the name".

to be tempted to engage in a battle of all against all, to claim the superiority of their own particular discourse over all other equally defensible discourses. In other words, a relapse into the old sins of modernity, where grand narratives have, more often than not, led to the installment of a rule of terror, is never far off. Or could it be that Lyotard, by his insistence on testifying to the sublime, has set himself the task of educating his pragmatic contemporaries to adopt a more reflective mind-set, in the conviction that only a reflective mind will, in the long run, be able to avoid the pitfalls of hegemonic thinking? Striking, at any rate, is his vivid interest in Kant's 'reflective judgement'. Yet his dealing with Kant has not only encouraged him to acknowledge the existence of an unfathomable noumenal ground beyond empirical reality, it also has led him to suggest that, instead of qualifying this ground as ungraspable 'ultimate unity' (as Kant still did), one would do better to refer to it in terms of 'ultimate heterogeneity'. The majestic void to which Lyotard wishes to bear witness takes on the form of an abysmal fountain-head, pregnant with alterity, from which all things flow in a rhythm of proliferating differentiation.

For Lyotard, difference, alterity, and heterogeneity constitute the all-pervasive milieu that gives birth to a non-unidirectional development of history. Incessant meandering is presented as the optimum ideal to live by, besides being the actual attitude shown by the intellectuals of advanced modernity. At the same time, however, there constantly seems to lurk the danger of retrogressing to homogeneous patterns of thinking, and hence to outbursts of intolerance. Thus, the dissident and the deviant, the transgressor of the rules, is staged as the new hero, whereas those who wager on mastering the whimsical twists of history by forcing them into the 'story line' of a straight finality geared towards the predictable future, are blamed for offering deceptive solutions. The question, however, is whether Lyotard's portrayal of these two opposing options is cogent or not. Some sociologists opine that Lyotard is more successful in exposing his readers to the strange sphere of virtual reality, than in advancing a tangible strategy to meet the problems of today's world. Anthony Giddens, to whom I now turn, offers a different account of the 'end of the grand narratives'.

b) Anthony Giddens

This author first points out that some of the debates on postmodernity "concentrate mainly upon institutional transformations" caused by our moving from a system based upon the production of material goods to one giving centrality to the ever new spreading of telematic information. But then, when philosophers set out to tackle this issue, they naturally tend to approach it from the standpoint of epistemology[75]. This helps them jump to the conclusion that, parallel to the replacement of heavy industries by electronics, substantial grounding must give way to a decentered dance of floating signs. But is this all one has to say about the matter? Giddens prefers to take another standpoint: "the disorientation which expresses itself in the feeling that systematic knowledge about social organization cannot be obtained,... results primarily from the sense many of us have of being caught up in a universe of events we do not fully understand, and which seems in large part outside of our control"[76].

What Giddens finds astonishing about modernity is that, in spite of its programmed critique of tradition, it continued for a long time to hold on to a disguised belief in providential guidance. The religious conviction, typical of Judaeo-Christianity, that God directs human history towards a definite end, had only been reshaped, but not displaced. Molded in a secularized form, providentialism made its most clear reappearance in the ideology of progress, modernity's favorite 'story line'[77]. Thus, the postmodern incredulity toward grand stories is nothing else but modernity's emancipation from tradition – carried out, this time, to the extreme. That is why Giddens prefers to characterize the postmodern phenomenon as a 'consequence of modernity'. More precisely, it is modernity that has come of age, modernity having acquired reflexive knowledge about the intrinsic radicalism of its own program. Engulfed in a process of erosion by postmodern reflexive thought, providentialism, the most long-lasting remnant of the old religious world view, had to collapse eventually, even

75. A. GIDDENS (n. 10), p. 2: "As he [Lyotard] represents it, post-modernity refers to a shift away from attempts to ground epistemology and from faith in humanly engineered progress. The condition of post-modernity is distinguished by an evaporating of the 'grand narrative' – the overarching 'story line' by means of which we are placed in history as beings having a definite past and a predictable future. The post-modern outlook sees a plurality of heterogeneous claims to knowledge, in which science does not have a privileged place".

76. *Ibid.*, pp. 2-3

77. *Ibid.*, p. 48: "Enlightenment thought, and Western culture in general, emerged from a religious context which emphasised teleology and the achievement of God's grace. Divine providence had long been a guiding idea of Christian thought. Without these preceding orientations, the Enlightenment would scarcely have been possible in the first place. It is in no way surprising that the advocacy of unfettered reason only reshaped the ideas of the providential, rather than displacing it. One type of certainty (divine law) was replaced by another (the certainty of our senses, of empirical observation), and divine providence was replaced by providential progress. Moreover, the providential idea of reason coincided with the rise of European dominance over the rest of the world".

in its secularized version. And this is what western civilization is experiencing now at large. True, some will assess this breakdown as a precipitation into nihilism, echoing hereby, with mixed feelings of dread and joy, Nietzsche's message of the death of God. Yet as Giddens points out: "the seeds of nihilism were there in Enlightenment thought from the beginning. If the sphere of reason is wholly unfettered, no knowledge can rest upon an unquestioned foundation, because even the most firmly held notions can only be regarded as valid 'in principle' or 'until further notice'"[78].

It is an actual paradox that the more unreservedly had rational thought dared to strip away the residues of tradition, the more it also had to ponder not only its own strengths and effectiveness but also its in-built limitations. Raised to independence, and left to its own, rational thought has been forced to increasingly engage in methodical doubt and to adopt scrupulous self-scrutiny as one of its basic principles. For to the extent that scientists have made huge advances in extracting accurate knowledge, they also felt the need to ask themselves critical questions, first, about the alleged reach and reliability of their scientific techniques at hand. They realize that a theory holds only until the moment it is falsified. Second, and more importantly, they have to consider the range of conceivable and unintended (minimal or massive) negative side-effects that unavoidably accompany even the most brilliant scientific achievements. No wonder then that this double-edged position ushers in a schizophrenic mentality: the unfettered human mind finds itself entangled in a web of riddles of which there are no easy solutions. Giddens puts it as follows: "modernity turns out to be enigmatic at its core, and there seems no way in which this enigma can be 'overcome.' We are left with questions where once there appeared to be answers, and... it is not only philosophers who realise this. A general awareness of the phenomenon filters into anxieties which press in on everyone"[79].

At this juncture, Giddens points out that the evaporation of the grand stories creates also new chances for the long-term survival of humanity. The so-called postmodern mood is half-described when being portrayed only in terms of resignation, as if the present generation's concern would consist only in the willingness to put up with every newly-emerging enigma beyond the reach of our mastery. Fortunately, there is also a positive aspect to the contemporary propensity to make progressive humanity assume a 'low profile', for owing to this propensity, people come to

78. *Ibid.*, pp. 48-49.
79. *Ibid.*, p. 49.

realize more and more that, first, they are living in a society with manufactured risks, and second, given this situation, a new ethics is required
which would make us attentive to the avoidance, as far as possible, of
risks that are our own making. For these ideas, Giddens refers to two
authors, namely, Ulrich Beck and Hans Jonas[80].

Ulrich Beck published an influential book on the *Society of Risk*, in
which he made it clear that our societies increasingly become risk-pro-
ducing, risk-monitoring, and risk-managing societies. Unlike Enlightenment thinking, which prided itself in its ability to increase knowledge
and to come to grips with the chaotic elements in nature, contemporary
ethicists have begun to call attention to the fact that our technical interventions in nature generate risks and damages that are affecting already
the very fabric of human life, but whose long-range effects cannot be
properly assessed. Especially among those who are concerned about the
well-being of the future generations, this situation breeds anxieties.
Things appear to get out of control precisely because of the expansion of
a production apparatus whose steady growth was deemed indispensable
for catering to the needs of the consumer society. The more the production apparatus expands in time and space, the riskier are the changes it
introduces into the balance of nature and the human community.

While these changes were still taken for granted in the hey-days of
modernity, serious warnings are now being issued: it appears that we
have definitely gone too far, and in the future, our primary tasks will
consist in clearing up the mess, in "seeking an exit from the havoc perpetrated by our actions of yesterday". The disorders we have been generating in performing our civilizing task now "reverberate far and wide;
their distant effects hit back as new dangers, new problems and thus
new tasks... We now begin to calculate the dangers of climatic change
caused by pollution, or of the depletion of soil and water supplies caused
by ever specialised fertilisers and insecticides"[81]. But still more items
can be listed: the depletion of the ozone-layer owing to the yearly addition
of hundreds of thousand of new vehicles to those already in circulation,
road accidents as a major source of mortality and disability, cancers
resulting from environmental factors, health risks arising from the 'ratio-
nalized' food industry, or the unforeseeable social effects of genetic
engineering on the coming generations, to mention a few of them. At any
rate, it is easy to understand that, in practice, the spreading awareness of

---

80. U. BECK, *The Risk Society*, London, Sage, 1992; H. JONAS, *The Imperative of
Responsibility*, Chicago, University of Chicago Press, 1984.
81. Z. BAUMAN (n. 66), p. 279.

manufactured risks has served as an eye-opener, encouraging people to become suspicious of modernity's grand story of steady progress. It has begun to dawn upon many of our contemporaries that our self-produced uncertainties "cannot be dealt with by age-old remedies; neither do they respond to the Enlightenment prescription of more knowledge, more control. Put more accurately, the sorts of reactions they might evoke today are often as much about *damage control* and *repair* as about an endless process of increasing mastery"[82].

Damage control, repair, and damage prevention have come to figure recently in the agenda of ethics. No wonder then that, in this context, the catchword in ethics is responsibility – for ourselves and for the future generations. Are we not getting frightening images of apocalyptic destruction from the distant future? Do we dare face up to the accelerating rhythm with which we are exhausting the quality of the biosphere? It is here that one sees the importance of Hans Jonas' methodological approach. The first duty of an ethics of responsibility, says Jonas, is "visualising the long-range effects of technological enterprise". Furthermore, he underlines that such an ethics must be guided by a "heuristic of fear", and by the "principle of uncertainty". This implies that, even when the ethical discussion would show that the argument of the pessimists and the optimists are finely balanced, "the prophecy of doom is to be given greater heed than the prophecy of bliss". To sum up his method, Jonas makes use of an updated – though far from logically self-evident – version of Kant's categorical imperative: "Act so that the effects of your action are compatible with the permanence of genuine human life". *If in doubt* – Jonas implies – *do not do it.* "Do not magnify or multiply the risk more than unavoidable; err, if at all, on the side of caution"[83].

To summarize this section: In his analysis of the postmodern aversion to 'grand stories,' Lyotard has focused mainly on the decentering trend in knowledge production, convinced as he is that humanity's happiness will grow to the extent that centralized agencies will give up their dominant control. Real progress in knowledge is possible only under the condition that specializing functions were to be given the freedom to proliferate. Giddens and Bauman give a different account; they point out that not even the maturation of differentiated knowledge is a guarantee of the survival of humankind on earth. What is needed then is an ethics of damage control and damage prevention. In their outlook, it is the awareness of manufactured risks and uncertainties – much more than the

82. A. GIDDENS (n. 54), p. 4.
83. Z. BAUMAN (n. 66), p. 280, who quotes from Jonas' work.

decentering of knowledge – which has undermined the success story of steady progress. The difference of the two assessments is evident, and this difference also comes to bear on one's understanding of the phenomenon of globalization.

4. Globalization and Cultural Change: A Threefold Reading

In this section, I shall examine the multilayered phenomenon of globalization, which is at the same time closely linked to processes of cultural change and the reinvention of local cultures. To treat this issue as exhaustively as possible, I shall give first a postmodern reading of it in the style of Lyotard and Vattimo. This will be followed by a reading of culture from the standpoint of the world system (Wallerstein). Finally, the section will expound Giddens' concept of the reflexive re-appropriation of traditions in the context of a world community that consciously faces up to manufactured risks. This threefold reading will uncover three seemingly unrelated foci, which on closer inspection, however, appear to be simultaneously present in the picture of the world as a global village.

a) Postmodern Mobility and the Globalization of Culture

As already stated, the transition from the modern to the postmodern mind lies in the awareness of the rapidity with which various specialized functions in society are growing apart, a fragmentation that commenced already in the hey-days of modernity. To typify this trend, Michael Walzer has coined the phrase "Liberalism is a world of walls, and each wall creates a new liberty"[84]. In modern times, this fragmentation had still been checked by counteracting tendencies such as state regulations and nation-bound legal structures. Yet postmodernity is weary of state-intervention, and wagers on mobile, ever-changing interactions between freely developing specializations across the borders of states and beyond regional alliances. It believes, moreover, that these interactions are to a great extent self-regulative and no longer directed to, or steered by, just one single model of what the good society should look like. Especially after the collapse of the East bloc, Marxism is ridiculed as reactionary because of its "desire for reproducing an undifferentiated organic whole"[85]. In what follows, I shall list some of the most prominent features of this development.

---

84. M. WALZER, *Liberalism and the Art of Separation*. in *PoT* 12 (1984) 315-330, p. 315.
85. M. SHAPIRO, *Reading the Postmodern Polity*, Minneapolis, University of Minnesota Press, 1992, p. 95.

(i) Postmodern mobility hinges on the growth and spread of mass media and 'immaterial' means of communication: electronically transmitted codes (fax, E-mail) and images (television). This leads to a time-space compression and to a dislocation of stable places, local habits, and forms of community life, in spite of the supposed lasting endurance (*'longue durée'*) of these forms. Advertising in view of consumption begins to fill the multilayered space of each one's life-world[86]. The media create desires and mimetic personalities. "Economists increasingly understand that in their new science it was not that useful things were desired, but that desired things were useful"[87].

(ii) The implication of this change in emphasis is clear: the once workable distinction between infrastructure (realm of production) and superstructure (realm of ideas, realm of culture) has begun to become nebulous. For the stylized commodities that are brought on the market as desirable things bear in their very shape and appearance the characteristics of the glamorous new culture. Postmodern attractive products perform the role of ambassadors of the ultra-developed world's refined consumer taste. Their production no longer needs to get the blessings of (local) organic intellectuals, who in their role as cultural *legislators*, used to make out what was and what was not in line with the 'objective hierarchy' of cultural values. From now on, it is the market which sets the standards for culture. But this market "recognizes no cultural hierarchy except the one of sellability; best-seller lists are the only recognized orders of cultural preference – and, indeed, the only criteria of excellence"[88]. What in fact has happened is that the cultural 'excellence' dictated by the market is making its inroads everywhere, and this globalization is carried out and publicized by the very circulation of fashionable commodities, which are offered to the buyers' mimetic desires. Whoever is going to buy the advertised brand-new products, is supposedly a man or

86. Hannerz gives the following striking example: "Switch on a television set in Kafanchan (a middle-sized, multi-ethnic, polyglot railroad junction town in Nigeria) at night, and you may see newscasts in English and Hausa, an old episode of *Charlie's Angels*, a concert by Hausa drummers, commercials for detergents, and bicycles, and a paid announcement of a funeral to take place in the nearest big city, where the TV station is located. The notion of funeral commercials struck me as an innovation at first, but obviously it is an extension of the concepts of full-page advertisements wealthy Nigerians take out in their daily newspapers to announce the burials of their loved ones. Death and conspicuous consumption often go together in Nigeria". U. HANNERZ, *Cultural Complexity: Studies in the Social Organization of Meaning*, New York, Columbia University Press, 1992, p. 24.

87. A. ORLÉAN, *Money and Mimetic Speculation*, in P. DUMOUCHAL (ed.), *Violence and Truth: On the Work of René Girard*, London, Athlone Press, 1988, p. 102; quoted in M. SHAPIRO (n. 85), p. 59.

88. Z. BAUMAN (n. 66), p. 237.

woman of taste and culture[89]. Flexibility and diversity, however, remain
the rules of the game. Contrary to the critical analysis organic intellectuals used to make in the 1950s, the advent of market domination over
culture has not led to the prognosticated 'mass culture' or 'cultural uniformity'. It rather turns out that the "cultural market seems to thrive on
cultural diversity and rapid succession of cultural fashions"[90].

(iii) Postmodern mobility is the motor behind the speed-up of the
process of globalization, which started in the second half of the 20th century. The various parts of the world are increasingly drawn into a tighter
configuration "through the increasing volume and rapidity of the flows
of money, goods, people, information, technology, and images"[91], to
form just 'one global village'. But again, one would be mistaken to
suppose that the process of globalization will end up in homogenization.
As David Harvey has pointed out, the shift away from modern Fordism
(highly centralized production systems) to postmodern flexible systems
of accumulation, contributed in fact to a profitable practice of giving
greater prominence to local places. This seems to go against the grain of
the logic of time-space compression. "The less important the spatial barriers, the greater the sensitivity of capital to the variations of place, and
the greater the incentive for places to be differentiated in ways attractive
to capital"[92]. What this flexible approach is all about is clearly shown
in the recent multinational conglomeration of enterprises: "A sports car
is financed in Japan, drawn up in Italy and constructed in Indiana (USA),
in Mexico, and in France; it contains the most recent electronic components developed in New Jersey and constructed in Japan... Which of

---

89. In a sense this constitutes a move beyond the Marxian concept of fetishism, which
attributed a fascination to commodities because of their market or surplus value (hereby
making abstraction of their use value, an abstraction which was made possible by the
abstract notions of money and labor). The new 'fetishism' in question is rather a cultural
fetishism, in so far as along with the marketed products also a specific type of culture
(and culture politics) is being sold and bought. See R. PEET, *World Capitalism and the
Destruction of Regional Cultures*, p. 194: "Indeed, the consumption of this working elite
has gone far beyond their physical need: this means that sophisticated persuasive advertising devices had to be invented to make consumers 'need' products in one year that
were unknown to them a few years ago. It meant *refocussing culture* on the consumption
of commodities – a new meaning adhered to commodity fetishism, the more conventional
sense of a perverse fascination with buying and owning objects". (italics mine). See also
R. LEE, *Modernization, Postmodernism and the Third World*, in *CS* 42 (1994) 1-63,
pp. 28-29: "The penetration of the cultural domain by advanced capitalism has unveiled
the workings of the postmodern commodity form as an aspect of the culture industry".
90. Z. BAUMAN (n. 66), p. 237.
91. M. FEATHERSTONE, *Undoing Culture: Globalization, Postmodernity and Identity*,
London-Thousand Oaks-New Delhi, Sage Publications, 1995, p. 81.
92. D. HARVEY (n. 60), pp. 295-296.

those products is a US one? Which one is not? How are we to decide? And is the answer really important?"[93]. A new world-wide division of labor – in terms of spatial repartitioning – is coming off the ground: "American airlines' tickets originate from the Bermudas, Swissair's accounting is done in Bombay"[94].

(iv) Authors who are specialized in the study of cultural change, begin to raise the question as to the extent to which local cultures, especially those in the 'Third World,' will be able to withstand their absorption into the commodification of culture which, under the impact of flexible economic systems, is going to grow global. Facing up to this question, most of them repel the prospect of a 'McDonaldization' of cultures – the uniform spread of fast-food chains and amusement theme parks around the world (Disneyland everywhere!). They instead expect the rise, all over the globe, of specific types of 'creolization' in which the particular (local culture) and the universal (the new international culture) in one way or the other will have come to merge[95]. This is an interesting approach, but still more fascinating would be an interpretive model inspired by an analysis of the postmodern condition. This is what Raymond Lee has successfully done in his essay, *Modernization, Postmodernism and the Third World*. (1) Lee, first of all, welcomes the fact that globalization has enabled Western entrepreneurs, through their dealings with Asian colleagues, to appreciate better the latter's personalities without labeling them as exotic. "The decline of the exotic other through globalization is a contributing factor to the gradual fading of Orientalist ethnography"[96]. Especially in various parts of Asia, people have begun to feel that they need not be westernized in order to reach a higher, or less 'barbaric', level of humanity. Orientalism, once used by colonial powers to remind the subdued of their cultural inferiority, is increasingly rejected since more and more intellectuals in the so-called Third World are convinced that, culturally speaking, they are at least 'equal' to those of the First World, whose political power is manifestly in decline[97]. (2) Lee goes on

---

93. R. REICH, *L'économie mondialisée*, Paris, Dunod, 1993, p. 103, quoted in F. HOUTART, *The World-Encompassment of the Economy*, in *CQ* 68 (1993-94) 2-10, p. 8.

94. *Ibid.*, p. 113.

95. U. HANNERZ (n. 86), p. 261.

96. R. LEE (n. 89), p. 21. The idea that 'Orientalism is fundamentally a political doctrine willed over the Orient because the Orient was weaker than the West' was launched by E. Said. See E. SAID, *Orientalism*, New York, Vintage, 1978, p. 204.

97. R. LEE (n. 89), p. 3: "There is hope that the 21st century will be recognized as the Asian century, particularly with the opening up of China in the post-Mao era to create huge markets catering to more than a quarter of the world's population. If modernity in the West needs revival, it may have to look towards Asia through trade and cultural exchanges to be instructed on what a revitalized modernity entails".

to observe that in postmodernity, according to Derrida and Baudrillard, the signifiers have been freed from the fixed meaning determined by their referents. He applies this to the global market situation: "The signifiers of the culture industry have no fixed referents. They float freely by virtue of their indeterminate exchange-values and are easily traded on the world market of leisure"[98]. From this, he concludes that the 'exchange signs' or 'symbolic codes' conveyed by the commodities no longer refer strictly to things typical of First-World culture and its hegemonic claims. It would be more accurate to state that the market products, presented as desirable, simply speak the language of the global world community, and this means that their signifying system can also be appropriated from, and harmonized with, an Asian or any other background: "Hypercommodification takes on local hues. This implies that the introduction and spread of Western commodity forms in the developing countries can be successful when they are culturally assimilated to local conditions"[99]. (3) Lee hereby refers to the new tigers of South-East Asia (Hong Kong, Singapore, Taiwan, South Korea) where this new synthesis between western high-technology and a revitalized local culture has taken place. Here, the local culture (Confucian frugality and self-control) has proven itself capable of assimilating western technology into its own layers of traditional meaning[100], and this is due to the rapidity with which modern technologies and labor-intensive production systems have been introduced. Sensualism, playfulness, and hedonism, which are easily transmitted through technology, could be kept within limits, checked as they were by traditional values. (4) When similar attempts at combining the culture of commodification with a revivification of the traditional lifeworld, will have proven successful also in other Asian countries and in the world community at large, then it will become evident that the 'global village' will be characterized by diversity. Globalization by no means implies homogeneity[101].

98. *Ibid.*, p. 29. Cf. also M. SHAPIRO (n. 85), pp. 56-60.
99. R. LEE (n. 89), p. 33.
100. *Ibid.*, p. 30: "It is because of the deep sedimentation of non-Western traditionalisms, that simulated modernity is mediated by layers of traditional meaning which may or may not be antithetical to it".
101. *Ibid.*, p. 37: "The simulation of modernity is however a complicated process that hinges on glocalization where the global is tailored to the local and vice versa. The outcome is not a simple local adaptation of the modernity paradigm, but possibly a revivification of traditional lifeworlds to alter modernity beyond its original image. Although the simulation of modernity may be considered a fateful reproduction of Western modernity, the power of traditionalisms in the developing world suggests that there can be no one modernity, and thereby exposes the falsity of *a* Third World modernization". See also M. FEATHERSTONE (n. 91), p. 91: "These 'third' cultures do not simply reflect American

b) Globalization and Culture Politics in the Context of the World-System

The alliance of postmodern sign exchanges and marketing has been forcefully criticized by Frederic Jameson and David Harvey, because this alliance creates a sphere of aesthetization which averts one's attention from the realities of political economy and the circumstances of global power. For these authors postmodernism is the cultural expression, if not the cultural logic, of late, or global consumer capitalism, which developed from modern monopoly capitalism and its tactics of profit-making and capital-accumulation. But instead of focusing on these hard facts, and how they come to bear on, and are tied to, the political-economic power constellations of the World-System, postmodern philosophers prefer to exalt the versatile meanderings of the system, and to take delight in the playful exchange of signs on the surface. Or as Harvey puts it: "Postmodernism has us accepting the reifications and partitionings, actually celebrating the activity of masking and cover-up, all the fetishisms of locality, place, or social grouping, while denying that kind of meta-theory which can grasp the political-economic processes (money flows, international divisions of labour, financial markets, and the like) that are becoming ever more universalizing in their depth, intensity, reach, and power over daily life... Meta-theory cannot be dispensed with. The postmodernists simply push it underground, where it continues to function as 'now unconscious effectivity'"[102].

Indeed, to the extent that, in postmodernity, surface and mirror effects have taken the place of substance, so too aesthetics has replaced ethics. This explains why the utopian grand stories, with their ethical impact and guilt-impressing character, are apparently gone. Yet this does not entirely mean the end of all-encompassing structures. In fact, as neo-marxist authors emphasize, we are left with an all-pervading fluidity of profit calculation, whose glamorous effects – a mixture of fiction and reality – are decidedly more discernible than the underlying hard-core constellations. Still, glitter on the surface, too, exerts power, especially when the power-centers from which the glitter emanates are difficult to identify. Moreover, the will to combat the enthrallment of the mirror palace has been enfeebled because of an astutely propagated reversal of ethical categories. Engineers of economic policies make people believe

---

values; their relative autonomy and global frame of reference necessitates that they take into account the particularities of local cultures and adopt organizational cultural practices which are flexible enough to facilitate this".

102. D. HARVEY (n. 60), pp. 116-117; he hereby refers to F. JAMESON, *Postmodernism, or the Cultural Logic of Late Capitalism*, in *NLR* 146 (1984) 53-93.

that those attitudes and actions that make the free market prosper, are to
be called virtues, whereas the things that thwart the market's expansion
are stigmatized as vices[103]. Yet in spite of this dissimulation, the 'total
market', as the globalization is called, is in its postmodern form, more
perhaps than in the days of classical national economies, the deity – or
the chance/fatality – which decides upon 'salvation' or 'damnation', not
just of individuals and social classes, but of entire nations and sub-con-
tinents. The adaptable game of profit enhancement, with its free-floating
codes and electronically steered mobility, is so to speak omnipresent,
omnipotent, and infinite in inventiveness. Thanks to the electronic media
of communication and to the dismantlement of state power, it meets no
more borders that restrict the inroads of its empire. It creates at will jobs
and unemployment, wealth and poverty, ordered life and crime, when
and where it wishes. It acts, thus, as a dark providence whose decisions
are not to be questioned.

The concealment of what is really going on in terms of power struggles has intrigued always the marxist schools of cultural studies[104]. In his
article, *Culture as the ideological battleground of the modern world-system*, Immanuel Wallerstein delves into the 'culture politics' promoted by
modern states, both taken in themselves as separate entities and in their
connections with the shifting interstate system. He examines how these
politics are intertwined with the dealings of the capitalist world-economy. Just as Bauman had already done[105], Wallerstein identifies culture
with modern, rational culture. He then examines, as his particular topic,
the ideological use that has been made – and is still being made – of this
notion, especially when "culture" gets globalized along with the development, without frontiers, of the capitalist world-economy. He, thus,
starts from the assumption that, to the extent that the spread of modern
culture goes hand in hand with the expansion of the capitalist world-system, it also must display, as well as conceal, the inherent contradictions
of the latter. Some of these contradictions and their cultural impact will
be examined more below. Suffice it to say that all of them revolve around
the tension between universality, peaceful coexistence, and homogeneity,
on the one hand, and inequality (unequal division of labor) and domination (master-servant relations), on the other.

The study of the world-system focuses on the link between inter-state
systems and the increase of capital on a world-scale. In Wallerstein's

---

103. F. HINKELAMMERT, *Capitalisme sans alternatives?* in *AS* 3 (1994) 43-63, p. 46.
104. A. MILNER, *Contemporary Cultural Theory: An Introduction,* London, UCL Press,
1994, p. 68.
105. Z. BAUMAN (n. 6), pp. 10-13.

analysis, "the rise and fall of the inter-state system is both the main cause and effect of the endless accumulation of capital"[106]. This means, in the first instance, that capitalism is an encompassing organization that allows various state systems to contribute to the endless accumulation of capital: "capitalism has been able to flourish precisely because the world-economy has had between its bounds not one but a multiplicity of political systems"[107]. 'Endless' capital accumulation is thus presented as the commonly shared, harmonious ideal beyond the divide of political systems. But this harmonious ideal fades away as soon as the aspect of competition comes in; for in view of upholding their competitive position on the world-market, states have to affirm and defend their separate dominions: "At the same time, the tendency of capitalist groups to mobilize their respective states in order to enhance their competitive position in the world-economy has continually reproduced the segmentation of the political realm into separate jurisdictions"[108]. There are, thus, two interacting poles at work: (i) the 'endless' accumulation of capital, to which in principle all the nations are invited to contribute, and (ii) the reshuffle of territorial power-positions as a result of economic competition. Some authors welcome this schema because it allows them to pragmatically study the evolutionary nature of the world-system, and also to understand the role played by successive hegemonic powers in establishing a relative stability in a world that is constantly deregulated by the spiral of the 'endless' accumulation of capital[109]. Wallerstein wants to show, in addition, that the efforts at creating stability, because they are carried out by historical actors, are also accompanied by ideological rhetorics: those in power make people believe that, if they really want social stability within the nation, then the extant unequal division of labor may not be changed.

Preliminary to the treatment of the ideological question, Wallerstein wants to clear up a "long-standing intellectual confusion" in the use of the term 'culture'. He even speaks of a "deliberate" confusion because,

---

106. G. ARRIGHI (n. 8), p. 32.

107. I. WALLERSTEIN, *The Modern World System, I, Capitalist Agriculture and the Origins of the European World-Economy in the Sixteenth Century*, New York, Academic Press, 1974, p. 348.

108. G. ARRIGHI (n. 8), p. 32; with reference to I. WALLERSTEIN, *The Rise and Future Demise of the World Capitalist System: Concepts for Comparative Analysis*, in *CSSH* 16:4 (1974) 387-415, p. 402.

109. G. ARRIGHI (n. 8), p. 33: "Only in this way can we fully appreciate the evolutionary nature of the modern world system and the role played by successive world hegemonies in making and remaking the system in order to resolve the recurrent contradiction between an 'endless' accumulation of capital and a comparatively stable organization of political space".

in his view, it can be explained by the particular logic of the world-system[110]. He begins with two definitions of culture. There is, first, 'culture I', which stresses what a particular group has in common such as "a kind of self-awareness" and "some shared patterns of socialization, combined with a system of 'reinforcement' of their values or of prescribed behavior, and some kind of organization". Under this definition falls a variety of cultures and subcultures such as 'national culture,' 'ethnic culture', 'linguistic culture', and even the culture of 'urban intellectuals', of the 'urban poor', of 'communists', and of 'religious fundamentalists'. But besides this typification in terms of shared characteristics common to a particular group, there is also the usage of a 'culture II', which highlights the prominence of "certain characteristics within the group, as opposed to other characteristics within the same group"[111]. Here, one sees binary distinctions that point to a division within the same group rather than to their unity. An evident example of this usage is the claim of some citizens of being cultured as opposed to those who are either ignorant or mediocre; there is also the disdain with which many intellectuals and technocrats look down on the labor of manual workers, housekeepers, and ordinary people involved in the informal economy (the mind is nobler than the realm of matter).

Asking himself, then, which of the two usages allows us to draw meaningful implications about real social situations, Wallerstein comes up with a dialectically constructed answer. Taken in itself, "culture (usage I) seems not to get us very far in our historical analysis", whereas "culture" (usage II) at least arouses one's suspicion that it functions as "an ideological cover to justify the interests of some persons (obviously the upper strata) within any given 'group' or 'social system' against the interests of other persons within this same group"[112]. Yet the strategy it uses to surreptitiously justify these interests is to throw dust in the eyes of the disadvantaged groups by appealing to their feelings of commonly shared habits in whatever form this culture (I) may present itself, provided it serves the purpose of creating feelings of unanimity. At times, an appeal to 'national culture' will do; other times, an appeal to 'ethnic'

---

110. I. WALLERSTEIN, *Culture as the Ideological Battleground of the Modern World-System*, in *TCS* 7 (1990) 31-55, p. 33: "It may be that not only the discussion but the conceptual confusion are both the consequence of the historical development of this system and reflect its guiding logic". The root cause of the deliberate confusion lies in the fact that the unequal division of labor, which is needed for the 'endless' accumulation of capital, is constantly played down in the current definition of culture and cultures (cultural groups are defined as a 'we' without internal class division).
111. I. WALLERSTEIN (n. 110), pp. 32-33.
112. *Ibid.*, p. 34.

or 'linguistic culture,' or even 'fundamentalist' or 'communist culture' will prove useful. This is at least the way I understand the 'deliberate' confusion Wallerstein has put his finger on.

To grasp the complex role of culture in relation to the world-system, it is important to understand, first, that culture is steered by "the idea-system of the capitalist world-economy", and second, that this idea-system is itself "the outcome of our collective attempts to come to terms with the contradictions, the ambiguities, the complexities of the socio-political realities of this particular system"[113]. Now, the strategy to come to grips with these contradictions consists in alternating the use of 'culture II' and 'culture I', realizing that 'culture I' is bent on asserting "unchanging realities amidst a world that is in fact ceaselessly changing", whereas 'culture II' intends to "justify the inequalities of the system", and "to keep them unchanging in a world which is ceaselessly threatened by change". To successfully achieve the latter – to keep the division of labor intact, even in a rapidly changing world – some backing from 'culture I' is needed, which can be brought about by making it clear to people how important one's collectively shared customs are as a moral support in the midst of change. This explains why "the very construction of culture becomes a battleground, the key ideological battleground in fact of the opposing interests within this historical system"[114].

From here, some retrospective light can be shed on Jameson's and Harvey's hint that the postmodern fragmented society, with its alleged respect for the otherness of the other, but also with its indifference to meta-theory, might in fact be entangled in the tentacles of the ideological apparatus of the world-system. Indeed, what matters to the ideologues of this system is that the unequal division of labor be kept unchanging in a world of change. And it is easier for them to obtain the consent of the masses by assuring the latter that their 'difference' and 'otherness' in terms of cultural identity (culture I) will be respected. This ideological strategy is facilitated by postmodern cultural dynamism, which encourages an endless proliferation of cultures and sub-cultures beyond any linkage that would bind them together, just as the free flow of heterogeneous language games has come to set the trend in scientific research. In this new situation, the term 'masses' sounds even obsolete since there are only fragmented islands each of which cherishes its own 'different voice', and in doing so, accelerates the drift away from what has once been the structuring metropolitan center. Has not Wittgenstein's metaphor

113. *Ibid.*, p. 38.
114. *Ibid.*, p. 39.

come true which says that language is "a maze of little streets surrounded by solitary islands of orderly and planned suburbs (...) of suburban sub-centres: visits between suburbs are rare, and no resident of the city has visited them all?"[115].

One of the good strokes of fortune that ever could have befallen the world-system is this cultural trend towards fragmentation which makes it is easy to persuade people to put up with their positions in the international division of labor. The age-old device 'divide and rule' (*divide et impera*) no longer ought to be implemented by force since no coercion is needed to keep groups of people apart, to keep people's lives fragmented. For the postmodern way of life achieves, without much ado, the dispersal of the masses, who head for their respective clubs to affirm there their cultural distinctness (usage I). So the world-system can afford to concede to the postmodern 'nomads' their illusion of cultural independence; it does not resent their pursuit for some consolation in face-to-face relations, which can be obtained in some socializing unit, whether this be a youth club, a Zen-Buddhist center, a charismatic congregation, a feminist discussion forum, a New Age group, the Society for the Conservation of National Parks, or the Society for the Revival of Indigenous Customs. In the postmodern condition, even socializing leads to fragmentation.

The logic behind this is consistent. First of all, the world-system comprehends the citizens' need to engage in a variety of cultural activities in order to construct some meaning for their lives, personally and in terms of social integration. The system understands also that cultural activities (culture I), to the extent that they are "decoupled from the structure of economic and political decision-making" (culture II), are in fact "systemically irrelevant", having no impact on the workings of the system[116]. The alleged 'autonomy' of the cultural sphere, including all the 'different voices' in it, poses no threat to the logic of capitalistic domination which, on the contrary, is thereby sustained. As Harvey puts it: "Worst of all, while it opens up a radical prospect by acknowledging the authenticity of other voices, postmodern thinking immediately shuts off those other voices from access to more universal sources of power by ghettoizing them within an opaque otherness, the specificity of this or that

115. Z. BAUMAN (n. 6), p. 38.
116. *Ibid.*, p. 38: "What has been left unexplored [in Lyotard's rendering of postmodernity] is the possibility that ... the novel freedom and independence of language games is in itself an outcome of the decoupling of the communicative sphere from the structure of political and economic domination". Because of this, "culture has become systemically irrelevant, shifting instead into the realm of social (as distinct from systemic) integration".

'language game'. It thereby disempowers those voices (of woman, ethnic and racial minorities, colonized peoples, the unemployed, youth etc.) in a world of lop-sided power relations"[117]. Considerations like this should invite one to be cautious about what some researchers report, namely, that "the world system is a source of cultural diversity", and that "the expansion of core economic and political influences promotes heterogeneity"[118]. This reported phenomenon may be correct as an observed fact, but the more crucial issue is how to interpret this fact in light of the world-system's hidden mechanisms of domination. It is here, I believe, that Wallerstein's analysis of ideological manipulations (culture II) continues to be an eye-opener.

If the cultural dynamism of postmodernity seems to have no serious impact on the hard core of political economy, the opposite is certainly not true. Political economy persists, on a world-scale, to lay down the lines for profitable conduct, and to pass judgement on culture-related matters from the vantage-point of what is functional to the world-system's consolidation. It goes without saying that these judgements are not value-free; they reflect the idea-system of capitalism. Wallerstein mentions two types of ideological reasoning which have a long history behind them; he also makes it clear that, irreconcilable as they may seem, they reinforce each other: "The two principal ideological doctrines that have emerged in the history of the capitalist world-economy – that is, universalism on the one hand, and racism, sexism on the other – are not opposites but a symbiotic pair"[119]. This symbiotic pair is used to resolve the antinomies of unity and diversity as these arise within the continuous zigzag of the system. To illustrate the workings of these two principles, six paradigmatic areas are selected in which the contradictions of capitalism are both visible and ideologically 'resolved'[120]. I limit

---

117. D. HARVEY (n. 60), p. 117.

118. U. HANNERZ (n. 86), pp. 224-225: "It is interesting to see that his (Wallerstein's) analysis leads him to regard the world system as a source of cultural diversity. Cultural differences within the system are not mere survivals from a past where cultural isolation and autonomy were greater; they can indeed be generated by pressures inherent in the world system itself. 'The expansion of core economic and political influence promotes heterogeneity'". With reference to Wallerstein, and to R. WUTHNOW, *Cultural Crises*, in A. BERGESEN (ed.), *Crises in the World-System*, Beverly Hills, Sage, 1983, p. 66.

119. I. WALLERSTEIN (n. 110), p. 29.

120. These conflictive areas are: i) pressure from the inter-state system versus coercion by the nation state; ii) modernization versus Westernization; iii) the logic of capital accumulation requires the producers to work more and to be paid less; iv) economic innovations lead to the fall and rise of nations; this poses the question of legitimation; v) capitalism is a polarizing system: tensions arise between real progress and human impoverishment; vi) limitless expansion ushers in a transition to uncertain futures: do we have to interpret this transition as 'systemic death' or as 'systemic birth'?

myself to reviewing some of them. The basic premise is that the capitalist world economy developed "by integrating a geographically vast set of production processes", thus establishing "one single division of labor" with unequal partners. What started in Europe as an interstate system that gave birth and legitimacy to a series of sovereign nation-states grew into a world-empire dictating the economic agenda for separate nations.

(i) A first tension that arises is that between 'economic' pressures coming from the international community (interstate system) and the geographically limited, 'political', coercive power of each nation-state. A nation-state has a limited range of action (particularity), while, at the same time it is compelled to act in accordance with the overarching whole (universality). Yet how can one explain and justify certain actions "nationally and internationally simultaneously?"[121] At this juncture, Wallerstein brings up the example of the Universal Declaration of Human Rights. These rights are advocated by the United Nations in universalist terms[122]. But no actual nation-state is able or willing to live up to this obligation in a universal manner for the simple reason that, within its territory, civil rights are based on citizenship (only citizens enjoy full rights). Moreover, it is no secret that 'equal rights' qualitatively vary from state to state. Nonetheless, each of those nations proclaim their loyalty to the Universal Declaration. Conclusion: the universalist ideology not only blurs these differences; it also disguises the fact that there "exists an hierarchy of states within the interstate system, and a hierarchy of citizens within each sovereign state"; it is precisely to cover up this inequality "that the ideology of universalism matters"[123]. But there is more to this. While the universalist ideology can still be seen as an incentive for climbing the ladder of the hierarchy, the other pair 'racism and sexism' sets out to justify the inequality in the division of labor. Some races, it is said, are 'genetically' or 'culturally' (usage II) better suited to perform certain tasks, while other races are not. In addition, this argument often takes on sexist overtones: "the dominant group is more rational, more disciplined, more hard-working, more self-controlled, more independent, while the dominated group is more emotional, more self-indulgent, more lazy, more artistic, more dependent"[124].

---

121. I. WALLERSTEIN (n. 110), p. 36.
122. *Ibid.*, p. 42
123. *Ibid.*, p. 43.
124. *Ibid.*, p. 44. Wallerstein adds that the sexist argument can be turned around and still justify world hierarchies: "The Moslems, it is argued, are not culturally capable of recognizing the same universal principles of man-woman relations that are said to be accepted in the Western (or Judaeo-Christian world) and from this it is said to follow that they are also capable of many other things".

(ii) The tension modernization-Westernization. Over 400 hundred years of successive expansions have transformed the capitalist world-economy "from a system located primarily in Europe to one that covers the entire globe"[125]. This raises the question whether it is enough for non-European populations to assimilate a world-wide modern culture, or it is imperative that they also westernize. The easiest way to resolve this difficulty is to declare that European culture is the universal culture. To justify this option, the ideology of universalism proves useful. It states that only western civilization is capable of evolving from pre-modern to modern culture, whereas the other cultures properly lack this capacity. The complex Eastern civilizations, e.g., are refined cultures yet incapable of evolving: "Inevitably, therefore, if one wanted to be 'modern', one had in some way to be 'Western' culturally. If not Western religion, one had to adopt Western languages. And if not Western languages, one had at the very minimum to accept Western technology"[126]. This argument can also be reinforced by its variant racism/sexism. Inferior races, which are not apt to westernize, should be educated in their native cultures to thus prepare them for specific tasks in the world economy[127]. The classic example is the former *apartheid*-regime in South Africa. Furthermore, whenever certain nations reaffirm their local traditions in a militant way, they ought to be given unequal treatment: "It becomes legitimate to treat Iran as a Pariah nation, not only because Iran uses 'terrorist' tactics in the international arena, but because Iranian women are required to wear the *chador*"[128].

(iii) Capitalism is a system based on the endless accumulation of capital; it requires workers either to get the same wages with more demanding work, or to be paid less. The question, again, is how this odd 'logic' can be marketed ideologically. Here, too, universalism will be used as a trick "in so far as the work ethic is preached as a defining centerpiece of modernity". Efficiency is presented as a value which is of universal merit and beneficial to all; consequently, all those who have not yet reached this stage of commitment will have to be blamed whether at an individual level or at the level of the hierarchy of states within the inter-state system. "Those who are worse off, therefore those who are paid

---

125. *Ibid.*, p. 36.
126. *Ibid.*, p. 45.
127. *Ibid.*, p. 45: "At the very same time that the universalist ideologues were preaching the merits of Westernization or 'assimilation', they were also (or others were also) preaching the eternal existence and virtue of difference... as a justification of educating various groups in their separate 'cultures' and hence preparing them for different tasks in the single economy".
128. *Ibid.*, p. 46.

less, are in this position because they merit it"[129]. Racism and sexism reinforce the universalist theme. Those at the lower scale (non-whites and women) are easily identifiable culturally. They are paid less because they work less, and they work less because there is something in their biology or 'culture' which conflicts with the work ethos. In so far as they cultivate their separateness as 'cultural groups', the assessment is only confirmed.

I have presented some of Wallerstein's case studies to make his point clear. His concern is the social consequences of the inbuilt unequal division of labor on which the capitalist system thrives and which capitalism seeks to justify through ideological contentions blended with cultural themes (racism, sexism). But equally important are his concluding remarks, which assert that the development programs set up to combat poverty in the Third World, as well as the socialist ideals that in practice were used to bolster these programs, apparently have not been able to break away from the basic patterns of the world-system: modernization and assimilation. Indeed, the developing countries have been encouraged to embark on the journey of modernization[130], and in order to reach this goal, they have been granted funds and investments from world financial institutions. But hardly has the question been raised whether or not modernization, in as far as it is entrapped in the ideology of unlimited progress, is as such a desirable good. The same is true for the 'anti-systemic movements' (marxism, socialism), which have wagered on transforming the capitalist system. Leftist militants have spent a lot of energy on the implementation of a more equitable distribution of wealth, without questioning the premises on which the world-system rests: the success story of science and the assimilation of all peoples into the modern way of life. Only from the 'cultural revolution of 1968' onward, Wallerstein adds, the new movements, or at least some of them, "have begun to evince doubts as to the utility, the reasonableness of 'science' and 'assimilation' as social objectives. These doubts have been expressed in different forms. The green movements, the countercultural movements have raised questions about the productivism inherent in the nineteenth

129. *Ibid.*
130. At the same time Wallerstein points out that the same ideological schemes of universalism and racism/sexism can be found also in 'developmentalism'. See *ibid.*, 49: "How can the underdeveloped develop? In some way, by copying those who already have, that is, by adopting the universal culture of the modern world, with the assistance of those who are more advanced. (...) If, despite this assistance, they are making no or little progress, it is because they are being 'racist', in rejecting universal 'modern' values which then justifies that the 'advanced' states are scornful of them or condescending to them".

century adulation of science. The many new social movements (of women, of minorities) have poured scorn upon the demand for assimilation"[131].

c) Globalization and the (Reflexive) Re-Appropriation of Traditions in the Context of Manufactured Uncertainties

Wallerstein's concluding remarks lead us to the domain Giddens considers important to explore: the reflexive re-appropriation of traditions in the context of a world community that has to face up to its self-produced risks. This topic, however cannot be isolated from Giddens' analysis of 'globalization', the post-traditional social order', and 'social reflexivity', three characteristics that he deems important in order to get a picture of what 'reflexive modernity' is all about. I start, thus, with a depiction of these three.

(i) 'Globalization'. In the context of Wallerstein's analysis, the world-system is nothing else than the capitalist system expanding beyond its birthplace. Under the pressure of its own objective, the endless accumulation of profit, this originally European system had to go global and establish itself as the 'total market', to use Hinkelammert's phraseology. In the context of the consumer society, the market orientation is viewed mainly under the aspects of sellability, advertizing, and the consumption of goods rather than the aspects of the production apparatus and the social relations involved in it. At the same time, it also is evident that the information society has come to play a significant role in the homogenization of the globe. Giddens mainly focuses on the spread of information, coupled with mass transportation. But instead of dwelling on the spell of ever-refined electronic tools, he delves into the transformative social effects of the communicated contents. He defines 'globalization' as follows: "Globalization is not only, or even primarily, an economic phenomenon; and it should not be equated with the emergence of a 'world system'. Globalization is really about the transformation of space and time. I define it as *action at a distance* and relate its intensifying over recent years to the emergence of means of instantaneous global communication and mass transportation"[132].

To understand what 'action at a distance' and 'the transformation of space and time' mean, one ought to recall the earlier discussion, in this article, about what Giddens says on the 'emptying of time' and the 'emptying of space' as two characteristic elements that explain the rise

---

131. *Ibid.*, p. 53.
132. A. GIDDENS (n. 54), p. 4. Emphasis original.

of the modern frame of mind. The mathematization of time has enabled us not only to program actions according to a precise time schedule but also to make these programmed actions work across various parts of the world. Control of time leads to control of space. Thus, modernity has acquired the capacity to transport technical and social influences to distant localities. There is also the modern 'emptying of space', which refers to the disembedding of social relations, as 'absent others' or absent decision-makers, from a distance, are able to routinely affect the day-to-day lives of people in their local contexts[133].

It goes without saying that the refinement and spread of means of instantaneous communication and mass transportation have decidedly intensified the globalization process to such an extent that these expanding large-scale systems seriously come to bear on our local and even personal contexts. Initially, the 'disembedding' of localities applied most relevantly to the way in which First World countries related to their colonies, but these days 'action at a distance' takes on the form of a two-way process. Owing to the availability of international networks of communication across the globe, decisions that are taken in one locality can be 'lifted out' and transmitted to very distant parts of the world, and then these can bounce back loaded with reactions from different social contexts: "Our day-to-day-activities are increasingly influenced by events happening on the other side of the world. Conversely, local life-style habits have become globally consequential. Thus my decision to buy a certain item of clothing has implications not only for the international division of labour but for the earth's ecosystems"[134]. For Giddens, globalization is a complex mixture of processes that often act in contradictory ways. For paradoxical as it may seem, the 'emptying of space'

---

133. A. GIDDENS (n. 10), pp. 18-19: "The 'emptying of time' is in large part the precondition for the 'emptying' of space ... For coordination across time is the basis of the control of space. The development of 'empty space' may be understood in terms of the separation of *space* from *place*. It is important to stress the distinction between these two notions, because they are often used as more or less synonymous with one another. 'Place' is best conceptualized by means of the idea of locale, which refers to the physical settings of social activity as situated geographically. In pre-modern societies, space and place largely coincide, since the spatial dimensions of social life are, for most of the population, and in most respects, dominated by 'presence' – by localized activities. The advent of modernity increasingly tears space away from place by fostering relations between 'absent' others, locally distant from any given situation of face-to-face interaction. In conditions of modernity place becomes increasingly *phantasmagoric*; that is to say, locales are thoroughly penetrated by and shaped in terms of social influences quite distant from them. What structures the locale is not simply that which is present on the scene; the 'visible' form of the locale conceals the distanciated relations which determine its nature".

134. A. GIDDENS (n. 54), p. 5. Emphasis original.

(the two-way process of communication through instantaneous action at a distance) ushers in a tremendous mobility in terms of social transformations or possible local resistances to them. This explains why also "the revival of local nationalisms, and an accentuation of local identities, are directly bound up with globalizing influences, to which they stand in opposition"[135]. "Globalizing influences are fracturing as well as unifying, create new forms of stratifications, and often produce opposing consequences in different regions or localities"[136].

(ii) 'Post-traditional social order'. Enlightenment aimed at destabilizing and discrediting traditions of all sorts. Yet it itself could not do without traditions. What in fact took place in the early phases of the development of modernity is that traditions were refocused, invented, or reinvented in view of consolidating the social order. In countries where the monarchy was abolished, new ceremonies were invented to cement the nation together. In some places, a civil religion was created, and above all, science began to acquire an unquestioned authority after the eradication of religion's revealed truth as the supreme judge of universal verities. Moreover, a close examination of modernity makes it clear that even "traditions of a more down-to-earth-kind were reconstructed, to do with, among other areas of social life, the family, gender and sexuality. Rather than being dissolved, these became reformed in such a way as to plant women firmly in the home, reinforce divisions between the sexes, and stabilize certain 'normal' canons of sexual behaviour"[137].

The reason why Giddens calls attention to the phenomena of the refocusing, the invention, and the reinvention of traditions in the course of 'simple modernity' (early phases of modernity) is to invalidate the slogan that modernity is averse to traditions. Traditions may regularly acquire new versions in accordance with the epoch's need for consolidation. However, what is typical of reflexive, post-traditional persons is that they require traditions to explain what they substantially have to offer and thus to open themselves to dialogic contact. Contrary to what one might expect, the 'post-traditional social order' "is not one in which tradition disappears, far from it. It is one in which tradition changes its status. Traditions have to explain themselves, to become open to interrogation or discourse"[138]. Giddens, thus, takes a reflexive distance both

---

135. *Ibid.*, p. 5.
136. *Ibid.*, p. 81: "These events and changes no longer pass just from the West to the rest. Thus the industrial development of the East is directly bound up with the deindustrialization of the older industries in the heart of the core countries in the global order".
137. *Ibid.*, p. 5.
138. *Ibid.*, p. 5. See also *ibid.*, pp. 184-185: "... welfare projects which don't respect local ties and modes of life can be almost as destructive as the market forces they seek to

from pre-modern and modern traditions, while being at the same time eager to learn lessons from them for the revitalization of life-politics. At times, one even gets the impression that he sets greater store by stimuli coming from pre-modern traditions than by motivations drawn from modern traditions, though in both cases, the inspiration is assimilated reflexively.

Illuminative in this respect is Giddens' discussion of our changing relation to nature. Before the Enlightenment, nature was a relatively 'fixed' landscape, "a physical environment of human action independently of that action". Enlightenment thinking and productivism have put an end to nature's independent status by reducing it to an immense inanimate resource to be exploited by modern technology. Human intervention almost led to a 'dissolution' of independent nature. But nowadays, in reflexive modernity, and owing to the environmental crisis, the awareness has grown that "the problems of environmental degradation which perturb us today come from the transformation of the natural into the social and cultural"[139]. This prompts us to revise our relation to nature and to engage in a renewed protection of the natural world, if necessary by drawing back from interventions that affect the environment, or by trying to eliminate side-effects. Yet Giddens is quick to add that this protection concerns not 'nature as nature' (this would be a naturalistic misapprehension, to be found among 'deep ecologists') but nature as an environment that since time immemorial has been and is still being "socially organized". As a consequence, "all ecological debates today are about managed nature", even when we judge that "some natural phenomena which we have influenced or could influence are best reinstated. Any such reinstatement is itself, at least obliquely, a form of management – the creation of parameters of 'protection'". In these debates, and this is Giddens' point, no appeal to nature as such can help us decide whether such reinstatement is appropriate in any particular case. The

---

counteract. When Glazer remarks that 'the creation and building of new traditions, or of new versions of old traditions, must be taken seriously as a requirement of social policy itself', he is surely correct. Yet such traditions should be understood in a post-traditional manner, as forms of conventional or ritual practice open to dialogic contact with others". With reference to N. GLAZER, *The Limits of Social Policy*, Cambridge, Harvard University Press, 1988, p. 8.

139. A. GIDDENS (n. 54), p. 47. Asking himself whether there is an affinity between radical ecology and leftist thinking, Giddens' answer is: not at all! See *ibid.*, p. 199: "In socialist theories (and in some otherwise quite opposing views as well) 'nature becomes for the first time simply an object for mankind, purely a matter of utility; it ceases to be recognized as a power in its own right; and the theoretical knowledge of its independent laws appears only as a stratagem designed to subdue it to human requirements, whether as the object of consumption or as the means of production'".

only appeal that can be made is to our moral option on the type of society we want for the future, and on the qualities of the socially organized nature we are going to hand over to the next generations: "The question, 'how shall we live?' is raised by any attempt to decide what to preserve – of nature or of the past – short of problems that bear in a brute way on global survival"[140].

Giddens' reasoning with respect to the preservation of elements taken from tradition develops along the same lines: "Tradition, like nature, used to be, as it were, an external framework for human activity which 'took' many decisions for us. But now we have to decide *about* tradition; what to try to sustain, and what to discard. And tradition itself, while often important and valuable, can be of very little help in this"[141]. This principle, which repeatedly comes back in Giddens' writings, summarizes what one has to understand by a post-traditional outlook. Traditions with their rituals, practices, and norms, admittedly, contain precious elements of human experience. But since the contexts wherein these experiences were functional, have gone, we have to determine ourselves which aspects of the 'wisdom' of tradition merit to be recovered as vehicles to help us cope with problems we are facing now in totally different constellations: "Traditions need to be saved, or recovered (...) in so far as they provide generalizable sources of solidarity"[142].

What, at any rate, must be avoided is an appeal to tradition in a traditional way, as if reflexivity did not matter. Such an attitude paves the way for fundamentalism. In current culture, fundamentalism is not just about defending "the purity of a given set of doctrines (...) and to set them off from other traditions"[143], but rather concerns the refusal to enter into "discursive engagements with a world of cosmopolitan communication". Nor is fundamentalism just a religious phenomenon; it may also include ethnic relations, nationalism, gender, and the family. "Religious fundamentalisms, as is well known, tend to overlap with these other contents"[144]. Giddens' point, thus, is that fundamentalist revivals, be they religious or cultural, are closely connected with the context of globalization and detraditonalization, which prompts people to interrogate their value system and to discursively explain what is constructive

140. *Ibid.*, p. 212.
141. *Ibid.*, p. 49. See also A. GIDDENS (n. 10), p. 38: "To sanction a practice because it is traditional will not do; tradition can be justified, but only in the light of knowledge which is not itself authenticated by tradition".
142. A. GIDDENS (n. 54), p. 48.
143. *Ibid.*, p. 6.
144. *Ibid.*, p. 85.

in it. A certain number of people shun this new climate of open dialogue which they feel is threatening them. They rather would opt for sticking to the unquestionable principles and certainties of their tradition, thus rejecting "a model of truth linked to the dialogic engagement of ideas in a public space. It is dangerous because edged with a potential for violence. Fundamentalisms can arise in all domains of social life where tradition becomes something which has to be *decided about* rather than just taken for granted"[145].

(iii) 'Social reflexivity'. Giddens uses this term to differentiate the current phase of modernity from anterior ones, and links it to the difference between simple and reflexive modernization. 'Simple modernization' is the period in which people wagered on the scientific predictability of events, and hence on the straightforward planning of a human-made society where there was no hesitancy as to the procedures to be used. 'Reflexive modernization', on the contrary, reckons with unpredictability and also knows about the ever-provisional character of acquired knowledge. The latter is not just the result of methodological doubt; it rather points to the dislocation brought about by the incessant flow of incoming information, as is typical in the era of globalization[146]. Pieces of information reaching us from various parts of the globe are constantly bombarding our closed shell of experienced knowledge, prompting us to widen our horizon and to respond to unsettling facts we would rather like to repel as unwanted intruders. Incoming information has a detraditionalizing effect because it makes us look at traditional certitudes as suppliers of answers that are no longer fit to make us come to grips with actual problems. As already mentioned, Giddens includes, in the notion of tradition, 'classical' modern institutions of knowledge: "When the claims of reason replaced those of (premodern) tradition, they appeared to offer a sense of certitude greater than that provided by preexisting dogma". But the reflexivity of modernity "actually subverts reason, at any rate where reason is understood as the gaining of certain knowledge.... We are abroad in a world which is thoroughly constituted through reflexively applied knowledge, but where at the same time we can never be sure that any given element of that knowledge will not be revised"[147].

Social reflexivity is not the same as nihilism, for rather than leading to despair, reflexivity makes people aware of their opportunities and

---

145. *Ibid.*, p. 6.
146. A. GIDDENS (n. 10), p. 38: "The reflexivity of modern social life consists in the fact that the social practices are constantly examined and reformed in the light of incoming information about those very practices, thus constantly altering their character".
147. *Ibid.*, p. 39.

responsibilities in ever changing conditions. Reflexivity realistically looks at the cultural situation in which the world is becoming one global village, and wagers on the interaction of various traditions, an interaction in which traditions declare what they have to offer to humanity's search for common survival. Giddens focuses hereby on social practices and experiences, and takes it for granted that knowledge and information are no longer the privilege of experts. Much relevant specialized knowledge is routinely made available to the wider public, and this gives many people the opportunity to make new experiences and to restructure their lives[148].

These three characteristics, 'globalization', 'post-traditionalism', and 'reflexivity', constitute the background against which Giddens tackles the problem of manufactured risks and uncertainties. He first of all observes that, since these risks present themselves as global threats, attempts at coming to grips with them must espouse also a global perspective. In other words, when one examines burning issues arising in the North, one ought to realize that they are related to burning issues present in the South, and vice versa. In *Beyond Left and Right*, various chapters are spent on the new social movements in Europe as well as on the crisis of the welfare-state and the search for Positive Welfare and life-values[149], yet these topics are examined in such a way that regular references are made either to what is happening or to what can be developed in the South in terms of life-strategies and economic activities. Giddens thus considers interdependence a two-way process, and links it to environmental questions that concern the whole world-population.

As far as the degradation of the environment is concerned, it is evident that high-consequential risks are created under the impulse of the western ethos of 'industry' (or productivism) along with consumerism[150]. Productivism and its negative side-effects, however, concern not only the North but also the South, which has embarked, with varying rhythms according to the regions, on the journey of development and productivism. The remedy, on a world-scale, would lie in the coming into being

---

148. A. GIDDENS (n. 54), p. 7 and p. 353.

149. Giddens attributes the crisis of the Welfare-State to the fact that it was meant to meet external risks, whereas nowadays a lot of manufactured risks are flowing in, which undermine the foundations and the functioning of the Welfare-State. Welfare-State is, in other words, a product of 'simple modernization', whereas 'reflexive modernization' is in search of new forms of welfare and life strategies of personalized happiness. See *ibid.*, pp. 134-150.

150. *Ibid.*, pp. 168-169: "Productivism, I shall assume, cannot be explained in terms of consumerism, the reverse is the case. Consumerism has its roots in, and indeed is a quite direct expression of, a productivist orientation to the world".

of a post-scarcity society, in which productivity will replace the 'ethos' of productivism: "I do not equate a post-scarcity society with an end to economic growth; and it is not a social order in which most people have become wealthy enough to do what they please. A post-scarcity order starts to emerge where continuous economic growth becomes harmful or manifestly counterproductive; and where the ethos of productivism begins to be widely called into question, creating a pressure to realize and develop life values."[151] For the North, this would involve a more frugal life-style, which leaves consumerism behind. But above all, it would involve an opting out of the compulsory work ethos[152], which only honors employment that is paid employment[153]. As for the South, a post-scarcity order would be tied to 'alternative development', i.e., the development of human potential from the bottom up and through participation in self-help groups and social movements. One of the desirable and probable results of this 'joint effort' would be a decrease in the life-style-choice distance between the 'wealthy' North and the 'poverty-stricken' South: "A positive move towards a post-scarcity system on the part of the global consumer class, coupled to an 'alternative development' for the world's poor, are the only plausible means of creating a more equal world"[154].

Giddens' blueprint for a post-scarcity society has, from the outset, a double objective: to limit environmental depletion and to bridge the gap between the affluent and the poor; its single strategy consists in persuading North and South of the utility and urgency of making a "life-style pact". He is deeply convinced that, in order to stop destructive economic growth, only life practices can be of any help[155]. One of Giddens' challenging statements in this respect is that the wealthy have much more to learn from the poor than vice versa. He does not question the significance of development aid, provided it goes to projects of alternative development. But what he objects to is the erroneous strategy that consists in the set-up of aid programs with the purpose of preparing Third World countries to eventually copy the wealthier states: "I want to

---

151. *Ibid.*, p. 163.

152. In Giddens' conviction, this ethos is morally impoverishing. See *ibid.*, p. 176: "Productivism, where work has become autonomous squeezes to the margins of social life most of those forms of moral experience which once linked human existence to tradition and to independent nature".

153. Giddens also treats the question of unemployment in western countries, as well as the plea for half time paid jobs to be complemented with unpaid work, in the family, or in 'third sector' employment, provided by the state and devoted to tasks of social and community care. See *ibid.*, p. 196.

154. *Ibid.*, p. 197.

suggest, however, a counterposed strategy – that a radical politics of welfare, North and South, has much to learn from the experiences of the most deprived"[156]. Giddens admits that these experiences are ambivalent. Poverty, combined with activities in the informal sector, may on the one hand demoralize the dispossessed in the inner cities and in the slum areas where they are "often terrorized by crime and in hock to the drug dealers"; on the other hand, activities and struggles in the informal sector may promote "the survival and perhaps recreation of local traditions, a bursting variety of activities carried on by neo-artisans, living off their locally developed skills, as well as catering to the needs of the neighborhood"[157].

When trying to give a more detailed account of what an alternative development program would involve, he lists the following traits:

(1) Furtherance of *reflexive engagements* in indigenous social movements and self-help groups. The Seventh Generation Fund (SGF), e.g., can serve as a model. This organization seeks to save the Iroquois Indians' cultural and economic heritage, in particular, by retrieving the practice of "considering, before policy decisions are enacted, their potential impact on the seventh generation". This leads to the use of renewable resources and local skills to provide goods and services.

(2) *Damage limitation* as a basic concern, whether this be in matters of local culture or the environment. Modernization, together with its many benefits, has also had harmful consequences; "in many situations we cannot expect further modernization to cope with these, since it helped bring them about".

(3) To regard *life-political questions* as "central to emancipatory politics, rather than simply working the other way around". Emancipation must, in a sense, be decoupled from simple modernity's cool rational planning. Questions of life-style become of vital importance since "a response to poverty today can no longer be regarded as purely economic". Life-style involves the question "of 'how to live' in a globalizing milieu where local culture and environmental resources

155. *Ibid.*, p. 163: "So far as economic growth is concerned, many critics are inclined to ask of the affluent countries today rhetorically, how much is enough? How much is enough? The question seems to be one of environmental limits, of how much the earth can bear, and so in some part it is. It is above all ... however, a question concerning life practices."

156. *Ibid.*, p. 157. Giddens is realistic enough to acknowledge that the 'North', symbol for the wealthy, has also its enclaves in the 'South'.

157. *Ibid.*, p. 167.

are being squandered". A battle for autonomy and self-reliance is also "a struggle to reconstitute the local as a prime way of avoiding endemic deprivation and despair".

(4) Promotion of *self-reliance and integrity* as the very means of development. Self-reliance entails the promotion of markets as well as the revitalization of local solidarities and support systems. An illustration is the Grameen Bank in Bangladesh whose system of granting loans to the poor is such that these do not expand into unpayable debts. Grameen aims to generate opportunities of development among the landless rural poor. "The majority of the borrowers are women; some villages do not accept men as members of the bank".

(5) Distinguishing *two different sources* of the ecological crisis. The major source of environmental disasters is the wealthy countries' wasteful pattern of production and consumption. The harmful practices of the poor are "more secundary and defensive". It is only when poor people are displaced[158] or marginalized that they adopt "more short-time and destructive practices in order to survive at all".

(6) Improving the *position of women* relative to that of men. Most of the differential found within the industrialized regions "apply in an even more acute way in more impoverished areas"[159]: women's paid employment is concentrated in peripheral sectors that have the worst working conditions, low take-home pay, and poor job security. Specifically in this case, emancipatory politics must be accompanied by life-politics. The issue is not only one of achieving greater equality between the sexes: "changes in femininity and masculinity, and in associated patterns of behaviour" are called for. As to the question of bringing down the population growth, more favourable results can be obtained from the local empowerment of women (their capaciy to make their own decisions in relation to reproduction) than from their mere involvement in labor markets.

(7) Primacy of *autonomous health-care*. Scientific medicine in very poor areas has to be regarded as one approach, among others, to health and sickness. Equally important is informed health care prac-

158. Giddens points out that the construction of large dams in impoverished regions of the South was one widely regarded as the major symbol of industrial development. These dams have certainly brought certain benefits to the wider economy, but at the price of the displacement of many local people: "Thus a study of more than fifty projects financed by the World Bank involving forced resettlement found not a single case in which those affected had reached the standard of living they had before" (*ibid.*, p. 164).

159. *Ibid.*, p. 161: "Women own less than 1 percent of the world's wealth; and earn less than 10 percent of the global income; yet they do two-thirds of the world's work".

ticed by ordinary people "provided with clear, simple information". These people "can prevent and treat common health problems in their own homes – earlier, cheaper, and often better than can doctors". Basic health care should not be delivered but encouraged as everybody's responsibility[160].

(8) Sustaining *family ties* while seeking to combat patriarchy and the exploitation of children. Although the family can often be oppressive to women and children, "for the very poor everywhere, family connections provide an emotional and material resource that no other institution can match." Family ties offer social insurance[161]; that is why people may want large families. But even when family size comes down and inequalities within the family are lessened, "the family remains an important protective mantle".

(9) Emphasizing not only rights but also *responsibilities*. Although the recognition of formal and substantive rights (such as the rights of women and children) is important, the shouldering of concomitant responsibilities is perhaps still more relevant because "responsibility accords closely with self-reliance".

(10) An alternative development cannot be organized purely in local terms. Such development "also depends on *intervention from 'big battalions'* – states, businesses, and international organizations". It is clear, however, that these interventions need to be sensitive to local demands and protective of local interests[162].

With this ten-point program, Giddens hopes to make a contribution to Third World development, which should be undertaken not only from a 'global' but also from a 'reflexive' perspective, and which looks at the 'consequences for the seventh generation'. He considers this life-policy program relevant to the 'culture of the poor'. Relying on two 'conservative' authors, Murray and Latouche, who are also deeply concerned about the future development of the world's societies, he puts forward two important questions: what is the ideal of human happiness? And

---

160. With reference to D. WERNER, *Where There Is No Doctor*, Palo Alto, Hesperian Foundation, 1977.

161. Cf. A. GIDDENS (n. 54), pp. 88-89: "The successful Asian countries do not rely on Western-style welfare state mechanisms to create equalization, but instead provide means for poorer groups actively to improve their life circumstances. Because of their sheer numbers, poorer people in the aggregate have much greater resources than the rich. Moreover, in the Asian economies poorer people 'save' by investing in others with whom they are closely linked in family or friendship networks. The payoff of 'investments' in this form is to be found in increased social solidarity – but these probably also have important implications for economic productivity".

162. The ten points are taken from *ibid.*, pp. 159-163.

what is the alternative to productivism? As to the first question, it is obvious that the possession of wealth is not necessarily a source of happiness. Happiness rather consists in "a lasting and justified satisfaction with one's life", which aside from the satisfaction of one's basic needs, flows mainly from 'security' and 'self-respect'. According to Murray, whose work has been influenced by experiences in rural Thailand, "not much more than subsistence is required in the way of material resources if one is to pursue happiness... after a certain quite low threshold, increasing levels of income do not lead to greater degrees of happiness or satisfaction with one's life. Security and self-respect, not wealth and income, are what count"[163]. If one adopts the perspective of a post-scarcity society, Giddens concludes, neither poverty nor wealth are the real enemies, but the ethos of productivism.

To substantiate this point, Giddens makes use of Latouche's study, which acknowledges the importance of the informal economy: "This sector makes up 60-80 per cent of urban employment in the Third World, even in those societies which do not rank among the poorest. How could one say that such a sector is 'secondary'?" In an attempt to understand the phenomenon, one should consider the hypothesis that the informal society represents an order on which modern institutions are in fact dependent. At any rate, from the standpoint of those living in it, the informal sector is a "set of strategies of global response to the spread of modern institutions"; it is a reaction of people "caught between lost traditions and an impossible modernity". There is something in this sector which Giddens greatly appreciates, namely, the fact that its informal activities obey a logic different from productivism. Where artisanal activities produce a surplus, it is not straightaway invested in expanded production but rather used to bolster local loyalties and solidarities. The 'economic' is not divorced from the rest of life. In Giddens' view, this ideal is the model that needs to be adopted for the emergence of post-scarcity economies in every part of the world[164]. The elements in Giddens' ten-point program are neither wholly pre-modern nor post-modern: "We couldn't say that the one comes 'before' modernity and the other 'after'; each constitutes a sort of partial repair and recovery of modes of life which modern institutions essentially destroy or repress". For those living in the First World and who would have to decide increasingly whether or not to engage in informal jobs, this step involves

163. *Ibid.*, pp. 165-6; with reference to CH. MURRAY, *In Pursuit of Happiness and Good Government*, New York, Simon and Schuster, 1988.
164. A. GIDDENS (n. 54), p. 167; with reference to S. LATOUCHE, *La planète des naufragés*, Paris, La Découverte, 1991.

'reflexivity'. For "a society of intensive reflexivity is not one where a compulsive attitude towards work can go unremarked"[165]. To give up this compulsive attitude may be rightly called (postmodern) emancipation.

VI. CONCLUSION

Some suspect that liberation theology's compliance with Roman pressures (*Libertatis nuntius*, 1984) has robbed the movement of its clout. For the last ten years, as J. Tamayo observes, Latin-American liberation theologians, perhaps partly for tactical reasons, have begun to develop a rather intra-ecclesial discourse on the meaning of suffering in the face of oppression. In doing so, they have moved increasingly into a direction that tacitly brackets off the once-extolled inclusion of socio-analytic mediation. Especially after the fall of the Berlin wall, some of them have felt the need to adopt themes from the social doctrine of the church to substitute for a radical socialist program, which is deemed no longer viable. And it seems that, even though in some quarters the interest is expressed as regards examining and appropriating recent developments in the social sciences (sociology, social anthropology, political science, group psychology, and economics), research programs with these perspectives hardly come off the ground[166].

1. I have presented a panorama of recent developments in the social sciences with the focus on how one can understand the transition from modernity (simple modernity) to postmodernity (reflexive modernity). Such an enterprise might appear quite limited, given the fact that it takes its starting-point from cultural changes that began in the 'First World'. It is, however, undeniable that these very changes are closely connected with the phenomenon of globalization and the challenges posed by it. Even before the term acquired widespread usage, globalization already had been brought to the attention of liberation theology in so far as dependency theory (and its concomitant strategies for liberation) took into consideration the subordinate position of Third World economies in the world market. Dependency theory and liberation theology stigmatized this subordination as a root cause of the perpetuation of poverty in the Third World. But apparently, globalization is too complex a phenomenon to be comprehensible within a framework that primarily distinguishes between central and peripheral economies.

165. A. GIDDENS (n. 54), p. 177.
166. J. TAMAYO (n. 15), pp. 132-134.

Indeed, a closer examination of the nature of globalization shows that the phenomenon cannot be separated from the politics of culture and the cultural issues that are generated by the very circulation of attractive consumer goods, which function all over the world as the ambassadors of the developed countries' 'good way of life'. At the same time, however, the continuing 'McDonaldization' of the globe must be viewed with distrust, for underneath the glamorous surface of the market, as Wallerstein has made clear, there still looms the veteran specter of the modern, unequal division of labor according to which certain ethnic characteristics or female features are considered incompatible with the capitalist and productivist work-ethos. The treatment of these targeted groups and subgroups reveals hidden mechanisms of racism and sexism; the 'inferior' are expected to put up with the lower positions they deserve within the inevitable hierarchy of the division of labor at both the national and international levels. Confronted with stark socio-economic realities, the postmodern appraisal of otherness and difference, publicly hallowed as the pre-condition for materializing greater diversification in knowledge-production, often boils down to lip-service paid to the ideal. Postmodern fragmentation means also ghettoizing the socially 'different' into an opaque otherness, where each ghetto is allowed to foster its own cultural identity as long as it keeps itself isolated from richer sources of power. In extreme cases, this also leads to a harsh exclusion from the benefits of the 'good life' offered by dazzling, postmodern society; cases of exclusion are not exceptional if we consider among them the many unemployed people even in the First World, the exploited workers in sweat-shops all over the globe, and the international abandonment of large regions or of a whole sub-continent, as in the case of sub-Saharan Africa.

The cultural consequences of postmodern civilization constitute a matter of concern also to the newly industrializing nations of the 'South,' South-east Asia in particular. Those booming nations are confident that the times of Orientalism have definitely gone. They expect that the racial discrimination inherent in the world system and in the global hierarchy of states would apply to them no longer. They strongly believe that it is possible to appropriate and develop western technology without having to give up the backbone of one's local cultural habits. Ancient popular wisdom is welcomed as an ally in resisting a globalization that ipso facto can westernize and thus alienate people from their cultural roots. In this perspective, it is hoped that limitless technological progress, as far as its cultural consequences are concerned, can and must be kept in balance by means of deep-seated, traditional values. To complete this picture, one should consider also Giddens' plea to 'save' aspects of traditional wisdom.

For him, globalization rests on the quasi-instantaneous information we get from all over so much so that we are well-informed about such high-consequence risks we are generating with our ethos of productivism: the depletion of ecosystems and the devitalization of the human life-world. In the face of these risks, we shall have to refrain from frantic industrial expansion. More in particular, groups of people alert to environmental questions are called upon to make use of their 'reflexive' habits and to selectively look for traditional resources for the formulation of life-policies. Apparently, various types of self-help groups have come to replace modernity's organic intellectuals, whose role seems to be finished.

Without doubt, a multi-layered analysis of globalization has added some new aspects to the view presented by a mere economic reading of history which emphasizes on the unequal division of labor. It has confronted us with the complex phenomenon of cultural changes and cultural domination. More in particular, it has shown that, as regards their respective futures, local cultures are finding themselves at crossroads. Some of them are going to be relegated to the fringes of public life, whose spatial area will be filled with the magic and the contradictions of the globalized postmodern way of life. Under specific circumstances, however, other cultures will prove successful in revitalizing parts of their common heritage and in making their voices heard in the public sphere. This differential diagnosis makes it difficult to sketch a blueprint for common strategies since much depends on the geographical, if not geopolitical, location. Geographical diversity inevitably comes into play. The respective life-styles in the suburbs of New York and Cape Town, or in the shanty-towns of Manila, Mexico City, and Sao Paulo show characteristics that are not found in rather isolated cultural enclaves in the Andes or in sub-Saharan, rural Africa, though even in these relatively remote regions, the media attempt to make inroads. Also, the dominant cultural patterns displayed in some of the booming cities of Japan, Taiwan, and South Korea present us with another shade of cultural behavior. Apparently, no direct prediction can be made with respect to the survival, adaptation, or erosion of a particular culture in the melting-pot of the global ecumene.

Studies dealing with the phenomenon of cultural changes, globalization, and the resistance to it confine themselves mostly to pointing out a set of actors from whose interplay a whole range of outcomes can be expected[167]. These actors are 'forms of life', 'market', 'state', and 'social

---

167. See U. HANNERZ (n. 86), p. 47: "For the four major frameworks which should take us at least a long way towards a comprehensive accounting of present-day cultural flow, then, I use the terms *form of life*, *market*, *state*, and *movement*. These do not work

movements'. These four frameworks have varying strengths and objectives. For instance, whereas 'forms of life' connote clusters of continuity, market and media usher in asymmetrical flows of leverage which can unleash nationalistic reactions ('state') or, perhaps, concerted actions undertaken by social movements. If one seriously considers this interplay, as well as the local components involved in it, a clear demarcation of a singular, historical 'actor of change' (e.g., the revolutionary class in Marxism) seems to be ruled out. The question then arises as to how liberation theologians, who used to wager on a singular (Christian) revolutionary movement, should react to this sort of 'dissipative' analysis. It was thought before that, to motivate people for collective action, definite and decisive language was needed. But today, straightforward lines of action have been obscured. In other words, the liberation of the poor does remain an urgent concern, but the manner to bring this about becomes more problematic when one realizes the fact that the poor are dispersed in various cultural settings. And in each setting, the poor face specific problems of personal and collective identity. For me, this is a vexed question, which I submit to the respondents for consideration.

2. Leaving this matter open, I now turn to an objection that might be raised concerning the theological pertinence of my paper. Indeed, much attention has been paid to the paradigm shift in the field of secular mediations (human and social sciences), and some might raise the question as to how all this could contribute to a valid interpretation of Christian faith. In short, is globalization a topic for theological reflection? Surely it is, as Cardinal Ratzinger has shown in *Christ, Faith, and the Challenge of Cultures*. In this article, a talk given in Hong Kong, Ratzinger pleas for a 'meeting of cultures', or more precisely, for an 'interculturality' in which various culturally-embedded religious traditions embark on a journey of development which, through a discovery of their potentials for universality, prepares them for intercommunication with one other. Ratzinger prefers the term 'interculturality' over 'inculturation' because the latter presupposes something like a disincarnated essence of (Christian) religion, an essence that, in a second step, has to be incarnated in some particular cultural pattern. More to the point, he asserts that Christianity is itself a culture that offers its cultural achievements to other peoples on the basis of its already-acquired universality. Furthermore,

---

in isolation from one another, but it is rather in their interplay, with varying respective strengths, that they shape both what we rather arbitrarily demarcate as particular cultures, and that complicated overall entity which we may think of as the global ecumene. Within each framework, there can be great variation, between instances as well as in any one instance".

Christianity's cultural achievements become available to enrich other religions, once these religions have developed, from their respective particularities, sufficiently universal perspectives. Now it is in this context that Ratzinger warns against the dangers of an inculturation that would consist in 'liberating' African or Amerindian forms of religiosity from a Christian universal culture that, for a long time now, they had espoused implicitly, if not explicitly. Such a step cannot be taken because it rests on an erroneous option, namely, to 'clothe' the abstract essence of Christianity with cultural forms of tribal religiosity or, as in the case of Latin America, with cultural survivals of the pre-Columbian religions. A reference to *teología india* is explicitly made[168].

What interests me, at this juncture, is the reasoning Ratzinger uses to rebuke the enterprise of a *teología india*, for this leads us to the field of globalization. This type of theology, it is said, has to be rejected because it involves a romantic return to the past. Such a return is totally unrealistic for two reasons: (i) The global spread of western technology and sciences is an unstoppable phenomenon; thus, it would be naive to think that some enclaves of 'primitive' civilization could be preserved. In fact, such pure enclaves exist no longer. (ii) One has to admit that western technology is making inroads into every part of the world, and thus it would be naive again to think that one could accept the achievements of the technological era and still keep one's 'primitive' indigenous religion[169]. Lower forms of religiosity in themselves lack instruments of theological reflection, and it is through their contact with Christianity that they, in a sense, can obtain and retain such reflexive instruments. On their own, these lower forms, sooner or later, will be overcome by the secularizing influence of western technologies and thus lose their

---

168. For more information, see *Teología india: Primer encuentro taller latinoamericano México*, México, D.F., Cenam., 1991.

169. J. RATZINGER, *Christian Faith and the Challenge of Cultures*, in *Origins* 24:41 (1995) 679-686, p. 683: "It is not only the case that the convergence of mankind toward a single community with a common life and destiny is unstoppable because such an inclination is grounded in man's essence, but also because the diffusion of technological civilization is irrevocable. It is a romantic dream to want to preserve pretechnological islands in the sea of humanity. You cannot enclose men and cultures in a kind of spiritual nature reserve. Virtually no one, whether in Latin America, Africa, or Asia, seriously wants to exclude himself from natural science and technology, which originated in the West. But since technology, like natural science, appear to be neutral, the thought suggests itself: Why not accept the achievements of the modern age while, however, at the same time keeping the indigenous religions? This seemingly so enlightened notion, however, does not work. For in reality modern civilization is not mere multiplication of knowledge and know-how. It deeply encroaches upon the basic understanding of man, the world, and God. It alters the interpretation of the world at its base. It changes standards and behavior. The religious cosmos is necessarily moved by it".

religiosity. A merger of technological culture with, say, African tribal religions, or with the survivals of Mayan religion, can only result in a composite whole of magic and cruelty, a cruelty that, moreover, can avail itself of sophisticated murderous weapons. At any rate, once these forms are purged of superior religious reflection, secular influences would eradicate the underlying religiosity, and they could not but fall prey to modern paganism[170]. On the other hand, Ratzinger holds in great esteem Asia's high religions, which in the course of history, have generated sacred texts and fonts of philosophical and theological reflection. These texts and resources have enabled them, first, to seriously question the materialistic world view that western technology is circulating, and second, to open themselves to dialogue with the universality of Christian faith[171].

One has to appreciate Ratzinger's emphasis on the necessity of religious reflection, which is a vital aspect in life and a useful instrument to realize where one stands and what one stands for, whether individually or as a religious community, in the market of religious world-views. Reflection paves the road for dialogue. This is true not only for religious reflection but also for reflection at the levels of philosophy and culture. Dialogue becomes easier for a reflexive person especially when reflection teaches one to look at one's particular tradition, from a distance, in order to uncover in it 'unreflected' elements that (even in Christianity as a reflexive religion) not only persist in everyday life but also once in a while threaten to carry the day. Although Cardinal Ratzinger does not venture himself into this direction, it would be appropriate not to close off this road, especially if we assume that a certain rapprochement can be brought about between Christian reflexivity and the type of reflexivity Giddens deems important for coming to grips with human-manufactured risks, or with the destructive side-effects of western productivism, whose

---

170. *Ibid.*, pp. 683-684: "In any case, it occurs more and more frequently that Christian faith is discarded as European cultural heritage and the former religions are religiously reinstated, while at the same time technology, though nonetheless Western, is passionately adopted and exploited. This division of Western heritage into the useful, which one accepts, and the foreign, which one rejects, does not lead to the salvation of ancient cultures. It can now be seen that what is great and forward-looking, I would say the adventistic dimension of the ancient religions, meets its downfall because it seems incompatible with the new knowledge of the world and man, while magic in the broadest sense of the word, everything which promises power over the world, remains intact and becomes for the first time life-determining. The religions thus lose their dignity because what is best in them is eliminated and what was dangerous in them alone remains".

171. Though encouraging the interreligious dialogue in the Asian context, especially with Buddhism and Neo-Hinduism, Ratzinger nevertheless rejects the solution proposed by R. Pannikar which holds that "Jesus is Christ, but Christ is not (only) Jesus" (*ibid.*, p. 685).

effects come to bear on the environment and on personality formation. Such a rapprochement, however, poses a lot of questions, not directly[172] as regards the essence of things (the essence of Christian life, on the one hand, and the essence of reflexive modernity on the other) but as regards this phenomenon: a variety of groups within contemporary Christianity can claim, and in fact are claiming, to be seriously reflexive in some matters within their 'specialty' of concern. And this also leads to a variety of approaches within the whole Christian body. Let me indicate what I mean through some questions.

(a) Can one maintain that the appropriation of social analysis by 'classical' liberation theology has made our Judaeo-Christian tradition more reflexive, less fundamentalist, and less idolizing? More in particular, did the use of social analysis in conjunction with biblical meditation and hermeneutics weaken the sense of fatalism among the poor? Did it also make them alert to manufactured risks that threaten the environment and the human quality of life? And if their sense of responsibility was strengthened, did this come to bear on community-building and on the (reflexive) preservation of vital elements of local culture related to it? Was this preservation something merely spontaneous, regressive, or highly reflexive?

(b) If liberation theology is expected to be enriched by integrating explicitly cultural themes, including racism and sexism and the clash between the new civilization (global culture) and local cultures, does this new encounter show more promise in making our Christian tradition more reflexive? Which new types of praxis are going to flow from it, both at the intra-ecclesial and extra-ecclesial levels? Does the persisting unequal division of labor in the economic domain still provide the overall scheme of interpretation for assessing asymmetrical cultural flows (in matters of gender and race)? Or has the socio-economic approach to disparities been superseded by new sensitivities? With respect to family structure? With respect to the abrogation of color barriers?

(c) If certain groups of Christians opt to give prominence to Christian culture (as defined by Ratzinger), what are the advantages of this type of reflexive commitment? It certainly will foster a personal and group piety founded on the contemplation of one's relationships with God, the neighbor, and the world; but will it create also an active openness to

---

172. By this I do not mean that this matter would not be worth discussing. My point is rather that first of all a 'fore-ground' question must be resolved, namely how one is going to reconcile with each other the various attempts at reflexivity which fill the spectrum of christian existence. Of course, I also submit this pragmatic stance to the assessment of the respondents.

social and cultural concerns? Or will it encourage aloofness from such concerns? Which social movements are going to be born from it? What will be their priorities? The conversion of hearts? The conversion of the cultural psyche? The transformation of unjust social structures? Is inter-religious dialogue important for them to enhance reflexivity?

(d) If there is a tendency within Christian popular religion to give prominence to autochthonous cultural habits, including traditional wisdom and a nature-caring religiosity, this will certainly preserve the contemplative and festive ethos of the devotional rural poor; but will this require also a return to premodern ways of life? How premodern could they be if well-informed choices would be involved? Could they, or should they, be secluded from the tentacles of the 'new civilization'? Will not sophisticated means of communication increasingly reach remote areas? On what basis should popular religion promote a responsible care for the environment? A traditional sense of wonder? Cognizance of manufactured, high-consequence risks? How can popular religiosity be stimulated to contribute to a realistic development and the making of a post-scarcity, non-productivist society with abundantly diverse, small, and informal markets and services?

3. There is still an issue that I would like to touch upon briefly, though its import is not negligible: the emergence of new social movements. In his attempt to devise a new agenda for doing liberation theology, J. Tamayo puts forward some programmatic points that, conceived independently of Giddens' analysis, show striking commonalities with the latter's 'alternative development program' (see above). Tamayo lists the following new features of 'poverty' to which various social movements have become alert, and which 'classical' liberation theologians have mostly overlooked: to combat racial, ethnic and cultural discrimination, indigenous and negro movements have emerged; to combat gender discrimination women movements have been created; to combat grave offenses against human dignity perpetrated by military dictatorships, human rights committees have been erected; confronted with the depletion of the environment, ecological movements have come off the ground; and in the struggle for material survival, popular organizations engaged in the informal economy have been created[173].

173. J. TAMAYO (n. 15), p. 95: "Las mujeres, los negros, los indios, la población excluida del sistema, los niños de la calle: he aquí algunas de las significativas formas – o mejor, algunos de los más significativos rostros – de la pobreza hoy en América Latina preteridas otrora por los teólogos de la liberación, a las que responden nuevos movimientos populares: 'Frente a la discriminación racial, étnica y cultural surgen los movimientos indígenas y negros; frente a la discriminación de género surgen los movimientos de mujeres; frente a los graves atropellos a la dignidad humana por las dictaduras militares

With the exception, perhaps, of the human rights committees, the other movements mentioned are all new, and they exhibit the new 'cultural awareness' that is being born in Latin America and, presumably, elsewhere in the 'Third World'. Associations formed to make the informal economy prosper are indeed part of popular culture, for as Giddens has made clear, they are culturally situated 'in between' premodernity and modernity in so far as the hard-working women and men in them are not slaves of the ethos of productivism. Instead, they work primarily to foster family and friendship bonds. Commitment to the informal sector, with its face-to-face relations, encourages the growth of self-respect and maturation in human dignity. The consequent feelings of self-esteem are dearly needed in situations of economic crisis and looming indigence. The feminist movements, too, have cultural repercussions; they further the empowerment and recognition of women against the background of the age-old legacy of patriarchy. The same is true for the indigenous and negro revival movements. After centuries of being objects of contempt, these groups are fighting to gain respect for their ethnic personalities. Finally, the ecological movements, in spite of their name, have cultural affinities also, for they seek to restore the balance between our human life-world and nature, if need be, by putting limits to the 'humanization' of nature.

What is typical about these new movements, however, is the fact that their new cultural awareness is not at all disembedded from material concerns. Even when one stresses their cultural contributions, as I have done, it is clear that their activities also come to bear on the 'infrastructure' of our societies. Besides furthering conviviality, the informal sector vigorously sees to it that provisions for material survival be supplied. In fighting for women's dignity, feminists are also eager to modify the classical division of labor, be it in the realm of paid labor or in the household. Indigenous movements are trying not only to reinstate their cultural habits and folklore but also to recover agrarian techniques and medicinal practices that once flourished in their native communities. And finally, it is not difficult to see the economic consequences involved in the activities of ecological movements especially when they try to preserve natural resources for future generations or to regenerate the environment to make it healthier.

surgen los movimientos de derechos humanos; frente al deterioro del medio ambiente, los movimientos ecologistas; frente a la lucha por la sobrevivencia, las diversas organizaciones económicas populares'. (Texto tomado del documento *Respuesta a pauta de consulta para la IV Conferencia general del episcopado latinoamericano*, elaborado por un Colectivo de teólogos y pastoralistas de Chile – Abril-Mayo 1990)".

Here too, I would like to finish with some questions. One may wonder why 'classical' liberation theology overlooked cultural trends, which also come to bear on the material setting of people's lives. Could it be that the discourse about unjust structures has been, in a sense, too abstract? Is not the cultural emphasis, especially when shouldered by the new social movements, a fresh way of tackling structural questions, a way that is more understandable to common people? Furthermore, does one do justice to these movements by accusing them of falling back to either exclusive concerns or private religiosity? And will it not be the case that these movements, as regards their religious impulses, will draw more inspiration from the biblical interpretations of grass-roots liberation theologians than from interpretations focused on inwardness like those put forward by Romanizers?

It is perhaps unusual to conclude an article with many difficult questions. I have done it in view of stimulating the discussion, and also to avoid the possible suspicion that the present author, from his armchair, is suggesting solutions to all sorts of problems he is not confronted with himself. Tensions between Third World and First World theologians are not new. Hopefully, they will diminish in the future since, as Giddens points out, thinkers in the First World are beginning to ask what they can learn from the Third World even as regards the domestic problems of the former.

WORKS CITED

ARRIGHI, G., *The Long Twentieth Century*, London-New York, Verso, 1994.

BAUMAN, Z., *Intimations of Postmodernity*, London-New York, Routledge, 1992.

—, *Life in Fragments. Essays in Postmodern Morality*, Oxford, Blackwell, 1995.

BECK, U., *The Risk Society*, London, Sage, 1992.

BETTO, F., *El fracaso del socialismo alemán y los desafíos a la izquierda latino-americana*, in *Pasos* 29 (1990) 1-7.

CELAM, *Réflexions sur Puebla*, Bogotá, CELAM, 1981.

ELLACURIA, I. & J. SOBRINO (eds.), *Mysterium Liberationis: Conceptos fundamentales de la teología de la liberación*, Madrid, Trotta, 1992.

ELLIS, M. & O. MADURO (eds.), *The Future of Liberation Theology: Essays in Honor of Gustavo Gutiérrez*, Maryknoll, NY, Orbis, 1989.

FEATHERSTONE, M., *Undoing Culture: Globalization, Postmodernity and Identity*, London-Thousand Oaks-New Delhi, Sage Publications, 1995.

FREIRE, P., *Education for Critical Consciousness*, London, Sheed & Ward, 1973.

FUKUYAMA, F., *The End of History and the Last Man*, New York, Free Press, 1992.

GIDDENS, A., *Beyond Left and Right: The Future of Radical Politics*, Cambridge, Polity Press, 1995, [1994].

—, *The Consequences of Modernity*, Cambridge, Polity Press, 1990.

GLAZER, N., *The Limits of Social Policy*, Cambridge, Harvard University Press, 1988.

GUTIÉRREZ, G., *A Theology of Liberation*, Maryknoll, NY, Orbis, [15]1988.

HANNERZ, U., *Cultural Complexity: Studies in the Social Organization of Meaning*, New York, Columbia University Press, 1992.

HARVEY, H., *The Condition of Postmodernity: An Inquiry into the Origin of Cultural Change*, Oxford, Blackwell, (1990), 1993.

HINKELAMMERT, F., *Capitalisme sans alternatives?* in *AS* 3 (1994) 43-63.

—, *Taking Stock of Latin-American Liberation Theology Today*, in *CQ* 76 (1995-96) 18-29.

HOUTART, F., *The World-Encompassment of the Economy*, in *CQ* 68 (1993-1994) 2-10.

JAMESON, F., *Postmodernism, or the Cultural Logic of Late Capitalism*, in *NLR* 146 (1984) 53-93.

JONAS, H., *The Imperative of Responsibility*, Chicago, University of Chicago Press, 1984.

KRUIP, G., *Die Theologie der Befreiung und der Zusammenbruch des realen Sozialismus. Eine unbewältigte Herausforderung*, in *ZMR* 80 (1996) 3-25.

KUDO, T. & C. TOVAR, *La crítica de la religión: Ensayo sobre la consciencia social en Marx* Lima: CEP, (1977), [3]1982.

LATOUCHE, S., *La planète des naufragés*, Paris, La Découverte, 1991.

LEE, R., *Modernization, Postmodernism and the Third World*, in *CS* 42 (1994) 1-63.

LEVINE, D.H., *Popular Groups, Popular Culture, and Popular Religion*, in D. LEVINE (ed.), *Constructing Culture and Power in Latin America*, Ann Arbor, University of Michigan Press, 1993, pp. 171-225.

LIBÂNIO, J.B., *Reflexiones a partir de la teología de la liberación. La impli-cación mutua de la doctrina social de la Iglesia y la teología de la libe-ración*, in P. HÜNERMANN & J.C. SCANNONE (eds.), *América Latina y la doctrina social de la Iglesia. Diálogo latinoamericano-alemán, 1: Refle-xiones metodológicas*, Buenos Aires, Ediciones Paulinas, 1992, pp. 169-183

LYOTARD, J.-F., *The Postmodern Condition: A Report on Knowledge*, Minnea-polis, University of Minnesota Press, (1974) 1984.

—, *The Postmodern Explained*, Minneapolis, University of Minnesota Press, 1992.

MARX, K., *Nationalökonomie und Philosophie*, MEGA, I,3, D 111-116, Frank-furt, 1929.

—, *Zur Kritik der politischen Ökonomie*, MEW, 8-9, G. 425-427.

MILBANK, J., *Theology and Social Theory: Beyond Secular Reason*, Oxford, Blackwell, 1995 [1990].

MILNER, A., *Contemporary Cultural Theory: An Introduction*, London, UCL Press, 1994.

MOLTMANN, J., *Die Zukunft der Befreiungstheologie*, in *Orientierung* 59 (1995) 19, 207-210.

MURRAY, CH., *In Pursuit of Happiness and Good Government*, New York, Simon & Schuster, 1988.

ORLÉAN, A., *Money and Mimetic Speculation*, in P. DUMOUCHAL (ed.), *Violence and Truth: On the Work of René Girard*, London, Athlone Press, 1988, pp. 93-105.

PEET, R., *World Capitalism and the Destruction of Regional Cultures*, in R.J. JOHNSTON & P.J. TAYLOR (eds.), *A World in Crisis? Geographical Perspectives*, Oxford, Blackwell, 1989, pp. 186-197.

RATZINGER, J., *Christian Faith and the Challenge of Cultures*, in *Origins* 24 (1995) 679-686.

REICH, R., *L'économie mondialisée*, Paris, Dunod, 1993.

SAID, E., *Orientalism*, New York, Vintage, 1978.

SANDOVAL, M., *Report from the Conference*, in J. EAGLESON & PH. SCHARPER, *Puebla and Beyond: Documentation and Commentary*, Maryknoll, NY, Orbis, 1979, pp. 31-37.

SCANNONE, J.C., *Doctrina social de la iglesia y teología de la liberación*, in *Medellin* 80 (1994) 546-565.

SEGUNDO, J.L., *Teología de la liberación: Respuesta al Cardenal Ratzinger,* Madrid, Cristiandad, 1985.

SHAPIRO, M., *Reading the Postmodern Polity*, Minneapolis, University of Min-nesota Press, 1992.

SOBRINO, J., *The Winds in Santo Domingo and the Evangelization of Culture*, in A. HENNELEY (ed.), *Santo Domingo and Beyond*, Maryknoll, NY, Orbis, 1993, pp. 23-27.

TAMAYO, J., *Presente y futuro de la teología de la liberación*, Madrid, San Pablo, 1994.

TAYLOR, B., *Modernism, Post-modernism, Realism: A Critical Perspective for Art*, Winchester, Winchester School of Art Press, 1987.

Teología india: Primer encuentro taller latinoamericano México, México, D.F., CENAMI, 1991.

TOULMIN, S., *Cosmopolis. The Hidden Agenda of Modernity*, New York, Free Press, 1990.

VATTIMO, V., *The Transparent Society*, Cambridge, Polity Press, 1992.

WALLERSTEIN, I., *The Rise and Future Demise of the World Capitalist System: Concepts for Comparative Analysis*, in *CSSH* 16 (1974) 387-415.

—, *Culture as the Ideological Battleground of the Modern World-System*, in *TCS* 7 (1990) 31-55.

—, *The Modern World System, I. Capitalist Agriculture and the Origins of the European World-Economy in the Sixteenth Century*, New York, Academic Press, 1974.

WALZER, M., *Liberalism and the Art of Separation*, in *PT* 12 (1984) 315-330.

WERNER, D., *Where There Is No Doctor*, Palo Alto, Hesperian Foundation, 1977.

WUTHNOW, R., *Cultural Crises*, in A. BERGESEN (ed.), *Crises in the World-System*, Beverly Hills, Sage, 1983, pp. 61-67.

Faculty of Theology, KULeuven
Sint-Michielsstraat 6
B-3000 Leuven

Georges DE SCHRIJVER

Note: In the following contributions, references to the Discussion Paper will be indicated by their respective page number enclosed in parentheses.

PART TWO

MAIN PAPERS

2

"AXIAL SHIFT" INSTEAD OF "PARADIGM SHIFT"

Twenty years after the first Meeting on liberation theology organized in Europe in El Escorial (1972), a second such meeting was held in the same place, in 1992[1]. I participated in both meetings, and a comparison of them illustrates at least an "axial shift" (*desplazamiento de eje*) from the socio-economic to the socio-cultural perspective, without, however, neglecting the former[2]. At the occasion of El Escorial II, Rosino Gibellini, editor of important works on liberation theology in Italy, told me, "You will be pleased to see that other positions have come closer to that of Argentinean theology". He was referring to the importance given in this meeting to cultural analysis, popular wisdom and religiosity, and symbolic reasoning. Does this shift deserve to be called, in the line of Thomas Kuhn's terminology, a change of paradigm?

In this presentation, I will first treat the Argentinean current of liberation theology, which from the very beginning attached importance to the historical-cultural analysis, and influenced on its adoption in Puebla, contrary to what happened in Medellín. Next, I will show why and how the axial shift referred to above took place within the main stream of Latin-American liberation theology. Lastly, I will point out how, in my opinion, the future of this theology is linked to this shift[3], insofar as it corresponds to a transformation in the reality of the poor and in the real possibilities of their liberation.

I. THE ARGENTINEAN CURRENT OF LIBERATION THEOLOGY

Gustavo Gutiérrez refers to this current – not too well known outside Latin America – as "a current with its own features within liberation

---

1. See the acts of both meetings: INSTITUTO FE Y SECULARIDAD, *Fe cristiana y cambio social en América Latina. Encuentro de El Escorial, 1972*, Salamanca, Sígueme, 1973; J. COMBLIN, J.I. GONZALEZ-FAUS & J. SOBRINO (eds.), *Cambio social y pensamiento cristiano en América Latina*, Madrid, Trotta, 1993. (I will refer to these as: *El Escorial* I or II).

2. Cf. P. RICHARD, *La théologie de la libération. Thèmes et défis nouveaux pour la décennie 1990*, in *FD* 199 (1993). This is a partial translation of an article that appeared in *Pas* 34 (1991).

3. In September of 1996, when I had already written the first version of this paper, I asked Gustavo Gutiérrez about his opinion on whether or not a paradigm shift took place in Latin-American Liberation Theology. His answer was that he preferred not to speak about a paradigm shift, but merely about a shift in emphasis, given the fact that the concern about culture had been present from the beginning.

theology"[4]. Roberto Oliveros, the historian of the origins of liberation theology, calls it "populist", while Alberto Methol Ferré, an opponent of mainstream liberation theology, has termed it "national and popular"[5]. Juan Luis Segundo, for his part, called it: "theology of the people"[6]. In a characterization that was later taken up by others, I called it, many years ago, "theology with its roots in the praxis of the Latin-American peoples" and "theology of popular pastoral ministry"[7]. Some question the inclusion of this current within liberation theology[8].

From the very beginning this current highlighted the importance of historical-cultural analysis without denying the value of structural socio-economic and political approaches. It gave preference, in its contextual-ized theological reflection and reading of the signs of the times, to the mediation by human sciences of a more synthetic and hermeneutic kind than are the social sciences, e.g. historical, cultural and religious sciences. Thus, it understood the people especially from the perspective of a shared *historical* memory, consciousness and project, and of *culture*, or common lifestyle, allowing, of course, for the importance of the leading role the poor and popular culture play in all this. So, special importance was given to the "*religion* of the people" as the incarnation of the faith in Latin-American culture, and which this theological stream saw as the new outcome of a cultural synthesis of the indigenous and the Iberian cultures (and, in many parts of Latin America, of the African cultures as well). Hence, in the confrontation with the socio-economic, political and cultural threats of a capitalist or communist modernization, and above all with secularism that goes hand in hand with them, special importance was given to the problem of the evangelization of culture, to popular piety as an inculturation of the Gospel, and to popular pastoral ministry[9].

4. Cf. G. GUTIÉRREZ, *La fuerza histórica de los pobres*, Lima, CEP, 1980, p. 377.

5. See, respectively, R. OLIVEROS, *Liberación y teología. Génesis y crecimiento de una reflexión 1966-1977*, Lima, CEP, 1977, p. 338; A. METHOL FERRÉ, *Da Rio de Janeiro a Puebla: 25 anni di storia,* in *Incontri* 4 (1982) 22.

6. J.L. SEGUNDO, *Liberación de la teología*, Buenos Aires, Carlos Lohlé, 1974, p. 264.

7. See my work: *Teología de la liberación y doctrina social de la Iglesia*, Madrid, Cristiandad, 1987. Therein, I take up again and re-elaborate on a study carried out in 1982. See pp. 61-74. See also J.B. LIBÂNIO, *Teología da libertaçâo. Roteiro didático para um estudo*, Sâo Paulo, Loyola, 1987, p. 260.

8. Cf. A. QUARRACINO, *Celam. Diálogo fraterno*, Bogotá, CELAM, 1984, pp. 54-69. On the other hand, in his presentation of the first Instruction on Liberation Theology of the Congregation for the Doctrine of the Faith, the actual Cardinal Archbishop of Buenos Aires, then a leading figure of CELAM, had included it within that theology, without any restriction (cf. *L'Osservatore Romano* [weekly edition in Spanish] Sept. 9, 1984).

9. See F. BOASSO, *¿Qué es la Pastoral Popular?*, Buenos Aires, Bonum, 1974; G. FAR-REL, J. GENTICO & L. GERA (eds.), *Comentario a la Exhortación apostólica de Su Santidad Pablo VI Evangelii Nuntiandi*, Buenos Aires, Bonum, 1978. Regarding the Argentinean

The difference in focus from other currents of liberation theology can be explained, at least in part, by Argentina's history and the social situation that this country lived after the Council. During this period, the Argentinean people placed their socio-political hopes in the Peronist movement due to the take over of the military regimes. On the one side, the Peronist movement – which had given self-consciousness to the working class and Argentinean unionism –, the revisionism present in Argentinean historical studies and the influence of the so-called "Cátedras nacionales de sociología" (opposed to both liberal capitalism and Soviet Marxism) given at the University of Buenos Aires, and, on the other side, a renewed analysis of the texts of the Council, especially *Gaudium et spes*, and of Medellín (1968) undertaken from their proper context, caused the Argentinean theological reflection to put an emphasis on categories like people-nation, culture, and popular religiosity, along with the existing themes of poverty, dependency and liberation[10].

As early as 1969, the Argentine episcopate applied Medellín to Argentina, using the focus sketched above, as it had been elaborated by the theologians of the COEPAL (Comisión Episcopal de Pastoral) [i.e., Episcopal Pastoral Commission], led by Lucio Gera. They published the so-called Documento de San Miguel, in which special importance was given to the chapter referring to Popular Pastoral Ministry which was no longer viewed, as it had been in Medellín, from the opposition "elites-masses", but from an understanding of a people-nation based on culture and on justice towards the poor[11].

strain, see also my books: *Teología de la liberación y praxis popular*, Salamanca, Sígueme, 1976, Ch. 4; *Teología de la liberación y doctrina social de la Iglesia*, mentioned above; *Evangelización, cultura y teología*, Buenos Aires, Cristiandad, 1990 (with bibl.); *Weisheit und Befreiung. Volkstheologie in Lateinamerika*, Düsseldorf, Steyler Verlag, 1992, esp. Chapters 3, 4 and 5.

10. Cf. S. POLITI, *Teología del pueblo. Una propuesta argentina a la teología latino-americana 1967-1975*, Buenos Aires, Castañeda, 1992. See also my article, '*Peuple*' et '*populaire*'. *Réalité sociale, pratique pastorale et réflexion théologique en Argentina*, in *NRT* 108 (1986) 860-877, and C. GALLI, *La encarnación del Pueblo de Dios en la Iglesia y en la eclesiología latinoamericanas*, in *Sedoi-Documentación*, 1994.

11. Cf. *Documento de San Miguel: declaración del Episcopado Argentino sobre la adaptación, a la realidad actual del país, de las conclusiones de la II Conferencia General del Episcopado Latinoamericano (Medellín)*, especially, *VI. Pastoral Popular*, in *Documentos del Episcopado Argentino 1965-1981. Colección completa del magisterio postconciliar de la Conferencia Episcopal Argentina*, Buenos Aires, CEA, 1982, pp. 66-101, particularly pp. 84-87. Among the numerous works by L. GERA, cf. *Cultura y dependencia a la luz de la reflexión teológica*, in *Stromata* 30 (1974) 11-64; *Pueblo, religión del pueblo e Iglesia*, in CELAM, *Iglesia y Religiosidad Popular en América Latina*, Bogotá, CELAM, 1977, pp. 258-283; and finally, *Evangelización y promoción humana*, in C. GALLI, L. SCHERZ (eds.), *Identidad cultural y modernización*, Buenos Aires, Boum, 1992, pp. 23-90, etc.

These perspectives, together with those of African and also Asian bishops and theologians, later influenced on the Synod of 1974, and through it, on the Exhortation of Paul VI, *Evangelii Nuntiandi*, especially with regard to the themes of the evangelization of culture and popular religiosity. Thus, it is not surprising that some time later, both themes were taken up again in the Puebla Document, as the intervention of Lucio Gera was decisive in the drafting of the chapter on the evangelization of culture, while that of the Chilean pastoral theologian, Joaquín Alliende (who was of the same mind with what he himself called the "Argentinean school of popular pastoral ministry"[12]), came to bear on the elaboration of the chapter on popular religiosity. In my opinion, it was at this particular point that the perspectives of Puebla – where the historico-cultural was taken into account, without abandoning the social – were decisively enriched and influenced by Gera's thought as well as by the theological insights that had been growing in Argentina, and, in dialogue with these, in other parts of Latin America.

In passing, it should be mentioned that, parallel to the theological current outlined above, the problem of culture also received a lot of attention within the Argentinean philosophy of liberation. This is especially true because Enrique Dussel had introduced the Heideggerian theme of "world" in the Latin-American historical and cultural context, and because Scannone, and with him, Dussel had applied to the poor the Levinasian phenomenology of ethical alterity, understood not only socially and structurally, but also culturally[13]. In this way, and coinciding with earlier works of Rodolfo Kusch[14], they discovered the philosophical (and even theological) relevance of popular wisdom and that of the Latin-American cultural *ethos* and their religious and cultural symbols, – those which "set us thinking (Paul Ricoeur) and tell us what to think". Moreover, at the time liberation philosophers were already speaking about "postmodernity", not exactly in its current understanding, but in

12. Cf. J. ALLIENDE (ed.), *Diez tesis sobre pastoral popular*, in *Religiosidad Popular*, Salamanca, Sígueme, 1976, p. 119.

13. See the two joint works of the first group of philosophers of liberation: *Hacia una filosofía de la liberación latinoamericana*, Buenos Aires, Siglo XXI Ed., 1973, and *Cultura Popular y Filosofía de la Liberación*, Buenos Aires, Siglo XXI Ed., 1975. Cf. Also my article, *Liberación. Un aporte original del cristianismo latinoamericano*, in J.G. CAFFARENA (ed.), *Religión* (tomo 3 of the Enciclopedia Iberoamericana de Filosofía), Madrid, Trotta, 1993, pp. 93-105.

14. For an almost exhaustive bibliography of this author, cf. M. MUCHIUT, G. ROMANO, M. LANGON, *Bibliografía de Rodolfo Kusch (1922-1979)*, in E. AZCUY (ed.), *Kusch y el pensar desde América*, Buenos Aires, Castañeda, 1989, pp. 185-194. It must be noted that Kusch collaborated from the very beginning in the joint works of Argentinian philosophers of liberation.

the sense that modernity's *Ego cogito* and its "I conquer" were dislocated by the Latin-American *difference* (Heidegger) and *alterity* (Levinas), understood from the perspective of the *wisdom of a poor people*.

Needless to say, the "Argentinean school" has also been changing during the last decades, not only because of other currents of liberation theology, but also, and more importantly, because of the changing historical circumstances. For instance, faced with the crisis of the modern Nation-State, it has increasingly taken into account the phenomena of globalization and regionalization (e.g. the Mercosur), although it had in a long standing tradition always brought up the ideas of a "Great Latin-American Mother Land", of the "People of God" and of "all the peoples of the earth". However, this new agenda does not diminish the importance of cultural analysis; on the contrary, it restates the issue of the relationship between universal culture in the age of globalization and the various cultural worlds[15]. Along this line, in the Santo Domingo Document, statements have been formulated not only on Latin-American culture (as in Puebla), but also, taking account of a kind of cultural unity understood analogically[16], on the cultures (in the plural) of Latin America and the Caribbean Islands.

II. THE SHIFT OF EMPHASIS (ACCENT) IN THE MAIN CURRENT OF THEOLOGY OF LIBERATION

1. *Foreshadowings before 1989*

Factors, other than those pointed to above also played an important role in the shift of emphasis in Puebla. For example, there were those who attempted to use the new focus ushered in by Argentinean theology and pastoral ministry, as well as by *Evangelii Nuntiandi*, not so much in order to enrich mainstream liberation theology, but rather to go against it. Nevertheless, I think that the document of Puebla itself, while not failing to integrate the structural analyses of Medellín, sheds a new light on the preferential option for the poor and their liberation, by framing them within a theological interpretation of the *history* of Latin-American

---

15. As an example of the new focus on cultural analysis, see the third part ("Dimensión sociocultural: nuevos tiempos, nuevas lógicas") of the joint, interdisciplinary work: D.G. DELGADO (ed.), *Argentina, tiempo de cambios. Sociedad, Estado y Doctrina Social de la Iglesia*, Buenos Aires, San Pablo, 1996.

16. See my work: *La inculturación en el Documento de Santo Domingo*, in *Stromata*, 49 (1993) 29-53.

evangelization, as well as in the pastoral mission to evangelize *culture*. Furthermore, it takes into account cultural changes[17].

In the discussions that were provoked first by the *Preparatory Document* for Puebla, and later by the interpretation of the Document of the Conference, the dialogue and interaction between the various currents of liberation theology became evident, especially between the Argentinean and the mainstream currents, the latter represented, among others, by Gutiérrez and Leonardo Boff. This explains that in writings of this period, Gutiérrez explicitly analyses the notion of people elaborated by Gera on the basis of the conjunction with "people-nation-culture"[18]. Boff, referring to Scannone, accepts the importance given to cultural analysis when dealing with the Latin-American reality, thus explicitly affirming that in this way "merely sociological analyses have to be transcended"[19].

As for the issue of popular religion, intimately linked with that of culture, undoubtedly some liberation theologians have criticized with some reason, as also Puebla does, its negative or alienated aspects. Nevertheless, already the first Meeting of El Escorial (1972) had pointed out its liberative aspects. In the particular case of Gutiérrez, he had clearly shown during this encounter his preoccupation with a popular spirituality of liberation[20], characteristic of a poor, religious and believing people.

Hence, there appeared in liberation theology, including in its main current, an ever growing interest in popular religion, departing from the Marxist characterization of its being intrinsically "opium of the people". This can already be noted in the works of Gutiérrez' disciples, like Raúl Vidales and Tokihiro Kudó, who discover an authentic, liberative religiosity in the "emergent popular class"[21], and most especially in the works of José Luis González, disciple of both Gutiérrez and the Peruvian cultural anthropologist Manuel Marzal, a specialist in Andean religiosity. However, whereas social analysis is still exclusively used in the first

17. Cf. CELAM, *Reflexiones sobre Puebla*, Bogotá, CELAM, 1979. See also Ch. 2 of my book, *Evangelización, cultura y teología* (n. 9).

18. Cf. G. GUTIÉRREZ (n. 4), p. 196-212. (An article first published in 1978, on the occasion of the Consultative Document for Puebla).

19. Cf. L. BOFF, *Cristo liberador. Una visión cristológica a partir de la periferia*, in *Sr* 14 (1978) 365-379.

20. Even if later surpassed by his own disciples, the Argentinian Aldo Büntig talked already then, in his article *Dimensiones del catolicismo popular latinoamericano y su inserción en el proceso de liberación. Diagnóstico y reflexiones pastorales*, of the "liberative values of the people which they express in sacral gestures of popular catholicism", in *El Escorial* I (n. 1), pp. 146-157. See also: S. GALILEA, *La fe como principio crítico de promoción de la religiosidad popular*, ibid., pp. 151-158. The work of Gutiérrez is entitled *Evangelio y praxis de liberación*, ibid., pp. 231-245.

21. Cf. R. VIDALES & T. KUDO, *Práctica religiosa y proyecto histórico*, Lima, CEP, 1975, pp. 111-116.

case [Vidales and Kudó], in the second case [González], due to the influence of Marzal, special attention is given to cultural-anthropological study. Thus, González recognizes – here he converges with Argentinean analyses – the role of *historical and cultural resistance* played by the Latin-American religion of the poor people, first against imperialist and later against capitalist oppression. For it [religion] helped the people not to disappear as cultural actors, and it even served as a vehicle for expressing alternative historical projects. It must be noted that such cultural analyses of the religion of the people are in line with the theological and social importance given, from the outset[22], by Gutiérrez, to liberative spirituality from the people.

Similarly compounding these influences were the comments received by the Latin-American theologians at the meetings of the EATWOT (Ecumenical Association of Third World Theologians) – from the theologians of Africa (especially in relation to cultures) and Asia (with regard to religion)[23]. Due to all this, attention was increasingly focused on cultural analysis, without neglecting socio-economic analyses.

On the other hand, one can neither underestimate the influence that Church documents, from both the Latin-American Episcopate as well as from Roman and Papal sources (e.g., the two Instructions of the Congregation for the Doctrine of the Faith: *Libertatis Nuntius* [1984] and *Libertatis Conscientia* [1986]), exercised on Latin-American theologians, so that they tried not to give the least bit of an impression of socio-economic or political reductionism. I think that it is unfair to attribute the said reductionism to the leading liberation theologians, with the exception, for example, of Hugo Assmann[24], who was active in a more radical theological current. However, because of the suspicions, even theologians who had not gone to such extremes, could not but state explicitly that they were talking of integral liberation, and this not only of the oppressed classes, but also of the oppressed races, sexes, nations, and *cultures*. Hence, the theme of culture was explicitly present.

---

22. Cf. J.L. GONZALEZ, *Teología de la liberación y religiosidad popular*, in *Pas* 7 (1982) 4-13. Among the numerous works of Marzal, one can consult *La transformación religiosa peruana*, Lima, CEP, 1983. On popular spirituality of liberation, cf. G. GUTIÉRREZ, *Beber en su propio pozo. En el itinerario espiritual de un pueblo*, Lima, CEP, 1983.

23. The acts of the various Congresses have been published. See also *Teología desde el Tercer mundo. Documentos finales de los cinco Congresos internacionales de la Asociación Ecuménica de Teólogos del Tercer mundo*, San José, DEI, 1982.

24. His main work is *Teología desde la praxis de liberación*, Salamanca, Sígueme, 1973 (the main part of the book had already been published in Montevideo, 1971). In this paper I refer to the position Assmann held then, not to his actual convictions.

2. *The Paradigm of "Classic Liberation Theology"*

Lastly, another factor that favored the axial shift can be located on a deeper level, i.e., on the level of the *paradigm* of understanding of reality itself and even of theology. Is the paradigm of liberation theology modern or postmodern? Does it surpass modernity?

Even if I agree with G. De Schrijver on various *modern* characteristics of what he calls "classic liberation theology" and with the reasons that he gives, I find positions like that of Juan José Tamayo, cited also by De Schrijver, more congenial to my thought, because he [Tamayo] discovers in liberation theology a kind of dialectical surpassing of modernity. I also agree with Franz Hinkelammert in that the said theology is not postmodern (in the sense that this word currently has), even if it criticizes not only capitalism but many features of Western modernity[25].

As a matter of fact, I especially agree with the analysis of Antonio González – an outstanding disciple of Ignacio Ellacuría – regarding what he calls "the philosophical meaning of liberation theology". In González' interpretation, liberation theology does not move in the ambit of classic theological categories (the paradigms of substance and subject), but in the ambit of contemporary philosophy, which could be called postmodern, in the sense that "it consists, to a large extent, of a dialogue with the intellectual situation in which Hegel has left us"[26]. Evidently, this is not a conscious philosophical choice of liberation theologians; rather, it only indicates the intellectual and cultural horizon in which they move.

On a cultural and philosophical level, this horizon is characterized by the primacy given to *praxis, difference, alterity, reality, having* or *being* as prior to their understanding from the perspective of the *logos*. González is convinced that this characterizes liberation theology more profoundly than its typically modern features. In this way one understands better liberation theology's *option for the poor* and the *world of the poor*, the emphasis it gives to praxis, its understanding of theology as a "*second act of liberative praxis*" (Gustavo Gutiérrez), or, finally, as "*intellectus amoris et misericordiae*" (Jon Sobrino), the *practical transcendence* of the other, the radical experience of evil "*beyond being*", etc.

25. Both authors are cited by De Schrijver, pp. 17.
26. Cf. A. GONZÁLEZ, *El significado filosófico de la teología de la liberación*, in *El Escorial* II (n. 1), p. 153. Without even referring to liberation theology, Marco Olivetti agrees with González to a large extent with regard to the latter's characterization of the three paradigms; see his article, *El problema de la comunidad ética*, in J.C. SCANNONE (ed.), *Sabiduría popular, símbolo y filosofía. Diálogo internacional en torno de una interpretación latinoamericana*, Buenos Aires, Siglo XXI Ed., 1984, pp. 209-222.

If this is so, then the axial shift (i.e., shift of emphasis) towards a greater consideration of Latin-American cultural *alterity*, so framed that it does not lose the *practical* and *material* (i.e., socio-economic) perspectives, as well as towards a more radical understanding *of the poor and their world* (social as well as *cultural*), and the emphasis placed, not only on the basic ecclesial communities but also on *basic neocomunitarianism* in general (where people live in a "post-traditional" way the gratuity, the alterity and the sense of communities that are traditionally Latin-American)[27], would be no other than *radicalizations* of the foundational paradigm, in the face of the changes in historical reality and new signs of the times. In this sense, the shift toward cultural analysis, without neglecting social analysis, would correspond to the deeper logic of liberation theology.

Hence, although one can speak of a shift of emphasis or axial shift, in my opinion, this is occurring within the radicalization of the same horizon or radical paradigm in which liberation theology from the very beginning had been moving, as far as its basic options are concerned, in spite of its other, clearly modern characteristics which it shared with other postconciliar theologies and with the dependency theory.

3. *Changes after 1989*

All the circumstances enumerated above contributed to this aforementioned displacement, but the decisive factor or the proverbial straw that broke the camel's back was the implosion of real socialism, as symbolized by the fall of the Berlin Wall. De Schrijver alludes to this, referring to the expressions used by Frei Betto and Leonardo Boff after the collapse of communism, pointing in the direction of the new approach[28].

This shift in perspective can be perceived more clearly in utterances by other theologians, also influenced by the events in Eastern Europe and the apparent non-viability of the socialist utopia on a short term basis. E.g., Pablo Richard, who had been an active member of the Christians for Socialism in Chile, coined the term already cited: "axial shift"

---

27. Concerning "basic neocomunitarianism", see D.G. DELGADO, *Las contradicciones culturales de los proyectos de modernización en los 80*, in *Le monde diplomatique* 27 (1989) 15-16, and its continuation: *ibid.* 28, pp. 17-18. On the "post-traditional" mode of assuming traditions, cf A. GIDDENS, *Más allá de la izquierda y la derecha. El futuro de las políticas radicales*, Madrid, Trotta, 1996.

28. Cf. F. BETTO, *El fracaso del socialismo alemán y los desafíos a la izquierda latinoamericana*, in *Pas* 29 (1990) 1-7; ID., *A Teologia da Libertação ruio com o Muro de Berlim?*, in *REB* 50 (1990) 922-929; L. BOFF, *A implosâo do socialismo autoritário e a Teología da Libertaçâo*, *ibid.*, pp. 76-92.

from the socio-economic and political to the cultural. He admits the revolutionary value today of reformism, and affirms that the "power of the poor in history" – which was previously conceived of as primarily political – is, before all else, ethical, religious, and cultural[29]. Only with this power can the people face up to today's strong neoliberalism.

The same perspective has been taken in several of the contributions to El Escorial II. In that meeting, social scientists like Manuel Antonio Garretón gave a positive appraisal of the actual cultural shift towards the valuation of everyday life and its joys (so different from the heroic idealism of Che Guevara). Or like Xavier Gorostiaga, they engaged in a self-critique of the Sandinista strategy for liberation – a strategy more focused on the accession to political power than on cultural transformation. For their part, theologians like Diego Irarrázaval proposed a theology starting from the popular wisdom of Latin America, and others, like Víctor Codina, gave primacy to symbolic reason over modern, enlightened reason. Still others like Pedro Trigo outlined the new alternative collective *imaginario*, about which I will speak shortly[30]. Gibellini was right in noting the rapprochement of these theologians to the positions of Argentinean theology on popular culture.

It seems to me that Pedro Trigo has been one of the liberation theologians who has best outlined and continues to outline the future of this theological perspective which, without abandoning the essence of liberation theology, situates itself in what Richard describes as an axial shift. For Trigo, the culture in the barrios of the big Latin-American cities exhibits a newness that the theologian has to consider; furthermore, this has to be interpreted as the action of God's Spirit among the poor, and as their positive answer to it[31].

Here a new collective *imaginario* is surging as an alternative not only to the *status quo* of late capitalist consumerist culture, but also to the politicized, revolutionary and socialist *imaginario* of the 1960s and 1970s. It revolves around everyday life, interpreting it not as a private

29. Cf. P. RICHARD (n. 2).

30. I refer, respectively, to the following contributions to *El Escorial* II (n. 1): M.A. GARRETON, *Transformaciones socio-políticas en América Latina (1972-1992)*, pp. 17-28; X. GOROSTIAGA, *La mediación de las ciencias sociales y los cambios internacionales*, pp. 123-144; D. IRARRAZAVAL, *Repercusión de lo popular en la teología*, pp. 181-197; V. CODINA, *Fe latinoamericana y desencanto occidental*, pp. 271-296; P. TRIGO, *El futuro de la teología de la liberación*, pp. 297-317.

31. Cf. P. TRIGO, *La cultura en los barrios,* and *El concepto de marginado. Sus usos y su realidad*, in J.C. SCANNONE & M. PERINE (eds.), *Irrupción del pobre y quehacer filosófico. Hacia una nueva racionalidad*, Buenos Aires, San Pablo, 1993, respectively, pp. 13-26 and pp. 45-70, and the theological works mentioned in the notes that follow.

matter, but rather in social and public dimensions, as it involves the creation of culture and a new social fabric[32]. This *imaginario* is the outcome of a new *cultural synthesis*, the subjects of which are many of the suburban poor of our subcontinent, – a synthesis of traditional Latin-American values and modern and postmodern contributions, which tends to take shape within different free organizations of the people[33].

We could call this new cultural "mestization", following Anthony Giddens' descriptions, reflexive and post-traditional, because it takes up the Latin-American communitarian tradition as a free, responsible and solidary response to the crisis provoked by the neo-liberal exclusion of great majorities of people from the socio-economic system, and because, from within traditional popular wisdom, it takes up (modern or post modern) criteria for efficiency, organization and flexibility. To Trigo, this is the communitarian emergence of a new type of human being, whose structural axis is the option for life, and a dignified life for all.

Life is being created amidst death. Dignity is being lived out in situations of humiliating injustice. Joyful celebrations take place in spite of extreme poverty. There is hope in God, against all hope. People live the gratuity of communitarian relations, even in the midst of social exclusion and competitive individualism. Institutions of freedom are created, even amidst oppression. In all of this and in the light of faith, one gets a glimpse of the creative and regenerative presence of the Spirit of God, and of the seed of a really possible future liberation[34].

According to Trigo, the Latin-American novel had already in some way, foreshadowed this, in literary figures like the Christ of the poor, in *Hijo de hombre* of the Paraguayan novelist Augusto Roa Bastos, or in outstanding characters like Rendón Wilka, the culturally mixed indio, in *Todas las sangres*, and in other urban, mestizo characters in *El zorro de*

32. Cf. P. Trigo's article in: *El Escorial* II (n. 1); id., *Imaginario alternativo al imaginario vigente y al revolucionario*, in *RT* 3 (1992), pp. 61-99.
33. Cf. J. SEIBOLD, *Imaginario social, religiosidad popular y transformación educativa. Su problematica actual en medios populares del Gran Buenos Aires*, in D.G. DELGADO (n. 15), pp. 323-388. See also my contributions: *Nueva modernidad adveniente y cultura emergente en América Latina. Reflexiones filosóficas y teológico-pastorales*, in *Stromata* 47 (1991) 145-192; *Les défis actuels de l'évangélisation en Amérique Latine*, in *NRT* 114 (1992) 641-652; *El debate sobre la modernidad en el mundo noratlántico y en el tercer mundo*, in *Concilium* 244 (1992) 1023-1033; *La nueva cultura adveniente y emergente: desafío a la doctrina social de la Iglesia en la Argentina*, in *Argentina, tiempo de cambios*, pp. 251-282.
34. See the description of these phenomena and their theological (or philosophical) interpretation in R. MUÑOZ, *El Dios de los cristianos*, Madrid, Cristiandad, 1987; P. TRIGO, *Creación e historia en el proceso de liberación*, Madrid, Cristiandad, 1988; J.C. SCANNONE, *La irrupción del pobre y la pregunta filosófica en América Latina*, in *Irrupción del pobre* (n. 31).

arriba y el zorro de abajo, – both novels from the Peruvian writer José María Argüedas[35].

For Trigo, the future of liberation theology is linked to this cultural shift of the collective *imaginario* and to the alternatives of the future which, within it, are being created among and for the poor. Nevertheless, the poor, even if they have to be the principal actors of their liberation, cannot liberate themselves by themselves alone. Rather, they have opted for life and the dignity of the human being in union with all those of other Continents, and with those belonging to different social strata. In this age of globalization, the network that they and their organizations form can become a new historical agent: the *international of life*[36].

III. THE AXIAL SHIFT, THE HISTORICAL VIABILITY OF LIBERATION AND THE FUTURE OF LIBERATION THEOLOGY

The axial shift in liberation theology is intimately related to the change in the cultural *imaginario* referred to, which is currently taking place among the people of Latin America, especially among the poor. Theology bears this in mind with the help of cultural analysis, when it reflects on today's signs of the times. However, it does not forget that this alternative *imaginario* takes shape in an alternative social phenomenon: *basic neocommunitarianism.* Hence, it does not give up social analysis either, even if certain overly rigid approaches inspired by Marxism have been abandoned.

Faced with globalization, structural unemployment and the crisis of the Welfare State – socialist, social democratic or populist – and faced with the failure of the self-regulated market to adequately answer the demands of human dignity and justice, a new event is occurring in all parts of the world: the *emergence of civil society*, as different from the State as well as from the market. This society organizes itself to carry out its objectives[37], without expecting to receive everything from the State or the market.

35. Cf. P. TRIGO, *La institución eclesiástica en la nueva novela latinoamericana* (doctoral thesis), Madrid, Cristiandad, 1980; ID., *Argüedas. Mito, historia y religión*, Lima, CEP, 1982, as well as his lectures.

36. See his works cited, in Note 35. His frameworks seem to coincide with some of Anthony Giddens and of Ulrich Duchrow. See his presentation *Dios o Mamón: economías en conflicto*, held at the IX Asamblea de la IAMS (Asociación International de Estudios Misionológicos), Buenos Aires, April 10-19, 1996.

37. See the work already cited, *Argentina, tiempo de cambios* (n. 33), and also D. DELGADO, *Estado y Sociedad. La nueva relación a partir del cambio estructural,*

Thus, also in Latin America, new multi-sectoral social movements similar to those of the First World (for human rights, "green" spaces, quality of life, justice in cases of concrete crimes, anti-corruption, etc.) are being born. But, above all, among the poor is emerging the so-called *new associationism*, or *neocomunitarianism*. This, and all the other movements referred to, are at the same time cause and effect of the above-mentioned alternative cultural *imaginario*, and they nourish it socially and materially.

In the religious sphere, we are no longer referring merely to basic ecclesial communities, as was the case for Puebla, but also to all kinds of religious groups that are not vertically structured. In these groups participate youth, adults, women, men, prayer groups, and also Bible study groups[38]. And the same phenomenon is happening at the economic level, both in the formal and the informal economy: popular economic organizations, micro-entrepreneurships, *pre-cooperativas*, small enterprises established by the workers themselves, communitarian vegetable gardens, "joint purchase" schemes. People organize themselves in order to survive in the most dignified way possible, generating jobs and even producing for the market[39]. In the social sphere, there are neighborhood initiatives (for health, road construction, town lighting, etc.), clinics, school cooperatives, soup kitchens for children or the elderly, mothers' associations, committees for the retired or the unemployed, and various kinds of free popular organizations. In the strictly cultural sphere, we come across not only with folkloric *peñas* or sports associations, but also with a wide variety of local community FM [frequency modulation] radios, and different forms of both formal and non-formal popular

Buenos Aires, San Pablo, 1994; P.H. ORDELAS, *La sociedad civil: su verdad y sus retos. La tercera revolución planetaria,* in *St* 62 (1995) 6-15. See also the entire issue of *Alternatives Sud* 1 (1994): on *"Les mouvements sociaux en Amérique Latine"*. In Brazil, the "Acción de la Ciudadanía" has been instituted: cf. Instituto Políticas Alternativas para o Cone Sul, *Açôes cidadâs no Brasil. Relato de Expêriencias de Comités da Açâo da Cidadania contra a Miséria e pela Vida,* Rio de Janeiro, CESEP, 1995.

38. See my article, *La religión en la América Latina del Tercer milenio. Hacia una utopía realizable,* in *Stromata* 51 (1995) 75-88.

39. On these popular economic phenomena, their interpretation, and the consequent reshaping of the economy and economic science, see especially – among the many works of L. RAZETO – *Economía de solidaridad y mercado democrático,* 3 Vols., Santiago, Academia de Humanismo, 1984-1985-1988; ID. (eds.), *Las organizaciones económicas populares 1973-1990,* Santiago, Academia de Humanismo, 1990; ID., *Empresas de trabajadores y economía de mercado. Para una teoría del fenómeno cooperativo y de la democratización del mercado,* Santiago, Academia de Humanismo, 1990. See also F. FORNI & J.J. SANCHEZ (eds.), *Organizaciones económicas populares. Más allá de la informalidad,* Buenos Aires, San Pablo, 1992; H. ORTIZ R., *Las organizaciones económicas populares. Semillas pequeñas para grandes cambios,* Lima, CEP, 1993.

education[40]. In this manner, a new social fabric is being woven, evidencing a shift in mentality and attitude towards the State and the market, and, therefore, a cultural change corresponding to the new *imaginario*.

Even if various authors differ in their interpretation of this phenomenon, not a few see in this cultural and social shift a *viable alternative* of liberation. Hence, economists like Luis Razeto and José Luis Coraggio see in the popular economy (the former, especially in the popular economy of *solidarity*) an alternative, not only for the micro-, but also for an important sector of the macro-economy (which would interweave with the capitalist and State sectors), constituting together as it were, a "democratic market"[41]. Razeto is rethinking economic science itself and development strategies from the perspective of the economic relevance of *factor "C"* ("community factor"), considered not only in the ethical and cultural dimension, but also as a factor of economic efficiency. It should be noted that the way this problem is set out is an example and an outcome of the emergent cultural synthesis discussed earlier. And this dovetails with other attempts in different parts of the world, and even with those of the UN, of an alternative *human* development, often emerging from the local and the small ("small is beautiful")[42].

These popular organizations tend to link up in the form of a network, i.e., based on a flexible, participative and self-reliant coordination. This seems to correspond to the new "postmodern"[43] cultural sensitivity, and seems to reinterpret the traditional values of solidarity in a post-traditional form (following the expression of Anthony Giddens already referred to). Well then, if in the past century, individual workers did not

40. On the topic of popular education, cf. J.L. CORAGGIO, *Desarrollo humano, economía popular y educación*, Buenos Aires, San Pablo, 1995; O. MONTES, C. LORA & R. BURNS, *Una experiencia de educación popular. La gestión del circuito metodológico en SEA*, Lima, Universidad de Lima, 1993.

41. Aside from the works of Razeto and Coraggio cited in previous footnotes, cf. L. RAZETO, *Propuestas de respuesta a la luz de la encíclica (SRS) a nivel socioeconómico*, in CELAM-CLAT, *Nuevo desarrollo con justicia social*, Bogotá, CELAM, 1990, pp. 349-396; *Para una proyección política del proceso de formación y desarrollo de la economía popular de solidaridad*, in F. FORNI & J.J. SANCHEZ, *Organizaciones económicas populares*, pp. 57-75; *Sobre el futuro de los talleres y microempresas*, in *RET* 2 (1994) pp. 51-75; J.L. CORAGGIO, *La construcción de una economía popular: vía para el desarrollo humano, ibid.*, pp. 29-48.

42. Cf. A. CAFIERO (ed.), *Desarrollo humano: un diálogo con la filosofía*, Buenos Aires, Castañeda, 1995, and the corresponding Informe sobre Desarrollo Humano of the Honorable Senate of Argentina in the context of the PNUD (Programa de las Naciones Unidas para el Desarrollo) [= United Nations Programme for Development].

43. Cf. The "network" metaphor corresponds to the new, more flexible and participative type of institutional organization, and to lateral (neither vertical nor hierarchical) post-modern thinking. Cf. B. WALDENFELS, *In den Netzen der Lebenswelt*, Frankfurt, Suhrkamp, 1985.

acquire political power until they united in unions and federations of unions, so in the same manner, the networking of these organizations (and with the NGO's and others in the different continents and social strata) can yield political power in order to dialogue, from a position of power, both on the national level as well as on the regional and international level, and so obtain a greater equity in an age of globalization. This would involve what Pedro Trigo calls – as I have mentioned – the international of life.

Today, the preferential option for the poor, foundation of liberation theology, is more vigorous than ever because the structural poor to whose ranks have been added the "new poor", or the impoverished middle classes, are facing the threat, no longer of exploitation, but of *exclusion*, in the form of marginalization and unemployment in a society more and more dichotomized between the included and the excluded, the winners and the losers, and fragmented by competitive individualism. On the other hand, the poor are developing a new cultural consciousness, "mestizising" their values with the contributions of modernity and postmodernity and creating a new cultural *imaginario* and a new social fabric, which is spreading, in the form of networks (in this society of communication), to other social sectors and geographic areas. All this cannot leave liberation theology indifferent. So, this theology is discovering here the liberative action of the Lord of history and that of the men and women who respond to Him with an option for life. And a life with dignity, to be sure.

Furthermore, in line with a revaluation of cultural pluralism (and the postmodern appreciation of heterogeneity and difference) *Indio* and *Afroamerican* theologies of a different type are surging. There too, liberation theology feels itself questioned and the need to open itself more and more to cultural and psycho-social analysis and to the anthropologico-cultural study of the ancestral myths of these peoples and cultures, as well as of the forms of syncretism that have appeared in history and/or are existing today. Not a few of these forms – according to important theologians and pastoralists – have been more or less successful attempts at an *inculturation of the Gospel*, made, not by the missionaries but by the indigenous peoples themselves[44].

Hence, the shift of emphasis in liberation theology is in basic agreement, as much with its hermeneutical and theological foundation in the

---

44. Cf. M. MARZAL (ed.), *O Rosto Indio de Deus*, São Paulo, CESEP, 1989, pp. 11-33. On Indio theology itself, see among other works, *Primer Encuentro de Teología India: Delegación mexicana, Teología maya. Conceptos fundamentales*, in *Christus* 58 (1993) 22-27.

option for the poor and of the poor, as with its goal of "critical reflection on the historical praxis in the light of the Word"[45], and with the essence of its method (elaborated through the mediation of the cultural and historical sciences, without neglecting the social sciences). As I have already repeated many times, the cultural shift has a social, and even economic base, even if it does not limit itself to this.

These displacements in approach and in the elaboration of the method exercise an influence not only in the first phase of the hermeneutic circle of liberation theology, i.e., in its critical interpretation of historical reality and praxis in the light of Revelation, but will also certainly have an influence on its rereading of Revelation, from the context interpreted in this way, i.e., in the second phase of the theological hermeneutic circle[46]. As the Instruction *Libertatis conscientia* No. 70 says, "a theological reflection developed from a particular experience can constitute a very positive contribution, for it permits to give witness to some aspects of the Word of God, the full richness of which has not yet even fully been perceived". Well then, the new, alternative cultural *imaginario* and the neocomunitarianism in which it finds its social expression, constitute a *new particular experience*, which, moreover, in my opinion, is being fostered by the action of the Lord of history.

In this way, the new cultural awareness links universal globalization, a new appraisal of particular cultures, and the simultaneous experience of particular, living communities influenced by the vigorous effect of factor "C". Also, because of its active, coordinating role in regional and international networks, it may contribute – in the light of the gift of the Spirit at Pentecost – to rethink not only the ecclesiology of communion, the Mystery of Trinitarian Love, its gratuitous communication in Christ or its concrete shape in the human being renewed by the Spirit of communion, but all and every single of the key theological realities, from the perspective of communion, community, and communication, in accordance with the new social context and the new emerging cultural *imaginario*, especially among the poor – the privileged of the Kingdom.

---

45. Cf. G. GUTIÉRREZ, *Teología de la liberación. Perspectivas*, Salamanca, Sígueme, ²1972, p. 38.

46. On the hermeneutic circle in liberation theology in general, see my book *Teología de la liberación y doctrina social de la Iglesia* (n. 7). On the second phase of this same circle after the axial displacement, see my articles: *Situación de la problemática del método teológico en América Latina. Con especial énfasis en la teología de la liberación después de las dos Instrucciones*, in *Medellín* 20 (1994) pp. 255-283; and *El futuro de la reflexión teológica en América Latina. El comunitarismo como alternativa viable*, to be printed in the forthcoming publication of the Actas del Encuentro del CELAM sobre, *El futuro de la reflexión teológica en América Latina*, Vallendar, CELAM, Septiembre, 1996.

Hence, with Pedro Trigo, I also think that the future of Latin-American liberation theology depends upon its ability to move within this new alternative, cultural horizon. This implies a continued deepening involvement in the axial shift from the socio-economic to the cultural, such that it would consist not of a mere substitution, but of a deepening and enrichment of perspectives. For liberation theology must not forget – as De Schrijver indicates – that the cultural is sustained by the socio-economic, even if the cultural transcends the economic.

In this way, Latin-American liberation theology will be able, in the light of faith, to respond theologically to the world of the poor, and contribute to its transformation in the love and justice that spring forth from the Gospel[47].

Facultades de Teología y Filosofía   Juan Carlos SCANNONE
Av. Mitre 3226
San Miguel, Buenos Aires, Argentina

---

47. This article has been translated by M.R. Pajarillo.

3

IRREDUCIBLE MULTIPLICITY
AND THE SEARCH FOR A COMMON PROJECT
A FEMINIST PERSPECTIVE

Beginning with the title of his work, G. De Schrijver's text indicates a paradigmatic change in the theology of liberation which was elaborated in Latin America in the decades of the sixties and seventies. According to De Schrijver, from a socio-economic analysis of Marxist inspiration, as a basis for the elaboration of theological thought, the theologians of liberation have begun to use a cultural paradigm for analyzing reality. This passage from one paradigm to another indicates a rupture point in this theological production.

In commenting on De Schrijver's proposition, I shall confine myself to the Latin-American situation, and then refer to sociology and feminism, the fields from which I shall react to the text.

I. Pertinence of the Proposition on a "Paradigmatic Rupture"

The current conception of a "paradigmatic rupture" refers to the concept elaborated by Thomas Kuhn, for whom "the term 'paradigm' is used in two different senses. On the one hand, it stands for the entire constellation of beliefs, values, techniques, etc. shared by the members of a given community. On the other, it denotes one sort of element in that constellation, the concrete puzzle solutions which, employed as models or examples, can replace explicit rules as a basis for the solution of the remaining puzzles for normal science"[1].

A change of paradigms presupposes two conditions: (1) the abandonment of the forms of elaboration of knowledge which were valid until then, and (2) their substitution with new formulations that are accepted by the academic community. In the present case of the theology of liberation, there is evidence that, at least in Latin America, neither of the two instances have been fully achieved. It is still premature to speak of the emergence of a clearly distinguishable, new paradigm. The current theological theory formation presents a lower degree of homogeneity in terms of methodological reference, compared with that which evolved

---

1. T. KUHN, *The Structure of Scientific Revolutions*, in *International Encyclopedia of Unified Science*, Chicago, University of Chicago Press, 1970, p. 175.

during the past two decades. A great diversity appears in relation to the constitution of the common ground from which the theological "liberating" theory emerged. Between 1995 and 1996, three meetings in Latin America have demonstrated this situation. The first occurred in Brazil and had as its discussion theme the very question of the "paradigm crisis". The preparatory texts that were furnished by theologians from various countries presented rather different perspectives.

The second meeting was also held in Brazil, and gathered theologians – men and women – from all over the country. The occasion was the annual meeting of the Society of Theology and Religious Sciences (SOTER). For the preparation of this meeting, various essays were written and compiled in a publication entitled "Theology and New Paradigms". Finally, in Costa Rica, a seminar was held with a small number of Latin-American theologians in order to discuss the tendencies of theological theory in the context of globalization. This seminar was followed by a meeting of women theologians, and the theme of the meeting was the inclusion of a gender perspective in theological theory.

The rapid sequence in which these meetings were held, and which gathered together significant male and female theologians of Latin America, points to the situation of perplexity and research in which theological elaboration finds itself today in our continent. In the case of the last seminar, the corresponding publication has yet to appear. The texts from the first two meetings, however, demonstrate the absence of a consistent corpus that is more or less homogeneous in terms of subject matter and methodology. This contrasts with the situation when liberation theology was in force. In this sense, more than a "passage" from one paradigm to another, LT finds itself in a situation of searching for new paradigms without having yet built a new "theological consensus" around an alternative proposition. Thus, we have before us a diversity of approaches.

Jorge Iulanelli, while admitting "a deep crisis of the Theology of Liberation"[2], affirms that "it is possible to admit that the Theology of Liberation faces a widening of approaches, adding to the socio-political question, that of economics, of plurality and cultural diversity and that of ecology. But, and for this very reason, I affirm it is a widening: there is no absence or loss of the socio-political approach"[3].

Franz Hinkelammert, however, argues that what is happening today is not a crisis of paradigms but the victory of one paradigm, that of the market. According to him, there is, in contemporary societies, a

---

2. J. IULANELLI, *Crise de paradigmas: Discutindo sobre a Teologia da Libertacao*, Sâo Paulo, CESEP/mimeo, 1995, p. 14.

3. *Ibid.*, p. 7.

"dogma" or a "taboo" that prevents the questioning of the dominance of the market, and this dogma acts to maintain such dominance. "There is practically no one who challenges this great dogma of our time: neo-liberalism, and its policy of globalization, its structural reorganizations and its ideological and theological susceptibilities. It is in the name of this paradigm that the idea of a crisis of paradigms is pushed onto all thinking beings. Therefore, the question does not seem to me to be a crisis of paradigms, but rather the fact that a sole paradigm has won and has imposed itself in an unquestionable manner. We see a great celebration of certainty, not at all that of fallibility. This victorious paradigm acts in name of the most absolute assurance. (...) It is understandable that this victory of one paradigm produces in the others the sensation of a loss of certainty, a loss of past paradigms, etc"[4].

Hugo Assmann, for his part, proposes a plurality of approaches: "Perhaps the moment has come for us to realize that the socially relevant Christian commitment, and the linguistic forms in which this can be expressed, require always, and simultaneously, *different articulating matrices* of theoretical thought and of the criteria for practice. (...) What we need today, in my view, is an interpenetration of many approaches... [which is] vital and fundamental to adequately come to grips with the complexity of reality. Any uniformisation would lead to misunderstandings". Assmann advances the following proposals to respond to the challenges of the current situation: a modern concept of ethics, the assumption of democracy, and the acceptance of a market economy. Instead of the definitive anathema that other theologians pronounce on the market, Assmann considers the possibility of a positive approach to the reality of a partially self-regulated market, without abandoning the criticism of "the idolatry of a messianised market", outside of which there can be no salvation. The dynamisation and creative diversification of the economy require the efficient mechanisms of a self-regulatory market. These do not produce exclusion alone but inclusion as well. Both logics of inclusion and exclusion coexist, and this allows for a consideration of the existence of a positive functionality of the market. It is possible, according to Assmann, to accept the market in a critical yet positive form, without relinquishing goals of solidarity[5].

A second element that is necessary to face the new challenges is a full adherence to democracy as an institutionalized form of facing uncertainties

---

4. F. HINKELAMMERT, *Comentario al texto provocativo presentado por el* CESEP, Sâo Paulo, CESEP/mimeo, 1995, p. 4.
5. H. ASSMANN, *Por una sociedad donde quepan todos*, Sâo Paulo, CESEP/mimeo, 1995, p. 1.

and differences of all kinds. For Assmann, "it makes a lot of sense, for example, to raise the question of the democratization of the international financial system, of the financial decision-making processes, of access to the market in general"[6]. A third element is introduced by Assmann: a modern conception of ethics which includes basic options and a normativity that finds adequate expression in institutions. This implies not only the existence of an organizing principle like, for example, the humane and pluralist society, but also the negotiation of a collective consensus that has criteria for the verification of the practical effects of this organizing principle. "Specifically in the economic field, there is no economic ethic capable of exercising a relevant influence if it remains confined to general principles and does not take the shape of mechanisms regulating the interaction between the economic agents and the society as a whole"[7]. At the end of his essay, Assmann proposes, as a "unifying reference", the reality of living bodies that entail human desires and necessities. "Living bodies are the source of verification criteria, in order to identify both the virtues and vices of capitalism as well as those of the unsuccessful 'real socialism.' It is also the key reference to link the acceptance of the market economy with the demand for political decisions concerning the planning of social goals that do not arise spontaneously from the market mechanisms"[8].

The various essays that compose the book "Theology and New Paradigms" are also indicative of a situation of research that characterizes current theological production in Latin America. For Leonardo Boff, the appropriation of ecological theory by the theology of liberation, while maintaining the oppression/liberation paradigm, allows for the elaboration of a theology that responds to the concerns of the North and the South of the planet, and permits "dialogue and convergence in diversity between the world's geographic and ideological poles"[9]. Among the other authors, there is no consensual proposition as regards a unifying element in the new theological approaches in Latin America. The journey of Libânio, a well-known Brazilian theologian of liberation, through no less than nine different paradigms that were chosen more or less by chance, and to which he does not attribute "the gravity" or "the weight of the great paradigms of science", is *paradigmatic* of this situation of perplexity in which LT finds itself today[10].

6. *Ibid.*, p. 5.
7. *Ibid.*, p. 4
8. *Ibid.*, p. 8.
9. L. BOFF, *Teología e Novos Paradigmas,* in MARCIO-FABRI ANJOS (ed.), *Teología e Novos Paradigmas,* Sâo Paulo, Loyola/SOTER, 1996, p. 88.
10. *Ibid.*, pp. 35-48.

In the foregoing set of texts in connection with the meeting on the "crisis of paradigms", it is significant that Assmann begins by referring, on the one hand, to a certain "rigidity of concepts" in the last decades among those Christians most sensitive to the cries of the poor and the excluded, and on the other hand, to the need currently felt to depart from schematic and definitive answers. "Precisely because of the great necessity for theoretical seriousness that the complexity of rapid changes occurring in the world demands, we find ourselves much more concerned with improving our questions than with accepting conclusions"[11]. And the "provocative text" of the 1995 conference on the "paradigm crisis" in Latin-American liberation theology not surprisingly ends with a series of questions: "From these premises, several fundamental questions arise: how is it possible to elaborate a project of radical change and the actions necessary for its realization, based on a fallible knowledge and a plurality of perspectives? How may we overcome the insecurity to act for the transformation of the world, based on fallible knowledge? How can we rediscover sense and coherence in the plurality of rationalities, interpretations, actions and meanings of life? Is it possible to find universal distinguishing criteria that allow for a fruitful dialogue between religions, cultures, sexes and classes? How can we reflect theologically the practices of resistance and liberation of the poor, assuming the fallibility of our knowledge and our projects?"[12]

Therefore, I believe that, rather than a passage from one paradigm to another, what characterizes the contemporary Latin-American theological production that claims to be a theology of liberation, is a process of a change of paradigms in which the possible alternatives have yet to be clearly defined. Exceptions to this situation are the case of Leonardo Boff, who has explicitly assumed, in his current works, an "ecological paradigm" that is closely associated with the liberation of the poor, and the case of some others like Hinkelammert who deny the existence of a crisis and remain within the scope of the paradigm(s) previously in force.

II. A New Agenda for Doing Liberation Theology

Chapter four of De Schrijver's text constitutes, in my opinion, the second part of his essay in which the author, after an analytico-critical presentation of LT in the first three chapters, puts forward some proposals

11. H. ASSMANN (n. 5) p. 1.
12. *Ibid.*

to help compose a "new agenda for doing liberation theology". The following are a few of my considerations relative to this second part.

In the first place, I shall express the propriety of the elaboration of a socio-analytical framework founded on Wallerstein's and Giddens' views, as the author suggests. The understanding of the "world capitalist system", in the terms these analysts propose, allows for a rigorous conceptual interrelation of the socio-economic, political, and cultural spheres, and illuminates the connections that ultimately shape global interdependence. However, great care must be taken to ensure that sexism and racism, as ideas, would not be treated as if they primarily are either "ideological doctrines" (50-52) or "cultural themes" (72-74).

In the development of feminist thought, a long and fruitful discussion with the Marxist postulates has indicated the need to consider gender and race relations as structuring social reality as much as class relations do. Feminist theories point to "the narrowing down of the concept of production to the production of food objects and commodities alone. This precludes an adequate understanding of traditional female activities like housework, care for the elderly and the sick, child-bearing and rearing"[13]. They affirm the social character of the relations established between men and women in all aspects of social existence, in family and in work, in politics and in culture or the symbolic sphere. They have discussed not only the simultaneity and the coextensiveness of different forms of oppression but also the irreducibility of the multiple orders of domination to a single hierarchy. They point critically to "the structural character of domination, which manifests itself in the relations of daily life (...) (demonstrating) that domination (is) at once occult and reproduced by way of powerful institutions such as the family, the separation between public and private, institutionalized heterosexuality, the gender-based division of work and employment, etc"[14]. A gender analysis thus requires more than either a simple widening of existing categories or the addition of the oppression of women to other supposed expressions of class oppression[15]. Gender social relations run through, limit, and orient all social practices, and constitute one of the organizing principles of society. Therefore, we do not postulate a pure and simple substitution of

13. S. BENHABIB & D. CORNELL, Introduction. Beyond the Politics of Gender, in S. BENHABIB & D. CORNELL (eds.), Feminisme as Critique. Essays on the Politics of Gender in Late-Capitalist Societies, Cambridge, Polity Press, 1987, p. 5.
14. E. VARIKAS, Refundar ou Reacomodar a democracia? Reflexoes críticas acerca da paridade entre os sexos, in EF 1 (1996) 69.
15. L. NICHOLSON, Feminism and Marx: Integrating Kinship with the Economic, in S. BENHABIB & D. CORNELL (n. 13), p. 28.

economic relations by gender relations, a substitution that turns gender
into a totalising explanatory category. What we propose is an attempt to
grasp the complexity of reality without an a priori hierarchization of
social relations.

As regards the questions posed at the end of the Discussion Paper,
I shall underline those that seem to me most pertinent to feminist considerations. In relation to authors of social change, De Schrijver investi-
gates the plurality of the poor "dispersed in various cultural settings"
(74). Beyond the considerations on the existing cultural diversity of
the poor, it seems to me that the question that ought to be advanced is
the following: how can we attend to or reckon with, simultaneously and
coherently, the constitutive diversity of humanity, its immanent unity,
and the possibility to build a collective project in response to a common
interest.

By choosing "the poor" as the main object of its theoretical elaboration, LT has elected them as sole subjects of change in close correla-
tion with the Marxist "working class". It ended up hypostasizing them
and constructing its homogeneity on the occulting of the multiplicity of
existing social relations. A pauper is not merely a member of an economically defined social class. He/she is also a man or a woman and
colored or white. And the exploitation and domination to which he/she
is subjected occurs in a differentiated form, according to his/her multiple
social identities. Feminist elaborations have criticized abstract universalism, which prevents the recognition of singularities. At the same time,
feminist thought does not give in to "the vision which is gaining ground
today, postulating the radical irreducibility of the single points of view,
closing individuals within homogeneous, static, essential identities, denying them the possibility to realize a common interest, despite all that dif-
ferentiates humanity"[16].

The consideration of the fact that not even "the poor" can be reduced
to their belonging to a social class allows, or mandatorily leads to, the
consideration of the situations of violence, domination, and exploitation
that occur inside particular social classes. Thus, it becomes possible to
think and express, for example, situations of domestic violence, which is
covered by an absolute silence in the pastoral speeches and propositions
of the *comunidades eclesiais de base*, the grass-roots church organizations, at least in Brazil.

Another question raised by De Schrijver refers to the challenges
that arise from the fact that "a variety of groups within contemporary

16. E. VARIKAS (n. 16), p. 75.

Christianity can claim, and in fact are claiming, to be seriously reflexive in some matters within their 'specialization' of concern. And this leads to a variety of approaches within the whole Christian body" (77). The author's observation is particularly appropriate in the case of Christian women. Daringly, they do not confine their claims today to a supposed "specific field", but aim, through the elaboration of a feminist theology, to redefine and transform all the intellectual institutions and academic disciplines including theology[17]. Thus, it seems to me that, more radically so than in the case of LT, feminist theology offers new paradigms in the elaboration of theological knowledge, as they reach the core of the question, and discuss the very concept of divinity through the necessity to go beyond the masculine representation of the Christian God. In harmony with a consistent portion of feminists, Christian women theologians refute the traditional understanding of "human nature", which confines women in a "specificity" in which maternity is destiny and not choice. This refutation of the practice to resort to biology in order to explain the social – and the religious – order of the sexes leads them to a radical criticism of the current hierarchical organization of ecclesiastical institutions particularly of the Catholic Church. By affirming individual autonomy, which is not opposed to the construction of collective ideals, but on which these ideals can be built, Christian women theologians come to recognize their condition as moral agents who are capable of ethical choices in all fields of life, including those relative to the control of their own capacity for conceiving new human beings.

These considerations are far from constituting an answer to the questions raised by the Discussion Paper. Rather, stimulated by the text itself, they perhaps deepen these very questions and perplexities, as we near a millennium's end that finds us facing challenges to which we have yet no solutions.

Institute for Religious Studies ISER   María José ROSADO NUÑEZ
Rua Rafael de Barros 174/113
São Paulo, S/P, Brazil

17. E.S. FIORENZA, *En mémoire d'elle*, Paris, Cerf, 1986, p. 8.

4

UNDERSTANDING LOVE:
THE BASIC PARADIGM IN LATIN-AMERICAN THEOLOGY

Doing theology today is sparked by a basic drama present in the human condition. Certain specific realities are obstacles to love. Concerning this drama, exhortations made by St. Paul seem most relevant: Christ's liberation does not reach us through a particular law and its enslavement; what matters is faith that makes itself felt through works of love, under the guidance of the Spirit (cf. Gal 5,1-26). In our Latin-American context, many persons are constrained by religious and theological padlocks. But when we enjoy degrees of freedom, we do envision a new heaven and earth. In a special way, this is due to relationships among and with the poor. We acknowledge the guidance of the Spirit in the hearts of the people of God and throughout creation. This fosters theology in the sense of an "intellectus amoris", a paradigm that is adequate for the Latin-American context.

When one makes an assessment of the three decades of liberation theology, one becomes deeply thankful for the courage and loyalty of fellow travelers. We have made mistakes, and at times, we have been undialogical and have invented new absolutes. On the other hand, there are fresh and urgent tasks ahead of us in the midst of the crisis of modernity and of the challenging signs of an unchartered epoch.

However, there are widespread misunderstandings: liberation theology is sometimes described as being socio-political, a product belonging to Latin America, and something that is done by a few experts who teach truths to ordinary Christians. Another caricature is to say that it lacks philosophical grounds and is partly or totally unorthodox, dangerous to church life, and a mere fashion that is dying out. May this presentation be a means to remove these misunderstandings. And what is most important, may we acknowledge the theological gifts that the Spirit of God places in the Church, which is a sacrament of salvation.

Why does LT generate a new paradigm? Latin-American and Caribbean theologies are special not because they nurture subversive ideas or because of their contextual spirituality. All good theologies include a critique of injustice and are prayerful ways of understanding. Our Latin-American model is due to persons and places of relationships. In epistemological terms, our model involves a radical interaction between spirituality, concrete acts of (historical) love, and reflecting on Christian faith within the Church and for the welfare of humanity. In practical terms, we are members of Christian communities that systematically examine their praxis of love in contexts of suffering and struggle for life. LT is done as a web of relationships that strength the perspective of faith of marginalized but hopeful peoples. All this is a way of doing theology; it is the soul of a revolutionary paradigm. Therefore, what really matters is neither a political option nor a conceptual construction but fertile relationships between humans and social sectors that are understood in critical and dialogical ways.

When one makes an assessment of a multi-faceted phenomenon, one usually underlines trends and issues. Since the eighties, this assessment on LT has been done from different standpoints[1]. One can also focus on a basic and fundamental question: what is changing in Third-World theologies? This is what this Symposium is concerned all about. My contribution outlines a Latin-American paradigm (first part), lays out certain questions and issues – not in apologetic nor nostalgic terms – (second part), and concludes by pointing out some elements present in our emerging agenda.

I. Words from the Edges

The wellsprings of the theologies of the Two-Thirds World are all those people excluded from centers of power and knowledge. Their cry and wisdom of faith denounces the ignominious suffering in which they

---

1. See general assessments: *Encuentro Latinoamericano de Teología*, in E. Ruiz (ed.), *Liberación y Cautiverio*, México, Clavería, 1975; R. Oliveros, *Historia de la teología de la liberación*, in I. Ellacuría & J. Sobrino (eds.), *Mysterium Liberationis, Vol. I*, Madrid, Trotta, 1990, pp. 17-50; F. Taborda, *Métodos teológicos na América Latina*, in *PT* 19 (1987) 293-319; J.C. Scannone, *La teología de liberación, caracterización, corrientes, etapas*, in *Stromata* 38 (1982) 3-40; P. Richard, *La teología de la liberación en la nueva coyuntura*, in *Pas* 34 (1991); J.B. Libânio, *Panorama de la teología de América Latina en los últimos veinte años*, in J. Combin (ed.), *Cambio social y pensamiento cristiano en América Latina*, Madrid, Trotta, 1993, pp. 57-78; A. Bentué, *Panorama de la teología de A.L. desde el Vaticano II a Santo Domingo*, in *TV* 34 (1995) 159-191; F. Hinkelammert, *Taking Stock of LA Liberation Theology Today*, in *CQ* 76 (1995-6) 17-31; D. Irarrázaval, *Nuevas rutas en la teología latinoamericana*, in *RLT* 39 (1996); V. Codina, *Une théologie à partir du Sud*, in *SEDOS* 28/2 (1996) 54-56; L. Boff (ed.), *A teología da libertaçâo, balance e perspectivas*, São Paulo, Atica, 1996; M.F. Anjos (ed.), *Teología e novos paradigmas*, São Paulo, Loyola-SOTER, 1996. See also dialogues with other forms of theology: two conferences in El Escorial (Spain) in 1972 and 1992, published as *Fe cristiana y cambio social en América Latina*, Salamanca, Sígueme, 1973, and *Cambio social y pensamiento cristiano en América Latina*, Madrid, Trotta, 1993; and the international dialogues organized by Eatwot, published in *Voices from the Third-World*, XVIII/1 (1995), 28-34; 59-78; XVIII/2 (1995) 38-42; 102-112; XIX/1 (1996), 37-51; 106-137.

find themselves constantly bordering between life and death. Why does good theology come from the margins of social and religious standards? Because there humanity comes to encounter the Saving God. The God who saves not because of our personal achievements but because of His unconditional divine love for the "last ones", for everyone at the open roads and hedgerows (cf. Lk 14,22).

What is the origin and character of theology in our Latin-American experience? What steers up this reflection is the irruption of the poor in our midst. On the grounds of this principle, LT is accurately described by Sobrino as *intellectus amoris*, that is, as an understanding embodied in concrete acts of "love for the poor of this world, as an understanding of love analogous to the reality of the revealed God"[2]. Theology deals with faith, hope, and ultimately love, since the latter is the definitive way of being (cf. 1 Cor 13,13). We know God as love in the Trinitarian relationship, as love in Christ crucified and risen, and as a preferential love that saves the poor. This mystical but concrete understanding of love is the soul of LT.

What is the theological status of the common people, of those on the borders between life and death? They are becoming participants in the process of understanding the Christian mystery. This is so because God hides the mysteries of the Kingdom from learned people and reveals them to the little ones (cf. Mt 11,25). Thus, LT is not done in their name, nor does it replace their contribution. Insofar as the marginalized respond to the guidance of the Spirit of God, they can be considered as real subjects doing theology[3]. Thus, their theological charism is sustained not by their cleverness but by God's grace. However, any idealization of the wisdom of the people distorts reality (oppression maims the poor). Every person needs to be open to salvation. In the following section, we shall return to these hermeneutics of the poor, women, indigenous, blacks, and all the marginalized.

What is then our paradigm? Is it an understanding of reality through the human sciences? Has it been more socio-economico-political and is it now focusing on culture, race, gender and ecology? The discourse

---

2. J. SOBRINO, *El principio misericordia*, Santander, Sal Terrae, 1992, pp. 49-50; 70-71. Likewise, Clodovis Boff points out that our point of departure is not an idea or methodology but, rather, compassion and struggle on behalf of all those who suffer: our "encounter with the poor as subject". See, *Epistemología y método de la teología de liberación,* in *Mysterium Liberationis, Vol. I* (n. 1), pp. 79-113.

3. As J.I. González Faus has stated: the poor are "a theological *locus* due to the action of the Spirit". In this way he summarizes the debate over the 'people' both as subjects in terms of inculturation and as objects of oppression in need of emancipation. See, *Cambio social y pensamiento cristiano en América Latina* (n. 1), p. 355.

about this paradigm belongs to the philosophy of science (even though many use – and misuse – it for any kind of model or project). It is a major vision with its values and actions. In contrast to a European classical and medieval ontological paradigm, a universal and modern paradigm is historical and subjective. As a part of this, we have the theological framework of the "history of salvation" which is the background for LT.

I state briefly the dimensions of our paradigm: 1) its *principle* is the irruption of the marginalized peoples of the world; 2) it has *hermeneutical features* provided by theological subjects (poor, women, blacks, indigenous, etc.) with the mediations of the social sciences and of symbolic, ecumenical, and inter-religious perspectives; 3) its *theological nucleus* is "understanding love" that is grounded on the revelation of God, to whom the Church responds with her faith, teaching, celebration, and service for universal salvation.

Is there a change of paradigms in today's world[4]? It seems to me that modernity is today a civilization present in all societies. It has a humanistic, rational, scientific, and technical paradigm (and several versions of this major paradigm exist in the First and Two-Thirds worlds). One phenomenon (not strictly speaking a paradigm) is the post-modern exaltation of the individual and a fragmentation of reality. Often and in an uncritical way, the modern world-view is assumed by most theological inquiries (e.g., seeing modernity through the eyes of the elates and not from the perspective of the underside of history).

A profound change has been taking place in all the so-called Third-World theologies (and not only in the Latin-American Catholic expressions of LT). During the sixties, theology began to be done in systematic communion with the marginalized (thanks to the "irruption of the poor", in Gustavo Gutiérrez' words). Together with Church leaders and with professional theologians, the poor began to take part in the process of thinking the faith. Since the eighties (and even earlier in some areas of the world), new types of hermeneutics begun to be developed in terms of gender, race, culture, ecology, and inter-religious dialogue. In our continent,

---

4. Philosophy of science offers the best discourse on paradigms. In simple terms, a paradigm is a major model of knowledge and action (and not merely any type of framework, as it appears in ordinary – and often misleading – language). Thomas Kuhn made the key distinction between science that accumulates knowledge, and, periods when paradigms change. See T. KUHN, *The structure of scientific revolution*, Chicago, University of Chicago Press, 1962. For first steps in a dialogue between science and theology (concerning changing paradigms), cf. F. CAPRA & D. STEINDL-RAST, *Belonging to the Universe, Explorations on the Frontiers of Science and Spirituality*, S. Francisco, Harper, 1992; L. BOFF, *Principio-Terra*, São Paulo, Atica, 1995. Therein, Boff spells out 10 characteristics of a new holistic paradigm, cf. pp. 76-80.

these silenced communities have also began to share their God-language: Afro-Americans, Indigenous peoples, *mestizos*, women, the youth, Asian-Americans.

All of this implies both a deeper and wider LT paradigm. The original accents on praxis and liberation are now enriched in terms of inculturation, ecology, gender, and inter-religious responsibility for our common Earth. So, in general terms, it is not a shift from the political to the cultural. What really matters is the historical and spiritual presence of the marginalized and loving peoples, with whom Church leaders and professional theologians are interacting and developing adequate methodologies. I want to stress this point: it is not a matter of one or another scientific mediation or of a set of religious concepts; much more important is the fact that relationships and understandings of reality shape a paradigm that better correspond to the hopes of the down-trodden. In our case, it is the day-to-day praxis of solidarity, compassion, struggle against hunger, and sharing of joy. In these concrete terms, we understand the Mystery of Love, which transforms and alleviates our historical journey.

Let me add some personal feelings and insights. When one is or opts for being in the margins, modernity looks not fascinating but repugnant and in need of salvation. In the course of many years among marginalized peoples, I have learned from them a critical participation in modernity and their alternative small paths. I admire their nuanced and non-unilateral view, as they select elements and accomplish a reconstruction of the modern human condition. Christian Parker calls it their hemidern logic[5]. So, with enthusiasm and a critical and reconstructive view, one faces modern challenges. The cultural-religious experience of common people may be seen as the heart and goal of this new construction. I share with others this acknowledgment of the political and symbolic meaning of the people's faith-experience. And certainly, LT has to continue being committed to be in dialogue with all these challenges.

Let us also recall that modernity is a universal model that historically establishes itself into a relationship of center-periphery (9-16)[6]. *Amerindia*, as one periphery, is at the origins of modernity. Thus, it may also become one source of modernity's re-orientation. *Amerindia* can be the source of a new paradigm arising from the margins.

5. See C. PARKER, *Otra Lógica en América Latina*, México, FCE, 1993, pp. 375-382

6. A global-critical vision is well drawn by E. DUSSEL, *Sistema-mundo, dominaçâo e exclusâo*, in CEHILA, *Historia da Igreja na America Latina e no Caribe*, Petrópolis, Vozes, 1995, pp. 46-58. Marginalization and exclusion are at the core of modernity. So, modernity is not only reason, science, technology, nation states, market and progress.

Nevertheless, I grieve to see how modernity maims common people, segregates others, and induces yet more individualism. It also distorts the identities of urban migrants. Everyone becomes more or less dizzy with illusions, with the "ideology of progress, modernity's favorite 'story line'" (40). Moreover, the poor are drawn either into socio-religious forms of fundamentalism or by fantasies supplied by economic publicity and political propaganda. All of this moves one to collaborate with the critique of modern realities.

Let me synthesize my convictions: fellowship with people on the borders of modernity has shaped the paradigm of LT. Instead of assuming uncritically the myth of progress, we believe and work within small alternatives. In terms of faith, we care for the seeds of the Kingdom and believe in the resurrection of humanity and creation. But hope is cautious since today's "fields of action" are fragmented and lack a unifying force (31). So, one again affirms the original and permanent thrust of LT: a holistic and pluri-dimensional liberation. Our paradigm, *intellectus amoris*, is characterized by praxis, a symbolic understanding of truth, and the people's life in the Spirit. This differs from *intellectus fidei*, which usually highlights concepts produced and communicated by the elite. Let us now continue examining the basic concerns of LT in our particular situations and in our dialogue among Two-Thirds World theologies.

II. QUESTIONS AND ISSUES

The process of LT is marked by the formulation of radical questions rather than by apologetics (which is more present when there is social-ecclesiastical misinterpretation and repression against this Christian reflection). This process is also characterized by hermeneutical guidelines rather than by closed statements. These guidelines constitute a praxis of love in the face of suffering and a spectrum of insights into God's transformation of life on this Earth. One must, however, be modest and realistic. LT exists on the edges of Church and society. It is produced by minorities who wish to reflect on the faith and wisdom of all peoples. If one examines the bulk of academic and pastoral theologies in Latin America, one will find the imitation and reproduction of First-World thinking. But bulky realities are often less important than new beginnings. In our continent, LT is like a small, intelligent child who is formulating and re-formulating the most challenging questions.

Some say that LT is in a state of comma or, furthermore, that it is dying. Has it abandoned its revolutionary orientation? Has it shifted from the socio-economic to the cultural (1, 9, 31, 71)? Some sectors of the Catholic church do emphasize (Christian) culture in order to replace the option for the poor. This emphasis was made explicit in the Puebla and Santo Domingo events. Yet this phenomenon does not represent the whole Church, and particularly, it does not take place in our theological tradition. For example, one of the architects of the paradigm of inculturation, Paulo Suess, has suggested "symmetrical social relationships, political participation, and, cultural differences in our societies, and also in theology, liturgy, evangelization and church institutions". Suess also underlines that culture is not a sector of reality, and that we are committed to the historical projects of the "other"[7]. Let us now examine key questions and hermeneutical issues.

1. How can LT be classified? Several types of evaluations (made by those who produce LT) have reached a consensus: since the 1980s, significant alterations in our regional and world contexts are posing new theological concerns and themes[8]. Some establish a sequence: foundation in the 1960s and early 1970s, development in the 1970s and 1980s, reformulation and plural ways of doing theology in the late 1980s and the 1990s (see R. Oliveros, J.B. Libânio, P. Richard, and others). One can situate LT within church renewal: the periods of Medellín, Puebla, and Santo Domingo (A. Bentué), or in reference to social options: a class analysis, a political revolution, people and culture (J.C. Scannone). Another typology emphasizes mutation and creativity owing to emerging subjects and themes women, ecology, etc. (V. Codina, P. Richard). Some acknowledge particular methods and a common concern: understanding and celebrating God through the reality of the poor (F. Taborda, myself, and others).

In these assessments, it becomes clear that LT is a process with plural developments. If we speak accurately, this means that a monolithic or compact LT does not exist as such. This is most evident today. LT is like a rainbow with different shades of colors.

2. We may reconsider the question: what is changing in LT in terms of historical vision and action? G. De Schrijver addresses four sets of good questions: (a) social analysis, (b) culture, race, and gender, (c) the proposal of a Christian culture, and (d) popular religion (77-78). It seems to me that theology today is exploring more dimensions of our intricate reality: LT does not abandon politics in order to concentrate on cultural

---

7. P. SUESS, *Evangelizar a partir dos prójetos historicos dos outros*, Sâo Paulo, Paulus, 1995, p. 217 and all chapter 10. Therein, Suess spells out the political agenda in the paradigm of inculturation.
    8. In this section I refer to assessments mentioned in n. 1.

and subjective concerns. Today, we are more critical towards interpretations that the social sciences offer to theological inquiry. Clodovis Boff honestly states that concrete mediations have to be modified since today there is no certitude as regards analysis, strategy, and the social project; nonetheless, our roots, God and the poor, do not change[9].

We are not naive in our discourse on culture in the context of globalization and of the totalitarian market and its idols[10]. De Schrijver summarizes a critical apprehension of contemporary phenomena: the cultural dynamics of post-modenity, globalization, the impact of the market on cultural diversification, the mingling of local and universal cultures, and other factors (44-59).

3. Let us now take stock of the deeper questions raised in our theological communities. They clearly point towards the roots of the paradigm. It is not a matter of clever arguments or of Church procedures. It is a matter of persons in all their lacerated and hopeful human condition. It is in their terms, and in a committed relationship with them, that theologians raise questions so as to walk forward together.

The basic question places our faith in the God of love *vis-à-vis* dehumanization. Gustavo Gutiérrez has asked, "In our Latin-American context, how do we thank God's gift of life in the midst of an early, unjust death? How do we express the joy of being loved by the Father, while our brothers and sisters suffer? How do we sing when people are in pain...?" And, "how do we speak of God who is revealed as love, in the midst of poverty and oppression?"[11] This shows how theology is born and sustained by love, not in sentimental ways, but by an authentic love with spiritual and political dimensions.

9. C. BOFF & L. BOFF (n. 1), p. 102.

10. Latin-American theologians can today be in dialogue with critical views of our global scenario: P. MORANDÉ, *Cultura y modernización en América Latina*, Santiago, U.C. de Chile, 1984; C. GARCÍA, (ed.), *Políticas culturales en América Latina*, México, Grijalbo, 1987; F. HINKELAMMERT, *Democracia y Totalitarismo*, San José, DEI, 1987; N.C. GARCÍA, *Culturas híbridas, estrategias para entrar y salir de la modernidad*, México, Grijalbo, 1989; J.J. BRUNNER, *América Latina: cultura y modernidad*, México, Grijalbo, 1992; G. BONFIL, *Identidad y pluralismo cultural en América Latina*, Buenos Aires, CEHASS, 1992; M.C. BINGEMER (ed.), *O impacto da modernidade sobre a religião*, São Paulo, Loyola, 1992; G. ARROYO Y OTROS, *Por los caminos de América*, Santiago, Paulinas, 1992; C. PARKER, *Otra lógica*, México, FCE, 1993; R. ORTIZ, *Mundialização e cultura*, São Paulo, Brasiliense, 1994; J. LARRAÍN I., *Modernidad, razón e identidad en América Latina*, Santiago, A. Bello, 1996.

11. G. GUTIÉRREZ, *Beber en su propio pozo*, Lima, CEP, 1983, p. 19; and *Hablar de Dios*, Lima, CEP, 1986, p. 19. Likewise: L. BOFF & C. BOFF, *Como fazer teología da libertação*, Petrópolis, Vozes, 1986, p. 11. For them, the most important question is "how do we live as Christians in a world of miserable people?". As for J.B. LIBÂNIO, the fundamental question is this: "*what is the meaning of the Christian faith in a world of oppression?*", in *Panorama de la teología* (n. 1), p. 59.

New strands of LT provide radical questions. The identities of the marginalized constitute the grounds of faith. In indigenous theology (a process in which I have participated since 1981) it is often said: "can we be indigenous people and be Christian?" In black theology one hears: "is it possible to be black and be a Christian?"[12] Women's theology formulates a radical question concerning God's gift of life in circumstances wherein women and men are denied, in historical terms, their human condition[13]. In ecological reflection, there is an explicit demand that Christian salvation is for the benefit of all living beings, instead of having an anthropo-centric religion. Here the sharp question is: "how is Christ and the Christian community a sign of holistic salvation?"

These questions of faith point to a way of understanding the Ultimate in reference to everyday concerns: being impoverished, black, indigenous, women, ecologically responsible, and members of God's people. Evidently, they are not questions arising from the "center" of today's world; they are ways of discovering truth on the "edges" where we are get to be free and joyful.

4. Furthermore, a survey of the main issues manifests how the irruption of the marginalized sets the course for theology. LT's manifold production is neither a list of rationalistic theses nor an encyclopedia of matters of faith. An adequate image is that of a *caminhada* (a Portuguese word that is used to refer to a concrete journey of God's people). It is the movement of a community in terms of solidarity, struggle against evil, common dreams, the forging of life, and understanding love. This reality (participation in the *caminhada*) is a pre-condition for any relevant theological work (on the part of those who are considered professionals). When this is the case, production is not logocentric (16)[14]. Theological production is a building of bonds as we name the Mystery who is revealed to us (in spiritual terms: we walk into the Mystery and respond to it in contemplation) and as we discover the rationality of being human and being cosmic in terms of science and philosophy.

---

12. A.A. DA SILVA, *Concientização, organização, fe e luta*, São Paulo, Asett, 1993, pp. 13. Likewise: M. RODRÍGUEZ: *Is it possible to be Back within the Catholic Church?*, in *GS* 48 (1994) p. 305.

13. María P. Aquino asks: "how is full life in God announced to those who live on the fringes... people who are denied their human integrity, with what language are they told about their being sons and daughters of God?", *Nuestro clamor por la vida, teología latinoamericana desde la perspectiva de la mujer*, San José, DEI, 1992, p. 33.

14. It may be said that we do not build on the cornerstone of modernity. G. De Schrijver reminds us that "the basic characteristic of modernity can rightly be called logocentrism". Neither is our cornerstone pre-modern nor post-modern; it is within modernity and goes beyond it.

I shall give an account of two levels of theological production. One is hermeneutical, and it may be compared to walking along those long and wide avenues. We have various hermeneutics, which are ways of understanding and communication, ways whereby Christian revelation is accepted in faith and put into practice in love and hope. The other level is confrontational, for there is a continuous dialogue and dispute with other forms of doing theology. This second level may be compared to walking along difficult paths. We draw lines and make distinctions, but we also receive insights from those who think differently. Then we learn to reformulate our points of view.

a) The hermeneutical production has universal and regional features. I would like to underline that the understanding of Christian praxis belongs to many communities throughout the world (done in Latin America neither for the first time nor better than elsewhere), that it has an ecumenical quality (barely present in our so-called Catholic continent), and that it is an eco-human and inter-religious responsibility (due mostly to Asian and African contributions).

This accomplishment forms part of the Two-Thirds World experience. It is a rich interaction that has formal moments. Allow me to focus on a pioneering series of international dialogues and the recent general assembly of the Ecumenical Association of Third-World Theologians[15].

In general terms, it comprises the hermeneutics of humanity's "irruption": "aspirations of the oppressed towards their full humanity", "historical irruption of the poor", "irruption of the Third-World", "irruption of the image of God from the standpoint of the poor"[16]. Theology is done within this fascinating and demanding historical and spiritual process. As regards sources and methods, these international dialogues show that theologians do not reduce their work to a highly specialized interpretation of sacred texts. Instead, they do contextual hermeneutics (listening to challenges that the social, political, economic, cultural, sexual, racial, and religious realities place before theology), and have as their sources

15. The first five international conferences took place in Tanzania (I), Ghana (II), Sri Lanka (III), Brazil (IV), India (V), between 1976 and 1981. See their statements in *Teología desde el tercer mundo*, San José, DEI, 1982. My quotes are from the paragraphs of this publication. The third and latest General Assembly of EATWOT (Kenya, 1992) has a moving document: *A Cry for Life*, the spirituality of the Third-World (my quotes are from the pages of the official publication following that assembly). Unfortunately, only a few persons can participate (due to financial limitations). More regreatable is the fact that a good number of Third-World theologians are not able to communicate with each other concerning their respective works.

16. *Teología desde el Tercer Mundo*, III (n. 15), pp. 28-30; IV, pp. 6-26; V, pp. 26-31; V, p. 52.

primarily the Word of God, the Church and its communities, the spirituality and praxis of liberation, and social, anthropological, and religious
signs in the world of today[17]. It is also noteworthy how the cultural and
religious go together with the social and political dimensions. One of the
Asian conferences calls for a synthesis between the religious-cultural
and the socio-economic aspects[18]. Assuming these hermeneutical principles, the Third General Assembly of EATWOT takes a great step forward
in terms of spirituality: the manifold cry for life (of the poor, women,
blacks, indigenous movements and religions, Hispanics in the First-World,
and the ecological movement) is read in reference to Christ and the
Spirit and as a "cry for God". Also, there is a realistic concern for alternatives: "we see the Spirit in our bonding... hope we offer each other;
visioning, struggling, empowering"[19].

Likewise, the hermeneutics done in Latin America is embedded in
new events: the down-trodden look for good human conditions, and
Christian communities grow spiritually as they work for peace and justice. These and other factors renew our theological inquiries. It is not a
mental exercise. What we seek to understand are the signs of the times
and, particularly, the irruption of what has been silenced. Here we need
the mediations of the human sciences. The heart of this process is to
be nourished by the sources of faith, the Word and the Spirit present in
human history and in the whole cosmos.

Methodologically, there is a common course, and there are several specific hermeneutical avenues. A good outline is drawn up by Clodovis
Boff[20]. Usually, there are three moments, three kinds of mediations:
human understanding of history (socio-analytical mediation), reflection
on faith and the living Word that moves us to personal conversion and
historical transformation (hermeneutical mediation), and liberating action
and contemplation (practical mediation).

A careful appraisal shows a plurality of hermeneutics. It is a spectrum of
different theological communities with their particular insights, concepts,

17. Concerning context and methods: I, pp. 3-14; II, p. 21; III, p. 5; IV, pp. 6-26; V,
pp. 9-31, emergent methodology: V, pp. 38-44. And concerning sources in the broad
sense of the word: II, p. 21; III, pp. 34-35; V, p. 42; II, p. 23; IV, pp. 19-26, 53-64, 74-
77; V, p. 49. Concerning use of social sciences, and social analysis: I, p. 7, 32; III, p. 33;
V. p. 43.

18. See V, pp. 44, 73. Therein, it is stated that "the socio-economic and the religious-
cultural are essential components of an integral liberation". And also pp. I, 6, 27; III,
pp. 25, 32, V, pp. 53-60. Regarding this point, several conferences admit the existence of
differences, together with common perspectives: I, p. 36; V, pp. 7, 44.

19. Nairobi, Kenya Document (n. 15), pp. 2, 3-6, 9-11.

20. C. BOFF, *Epistemología y método de la teología de liberación*, in *Mysterium Liberationis*, I (n. 1), pp. 79-113.

symbols, and celebrations. Each hermeneutics is an understanding and communication of the response in faith to God's mysterious revelation and salvation given to humanity. (Some speak of hermeneutics only as a way of interpreting the Bible. As for us, here we are speaking of a wider concept.)

It seems to me that LT has developed four main avenues, while others are being built such as eco-hermeneutics and a *mestizo* perspective. All of these four are generated by specific communities of faith with their respective ways of understanding God, celebrating the Sacred, and being in Love. Among all of these, there is a common option for life, feelings, concepts, and projects. Unfortunately, there also exist obstructions to communication and the lack of a common theological agenda. Allow me to briefly present these four major hermeneutics[21].

i. Common people, whether Evangelicals or Catholics, are systematically reading the Word. They joyfully discover God's power to change their lives and their environment. With the assistance of exegetes (notably Carlos Mesters and innumerable "biblical teams"), these communities develop a method of prayer, biblical reflection, and human commitments.

ii. Women have constructed their hermeneutics from the grounds of everyday experiences and liberating relationships and praxis. In this response to God's Presence, andro-centric reality is confronted, and a full humanity is affirmed. A gender perspective reconstructs political, sexual, artistic, ecumenical, cosmic, and mystical dimensions, which are relevant for women and men.

iii. Black communities – inspired by African and North American theologies – are examining their history of salvation. In spite of racism and the self-denial of their identity and religion, black Christians generate a christological, ecclesial and spiritual understanding that has its own dynamics and symbols.

iv. Indigenous reflection – according to its representatives – is concrete, holistic, symbolic, mythical, and communitarian, and builds life

---

21. These hermeneutics are described in my *Nuevas rutas*. May I recommend some basic works. C. MESTERS, *Peoplés biblical hermeneutics*, in *La biblia, el camino de un pueblo*, Buenos Aires, Paulinas, 1987; G. MARCHAND & J. MIZZOTTI, *Metodología, lectura pastoral de la biblia*, Lima, Centro Mariano Montfortano, 1992; and the journal *Revista de interpretación bíblica latinoamericana* (published since 1989). Womens theology and gender perspective: U. KING, *Feminist Theology from the Third-World*, SPCK, London, 1994. A. HERRERA, *Teología afroamericana*, Quito, Centro C. Afroamericano, 1994; *Indigenous Theology: CENAMI, Teología India I*, Quito, Abya Yala, 1991; M. MARZAL (ed), *Rostros indios de Dios*, Lima, PUC, 1991; V. DELORIA, *God is Red*, Golden, North American Press, 1992; A. PEELMAN, *Christ is a Native American*, Maryknoll, NY, Orbis, 1995.

for all. Ritual and communion with the Earth is an essential component of reflection. Indigenous wisdom is relational, and affirms reciprocity between different elements.

Thus, we have plural, emergent, and open hermeneutics. It is neither a system to be learned and reproduced mechanically nor a new monolithic "summa". It is rather an ongoing and beautiful mosaic, the fruit of compassionate and intelligent work done by women and men.

b) A confrontation with other types of theology takes place in a global scenario. Its immediate context is the internal church struggle, but it is mainly due to ideological and religious conflicts within our societies. So, the inter-theological dispute is secondary; what is most important is the Christian responsibility *vis-à-vis* evils that harm humanity.

Third-World dialogues are mostly concerned about colonialism and every form of oppression, including racism, sexism, and religious and cultural domination. A critique is addressed to churches and theologies insofar as they are complacent and have become collaborators with these evils. In the Conferences previously mentioned, African theologians opt for methodologies that are different from the dominant ones in the West, while Asian theologians question instruments and concepts closely linked to Western culture and capitalism[22].

In our Latin-American context, the first series of polemics were with liberal, progressive forms of thinking, while from the eighties onward, there arose more controversy with the neo-conservatives (in the historical churches and in new Christian movements). Both of these discussions deal rather with the social implications of faith and theology and scarcely with biblical and doctrinal issues. G. Gutiérrez made the famous distinction between a theology in dialogue with the modern spirit (the effort by progressives to speak of God in an adult world) and a theology in dialogue with the oppressed, those considered non-persons (the perspective of the poor)[23]. P. Richard points out that, within our continent, there is a strong theology of oppression, and he draws a sharp contrast between thinking from the center – with its salvation through law and concepts – and thinking from the periphery – with its salvation through faith and resurrection[24]. To these we have to add internal debates, mainly about ecclesiology, and about social mediations such as the following: the use

22. See *Teología desde el tercer mundo*, II (n. 15), pp. 22; V, pp. 32-37.
23. G. GUTIÉRREZ, *La fuerza histórica de los pobres*, Lima, CEP, 1979, pp. 307-365. In facing all of these debates, he says that what matters is not theology but that people be free, p. 393.
24. P. RICHARD, *La iglesia latinoamericana entre el temor y la esperanza*, San José, DEI, 1980, pp. 17-33.

of Marxist categories and strategies, the meaning of poor and people, cultural and political priorities, patriarchalism, racism, and ecological categories.

It seems to me that all of these discussions, although at times very painful, have strengthened LT and motivated a critique among ourselves and within our faith communities. I also see much work ahead of us in a crucial debate: the Christian response to modern forms of socio-economic-cultural idolatry and the problem of the theological sustenance of the "total market". An Ecumenical Institution in Central America, DEI, and especially Franz Hinkelammert and Jung Mo Sung are opening up this urgent debate[25]. It is not the case of making the modern market economy synonymous to evil, yet we need a critique of economico-religious factors and a design of human alternatives with the depth of Christian liberation.

III. CONCLUSION: AN OPEN AGENDA

In the process of LT, we walk in the rhythm and the fellowship of the marginalized. Our basic agenda arises from the people's voices and wisdom, from their silence, from their cry for life and joy. One critically and openly listens to these voices. One reads the signs of our times, and relies on the guidance of the Spirit of God. We also have specific tasks within Christian communities and church structures and tasks as professionals who place our leadership at the service of human salvation. Allow me to conclude with some elements present in the agenda of our paradigm, *understanding love*, as we continue to join innumerable efforts against oppression and for the sake of a holistic liberation. All of this is, if we speak from the heart, a way of doing theology for the glory of God.

This agenda is organized according to the three dimensions of our paradigm: its principle, hermeneutics, and theological nucleus.

First, peoples, in particular contexts and within a universal modernity, have concrete life-projects. Here we find concrete signs of global alternatives. They are like seeds in rocky land which are small and fragile but growing and hopeful. They are signs of a new humanity insofar as they

---

25. See DEI, *La lucha de los dioses*, in *Los ídolos de la opresión y la búsqueda del Dios liberador*, San José, DEI, 1980; F. HINKELAMMERT, *Teología del mercado total*, La Paz, HISBOL, 1989; J. MO SUNG, *Deus numa economía sem coração*, São Paulo, Paulinas, 1992. Hinkelammert warns that philosophy speaks of a crisis of paradigms, but reality shows there is one universal paradigm: the market. See *Determinismo y auto-constitución del sujeto*, in *Pas* 64 (1996) 18-25.

are ways of sharing basic human needs, instead of destroying each other and our environment (as it now happens in our "world order").

In many ways, as persons and communities, we affirm and transform life for ourselves and others. These life-projects are potential contributions to larger alternatives; they have to establish links with one another and jointly carry out a holistic program. This open agenda demands intelligent imagination and no fantasies. The planet where we live and our human condition seem to be going towards a dramatic future. This reality summons our responsibility for the survival of everyone and everything.

In our world, future scenarios are not grey. Common options have a variety of colors. Even the (supposedly) universal framework has different versions. People say that there is one technology, educational system, market, system of mass media, and organization of modern society. Certainly, there are world-standards, but at the same time, one sees pluri-formity within the dominant framework. On the other hand, there is widespread malaise since progress does not satisfy the human heart. At times, this malaise goes together with a longing for realistic alternatives. This is expressed by religious language, humanistic ethics, art, and new social movements.

There are also reasonable global proposals. Anthony Giddens argues for a "post-scarcity order", and a "life-style pact" between North and South, spelling out a viable development program (64-69). This program takes into account local and global issues on politics, the family, health, women, ecology, economics, and self-help groups. Leonardo Boff correlates a planetary concern with the point of view of the poor and excluded. We have to change the course of civilization, with the logic of the well-being of all the Earth. This may be done according to an emerging paradigm[26]. Paulo Suess explains political aspects in the church's strategy in terms of an inculturated liberation: democratic participation, different human projects, ethics in politics, economic rights, people's identity and autonomy, structural changes that go hand in hand with socio-cultural alternatives, and a struggle for justice with the logic of hope[27]. These and other blueprints show an intelligent imagination, and disagree with post-modern skepticism.

Another realm for open discussion is the staggering question about modernity. Has the market-society become a monolithic paradigm? Or

26. See L. BOFF, *Da libertaçâo e ecología: desdobramento de um mesmo paradigma*, in M.F. DOS ANJOS (ed.), *Teología e novos paradigmas*, pp. 75-88; L. BOFF, *Principio-Terra*, pp. 76-80.
27. See P. SUESS (n. 7), pp. 234-235.

do we in fact have economic-political-ethical plural possibilities? Is modernity in such a radical crisis that we have to move into another paradigm: a new spirituality?[28] I share the opinion that, considering modernity's two basic orientations (material progress and instrumental logic) and the dimension of human freedom and its rationality, if the latter sets the pace for the former, then we may reconstruct a healthy modern agenda[29]. Another key question is how cultures are transforming modernity. J.C. Scannone speaks of "a synthesis between people's wisdom and modernity that transforms each of them from within"[30]. In all of this, we are reshaping a principle: the irruption of the poor in modern contexts. This principle is a fertile ground for a liberating paradigm.

A second conclusion deals with hermeneutics. A rich spectrum is being developed in Two-Thirds World theologies and in our particular Latin-American reflections. This is due to classical LT and to new theological communities that are working on challenging themes and perspectives. Paulo F.C. de Andrade and others are emphasizing gender, ecology, rituals and celebrations, art, healing, death and life, subjectivities (identity and relationships according to each economic-cultural milieu), day-to-day experiences and utopias, mysticism, and people's wisdom and their symbolic production[31].

Theology as "understanding love" is nurtured by communities of believers according to the construction of one's particular identity, history, and spirituality. This is happening in the people's biblical hermeneutics, in communities of Afro-Americans and Indigenous peoples, and in the explicitly holistic way generated by women. Let me underline this last point. Pilar Aquino presents a synthesis of Latin-American women's work as a "logic that gives life...that faces universal problems and seeks well-being and justice in the whole world"[32]. In this sense, epistemology developed by women tends to be both concrete and universal, and thus offers a foundation for other hermeneutical projects.

28. Concerning this point, see L. BOFF, *Nueva Era: la civilización planetaria*, Burgos, Verbo Divino, 1995, pp. 85-122.

29. See I. WALLERSTEIN, *¿El fin de qué Modernidad?*, in *Pas* 64 (1996) 10-17; and J. LARRAIN, *Modernidad, razón e identidad en América Latina*, Santiago, A. Bello, 1996. Following Habermas, he argues that communicative reason has to give direction to instrumental reason; both are necessary, but the former has to be cultivated more; See pp. 247-248.

30. J.C. SCANNONE, *El debate sobre la modernidad en el mundo nordatlántico y en el tercer mundo*, in *Con* 244 (1992) 124-125.

31. P.F. CARNEIRO DE ANDRADE, *Novos paradigmas e teología latinoamericana*, in M.F. DOS ANJOS (n. 1), pp. 61-62. See also P. RICHARD, *La teología de la liberación en la nueva coyuntura, temas y desafíos nuevos para la década de los noventa*, in *Pas* 34 (1991).

Urgent debate and inquiry has to be carried out in neglected areas: a pluri-cultural Church, symbolic thinking, and inter-religious dialogue. Insofar as the church acknowledges its pluri-cultural constituency and mission, hermeneutics may not remain mono-cultural. How can the people of God and its authorities promote different interpretations of God's message to humanity?[33] Another urgent task is to leave room for symbolic knowledge in our professional work. The people's wisdom is character-ized by insights on rituals, icons, narratives about day-to-day experience, biblical imagery and art. This enriches other forms of understanding because compared to conceptual frameworks, symbols touch the hearts and minds of people. Symbols are better mediations for an understand-ing of God's mystery in history and the cosmos[34]. Moreover, we need some hermeneutics of salvation which take into account sensibilities and ideas of different religions and which can also be enriched by the pluri-religious reality within the Christian tradition[35]. In these three areas, it is possible to discover holistic, ecumenical, and Catholic perspectives.

A third conclusion refers to the heart of the paradigm: understanding love. Two-Thirds World theologies blend the human and the divine: "love among the poor and towards its enemies... shows the presence of the Father's love..., the commandment of love among brothers and sisters means being disciples of the Lord". As churches, we have "the mandate of Jesus to take the message of love and service to all the peo-ples of the world"[36].

This is not an emotional enterprise that abstains from holistic praxis and promotes closed human and spiritual relationships. Nor is it an empty call for a "civilization of love" (without a critique of contemporary idols). Rather, it is a paradigm that creates and transforms life. Doing theology is one expression of "following Christ by loving" (Eph 5,2). As St. Paul draws concrete implications for this "imitation of God", so it may be said that the work of understanding revelation and salvation today is

32. P. MARIA AQUINO, *Teología feminista latinoamericana* (manuscrito), 1996, pp. 5 and 24.

33. Marcelo Azevedo rightly says: "we may no longer justify a mono-cultural Chris-tianity. Rather, the results of an inculturated evangelization will be a multi-cultural Chris-tianity". See M. AZEVEDO, *Cristianismo, una experiencia multicultural*, in *REB* 220 (1995) p. 779.

34. On symbolic thinking, see V. CODINA, *Creer en el Espíritu Santo*, Santander, Sal Terrae, 1994, pp. 175-179; and my *Repercusión de lo popular en la teología*, in *Cambio social y pensamiento cristiano en América Latina* (n. 1), pp. 186-191.

35. Faustino Teixeira gives a deep, radical proposal: *Novos paradigmas resultantes do diálogo inter-religioso*, in M.F. DOS ANJOS (n. 1), pp. 105-133.

36. *Teología desde el tercer mundo*, IV, (n. 15), pp. 42, 52, and *A Cry for Life* (n. 15), p. 11.

done "by loving". For example, by loving-thinking oneself in Christ as *mestizo*, indigenous, white, and black; by loving-thinking Christ as woman and man since we are all part of the body of Christ; or by interpreting the communion of the saints in terms of ancestors especially in the African or Amerindian perspective.

Living and thinking in this way may be seen as a gift of God's Spirit. What does "the Spirit of him who raised Jesus from the dead... living in you" (Rom 8,11) imply for theology? In LT – as in other forms of reflection – it implies that we receive new life and understand such a life. When we think and live in the Spirit, there is no spiritual enclosure because each believer-receiver of life also becomes a believer-giver of life. This pneumatology is present in women's interpretation of the divine Presence (as well as in other interpretations about Life).

All these languages of faith are revealing old-new dimensions. Black theologians see God as community[37]. Indigenous peoples acknowledge the divine as Mother Earth[38]. People's hermeneutics understand discipleship in day-to-day *caminhada* towards the Ultimate celebration. Women do theology, as Ana María Tepedino says, with "another music", with a "praxis of love"[39].

A polyphonic humanity is naming God. This sustains our paradigm, "intellectus amoris". Theology is first and primarily the way a community speaks to God, who is all in all. No concept or symbol about the divine can be a final word. What really matters is mutual communication, and silence, when we enjoy love.

Instituto de Estudios Aymaras   Diego IRARRAZAVAL
Apartado 295
Puno, Perú

---

37. M. RODRÍGUEZ (n. 12), p. 123

38. *Teología India II* (n. 21), Final Document: "at this propitious hour for the Amerindian peoples and for all the peoples of the world, we wish that Mother Earth be again full of flowers... (and the Catholic Bishops present in this meeting add) ... that Christianity may be enriched, thanks to to the indigenous religions, with a respectful relationship with Mother Earth". See pp. 184-187.

39. A.M. TEPEDINO and M.L.R. BRANDÂO, *Teología de la mujer en la teología de liberación* (n. 1), pp. 293-294.

5

THE POLITICAL AXIS OF AFRICAN LIBERATION
THEOLOGY

I. Methodological Considerations

1. *Justification for a Personal Reading*

A personal reading of G. De Schrijver's (hypo)thesis seems appropriate at the beginning of this response. Indeed, this is a necessary step, even if difficult and risky. Any attempt at understanding another person's 'speech,' – particularly written speech – involves interpretation. For as hermeneuticist Paul Ricœur has argued, compared to the spoken word, written speech is at some disadvantage in many ways. "Written speech", he notes, "cannot be 'rescued' by all the processes by which spoken discourse supports itself in order to be understood – intonation, delivery, mimicry, gestures". In the absence of all these 'supports' for understanding, therefore, only the meaning within the written text can save the meaning of the text. In Ricœur's words: "Henceforth only the meaning 'rescues' the meaning without the contribution of the physical and psychological presence of the author. But to say that the meaning rescues is to say that only interpretation is remedy"[1]. Yet it is precisely here – namely, where does the meaning intended by the author lie? – that the difficulty and risk involved in textual interpretation become evident. And given the length and scope of the essay in question, these elements are formidable.

Where a response is the task, however, interpretation becomes all the more unavoidable because a reaction to, or assessment of, an idea or position needs to proceed in the light of the issues raised by the original question. It needs to address and even test the (hypo)thesis as presented. It is in this sense that it has been said that, in an exercise such as this one, the understanding of the question becomes at least as important as the response. This means that, if the response is erroneous, the error will more often than not reflect some inadequacy or failure of analysis and understanding as regards the issues involved in the question, assuming that the question is well articulated (which in this case it is).

---

1. C. MYERS, *Binding the Strong Man: A Political Reading of Mark's Story of Jesus*, Maryknoll, NY, Orbis, 1988, p. 4.

The exercise we are undertaking, then, is clearly not superfluous: the immediate point facing us is to try to see what the issues are that are explicated in the essay we are concerned about here. Not to be overly repetitious, however, I shall be brief. I might be ridiculously simplifying, but for the purpose of this response, I shall present in a few paragraphs the thrust of the essay's argument as I read it, and explain from what perspective I do so. Then I shall spend the bulk of my presentation reacting to the essay's argument from that particular viewpoint.

2. *The Issues*

The central issues addressed by De Schrijver's essay revolve around the influence that the phenomena called 'modernity' and 'postmodernity' have brought to bear on our universe in general and on the theologies of liberation of the 'Third-World' (hereinafter the 'South') in particular. Aided by the work of various authors, De Schrijver discusses the meaning of these phenomena and how they have emerged in history. His main discussion intends to demonstrate that, though manifestly European (or Western) in origin, the effects of modernity, through its five mainstays or 'pillars' of science and technology, rationality, the profit motive, faith in unlimited material development, and the autonomy of the nation state have come to take hold of the whole world. Their protagonists presented these pillars of modernity as 'grand stories,' realities that could be appealed to so as to supply 'objective' answers to the world's perplexing question in their respective areas. But these grand stories that constituted modernity were eventually found to be wanting; they did not lead to the fulfillment of the longings of the human soul and psyche. Instead, doubt eventually emerged concerning their efficacy as sources or foundations for 'universal' order.

This disillusionment towards 'metanarratives', as some of De Schrijver's authors call the grand stories, appeared both as a subjective feeling among individuals and as empirical factors of change. Rather than science being seen and understood as a tool of objective validity, for instance, it came to be generally understood in the sense of efficacy: what is scientific is 'whatever works' for me/us here and now. The question for science no longer was what is the objectively valid; it became, rather, what is useful or what succeeds in meeting the needs and desires of the moment. Thus, now, we do not have singular, objective or universal answers to questions that arise as a result of scientific investigation; we do have, on the contrary, "an indefinite number of meaning-generating agencies,' each of which is pragmatic and self-referential" (34).

At this point, modern science dies. This 'death' of science, understood as the universal supplier of educated meaning, if I understand De Schrijver correctly, has been helped along by the multiplication of "specialized branches of knowledge" – a consumer market-like situation – instantly made available worldwide by the mass media. It is then "up to the consumers to make their choice or choices and to make out which messages sound the most convincing, at least for the moment" (35). It has also been accelerated by the end of European colonialism or Eurocentrism. If European colonialism meant "the unquestioned western dream of molding the whole world into a pattern with just one center of universal significance", the independence of the colonies put an end to this dream. It forced home the realization, if not necessarily the recognition, of the 'otherness of the other', the African, the Asian and the Latin-American. With these and other developments, modernity became mature. It came into full awareness of itself. Thus simple modernity developed into 'reflexive' modernity or, in a word, 'postmodernity.'

3. *Paradigm Shift in Theology*

The question of how these changes in the secular world have impacted theology or, more precisely, theological method, cannot be escaped. That major world developments shape the way human beings perceive their relationship with the Divine is accepted and is not debatable today. These events, modernity and postmodernity, have clearly influenced doing theology both in the North and South. Our concern here is with the theologies of the South and particularly with theologies of Africa.

In the early 1970s, after decades and, in some places in Latin America, centuries of being fed with western theology as universal theology, theologians from the South began to question the validity of this centralization of the theological enterprise. Convinced that this was not in the interest of the development of the faith of their peoples, they began to develop what they called 'a new way of doing theology', with the situations and histories of their peoples and countries in mind. The emerging reflections that, initially with the help of Marxist social analysis, placed the poor and marginalized at the center of theological thought, came to be known as 'liberation theology'. Thus at first, the central concern – or what I characterize as axis – of the liberation theologies of the South was the economic emancipation of the masses. This was already a shift from the former, western method of theological reflection where the poor hardly featured as privileged subjects in the discussion.

It is De Schrijver's major thesis that. because of the impact of post-modernity, the point of departure for these theologies of the South has again shifted. He argues that the analysis required in these new circumstances is no longer socio-economic but cultural. This shift, he claims, is exemplified by the reflections of the conferences of the EATWOT since the 1980s. But a clearer illustration he cites are the reflections of the conferences of the bishops of Latin America CELAM in Medellín (1968) and Puebla (1979). The Latin-American bishops themselves signaled this paradigm shift, as they remarked, "if Medellín has offered a primarily socio-economic analysis, Puebla completes this analysis presently with socio-economic data in an anthropological and historico-cultural, and thus more global perspective" (5). This means that the emphasis for theological reflection has moved from being exclusively economic. New developments make cultural liberation the more comprehensive point of departure for theological analysis. "The revival of cultural roots is presented [by Puebla] as the actual incentive to liberation... the religiosity of the Latin-American people is turned into a cry for true liberation,... In short, Puebla propounds a cultural approach to the people's resistance, a strategy meant to replace the Marxist socio-economic analysis and its distrust of religion and popular culture" (6-7).

According to De Schrijver's description of claims from Asia, theological efforts there also preserve "deep seated, traditional values" amid, and as a counterbalance to, rapid and vast technological changes that are taking place in some regions of that part of the world. As De Schrijver sees it then, the shift in Third-World theologies of liberation from socio-economic to cultural analysis is evident and incontrovertible. As he barely refers to Africa, however, we are bound to ask whether or not this claim holds true for the situation in the African continent as well. Does the African theological literature of liberation bear out his contentions? Here we need to digress and point out a weakness (even if perhaps an unavoidable one) in De Schrijver's discussion and then to spell out our own orientation in this reply.

4. *Different Contexts and Content*

If De Schrijver's analysis is an unquestionably able, serious, and sober analysis of the elements conditioning, as well as the questions facing, liberation theologies of the South, one must nevertheless submit right away that it proceeds from a thoroughly European grounding. The literature used to back up the arguments of the essay is an ample indication of this. Consequently, the essay approaches the influence and effects of modernity and postmodernity from the same perspective. In other words, it views the situation of the whole world from the point of view of the 'actor' and not really of the recipient, which is the image of the South in his analysis. It is not our contention that the conclusions reached by De Schrijver are wrong from that particular perspective; we want to point out that it is possible to show cogently that the actual effects of modernity and postmodernity may be seen in a different light by the 'victims' or 'sufferers' of these effects in the South. What is more to the point of the present discussion is the probability that these effects create a different base or axis for theological reflection there.

At the same time, however, a warning must be sounded with regard to this criticism. Our author must not be overly blamed for his "bias"; we will soon set forth our own Afrocentric bias in this reply. What Michael Novak, a diplomat and critic of Latin-American liberation theology, has remarked about approaches to fundamentally different cultures needs to be kept in mind. He terms the task "inherently invidious" and continues: "One cannot truly compare dissimilarities. And when the dissimilarities have to do with values and ends, as invariably they do (for values and ends shape, as it were, the 'cult' in culture), there is no neutral Archimedean point on which to stand to compare them"[2].

Nevertheless, this difficulty ought not to lead to paralysis. When perspectives are respected as such, while points of contact are sought between them, they can lead to enlightenment. My bias in this response, as I have mentioned, and as will be readily apparent, is the African experience, the African view of the universe and the African peoples' relationships to other peoples of the world. If culture molds people and makes them "what they are or almost what they are", as K.C. Anywanu, the Nigerian scholar argues, it is because they have first fashioned it through experience. "Culture cannot be separated from human experience, and it is this experience that produces it. In other words, experience constitutes the root of all cultural activities, and understanding culture entails understanding of the philosophy of experience"[3]. However, I will be concerned here not so much with the philosophy as with the empirical reality of African experience, that reality which has made them 'what they are' and thus conditions their response in the midst of the circumstances of our modern or postmodern epoch.

2. M. NOVAK, *Will It Liberate? Questions About Liberation Theology*, New York/Mahwah, Paulist Press, 1986, p. 4.
3. K.C. ANYWANU, *The African Experience in the American Marketplace*, Smithtown, New York, Exposition Press, 1983, p. 21.

Africa and its inhabitants have of course developed and changed through contact with the realities the whole world is experiencing. But our Afrocentric conviction is that Africans are still a distinctive people despite all that, and with reference to deeper realities than what appears on the surface. There is more to culture than its material side. There is also the 'soul' of a people, or what theologian John S. Mbiti has described as "the side of the thinking pattern, language content, mental images, emotions, beliefs and responses in situations of need"[4]. These often are barely changed even by the strongest stimuli. With regard to Africa, scholars have noted some of these 'essentials of African personhood' which have withstood the assaults of 'modernization' in the form of, among other things, the colonial and western missionary enterprises. They may be summarized in the words of Marimba Ani as follows:

> The universe to which they [Africans] relate is sacred in origin, is organic, and is a true cosmos". Human beings are part of the cosmos, and as such, relate ultimately with other cosmic beings. Knowledge of the universe comes through relationship with it and through perception of spirit in matter. The universe is one; spheres are joined because of a single unifying force that pervades all being. Meaningful reality issues from this force[5].

Thus, what Africanist Aylward Shorter has pointed out is significant. Christianity, for example, "has really had little to say about African Traditional Religion in the way of serious judgments of value". Given this situation, "the African Christian operates with two thought systems at once, and both of them are closed to each other. Each is only superficially modified by the other"[6]. We mention this observation of Shorter because it raises the question whether or not modernity and postmodernity have influenced Africa in the same way as they have their regions of origin, or even other parts of the South. Perhaps the context of African experience has been different from these other areas of the world so that the result or content has differed as well. What is the experience of Africa under modernity and postmodernity? It is to this question that we must turn.

---

4. J. MBITI, *African Religions and Philosophy*, London, Heinemann, 1969, p. xi.

5. M. ANI, *Yurugu: An African-centered Critique of European Thought and Behavior*, Trenton, NJ, Africa World Press, 1994, p. 29.

6. A. SHORTER, *Problems and Possibilities for the Church's Dialogue with African Traditional Religion*, in A. SHORTER (ed.), *Dialogue with the African Traditional Religions*, Kampala, Gaba Publications, 1975, p. 7.

II. AFRICA'S EXPERIENCE UNDER MODERNITY AND POSTMODERNITY

1. *The Current Situation*

The contemporary situation of sub-Saharan Africa is well-known to all who have cared to follow world events in the past several decades. The region has been described variously as "a human and environmental 'disaster area', 'moribund', 'marginalized', 'peripheral to the rest of the world'"[7]. Even the most adamant of Afro-optimists, while emphasizing, it is true, that the case for Africa is not irredeemably lost, nevertheless concede that the continent is in a very bad shape indeed.

Things have not been made any better by the recent collapse of the Eastern ideological bloc. Instead of a bipolar political and economic power-arrangement in which the political and economic systems of Africa had some room for maneuver, there is now a unipolar world in which Africa counts for less and less on the world scene. This is because of several factors. For one, whereas other areas of the world are comparatively politically stable – a situation which favors economic growth – Africa is experiencing a growing number of cases of civil unrest in many countries, and some of these cases have frustrated the efforts of the international community to prevent or control them. Rwanda, Somalia Liberia and Burundi are current examples. Moreover, by far the greatest number of refugees and other displaced persons in the world are in Africa. And socially, the picture seems to be just as devastating, and discourages economic investment. While many countries of the continent have some of the fastest growing rates of population in the world – "demographers forecast that Africa's population in 2025 could be nearly three times that of today"[8] – they also have the highest infant mortality. Deaths by controllable and preventable diseases such as malaria and various forms of dysentery are also among the highest in the world. Africa is likewise experiencing the highest incidence of HIV infection and death by AIDS anywhere. Thus economically, according to the World Bank, "virtually everywhere else in the world is likely to experience a decline in poverty by the year 2000 *except* Africa, where things will only get worse"[9]. Where does the origin of this situation lie?

2. *Slave Trade and Colonial Experience*

As briefly portrayed above, the present African predicament has deep roots in history. In order to appreciate how modernity and postmodernity

---

7. P. KENNEDY, *Preparing for the Twenty-First Century*, New York, Random House, 1993, p. 211.
8. *Ibid.*, p. 213.

have impacted the continent, it is essential to understand some of the most crucial of these historical events and how they are, in a real sense, a culmination of developments outside the continent itself. The transatlantic slave trade was one of these events.

The brutal facts of slave trading in Africa since the sixteenth century, the consequent passage of captured slaves across the Atlantic Ocean and the suffering of the slaves in North and South America and the Caribbean islands need no recounting. The devastating effects of the trade on the political, social and economic institutions of the African peoples concerned are familiar as well. If Africa is poor, sick, alienated, and its humanity not very much respected or valued, it is to a large extent due to the negative foundation laid down during the slave trading days. It was then that a great number of the able-bodied population of the continent (an estimated 200 million people in all) was dispersed to other lands and displaced within Africa itself. Thus, lacking the cohesiveness and stability that are prerequisites for cultural development, among other things, these societies became culturally stymied. As a result, they tried to adopt ways of living and doing things that alienated them from themselves, from their fellows and from their indigenous institutions. What Cameroonian theologian Jean-Marc Ela has called Africa's "anthropology of misfortune" begins here, and it is "tied to the domination of this region of the planet by the West since the Renaissance"[10].

> At the beginning of our [African] historical experiences, there has been since the Renaissance this incapability of Western civilization "to recognize and accept the Other as such, its refusal to let live that which is not identical with it.' Ever since the West launched its technical know-how, its culture, and its faith for the conquest of the tropics, the different peoples that it met on its way have been given up to extinction and death. A sort of specific suffering is tied to the condition of peoples who clash with Western expansion beyond its frontiers. Deprivation of one's own self, massacres, annihilation of indigenous cultures, systems of exclusion or destruction do not constitute abnormalities of the system. They belong to this form of savagery that the West carries along with itself from a 'culture of intolerance and violence' that belongs intrinsically to it[11].

The African slave trade was facilitated by, and indeed was a result of, these constitutive elements of the Renaissance in Europe since the 15th century: the emergence of the nation-states, European 'exploration' of other lands, and an unprecedented increase in commerce. It is worthwhile to recall the political theories of Renaissance philosophers such as

9. *Ibid.*, p. 212.
10. J.-M. ELA, *Afrique, l'irruption des pauvres*, Paris, L'Harmattan, 1994, p. 21.
11. *Ibid.*, p. 22.

Niccolo Machiavelli (especially in his *The Prince* of 1532) that, I hold, helped in the process of the subjugation of the peoples of Africa for Europe's own self-interest.

As economic activities grew among nation-states, European 'explorers' venture to 'discover' other lands for the same purpose of acquiring new and more materials for trade. The Enlightenment (18th century), which roughly coincided with the Industrial Revolution (late 18th to 19th centuries), reinforced the trend begun by Renaissance thought and attitudes as far as Africa is concerned. All of these developments seemed bent to "exclude Africans from the status of the human in order to throw them back to the status of animals, locked within biological and basic needs"[12]. The massive enslavement of Africans since the sixteenth century had thus a long process of legitimization in European intellectual and practical history.

Competition among European nation-states, spurred on by the other elements of modernity (technology, the profit motive and material progress), led inevitably to European imperialism. Expansion in the form of acquiring colonies was the only thing that could save the European nations from mutual destruction through competition for resources, labor and markets. The Berlin Conference, which partitioned Africa among the European nations, acted on this realization. But as a justification for this step, 'rationality' played a decisive role; anyone who relied on anything other than European processes of reasoning, as source of knowledge, was deemed inferior and was to be 'civilized'. The Christian missionary movement of the nineteenth century was thoroughly part and parcel of this story. Though its purpose was not to acquire territories for *political* domination, it did acquire them for *spiritual* domination and, given the close collaboration then between the colonialist and missionary movements, they both appeared hardly distinguishable in the eyes of many Africans. At any rate, their negative effects on the psyche and culture of the people were very similar indeed.

The African slave trade and the colonization of Africa could not have happened except as a result of modernity's 'monolithic', 'universal,' 'grand stories' of inevitable, 'steady' progress of capitalism which De Schrijver describes. But Marxism or scientific socialism, as also a child of modernity, did not escape this trend: it too propagated its own grand story of the total emancipation of the masses. It is a story whose limits became clearly evident with the collapse of the Berlin wall and the disintegration of the socialist (Eastern) bloc in the late 1980s.

12. *Ibid.*, p. 26.

3. Postmodernity and Globalization

Marked by the 'reflexive' character of people and systems today or by the ability of "realiz[ing] from within what the acceleration process of modernization is all about" (33), and by the 'performative', pragmatic view of science rather that the 'denotative', universalist one that characterized modernity, postmodernity affects Africa substantially in the same way as the slave trade and colonialism did. If in Africa the slave trade and colonial subjugation were the socio-political, economic and moral manifestations of modernity, what is generally known as neocolonialism is their equivalent in postmodernity and the global era, the era of de facto universal linkage and interdependencies that intertwine and affect the lives of people worldwide[13]. The 'anthropology of misfortune' that Ela has described in reference to African slavery and colonial experience continues today in new forms. Among the most significant of these are stateless TNCs, which often do not pay much attention to the implications of their activities in human and social terms, namely, unemployment, crime, environmental degradation and so on. There are also the IMF and World Bank credit, aid or loan conditionalities which, in general, demand a reduction of the protection of local industries while promoting unsubsidized export commodities. They also undercut domestic policies designed to promote affordable education and health services for the majority of the people in any African country. This, as African elder statesman Julius K. Nyerere argues, is "an impossible situation" for African governments.

> It is easy to criticize African governments of any party or none. And I am certainly not unaware of all their mistakes deliberate or otherwise – or the frequent corruption. But these things make worse an impossible situation; only in the most extreme cases are they the major causes of it. The prices of copper, cotton, coffee, bauxite, cocoa, and so on are not in the slightest affected by African elections; any government revolutionary, reactionary, or a model of good governance – has to face the fact that when the price of its exports goes down, the wealth of that country goes down[14].

When the wealth of any African country goes down, it means in real terms is that HIV infection increases exponentially due to lack of both information (education) and medication; children slowly starve to death; educational levels fall for lack of books and good teachers; and health services decline radically. These are not academic issues worked out in

13. C.J. COLLINS, *Reshaping Africa. Effects of Economic Globalization*, in *AFJN* 401 (1996), p. 1.
14. J.K. NYERERE, in V. MORTENSEN (ed.), *A Just Africa: Ethics and the Economy*, Geneva, Lutheran World Foundation, 1994, p. 22.

studies; they are realities affecting millions of Africans every day as a result of postmodernity and globalization, the world as "a global village", which is an "evocative image", as R. Cranford Pratt has pointed out, but also enormously misleading". For the truth is that "we can claim to be a global village only in the sense that the industrialized countries are able to reach out globally to find the resources they need and sell the products they manufacture. However, our world has neither the institutions of self-rule nor the sense of community and mutual responsibility the image of a global village suggests. Our world, dominated as it is by the nation-state system, with that system in turn dominated by the rich and powerful within it [the United States and European Union, for instance, have the most say in IMF decisions because they contribute the highest 'quota' to the Fund], has developed neither the will nor the institution to ensure that global economic (and hence political and cultural) interdependence operates with tolerable fairness"[15]. Globalization is therefore "one of the most powerful and complex processes reshaping the lives of Africans and people in all the regions of the world"[16]. In Africa "it erodes or reinforces or, to borrow a term from Ivan Illich, modernizes social and economic injustice and poverty"[17].

At this point it is useful to touch specifically on one of the major 'agents' of postmodernity and globalization: the mass media. If the three 'webs' of globalization that Collins speaks about[18] namely, "global trade", "global financial networks" and "global workplace" are able to function and affect Africa the way they do, it is mainly thanks to the fourth web, that of the proliferation of information technology and information itself. In Africa, the main source of information has been and to a large extents still is the radio. Increasingly now, there is also the influence of television and film, particularly among the youth. But in this explosion of information, Africans are largely *consumers* and not producers. Even news on and about Africa is 'produced' or processed from outside the continent. Already in the 1970s, a claim by Third-World countries for a restructuring of sources of information so that news on Africa would originate in Africa (that is, the formation of a New International Information Order – NIIO) was rejected by the North.

What has usually been stressed in discussion is the effect this Northern-tailored information has on African culture: low self-esteem and self-doubt

15. R.C. PRATT, in J. TORRIE (ed.), *Banking on Poverty: The Global Impact of the IMF & World Bank*, Toronto, Between the Lines, 1983, p. 55.
16. C.J. COLLINS (n. 13), p. 1.
17. *Ibid.*, p. 1.
18. *Ibid.*, pp. 2-4.

and mimicry of foreign ways of doing things without sufficient analysis
and judgment. Its impact on political and economic development are, however, just as significant. One wonders what *kind* of democracy and democratic institutions African states and peoples are aspiring for. Similarly, the confusion of economic development with Westernization has very deep roots
in the psyches of many Africans, a confusion that is reinforced by the
information that constitutes a pillar of postmodernity and globalization.

4. *The Otherness of Africa*

One of the most important issues raised by postmodernity relates to
the survival of traditions. As De Schrijver points out, "authors who are
specialized in the study of cultural change begin to raise the question as
to the extent to which local cultures, especially those in the 'Third-
World', will be able to withstand their absorption into the commodification of culture which, under the impact of flexible economic systems, is
going to grow global" (47-48). The question that may be asked then is:
will globalization have the effect in African societies of freeing them
from their traditional ways of viewing and doing things, or will it result
in a kind of "'creolization' in which the particular (local culture) and
the universal (the new international culture) in one way or the other will
have come to merge" as, according to R. Lee, may be the situation in
Asia (47)? Even seriously considering I. Wallerstein's point on this matter (50-59), it is still difficult to see how these two alternatives (that is,
either the elimination of African culture or its 'creolization') strictly apply
to the fundamental cultural reality of the continent. Rather, Africa is gov-
erned by the 'two thought-systems' that we noted at the beginning of this
response and, despite the influence of modernity and postmodernity on it,
the 'essentials of the African personhood' retain the upper hand. This is
evident in the many situations of crisis that postmodernity brings with it.

If this is the reality, a further and perhaps more fundamental question
for our discussion is whether or not this essential otherness of Africa is
respected by postmodernity's manifest elements, for example, the mass
media. In the South-East Asian region, Lee argues that a "new synthesis
between western high-technology and revitalized local culture has taken
place". The "sensualism, playfulness, and hedonism, which are easily
transmitted through technology" have been kept in check by traditional
Asian (Confucian) values of 'frugality' and 'self-control' (48). In the
case of Africa, the international mass media pay scant if any attention at
all to African values of solidarity and sharing. In other words, these values command little respect.

III. Politics as the Basic Paradigm in the African Theology of Liberation

1. *The Political Axis*

Given the predominant situation of alienation by the western-dominated environment of modernity and postmodernity in Africa, what has been the theological response, indeed, the religious response there? In other words, what has been the basic axis or principle tool of analysis of the situation by theologians? Furthermore, what has imperceptibly guided the great majority of African Christians in living out their faith?

Social, economic and political elements are always factors in any theological analysis and general response to empirical situations and to Christ's call to follow him in these contexts. Modernity and postmodernity are a combination of all of these elements as they impact Africa and the rest of the world. But at any one time, one or another element, or a certain combination of them, stands out as the dominant element. This holds true also with regard to how people or groups of people or even societies relate to them. Latin-American theology of liberation, while certainly not ignoring completely social and political factors, chose to make economic analysis the controlling paradigm of its reflection. I wish to suggest that, for much of Asian liberation theology, the paradigm was social-cultural, as a quick survey of titles dealing with liberation themes there will confirm. In sub-Sahara Africa, the basic paradigm for theology and religiosity (i.e. how people conduct their everyday, Christian lives) is clearly 'political'. I will describe what this means below, but whether evident in clear analysis as a tool or, more often, simply assumed, the political element has been the basic factor in all three branches of African Theology: Liberation, Inculturation and Popular-charismatic.

To simplify the discussion, I will show how the political element influences the work of some representatives of each of these branches of African Theology and indicate how, despite reservations of the Vatican, it has emerged as a basic paradigm in the reflections and conclusions of the recent African Synod. But first we need to understand what is meant here by "politics" and "political response".

2. *Politics and the Reality of Power*

Politics, as we will use the term, is always associated with the reality of power. When people organize to dispossess others of their ability to govern or simply define themselves, they are engaging in a political process. And when, in response, the dispossessed organize to recover their rights of self-determination and self-definition as individuals, as groups, or as societies, they are likewise engaging in a political process. In this sense, there is much politics in the social, economic, cultural and religious activities of peoples throughout Africa.

African experience ever since slave-trading days is replete with politics as a struggle for power. Even though the most visible element was economic, the slave trade was fundamentally a question of acquiring power *over* the dark peoples of Africa so that their seemingly superior energy to produce wealth could be used by their 'masters'. As an extension of slavery, or slavery in a new form, the rationale for colonialism was the same. It was to acquire the economic power which African natural and human resources could provide. Today with postmodernity, neocolonialism does the same thing in a subtle way before the collapse of the Berlin Wall and in an open and quite shameless manner after the collapse.

The African reaction to their subjugation by the slave traders and colonialists was no less political. The slave-merchants were often resisted through military action by the persons and societies they invaded to procure slaves. Attempts by slaves to escape were similarly political struggles – attempts to regain power over oneself and one's life.

We have mentioned the call by Third-World countries for a New International Information Order. There was also the call for a New International Economic Order (NIEO) before the collapse of the Berlin Wall. The western countries sabotaged these calls so that they did not take effect.

Yet the huge African 'debt' and the World Bank's conditionalities as prerequisites for loans or grants continue to make Africa's response a political one. What concerns many African states now is how to strategize to get out of the grip of the Bretton Woods Institutions. Whether or not this is a losing struggle on their part is not the point here; the point is that they are concerned about the *power* to control and direct their own national lives.

These are, however, not strictly theological responses even though they constitute theological loci. Per Frostin has illustrated how these loci have given rise to distinctive theological reflections in Tanzania and South Africa[19]. In what follows, I now wish to indicate the political axis in the theology of Jean-Marc Ela and Mercy Amba Oduyoye (the African liberation and feminist schools), Charles Nyamiti (the African inculturation

19. P. FROSTIN, *Liberation Theology in Tanzania and South Africa: A First World Interpretation*, Lund, Lund University Press, 1988.

school), Emmanuel Milingo (the popular-charistmatic trend), and finally, the conclusions of the African Synod (the official stance). This discussion will substantiate the claim I have made that African liberation theologies are attempts of the dispossessed to regain 'the right of self-determination and self-definition' in the context of the prevailing hostile world-influences and pressures.

3. *African Liberation Theology: Jean-Marc Ela and Mercy Amba Oduyoye*

For Ela, "every manifestation of our faith today [in Africa] takes place in a world of domination and injustice. Can we remain untouched? Or must we live with our people? In what way? How can we feel ourselves genuinely involved in this situation?"[20] As Ela sees it, African theologians and the Church in general must commit themselves to the aspirations of the African people and their welfare: "to see their people free themselves from oppression, from slavery, poverty and hunger"[21]. Only "solidarity with the poor and exploited in our societies" will constitute the true manifestation of the Christian faith. This solidarity is a *political* act both in the sense of communion (of the people of God/Church) and in the sense of organization and struggle against whatever prevents the self-affirmation of Africans.

> The growth inequalities of every sort, the degradation of the African peasantry, repression, dependence, including dependence on foreign interests, with all its legacies and its ideological apparatus challenge African Christians. Under the influence of our mother-churches, our faith has long been committed to a strategy of aid, based on a reading of Matthew 25:31-46 that emphasizes charity. Today we must move on to a strategy of liberation as we follow the crucified one of Golgotha who confronted everything that did not conform to God's plan. Today, as yesterday, we encounter the living God when and where God hears the cry of the poor and remembers the covenant. If we view the Eucharist itself as a sign of mutual exchange and as a political act, we must turn away from a world that prevents us from sharing. The Eucharist celebrates and anticipates that relationship of communion among human beings willed by God. It calls us to question radically all structures of injustice throughout the world[22].

The question here involves, on the one hand, an analysis of the political substructures and motivations that drive and have driven the economic and cultural manifestations of the domination of Africa. On the other hand, it calls for strategies to counteract these forces. "It is no

20. J.-M. ELA, *My Faith as an African*, Maryknoll, NY, Orbis, 1988, p. 98.
21. *Ibid.* p. 99.
22. *Ibid.* p. 98.

longer a matter of having our rights acknowledged", stresses Ela. "It is [now] a matter of exercising them"[23]. Even within the church itself, Africa Christians need to assert their 'right to be different': "We feel the need to rethink the church, then with the conviction that those who claim the church as their own will be able to deliver themselves from the many yokes under which they labor by taking full account of daily reality as it is lived by the majority of human beings in African society"[24].

The political paradigm is even clearer in feminist theology in Africa (and obviously elsewhere in the world). As many women realize today, sexism is nothing but a struggle for power and control. Under various pretenses, men in many cultures have sought to control women totally, their bodies as well as their minds, and for a long time they succeeded. They did so by institutionalizing this oppression and discrimination as culturally acceptable or even culturally required. The feminist movement all over the world, however, as was the struggle against the slave trade and slavery itself, and the movement against colonialism in Africa in the 1960s, seeks to change this. The need for equitable demands, expectations, rights and responsibilities between the sexes is clearly a question of the 'self-affirmation' of women. Admittedly, it is a cultural issue, but the controlling motif is political. It concerns power, and as such it is by no means an easy matter for all concerned, not least for the women themselves.

As Cameroonian feminist theologian Louise Tappa declares: "Self-affirmation is very difficult in our context today, especially for women, since, in our context, women have so interiorized the ideology of self-denial that they feel it is illegitimate and presumptuous to demand things for themselves!"[25] Of course, African men quickly exploit this weak link in women's thought. They therefore argue, as Tappa herself notes that "'the women's liberation movement is not a response to a genuinely African need' or 'the African woman has always been one to give of herself', as if self-giving and self-affirmation as a human being of equal worth with all the others were intrinsically contradictory!"[26].

This summarizes the thrust of the thought of Mercy Amba Oduyoye, one of the foremost representatives of African feminist theology. Emancipation is for her the present and future task of the African woman. She must seek economic, religious, cultural and political liberation so as to

23. J.-M. ELA, *African Cry*, Maryknoll, NY, Orbis, 1986, p. 128.
24. *Ibid.*, p. 110.
25. L. TAPPA, in V. FABELLA & M.A. ODUYOYE (eds.), *With Passion and Compassion: Third World Women Doing Theology*, Maryknoll, NY, Orbis, 1988, p. 33.
26. *Ibid.*, p. 33

effect just gender relationships. In this task, the African woman must be persistent and relentless. "I do not wish", says Oduyoye, "to be pushed to the point where I must bare my breasts, throw off my clothes, or beat pots and pans in the streets, but as an African woman I do want to be given a hearing"[27].

4. *African Inculturation Theology: Charles Nyamiti*

The political paradigm or motif is most difficult to establish where inculturation theology is concerned. After all, 'inculturationists' in Africa have in the past accused 'liberationists' of being overconcerned with 'political' or economic issues at the expense of addressing the issue of culture which, as they perceive it, suffered the most serious denigration since the advent of the slave trade. Similarly, as inculturation theologians argue, with modernity and postmodernity, it is culture that is being invaded and that has to be defended without, however, neglecting the economic and political elements. Tanzanian inculturation theologian Charles Nyamiti makes this point most strongly. His criticism of South African liberation theology for not paying enough attention to the cultural issue during the apartheid era was unequivocal, and his major writings have dealt with the question of how to relate African cultural values to Christian doctrine.

Yet even though his writings are concerned with the issue of relating African culture to Christianity, the question remains as regards his fundamental reason for doing so. Nyamiti does not spell this out in so many words, but his concern with culture is in implicit criticism of Western Christianity in Africa. By not taking Africa culture seriously, and only adopting certain African expressions and values into its expressions of the faith, Christianity in Africa seems to impoverish itself. It impoverishes the African person even more because she feels alienated from her own church. The theological struggle for the African person to 'feel at home' in the church – a struggle in which Nyamiti is engaged – is one in which the question of mutual recognition between African culture and the western expression of the Christian faith predominates. African culture seeks to regain its rightful place as also a valid statement about things divine, at least in part. Even though on the surface this appears to be an exclusively cultural-religious matter, our understanding of politics above indicates that the reality is deeper that that. Deep down it is an

27. M.A. ODUYOYE, *Daughters of Anowa: African Women and Patriarchy*, Maryknoll, NY, Orbis, 1995, p. 157.

attempt to attain emancipation from a form of oppression. As always, emancipation is fundamentally a political process. As Frostin notes, "In Nyamiti's exposition there is an explicit parallel between the concept of God and politics. The triune God is presented as a model of African socialism, since in God there is 'perfect harmony, equality of persons, solidarity through unlimited sharing of life, and participation'. On the basis of this theology Nyamiti advocates a society based on dialogue and mutuality without economic, sexist, or racial oppression. Generally, there is a strong egalitarian ethos in his writings where the commitment to liberation and the common good are central issues"[28].

What has been called 'popular inculturation', that is, the synthesis of faith and culture made by the majority of the faithful in their day-to-day process of living out their faith in Christ as Africans shows very clearly the political axis of inculturation. Popular inculturation 'rebels', so to speak, against the formal, dogmatic interpretations of the faith as spelled out by the official church. It opts to live the faith in a way more consistent with the demands of the prevailing realities. This is the basic political point regardless of what the very same people may otherwise verbally claim to profess.

5. *Popular – Charismatic Theology: Emmanuel Milingo*

Popular-charismatic 'theology' in Africa is not so much thought out as lived. In this sense it is personalized, and is evident mostly in the life and work of its representatives such as Emmanuel Milingo (former Archbishop of Lusaka). In the case of Milingo, as in many other cases of this school, one of the central areas of activity involves healing. And it is here that the conflict between cultures, and the struggle on the part of Africa for self-definition and self-appropriation, arises. Gerrie Ter Haer describes the context of the Zambian prelate's work as one of tension between "the white 'mother church' in the West and the Black 'daughter churches'" of Africa[29]. Basic to the tension is the question of belief where the 'mother church' holds one thing and Africa holds another. According to Ter Haer

> It is Milingo's firm conviction that Africa must be accepted as a continent with its own spiritual identity. He also believes that the people of Africa can effectively communicate with a world of spirits beyond the visible

---

28. P. FROSTIN (n. 19), p. 56.
29. G. TER HAER, *Spirit of Africa: The Healing Ministry of Archbishop Milingo of Zambia*, London, Hurst & Company, 1992.

world. He has come to these conclusions on the basis not of dogma but of his pastoral experiences in Zambia[30].

Are these evil spirits? What kind are they? What must be done to deal with them? These are the questions that occupy Milingo's healing ministry, whose response to these questions has estranged him from the Western-dominated church. Yet having discovered through experience the truth of the African cosmology, Milingo refuses to be alienated from it owing to doctrinal formulations that are foreign and academic[31]. His concern is there-fore not much different from that of all other types of African theology: the acceptance of the otherness of Africa particularly by Africans themselves. Again on the surface, this has to do with culture, but essentially, it is a political process of change. Milingo underlines this to the members of the congregation of Sisters he founded, the Daughters of the Redeemer.

> He wanted them to serve as an example to other Zambians, who should learn to be themselves and live at ease with their own identities, and to show them that God accepts people the way they are, which is the way He made them. Milingo once remarked: 'to convince me that I can only be a full Christian, when I shall well be brought up in European civilization and culture, is to force me to change my nature. If God made a mistake by creating me an African, it is not yet evident. My antagonists have not yet given me summons to call me to the high court of God, where He promised to undo me as an African in order to make me a European as a process and a *conditio sine qua non* to become a full Christian[32].

If the political element is implicit in all this, it was explicit in the for-mative years of Milingo's ministry. In 1970, for example, he criticized the regimes in Angola and Mozambique, and the church's support for them, for not respecting the human dignity of Africans[33]. As Milingo continues his healing ministry in exile in Europe, he has not given up this political basis for change in Africa.

6. *Official Position: The African Synod*

Couched in theological language, the documents produced at the beginning, during, and at the end of the African Synod are some of the clearest examples of the political axis of African theology. No African bishop can be accused of being a radical liberationist. Indeed, for most, the opposite is true: they are more accurately described as 'conservative'

---

30. *Ibid.*, p. 138.
31. *Ibid.*, p. 94.
32. *Ibid.*, p. 178.
33. *Ibid.*, pp. 11-12.

in the sense of not being quick to read the signs of the times and to offer pertinent interpretation. So, the political streak in many of these documents can be said to arise not because of, but truly *in spite of*, the official church's fundamental orientation. How can this occur? Why? The only plausible explanation is that the bishops instinctively reacted against many of the consequences of modernity/postmodernity, while they were psychically unconscious about the nature of their reactions. One of these consequences of globalization is the burden of the international "debt" which all African countries bear. Without much analysis of the conditions which bring about this situation, the bishops at the Synod wrote to their fellow bishops in Europe and North America to help them persuade their governments to write off this debt. They instinctively justified this request in political terms:

> The right of the Church to intervene in political and economic affairs is limited in any part of the Church. Yet the social teaching of the Church is part of her mandate to go and teach all nations. These are times when justice compels us to speak publicly on these matters. If we remain silent and inactive, whether in Africa or the countries of the North, we may appear as cowards or accomplices rather than as champions of justice. We have the right and duty to enlighten the consciences of the decision makers. The question of African debt offers an opportunity for the bishops of Africa to work in partnership with their fellow bishops in Europe and America to seek a just speedy way of resolving it[34].

Pope John Paul II, in the post-Synod Apostolic Exhortation *The Church in Africa*, speaks of the Synod as an occasion for resurrection and hope. In what sense is it so? In the sense that the continent must arise from the present situation of "misery, wars, despair", and of being "controlled by rich and powerful nations"[35]. It must affirm itself and its culture if it wants to save itself from this situation brought about by modernity, he suggests. Many prominent Northern theologians take up the same theme by confessing their and their countries' complicity in the current alienation of Africa. "In grief and pain", they wrote at the beginning of the Synod, "we acknowledge the countless wrongs inflicted on African people. We are ready to identify ourselves with the sins of our ancestors. We have begun to examine the ways in which we ourselves up to this day have taken part in the oppression of and contempt for your dignity and self-determination, politically, economically, ecologically, culturally, and even ecclesiologically"[36].

34. AFJN (Africa Faith and Justice Network), *The African Synod: Documents, Reflections, Perspectives*, Maryknoll, NY, Orbis, 1996, p. 115.
35. *Ibid.*, p. 245.
36. *Ibid.*, p. 71.

Indeed, the entire history of the Synod shows that, from the point of view of those who were its main protagonists – particularly African theologians – the Synod was meant to be an event whereby the African church and society in general would be helped to recapture their own identity, to regain their power for self-definition. This underlying motif is what the Roman church authorities were uncomfortable with all along. It is, in fact, what made them downgrade the assembly from a deliberative 'council' – as had been proposed by African theologians and some bishops – to an advisory synod. Nevertheless, in the documents produced, at least, the political element, as a question of who exercises power, could hardly have been avoided.

IV. Conclusion: Summary Remarks

1. *Reflexivity*

Concluding his essay, De Schrijver poses some penetrating questions to which he invites his respondents to react. Instead of addressing them one by one, however, I wish to offer a summary consideration of some of the points contained therein and which are in line with the argument I have presented in the foregoing pages, a summary which will serve also as my concluding remarks.

De Schrijver explains in the body of the essay that postmodernity is reflexive modernity, that is, modernity that has reached maturity. Reflexivity is therefore central to understanding the circumstances of our world today. It seems to be, among other things, the criterion which distinguishes 'higher' from 'lower' or 'primitive' forms of religion. De Schrijver writes that, for Cardinal Ratzinger, "Christianity is... a culture that offers its cultural achievements to other peoples on the basis of its already-acquired universality. Furthermore, Christianity's cultural achievements become available to enrich other religions, once these religions have developed, from their respective particularities, sufficiently universal perspectives", that is, once they have become sufficiently reflexive (74). In this sense, then, reflexivity plays a major role in the process that is globalization.

Faced with this emphasis on reflexivity, Africans have reacted in several ways which have an implicit but fundamental bearing on their self-definition. In religious matters, the reaction has taken the form of fundamentalism, pentecostalism, the founding of indigenous churches and a renewed reappropriation of traditional values. In the secular sphere, it emerges as corruption and irresponsibility.

2. *Fundamentalism*

Religious fundamentalism and pentecostalism in Africa constitute mainly a rejection of rationality as the West conceives it. By and large, it is an acceptance of 'divine order' as it is. Not every mystery can be explained or explained away; this is the message of fundamentalism. The same thing is what pentecostalism in African Christian churches involves. To the human mind, it says, what the Holy Spirit does or prompts a person to do may appear senseless. "Making sense" is, for pentecostalism, certainly not the only way in which God acts. As it sees things, 'reason' is not always the best counselor.

This unquestioned acceptance of the holy, without necessarily enjoying the support of reason, is also at the root of the founding of the numerous indigenous churches in many parts of the African continent. And in this, it finds fertile ground in the religious beliefs and practices of African religions. There are no doubts raised in this tradition about the existence of spirits; their influence on human life and on the universe in general is taken for granted. As it may easily be seen, African popular-charismatic theology derives from this conviction.

3. *Corruption and Civic Irresponsibility*

One may say that corruption is one of, if not the major, social problem facing African civil societies today. It is a perplexing issue which is explained in many ways. It is often said that corruption arises because of poor remuneration for workers and others engaged in productive labor. Another reason advanced to explain this situation is the African family structure, whose extended membership puts a strain on any one individual's resources. Yet another reason is that the appreciation and workings of the cash economy needs time to develop and mature in African societies, which are not yet attuned to it. Be that as it may, what cannot be ignored is also the fact that civic irresponsibility is at bottom also a rejection of western notions of order and efficiency. This rejection is so strong that it blinds many people against recognizing the injustice involved in corrupt practices.

4. *The Future*

The political undercurrent that characterizes African Liberation theology has its own dangers, one of which may be the lack of sufficient consideration of the other elements that shape theological reflection and the practice of religion. Yet the need for the founding and maintenance of the authentic self of the African person and the continent as a whole makes this axis in theology a necessity in Africa. Theology can help guide its proper development in small communities of faith.

Bukama Parish   Laurenti MAGESA
PO Box 70
Tarime, Tanzania

6

GLOBALISATION ET PAUPÉRISATION
UN DÉFI À LA THÉOLOGIE AFRICAINE

Au mois d'août 1976, s'est tenu à Dar-es-Salaam, en Tanzanie, un Colloque regroupant une vingtaine d'africains, d'asiatiques et de sud-américains engagés dans la recherche théologique. Au cours de ce Tricontinental d'un nouveau genre, ces théologiens ont découvert que leurs peuples avaient un passé commun d'exploitation coloniale et néo-coloniale. Ils ont aussi pris conscience que la problématique de la libération s'appliquait à l'ensemble des pays du Tiers-Monde. Le Colloque de Dar-es-Salaam marque un tournant capital dans l'histoire du christianisme contemporain. Lieu d'une nouvelle prise de parole réclamant le droit à l'émancipation et à la liberté, ce colloque est aussi l'affirmation claire que l'avenir des peuples du Tiers-Monde passe par une transformation radicale du système international. Ce défi gigantesque met en cause la pratique de la théologie elle-même: «Comment se situe la théologie chrétienne devant l'exploitation qui continue aujourd'hui dans le monde? Quelle est sa contribution à l'édification d'une société mondiale juste? Quelle sera la contribution de l'Église à la libération des peuples opprimés qui souffrent depuis longtemps la domination de sexe, de la race ou de la classe»[1]?

Depuis vingt ans, les questions du Manifeste de Dar-es-Salaam n'ont cessé de travailler en profondeur les hommes et les femmes qui prennent le risque d'arracher l'Évangile au drame de l'insignifiance afin de lui redonner toute sa pertinence et sa crédibilité en repensant l'essentiel de la foi à partir des espoirs de libération qui habitent le cœur des pauvres et des opprimés. Toute cette expérience de recherche, de réflexion et de réinterprétation du noyau de sens inhérent au message chrétien, est aujourd' hui remise en question.

Au moment où nous assistons au «retour des certitudes», tout se passe comme si les théologiens du Tiers-Monde n'avaient plus qu'à commenter le nouveau catéchisme de l'Église catholique. Éblouis par la «splendeur de la vérité», il ne leur resterait plus qu'à reproduire les discours institués comme ces perroquets que l'on capture dans les forêts vierges. Ce qui me paraît aussi important, c'est que la théologie de la libération qui a surgi dans les peuples du Tiers-Monde n'aurait plus de raison d'être.

---

1. Voir *Manifeste de Dar-es-Salaam*, dans *Théologies du Tiers-Monde. Du conformisme à l'indépendance*, Paris, L'Harmattan, 1977, p. 250.

Après la chute du mur de Berlin, nous n'aurions plus qu'à reprendre à notre compte les grands thèmes de la doctrine sociale de l'Église. Le tournant est grave. Pour mesurer l'ampleur des défis porteurs d'avenir, une question fondamentale doit revenir au centre des débats qui nous rassemblent: Faut-il jeter dans les poubelles de l'histoire les approches socio-économiques qui sont restées jusqu'ici le cadre de référence de toute la démarche de la théologie de la libération? Ces approches sont-elles devenues anachroniques? Dans ce cas, devons-nous les abandonner pour assumer dans l'espace de notre réflexion le rapport à la culture comme lieu privilégié de toute intelligence de la foi?

Ces questions sont d'importance car elles nous invitent à réexaminer les postulats de base, les modèles d'intelligibilité de notre «être au monde» et de la réalité dans laquelle nous vivons dans les pays du Tiers-Monde. En fin de compte, il s'agit de redéfinir notre manière de faire la théologie, de reconstruire d'autres grilles de lecture de la révélation, de fonder à nouveau notre pratique de l'intelligence de la foi à partir d'une rupture épistémologique. En nous invitant à changer de paradigmes, on se demande si, à la limite, l'on n'exige pas des Églises du Tiers-Monde un autre regard sur Dieu lui-même, une autre écoute du verbe et une autre manière d'être l'Église hors de l'Occident. Il me semble important de situer le débat à ce niveau, si l'on veut saisir toutes les implications concrètes, ecclésiales et historiques de la pratique théologique en cette veille du XXIe siècle.

Pour situer les réflexions qui vont suivre, nous tenterons d'abord de cerner les enjeux théoriques de la question qui s'impose à notre examen. Nous nous pencherons ensuite sur les défis théologiques qui ouvrent de nouvelles perspectives à l'intelligence chrétienne à partir de «l'irruption des pauvres»[2] dans le contexte africain. Après l'évaluation critique des tendances actuelles de la recherche, nous nous interrogeons sur l'actualité et l'urgence de la théologie de la libération dans la crise du monde contemporain. Précisons d'emblée le cadre de référence des discussions sur le thème qui nous occupe.

I. FAIRE LA THÉOLOGIE À L'AGE DE LA PLURALITÉ DES CULTURES

Le retour à la culture est un phénomène majeur qui caractérise les «déplacements théologiques» de l'Église de Vatican II. Ce phénomène

---

2. J.-M. ELA, *Afrique, L'irruption des pauvres: société, contre-ingérence, pouvoir et argent*, Paris, L'Harmattan, 1994.

ne doit guère nous surprendre. Dès le deuxième Concile du Vatican qui, il faut le reconnaître, apparaît comme le dernier Concile de l'Occident, l'on a pris conscience de la nécessité du pluralisme dans les différents domaines de la vie chrétienne. Cette exigence s'est imposée notamment dans la réflexion sur la célébration du mystère chrétien dont on a reconnu l'importance dans la vie de l'Église. Au-delà de la question de la langue liturgique qui se pose dans un contexte nouveau où le latin a perdu son monopole de langue unique dans le catholicisme, le Concile amorce une ouverture sur la diversité des rites compte tenu des particularités propres à chaque peuple: «l'Église, dans les domaines qui ne touchent pas la foi ou le bien de toute la communauté, ne désire pas, même dans la liturgie, imposer la forme rigide d'un libellé unique; bien au contraire, elle cultive les qualités et les dons des divers peuples et elle les développe»[3]. Sans doute, l'on réaffirme la fidélité à «l'unité substantielle» du rite romain. Mais, l'approfondissement du mystère de l'Église qui s'opère dans les débats conciliaires s'oriente vers la reconnaissance des différences légitimes. «La Pentecôte des Nations» est un événement qui, comme au début du christianisme, bouscule et pose des questions vitales qui ne peuvent être résolues que par le refus de toute forme d'assimilation ou d'uniformisation. Tel est l'enjeu de l'articulation des rapports entre l'Église universelle et les Églises particulières: «Tout en sauvegardant l'unité de la foi et de la structure divinement instituée de l'Église universelle, les Églises jouissent d'une discipline propre, d'une coutume liturgique particulière, d'un patrimoine théologique et spirituel qui est le leur»[4].

Dans cette perspective, le ministère de Pierre doit lui-même être repensé de telle manière qu'en présidant à l'Agapè, il devienne ce centre visible de la catholicité «qui protège les légitimes diversités et, en même temps, veille à ce que les différences ne nuisent point à l'unité, mais la servent»[5].

La légitimation des différences est une nécessité qui concerne la théologie chrétienne. C'est pourquoi, dit le concile, «il est nécessaire que dans chaque grand territoire socio-culturel, comme on dit, une réflexion théologique de cette sorte soit encouragée, par laquelle, à la lumière de la Tradition de l'Église universelle, les faits et les paroles révélés par Dieu, consignés dans les Saintes Lettres, expliqués par les Pères de l'Église et le Magistère, seront soumis à un nouvel examen. Ainsi, on saisira plus nettement par quelles voies la foi, compte tenu de la philosophie et de la

---

3. *La Sainte Liturgie* III, (37).
4. *LG* III, (23).
5. *LG* II, (13).

sagesse des peuples, peut «chercher l'intelligence», et de quelles manières les coutumes, le sens de la vie, l'ordre social peuvent s'accorder avec les mœurs que fait connaître la révélation divine»[6]. On reconnaît ici le poids des peuples du Tiers-Monde dont la prise de conscience s'est manifestée au Concile par un nouvel examen des tâches de l'intelligence chrétienne dans un monde aux multiples visages. Vatican II renonce à parler de «culture» au singulier. Il redécouvre «la pluralité des cultures». Car des styles de vie divers et des échelles de valeurs différentes trouvent leur source dans la façon particulière que l'on a de se servir des choses, de travailler, de s'exprimer, de pratiquer sa religion, de se conduire, de légiférer, d'établir des institutions juridiques, d'enrichir les sciences et les arts et de cultiver le beau. Ainsi, à partir des usages hérités, se forme un patrimoine propre à chaque communauté humaine»[7].

Faire la théologie à l'âge de «la pluralité des cultures»: tel est l'un des défis majeurs auxquels sont confrontés les Églises chrétiennes dans un monde en mutation. Le besoin d'une Évangélisation en profondeur a permis de mesurer l'enjeu de l'inculturation qui conduit le chrétien sur la voie d'une véritable conversion devant l'amener à dire et à vivre l'universalité du Christ de façon radicalement différente. Bien avant les transformations du monde d'après-guerre froide, les théologiens du sud ou du nord tentent cette expérience cruciale. On le voit en Afrique où, Engelbert Mveng, Mgr. Tshibangu, Patrick Kalilombe, Oscar Bimwenyi-Kweshi, Mgr. Sanon, Meinrad Hebga ou Benezet Bujo, ont investi leurs capacités de réflexion théologique dans l'axe des rapports entre l'Évangile et la culture dans les sociétés africaines. L'on doit bien se garder de voir ici une sorte d'exceptionnalisme des théologies d'Afrique Noire.

Le défi de l'inculturation est au centre des préoccupations sur l'évangélisation de l'Amérique latine comme le montrent bien les documents de Medellín, de Puebla et de Santo Domingo. Si l'attention accordée à la religiosité populaire permet de renouer avec les fondements culturels des stratégies de résistance des pauvres, le choc provoqué par la rencontre avec l'Indien et les descendants d'esclaves noirs qu'on retrouve dans de nombreux pays d'Amérique latine comme on le voit au Brésil et au Pérou, au Vénézuela, au Panama, en Colombie, à l'Équateur ou au Honduras nécessite une reformulation de la foi en fonction des cultures non occidentales qui ont survécu à la conquête et à l'esclavage dans le sous-continent. Tel est aussi le défi de l'Église face aux cultures amérindiennes comme on le voit au Canada où Peelman se réapproprie le pro-

6. *AG* III, (22).
7. *GS* II, (3).

jet d'inculturation en s'interrogeant sur le Christ amérindien. Il n'est pas nécessaire d'insister sur l'ampleur des défis analogues en Inde, au Japon et en Chine où les chrétiens vivent en permanence au milieu des peuples profondément marqués par des cultures et des spiritualités différentes.

Au sein des Églises occidentales elles-mêmes, la question culturelle est devenue incontournable dans la mesure où, avec la crise de l'humanisme greco-latin, l'on assiste depuis la révolution industrielle à l'émergence de nouveaux styles de vie et de pensée qui, par-delà la science et la technologie, mettent en lumière l'avènement de nouveaux repères socio-culturels et de nouveaux paradigmes. Au cœur de la modernité, ces mutations profondes qui affectent la sensibilité et l'intelligence occidentales interpellent les théologiens. Pour la première fois, sans doute, les Églises sont confrontées à un problème commun: «Dire Dieu dans l'horizon de la rencontre des cultures»[8]. Soulignons l'intérêt et la profondeur des bouleversements que ces choix de recherche entraînent. Assumer le risque de l'autre dans l'intelligence de la foi engage l'avenir du christianisme dans une direction où les schémas de pensée, les structures et les institutions religieuses, le système des valeurs et les formes de spiritualité peuvent être totalement modifiés. À travers ce projet global qui peut-être considéré comme l'une des tâches fondamentales de la foi chrétienne aujourd'hui et demain, il s'agit de réinventer l'Église elle même.

Ce qui se cherche, en effet, c'est une reprise en charge des questions centrales de l'Évangile au-delà des controverses de la réforme et de la contre-réforme. Toute la théologie moderne s'est développée à partir des débats soulevés par la lecture de l'Épître aux Romains. «Inculturer l'Évangile», pour reprendre le mot d'ordre officiel de Jean-Paul II, exige des déplacements théologiques qui redonnent toute leur importance aux questions radicales laissées sans réponse par le développement de l'intelligence chrétienne qui s'est réalisé autour de ces grands piliers de l'univers de la contre-réforme que sont la foi, la grâce et les sacrements, l'Écriture et la Tradition. Reconnaître que l'inculturation est «une exigence de foi» comme l'a dit récemment l'Assemblée spéciale pour l'Afrique du Synode des évêques, c'est admettre l'existence des lieux théologiques autres que ceux dont Rome a la mémoire dans l'histoire de la pensée chrétienne. Cette reconnaissance impose un véritable dépaysement mental et religieux. Il s'agit d'une «révolution copernicienne» au sens propre du terme.

---

8. Nous avons développé ce thème dans la Conférence d'ouverture de l'année académique de la Faculté de théologie, d'éthique et de philosophie de l'Université de Sherbrooke, Sherbrooke, Août, 1996.

II. Décentrements salutaires

On devine les troubles que suscitent les perspectives d'une inculturation véritable. Se croire le centre de toute intelligibilité de la foi et apprendre brusquement que le centre est peut-être ailleurs ou autrement est inconfortable et insécurisant. Comment accepter d'être dérouté, de se voir renvoyer hors des routes bien connues et des chemins que l'on pensait avoir définitivement balisés? Depuis des siècles, les gardiens du temple et les maîtres de vérité sont persuadés que l'essence du christianisme a été pensée dans les limites et les formules fixées une fois pour toutes par l'orthodoxie romaine. Le choc des humanités différentes exige des décentrements salutaires. Car, à moins de n'être qu'un hochet, l'inculturation entraîne nécessairement déplacements et décentrements. Rien ne prouve que tous les gestionnaires de la curie romaine soient disposés à assumer les risques que doivent prendre les théologiens qui s'engagent à repenser avec courage le modèle d'Église que nous avons reçu.

Ce n'est pas le lieu d'examiner les blocages auxquels l'on est confronté dans les Églises du Tiers-Monde lorsqu'il s'agit de passer à l'acte dans le domaine de l'inculturation. Contentons-nous d'évoquer les difficultés que provoque la simple éventualité d'utiliser une autre matière que le pain de blé et le vin de la vigne dans l'Eucharistie sous les Tropiques alors que la foi n'est nullement en cause dans la réappropriation des gestes du Christ à travers une symbolique du repas propre aux peuples qui ont leurs manières de manger et de boire[9]. Ce problème peut sembler un détail banal. En réalité, il révèle un état d'esprit que n'ont pas changé les discours sur l'urgence et la nécessité de l'inculturation dont parle Jean-Paul II dans l'exhortation apostolique sur l'Église en Afrique[10]. Chaque fois qu'ils se rassemblent pour se souvenir du Christ mort et ressuscité, les hommes et les femmes du mil comme on le voit chez les Kirdis du Nord-Cameroun doivent recourir à des nourritures étrangères qui ne leur disent rien. Par obéissance, ils doivent consentir à une rupture symbolique et culturelle dans l'acte même où la communauté des disciples de Jésus veut exprimer le meilleur de sa foi naissante.

Prendre en compte les rapports entre l'Évangile et la culture suppose que l'on accorde aux Églises locales la confiance et la liberté nécessaire

9. Sur ce sujet, lire J.-M. ELA, *Le cri de l'homme africain*, Paris, L'Harmattan, 1980, pp. 9-17. Lire aussi la thèse de R. JAOUEN, *L'Eucharistie du mil. Langages d'un peuple, expression de la foi*, Paris, Karthala, 1995.

10. Exhortation apostolique de JEAN PAUL II, *L'Église en Afrique*, dans *DC*, 21-23 (1995) 831-832, III, (59).

pour réaliser l'inculturation qui doit laisser la place à des essais et à des erreurs, avec tous les risques que cela comporte. Le spectre du syncrétisme qui hante les dicastères romains et nourrit leurs inquiétudes repose, en fait, sur la peur de passer du centralisme ecclésiastique et uniformisateur à la décentralisation sans laquelle l'inculturation reste un vain mot.

On peut dissimuler les tourments que suscitent les efforts d'inculturation par un intégrisme inavoué que justifient les dangers de déviation que l'on exhibe en refusant aux chrétiens du Tiers-Monde le droit à l'erreur reconnu par toutes les théories de l'apprentissage. Des esprits avisés masquent aussi leur résistance aux efforts d'innovation en s'appuyant sur les dédoublements de personnalité que l'on observe dans les Églises où l'univers culturel et symbolique des chrétiens indigènes n'a jamais été pris au sérieux dans la manière dont l'Évangile leur a été présenté. Parlant des chrétiens africains, le Cardinal Poupard écrit: «Pour beaucoup, une partie de leur être et de leur vie reste en marge de l'Évangile, d'où une duplicité, véritable écartèlement entre deux modes de vie, partagée entre les pratiques traditionnelles de la coutume et la foi au Christ»[11]. Ce constat de la dichotomie dans la vie de certains chrétiens devrait pourtant stimuler les recherches en vue de l'évangélisation en profondeur. Mais cela suppose que l'on accepte de revoir radicalement la façon dont on comprend l'universalité du christianisme.

Pour guérir les chrétiens africains de leur schizophrénie spirituelle, les instances régulatrices de la foi ne cessent de se méfier du concret. Malgré des avancées verbales, elles ne laissent les Églises locales faire les expériences d'inculturation que dans les limites de ce qu'il convient d'adapter et qui se réduit, en somme, à l'utilisation des langues vernaculaires et l'introduction des tam-tams et des tambours. Mais en ce qui concerne l'essentiel, comme le rappelle la célébration des sacrements en l'état actuel de l'inculturation de la foi, l'Église assume difficilement les différences légitimes. Tout effort dans ce domaine est bloqué par une vision du christianisme où les chrétiens de cultures différentes ont tout à recevoir, rien à apporter. C'est ce que nous enseigne aujourd'hui le Cardinal Ratzinger. Les africains sont particulièrement visés par cette approche.

Le Président de la Congrégation pour la Doctrine et la Foi ne trouve en Afrique que des religions primitives et tribales qui ne peuvent résister et survivre aux assauts de la science et de la technologie occidentales. C'est seulement au sein du Christianisme que ces formes inférieures de religiosité trouvent les instruments de réflexion théologique qui leur manquent. Dans cette perspective, l'adhésion au christianisme apparaît

---

11. Cité dans *AR*, 15 octobre (1995) 56.

comme la seule voie d'accès à la modernité dans le processus actuel de la globalisation. Car, le Christianisme lui-même est une culture qui offre sa plénitude culturelle à d'autres peuples à partir des fondements d'une universalité déjà là, définitivement acquise et établie[12]. Sans nous arrêter sur les caricatures des cultures africaines dont Ratzinger donne une image qui reproduit les clichés de l'ethnologie coloniale et réactualise le portrait de l'homme africain esquissé par Hegel[13], relevons les limites d'une conception de l'universalité qui exclut la participation active des peuples évangélisés dont l'avènement est un événement qui apporte, précisément, ce qui manque à l'épiphanie de la catholicité.

Toute l'ecclésiologie contemporaine à travers l'œuvre de H. De Lubac, de J. Daniélou ou de Y. Congar n'a cessé de rappeler cette aptitude de l'universalité chrétienne à s'accomplir par la diversité des apports qui trouvent en Jésus-Christ leur plénitude. Faut-il le redire: comme révélateur ultime[14], qui nous livre le dernier mot de Dieu[15], Jésus Ressuscité est Seul Universel. Qui peut prétendre qu'une figure historique du Christianisme soit en mesure d'épuiser le potentiel de son mystère dans la singularité de ses formes d'expression? Le concept d'une universalité «déjà acquise» relève de l'intégrisme qui hante les milieux habités par l'imaginaire préconciliaire. Croire que les cultures indigènes ne peuvent échapper au risque de demeurer des «enclaves» d'une «civilisation primitive» ou des «réserves naturelles» appelées à disparaître dans le vaste mouvement qui porte l'humanité vers une culture et une science-monde, ne prend pas en compte les dynamiques historiques.

Les crises identitaires et la revanche des religions traditionnelles dont la vitalité est un fait notoire oblige à reconsidérer les enjeux culturels dans les mutations contemporaines. En luttant contre ce qu'il considère comme «les dangers de l'inculturation», Ratzinger redonne toute son actualité à l'alliance tragique entre révélation et domination.

III. CHRISTIANISME SANS FÉTICHE:
FAIRE FACE À LA GLOBALISATION DES FORCES DU MARCHÉ

Pour dire le «Christ aujourd'hui et demain» dans l'enracinement de notre culture et de notre histoire, seule une Église semper purificanda

---

12. J. RATZINGER, *Christian Faith and the Challenge of Cultures*, dans *Origins* 24 (1995) 679-686.
13. Sur ce sujet, lire F. HEGEL, *La raison dans l'histoire*, Paris, Hatier, 1987, pp. 10-18.
14. *DV* I, (4).
15. *Heb*, I, 1-2.

peut poser les conditions d'une universalité libérante qui nous conduirait
à ce qu' Éboussi a appelé un «Christianisme sans fétiche»[16]. C'est pourquoi, il nous faut reprendre le débat sur la globalisation escamoté par
Ratzinger. Le défi que pose ce phénomène reste entier. Il doit être posé
ici dans toute sa radicalité. Car, il présuppose un modèle de développement qui s'impose comme universalisable à l'ensemble de la planète. Il
renvoie à ce que Albert Jacquard appelle un «intégrisme aussi ravageur
que les intégrismes religieux»[17].

Pour le théologien africain, une relecture du message central du Nouveau Testament doit tenir compte du contexte actuel où s'impose la
croyance aveugle au règne de l'argent. Notre manière de comprendre Dieu
et son règne est mise à l'épreuve par les fondements du «système-monde»
qui structure le quotidien des hommes et des femmes de notre temps.
Comme le disait le Père Engelbert Mveng, «il faut se rendre à l'évidence:
l'Évangile est incompatible avec la conception du monde propre à l'Occident actuel»[18]. Il nous faut considérer attentivement ce fait afin de saisir
l'urgence et la nécessité de la théologie de la libération au seuil du troi-
sième millénaire. Cette réflexion paraît nécessaire lorsqu'on cherche à
approfondir le sens de la révélation en assumant les questions concrètes que
pose à la foi et aux Églises chrétiennes l'état actuel du monde africain.

1. *Réappropriation théologique des défis posés par la globalisation: les
    pièges de l'inculturation.*

Une réappropriation théologique des défis de la globalisation exige un
certain nombre de précautions et de préalables théoriques. Rappelons
d'abord cette banalité: personne ne parle de Dieu de nulle part. Toute
exploration intelligente de la foi se fait toujours à partir d'un lieu déterminé dans un temps précis et à la lumière des schémas d'intelligibilité
et d'interprétation de l'homme et du monde. Bref, toute théologie est située
au cœur de l'histoire. Elle s'élabore à partir d'un contexte spécifique.
Remarquons que la contextualisation de la théologie n'est pas une mode pas-
sagère, mais elle appartient à la nature même de la théologie[19]. Se demander
si l'heure n'est pas venue de renoncer aux analyses socio-économiques

16. F. Éboussi Boulaga, *Christianisme sans fétiche. Révélation et domination*, Paris,
Présence africaine, 1981.
17. A. Jacquard, *J'accuse l'économie triomphante*, Paris, Calman-Lévy, 1995, p. 88.
18. E. Mveng, *De la mission à l'inculturation*, dans J. Ndi-Okalla (dir.), *Inculturation et conversion: Africains et Européens face au synode des Églises d'Afrique*, Paris,
Karthala, 1994, pp. 15-16.
19. B. Stephen & B. Bevans, *Models of Contextual Theology*, Maryknoll, NY, Orbis,
1992.

pour privilégier l'analyse culturelle suppose un choix de recherche dont il faut mesurer les conséquences pour l'avenir de la théologie elle-même. Car, ce choix vise manifestement à promouvoir une nouvelle façon de faire la théologie qui présuppose que le seul contexte qui doit préoccuper le théologien est celui où le rapport à la culture est le vrai défi de la foi. Dès lors, la théologie de l'inculturation récapitule toute théologie contextuelle.

Dans les Églises d'Afrique, l'on est tenté d'enfermer la théologie africaine dans la problématique de l'inculturation. On se souvient de l'intervention de Mgr. Tshibangu au Synode romain sur l'Afrique: «Le propos de la théologie africaine a été déterminé délibérément, au moins pour le stage et dans les circonstances actuelles, comme une théologie de l'inculturation»[20]. Nous comprenons cette préoccupation dans les communautés locales où la relation à l'Invisible, la Communion avec les ancêtres, le monde des esprits et les problèmes de guérison ouvrent un espace d'interrogations et de recherches et doivent mobiliser l'attention des théologiens africains. Nous ne reviendrons pas ici sur leurs contributions à la redéfinition des rapports dynamiques entre la foi et les cultures. Ce qui fait problème, c'est de savoir si le modèle de théologie contextuelle qu'on veut promouvoir en faisant croire que tous les problèmes de l'Afrique contemporaine se réduisent à des problèmes d'identité culturelle ne conduit pas à des impasses tragiques.

Les turbulences que vit l'Afrique depuis les années 1990 n'invitent-elles pas le théologien à des révisions déchirantes? À Kinshasa, la marche des fidèles qui s'est heurtée à la violence du pouvoir à la sortie d'une église n'a pas été organisée au nom de l'authenticité. Il s'agissait de «libérer la démocratie» et de refonder la société sur la base des nouveaux rapports entre l'État et le peuple. Plus de trente années après les indépendances, le bilan économique, les problèmes de société et l'effondrement des mythes fondateurs de l'État post-colonial constituent autant de défis graves à partir desquels les Églises chrétiennes doivent s'interroger sur leur apport à l'Afrique contemporaine. Dans ce contexte, comment résister à la tentation du lévite de la parabole qui «prit l'autre côté de la route et passa en laissant l'homme tombé aux mains des brigands» (Lc10,32-36)? La seule réponse crédible à cette question est la suivante: tout faire pour échapper aux pièges de l'inculturation en assumant dans un vaste mouvement théologique ce que j'ai appelé «Le cri de l'homme africain»[21].

---

20. Cité par M. CHEZA (ed.), *Le synode Africain, histoires et textes*, Paris, Karthala, 1996, p. 158.
    21. J.-M. ELA (n. 9).

Au-delà du culturalisme irénique, qui triomphe dans «l'ère du vide» ouverte par la «fin des grands récits»[22], examinons les conditions de possibilité d'une démarche susceptible de répondre aux nouvelles demandes de l'intelligence de la foi. Il faut ici revenir à Vatican II pour reconstruire les bases d'une théologie à l'écoute des sciences de l'homme en plein essor. «En effet, dit le Concile, les plus récentes recherches et découvertes des sciences, ainsi que celles de l'histoire et de la philosophie, soulèvent de nouvelles questions qui comportent des conséquences pour la vie même, et exigent de nouvelles recherches de la part des théologiens eux-mêmes. Dès lors, tout en respectant les méthodes et les règles propres aux sciences théologiques, il sont invités à chercher sans cesse la manière la plus apte de communiquer la doctrine aux hommes de leur temps: car autre chose est le dépôt même ou les vérités de la Foi, autre chose la façon selon laquelle ces vérités sont exprimées, à condition toutefois d'en sauvegarder le sens et la signification»[23]. À moins de faire œuvre d'antiquaire, le théologien africain ne peut se situer en marge des savoirs élaborés par les disciplines qui permettent de comprendre la complexité de la réalité dans laquelle nous vivons. En travaillant à la promotion d'un christianisme africain, la plupart des recherches n'hésitent pas à recourir à l'anthropologie. Notons l'apport de cette discipline dans les réflexions sur les rapports entre le message chrétien, les croyances, les coutumes et les religions traditionnelles en Afrique Noire.

Si l'on considère les tendances qui dominent, on constate une sorte de méfiance à l'égard des autres sciences sociales. Tout au plus, l'on conçoit leur importance pour la pratique pastorale, comme le recommande Vatican II: «Que, dans la pastorale, on ait une connaissance suffisante non seulement des principes de la théologie, mais aussi des découvertes scientifiques profanes, notamment de la psychologie et de la sociologie, et qu'on en fasse usage: de la sorte, les fidèles à leur tour seront amenés à une plus grande pureté et maturité dans leur vie de foi»[24]. Les nouveaux défis de la pauvreté et de l'oppression qui sont désormais au centre de l'engagement missionnaire de l'Église en Afrique exigent une véritable révision des méthodes d'analyse des problèmes de la Foi. Si comme l'ont affirmé les Pères synodaux, l'Église d'Afrique «doit continuer à jouer son rôle prophétique et à être la voix des sans-voix»[25], l'on voit mal comment le théologien peut se passer des apports de l'analyse

---

22. Voir J.-F. LYOTARD, *La condition post-moderne*, Paris, Éd. de Minuit, 1988.
23. *GS* II, (62), 2.
24. *GS* II, (62).
25. L'exhortation apostolique (n. 10) 70.

socio-économique qui, en élargissant l'espace du regard, peut permettre de ré-entendre la parole de Dieu à partir de la situation actuelle de l'Afrique dans le système-monde.

Dans ce sens, nous ne pouvons nous contenter d'une relecture de l'Évangile à l'intérieur du contexte africain réduit à la seule prise en compte de l'héritage ancestral. Il s'agit de nous mettre à l'écoute du Verbe en nous replongeant dans les dynamiques historiques à partir desquelles des logiques de permanence et de rupture sont à l'œuvre dans les sociétés africaines qui réexaminent leurs modes de pensée et de vie, leurs normes de comportements et de valeurs à travers les stratégies qu'elles inventent pour réagir et répondre aux défis du présent. «Les risques de la créativité dans le domaine de la réflexion théologique» dont parle Robert Sastre[26] nous ramènent au cœur des tensions entre la tradition et la modernité dans cette Afrique qui passe du rural à l'urbain. Une «théologie inculturée» ne peut nous suffire pour assumer ces risques en vue de faire face aux défis de la foi provoqués par les crises et les mutations des sociétés africaines qui vivent aujourd'hui sous les contraintes de la globalisation.

Le Synode africain a pris conscience des enjeux socio-politiques de ces défis en s'interrogeant sur les tâches de l'évangélisation dans les pays du Continent soumis aux régimes autoritaires et oppressifs. L'on s'est rendu compte du poids de la dette, des conséquences du trafic des armes et de l'utilisation de l'Afrique comme dépotoir des déchets du Nord. L'on a mesuré aussi l'ampleur des conflits qui déchirent des peuples. L'on a également perçu les ravages dus à l'exploitation des pauvres par les riches. Derrière l'Afrique qui vit dans une situation économique de pauvreté, on a retrouvé les puissances d'argent qui oppriment l'hémisphère Sud. En cette veille du XXIe siècle, une évidence s'impose à la conscience de l'Église: «Dans un monde contrôlé par les nations riches et puissantes, l'Afrique est pratiquement devenue un appendice sans importance, souvent oublié et négligé par tous»[27].

Pour repenser l'évangélisation de l'Afrique dans ce contexte, les mécanismes de société doivent être repris en compte. Au-delà des approches idéalistes et moralisantes, ces mécanismes nécessitent une analyse rigoureuse qui fait appel à plusieurs disciplines de recherche. L'histoire, la sociologie, les sciences économiques et politiques peuvent ici offrir les instruments d'analyse dont le théologien a besoin pour approfondir le sens de la révélation vivante. Si l'importance accordée aux défis de la

---

26. M. CHEZA (n. 20), p. 82.
27. *Ibid*. p. 296.

modernité africaine en gestation, constitue désormais l'une des priorités de l'Église en Afrique, l'on ne peut donner un signe d'espérance à l'homme africain sans recourir aux analyses socio-économiques qui nous éclairent sur la gravité de ces défis.

2. *Effets de la globalisation: Économie de prédation et programmes d'ajustement structurel.*

Après la décennie perdue, l'on prend conscience des nouvelles stratégies du capital à travers les «habits neufs de la domination néo-coloniale»[28] dans un moment de l'histoire où le développement est en question tandis qu'il n'existe plus «qu'une seule politique: l'ajustement structurel»[29]. On ne peut rien comprendre à la situation actuelle des millions d'africains sans découvrir les effets pervers des mesures imposées par les forces du marché dont l'intervention se traduit par la destruction de tout potentiel futur du développement en Afrique. En utilisant l'arme de la dette, les pays du Nord obligent les états d'Afrique à sacrifier l'éducation et la santé dans les pays ruinés par «l'économie de prédation» entretenue par les classes dirigeantes qui ont fait de la violence une méthode de gouvernement. La pauvreté qui explose dans ces pays est le résultat d'un ensemble de contraintes aggravées par les programmes d'ajustement structurel qui ont pour objet l'intégration des sociétés du sud dans l'économie du marché mondialisé. L'Afrique est sous l'emprise des mécanismes de «l'argent fou»[30].

Certes, la gravité de la situation varie selon les pays. Mais dans l'ensemble du Continent, tout se passe comme si la recolonisation programmée était une partie intégrante des mesures mises en place sous l'égide du FMI et de la Banque mondiale qui enferment l'État dans leur tutelle, compte tenu des contraintes qui lui arrachent tout espace de décision au niveau de l'application des principes destinés à démanteler l'État en vue d'accroître l'emprise des forces du marché. Le poids des blocages structurels qui résultent de cette situation ne fait qu'engendrer appauvrissement et enfoncement sans que se matérialise le scénario de crise si souvent annoncé par les organismes internationaux: «Face aux faibles perspectives ouvertes par ce processus d'ajustement imposé de l'extérieur, de nombreuses stratégies de résistance se sont fait jour, qui tendent à le dévoyer. Dans cette situation d'étranglement, l'ajustement

---

28. Sur le thème, voir l'article de G. CORM, *Le monde diplomatique*, février (1989).
29. C. COMÉLIAU, *Le monde diplomatique*, février (1989).
30. A. MINC, *L'argent fou*, Paris, Grasset, 1990.

fait place à l'enlisement»[31]. À l'échelle planétaire, cette situation paraît bien dramatique. Comme le souligne Samir Amin, le «quart-monde africain ne représente déjà plus la 'périphérie typique' mais les vestiges en voie de destruction de la périphérie d'hier»[32].

La violence de l'argent qui étrangle l'Afrique prend des formes cyniques en préparant le monde à accepter dans l'indifférence et la passivité la disparition des millions d'hommes et de femmes dans les pays du Continent où tous les ressorts de la vie sont brisés. Les dégâts humains sont énormes dans les sociétés que le FMI et la Banque mondiale obligent à s'ajuster pour accéder à la «modernité émergente» qui se confond avec la rationalité capitaliste. En effet, le nouvel ordre social dans lequel l'Afrique doit s'acheminer est «capitaliste non seulement dans son économie, mais dans ses autres institutions»[33]. À partir des contraintes de l'ajustement vécu au quotidien, l'Afrique en transition vers l'économie de marché doit payer le prix de cette transition par la subordination aux forces du marché.

Il faut avoir l'honnêteté de reconnaître que cette dépendance est à l'origine de la pauvreté qui n'est pas autre chose que l'expression des ravages du capitalisme-tueur. F. Houtart l'a rappelé avec force lors d'un séminaire récent sur l'avenir du développement au Sud. «Loin de répondre à la logique de la main invisible, l'économie du profit construit au contraire un rapport social de domination. Ce même rapport qui présidera à la Conquête des Amériques et au génocide des Indiens, au libre commerce des esclaves et au blocage politico-social de l'Afrique, à l'exploitation du prolétariat industriel, à la colonisation mercantile d'abord et l'exploitation des richesses ensuite, à la guerre de l'opium et à la révolte de Tou Pei, à l'intégration de l'ancestrale infériorité des femmes dans des rapports sociaux générateurs d'avantages économiques, à l'émigration massive des Européens vers d'autres continents et à la fermeture des frontières quand le flux s'inverse, à l'échange inégal entre le Nord et le Sud, à l'informatisation du Tiers-Monde et à ce qu'on appelle aujourd'hui dans les sociétés industrielles l'exclusion»[34].

En Afrique Noire, si l'on veut bien constater l'emprise du FMI et de la Banque mondiale sur les choix de société imposés aux États endettés qui

---

31. G. DURUGLÉ, *L'ajustement structurel en Afrique (Sénégal, Côte-d'Ivoire, Madagascar)*, Paris, Karthala, 1988.
32. S. AMIN, *La faillite du développement en Afrique et dans le Tiers-Monde*, Paris, L'Harmattan, 1989, p. 107.
33. A. GIDDENS, *Les conséquences de la modernité*, Paris, L'Harmattan, 1994, p. 20.
34. F. HOUTART, *L'avenir du développement au Sud. À la recherche d'une alternative de Gauche*, Séminaire à l'occasion du XXe anniversaire du Centre Tricontinental (CETRI), Bruxelles, septembre 1996.

ont perdu toute souveraineté, l'on doit aussi admettre la nécessité d'une reprise et d'une réactualisation des modèles d'analyse qui n'ont cessé de mettre en lumière la misère des peuples du Sud en privilégiant le poids des structures de domination et de dépendance enracinées dans l'histoire depuis l'esclavage et la colonisation. Au cœur d'un ordre mondial en crise où la mort du pauvre est devenue une chose facile, il importe de cerner l'ensemble des efforts de restructuration des rapports entre le capital en expansion, l'État et la société pour comprendre le drame des peuples contraints de passer à l'économie de marché.

Au-delà des stéréotypes inopérants qui dissimulent la réalité, ne faut-il pas réapprendre l'Afrique? Écarté des échanges mondiaux, dévalué et soumis aux diktats des institutions financières internationales, le Continent noir est sous l'emprise d'un capitalisme sans état d'âme et sans entraves. Car, le processus de globalisation se traduit par un élargissement de l'espace du capital au prix d'une aggravation des distorsions, des déséquilibres et de la dépendance, d'une marginilisation accrue et d'une paupérisation croissante du monde africain. Soyons clairs: la réappropriation du débat sur les paradigmes qui fondent la démarche du théologien nous oblige à affirmer le caractère central des rapports sociaux de production dans l'Afrique ajustée. Compte tenu des ravages du néo-libéralisme, la conscience de la complexité des réalités africaines amène à faire des choix théoriques et à redéfinir les cadres conceptuels en vue d'analyses nouvelles mieux appropriées aux situations concrètes des sociétés africaines contemporaines. Si les dogmes sacralisés n'ont guère de signification pour ces sociétés, la réalité vécue des peuples opprimés exige une radicalité dans l'approche des défis du Continent noir.

Il nous faut aujourd'hui sortir d'une attitude de réserve pour assumer les tâches de la pensée critique en cette fin de siècle où la recherche d'alternatives s'impose aux acteurs socio-historiques. Pour répondre aux nouvelles demandes des générations sacrifiées, il ne faut pas hésiter d'aller à la racine dans l'analyse, face à des situations qui deviennent de plus en plus intolérables. L'énorme défi des peuples transformés en haillons dans un continent qui constitue une véritable jachère géopolitique nous pousse à revoir en totalité les conditions d'exercice de notre métier de théologien. Il nous faut ré-examiner en profondeur l'objet et la finalité de notre discipline en ayant le courage de sortir des filets de la pensée unique pour mesurer dans quel sens le renouvellement des structures d'oppression à l'ère de la globalisation est, peut-être, le seul vrai défi à la théologie chrétienne à la veille du XXIe siècle.

3. *Globalisation et structures d'oppression: Opposer à la Théologie de l'empire une Théologie de la vie.*

Dans cette perspective, l'on doit considérer la crise de Dieu qui est l'objet du discours théologique au moment où l'on assiste à l'étrange déplacement du sacré à partir du marché et de sa mondialisation. Ces métamorphoses donnent à penser sous le règne de «l'argent-dieu» auquel toutes les sphères de la vie sociale et des activités humaines sont désormais soumises. Dans les mutations en cours, comment ne pas observer le basculement du marché et des structures dans la sphère du religieux? Dans un livre impertinent, Susan George n'hésite pas à comparer la Banque mondiale à une Église et à considérer ses fonctionnaires comme des prêtres cooptés plus que recrutés, dotés de nombreux privilèges moyennant une fidélité absolue à l'institution[35]. Leur dogme, c'est la toute-puissance du marché hors duquel il n'y a pas de salut. Les chefs d'entreprise sont assimilés aux grands prêtres et les économistes aux théologiens tandis que les banques ou la bourse fonctionnent comme des temples. La publicité elle-même joue le rôle de la prédication dans le nouveau culte de l'argent-roi. Dans cette nouvelle religion, s'il faut se soumettre aux lois du marché auxquelles on adhère comme à des dogmes intouchables, l'on doit reconsidérer le péché comme la désobéissance à ces lois. La sacralisation de l'économie marchande affecte les comportements, les individus et des groupes sociaux auxquels on demande de se serrer la ceinture et d'assumer les coupures et la réduction des dépenses sociales de l'État comme des pénitences et des sacrifices nécessaires à l'assainissement des finances publiques. On parle d'effacer la dette comme on efface un péché.

Le credo de cette religion séculière revendique le droit d'universalité dans la mesure où il est rigoureusement identique pour tous les pays du Sud: il faut passer par l'ajustement structurel. C'est à l'intérieur de ce programme que l'Occident guère la crise des pays qui s'enfoncent dans l'enlisement. Comme l'observe F. Houtart, «Les puissants de plus en plus dérangés par la dangereuse dégradation des conditions naturelles et humaines, mettent en place des programmes d'allégement de la pauvreté qui s'avèrent aussi pertinents et efficaces que la charité du XIXe siècle, pour résoudre la 'question ouvrière'. Ils ont la même fonction: entretenir la bonne conscience de leurs auteurs et construire l'image de l'altruisme. Si dans une société pré-capitaliste comme la Palestine du 1er siècle, Jésus-Christ avait déjà dit, qu'il était plus difficile à une riche d'entrer

---

35. S. GEORGE & F. SABELLI, *Crédits sans frontières. La religion séculière de la Banque mondiale*, Paris, La découverte, 1995.

dans le royaume de Dieu qu'à un chameau de passer par le trou d'une aiguille, que dirait-il aujourd'hui, face aux capitaux spéculatifs qui dominent les marchés monétaires, face aux pouvoirs économiques trans-nationaux qui décident des politiques énergétiques, alimentaires ou pharmaceutiques à travers le monde, sans contrôle démocratique et face aux pouvoirs politiques qui n'hésitent pas à utiliser les armes pour imposer ou maintenir des rapports économiques avantageux pour leurs classes sociales privilégiées? »[36]

En tenant compte de ces rapports inédits entre le marché et le sacré, on voit les nouveaux champs qui s'ouvrent à l'intelligence de la foi, au-delà des liens traditionnels entre la théologie et la philosophie. Pour la première fois dans l'histoire de la pensée chrétienne, il va falloir redéfinir les tâches de la théologie à partir des défis de l'économie dans le processus actuel de la mondialisation. Face à l'idolâtrie du marché, il s'agit, en effet, de s'interroger sur la manière de s'y prendre aujourd'hui pour laisser Dieu être Dieu. À l'exemple de la Bible qui parle de Dieu et de l'homme d'un même souffle, nous avons besoin de découvrir l'actualité et la profondeur de cette révélation bouleversante: «Exploiter le pauvre, c'est outrager son créateur (Pr 14,31)». La portée de cette affirmation centrale doit être soulignée dans le contexte des sociétés affectées par le «colonialisme global» dont les mécanismes sont à l'œuvre à partir du «consensus de Washington». En effet, la totalité du sens de la révélation divine est mise à l'épreuve par la mondialisation que Petrella considère comme «le cheval de troie qui permet de réduire le monde en un immense marché»[37].

Confronté à «l'Évangile de la compétitivité» dont parle aussi Petrella, le théologien doit revenir à Celui qui est la Vérité, Jésus-Christ qui exige la conversion et nous somme de résister aux logiques néo-libérales qui sont un instrument de domination du Nord sur le Sud et affectent de plus en plus un grand nombre de citoyens des pays industrialisés. Au cœur de l'histoire où le mystère d'iniquité agit en profondeur par les structures qui oppriment, toute réflexion sur l'alliance de Dieu avec l'homme en Jésus-Christ exige la remise en question de l'économie-monde où l'esprit de profit évacue «l'esprit du don»[38]. Dès lors, la grande transformation qui s'est opérée avec le passage à l'économie de marché pose un problème dont on doit retrouver la place centrale dans l'effort de réappropriation de l'Évangile dans le monde de ce temps.

36. F. HOUTART (n. 34).
37. R. PETRELLA, Le Devoir, 10 juin (1996).
38. J.T. GODBOUT, L'esprit du don, Montréal, Boréal, 1995.

Si le marché est cette «idolâtrie» (Éph 5,3) dont la logique fonde une économie barbare qui ne peut prospérer que sur la ruine de la société, l'on est tenté de revenir à l'Apocalypse pour comprendre l'empire totalitaire dans lequel l'humanité est enfermée par un système économique qui cherche à s'imposer comme une loi inexorable de l'histoire. En un sens, le «capitalisme total» dont parle Friedmann est ce monstre géant aux pieds d'argile dont la chute doit ouvrir l'avenir à la réalisation d'alternatives. Face à l'empire qui ne laisse aucune issue et dont le FMI et la Banque mondiale impose la théologie, il nous faut retrouver l'audace de l'Évangile pour créer des espaces de vie en brisant l'interdit qui conduit à la «culture de mort» imposée par la rationalité marchande. Opposer à la théologie de l'empire, une théologie de la vie, tel est le défi à relever dans la nouvelle Babylone où Dieu nous appelle à le découvrir et à comprendre sa volonté à partir des pauvres et les opprimés.

IV. Repenser la Théologie à partir des «damnés de la terre»

Les temps sont mûrs pour fonder une nouvelle démarche de la théologie chrétienne à partir de l'enjeu de Dieu qui se révèle hors des temples, sur les chemins d'indignité où nous rencontrons le crucifié du Golgotha qui s'est identifié avec l'homme dépouillé, humilié et asservi (Ph 2,6-8). Dans la mesure où en Jésus-Christ, Dieu établit sa demeure dans le monde des pauvres et des opprimés (Mt 25,31-46), l'incarnation apparaît ici comme le chemin de tout engagement en faveur des laissés pour compte de notre temps. En nous rappelant que Dieu se dit dans l'histoire, il nous faut apprendre à le rencontrer dans les luttes et les combats où le Royaume qui est au centre du message de Jésus-Christ (Mc 1,14-15; Mt 4,17), se donne à voir et entendre dans les transformations globales de la structure de la société, les signes annonçant le monde nouveau où il n'y aura plus ni mort, ni cri (Ap 21,5).

Ces réflexions nous amènent à découvrir comment s'actualise le regard de Dieu sur la misère de son peuple aujourd'hui (Ex 3,7-9; 6,6-7). Elles nous invitent à affronter ce regard pour retrouver cette tradition d'attention aux faibles et aux petits qui est une marque spécifique de la compassion de Dieu. En s'exposant à voir le pauvre qui se tient à la porte de l'homme riche, l'on doit faire preuve de lucidité critique face à l'urgence et à l'énormité des situations de sous-humanité dans lesquelles vit la majorité des peuples que S. Latouche appelle «La planète des Naufragés». En accordant une place prépondérante à ces situations, le théologien est condamné à prendre l'économie au sérieux. S'il ne veut pas se tromper de problématique au sujet de Dieu, il doit repenser la révélation à partir des «damnés de la terre» et remettre en valeur la force subversive de l'Évangile. L'enjeu est considérable puisqu'il s'agit de la reconnaissance de l'autre, notamment celle des exclus de l'histoire qui peuplent les pays du Sud où la pauvreté s'aggrave. Ce qui fait de la théologie de la libération une théologie qui dérange, c'est sa remise en question radicale de la manière dont la question de l'autre est traitée depuis la Renaissance à travers des formes de violence, de génocide et d'oppression qui se renouvellent.

À partir de cette question provoquante, toute la mission de Jésus-Christ est en jeu. Pour dire Dieu dans le «hors-monde» où se trouve l'homme africain, nous devons reprendre à notre compte cette question par laquelle Dieu nous rencontre sur les chemins de notre histoire. Il faut revenir à l'évidence: la sacralisation du «marché total» est le lieu où Dieu interpelle aujourd'hui notre «foi d'Africain». C'est là qu'il nous faut résister à la violence séculière qu'exerce ce que d'aucuns prétendent être le meilleur système au monde. En ce qui nous concerne, ce système impose une logique de mort qu'il nous faut considérer comme l'expression de l'idolâtrie. Pour croire et faire la théologie dans les pays d'Afrique où l'on exige des millions d'hommes et de femmes de s'ajuster ou de crever, l'économisation marchande nous oblige à porter notre attention aux situations d'oppression qui résultent de ce que l'argent est devenu la nouvelle souveraineté qui se fonde sur la violence de l'ordre marchand.

Cet ordre identifié à l'idéal social détourne l'humanité contemporaine des voies d'accès aux conditions de bien-être. L'argent-dieu est incapable d'assumer le défi primordial de l'Évangile qui commande le partage et la solidarité. Chaque jour, nous voyons le modèle de développement qui domine s'opposer au projet de Dieu qui, face au frère démuni, nous rappelle cet impératif catégorique: «donnez-leur vous-mêmes à manger (Mc 6,37)». La réponse à ce défi est impossible aujourd'hui car, le désir qui investit l'argent crée la rareté et la pénurie. Il conduit à la marginalisation des individus et des peuples. Il leur interdit de prendre part au grand banquet de la vie. Le Christ est en procès à travers le drame des groupes humains qui meurent à petit feu dans un système qui identifie la violence et l'économie, la compétitivité et le meurtre du frère. Si l'Évangile doit prendre sens pour l'homme et la femme en milieu africain, il faut retrouver Dieu lui-même parmi les victimes du capitalisme en marche.

Dans ce contexte, les combats pour un christianisme africain, si nobles soient-ils, ne sauraient absorber toutes les forces de l'Église en Afrique. Osons reconnaître que face au meurtre fondateur qui réactualise

le drame d'Abel au cœur de la violence de la monnaie, la priorité de la
mission de l'Église en Afrique n'est pas l'inculturation liturgique, caté-
chétique et théologique. Il nous faut retrouver la véritable priorité du
Royaume de Dieu à travers la refonte d'un système global qui pousse
l'Église à vivre en solidarité avec toutes les personnes qui subissent
aujourd'hui des situations d'injustice et d'oppression inacceptables au
nom de notre foi.

V. LE GÉNOCIDE DU MARCHÉ COMME DÉFI PRIMORDIAL À LA THÉOLOGIE AFRICAINE

Au terme des réflexions qui précèdent, nous entrevoyons l'ampleur
des nouveaux défis d'une théologie qui s'élabore dans les turbulences
de l'histoire de l'Afrique contemporaine. Si la légitimité d'une théologie
africaine n'est plus discutée au sein de l'Église, le débat s'est déplacé
dans la mesure où au moment où il faut faire cette théologie, nous
nous rendons compte des choix d'analyse et des cadres de référence
qui conditionnent la réflexion théologique dans les Églises d'Afrique.
Jusqu'ici, la tentation a été grande de ne voir dans le christianisme que
l'accomplissement de ce qui s'annonçait en germe dans les religions traditionnelles. Le théologien africain ne ferait que nommer une présence
cachée sans souci de mettre en cause une situation sociale et politique
infiniment contestable. En marge des courants mettant en œuvre une
théologie critique qui soit réellement prophétique comme on l'a vu en
Afrique du Sud ou chez les Noirs des États-Unis, les chrétiens d'Afrique
Noire se mobiliseraient autour d'une théologie de l'inculturation.

Au Colloque d'Accra, la théologie africaine s'interroge: libération ou
adaptation? Aujourd'hui, cette question est devenue anachronique. L'on
prend conscience de la nécessaire articulation entre la problématique de
l'inculturation et de la libération. Au tournant de l'an 2000, peut-être
l'avenir de la théologie africaine se joue autour de l'interprétation
vivante de l'Évangile en fonction de la situation globale du monde africain et de son rapport critique avec la théologie des hommes et des
femmes opprimés qui, dans le monde, confessent le Dieu Libérateur. À
l'ère de la mondialisation de la pauvreté qui résulte de la restructuration
du capitalisme dans une nouvelle phase de son expansion à l'échelle de
la planète, c'est devenu une nécessité urgente de susciter un vaste cou-
rant de réflexion chrétienne à partir de la pauvreté, du chômage et de
l'exclusion dans les pays du sud contraints de s'ajuster à un système
économique mondialisé. Dans ce contexte, le théologien africain n'a pas

de choix: face aux nouveaux maîtres à penser qui voient dans le marché et sa mondialisation la seule réponse à la crise des sociétés du Sud, il faut remettre en cause au nom de l'Évangile un système mondialisé qui est la forme post-moderne de la servitude et de la barbarie.

La théologie africaine doit se redéfinir en fonction du débat avec ce système auquel elle est confrontée en permanence lorsqu'en ouvrant la Bible, elle entend cette parole de Dieu: «J'ai vu la misère de mon peuple» (Ex 3,6). Ce dont il s'agit en profondeur, c'est de mettre en lumière la pertinence et l'actualité de la révélation de Dieu dans un contexte socio-historique où la découverte de la figure de l'autre oublié, écrasé, méprisé et opprimé nous ramène à la question centrale de Dieu à l'être humain: «Qu'as-tu fait de ton frère? La voix du sang de ton frère crie du sol vers moi» (Gn 4,8-12). Le paradigme d'Abel n'est-il pas aujourd'hui le modèle de référence obligé pour toute théologie qui veut repenser la mémoire du crucifié en se mettant à l'écoute des autres voix de la planète compte tenu de la complicité secrète de Jésus de Nazareth avec les victimes du capitalisme triomphant? Pour découvrir ces liens, la théologie a besoin de recourir à des instruments d'analyse permettant de mettre à nu les situations concrètes qui exigent une radicalité dans les efforts de compréhension du tissu humain et social où Dieu nous fait signe pour le rencontrer à travers des visages et des dignités bafoués, des corps meurtris, des vies brisées ou fauchées. Bref si l'échec du néo-libéralisme à faire le bonheur de l'humanité n'est plus à démontrer, le génocide du marché apparaît comme le défi primordial à toute théologie qui s'élabore en solidarité avec les peuples laissés en bordure du monde.

Si, comme a dit le théologien allemand J.B. Metz «on ne peut faire de la théologie en ignorant Auschwitz»[39], on peut se demander de quel côté se situe véritablement l'Église lorsqu'on réfléchit sur les tracasseries romaines à l'égard de la théologie de la libération. Comment marquer la rupture entre Rome et le Département d'État américain qui voit dans la théologie de la libération une menace pour les sociétés multinationales qui redoutent que le christianisme soit vécu comme un ferment de libération? L'offensive de Rome contre la théologie de la libération est-elle justifiée par un souci d'orthodoxie? Ou bien, en contrôlant la réflexion théologique et en cassant les secteurs de l'Église vivante, le Vatican ne risque-t-il pas de jouer le jeu de la dictature de l'argent? Au temps de la guerre froide où les peuples du Tiers-Monde ont pu trouver des appuis du côté de l'Est alors que les puissances occidentales n'hésitaient pas à porter à bout de bras les régimes oppressifs et corrompus, le rejet du

---

39. Voir G. Baum, *Compassion et solidarité*, Montréal, Bellarmin, 1992, p. 106.

marxisme athée et la propagande anti-communiste sont apparus comme un moyen de faire accepter aux opprimés la perpétuation de leur oppression.

Aujourd'hui, la propagande contre la théologie de la libération ne risque-t-elle pas de faire jouer à l'Église le rôle de légitimation de la servitude et de la domination? Pour les classes possédantes obsédées par le caractère révolutionnaire de l'Évangile, Rome serait un puissant facteur de conservatisme social. Quelle crédibilité Rome donne-t-elle à l'Église lorsqu'elle réduit au silence les théologiens qui s'efforcent d'aborder les vrais problèmes de leur société à la lumière de l'Évangile? Si le christianisme n'est pas une mystification d'envergure, la théologie de la libération est un fait d'Église. Elle est devenue l'âme de toute évangélisation qui veut relever le défi incontournable qu'adresse aux chrétiens la pauvreté structurelle des pays du Sud. Elle nous rappelle que le destin des pauvres est au cœur du mystère chrétien.

Au moment où l'on assiste au déplacement du centre de gravité du christianisme du Nord vers le Sud, l'enjeu principal de la théologie n'est-il pas de permettre à l'Évangile de rester aux mains des pauvres? Dans cette perspective, en contextualisant son point de départ qui demeure les pauvres et leur libération, la théologie qui prend en charge ce choix d'Église doit diversifier ses approches en s'ouvrant aux nouveaux champs d'analyse. Car, les pauvres aujourd'hui, notamment dans les pays d'Afrique, ce sont aussi les jeunes, les femmes, les enfants de la rue, les paysanneries aux abois, toutes les victimes des programmes d'ajustement structurel, les penseurs et les créateurs, les artistes et les écrivains, les intellectuels contraints à l'exil par les pouvoirs qui tuent. Le retour en force des dictatures dans les pays du Continent met en évidence l'ampleur des défis socio-politiques dans un contexte nouveau où l'annonce du Royaume de Dieu ne peut être séparée des combats pour l'homme.

Un fait nous paraît certain: la théologie qui se cherche dans les pays du Sud ne peut plus se résigner à une approche spéculative de la foi. Pour les chrétiens du Tiers-Monde, la question théologique primordiale n'est pas: «Dieu existe-t-il?» Coupée de toute action, cette question engage un débat purement théorique où le vrai partenaire du théologien est le philosophe en chambre. Le théologien du Tiers-Monde se pose au contraire la question radicale: «Quel est notre Dieu?» Cette question prend racine dans une expérience de solidarité avec le peuple des pauvres. Le scandale de la pauvreté dans un monde où il n'y a jamais eu autant de richesses impose la rupture avec tous les discours qui empêchent le chrétien de redécouvrir Dieu dans les marges de l'histoire à partir des situations de domination et de malheur où l'Évangile est une force de vie capable d'inventer des chemins de libération. Comment contribuer à la sortie de l'étranglement et de l'enlisement où se trouve l'Afrique? Telle est la question-mère qui doit habiter la théologie africaine à la veille du siècle qui vient. Cette question ouvre des pistes fécondes qui restent à explorer pour redonner à l'Évangile sa crédibilité et sa pertinence dans cette partie du monde où, depuis de nombreux siècles, «la création gémit dans l'attente de la délivrance» (Rm 8,22).

Faculté des Sciences Sociales   Jean-Marc ELA
Université Laval, Cité Universitaire
Quebec GIK 7P4, Canada

7

THE FUTURE OF THE THEOLOGY OF LIBERATION
IF IT HAS A FUTURE

G. De Schrijver's paper is undeniably a stimulating one. It asks many important questions explicitly and many others implicitly. It is also highly academic and intricately philosophical. However, even though today it is not fashionable to quote him, the paper never forgets Marx's eleventh thesis on Feuerbach: "The philosophers have only interpreted the world in various ways; but the point, however, is to change it". Already in the Introduction of his paper, De Schrijver makes it clear that he engages in liberation theology for "the conscientization of the poor towards social transformation".

I. STARTING-POINT FOR DOING LIBERATION THEOLOGY

1. *Change is Imperative*

Social transformation or social change is imperative: a total and radical change of the world order as it exists and is getting worse these days. The change must be courageously, yet hopefully, pursued. For us in the Third-World, the necessity of change is a categorical imperative of both the theory and the practice of social action.

The bare facts have often been stated. But they bear repeating at the beginning of this response to De Schrijver's paper.

In 1960, the countries of the North were about 20 times richer than those of the South. In 1990 – after a great increase of trade, grants and loans – the countries of the North were 50 times richer that those of the South. The wealthiest 20% of the world's population in 1992 had 83% of the world's income; the poorest 20% only 1.4%. The GNP per capita in Belgium in 1989 was US $ 15890, in India US $ 350, in Sri Lanka US $ 430. In the same year, Belgium had one physician for every 309 persons, India had one for every 2418 persons, and Sri Lanka for every 7161 persons. Energy consumption per capita in Belgium in 1989 was 6532 kw hrs, in India 313, in Sri Lanka 168. Every day 1500 of the world's women die during pregnancy or childbirth. Every year 500 thousand children die from neo-natal diseases. Today 128 million children, mainly in South Asia and Sub-Sharan Africa, are denied primary education. Nearly

1000 million adults are illiterate. Around 1000 million human beings remain in absolute poverty. One hundred and ninety million children are chronically undernourished. Twelve and a half million children below five years of age die each year. In 1988-89, the industrial countries put into the atmosphere an average of 3.5 tonnes per capita of carbon dioxide or the equivalent of other greenhouse gases, the USA alone 5.3 tonnes per capita, while developing countries only 0.9 tonnes. Thus the 1.2 billion people in the First-World produce as much carbon dioxide as the 4 billion people of the Third-World. And thus, the dismal story goes on and on[1].

I distinctly remember an incident in the early 1950s when one of my Jesuit co-students in our theologate in Europe adduced figures much less startling than these in a dining-room practice sermon. The Rector, a kind and well-meaning man, called him up to his room the next morning and told him: "Be careful, brother. By this kind of sermon you will stir the jealously and the hatred of the poor against the rich. So desist".

Yet we know the system can be changed. Smallpox, a scourge for 6000 years, and which killed some two million people a year only 30 years ago, has now been eradicated. Deaths from childhood measles have been brought down from 2.5 million a year in 1980 to just over one million today. Polio is now in retreat. Life expectancy in India in 1941 was 32.4 years for males and 31.7 for females. In 1989, it was 58.1 for males and 59.1 for females[2].

We have also to remember that Marx and Engels knew that, with the development of productive forces after the mid-18th century, the world already in the mid-19th century had the capacity for the first time in human history to give all women, men and children an existence worthy of their humanity. If the world has the capacity, yet did not use it, this was because of the inequity of the existing social system. It was for this reason that Marx and Engels, and hundreds of Marxists after them, turned against the existing system with such ferocity. Socialism is a social system for a time of abundance. Yet with such nearly limitless abundance, capitalism and the exploitation it entails continues its rampage around the world.

Already in the first paragraph of his paper, De Schrijver points to the struggle against injustice as being the central focus of liberation theology. If injustice is the focus, the struggle against it is the praxis. The injustice is both economic and cultural. Whether liberation theology sees

1. K. SOOD, *Un-Wider*, 1995; Britannica. *Year Book*, 1992; *The Reality of Aid*, 1995; SINGER & JOLLY, *IDS Bulletin*, Oct. 1995.
2. SINGER & JOLLY, *IDS Bulletin*, (October, 1995); DATT & SUNDHARAM, *Indian Economy*, New Delhi, 1991; Britannica, *Year Book*, 1995.

cultural injustice as being a different item on its agenda, and whether cultural and economic injustices are both joint aspects of the single reality of injustice, are questions we shall consider later. At present, what is to be noted is that liberation theology shows a face of inflexible steel towards injustice in whatever form and in whatever place it dares to make its appearance in human society.

2. *Relevance to Theology and Faith*

Towards the end of his paper, De Schrijver raises the question of its relevance to theological reflection and Christian faith. How far does an examination of the suggested paradigm shift from socio-economic to socio-cultural analysis, the transition form modernity to postmodernity, enter into the discourse of theology as theology? How far do the four concepts so central in De Schrijver's paper – economics, culture, modernity, and postmodernity – enter into the living faith as faith? De Schrijver, citing Ratzinger, sees the nexus in the critique of globalization. I would rather look for it in the concept so fundamental to liberation theology, namely, justice.

We recall the statement of the Second General Assembly of the Synod of Bishops of 1971. "Action on behalf of justice and participation in the transformation of the world appear to us a constitutive dimension of the preaching of the Gospel". It is probably not necessary to labour this point in this assemblage of committed social activists and theologians.

However, I still find it such a stumbling block to many good Christians genuinely seeking to live the Christian life, and even to many theologians, that it seems necessary to establish the essential and inseparable link between faith and justice. Some recent theological papers speak of justice as an "essential dimension" of faith, others as an "integral part" of faith or as an "absolute requirement" of faith. It is possible to make nice logical and semantic distinctions among the various formulations. To liberation theologians of the Third-World, the making of these distinctions is a luxury that they cannot afford. To them, it does not matter what phrase is used provided it is understood that there is no service of faith where there is no concern for the promotion of justice.

My starting-point always is the incident in the life of Jesus recorded in Luke 4. It never fails to inspire once one seeks and begins to understand it. Jesus is a young man in his late twenties. He has obviously created already a name for himself as a rousing leader of the people. He returns to his hometown synagogue in Nazareth and delivers a homily as part of the usual Saturday synagogue service:

> The Spirit of the Lord has been given to me
> for he has anointed me
> He sent me to bring the good news to the poor,
> to proclaim liberty to captives
> and to the blind new sight
> to set the downtrodden free,
> to proclaim the Lord's year of favor.

Being filled with the Spirit, and the mission to bring the good news to the poor, are presented as intricately linked with each other, each being both cause and consequence of the other. The Spirit of the Lord which fills him leads him inexorably to seek to bring liberation to the poor. In order to sustain him in his mission, he is given the gift of the power-filled Spirit of Truth and Justice.

The socio-political situation of the people in Palestine at the time Jesus spoke at Nazareth – external oppression by the foreigner and internal oppression by the social classes represented in the Sanhedrin – makes it impossible for Jesus to use his heavily loaded language about freedom and expect to be understood in an other-worldly sense of spiritual liberation only. Jesus here says that it is his mission to bring interhuman justice to his people or what we today more commonly call social justice.

The disciples of Jesus are to do the same. The life of the Spirit to which we are called can never be detached from the summons to justice which each one of us receives. The struggle for justice is not something to be merely added to the primary task to live the life of the Spirit. It is the very life of the Spirit driving the disciples of Jesus to commit them-selves relentlessly and untiringly to the task of making human life and society what in God's plan it is meant to be. Hence the depth and intensity of the life of the Spirit is not endangered by one's all-absorbing passion for justice. Commitment to justice strengthens and ensures existential relevance to the life of the Spirit. The fire for justice with which one is consumed makes it impossible for the Christian not to have the desire that that fire be kindled all over the earth. There is only one proviso. The passion for justice must spring from the life of faith. It must constantly be nourished by the Spirit of God, for what is faith but a commitment to the God who appears to us in Jesus and calls us to work with him for the liberation of his people?

So does Psalm 10 say:

> Yahweh, you listen to the wants of the humble,
> you bring strength to their hearts you grant
> them a hearing
> judging in favor of the orphaned and exploited
> so that earthborn men may strike fear no longer.

Or in the powerful Sinhalese poem of the contemporary Sri Lankan poet, Yagama Sekera, brilliantly translated into English by Ranjini Obeysekere:

> If there is a god
> O god!
> Before you descend
> a fireball
> on this
> fearful, doubting, famished world,
> weighed down in unrighteousness
> examine it well.
> Take this my life
> wasting away useless
> make it your tool
> work it to the last dregs.

Rajini spells "god" with the simple "g". But faith reveals to us and experience teaches us that God with the capital "G". That God is the God of love and justice, the Lord of history, moving ceaselessly towards the Parousia, where we shall all be forever one. We shall no longer be divided as we now are into Christians and Jews, Buddhists, Hindus and Muslims, into rich and poor nations, into rich and poor individuals, into blacks and whites and colored, but be the society that God intended it to be. There each one lives for the other, and all live for each one. From each according to ability, to each according to need.

And, finally, let us conclude this brief excursus into Scripture by one who is neither scriptural exegete nor professional theologian but merely one who is concerned about Justice and Equality. If one reads the Bible without any commentary more sophisticated than the foot notes of the Jerusalem Bible, and lets Scripture hit one full in the face, one sees that the central event linking together the books of the Old Testament, and even linking the Old and New Testaments, is the theme of the release from injustice by the God of Justice. The central event in the Old Testament is the Exodus, and later in the history of God's people, the Exile. The central idea behind the central event is that God is the God of the Oppressed. The key to the New Testament and to the linkage of the New with the Old is the Lucan programmatic manifesto of chapter 4 in which Jesus quotes Isaiah. God stands firmly on the side of the unjustly treated. God does not waver in the stand taken. God is with the poor not because they are better and more faithful than their oppressors but because they are poor. The God of the Bible is a God partial to the poor. Ultimately, God leads the People to their release from oppression. The final word is theirs, and it is the word of freedom, liberation.

II. Paradigm Shift?

Have we departed too far from the concerns expressed in De Schrijver's paper? I hope not, for the main concern of the paper, as I understood it, is justice: socio-economic justice and socio-cultural justice.

Is there a paradigm shift from socio-economic analysis to socio-cultural analysis and, consequently, a shift from a paradigm in which interhuman justice is central to one in which culture is the center?

The word paradigm comes to the social and theological sciences from other sciences. In the social and theological sciences, I understand the word to mean today the basic framework of the underlying structure that then determines the entire construct that rises upon it and out of it. If that is so, is there a paradigm shift or rather only a transition or a difference of emphasis springing from the search for fullness and completion in the understanding of justice and injustice? Is it not so much a movement away form socio-economic analysis as a movement to socio-cultural analysis?

1. The Shift from John XXIII to John Paul II

My own view is that it was not the liberation theologians of Latin America but Pope John Paul II who promoted the paradigm shift from justice to culture. Indeed, if it was possible, he would issue a veto on theologians as theologians talking about the release from injustice and oppression and asking for social change. Instead, in his mind, theologians should turn from justice to culture. He knows that the talk about justice has to be direct, with no holds barred. That talk about culture can afford to be much more nebulous. The talk about justice has also to be political. The talk about culture can be merely philosophical. And we know that this pontiff in theory and in practice discourages any political activism of priests and religious, though he himself has probably been the most political of the popes since the Reformation. His defense of this contradiction would be that anything to counter socialism is not political but religious, while anything to change the existing social order is' not religious but political.

Knowing the pontiff's views, and the power he had to enforce them, and his actual use of that power, the theologians of liberation faced a choice. They could either opt out of hierarchical control or temporarily change gear from justice to culture remembering that no Pope is immortal. Here is where the hand of Providence has probably acted. During the first glorious phase of liberation theology, the talk was almost entirely about the sinfulness of interhuman or social injustice and unjust national and international socio-political structures. In the second phase, the talk has to be about the injustice of hegemonic cultures and the values of the indigenous cultures of Latin America, Africa, Asia and the Pacific Islands. In this way will the task of liberation theology be more holistic and all-encompassing. What John Paul II intended to be a veto has become an opportunity.

There was therefore no paradigm shift from justice to culture but only the shift from John XXIII to John Paul II . John XXIII was certainly not a liberation theologian. But he paved the way for liberation theology by the seminal "punto luminoso" of his radio message on 11 September 1962, exactly one month before Vatican II was due to begin. He said: "There is another point of shining significance. Facing the underdeveloped countries, the Church shows itself as it is, and as indeed it wishes to be, as the Church of all, but particularly of the poor"[3].

But there are other reasons for what De Schrijver calls a paradigm shift but which I prefer to consider a transition motivated by the search for wholeness or to call an accentual shift.

2. *Spiritual Undergirding of LT*

One such reason is the growing realization of the need for a deep and genuine spiritual undergirding for the theology of liberation. It began to be understood that the movement from the traditional scholastic theology to the theology of liberation was not sufficiently supported by the necessary parallel movement from the traditional spirituality to the spirituality of liberation. Some may also have erred by throwing away the baby of any spiritual undergirding together with the bath water of the traditional sterile theology. If this happens, what results is not a theology, but a sociology. Hence what is needed is spirituality, but it had to be a new spirituality, one that moved from the pews to the market place. The most intense prayer had to occur not in the chapel but at the bus stands and railway stations. God had to be seen not in the sky but moving, as Jesus' God did, among the People, the so-called ordinary people. I have sometimes said that the task for liberation theology in Asia today is not to say that Jesus is God but that God is Jesus of Nazareth. The former phrase takes Jesus to Heaven, the latter brings God to earth. So it should be said that liberation theology, far from being a suspect theology, is the only orthodox and relevant theology. All other theologies miss the main

3. *AAS* 54 (1962) 682.

theme of our Scriptures that God loves the people and wants justice for them. Texts may be multiplied, but let this one from Jeremiah suffice:

> your father ate and drank, like you,
> but he practiced honesty and integrity,
> so all went well with him.
> He used to examine cases of the poor and needy,
> then all went well.
> Is this not what it means to know me? – it is Yahweh who speaks (Jer 22,16).

We come to know and encounter God in the pursuit of justice. But there was the danger that the pursuit of justice would be divorced from the pursuit of God. Liberation theologians, self-critical of their own work and of its effects on those whom they influenced, began to experience the need for a deep spirituality to sustain themselves and their followers in the pursuit of justice. To fulfill this need, they thought it was wise to move forward from accentuating justice to accentuating the ancient religious experience of their people as expressed in their pluriform culture. Doing this, they were also able to meet the desires of the majority of the Bishops who were fearful of too radical talk about justice. Justice is too perilously close to political action and maybe to Marxism. Culture is altogether a safer exercise.

In the 1990s there is an added reason not to speak so much of justice. There was the fall of the communist regimes in the Soviet Union and in Eastern and Central Europe. And to further increase the pressures from the right against the left, the center stage continued to be occupied by Thatcherism, Reaganomics, and the Structural Adjustment Programs imposed on Third-World Countries by the World Bank and the IMF. Logically, there is no reason to mute the talk about justice just because state socialism, hardly indistinguishable from state capitalism except in the rhetoric, failed in certain countries. And logically there is even more reason to talk about justice in the context of the rampage around the world of International Capital. But there is more to life than logic!

3. Faith, Justice and Social Analysis

The movement from political economy to culture, as the new locus of liberation theology, can be used to the discomfiture of the conservatives and to the advantage of a radical theology of liberation. In this way, a weapon of destruction may be made to boomerang to the dismay of those who invented it. Much depends on the way that cultural analysis is used. Talk about culture can be as explosive in liberation theology as justice ever was or might be.

It needs to be observed, however, that to approach the struggle for relevance in religion through inculturation runs the risk of deradicalizing the struggle without radicalizing culture. Contrarily, to approach it through justice has the potential to radicalize both religion and justice. What is needed therefore is the twofold approach through both Justice and Culture in a pincer movement of the theology of liberation.

In so far as liberation theology by its very raison d'être gives primacy to contextual relevance and the consideration of human interrelationships, it uses, more or less explicitly and deliberately, social analysis. It is on this analysis that the theologians of liberation seek inspiration for their theology.

It is a frequent mistake to think that social analysis is only or mainly socio-economic analysis. In fact, economic analysis is only one element of social analysis. On the foundation or the economic infrastructure of society – either macro-society or micro-society – the superstructure rears itself: religion, politics, education, family, welfare, and management. All these superstructural elements together with their economic base form culture, which may then be briefly and simply defined as the way of life, the mores and values of a people, as manifested in the superstructural institutions of the social system. Culture is therefore complex and pluriform. The more common mistake is to think that those who build their theology or even their activities in the world on the foundations of economics believe that economics is the sole determinant of society. The superstructure, including religion, is then of little importance since its elements are determined solely and entirely by economics, and are destined to disappear or to change substantially when the economic base changes.

Nothing is farther from the truth, as Engels himself explained clearly in his letter of September of 1890 to Joseph Bloch:

> According to the materialist conception of history, the ultimately determining element in history is the production and reproduction of real life. More than this neither Marx nor I have ever asserted… The economic situation is that basis, but the various elements of the superstructure: political forms of the class struggle…, judicial forms, and then even the reflexes of all these actual struggles in the brains of the participants, political, juristic, philosophical theories, religious views and their further development into systems of dogmas, also exercise their influence upon the course of the historical struggles and in many cases preponderate in determining their form… Otherwise the application of the theory to any period of history one chose would be easier than the solution of a simple equation of the first degree[4].

4. K. MARX & F. ENGELS, *Collected Works*, *vol. 37*, Berlin, Dietz Verlag, 1967, p. 463.

Social analysis, therefore, even in its Marxist formulation, does not reduce everything to economics.

Cultural analysis can undoubtedly be used, as has been indicated earlier, in a way that blunts the sharp edges of social analysis and, in so far as social analysis influences liberation theology, of that theology too. In fact, even the word "analysis" is not used probably because it raises specters of Marxist social analysis. In ecclesiastical documents, the talk is only about culture and only Christian culture is held to be complete. Other cultures need the inculturation of the gospel which

> brings to each culture the gift of purification and plenitude. All the cultural values and expressions that can be oriented to Christ foster what is genuinely human. What does not go by the way of Christ will not be redeemable.

> By becoming incarnate [in non-Christian cultures], faith seeks to correct their errors... Properly applied, inculturation must be guided by two principles: compatibility with the Gospel and communion with the universal Church[5].

These are only assertions about culture and the primacy of Christian culture. There is no cultural analysis.

4. *Three Missed Opportunities*

Only grudgingly and very rarely are admitted the grave errors and criminal injustices of the institutional church's own cultural history of thought-control, alliance with secular power, the adoption of the pomp and panoply of secular rulers, and the distancing of the hierarchy of the Church of God from the People of God. The horrors of the Inquisition and the genocide of whole peoples in the name of Christian civilization in what is now called Latin America are not confessed as crimes against culture and against basic humanity. The church then as now is simply not given to confessing that it has erred, nor does it apologize for the sins against justice it has committed.

The Columbus quincentenary in 1992 was indeed one unrepeatable occasion for the institutional church to demonstrate how the cultural approach might lead to the promotion of justice. To achieve this, of course, the cultural approach had to be supported by cultural historical analysis, which the Vatican did not want. Instead, the Curia wanted to celebrate it in an air of triumphalism. It was fortunately stopped in its tracks by dissident voices from Latin America, especially from the indigenous

---

5. *Santo Domingo Conclusions*, Secretariat Bishop's Committee for the Church in Latin America, pp. 129-130.

peoples for whom the quincentenary gave no cause for celebration but for sorrow and shame. That was in 1992. Yet on 4 September 1996, on the occasion of what the Vatican hails as the fifth centenary of the first baptisms in what it calls the New World, the pope addressed a special letter to the church in the Dominican Republic in which the customary Vatican triumphalism breaks out again. In it he suggests that, among the great achievements of the second Columbus voyage, "twelve missionaries accompanied Friar Bernardo Boyl and the *Instrucción Real* ordered the Admiral to see that 'they worked to bring the inhabitants of the island to embrace the Catholic Faith'"[6].

Another opportunity was the centuries-overdue vernacularization of the liturgy after the 1939-45 war and the liberation of several colonies and dependencies from direct western control. If cultural analysis was seriously employed, the vernacularization should have been the beginning of a whole movement of making the church truly incarnate in the ancient cultures of the decolonized nations. But such analysis did not take place.

Let me cite just one simple instance. When the translation of the words of the Eucharistic consecration was made, some of us pleaded for a genuine translation and not a mere transliteration. My Jesuit colleague, Aloysius Pieris, for instance, suggested that "taking the bread into his holy and venerable hands" should be rendered "taking the bread into the lotus of his hands". This was of course too much inculturation to be tolerated by the church authorities both locally and in the Vatican, who preferred to talk unsurely about inculturation but in reality do nothing to weaken the hegemonic control over the churches in the Third-World by the Roman church.

A third opportunity which the Church is squandering is the challenge to oppose the model of development without cultural roots or whose cultural roots are only the making of money and profit, and ever more money and ever more profit. Engels is said to have once told a Manchester manufacturer: "I have never seen so badly built and filthy a city". The manufacturer listened to the end and, at the corner of the road where they parted, replied: "And yet there is a great deal of money made here: good morning, Sir". A well-known French Marxist economist told me personally that he didn't know what was meant by the quality of life. All that the Third-World needed he said was a higher GNP per capita. Bad Marxism! Poor Frenchman! The World Bank is presently engaged in giving gratuitous advice to the people of Sri Lanka to downgrade the

6. *International Fides Service*, (September, 1996), p. 4020.

domestic production of rice in favor of production for export. Besides the economic and political stupidity of such advice, the World Bank trivializes the age-old place of the planting, harvesting and eating of rice in the culture of our people. To touch paddy is to touch the deepest cultural sources of our people. On this ground alone, the World Bank and the culture it represents should be consigned to a bonfire of all institutions, ideas and programs that would destroy the world and the cultural wealth which the peoples of the world have accumulated over the cycles of human history.

It seems to me that I have spoken so far in my presentation of the lost opportunities of the shift. It is now time to speak of the chances, for there are chances. But these chances can be seized only if the cultural approach is based on a cultural analysis that will proceed with the same seriousness and depth as economic analysis. The latter, as we know, examines in depth the mode, the relations and the forces of production and distribution. So also should cultural analysis examine in depth the roots of culture in history, in the psychology of the people, in the forces that have made them through history either succeed or fail in providing the conditions for creative and humane human living. It should also examine the interactions of cultures whenever they meet one another and the reasons why at certain historical times and in certain places the meeting of diverse cultures enriched each of the separate cultures, and why at other historical times and places the meeting led to cultural hegemony and even to the ruin of the cultures that were not backed by power.

When this is done, cultural analysis will move into the mainstream of a multi-faceted social analysis which precisely moves forward from the analysis of the economic infrastructure to the analysis of the cultural superstructure of religion, theological and philosophical ideas, and the pursuit of knowledge and happiness.

A final remark has to be made. This cultural analysis, like the economic analysis which should be concurrently conducted, should be accompanied by a deep spirituality. The basic mark of this spirituality is respect for the Other, and then seeing in this Other the eternal and cosmic Christ, who is also the Christ in Jesus of Nazareth. Without such spiritual undergirding, cultural analysis will not be a continuing effective process but a mere fad to be given up nearly as soon as it begins.

I have already stated that, in my opinion, there was no paradigm shift from, but only a natural evolution of, socio-economic analysis to socio-cultural analysis within the framework of a multi-faceted social analysis.

III. Modernity and Postmodernity

It is now time to move to the other paradigm shift discussed in De Schrijver's paper: from modernity to postmodernity. For us in the Third-World, much more significant than the shift form modernity to post-modernity is the shift from the legal political status of dependency to the legal political status of independence. [Whether the independence we received was real and not merely legal is a problem that need not detain us here.]

1. *Modernity and Colonization*

In the First-World, the shift to postmodernity gives you the chance to rethink the results of modernity, in so far as postmodernity gives you what Santo Domingo calls "a space open to transcendence". The space certainly enables First-World theology to adopt a constructive and positive, but also a critical and skeptical, stance towards the results of modernity over the past four centuries in order to aid in the formulation of a new world order. In this new order, the positive achievements of modernity in all spheres can be made to coexist with the other aspirations of the human spirit such as aspirations for beauty, creative leisure, and time to be oneself in community with others.

In the Third-World, however, neither modernity nor postmodernity is of much interest, not the latter because we did not experience the former. The Third-World did not receive anything much more than the throw-aways of western modernity, its refuse and its power to destroy the past without replacing it with a more human future. Much of the Third-World was, before 1945, under the direct control of western imperial powers. In the eyes of the colonialist First-World, the Third-World has no self-existence but for the sake of the First-World. The attitude persisted, for even though colonialism disappeared, neocolonialism took its place. However, rarely is this attitude of the First-World stated so openly and bluntly as in a leaked "internal memo" of Lawrence Summers, described as "Chief Economist" of the World Bank in 1992. He stated,

> I think the economic logic behind dumping a load of toxic waste in the lowest wage countries is impeccable and we should face up to that[7].

It is sufficient to recall a passage from Marx's brilliant pages on imperialism in India in which Marx himself quotes Stanford Raffles, the English

---

7. *World Bank Report*, 1992.

Governor of Java. Raffles speaks of the Dutch East India Company. Marx says correctly that the British East India Company merely followed in the footsteps of its Dutch predecessor, and we may say that later imperialism in the colonies of all the western colonial powers was a faithful follower of the traditions handed down by the Dutch and the British Companies. Marx pointed out that the Dutch company, motivated solely by profit, used the existing machinery of despotism to squeeze out the last dregs of the people's labor, exploiting the weakness of the existing government, in order to serve their selfishness. At the time when the British consolidated their stranglehold on India in the middle of the 18th century, we have also the authority of a British historian of India, Sir Percival Spear of the University of Cambridge, to say that:

> Taking it all in all, Mughal India, with an estimated hundred million inhabitants, had for about a century and a half a standard of life roughly comparable with that of contemporary Europe, though arranged on a different social and economic pattern. The peasant had a little more to eat, the merchant less opportunity of spending. Most European travelers commented on the dire poverty of the countryside but we must remember that before the agricultural revolution there was also dire poverty in the European countryside[8].

After the British conquest of India, Britain raced ahead in the acquisition of wealth, while India lagged behind. The same happened with the other colonizing countries in relation to their colonies and dependencies. The reason for unprecedented wealth in the West and abiding poverty in the dependencies was colonialism.

2. *Form Dependency to Independence*

It should therefore surprise nobody that, for us in the Third-World, the paradigm shift from modernity to postmodernity can only be of academic interest to a few of our scholars unless it is fully subsumed in another shift. This is the paradigm shift that occurred after the end of the world war in the 1940 and in the 1950's, namely, the shift from dependency to autonomy. The shift has been from a eurocentred world to a wealth-dictated one (centered in the First-World) and then to the polycentred world in which the countries of the Third-World are demanding positions of equality with the great giants of the past.

The sooner the First-World takes serious note of this the better. The Third-World, as certain crucial sessions of the United Nations have

---

8. P. SPEAR, *A History of India*, Middlesex, Penguin Books, 1973, pp. 47-48.

shown, can no longer be silenced. Already in his History of Western Philosophy, Bertrand Russell has argued:

> I think if we are to feel at home in the world... we shall have to admit Asia to equality in our thoughts, not only politically but culturally. What changes this will bring about I do not know, but I am convinced that they will be profound and of the greatest importance[9].

If the four centuries before the 20th were the centuries of Europe, the twentieth the century of the United States, the next centuries may well be the centuries of Asia and Africa. As for Latin America, so close as it is to the US, one wonders how many of the countries there will feel strong enough to pursue independent political, economic and cultural paths, as Cuba has already done despite fearful and tremendous odds. They will also to have to face the might of the conservative bishops appointed by John Paul II.

What then are the tasks for liberation theology in the context of the paradigm shift from subservience and dependence to constitutional independence?

I would divide my answer into two sections: (i) the tasks common to the theologians of liberation in both the First and the Third-Worlds and (ii) the specific tasks, as I see them, for those concerned with liberation theology in Centers such as the Centre in Leuven. I attempt the second answer not without trepidation and only because it is one of the questions posed by De Schrijver in his discussion paper.

3. *Tasks for Libertation Theologians: Economic and Cultural Independence*

First, it would be necessary for the theologians of liberation to examine the theological significance of the change of status from one of subjugation by a foreign, mostly western, power to a status of independence. Liberation theologians would, I believe, wholeheartedly welcome the change. In the event of independence, they would see a repetition of the Exodus experience and the experience of the return from the Exile, both recorded as central themes in the books of the Old Testament. I see the change of the status as potential for the realization of the Beatitude, Blessed are the meek, for they will inherit the earth.

Is not the right of self-determination a basic human right both of individuals and of nations? The theology of liberation should seriously consider this question. Fifty years ago, an undergraduate colleague asked:

9. B. RUSSEL, *A History of Western Philosophy*, p. 420.

what is the theological and moral basis for colonialism? We received no answer. Maybe this Centre should try to give us one.

Second, the theologians of liberation in the First-World should exploit to the utmost the advantage of being in the First-World in order to help translate the constitutional independence of Third-World countries into full economic and cultural independence.

Let us begin with the task of cultural independence. The deculturation of the Christian Community in Asia is well-known. In Sri Lanka, it appears possible to put forward two clear hypotheses about the deculturation-inculturation process of the Christian group.

First, for four preceding centuries until about the 1950s, the role of the Christian Church, led by western bishops and clergy and superiors of female and male religious congregations (into which local recruits were only reluctantly admitted), was to achieve, preserve, and confirm the specific identity and distinction of the minority Christian group. The identity had to be maintained not only in relation to all other religious groups but even in relation to the nation (however difficult the former and myopic the latter enterprises). The second hypothesis is that only after independence, in the late 1950s, was the role increasingly viewed as an outward and adaptive one in terms of the achievement of a national socio-cultural equilibrium. To this end, there began the fostering of creative interaction, on the one hand, with the Buddhists, Hindus and Muslims and, on the other, with the ideologies of secularism and Marxist socialism.

Maybe it will take several decades before the sincerity of the Christian Church, especially of its major Roman Catholic component, is accepted by the three other religious groups in the island and by the nation. Still, it is not rare to hear very ordinary people spontaneously say: "Oh no, that family is not Sinhalese. They are Christians".

Full acceptance by the Buddhists, who are 69 per cent of our population and 80 per cent of our Government, is also hindered by two factors. The first is that, in the minds of the majority of the Buddhists led by the monks, Sri Lanka is and must remain a Sinhala Buddhist country in which the Sinhala Buddhists coexist with other ethnic and religious groups only because of that ancient traditions of Buddhist tolerance and kindness to all human beings.

The second is the triumphalism of the Vatican as it approaches the year 2000. This triumphalism was conspicuous on the occasion of the pope's visit to Sri Lanka in January 1995. The Buddhist monks, despite prior preparations for a most hospitable welcome, boycotted the event when they came to know of the blatantly incorrect assertions the Pope had made about Buddhism in the book *Crossing the Threshold of Hope* and his predictable refusal to admit error. Instead, he patronizingly said in his address on the occasion:

> The Catholic Church rejects nothing of what is true and holy in other religions for she sees in them a ray of the Truth which enlightens them all[10].

The more discerning were quick to see that, while the pope conceded a ray of truth to Buddhism, Hinduism, and Islam, he, with the usual Vatican triumphalism, held that the Church he led had the whole constellation of truth and light. If this is the way the Vatican understands inculturation, it will not be too much to hope that First-World theologians in collaboration with their Third-World colleagues will resolve to show its farcicality to all in the Church but especially to those in the Vatican.

4. *The New World Order*

But there are tasks which First-World theologians are in a privileged position to perform just because they live in the First-World. There is the task to undertake the theological buttressing of the imperative for a new world order of genuine solidarity where all nations can meet in a climate of justice and equality.

The idea of a New Just World Order first came up at the Fourth Conference of Non-Aligned Countries in Algiers in September 1973. On 1 May 1974, the sixth special session of the United Nations General Assembly, in the wake of Algiers, adopted the Declaration on the Establishment of a NIEO.

The rich industrialized countries felt seriously threatened. If allowed to proceed unchecked, it would endanger the entire political and social edifice of western (and Japanese) neocolonialism. The then US Secretary of State, Henry Kissinger, led the campaign against the NIEO at the UN Special Session held in September 1975. While pretending to show understanding of the aspirations of the Third-World countries, early in his long speech, he made his real intentions clear:

> It is also ironic that a philosophy of non-alignment, designed to allow the new nations to make their national choices free from the pressure of competing blocs, now has produced a bloc of its own. Nations with radically different economic interests and with entirely different political concerns are combined in a kind of solidarity that often clearly sacrifices practical interests. And it is ironic that the most devastating blow to economic devel-

---

10. *The Messenger* 1 (1995) 29.

opment in this decade came not from "imperialist capacity" but from an arbitrary, monopolistic price increase by the cartel of oil exporters... (Note the age-old imperialistic tactic, *Divide et impera*).

So let us get down to business. Let us put aside the sterile debate over whether a new economic order is required or whether the old economic order is adequate. Let us look forward and shape the world before us.

Twenty-one years have passed since Kissinger performed on the international stage. The world order remains as iniquitous as it has ever been since today's Third-World countries were first forced to submit to the military and economic might of the today's First-World countries. We agree with Kissinger that there is no need to debate whether a NIEO is necessary. It is necessary as daybreak at the end of the night.

What might First-World Theologians do? Some areas may be singled out. First, they can place the NIEO high on the world's theological agenda. So far, no suggested alternative can take its place. The World Trade Organization (WTO) set up at the Uruguay Round of the GATT is not even a caricature of the NIEO. It negates nearly everything that the NIEO envisaged. Similarly, the Structural Adjustment Programs of the World Bank and the IMF, far from eliminating or even alleviating poverty, actually makes things worse for the poor.

Second, First-World theologians should bring their research and their theological reflections to bear on the injustice of present systems of world trade. Primary commodity exports of the Third-World fetch low prices, while their essential imports of First-World commodities have high prices. Furthermore, the real terms of trade made available to Third-World countries continually deteriorate.

Let me cite an example of what may be achieved by fair trade. Sri Lanka exports over 200,000 metric tonnes of tea each year. If we get 2 more British pounds per kilo (and the price will still be low compared to any beverage produced in the rich countries), we shall receive 400 million pounds or 620 million US dollars more than we now get in foreign exchange each year. At 500 cups of tea per kg of tea, the price of a cup of tea in the rich countries will increase by 0.4 pence, and there will be no coin in all Europe or America small enough to pay for the increase. Yet it would mean much for Sri Lanka. The total foreign aid that Sri Lanka has received from all sources in the last two or three years has been less than 1000 million US dollars per year. What we need therefore is real fair trade, not aid. We think of what the strikers said during the general strike of 1926 in England, "Damn your charity, give us justice".

I recall the evening when a good Belgian Communist friend and I were driving in his car from Brussels through the Ardennes. We were on one of Belgium's great highways, which are said to be the best-lit highways in Europe. They were so well-lit that I told my friend I felt I could read a book in their light. Suddenly our conversation stopped. There was perfect silence, if not for the purr of our slowly moving car. After a few minutes, my friend asked, "what are you thinking about?" "Probably what you are thinking about", I answered. "I am thinking of the waste of all this electric light. I am thinking of our plantation line-rooms, dark even at noon. I recall Gandhi saying that while there is enough for everyone's need, there isn't enough for everyone's greed". "Sure", my friend replied. "The world must change".

Third, the First-World theologians can help expose the myth of foreign aid. The original target was 1 per cent of GNP. In 1963, the Development Assistance Committee of the OECD counties lowered the target to 0.7 per cent. Yet even this target has not been reached, and most years it has not exceeded 0.4 per cent. Among the traditionally generous donor-countries, only the smaller ones – the Netherlands, Norway, Sweden, and Denmark – have come close to the 1 per cent target or even slightly exceeded it. Furthermore, if we set off total inflows of foreign exchange against total outflows, in many years the annual net transfer of resources from North to South will prove to have in fact been negative. The outflows of foreign exchange arise from payments of interest on, and amortization of, previous loans and from the repatriation of profits on private foreign investment in poor countries. If we include losses from worsening terms of trade and restrictions on exports from the developing countries, the picture that emerges is one of stark injustice. Finally, one has to take account of the compulsory aid given by the colonies for the development of imperialist countries during the heyday of direct colonialism. If this is included, then what is being made available today will be reckoned not as aid but as partial restitution.

Fourth, First-World theologians should work in collaboration with the new theologians of Asia, Africa and Latin America to work out a theology of a just world order. Institutes such as this one should establish working links with similar institutes in the Third-World. Books and international seminar papers are hard to come by in the Third-World, even if money can be found to buy them. Could not First-World theological institutes be of assistance to the Third-World in this field?

Let me insist. The tasks outlined are not only for economists and sociologists. If the preferred locus for theologians of liberation is the real world, they cannot ignore these most pressing tasks.

IV. CONFRONTING THE REAL WORLD

1. *Liberation Theology and Traditional Theology*

The world of today poses a challenge to liberation theology. But in order that liberation theology might accept the challenge that comes to it from the world, it has itself to continue to challenge traditional theology. Theology, whether traditional or liberational, cannot but be the word about God: God's Word in Jesus, God's Word in Scripture, and God's communication with People through grace, God's Church, the sacraments, and the experience of the Church since Jesus died. Only nominally are the themes of liberation theology the same as those of traditional theology. For each of the themes in liberation theology passes through the prism of liberation, of the breaking of the fetters of injustice, of whatever shackles the mind and the heart and whatever oppresses the body. The theme of theology is God. But the theme of liberation theology is the theme of God the Liberator. Soon after Jesus was killed, the early Christian community has this as their theme:

> God has shown the power of his arm.
> He has routed the proud of heart.
> He has pulled down princes from their thrones and exalted the lowly.
> The hungry he has filled with good things, the rich sent empty away.
> He has come to the help of Israel his servant, mindful of his mercy.

We should seek to experience the joy and the hope of those early Christians, drawn from the ranks of the lowly and the despised, as they sang this song of the revolutionary victory.

The question that arises in my mind is how, for many, many years, we of my generation read and re-read these texts – the Magnificat, the Beatitudes, the Benedictus, the Parables of Jesus, Luke 4, the Lord's Prayer itself, the Prophets and the Psalms of the Old Testament, and some of the Fathers of the Church – and did not see in them the message of liberation which now seems so primary and obvious. We had to wait for Pope John XXIII, Vatican II, and the first stirrings of liberation theology in Latin America to understand these texts in the only way that they can be understood and, through them, to proclaim the freedom of God to ourselves and to our peoples.

It took seventy years for the papal social encyclicals, which began with *Rerum Novarum* in 1891, to make mention, as in Pope John XXIII's *Mater et Magistra*, of the Third-World. But surely an even bigger scandal is the fact that it took several centuries for Christian theology to take serious note of the huge areas of the world that lay under the heel of western colonialism. Bartolomé de las Casas, Roberto de Nobili, and Matteo Ricci should never have been the exceptions regarded as eccentrics but should have been seen as indicative of the rule for a Church that professed to preach its message to the whole world.

The all-important task of liberation theology, wherever people have begun to live it, is to work for a world-society in which persons and nations can again be free. To say that history ended with the collapse of the Berlin Wall in 1989 is nonsense. It is an entirely western capitalist understanding of history. Much more resounding than the fall of that wall was the rumbling of crumbling empires which people like Nehru, Mao, Soekarno, Che Guevara and Castro heard after the end of the 1939-45 war. It indeed was the end of the period when the winners were always in the First-World and the beginning of the period when the Third-World is demanding its rightful place in the assemblies of world peoples.

2. *Broken Reality*

Yet fifty years later, there is still the broken reality of Asia, Africa and Latin America, so broken that we are so stunned as to be in danger of being paralyzed into inaction. We sometimes feel that there is nothing that we can do to put the pieces together, to bring wholeness to a body so badly damaged. The principalities and the powers of International Capital, the largest two hundred transitional Mega-Corporations, the World Bank, and the IMF are arrayed against us like the Great Harlot of the Apocalypse. If the devil of colonialism has been driven out, it returns with seven others in the form of neocolonialism. Yet the Third-World is a huge reality. It is not, as Neville Chamberlain once said of Czechoslovakia, a faraway place of which we know nothing. Asia alone holds more than half the world's population, though it has less than one-third of the world's land area.

It is here that liberation theology comes to our rescue with its voice of prophecy, urging us to be relentless in analyzing reality and seeing it as God sees it, and in the power of God to seek to change it. It is inherent in prophecy that it runs the risk of not being heard, then in the Sanhedrin, today in Episcopal palaces around the bleeding world. But it is also inherent in authentic prophecy that it refuses to be silenced.

So should the numerically small minority of Christians in Asia raise their prophetic voices as regards the economic scenario that is unfolding itself before their eyes. They must speak boldly of its evils and say that, if unchecked, these evils can destroy whole peoples or maim them spiritually and physically for ever. It must then prophetically suggest an alternative.

But it is not only the Third-World. The whole world presents a picture of fractured reality. On the one hand, stupendous progress in science and technology. On the other hand, progress not only against basic moral values but contrary to all moral sense. On the one hand, the whole range of telematics brings the whole world to anyone's doorstep. On the other hand, racism, crude color bars, ethnic intolerance divide people not only between countries but also within countries. On the one hand, internationalism; on the other, the worst forms of nationalist exclusivism. There is unemployment, homelessness, alienation and, even in the rich countries, malnutrition and hunger. Sport becomes increasingly commercialized, the playground of business tycoons, advertising firms, and the transnationals.

The Golden ABC, a popular Finnish children's reader, now in its 12th edition, says: "The Negro washes his face but it never gets any whiter". A recent British official report, *Social Focus on Ethnic Minorities*, says that minority groups are statistically more liable that whites to be victims of both personal and property crimes. Yet economic migration has been a fact from the very beginning of human history. Indeed, there has been more economic migration of white people into the lands of non-whites than the opposite, and the colonial migration of whites was often supported by a military power that resulted in the decimation of indigenous peoples. Yet today, anyone from Asia or Africa asking for a visa to enter the white people's land is suspected of being an economic migrant and hence made to look like a rogue. Economic migration before was held up as a triumph of human daring. Today it is a badge of shame.

An important aspect of contemporary scientific and technological inventions is corporate or group endeavor. It is no longer possible to assign an invention to one single inventor. Who invented the word processor, the fax, the E-mail? Who first made travel to outer space possible? Often, many individuals working together, sometimes in different parts of the world. Yet in other places, there is selfish private appropriation of the social gains of invention. Intellectual Property Rights are meant to block the advancement of the poorer nations. Plant genetic technology is jealously guarded by First-World holders of genetic resources, often stolen from the fields and forests of the Third-World. On the one hand, environment protection groups press their case as never before in the history of the planet. On the other hand, every year, an area of tropical forest nearly the size of Korea is destroyed for short-term commercial gain. Millions of new books, journals and seminar papers gush forth from world printing presses each year, yet more than one billion persons, most of them women in the Third-World, are still illiterate. Medical science has progressed incredibly, yet millions remain without basic medical care and, even in the rich countries, many have to wait in long queues for surgical treatment in state hospitals because they cannot afford private surgery. Many may think this is mere demagoguery or an overdose of missionary zeal. But it is neither.

3. *Search*

We have to search for a saner and just world. Even existing Asian Models – OPEC, the strong state model of China and Vietnam, the private enterprise model of the four tigers of Southeast Asia, the Japanese model – do not suit the immense lands of South Asia. Even China has still to search.

The main lines of search are given to us by Aimé Cesaire in his Discourse on Colonialism: "It is a new society that we must create... a society rich with all the productive power of modern times, warm with all the searching of olden days". Or, as Marx said in the last lines of his brilliant essay on imperialism in India, speaking of the undeniable productive power of those modern times:

> when a great social revolution shall have mastered the results of the bourgeois epoch, the market of the world and the modern powers of production, and subjected them to the common control of the most advanced peoples, then only will human progress cease to resemble that hideous pagan idol, who would not drink the nectar but from the skulls of the slain.

Both Cesaire and Marx welcome the modern developments of the productive powers. But Cesaire, being a Third-Worlder in a way denied to Marx, is also very conscious of the ancient values held dear by our people. I agree that the past is another country. Our country is the present and the future which becomes present even as we speak. I even agree with Professor Masao Maruyama who wrote and spoke of the Japanese notion that "the beginning of the heaven and the earth is in the present". If the present is forever the beginning of history, we have to take into our minds and hearts and hands and feet all the productive power of modern times, the technological progress, telematics, mechanization of tasks that for nearly the whole of human history were performed by human hands, foreign trade, and the instruments of finance. Not to do so would be to retreat into another country and another world. Yet, as Maruyama himself fully understood, this absorption of modernity must be on our own terms, into the substratum of our own indigenous history, and culture, and ways of thought and life in which there is so much of priceless value. To be oblivious of the past, which the present has inherited and which contributed to make the present what it is, is as fatal a mistake and as much a betrayal of the human heritage as a refusal to accept the changes that have taken place from the time modernity began.

The superstructure of liberation theology, through the pincer movement of economic justice and inculturation, can powerfully influence the direction of world history and the evolution of peoples and states. If there was no liberation theology, theologians would have to invent it, for it is the only theology that can be relevant to the tremendous times in which we live. The darkness is intense. A thousand liberation candles can shine through it. The light is also terrific. Liberation theology can ensure that it does not make us blind. The task is immense, but never too immense for the God of Truth and Justice who works in us and through us.

Satyodaya Centre   Paul CASPERSZ
30 Pushpadana Mawatha
Kandy, Sri-Lanka

8

ATTENDING TO THE CULTURAL
IN CONTEMPORARY FILIPINO THEOLOGIZING

Among the areas of our humanity within which the historical dimension of salvation is to be made concrete in human experience is that of
the conditioning of persons and people by culture[1]. To be whole (that is,
"saved") people need cultural identity and integrity. Rightly has Vatican II
in Gaudium et Spes, article 53 said that "it is a fact bearing on the very
person of [human beings] that [they] can come to an authentic and full
humanity only through culture…".

If Christianity proclaims a message of salvation, and undeniably it does,
then the promotion of the gospel must necessarily include the furtherance of
a people's culture. Without meaning to equate it with the totality of salvation,
we can still rightfully say that cultural identity and integrity is a soteriological
issue. Their promotion is essential and constitutive in the proclamation of
the Gospel of salvation. From this soteriological perspective, the fostering, or in situations of threat, the defense of cultural identity and integrity
of a people is a real though partial advancement of the Gospel message.

Discussions regarding modernity, however, indicate that this process
has not been truly congenial to particularity and traditions linked with
such particularity. It tends to disrupt local cultures, questions a group
identity and de-stabilizes its sense of security and continuity. And where
particular cultures seem to be encouraged and supported in a context of
"globalization", the promotion turns out to be an ideological ploy of
power brokers. The apparent interest is really a way of ensuring the
exclusion of people in the set goals and socio-political and economic
structures already in place in society (15-16).

When viewed as a force of change, modernity is in spirit and in fact
directed to the spread of a way of thinking and living which is aggres-
sively and powerfully advertised as the inevitable and the desirable. It
envisions one homogeneous global village designed and being realized
by the West. In this way this process can be likened to the stance of
the classical conception of culture: There is only one universal culture,
Western civilization, and that is normative for all[2]. Its spread to other

1. E. SCHILLEBEECKX, *Christ: The Experience of Jesus as Lord*, New York, Crossroad,
1983, pp. 734-743.
2. B. LONERGAN, *Method in Theology*, New York, Herder & Herder, 1972, pp. 124,
301, 362-363. A classicist, writes Lonergan, "would feel it was perfectly legitimate for

peoples, and even its imposition on them, ought to be seen by one and all as a blessing.

When we consider the economic, social and religious motives underlying the phenomenon of colonization and the amount of horrendous suffering that this history had caused to the natives, this expression of the classical notion of culture may be a tame theory when compared to what modernization is causing today. It was in a way the same classical understanding of culture, after all, which provided Spain and the United States an overarching reason to invade, take over, and exploit the resources of the Philippines. Today, this so-called emerging global culture is doing the same thing, but more widely and with more sophisticated means. Perhaps, modernity is at least partly the continuing thrust of a classical interpretation of culture that refuses to die. But now that the existence of a diversity of cultures can no longer be denied, such pluralism is neutralized either through cultural homogenization or ideological co-optation (49-50).

I. PARTICULARITY OF CULTURES: "OUR CUP OF LIFE"

Diversity has always been part of life. Being and becoming human requires specificity. Through such a specific way of thinking, feeling and behaving, people participate in life; through culture people live life. The Digger Indians (as the Californians call them) have a picturesque way of expressing this thought: "In the beginning God gave to every people a cup, a cup of clay, and from this cup they drank their life. They all dipped in the water, but their cups were different"[3]. With our own respective cups, we drink of life. Because of this cup, we are able to experience life concretely and meaningfully. Culture, we may wish to add, is the set of meanings which people create, and which create people, as members of societies.

This "cup of life" covers (i.e., influences or affects) everything in life. Culture is not everything in life, but it does touch all the areas of life. Even a very simple description of culture as an integrated system of beliefs, values and customs and of institutions which express these beliefs, values and customs and which provide a group of people with

---

him to impose his culture on others. For he conceives culture normatively, and he conceives his own to be the norm. Accordingly, for him to preach both the gospel and his own culture, is for him to confer the double benefit of both the true religion and the true culture".

3. R. BENEDICT, *Patterns of Culture*, Boston, Houghton Mifflin Co., 1934, pp. 21-22. See also D.M. MIRANDA, *Outlines of a Method of Inculturation*, in *EAPR* 30 (1993) 149-151.

a sense of identity, security and continuity, implies this truth. The way we think, feel, value and behave as a group is culturally conditioned. It means that our experiences are in a very true sense cultural experiences. Experiences are constituted by some form of contact with reality together with interpretations. Since most, if not all, of these interpretations are drawn from culture, it would be reasonable to assume that our experiences are indeed influenced by culture in one way or another. To understand the economic and political underpinnings of globalization, for instance, we need to study culture[4].

Singularly relevant to our discussion of culture is the fact that it is second-nature to us. Through the process of socialization or of enculturation, we internalize the culture of the particular group of people we are a member of. If we follow the insights of the psychological theory of transactional analysis with regard to imbibing external influences, then we are cultured by the time we are seven years old[5]. Our major cultural orientation is somehow set. By that age, our culture is us; we are our culture. It is thus not misleading at all to think of culture as an identifiable group of people who share beliefs and experiences, feelings of worth and value attached to those experiences, and shared interest in a common historical background.

We think, feel, value and behave the way our culture has conditioned us to think, feel, value and behave as well as assume these to be "the way things are" and "the way they are supposed to be". Reality for us has become culturally mediated reality. So deep and pervasive is this conditioning that most of the time we are not aware of it. Rightly has it been said that "culture hides much more than it reveals, and strangely enough what it hides, it hides most effectively from its own participants"[6].

Although not determined by culture, we are inextricably cultural. Ethnocentricism remains a temptation because of the deep and pervasive conditioning by culture. We who are engaged in the theological enterprise may do well if we examine our theological positions to see how cultural

4. "To study culture is to study ideas, experiences, feelings, as well as the external forms that such internalities take as they are made public, available to the senses and thus truly social". U. HANNERZ, *Cultural Complexity: Studies in the Social Organization of Meaning*, New York, Columbia University Press, 1992, p. 3. Cf. also F. WILFRED, *No Salvation Outside Globalization?*, in *Euntes* 29 (September, 1996) 135-144.

5. Transactional Analysis in discussing important influences in our lives states that the "basic plot" of our "life story" is written during our infant years before we are old enough to talk a few words. By 7 years of age most of our "life story", although not final, has already been "written". See I. STEWART & V. JOINES, *TA Today: A New Introduction to Transactional Analysis*, Nottingham, Lifespace Publishing, 1987, p. 5.

6. As quoted in P. CASSE, *Training for the Cross-Cultural Mind*, Washington, DC., The Society for Intercultural Education, Training and Research, [2]1981, p. 252.

they might be. We just may discover that some of our problematic theological differences or even conflicts are really cultural differences masquerading as theological difficulties. One, for example, may raise the question whether claims of superior theologizing are in reality latent presuppositions of cultural superiority.

Culture is precious because it is a tradition of time-tested experiences created by people. It is a hard-earned product of people's efforts through several generations to cope with the demands of their total environment, first, in order to survive, and then to enhance life. Not only is it a resource for a people's identity, it also provides a communication system that creates continuity, and offers means to incorporate innovation into the community. Cultural tradition, and any tradition for that matter, is not static. We know that the progress witnessed yesterday is the tradition we claim today. And tomorrow's tradition will be what we have managed to advance culturally today. The historical imagination "is refreshed by each new generation, whose efforts do not erase what went before but, rather, build on it, adding new voices and opening new connections"[7].

Such way of life does not come to existence all at once. It requires time. Repeated occasions for creating and testing appropriate (life-giving) responses to such demands make for a tradition. We are surely aware of how long it takes persons to learn a language, other than their own, well enough to be comfortable with it; we are, however, not in a position to say just how long it will take us to develop a new language if we were to start from scratch. How much time will we need to work out a system of communication if from this moment onwards we decide that the words (which really are sounds) we use did not have the meanings we now assume they have?

Positing the importance of culture as a tradition is recognizing the value of learning from repeated experiences of a group as well as of systematizing such learning[8]. It would be arrogance on our part to assume that just because we come later we and our cultural innovations are better. History is not necessarily a forward movement. For a tradition to become a genuine and welcomed tradition, it must make sense precisely because of experience that has been tested by time. Rapid and engineered

---

7. D.H. LEVINE, *Constructing Culture and Power*, in D.H. LEVINE (ed.), *Constructing Culture and Power in Latin America*. Ann Arbor, The University of Michigan Press, 1993, p. 24.

8. Culture is seen here psychologically as "a set of techniques for satisfying needs, for solving problems, and for adjusting both to the external environment and to other people. Cf. J. GOULD & W.L. KOLB (eds.), *A Dictionary of the Social Sciences*, London, Tavistock Publications, 1964, p. 166.

changes aimed at the creation of a so-called "global culture", however, are not a respecter of traditions. If progress is to be achieved, the Third World countries are taught to believe, they must either discard or, at least, marginalize their respective cultural heritage (49-52)[9].

1. *Culture and Evangelization*

Culture was regarded as indispensable for evangelization by the first generation of foreign missionaries in the Philippines during the sixteenth century. Although obviously operating from a classical understanding of culture in general, this group manifested a sensitivity to the culture not unlike the attitude displayed by the Italian Jesuits Mateo Ricci, Roberto de Nobili, and Alessandro Valignano[10]. For one reason or another, these preachers of the Gospel somehow realized the importance of language as the expression of culture. An eloquent testimony to this exceptional respect and appreciation for the culture in Philippine ecclesiastical history is the text of the Lord's Prayer in the *Doctrina Christiana* of 1593[11] which had been written in our almost extinct native script as well as in a Romanized form[12]. Below, a quite literal translation of the original Tagalog text[13] into English more than suggests the attempts of those early missionaries at genuine inculturation, especially when we bear in mind that language "is the reservoir of tradition and the medium in and through which we exist and perceive the world"[14].

9. Cf. also *And God Said, "Bahala Na!": The Theme of Providence in the Lowland Filipino Context,* Maryhill Studies 2, Quezon City, Maryhill School of Theology, 1979, pp. 40-44.

10. A. ROSS, *A Vision Betrayed: The Jesuits in Japan and China, 1542-1742*, Maryknoll, NY, Orbis, 1994.

11. The *Doctrina Christiana* was based on the Nahuatl catechisms previously compiled for Mexican Indians.

12. The translation in the late 16th-century of the *Doctrina Christiana*, the first book printed in the Philippines, is attributed to the Franciscan, Juan de Plasencia, who is perhaps the most noted of the Franciscan friars in Philippine history. Cf. O. ANTE, *Contextual Evangelization in the Philippines: A Filipino Franciscan Experience*. Kampen, J.H. Kok, 1991, pp. 46-47. The synod of Manila in 1582 approved this translation for use as the standard catechism in instructing the natives. See M. A. BERNAD, *The Christianization of the Philippines: Problems and Perspectives*, Manila, The Filipiniana Book Guild, 1972, p. 232.

13. *Ama namin, nasa langit ca; ypasamba mo ang ngalan mo; moui sa amin ang pagcahari mo. Ypasonor mo ang loob mo dito sa lupa parang sa langit. Bigyan mo cami ngaion nang aming cacanin para nang sa araoarao at pacaulin mo ang aming casalanan yaiang uinaualan bahala namin sa loob ang casalanan nang nagcacasala sa amin. Houag mo caming iiwan nang di cami matalo nang tocso. Datapouat yadia mo cami sa dilan masasama. Amen. Jesus.*

14. H.G. GADAMER, *Philosophical Hermeneutics*, Berkeley, University of California Press, 1976, p. 26.

Our Father, you are in heaven.
Make your name be worshipped.
Make your kingdom *come home* (= *mauwi*) to us.
Make your *most authentic self* (= *loob*) be followed
here on earth as in heaven.
Give us today our daily *rice* (= *kakanin*).
And release our sins
As we are completely indifferent within our *most authentic self* (= *loob*)
to the sins of those who have sinned against us.
Do not leave us (= *huwag mo kaming iiwan*) so we are not overcome
by temptation.
But deliver us from every evil.
Amen. In the name of Jesus.

Allow me to comment on just two very meaningful themes in the lowland Filipino culture found in the text: relationships and food.

a) *Relationships*

The choice of the essentially relational concept *loob* to render God's "will" and to indicate what forgiveness implies was a stroke of genius. For *loob,* which literally means "the inside" or "the inner self", is one of the richest concepts, content and value-wise, in the Filipino way of thinking which was, curiously, not explored by local theology until recently[15]. *Loob* is a wholistic understanding of the most authentic self of a person in relation to God, others and the world. Thought, feeling and behavior are all situated in the *loob*. That is where freedom, initiative, reflection, gut feeling and decision emanate. In this Tagalog translation of the Our Father to do the will of God, with whom we are intrinsically related, is not simply to follow a divine imperative; it is "to *be* (wholistically) perfect as your heavenly Father is perfect", "to *be* (in all the aspects of life) merciful as your heavenly Father is merciful". "*Ipasonod mo ang loob mo*" is a petition to God to transform our innermost selves, where the true worth of our personhood lies, through the interiorization of God's own *loob*. The pastoral decision to use the term *loob* among other possible and similar terms for will, wish, desire, intention and plan like *nais, ibig, mithi, bilin, nasa, pasya, balak, layunin* and *pakay* was truly significant.

Homecoming *(mauwi, pag-uwi),* our second relational theme, is socially, personally and emotionally loaded for lowland Filipinos. They

15. See A.E. ALEJO, *Tao po! Tuloy!: Isang Landas ng Pag-Unawa sa Loob ng Tao,* Quezon City, Office for Research and Development, Ateneo de Manila University, 1993. See also D. MIRANDA, *Loob: The Filipino Within: A Preliminary Investigation into a Pre-Theological Moral Anthropology,* Manila, Divine Word Publications, 1989.

manifest an almost compulsive inner desire to go home to where their families are, especially during important social occasions as Christmas, the Holy Week and the town fiesta, or personally significant events such as a marriage or a funeral. So emotive is the mood and imagery of coming home that a telephone company once took advantage of this cultural phenomenon by advertising long distance calls as bringing the people one loves home on the telephone. Thus to present God as yearning to come home to us is surely affectively effective for Filipinos (cf. also Rev 21,3).

Finally, the phrase "do not leave us so we are not overcome by temptation" ("*huwag mo kaming iiwan*"). Sociologists in the country are wont to point out that Filipinos are not inclined to being alone. They are never alone when they are born, wedded and buried. In general they do not want to be left alone. Companionship is desired even in simple activities of life. Happiness is found in being together in relationships. While seemingly amusing, the remark that a gathering was a happy one because there were so many people is indicative not only of the Filipino propensity for gregariousness, but of the importance of relationships too[16]. Being left alone, which may be regarded as a right or a privilege in other cultures, is construed in the Philippines as a punishment or as an exclusion. In this translation of the Our Father, God is perceived as the God who never leaves us alone.

b) *Food*

Food and the sharing of food is a major symbol truly alive in the culture. This is probably why the *fiesta* is such an important occasion for Filipinos. In such a celebration in honor of the patron saint of the locality, there is an abundance of food which is shared with all the guests. Living and living with others are more than enough reasons to celebrate. But the sharing of food is more than that. It strengthens existing bonds and creates new ones. An investment, if you will, but in human relationships. It is even apropos to talk about such sharing as transformative. The memorable February event of 1986, which toppled the power of a dictator through non-violent action and which drew world attention as well as admiration, was characterized by spontaneous food sharing.

It would be unthinkable in the Filipino setting to talk about food without mentioning rice. Although bread is available, it cannot replace rice.

---

16. Cf. F.M. LEON, JR., *Cultural Awareness: Keystone to National Development*, Series on Filipino Spiritual Culture, 9, p. 10. The series is privately published.

Bread for Filipinos is not "the food". It may just be as filling, but it is not perceived to be truly satisfying. Hence, asking for rice on occasions when bread is served for the meal is rather common. Rice is staple, and it is a very rich indigenous symbol for nourishment, especially when we consider the different ways rice is prepared. The decision of the author(s) of the *Doctrina Christiana* to utilize the term "rice" in the Lord's Prayer gives us a glimpse of the missionaries' grasp of the culture. To petition God to provide us with our daily rice is a most meaningful supplication indeed.

The use of the vernacular was part of the Spanish missionary policy in the beginning. But in the seventeenth century, the royal policy encouraged the natives to become bilingual, and in the next century, frantic efforts were made to compel the natives to adopt Spanish because the native tongues were regarded as not sufficiently well developed to transmit the mysteries of the Faith. The civil authorities feared that idolatries and superstitions would continue until the natives abandoned the languages of their pagan past. State policy dovetailed with western cultural assumptions of the time[17].

The developments of the seventeenth through the nineteenth centuries were in line with the prevailing mind-set. Culturally speaking, they witness to the consistent belief and propagation of a civilization both by Spain and the United States which was presupposed to be superior and normative. This "classical" way of thinking about culture betrayed itself in its advocacy of Spanish Catholicism and its structures, and the promotion of American Christianity and system of education[18].

Within the institutional church specifically, scholastic and, later, neo-scholastic theology became the official theology. Like any theology, scholasticism was really culturally conditioned and historically rooted. It was in its own way a contextualized theology. But considered as "*theologia perennis*" by its advocates and propagators, this school of theology dominated the theological scene. Its study was obligatory for those preparing for ordination and highly recommended for those engaged in the spread of Catholicism in one way or another. At any rate, the faithful who were reached by the pastoral care administered by the institution became familiar with scholastic categories through the catechism.

But notwithstanding the efforts at instilling such theological thought, scholasticism remained both in content and methodology alien to the

17. See J. PHELAN, *The Hispanization of the Philippines: Spanish Aims and Filipino Responses 1565-1700*, Madison, The University of Wisconsin Press, 1959, pp. 51, 131.

18. *The Challenge of Nationalism in the Philippines to the Church and the State in the 21st Century*, EAPR 28 (1991) 140-146.

cultural way of the Filipinos. Catholicism in this form only made sense to the few who had been initiated into its scholastic subtleties and complexities. The situation in general was to remain like this until the mid-sixties, having very little impact because its content was unrelated to the experiences of the people and its language largely unintelligible. Could it have been that those who presupposed the superiority and normativeness of scholasticism did not even realize that this view of theirs was but a theological expression of the classical interpretation of culture?

2. *Vatican II and Culture*

Among the many things that Vatican II will be remembered for is its rediscovery and recovery of the importance of particular cultures in the life and mission of the church. Precipitated, most likely, by shift from the classical to the empirical understanding of culture during the early part of the present century[19], the church remembered its original vision of embracing all existing cultures (cf. Acts 2,6-8,11). The realization in society that there is not only one culture which is normative for all, but a plurality of cultures with a variety of perspectives reminded this faith community of a diversity willed by God. The Council of Jerusalem acknowledged and articulated the principle of cultural catholicity. God was actively present in all cultures. The gospel of salvation could be lived and thought in a plurality of cultural ways; it can be embodied in different designs for living life. Reiterating this sentiment from the New Testament, Vatican II affirmed that "the church, sent to all peoples of every time and place, is not bound exclusively and indissolubly to any race or nation, nor to any particular way of life or any customary pattern of living, ancient or recent. Faithful to her own tradition and at the same time conscious of her universal mission, she can enter into communion with various cultural modes, to her own enrichment and theirs too" (GS 58).

This retrieval of cultural sensitivity had an increasing impact on the consciousness of the church's leadership. After Vatican II, terms like "radical adaptation" to the culture, "indigenization" and "localization" became commonplace within theological circles. The meeting of Asian bishops in Manila in 1971, during Paul VI's visit, used the word "inculturation". The Synod of 1974 and *Evangelii Nuntiandi* were convinced that "what matters is to evangelize culture and cultures" (EN 20).

---

19. This classical perspective on culture has largely been abandoned thanks to the efforts of social scientists, who brought to the attention of contemporary society the fact of plurality of cultures. Cf., for example, R. BENEDICT (n. 3); E. HALL, *The Silent Language*, Conn., Fawcett, 1959.

Subsequent synods did not fail to consider inculturation as an integral dimension of the church's life and mission. More recently, our very own Second Plenary Council of the Philippines (PCP-II) also re-echoed in 1991 the sentiments of Vatican II with regard to culture. It stated that "faith must take root in the matrix of our Filipino being so that we may truly believe and love as Filipinos. But for this to happen, the Gospel must be presented with tools, methods and expressions coming from the culture itself. It must be accepted within a person's cultural heritage"[20].

II. THE SHIFT TO LOCAL EXPERIENCE IN THEOLOGIZING

Conciliar and post-conciliar theological developments, especially the renewed understanding of revelation-faith, church and mission as well as theological method, converged with a growing sense of nationalism to effect a paradigm shift in theologizing in the Philippines. It was the shift from the neo-scholastic method of theologizing, which starts from a doctrinal statement to one which begins with experience[21]. It was paradigmatic because it did not merely affect an aspect of theology and theologizing, but theology as a whole starting from the way it is done. The closed and seemingly immutable manner of thinking about the faith began to be questioned and gradually set aside. Theologians began to work out the implications of the change. A major consequence of this paradigm shift was the development of different foci and approaches which explicitly begin with contemporary experiences, not with just any experience from anywhere or experience in general, but with *the locally significant* ones. Theological language in the Philippines, in order to be meaningful, needed to have a recognizable reference to the lived-experience of Filipinos. Theology and the doing of theology had to be localized, perhaps in a manner already discernible in folk Catholicism. It is interesting to note that it is around this time that the Federation of Asian Bishops' Conferences (FABC) also spoke of the building up of a truly local church as the primary focus of the task of evangelization. In their thinking, the local church is "a church in continuous, humble and loving dialogue... with all the life-realities of the people in whose midst it has

20. *Acts and Decrees of the Second Plenary Council of the Philippines*, Manila, Catholic Bishops' Conference of the Philippines, 1992, p. 30, No. 72.
21. In its oft-quoted opening lines, *Gaudium et Spes* recognizes the indispensability of seriously taking into account contemporary human experiences. More precisely, it asserts that the number of particularly urgent needs characterizing the present age needs to be considered "in the light of the gospel and of human experience" (GS 46).

sunk its roots deeply and whose history and life it gladly makes its own"[22].

A possible reading of what had occurred suggests that it is the shift from the universal (or, at least, the allegedly universal) to the local that is significant in the context of Filipino theologizing because of the change of understanding of culture from a classical interpretation to an empirical one. While affirming that the Tradition was essential and constitutive also in the doing of theology, the preferred starting point had become the local experience rather than an absolute doctrinal formulation or, in some instances during the initial period of the shift, the Euro-American set of contemporary experiences. It was not for nothing that someone made the remark that when Europe catches cold, Asia sneezes.

One can read the events thus: The movement from a "universalist" perspective of culture (classical) to a "local" (empirical) one is paralleled in theology by a movement from a "universalist" articulation of the Faith to a "local" theology. From this development arose more specific concerns and more focused theological approaches. Thus, in positing that "the joys and the hopes, the griefs and the anxieties of the people of this age, especially those who are poor or in any way afflicted, these too are the joys and the hopes, the griefs and the anxieties of the followers of Christ", one is thinking in terms of the concretely local situation, where people speak a particular language, the poor have a particular complexion, and the afflicted have their own way of coping with life's challenges. Theologizing had gained a human face.

1. *Attending to the Local Culture*

The early post-Vatican II efforts at indigenization was and is an acknowledgment of the importance of a people's local culture. Against the historical background of the tandem colonization-evangelization which had stigmatized the culture, the efforts to clarify cultural identity as well as the attempts to recover legitimate pride over the riches of the indigenous cultural heritage were justifiable[23]. Besides, the church in the

---

22. Federation of Asian Bishops' Conferences, *Evangelization in Modern Day Asia: Statements and Recommendations of the First Plenary Assembly*, Taipei, Taiwan, 27 April 1974, in G. ROSALES & C.G. AREVALO (eds.), *For All Peoples of Asia: Federation of Asian Bishops' Conferences Documents from 1970 to 1991*, Quezon City, Claretian Publications, 1992, p. 14.

23. The de-stigmatization and re-valuation of the culture remains to be one of the major tasks in the Philippines. See *Cultural Analysis and Inculturation in the Lowland Filipino Context*, in C. CORNILLE & V. NECKEBROUCK (eds.), *A Universal Faith? Peoples, Cultures, Religions and the Christ* (Louvain Theological and Pastoral Monographs, 9),

Philippines has still to rethink Catholicism in indigenous categories. It needs a working "up" to explanation about the faith from the categories people use in daily life, not unlike those already operative in local popular religiosity. But the widespread impression that indigenization gloried in the traditional culture of the past did not help the attempts to instill the significance, even indispensability, of culture in matters theological and ecclesiastical. Somehow, in striving to come to terms with what was genuinely native, the fact of socio-cultural change was also largely over-looked[24].

For instance, in the socio-cultural changes which had come to pass within the lowland Philippines due to western influences, it has been noted that two yet unintegrated and at times conflicting cultural systems are currently operating: the traditional and the modern, the native and the foreign or the indigenous and the exogenous. This fact not only signals the arrival of "modernity", but it also harbors a conflictual situation and implies the issue of social justice. A small but socially and economically dominant group of people have a tendency to align themselves with the western Euro-American culture (modern), while the majority, who are mostly poor, usually remain in tune with the way of thinking and behaving stipulated by the traditional cultural heritage[25]. The development and furtherance of an industrial and technological society and the concomitant changes in social relations had become urgent issues which theology could not afford to ignore.

2. Broadening the Traditional Understanding of Culture: Contextualization and Liberation

The doing of theology which was beginning to claim local experience as its starting point had to recognize the social changes happening before its very eyes. To remain consistent, it had to also reckon with contemporary developments. Where "indigenization" was found wanting, "contextualization" supplied for the inadequacy. Coined by the Theological

Louvain, Peeters Press, 1992, pp. 119-123; V.G. ENRIQUEZ, *Pagbabangong-Dangal: Indigenous Psychology and Cultural Empowerment*, Quezon City, Akademya ng Kultura at Sikolohiyang Pilipino, 1994; and F.L. JOCANO, *Issues and Challenges in Filipino Value Formation*. Punlad Research Paper No. 1, Quezon City, Punlad Research House, 1992.

24. There were exceptions. Cf., for example, V. GOROSPE, *The New Christian Morality and the Filipino*, in V. GOROSPE & R. DEATS (eds.), *The Filipino in the Seventies: An Ecumenical Perspective*, Quezon City, New Day Publishers, 1973, pp. 309-385 and E. NACPIL, *A Gospel for the New Filipino*, in G. ANDERSON (ed.), *Asian Voices in Christian Theology*, Maryknoll, NY, Orbis, 1976, pp. 117-145.

25. M. RAMIREZ, *Reflections on Culture*, Occasional Monograph, 2, Manila, Asian Social Institute, 1991, pp. 17-18.

Education Fund of the World Council of Churches in the early seventies, "contextualization" acknowledged the importance of indigenization, but it sought to press beyond indigenization by also taking into account "the process of secularity, technology, and the struggle for human justice, which characterize the historical moment of nations in the Third World"[26].

While the challenges of modernity were not neglected, it was much more the question of social justice that occupied the attention of many and for good reason. More than contextualization within an increasingly modern society, theology needed to face the challenge of liberating people from socio-economic bondage aggravated by modernity. The large majority of the population were (and are) poor because of, among a few other reasons, structures of inequality. Institutionalized social relationships were (and are) heavily and unjustly tilted in favor of the few rich and powerful. Class interests were at loggerheads. So obvious is this situation that even the Second Plenary Council of the Philippines had to mention it in its conciliar document:

> The poverty and destitution of the great mass of our people are only too evident, contrasting sharply with the wealth and luxury of the relatively few families, the elite top of our social pyramid... Power and control are also elitist, lopsidedly concentrated on established families that tend to perpetuate themselves in political dynasties[27].

In response, social action, a church movement aimed at social transformation, was born. Theologies of liberation and of struggle were developed, with the latter being the local version of the former[28].

Together with, as well as within this development, there was growth in consciousness regarding humanly created social structures[29] through

26. TEF Staff, *Ministry in Context: The Third Mandate Programme of the Theological Education Fund 1970-1977*, Bromley, The Theological Education Fund, 1972, p. 20.

27. *Acts and Decrees of the Second Plenary Council of the Philippines*, p. 12.

28. For information on liberation theologies in the Philippines, see R.G. Musto, *Liberation Theologies: A Research Guide*, New York, Garland Publishing, Inc., 1991, pp. 162-167; *Liberation Theology and the Vatican Document, II: A Philippine Perspective*, Quezon City, Claretian Publications, 1986; R. Tano, *Theology in the Philippine Setting*, Quezon City, New Day Publishers, 1981, pp. 87-115; B. Dominguez, *A Theology of Struggle: Towards Struggle with A Human Face*. Kalinangan Book Series II, Quezon City, Institute of Religion and Culture, 1992.

29. From around 1935, many British social anthropologists have tended to use the concept "social structure" rather than culture, deprecating the latter and avoiding its use. For instance, R. Firth, who represents this school of thought, says, "If society is taken to be an aggregate of social relations, then culture is the content of those relations". Further, he writes, "In the types of society ordinarily studied by anthropologists, the social structure may include critical or basic relationships arising similarly from a class system based on relations with the soil. Other aspects of social structure arise through membership in other kinds of persistent groups, such as clans, castes, age-sets, or secret societies. Other basic relations again are due to the position in a kinship system...". See Gould & Kolb (n. 8), pp. 167-169.

the use of social analysis which probed into the historical and structural dimensions of such structures. Not without the influence of social
anthropologists, the concept of "social structure" became more important
than culture. Social analysis broadened and sharpened our traditional
understanding of culture[30]. It also exposed local and foreign ideological
currents at work to maintain the present structures to the advantage of
the elite but at the expense of the majority, especially the poor. While
differing social classes might have shared many cultural similarities, it
was undeniable that there were class conflicts as well. Within an anthro-
pologically defined culture, we were able to sociologically pinpoint
the existence of yet another kind of culture in which the importance of
social relations, particularly their conflictual aspects, are attended to (51-
53)[31]. Clearly influenced to a great extent by the Latin American manner
of theologizing, practitioners of liberation theology in the country utilized social analysis (often referred to as structural analysis with
synchronic and diachronic aspects) to conscientize people about their
plight and to reflect on their faith as Catholics in the light of their experiences[32].

Probably because of a lack of an integrating vision the two experienced-
based theological trends (indigenization/inculturation and liberation/
contextualization) in general went on their separate ways. Focus and
emphasis became sources of tension: liberation-oriented theologies
regarded indigenization/inculturation as past-oriented and domesticating;
inculturation-based theologies considered contextualization/liberation
as being out of touch with the Filipino soul. A synthesis could have
brought together the strengths of each approach, type of analysis and
specific reflection to effect social transformation. Doing theology with
combined cultural and social analyses would definitely have been a gain.
Inculturation with its cultural analysis, for example, could have been
more attentive to what was currently going on in society by taking into

30. Definitions of culture fall into six major groups (i.e., enumeratively descriptive,
historical, normative, psychological, structural and genetic) depending on what points are
emphasized and which elements a particular social scientist feels it necessary to make
explicit. GOULD & KOLB (n. 8), pp. 166-167. Social analysis emphasizes the structural
aspects.

31. RAMIREZ (n. 25), p. 17 See also De Schrijver's discussion of the two definitions of
culture drawn from I. Wallerstein. The question of gender, especially in male dominated
societies, is regarded as an important aspect of the concern for justice and equality in
society as well as in the church. This gender issue is a conflictual issue.

32. See the entire issue of *Pulso* I:1 (1984) on "Analysis and Society" especially
R.A. OCAMPO, *Structural Analysis in the Philippines: Its Usefulness and Limitation in the
Context of Social Transformation*; J.J. CARROLL, *Social Theory and Social Change in the
Philippines*; and F.F. CLAVER, *Cultural Analysis Towards Social Change.*

account insights derived from social analysis[33]. And liberation with its use of social analysis could have had more impact on people through its incorporation of cultural analysis[34]. But for one reason or another, the integration did not happen, or perhaps, did not happen enough although there were indications of awareness of the connection between the two[35].

3. *Towards the Integration of Cultural and Social Analyses*

The development of both inculturation and liberation theologies in the Philippines, albeit far from ideal in terms of mutual influence, has also something positive to contribute to local theologizing. When one takes a broader view of culture than each of the approaches presently bears, it is possible to suggest their complementarity or even an integration.

I am not insinuating in any way a facile bringing together of these two forms of analysis. Juxtaposition will not do, for this supposes that there is no inner connection between the two. Neither will co-optation of one by the other. For while it is true that both examine local experience, each has a certain autonomy because of focus and approach to reality. Cultural analysis largely deals with culture as a symbol system or a web of meaning. Social analysis, for its part, mainly tackles the more institutional/structural aspects of the same culture. Since each has something distinctive to offer in the understanding of reality, the suggestion to dialogue has merit and deserves a hearing. A formula like "in the light of" can be useful when appended to each of the approaches to culture. Cultural analysis in the light of social analysis and vice-versa. Cultural analysis should be done in such a way that it wakes up to the fact that what is considered "traditional" and "indigenous" is not necessarily life-giving. If culture is for the enhancement of life, consciousness and action against death-dealing elements in the culture must be fostered. Social analysis ought to be carried out in a manner that utilizes indigenous cultural constructs rather than importing other models which are foreign. The indigenous culture should not be assumed to be bereft of analytic rationality just because it is not western. In this way social analysis can systematically yet affectively (inculturally meaningful terms) examine institutions in society.

---

33. See J. UKPONG, *Towards a Renewed Approach to Inculturation Theology*, in *JIT* I:1 (1994) 8-24 as an attempt towards a more integral inculturation.
34. F.F. CLAVER (n 32), pp. 50-51, 60-61. We are reminded here of the sociological truism that says "class position does not translate in any direct way into collective action or shared identity". See D. LEVINE (n. 7), p. 7.
35. F.F. CLAVER (n. 32), pp. 48-63; RAMIREZ (n. 25), pp. 17-18.

Searching for broader and commonly shared categories of thought and discourse may be a first step in this dialogue. A *sine qua non* for the dialogue is that it is done in the vernacular (the language of the majority poor), not in and through a foreign set of concepts (the preferred expression of the elite)[36]. Such, as I will talk about in detail later, is *"loob"*, one of the key cultural concepts in lowland Philippines. Not only does it point to a major indigenous thought category, it provides space for symbol and institution to encounter one another. *Loob* is a symbol for the authentic self; *loob* structurizes relationships both by the orientation and the patterning it provides to the "outside" world.

Moreover, we ought to remember that analysis within the theological process is not merely analytically descriptive, but also prescriptive. It is at the service of the Kingdom. Its purpose is the announcement of the Gospel of salvation in word and deed and of transforming humanity from within. This faith perspective is to be seen as a particular point of view orienting the analysis being utilized in the same way any pre-understanding functions within an examination of reality.

III. INCULTURATION:
DRAWING ON THE RESOURCES OF THE LOCAL CULTURE

1. *The Future of the Local Culture*

In the context of the spread and intensification of globalization, the issue of the role of culture in people's lives, especially the political and the economic aspects of it, is going to be increasingly crucial. Wallerstein considers the construction of culture to be the key ideological battleground of opposing interests (53), while Paul VI believed that culture will be an essential element in the drama of our times (EN 20). Even

---

36. My suggestion for the use of the vernacular comes from the fact that it is the majority poor who use it in contrast to the elite who prefer to use English in their discourse. Cf. RAMIREZ, (n. 25), pp. 8-11. In the case of the Philippines the task of inculturation, Miranda contends, "must take the majority poor as its responsibility and its resource". He says that "it is they who have endured basically untouched through the most visible transitions of elite culture. It is they who will survive to carry the basic traits of the culture beyond all economic, political, social and religious arrangements. It is they without whom there will be no meaningful Filipino culture to speak of. It is they who are the principal bearers of the culture, and it is on them rather than on the ambiguous middle or alienated upper classes that the future of this country will hinge". D.M. MIRANDA, (n. 3), p. 158. A word of warning about translation into another language is expressed by K. SURIN in *A Certain 'Politics of Speech': 'Religious Pluralism' in the Age of the McDonald's Hamburger, MT* 7:1 (1990) 83.

more fundamentally, one may raise the question as to whether globalization will relegate local cultures to the fringes of public life or whether it will lead to the revitalization of part of their common heritage[37]. These concerns are most important to inculturation. For if culture has no future in the face of globalization, then inculturation will not only be a useless endeavor, it will also be a distraction to what the church should be preoccupied with in such a situation. Yet this reasoning, will not do in order to decide whether to attend to or dismiss culture in doing theology. Cultural identity and integrity are soteriological concerns and, therefore, cannot be dispensed with. Still, no *a priori* answers can be given to the questions about culture; "no direct prediction can be made with respect to the survival, adaptation, or erosion of a particular culture in the melting-pot of the global ecumene" (73).

There is no knowing for sure what will happen to the local culture(s) of the Philippines as globalization becomes more a fact we have to live with than prognosis. But if past experience were a gauge, then chances are that the local lowland Filipino culture[38] will more than survive. While introducing new elements into the native culture, Spanish and American influences did not simply replace indigenous elements. The foreign elements were assimilated and modified into the native pattern. So while these intrusions did something to the native culture, the natives, in turn, did something to the intrusions; they assimilated and changed them.

In other words, the natives were not only critically receptive, they were also creative. The degree and the rate of assimilation varied from place to place and from group to group, but there is no doubt whatsoever about the assimilation taking place[39]. And in this process, the indigenous Malay cultural stratum not only withstood as a whole the damaging effects of the two acculturation processes, but also benefited from the enriching aspects of these dual cultural contacts[40].

37. Attention to the local culture is a way of standing up against "the amnesia of the local" which globalization engenders. F. WILFRED (n. 4), pp. 141-142.
38. The lowland Filipino culture is made up of eight major linguistic groups in the country. Nine out of ten Filipinos are lowlanders.
39. By way of generalization, it can be said that from the earliest times the islands have been subjected to an almost continual stream of cultural influences from without. Filipinos reacted to these influences not by rejecting them or simply imitating them but by assimilating them, more or less successfully into their cultural heritage. Cf. H. DE LA COSTA, *The Background of Nationalism and Other Essays*, Manila, Solidaridad Publishing House, 1965, pp. 25-26.
40. The flexibility of the Filipinos has enabled them to be selective concerning cultural influences. Hence, they have never lost the Malaysian stratum which to this day remains the foundation of their culture. See J.L. PHELAN (n. 17), p. 26. Cf. also T.A. AGONCILLO & M.A. GUERRERO, *History of the Filipino People*, 4th ed.; Quezon City, R.P. Garcia Publishing Co., 1973, pp. 111-112.

Interestingly, there is at the present time a strong resurgence of the desire to define the Filipino cultural identity when, as a matter of official policy, the government wants and is doing all it can to attain the status of "newly industrialized country" (NIC) by the year 2000. Asia is experiencing economic ferment and great technological change, and the Philippine government does not want to be left behind by Japan, Taiwan, Korea and Thailand[41]. "Philippines 2000" is a slogan used by the government to persuade or motivate people to toe the line towards a full participation of the Philippines in the globalization process so that it can be an "economic tiger" in the region. This hankering after clarity of cultural identity was also true during the period of anti-colonial struggle in the late nineteenth and early twentieth centuries as well as during the time of the anti-imperialist movements of the late 1960s and early 1970s. These three instances have one thing in common: the felt need to re-define the culture vis à vis new situations.

This coincidence can be explained in a variety of ways, each of which embodies its share of truth. First, the deliberately conscious reinterpretation of culture is a way of resisting threatening onslaughts to corporate self-identity. Because it is a re-thinking on its own cultural terms, the reception of new influences is filtered through what is already indigenous. Second, the commonality of the three periods is also an expression of the dynamism of a living culture to re-define itself with elements it did not possess before. Uncertainty brought about by a new situation, especially if unprecedented, can surely elicit such a reaction. A third way of reading consists in explaining the similarity of the three moments in our history within a continuum. Each of the three overlapping periods represents a stage of the cultural maturation process of the Filipinos as to who they are as a people, and not just a loose aggregate of barangays (groups under particular chieftains): the stage of being defined by others (colonization), the stage of self-definition in reaction to others (psychosocial distancing) and the stage of self-definition[42].

---

41. See FABC, Office of Evangelization, *Conclusions of the Theological Consultation in Hua Hin, 10 November, 1991*, in ROSALES & AREVALO (n. 22), pp. 335-336.

42. I am assuming that consciousness of being a Filipino people was not yet present before the coming of the Spaniards. In no way does this imply that the natives inhabiting the islands did not have a distinct culture of their own. For some information about the pre-colonial culture, see *Providence as God's concern for His People in the Lowland Filipino Context: An Attempt at Theological Re-rooting of A Gospel Theme*. A dissertation for a Ph.D. in Religious Studies presented to the Faculty of Theology, Katholieke Universiteit Leuven (1978), pp. 4-11. See also P.R. COVAR, *Unburdening Philippine Society of Colonialism*, (Unplublished manuscript), pp. 1-3.

Awareness of a common cultural identity among lowland Filipinos historically began and thereafter developed during the colonial periods. During these times, Filipinos as a whole were defined by others in a way that made them lose confidence in their own selves. After all, what can one expect when, for almost four hundred years, we were characterized to the likes of "those wretched beings are of such a nature that they live a purely animal life, intent solely on its preservation and convenience, without the corrective of reason or respect or esteem for reputation". We were said to be laboring under the defects of extreme shallow-mindedness, uncontrolled propensity to the vices of the flesh, and yes, narrowness of soul that reduced us to almost nothing in the estimation of any European[43]. It seemed that the colonizers did not consider subjugating the Filipinos enough to rule over them; they also had to be insulted to impress on them their inferiority.

The late 1960s and the early 1970s were a period of self-definition in reaction to others. It was the time to know who we were as Filipinos in relation to the American colonizer. While comparison (in which the Filipino often lost out) was a recognized way of self-definition, there were also those who sought to understand the Filipino over and against the American. It was a time of spelling out who we were by focusing on who we were not. We were not brown Americans. We have our own culture and we can manage our affairs in our own way. And this could only happen if the Americans would leave the country they have invaded and colonized, and no longer interfere in any manner. In the context of Marxist thought and of anti-imperialist sentiments, this self-definition vis-á-vis the colonial master was best expressed by left-leaning student radicals (as they were called) in their oft-chanted slogan of the time: "*Makibaka, huwag matakot*"!; that is, "Struggle and fight, do not be afraid"! As we have noted earlier, this was also the time when our understanding of culture was broadened by incorporating a consciousness regarding social structures.

The late eighties and the first part of the nineties appear to be once again stamped with a strong interest in our cultural identity, with an intense desire to create space for ourselves in our own terms. We get a glimpse of this spirit in certain events and movements in the country. No less than the Philippine Senate, for example, legislated for a mandatory moral recovery program through a cultural values

43. M. BERNAD (n. 14), pp. 162-170, especially p. 168; Q. GARCIA & J. ARCILLA, *Acts of the Conference of the Bishops of the Philippines held in Manila under the Presidency of the Most Reverend Apostolic Delegate, Monsignor Placide de la Chapelle, 1900* in *PS* 26 (1974) 315-317.

education[44]. This program is being systematically implemented by the Department of Education nationwide. Politically, this same body voted "no" to the continuing presence of American bases in Clark and Subic in 1991. This daring act provided a much needed psychological and social boost to continue the process of our self-definition. A group of Filipino psychologists have initiated a program of "*pagbabangong-dangal*" (raising of dignity) aimed at restoring Filipino honor and cultural pride in the country and in the world. Through a concerted effort of consistently adopting the indigenous perspective in the social sciences, it also wants to end the continuing western cultural domination of the Filipino mind in our modern times[45].

Another group of social scientists from various disciplines have come together to explore the Filipino spiritual cultural genius and share their findings with the wider public[46]. While a school of theology is engaged in collecting and re-publishing early manuscripts of and writings on Filipino culture[47], an institute of sociology and economics is experimenting with a "tent-school". In this "school", grassroots leaders from the urban (rural areas affected by urban influences) and urban areas reflect on the assumptions of the Filipino language in order to take hold of themselves[48]. A religious congregation of women have adopted, for all their communities and schools throughout the country, a program developed for ecology and simplicity of life based on the indigenous concept "*sapat*" (that which is enough). Have only what is needed; consume only that which is necessary. In this way everyone will have enough, and our natural resources will continue to be available for the future generations[49]. "*Sapat*" seems to be an indigenous notion that contains elements similar to the characteristics of a "post-scarcity society" proposed by Anthony Giddens to combat the ethos of productivism (62-67).

---

44. Cf. P. LICUANAN, *A Moral Recovery Program: Building a People – Building a Nation*, in A Study Submitted to the Senate Committees on Education, Arts and Culture and on Social Justice, Welfare & Development, *May*, 9 (1988).

45. Cf. V.G. ENRIQUEZ, *Pagbabangong-Dangal: Indigenous Psychology and Cultural Empowerment* (n. 23).

46. See Series on Filipino Spiritual Culture, ed. A.R. ENRIQUEZ. The series is privately published.

47. "Pulong" research office of the Loyola School of Theology in Quezon City, Philippines.

48. RAMIREZ (n. 25), p. 12. The experiment might be characterized as theorizing "from below".

49. Conversations with the person who developed the program and the Franciscan Missionaries of Mary in the Philippines.

2. *"Pagbabalik-loob" : Strengthening Identity and Solidarity*

The third stage in the development of our cultural identity is a time of deliberately conscious self-definition in our own terms: our perspective, our categories of thought and our process. In this phase of our collective cultural maturation, we are going back to our real selves because a long time ago, at least as early as 890 BCE, our ancestors have already "defined" themselves. Long before we discovered the Spaniards, we already knew who we were and did not need colonizers to tell us about it, much less for them to insist that they knew us better than we ourselves. To lowland Filipinos, this re-definition of the collective self requires a "conversion". This is what the indigenous term for conversion – *"pag-babalik-loob"* – means: a return *(pagbabalik)* to the most authentic self *(loob)* where the true worth of a person lies. Rather than rupture, the intent of this conversion is to get in touch, to affirm, to connect, to be nourished by the wisdom and genius of the culture. It is less a matter of defending tradition than of creating a new identity and exploring new possibilities. *"Loob"*, our inner self, is the core of one's personhood, the organizing center of human reality and the substratum of ideas, feelings and behaviors. This "return" is not an escape to the security of the familiar, a retrogression to a world that no longer is. *"Loob"* in *"pagba-balik-loob"* is not inwardness in the sense of withdrawal and seclusion, but rather the movement of journeying to the very depths of reality to be in continuous touch with it. While such depths are not static, cultural identity is not shallow either.

We have to realize, in this connection, that even in an appreciable change in culture, there is nothing like a synchronous development occurring in every sector of it at the same pace and rhythm of acceleration. For within the one historical process, there are at least three discernible planes, which enfold and interpenetrate one another. Together they constitute the history of a given culture. First, there is "ephemeral history" with its fast and superficial changes of everyday life. Then a level of "conjunctural history", which is more expansive and has a more profound reach, but also a slower pace of change. Lastly, there is "structural history", where basic structures of a culture are located. The pace of change on this level borders on what changes and what does not. Basic cultural structures – call it the world-view, if you will, or fundamental mind-set, if you prefer, survive the most radical of revolutions[50].

---

50. Some analysts of culture have shown that, even after a successful political and social revolution, eighty percent of the old, rejected structures "recur" in one way or another. See E. SCHILLEBEECKX, *Jesus: An Experiment in Christology*, New York, The Seabury Press, 1979, pp. 577-582.

The return to our roots is in function of moving forward in full awareness of the difficulties and risks conjured by globalization, but also with
the confidence that only a strong cultural identity can bring[51]. In order
to build a society worthy of human beings, the native tradition must be
honored[52]. The building of a humane and life-giving society begins in
the heart – in the sentiments, attitudes and behavior of the people desiring to build that society – before it is rooted as intellect in the mind or
expressed as skills of the hand.

The most important social sources, to follow the thinking of sociologist Robert Bellah, are symbolic and cultural, the great collective symbols of social life. To him the most important social changes are also
symbolic and cultural. As he puts it, "We are used to thinking of change
in economic and political terms but it is the symbolic change that goes
the deepest and lasts the longest". (Not to mention, the hardest and
longest in terms of time to achieve!) Moreover, "no one has changed a
great nation without appealing to its soul, without stimulating a national
idealism". Bellah believes that "culture is the key to revolution; religion
is the key to culture"[53]. Retrieving the life-giving resources of the culture is not romanticizing the past, it is equipping one's self for the challenges ahead. This rather sophisticated articulation of what is important
is simply a particular reformulation of an old and wise Filipino saying:
"Those who do not know where they have come from will never reach
their destination". The culture indeed calls us to a "pagbabalik-loob", a
conversion to itself and, therefore, to who we really are[54].

If the above is beginning to sound as if the broadening of the understanding of culture has been futile, let me assure you it does not. Culture
as a way of feeling, valuing, thinking, and behaving of a people is not
divorced from culture as the set of institutionalized relationships. The

51. Indian theologian Felix Wilfred says something similar: "No Nation, no people,
no country can make progress on the basis of a borrowed identity...This rootedness [in
their culture] is not simply a matter of culture and tradition alone. It is the foundation as
well for a healthy all around growth. I mean to say also economic growth" (n. 4), p. 142.
Ramirez also states that "to develop one's cultural identity does not mean a retrogression
to a world that has gone by. Rather, it is an awakening of the hidden dimension of a culture, the values lying latent within a culture to which can be imputed new meanings based
on the conditions of the present. It is bringing together of the past and the future into the
present, recharging the present with new energies that constantly recreate and renew the
world, and developing, in a humane way, persons in the process". RAMIREZ (n. 25), p. 13.

52. F.L. JOCANO (n. 23), pp. 20-21.

53. J.A. COLEMAN, The Renewed Covenant: Robert N. Bellah's Vision of Religion and
Society, in G. BAUM (ed.), Sociology and Human Destiny, New York, The Seabury Press,
1980, pp. 89-90.

54. Anthropologist P. Covar suggests "pagbabalik-loob" as one of the key values necessary for a genuine independence as a nation beyond 1998. Kaalamang Bayang Dalumat
ng Pagkataong Pilipino, Quezon City 1993, pp. 17-18.

use of the concept *loob* in *pagbabalik-loob* prevents us from separating the two complementary meanings of culture. As a consequence, it also deters us from an either-or solution when it comes to cultural and social analyses.

Loob, the most authentic self, is essentially a relational concept with constitutive and strong links with God, others and even nature. *Pagbabalik-loob* is at least an invitation to strengthen not only cultural identity, but also openness and solidarity or what some prefer to call universality[55]. Healthy cultures combine self-identity and bondedness to others. Incidentally, we normally do not refer to other people in the Filipino language as "the others", they who are different from us, but as those who are *as we are*. "*Kapwa*", we call them; they who are the same as we are. The intrinsic linkage of one group of human beings to any other group of people is part and parcel of the concept of *loob*. It has also been persuasively shown in a study that *loob* has ecological implications because it is essentially linked with nature[56]. So *pagbabalik-loob* lends itself not only to cultural analysis, but also to social analysis. But what the foregoing discussion does say is that cultural analysis (what Wallerstein would relate to culture I) may be the better point of departure as well as emphasis towards genuine and life-giving social change (especially in the area of Wallertein's culture II) in the Philippine setting today. Such a move will not only ensure the taking of the indigenous cultural point of view in examining reality, but also of the procedure from a consciousness of one's basic cultural identity and a willingness to dialogue with new influences.

IV. ATTENTION TO THE CULTURAL AS STARTING POINT AND EMPHASIS

There are reasons in the cultural situation itself of the Philippines to suggest that, by way of starting point and emphasis, priority should be given to cultural analysis over social analysis in local theologizing. One is related to the concept of *loob,* which we have already seen, and the other has to do with the Filipino understanding of experience.

---

55. Apart from the relational element which characterizes *loob* it is also helpful to bear in mind that "language is an irreducibly social activity, and is therefore dependent on social relationships. Speakers are thus always active participants in a virtually unending chain of communication, a continuing and extended social process into which they are inserted at birth and which in principle shapes them just as much as they shape it". Cf. K. SURIN (n. 36), p. 80.

56. E. GUZMAN, *Creation as God's 'Kaloob: Towards an Ecological Theology of Creation in Lowland Filipino Socio-Cultural Context.* A dissertation for a Ph.D. in Religious Studies, Katholieke Universiteit Leuven (1995).

1. *The Filipino Person:* "Loob", "Labas", *and* "Lalim"

A metaphor suggested for the Filipino person is a jar, and like the jar, a person has the dimensions of the "inside", the "outside" and "depth". In the complementarity of the within *(loob)* and the without *(labas),* every element found "inside" normally has a counterpart located "outside" and vice-versa. Thus "the heart" inside *(puso)* is paralleled by "the breast" outside *(dibdib),* "the mind" *(isipan)* has an external partner in "the face" *(mukha)*[57]. "*Loob*" (inner self) and "*labas*" (outer self) are not antithetical to each other. They are two sides of the total reality, complementary but not identical.

In the "*loob-labas*" (inside-outside) relationship and complementarity, the culture is inclined to value the former as more important than the latter. What emanates from the *loob* (inner self) is what is regarded as authentic or true, while that which is perceived as the *labas* (outer self) can be ambivalent. It may either disclose what is within or conceal it. This way of thinking arises from and is an extension of the cultural presupposition that, in order to know a person, it is necessary to get a hold on that person's *loob*. External manifestations may or may not be faithful expressions of what is in the *loob*.

There ought to be a continuity between the *loob* and the *labas* because the *labas* is the visible manifestation of the *loob;* it takes its cue and substance from the *loob*. So what motivates people and drives them to carry out something comes from the *loob*. In a study of the *Pasyon* in folk Catholicism, a popular account of the passion of Jesus sung during Lent in houses, it was discovered that, since the state of the inner self is traditionally perceived as the determinant of overt political phenomena, the state of a people's *loob* has an immediate effect in this world *(labas)*. As illustrated in the *Pasyon*, for instance, those whose *loob* are pure, serene, and controlled have "special powers" granted to them by Christ. They can control the elements, cure the sick, speak in different tongues, interpret signs, and foretell the future"[58].

In the context of this understanding of *loob* and *labas,* we can formulate a reason as to why priority ought to be given to cultural analysis. In the historical development of social analysis in the Philippines, it has emphasized the external factors *(labas)* in situations of injustice in a couple of ways. First, in terms of structures of relationships (or institutionalized

---

57. P.R. COVAR, *Kaalamang Bayang Dalumat ng Pagkataong Pilipino* (n. 54), pp. 3-12.

58. R. ILETO, *Pasyon and Revolution: Popular Movements in the Philippines, 1840-1910*, Quezon City, Ateneo de Manila University Press, 1979, pp. 20-21, 25-26.

relationships) imposed from the outside by those who have the power and/or the wealth to push their interests. Second, in terms of modes and categories of analysis brought in from the outside (Marxism, Leninism, Maoism, capitalism) rather than those developed in the country from indigenous cultural resources[59]. Thus social analysis was associated with exogenous elements impinging on the indigenous. The more "internal" and, therefore, indigenous reasons as to why structural injustices existed, and which cultural analysis could have uncovered, were hardly given attention. The realities coming from the *labas,* which are culturally construed as subordinate to what comes from within, were dealt with more than those arising from the *loob.*

Bishop F. Claver, whose theological thought has been regarded in the Philippines as liberational, illustrates with a personal experience the "internal" role cultural analysis plays. While listening in an international conference to some well-known Latin American liberation theologians on the social problems of their continent and their solutions, he noticed that the blame for the sad state of their countries was being consistently put on forces and powers outside of themselves such as North American economic and political imperialism or national security states. He conjectured that, even if the United States and their own governments would cease the oppression these were charged with, the countries concerned would probably still not have the freedom they wanted. There are, after all, strands within the local cultures to which bonds of external oppression are tied and which make it possible for oppression to take hold in the first place[60].

While the above incident shows how cultural analysis can be of critical help to the culture which is not exactly innocent, it must also be said that this type of analysis can also be of immense help in making people truly aware of the wisdom and genius of their culture. Against the background of colonization, cultural analysis can surely help the culture find its own voice or articulate its authentic speech, enabling it for dialogue. Our analysis of *pagbabalik-loob* is already an indication of this as well as a signal for developing a cultural hermeneutics of appreciation in local theologizing.

The third dimension of *loob* may also be a source of justification for giving priority to cultural analysis in the doing of theology in the Philippines. The relational character of *loob* we noted has also something to do with God. This is what we find in the depths *(lalim)* of the *loob*: the

---

59. J.J. CARROLL (n. 32), pp. 46. It is worth asking whether there was or is an indigenous form of social analysis. Ileto's work on *loob* may be a good starting point.
    60. F.F. CLAVER (n. 32), pp. 50-51.

truth that our most authentic self is a gift from God ("*kaloob*"). In the process of returning to our innermost selves *(pagbabalik-loob)* we affirm that being a genuine person is being related to God. This point is further deepened when seen in the light of the Christian faith.

Because we are made in the image and likeness of God, our *loob* is constituted by being related to God. So conversion, that return to our most authentic self, is primarily an affirmation of who we truly are before God: recipients and traces of the Divine *Loob*. Here we not only see how integral religiosity is to the culture, but also how faith throws light on culture[61]. Culture and religion are vitally related to each other. If "depth" in *pagbabalik-loob* puts us in conscious touch once more with the God with whom we are essentially related, then cultural analysis has become in truth an instrument of faith. To begin theologizing from the perspective of cultural analysis can serve as a reminder that theology is "*fides quaerens intellectum*". In comparison, social analysis does not have this advantage of drawing directly from cultural wisdom and religiosity.

2. Filipino Understanding of "Experience"

We saw earlier that the significant shift in Filipino theologizing was in terms of its starting point: from doctrine to local experience. We moreover noted how starting from local experience led theologizing to concentrate either on culture as meaning or culture as system. But even in a broadened comprehension of culture, there may be a further reason as to why beginning from culture as meaning should be the preferred starting point.

If we recall that culture as a way of feeling, valuing, thinking and behaving is second-nature to us because of the socialization process, then we can speak of the very notion of experience itself as culturally conditioned. What precisely does "experience" mean to a Filipino? In the Filipino hermeneutics of experience, it has been noted that Filipinos have a tendency towards "what is felt" over "what is cognitively grasped" in their interpretation of reality. The interpretative element known as "*pagdama*" can be translated either as sensuous cognition or integrated sensing, where feeling is part of thinking and thinking part of feeling. Although *pagdama* combines both the elements of the affective-intuitive *(damdamin)* and the rational-cognitive *(isip)*, Filipinos demonstrate a propensity towards the affective-intuitive. The possibility, state and quality of

61. A.E. ALEJO (n. 15), pp. 29-33.

relationships are gauged in terms of feelings *(pakiramdaman)*. We speak spontaneously of a "felt love" *(damang pagmamahal)* which the younger generation would most likely refer to as a love that is "feel and feel". It would not be a misrepresentation of the Filipino manner of perceiving to refer to what has been experienced as what has been felt. If experience is necessarily interpreted experience, then for Filipinos the "felt experience" is what counts first and what matters most. It must be insisted upon that in no way can we equate this "felt experience" with experience devoid of rationality and cognition. It is also knowing but in a way that a mother knows the presence of her love for her child but is unable to immediately explain it, or in the way that two lovers both know that something is wrong between them by subtle and unspoken communications in silence and eye contact. For both the mother and the lovers, trusting the feeling is important in experience[62]. I once heard an anthropologist describe culture in terms of feelings. He insisted that to understand culture, this web of symbols, is to understand it as our shared and spontaneous feelings towards life's realities. Allow me to elaborate with a personal "felt experience".

When one considers the Filipino catholic religious landscape, it is not difficult to get the impression that the most important figure, in terms of attention and devotion, for ordinary believers, is Mary, a woman and a mother. God, Jesus tend to get secondary attention from Marian devotees. One local theologian even finds it necessary to challenge his theology students in class to reflect as to whether they are Christians or Marians. A quick comparison reveals that we are dealing here, among other things, with a male image (God the Father or Jesus) on the one hand, and a female image (Mary) on the other. If culture provides us with our spontaneous interpretations of reality, it is at least possible that people perceive God and Jesus with the cultural meanings and connotations of the male (particularly the Father) in the culture and Mary with the cultural meanings and connotations of the female (particularly the mother).

---

62. See J.J. MUELLER, *What Are They Saying About Theological Method?*, New York, Paulist Press, 1984, pp. 49-50, where this integration of feeling and thinking is seen as advantageous in grasping data. *"Pagdama"* seems to have some similarities with Newman's "Illative sense" which expresses in one composite term "the togetherness polarity of two movements of the mind: reasoning and intuition". The two functions of the illative sense "spring from an antecedent unity, the living personal mind, and by their very nature they are opposed to one another". "Their inherent inclination to exclude and dominate one another is... proper to the situation of polarity". See T. MERRIGAN, *Clear Heads and Holy Hearts: The Religious and Theological Ideal of John Henry Newman* (Louvain Theological and Pastoral Monographs, 7), Louvain, Peeters Press, 1991, pp. 227-228.

Though the following are stereotypes, they hint at how the Filipino feels about his or her father or mother. The father very often symbolizes authority and suggests authoritarianism, while the mother stands for understanding and compassion. The father is the cold and strict disciplinarian, while the mother is the warm and forgiving person in the family. The father, who is the one who works outside the home, is normally distant, while the mother, who makes the home, is always near. The father is rational, and the mother is affective. When in need, therefore, a child would prefer to approach his or her mother precisely because, of the two, she is the one approachable and understanding where the father tends to be stern and unbending.

This was brought home to me by the following story which I heard many years ago and which struck a cord in me. A certain son, so the story went, was so heartless and wicked that he killed his mother in the upper story of their house. As if this evil deed were not madness enough, he chopped the dead body of his mother into small pieces and threw them all out of the window onto the ground below. After doing that, he went down the stairway which led outside the house. But as he was doing so, he tripped and tumbled down the stairs. He found himself lying on the ground beside the heart of his mother and heard it solicitously say, "Son, were you hurt?"

I have never really understood (or should I say "felt"?) the parable of the merciful father in the gospel according to Luke (15,11ff) until I heard a Filipino singer's version of it[53]. In Luke we read of a son who not only broke relations with his father, but also squandered, in loose living, his part of the inheritance which he got from his father. Coming back to his senses, he decides to return to his father who warmly welcomes him back as if nothing had ever happened between them. While my religious intellectual training persuaded me that I had understood the point of the parable, my feelings somehow remained unconvinced that God could be that forgiving, that compassionate.

My cultural conditioning kept insisting that if the prodigal son went back to his father in the Philippines, he would have gotten it. I could picture the son cowering before his father who is bawling him out with expletives such as, "How dare you come back; you're so shameless! Go away"! or "You still have the nerve to show your face after what you've done"! After all God, according to popular belief in the Philippines, does punish humanity for its wickedness: personal and social tragedies,

---

63. The title of the song, which was written, sung and recorded by Freddie Aguilar, is "Anak" meaning child.

disasters and natural calamities are God's punishment for human sinfulness. Despite the catechesis on the good Father in heaven, God is still
primarily the authority figure whose will is surely carried out. God is not
only powerful, he also tends to be overbearing.

In contrast, the Filipino singer I referred to replaces, in a master stroke
indicative of sensitiveness to culture, the father with the figure of the
mother in his song. The son, like the prodigal son in Luke's gospel,
strayed from the right path. Desiring to return home, this son decides to
turn to the person who, he is sure, would show compassion – his mother,
who asks him in tears, "Son, what happened to you"? And like many
local stories that evoke people's sentiments and draw their sympathy,
the song ends with the son crying as well.

A need to emphasize the cultural in the above sense has also not
escaped the attention of a theologian from Latin America who thinks
that "it is necessary to break the chains of pure reason as the supreme ruler
over society and humankind" and that "it is necessary to reincorporate the
symbolic, what has profound dimensions in human existence...". To him
"the problem with liberation theology was not being infiltrated by Marxism, but its inability to infiltrate grassroots logic" so that, though liberation theologians were talking about the poor and liberation, the discourse
was "like a stranger to the people". He reckons that there is a "need to
abandon excessive rationality and recover the subjective, which has profound dimensions in human existence"[64].

V. CONCLUSION

There is no gainsaying that culture is important in peoples' lives. That
is how they concretely "drink of life" with their very own "cup".
Always particular, culture provides people with specific ways of feeling,
thinking and behaving. It gives them a sense of identity, security, and
continuity amidst the changes in their societies. Change is no stranger to
cultures, for that is how they develop. But today, perhaps more than ever
before, cultures are not only being subjected to changes which are rapid
and which have far-reaching consequences, they are being threatened
with debilitation, marginalization and even destruction by a process
known as globalization. Because cultural identity and integrity are soteriological concerns, theological reflection can only disregard them at the

---

64. A. ECHEVERRY, *Liberation theology: A Necessary Revision*, in *Euntes* 29 (1996)
184-185.

risk of betraying its commitment to be at the service of the Good News of salvation.

For this reason, we reviewed the role of culture in the life of the church in the Philippines from the sixteenth century up till the present. We noted how, despite a promising beginning, the church followed the classical understanding of culture and manifested it theologically in its promotion and use of scholastic and neo-scholastic theologies. It was not until the perception of culture shifted from the classical to the empirical, and Vatican II began to promote the inculturation of the Christian life, that a significant change occurred in Filipino theologizing. This paradigm shift could be located in the change of starting point in theologizing: from a neo-scholastic formulated doctrinal statement to locally significant experience. The shift encouraged attention to the local culture as well as the broadening of the understanding of culture (social structures) in matters theological. It also led to theological attempts at indigenization, contextualization and local versions of liberation theology. This whole development points towards an integrated use of cultural and social analyses in the doing of theology.

For reasons arising from the cultural situation of the Philippines itself, we are suggesting further that cultural analysis, in the sense of systematically inquiring into a people's design for living, be the starting point and emphasis within the integrated cultural-social analysis as well as within the process of theological reflection. In this way, inculturation as the cultural re-appropriation and expression of the Gospel into the totality of life in society by a particular group of people will be realized from the very "cup" that they drink of life, their culture.

Ateneo de Manila University   José DE MESA
PO Box 221, 1101 UP Campus
Quezon City, Philippines

PART THREE
OFFERED PAPERS

ASSESSMENT OF THE SYMPOSIUM

9

THE RETURN TO IDEALISM

"Postmodernism" has become the intellectual fashion accessory of the decade. Has analysis of the contemporary novel become insipid? Then spice it up with a dash of postmodernism. Have the plastic arts become absurd? Then pretend they are deeply significant expressions of the postmodern condition. And now liberation theology receives the same treatment. Has it lost its way? Then let it follow the Yellow Brick Road to the magic kingdom of postmodernism.

That was my immediate response on reading the Discussion Paper prepared by G. De Schrijver. And if I as a European took this view, it was with some anticipation that I looked forward to hearing more detailed and penetrating criticisms from participants from other parts of the world. The Symposium itself was intellectually stimulating but I found it disappointing in two respects. Firstly, the Discussion Paper was not properly discussed. Seven theologians from different parts of the world were asked to (a) evaluate the Paper, (b) indicate at what points they rejected it, (c) show how those aspects which remained could be applied in the local situation, or (d) propose an alternative analysis. Presumably they had agreed to participate in this process, but in the event they did something else. We are all familiar with conferences in which speakers simply say what they want to say (and have often said), regardless of the specific conference theme. Secondly, and as a consequence, there was no sense of how we might proceed after the Symposium. Anyone who has a dialectical view of history will understand why. The Discussion Paper – even for those of us who were deeply critical of it – provided the occasion for discussion, debate, even conflict. And from that positive and creative experience we might have expected to find a new way opening up to us, a new analysis which led to a new parxis. That outcome of course would have left the Discussion Paper behind; such pieces have a limited shelf-life. But in coming to terms with it we should have clarified the present situation, which is one of frustration and confusion. The Discussion Paper was not properly discussed and therefore did not play its potential catalytic role. Even I, without great sympathy for the Discussion Paper, was disappointed that the time and careful study which had gone into its production were not better rewarded.

However, having said that, we are all familiar with another conference experience, namely time-lapse. Thus a paper is not well discussed when it is delivered, but its main themes reappear later in the week. The issues raised in the Discussion Paper reappeared in a surprising way at the end of the Symposium, and I have no doubt, will suddenly appear on the agenda of other such gatherings throughout the world in the next few years. This present contribution is therefore divided into two parts. The first is a criticism of the Discussion Paper, the kind of criticism which I found lacking in the Symposium itself. The second part will reflect on how the main thesis of the Discussion Paper, having been unceremoniously (and rudely) pushed aside as irrelevant, suddenly took hold of the closing session of the Symposium.

I. PRE-SYMPOSIUM RESPONSE

The Discussion Paper deals with liberation theology, modernity and postmodernity. I shall consider each in turn.

1. *Liberation Theology*

The Discussion Paper begins by simply assuming that a paradigm shift has taken place in theologies of liberation, from economic analysis to cultural analysis (which includes economic aspects). On closer inspection two very different movements are reviewed, one within liberation theology, the other outwith.

a) In the first, liberation theology, as it originated in Latin America, has been supplemented by other liberation theologies, notably feminist theology, and black theology, but also those concerned with ecology and indigenous movements. During the 1980s a very positive (and frank) exchange took place among these interest groups. Latin-Americans accused North-American blacks of having no economic analysis; blacks accused *latinos* of failing to acknowledge the importance of race, even within Latin America itself. Feminists broke in to accuse both sides of a lack of awareness of the oppression of women by *latino* and black men – often the very men who claimed to oppose oppression in the form which most affected them. And while these white middle class North-American women were congratulating themselves the *mujeristas* broke in to say that such feminist analysis did not describe their situation at all. The white feminists were part of their problem, not its solution.

Yes, all very fascinating, but I do not believe this can be described as a paradigm shift from economic analysis to cultural analysis. What all of these other theologies of liberation have lacked is an ideological analysis of oppression which addresses the roots and not simply the symptoms. Liberation theology took its name from liberation movements which were intent on the revolutionary overthrow of undemocratic and morally unjust regimes. 'Liberation' from the outset entailed the acceptance of some form of Marxist analysis of the relationship between the economic modes of production in the country, and the social institutions and relationships following from it. It was for this reason that the term 'liberation theology' was a cause for hope among the poor and a source of anger and dismay among the ruling class (including the religious leaders who had assumed a commonality of interest with that class). Nothing could suit the latter's interests more than a paradigm shift which downgraded or eliminated the fundamental importance of economic analysis within liberation theology. I do not believe that such a paradigm shift has taken place. Yes, liberation theology has moved to take on board criticisms about its limitations, but the other theologies, important as they are, are not liberation theologies in the original sense. They are idealist movements. Liberation theology is in crisis; it has lost its way, but the way forward does not lie in a paradigm shift which distracts it from its analysis of capitalism. How should it proceed? To this question I shall return after examining the second movement which the Discussion Paper deals with in discussing the paradigm shift.

b) This second movement is not within liberation theology, but rather is traced through the sequence of episcopal conferences (CELAM) from 1968-1992. It might be regarded as a paradigm shift from economic analysis to cultural analysis, although Medellín was hardly dominated by economics and Santo Domingo was not concerned primarily with popular culture. The Discussion Paper is critical of the movement, particularly the initiatives which can be attributed to the Vatican. The motive behind this second movement towards culture lies not in the strong desire to deal with oppression through gender or race, but rather the intention to reassert Roman Catholic hegemony over society as a whole. In this respect I am always surprised that discussions of CELAM invariably begin with the second conference. The first conference, in 1955, laid down markers which have not been rejected; it was concerned with the dual threats to the Catholic Church posed by Protestant evangelical missions, and related modernity. These two issues have become if anything

more not less pressing in the intervening years. It is not surprising therefore that the Discussion Paper sees CELAM, under Vatican direction,
attempting to re-establish a Catholic culture to oppose modernity. The
emphasis on culture has been taken as a rejection of liberation theology,
but it is in reality the continuation of a pre-Vatican II policy by other
means. Gutiérrez began his exposition of liberation theology by observing
that the Christendom movement was dead. After thirty years resurrec-
tionists can be seen at work.

As the Discussion Paper describes it this movement is in fact ambiguous towards modern culture and popular culture. It wishes to reject the
trend towards secularism, hedonism and atheism, while at the same
time accepting some elements of modern culture (which if truth be told
could only arise in a secular culture). The old Catholic ethos is to replace
Marxist analysis. With regard to popular culture the Church would like
to promote those element in indigenous culture which can develop
towards Catholic practice and belief. But this is hardly a joyful and liberating affirmation of popular culture.

There may have been something of a paradigm shift in the CELAM
succession though if the first conference is taken into account the continuity is more striking than the discontinuity. However, from this perspective
the change does not reflect a development within liberation theology,
but precisely against it. It therefore does not contribute to the thesis of
the Discussion Paper, but it does throw some light on the second topic
covered in the Paper, namely, modernity.

2. *Modernity*

At the beginning of this century the Vatican's long-standing hostility
towards the modern world was evidenced in the excommunication of
Catholic Modernists. Indeed it might be argued that with the exception
of the period 1959-1979 hostility towards the modern world has continued to be the attitude of the Vatican. The characterisation of modernity
in the Discussion Paper does not really bring out the basis of this hostility.
I draw attention to two features.

a) The term "secularization" is not mentioned in the Paper. It represents that movement in European history by which social institutions
passed from the sphere of religious control to that of the political and the
civil. Perhaps more importantly, these issues, such as education, health
and welfare were given a non-religious interpretation and meaning.
Indeed by the end of the process, in the 1950s, religion itself had become

an institution subject to secular norms of management and meaning. This was not 'secularism', an atheistic ideology with a reductionist, dismissive view of religion, but a historical process whose roots were themselves arguably religious. In 1972, I gave my first lecture on the work of Gutiérrez. At that time I had been writing on Secular Theology, and was struck by the fact that liberation theologians had no interest in such matters: they were dismissive of the project. Worse, they regarded it as somehow a betrayal of the poor and symptomatic of capitulation to the values of a dehumanising culture. The Spanish theologian Alfredo Fierro was to describe their position as "leftist orthodoxy". They were radical on non-religious matters, but very orthodox in doctrine and loyal to their own tradition. That is to say, on the matter of modernity the Vatican did not realise how much it could count on the support of these troublesome priests. 'Counter-culture' is a phrase of the 1960s describing a movement intent on going beyond the restrictions of the modern age. As described in the Discussion Paper, the Vatican has revived the attitude of counter-culture in the opposite direction. Like King Canute it wishes that the tide of secularization could be rolled back to the point at which (the true) religion could be the fabric of society once again. Few liberation theologians would object to this ideal. I make this point, since it is relevant to the conclusion of the Discussion Paper on liberation theology and *post*modernity.

b) There is a second feature of modernity which is touched upon by the Discussion Paper, but once again without gathering up its implications. Yes, there was a revolution in science and in mathematics, but these discoveries were thinking the thoughts of God after Her. However, modernity taken together provides a world-view which has features which alienate people from a religious perspective. It is not just 17th century science, it is 18th century political economy. With capitalism something new had appeared in the world, the ability to create wealth. This was so potentially revolutionary that it was necessary to discover the laws governing the "nature and causes of the wealth of nations". This was the title of the book which Adam Smith published in 1776, and when Marx decided to become an economist it was to a French edition of this work that he turned (see the extensive quotations in the Paris Manuscripts of 1844). And if Marx was to compare his historical materialism to Darwin's work in biology, we should know that the theory of evolution itself is dependent on Hegel, Marx's mentor, the great seculariser of the Christian view of history. When liberation theologians took over Marx's analysis they did so selectively. They could never come to terms with his commitment to modernity. I have discussed this at length in *Marx and the Failure of Liberation Theology*. Their inconsistency does not lie in anything as superficial as his atheism (which Marx, unlike Bakunin, regarded as a personal matter), but in their ambivalence towards modernity. What then does the Discussion Paper say about liberation theology and modernity?

3. *Liberation Theology and Modernity*

The Discussion Paper points to the ambiguity: liberation theology began by accepting Marx's critique of capitalism, Marx was a supporter of modernity, the liberation theologians were critical of modernity. However, I believe that behind this ambiguity lies the fact that there is virtually no interest in historical materialism among liberation theologians. They showed more interest in Marx's critique of ideology and his analysis of 'interest'. There can be no doubt of Marx's commitment to and admiration for modernity. Because of his historical materialism he could afford to be fulsome in his praise of capitalism. It destroyed feudalism and rescued the industrial workers from "the idiocy of the rural life". Given his admiration for western urban industrial life it is amazing that Marxism has been so popular in this century in the countries of the third world.

According to historical materialism it is necessary to go through the capitalist phase in order to revolutionise not simply economic relations but social institutions and of course human consciousness. Only then is society ready for socialism. The ambiguity among liberation theologians arises from their entirely un-Marxist project to choose between capitalism and socialism, to proceed to socialism without going through capitalism. The history of the USSR and China demonstrates the impossibility of such attempts to omit phases in the historical process. Socialism (in contrast to primitive communalism) presupposes modernity. If they reject modernity they are rejecting Marx and aligning themselves with the Vatican's struggle to reassert its control over third world societies.

The Discussion Paper deals briefly with dependence theory, theology and praxis, and conscientization. In each of these liberation theology relates to modernity. What is not discussed is the criteria for evaluating modernity. Is modernity intrinsically bound up with the history of Europe and North America? Or is it possible to modernise according to a different model? That would indeed be a paradigm shift of some consequence. Or again, which of the values of modernity are accepted, and on what basis? Instead this discussion comes to an end with reflections on the situation after the fall of the Berlin Wall. Two aspects are of particular importance.

a) The first concerns the development of the social sciences beyond
Marxist analysis. Anticipating the final section, there is the death of the
meta-narrative and the end of utopian visions. But what conclusions
should we draw from this? There are of course some social scientists who
are completely besotted with neo-liberalism and affirm it as a religious
faith. But liberation theologians are being encouraged by others to affirm
social democracy. And what is social democracy if it is not a longing for
something better than (in a moral sense) capitalism? Let us set aside the
idea that Marx in the middle of the 19th century could predict the form
of a post-capitalist social system which built upon capitalist achievements but put a consensus of moral and humane values above its purely
economic logic. Those who write now of social democracy have not lost
the capacity for meta-narrative or the capacity to dream dreams of what
might be, what should be. b) The second aspect of this section of the
Discussion Paper begins with a reference to Leonardo Boff who now
recognises the oppression and exploitation beyond the context of the
(male) labour market. I do not believe for a moment that liberation theologians ever took such a restricted view, but the categories used here
– 'gender, race and culture' – actually presuppose modernity. The analyses of oppression in these constituencies actually arose within the modern, capitalist societies. Arguably oppression in these three contexts is
worse in Latin America today than in Europe. Sensitivity to the issues
has come with modernity, not as a protest against it. If the movement for
liberation now incorporates such sensitivity that is to be applauded, even
at this late stage, but it is not evidence of a turn from modernity. To the
contrary it presupposes the modern meta-narrative and the moral consensus of utopian visions.

4. *Postmodernity*

I noted at the outset that postmodernism has become the intellectual
fashion accessory of the decade. It is frequently used to describe phenomena which are actually features of modernity itself. The revolution
in technology, for example, has enabled us to see places which we have
never visited, speak to people we cannot see, access information more
extensive than previously existed more quickly than we can ourselves
imagine. This is the outworking of modernity. To call it postmodern is
to devalue the important critical dimension of postmodernity. Modernity
continues in its merry self-confident path, unaware that its very foundations have been undermined and largely removed. No one understood
this better than Nietzsche. Like the madman of *The Gay Science* he came

too early; he described a situation which would not exist for another century, that is until our present time. To describe the qualitative leap achieved through technology as somehow postmodern would be to reduce the term to a fashion note, but more importantly it would be to distract us from seeking out, identifying and coming to terms with the very real and alarming implications of living far out over infinte space with no continuing means of support for our world-view, moral judgments or even self-understanding. It was to alert us to such distractions that Nietzsche wrote with such power, originality, clarity and honesty. His contemporaries could be forgiven for not understanding his prophetic analysis or seeing its relevance for them. We in Europe today have no such excuse. I say in Europe, since just as it is necessary to go through the capitalist revolution to achieve a postcapitalist order, it is necessary to fully embrace modernity before being confronted by what Nietzsche called "the logic of terror" – the postmodern condition. The precapitalist third world was never in a position to choose socialism; cultures which have not been revolutionised by modernity cannot be confronted with postmodernism. In passing we should note the danger of a return to idealism. Previously history was described as a series of epochs characterised by changing ideas, such as the age of reason, the age of romanticism, the age of anxiety. We see here a tendency to fall into the same pattern, history characterized in terms of ideas: modernism, postmodernism. Modernism did not create capitalism: capitalism created the social institutions and the common consciousness which we now call 'modern'. Nor does postmodernism supersede modernism. Modernity will continue as long as capitalism continues: postmodernism refers to the dawning recognition of the implications of this new epoch for such matters as the meaning and value of life.

Turning to the Discussion Paper we find some of these issues brought to our attention: a variety of world-views, the end of absolutes in knowledge, the loss of credibility in the grand narratives within which life had meaning and significance even in an alienated form, the loss of belief in the goodness of progress (= unbridled exploitation of the natural world). This last sobering point has generated a debate which presupposes certain ethical values and a consensus on what constitutes human and humane life. This is encouraging and hardly surprising. After all, Nietzsche's goal was not nihilism but the proper founding of a new and more natural morality. We are presented with these issues arising from a brief account of modern experience, a snap-shot of western life at the present time. This is modernity, at its current point of development. It will continue to develop and that too will be modernity. Postmodernity, by

contrast is a reflexive form of consciousness which is beginning to grasp
the implications of this development. Postmodernity does not describe
new forms of technology, rather it struggles to grasp their implications –
sometimes exciting and liberating, as often alarming and debilitating. It
is all the more surprising therefore that the second half of the Discussion
Paper, indeed 50 pages out of a total of 80, is given over to an examination of postmodernity and globalization. There could hardly be a better
example of *modernity* than globalization. As indicated earlier, political
economy as a (social) science began with Adam Smith. His work was a
sustained criticism of mercantilism, the direction and control of the
national economy by central government. The criticism is based on the
assertion of the superiority of economic liberalism (*laissez faire, laissez
aller, laissez passer*). It is for this reason that the eighteenth century
debate has such a modern ring to it. Liberalism, or neo-liberalism was
revived in this century by Hayek and sold on by the Thatcher-Reagan
partnership. Globalization of markets, or the marketization of all economies,
is the goal and logical outworking of neo-liberalism and as such one of
the most paradigmatic examples of modernity at work.

II. POST-SYMPOSIUM PROSPECT

At the evening session on the penultimate day of the Symposium it
seemed as if the Discussion Paper had no support whatsoever outside the
group responsible for its production. It had not been properly discussed,
but the general attitude was that it was not relevant enough to warrant
engagement. It therefore looked as if the session planned for next morning, the final session, would be pointless: we were scheduled to discuss
globalization. In the event the groups went very well. The theme was
taken up with enthusiasm, examples piled up, the application was
clear. At last the Symposium came alive. How strange, reminiscent of
the gospel parable. The concept which the participants had rejected had
become the chief cornerstone of their deliberations. Those who had
come with their own local situations and circumstances in mind had
found little to which they could relate. But now globalization threw
light on these situations. Like all timely analyses it enabled them to
understand what was happening to their people, it disclosed coalitions of
politico-economic forces and interests hitherto disguised, it provided a
picture of future trends which would overwhelm the unwary. The universal and the local: glocalization! I fully expected it to be set to music,
our hymn of hope as we marched to the reception at the Town Hall. As

indicated above, I believe that globalization is a feature of modernity, and the majority of individuals and societies experiencing it do so as a modernist and not postmodern challenge. (In any case this important distinction becomes blurred towards the end of the Discussion Paper when, rather disarmingly modernity is defined as "simple modernity" and postmodernism is defined as "reflexive modernity". As indicated earlier, this is to devalue postmodernism and distract us from its critical stance over against modernity. As the Paper makes clear, globalization is an ambiguous phenomenon. For example it does not necessarily overwhelm local cultures; by featuring such differences the historical division of labour can be promoted under a different and apparently benign guise. Aesthetic concern with local culture can be to the detriment of the ethical struggle. I am therefore less sanguine than the Paper about any change of paradigm from economics to culture. Cultural analyses can neither comprehend capitalism nor provide any defence against it.

My own analysis of the situation is therefore rather different from that of the Discussion Paper, though there is a convergence at the end. As one who has been inspired and heartened by liberation theology over many years, I am disappointed that it has not been able to respond to the new reality after 1989. After the end of the Cold War the USA lost interest in maintaining in power all anti-communist regimes, regardless of their undemocratic or anti-democratic character. Instead the USA turned to another long term project, the marketization of all national economics. Globalization is one aspect of the neo-liberalism which is sweeping the world. On a recent visit to Central America I was disappointed that no answers to the problems were on offer, but I was more disturbed that the problem itself was rarely addressed by liberation theology.

Yet, it is being addressed by necessity by those who are experiencing the effects of neo-libealism on their communities. I give one example. I am an editor for the *Cambridge Series on Ideology and Religion*, and I have recommended that a manuscript be published this year. It is by Manuel Vásquez and is based on empirical studies he has done on the popular church in Brazil, which suggest that people in towns and villages have had to find their own way, since the repetition of the old themes from liberation theology by the lay leaders of the ecclesial base communities is of no help to them.

For me the Discussion Paper misreads the situation in two important respects. The first is that there has been no paradigm shift. I regret that there has been so little movement, though I do not think a shift towards culture would be the way forward. Secondly, the phenomenon of globalization makes it urgent that liberation theology comes to terms with modernity, not postmodernism. There has been a shift – in reality, not in theology. Globalization is the name of a new experience which is impacting increasingly on every society and reaching into the most remote and enclosed communities around the world. Liberation theology has always maintained that like Minerva's owl it arises from and reflects upon the experience of the poor. Liberation theology must therefore begin from this new experience in all its ambiguities. Whether it needs a new 'paradigm' I very much doubt. This new reality has an economic base, it is the next phase in the capitalist revolution, which after 1989 has free rein throughout the world. Its possibilities and its dangers will not be realized or resisted by culture analysis. As we have seen, the romantic revival of antique rituals and relationships is no response to globalization, which will simply gather them up as new commodities, new markets for its infinite imagination. Alternatively, the broadening of culture to incorporate considerations of gender, race, and ecology ensures that globalization proceeds unchecked. Far from providing a bulwark against it, such culture analyses speak its language: throughout the world it hears the same clichés imported from western modernity. How comforting. The paradigms of culture analyses, whether antique or modern, mark a return to idealism, a false and romantic hope in a time when the vision of liberation has been lost.

The Symposium presented a paradox, the Discussion Paper a challenge. The paradox lay in the contrast of the last two sessions. The thesis set out in the Paper was that there had been a paradigm shift in liberation theology, and that this paradigm is to be understood in terms of postmodernism. Both propositions were rejected. Throughout the Symposium it was denied that there has been a paradigm shift, and postmodernism was rejected out of hand. In the final session however, globalization was suddenly accepted as a matter of course. The paradox highlights the Discussion Paper's final challenge. The conclusion seems clear. Globalization is indeed a reality. Whether there has been a paradigm shift or not, there has been no serious response. If liberation theology has not addressed the new reality – then by this time it should have. This to me is the value of the Discussion paper and it is for this reason that I believe its challenge will haunt EATWOT type conferences until the problem is confronted head on.

University of Edinburgh   Alistair KEE
New College, Mound Place
Edinburgh EH1 2LX, Scotland

10

GHOSTS IN THE SYMPOSIUM: A PERSONAL REPORT

The international Symposium on the paradigm-shift thesis was a laudable event, for it enabled the key-respondents and the official participants to unrestrainedly express significant qualifications and corrections to the thesis. The Symposium discussed the Discussion Paper of G. De Schrijver, who asserts that a paradigm shift from socio-economic analysis to cultural analysis has occurred in Third-World theologies of liberation and that this shift reflects an ongoing transition from modernity to postmodernity in the contemporary world. In my view, the majority in the Symposium have concluded that the term "paradigm shift" does not sufficiently acknowledge the profound continuities that they perceive throughout the significant changes in the reflections and analyses of liberation theologians. Besides this criticism of the thesis, however, the Symposium has affirmed that globalization is a complex reality that affects all contemporary societies and which liberational theologians have to reckon with.

As for the more colourful side of the Symposium, there were some tense moments and harsh words during the discussions, yet the participants from the Third and First-Worlds were able to perceive and confirm a common liberation concern and a will to solidarity among them. Also, several participants expressed a common unwillingness to accept the current state of our world as it is.

Owing to a shared liberation concern, the Symposium did not become an arena for a gladiatorial combat between, on one side, the Third-World theologians who favour socio-economic analysis and, on the other side, those who favour cultural analysis. Early in the conference, during the open forum after the lecture of the first key-respondent, the prospect of a gladiatorial spectacle increased when another key-respondent expressed vigorously his dissatisfaction as regards the conclusion of the lecturer that cultural analysis ought to be the starting-point and emphasis within an integrated cultural-social analysis as well as within the process of theological reflection. There followed critical comments from two other Third-World participants, one of whom objected to the lecturer's statement that culture, including patriarchal culture, is passed on from one generation to the next primarily through the mothers.

Fortunately, a gladiatorial spectacle, which could have provided some amusement to bored academics, did not occur. The non-event was perhaps disappointing to those who believe that only a head-on clash either will show who is victoriously right or will produce the starlight of higher illumination.

In retrospect, I believe that most of the Third-World participants, who constituted approximately one-fourth the number of official participants, came to tacitly and rightly realize that to argue with each other in front of a predominantly First-World audience, would only weaken the struggling and critical state of Third-World theology in the face of the continuing dominance of First-World theology. In the last session of the second day, one of the key-respondents said that, at the beginning of the Symposium, he was worried that there would be a divergence of approach between the Third-World participants from the continents of Asia, Africa, and Latin America. Instead, he was comforted when he perceived that there were more points of convergence than divergence, as all three of the continents are going through the same agony – the agony of mass poverty that arose from colonialism.

As in similar forums that brought together liberational theologians from the Third and First-Worlds, a spectre haunted the Symposium – the spectre of colonialism. Four of the seven key-respondents emphasized the continuing effects of colonialism on the ravaged cultures of Third-World peoples. Their nation-states are politically independent, yet the foul colonialist spirit has returned with the group of seven (G-7) neocolonialist spirits that are even more wicked.

In private conversations, a few First-World participants expressed their surprise that colonialism was still regarded as a major issue. Someone even remarked that most of the adverse references to colonialism were no different from those he heard in an international Symposium he attended twenty years ago. Is it a case of time standing still or of ears that are dull of hearing?

Also on the second day, a protest statement was read out by five feminist participants. They asserted that the Symposium was in error when it did not question definitions of culture that failed to give attention to the patriarchal elements contained in culture. They expressed their distress at the "casual, facile, and careless manner in which women have been mentioned in many of the presentations", and for them, the inclusion of only one feminist lecture in the whole programme "amounts to tokenism, a most humiliating form of sexism". One participant privately remarked that, in every theological conference he recently attended, feminists made a protest against the organizers and the presentations. For him, the frequency and predictability of these protests are making them "cheap". I personally heard this remark, and I was inclined to ask:

what has to be rebuked here? A touchy spirit or a deaf spirit? Is it a case of howling they gain nought, or hearing they hear not?

The spectre of colonialism was a major reason for what appeared to be a united front of the African and Asian participants against the paradigm-shift thesis and the modernity-postmodernity framework propounded by the Discussion Paper, which was dismissed as either "irrelevant" or "Euro-centric". They indicated that a colonialism-neocolonialism framework would have been much more apt for their contexts, as modernity and post-modernity basically are both Western economic and cultural invasions.

As for the Latin-Americans, one of them suggested that the language of the Discussion Paper is quite intellectual in comparison with the more figurative language of liberation theology, yet he also said that it is not fair to call the Paper Eurocentric. Another Latin American acknowl-edged but qualified the paradigm shift as an "axial shift" within the main current of liberation theology. One Argentine theologian shared her reflections on her encounters with the excluded and the "mad" peo-ple and children of the streets whose day-to-day survival strategies and chaotic practices can relevantly be called postmodern and postcolonial, for they are deconstructive of the the social grand narratives of Father-land, (patriarchal) family, (authoritarian) tradition, and national security. Postmodern phenomena in the streets of Third-World mega-cities seem to be more authentic and more liberational than the postmodernist epistemological emissions from the self-stimulation of some spoiled and bored academics in affluent societies.

The African and Asian participants inferred that the Discussion Paper did not adequately treat the fact of colonialism and its connection to modernity. Colonialism should have been acknowledged as a major dimension of the under-side of European modernization, which entailed the violent conquest of non-European peoples and the stigmatizing of their cultures. From the colonial period down to this day, the tribal and agricultural practices and habits of Third-World peoples have been directly and indirectly stigmatized as indolent, irrational, or idiotic. Should their local specialists then believe in the possibility that the First-World cultures that invaded and vilified the Third-World could also pro-vide intellectual or analytic resources for their cultural liberation?

If postmodernism is indeed a reflexive consciousness of both the lib-erating and life-threatening implications of modernization, and if post-modernists have come to realize from within what the acceleration process of modernization (with its under-side) is all about, then they will have to acknowledge categorically that decades or even centuries of injustices and indignities have been inflicted on colonized peoples. In their writings and lectures, have First-World postmodernists sufficiently expressed a heartfelt regret for the sins of their colonialist ancestors?

As for the Vatican, despite its criticisms of modernity's reductionist pretensions and ideologies of progress and individualism, it is certainly not postmodern. One of the key-respondents pointed out that, at the quincentenary celebration of the coming of Columbus to America, the Vatican missed a historic opportunity to officially apologize to the indigenous peoples for its historical alliance with the Iberian colonial powers, and for the blessing and ultimate legitimation it provided to the colonial enterprise. No Vatican document, and none of the social encyclicals, has offered a critical analysis of modern colonialism, nor has any official document contained sufficient self-criticism of the church's actions during the colonial period.

After the last plenary session in the evening of the second day, I believe that the foul colonialist spectre was partially exorcised from the Symposium. A very difficult but well-meaning dialogue took place. The author of the Discussion Paper concluded the session with a straightforward sharing of his standpoint, the personal worry and liberation concern that steered his writing, and he admitted that it would have been better if he had consulted additional sources especially from the African, Asian, and feminist standpoints.The sharing had enough authenticity, sobriety, and sympathetic humour, and it never came close to a masochistic self-denunciation.

The next morning, the five workshop groups favourably took up the issue of globalization, which is a key-issue in the Discussion Paper. A secretary of one group reported that not only is globalization a reality in both the First and Third-Worlds but it is also linked with localization and with postmodernism. The current process of globalization has a somewhat postmodern aspect, for there is no mastermind, singular state, or centralized organization that is ultimately controlling the process. Only in the improbable event of the formation of an actual world government will globalization perhaps lose its postmodern aspect. The secretary said that his group apparently were contradicting their previous report, for they were now saying that postmodernism is relevant to Third-World contexts, where some emergent trends and groups are analogously postmodernist as they promote an enriching plurality of cultures and life-styles. Yet there were those who maintained that postmodernism does not deal with the hard economic issues. The group also brought out the term "glocalization", which refers to the inseparable interconnection of the global order and the local situation, and challenges us to analyze, act, and organize both globally and locally.

In another group report, it was said that, in general, First-World theologies do not reflect a genuine interest in Third-World issues, and thus, acute differences often emerge whenever First and Third-World theologians meet for formal discussions. But the common opinion of the group is that the Discussion Paper does not reflect the dominant type of First-World theology, the type that is idealistic and overly abstract. In their perception, the First-World theologians behind the planning and organization of the Symposium do share similar if not the same liberation concerns with those from the Two-Thirds World. As regards globalization, negative and positive views of it were reported. Some mentioned the possibility that it could lead to the homogenization of cultural identities or to hegemonic control since the First-World has more access to means of communication. Thus, fragmentation might be good as a form of resistance. Others pointed out that globalization could lead to a widened reflexivity wherein persons and groups could discern and discuss those aspects of their local culture which ought to be preserved and enhanced, the aspects that ought to be changed, and the aspects of other local cultures which are beneficial to borrow and combine with their culture.

Here are some of the notable views of the other groups. It was asserted that globalization is a form of neocolonization that is more insidious than formal colonization, and globalization is at present a predominantly negative process from the perspective of the majority who continue to be oppressed and excluded. The positive aspect is its potential to promote a dialogue of cultures. There were those who stressed that globalization is primarily an economic phenomenon, namely, the triumph of the total market. Someone asserted that globalization is ultimately controlled by the World Bank. Yet there were those who preferred to view globalization as the emergence of an information world where the flow of information and opinions is becoming more difficult to censor. There was also the suggestion that another form of globalization is possible, the globalization of resistance through domestic and international networks of liberational groups against the new world system that has arisen after the decline of communism.

In that final morning, the general character of the group discussions and the plenary session showed that the foul spectre had not overcome the common spirit of liberation and solidarity. Perhaps most of the Third-World participants scented the essential commitment of the persons behind the making of the Symposium and the Discussion Paper. They had tested this commitment, and discerned whether it was authentic or not. One key-respondent said that Third-World critics ought not to be dismissive of the real growth in liberational consciousness in the

First-World. Thus, the significance of the struggle of some First-World intellectuals against a money-culture has to be acknowledged, and their struggle has to be encouraged.

As I see it, the Discussion Paper is not an affirmation of West-European cultural or intellectual superiority. It is not the paper's aim either to rob Third-World men and women of their right to self-definition and self-analysis or to reduce liberation theologies to an epistemological game of the mind.

The Discussion Paper indicates modernity's positive and negative dimensions and consequences, which include the ideology of steady progress and limitless innovation, the compulsive disruption of local cultures, and the rationalistic stigmatizing of rural customs and popular beliefs. Furthermore, the paper affirms that productivist, consumerist, and progressive modernists in affluent societies have much to learn from the life-giving values of many poor and excluded persons and sectors in the Third-World. It approvingly refers to some authors who maintain that the unpretentious men and women of the informal economic sector and the rural communities in the South generally seek wholesome family and friendship ties and self-respect more than the private accumulation of wealth.

Since the decade of the nineties appears to be a period of frustration and confusion especially for the liberational militants and intellectuals all over the world, the Discussion Paper represents a daring attempt or, for some critics, an over-daring attempt, to propound a general analytic framework to interrelate and shed some more light on the various liberational struggles of the Third and First-Worlds. The possibility of interrelating validly these different struggles has become more admissible in view of the current process of globalization, which is a complex, interactive, and discordant process in which, on the one hand, our day-to-day activities are influenced strongly by global systems and distant events, and on the other hand, local life-style habits have become globally consequential. In this current period, more than ever, the futures of all our societies have been firmly conjoined.

Globalization is not only an economic process. It has communicational and ethical aspects, and contributes immensely to social reflexivity. Through globalization, a diversity of expert systems of knowledge, traditions, and even lay opinions can confront one another regularly. This day-to-day flurry of data and discussion from familiar and strange places stimulates a periodic self-interrogation about social practices, local life-styles, personal habits, and self-identity. The enhancement of social reflexivity is both a cause and an effect of the deconstruction of the grand narratives of progress. Every progressivist narrative has propagated the ultimately sectarian belief that there is a singular, primary, or central character among the other characters in the grand narrative. The central character might be the economic infrastructure, the invisible hand of the market, the party of the people, or the inner nature or cultural genius of the people. Information and communication globalization helps expose the sectarian, prohibitive, and potentially totalitarian character of progressivist narratives.

I think that it is fair to say that the Discussion Paper as a whole, and in spite of flaws that might be found in it, represents a commendable attempt at encouraging and helping the different liberational theologies to include a global outlook in their analyses and praxes. It is a legitimate worry that, without a global outlook, localized liberational struggles pursued by different groups or movements might become isolated from each other, or worse, turn into either a destructive competition or a clash of fundamentalisms.

A possible degeneration into a noisome head-on clash, whether between Third-World theologies, or between Third and First-World theologies, was avoided by the Symposium. The Spirit of solidarity among the participants and organizers was not overwhelmed by grim ghosts whose presences were felt in the sessions.

Maryhill School of Theology   Dennis GONZALEZ
PO Box 1323
Manila, Philippines

10

THE HERMENEUTICS OF TRANSGRESSION

I. TIME AND THE CHILDREN IN THE STREETS OF BUENOS AIRES

– How long have you been living in Buenos Aires?
– A month, I think; well, some time… I think I was 10 when I arrived here.
– And how old are you now?
– 15 years old, I think… *Maa, qué sé yo!* (It's the same; what do I know? /
I don't care…)

1. *Talking* some *Bataille under the Bridges of Buenos Aires*

The above dialogue between myself and Carlos, a child of the street
in Buenos Aires, Argentina, happened in July 1996. We spent a month
talking and occasionally sharing *mate* (a traditional herbal tea drunk in
Argentine, South-East Brazil, Paraguay and Uruguay). He had sad eyes
and the expression of what Bataille would call the presence of what is
lost, the past without resurrection, "the irrecoverable" in our lifetime.
Carlos was perhaps fourteen years old although he did not know it in
that way, because he knew his age using a different conceptual frame.
Children who do not go to school or celebrate annual festivities such as
Christmas, New Year's Eve and New Year's Day or birthdays, nor are
they involved in any domestic or public ritual celebrations, count time
according to the significant events in their lives. If you have had just a
few significant events in your life you are always younger than anybody
who can recall many meaningful life experiences. Carlos told me that he
had been in Buenos Aires for "some months" when, according to the
counting of the social worker, he had been in the big city for at least 4
years, and 4 years living in the streets, or under the bridges – as we say.
What we are confronted with here is a sort of Nietzchean Mathematics,
dismissing the surplus of accumulative reason, in this case the counting
of non-significant events. Accumulative reason produces what we understand in Latin America as realidad ("reality" but as a concept which combines past and present; it is a combination between present circumstances

and the historical processes which led us into that present). But realidad, although it is presented as "truthful appearance", is only a by-product of a restricted economy. This is an homogenous realidad, with its clear delimitation of time and space. From Carlos, we receive instead a glimpse of a realidad which comes from a more unrestricted economy, born as Bataille would say, from violence; the violence of hunger and repression, and the violence of peace (the *Pax Romana*) which supports the miserable living conditions of the children of the streets. The violence manifested in the mutilation of memories and the irrecoverable loss of history in their lives. Since we do not exist except in the eyes of the Other who looks at us, this is also our mutilation and our violent loss.

This is what I call "talking *some* Bataille under the bridges", as a form of criticism of modernity from the people in the streets of Buenos Aires. They are post-modern critics because they embody the *turbulence*[1] of Savage Capitalism in Latin America. This turbulence, in Bataille, is an excess of the excess of poverty. In Latin America, we no longer consider the poor to be the option of Liberation Theology, because after the partial collapse of Socialism we are confronted with the new Global Order and also with new frontiers of misery and human degradation. These are the frontiers of those for whom to be poor would be a privilege. These are the excluded masses of Latin America.

The turbulent poor such as Carlos belong to a community which deconstructs the social system by dislocating the time of our nation. While the government does things with numbers, by budgeting in advance, controlling the rise of hyper-inflation or predicting year by year the results of the Currency Convertibility Plan, the excluded masses are getting younger, in a counting of history slowed down by the lack of meaningful, transformative events. Madness, hunger and violence without substantial changes.

2. *The Excluded are not the Poor*

The excluded are not the poor. The poor have a space in Latin America, even if it is a space of exploitation. The poor manage somehow to be part of society; their spirituality is basically Primal although read through Christian lenses. The excluded are not the marginalized either because the marginalized still have the privilege of occupying the space on the borders of society, with one foot in and the other out. The excluded are those who are outside, such as Carlos, for whom to be exploited would be a dubious but real privilege. The excluded are those people in whom all

---

1. Cf. G. BATAILLE, *La part maudite*, Paris, Éditions de Minuit, 1967, 67 ff.

the co-ordinates of marginalization coexist, that is, poverty, violence and madness. The main characteristic of these excluded masses is usually summed up in Capitalistic terms with the expression, "they are non productive". This lack of productivity is manifested in the fact that they do not occupy either space (they live in the city, invisible, nomadic) or control time (they do not have history). Moreover, they do not occupy political, philosophical, theological or legal spaces. This becomes obvious when we realize that there is a lack of research, for instance, on the economic policy in Latin America and the transition to exclusion. We do not have an epistemological corpus centered on "exclusion knowledge". We ignore that the ultimate degradation of the Grand Narratives is an active part of the praxis of the excluded, and theology has not yet discovered who are the gods that ally with them.

The point is that the excluded have an invisible existence because they do not occupy the legal spaces of the construction of the social system. For instance, Carlos is not called Carlos. His name is not a name, but his own delusion of existing in a society where your name is accepted after an identity card establishing that your name is Carlos has been shown to the police. In a society where the state and the main church have been at war with their own people, to say your name does not mean that that is your name. Your name can only be said by a card with your picture and an official signature on it. Since the births of the excluded masses are generally not legally registered, and they do not have ID-cards saying their names, Carlos is not Carlos. Moreover, the street children generally do not have names but nicknames which refer to their physical features, such as "Skinny" or "One-Eye". Carlos is the name of a famous boxing champion whom he admires. As it is well known, in the Savage Capitalism we are living in, not only the identity of the excluded is erased but even the borders between life and death are blurred. Children can be executed in the streets of Latin America without leaving a trace/memory of their presence just some hours later. Time works in reverse. Seldom do they get older. In theology, the excluded are considered as "the disposable people".

When we say that the excluded represent the excess of the excess, we refer to the excess of degradation to which human lives can be subjected; the excess of anonymity and invisibility, too. A child from the street recalled how one lunch time, in a busy street of Buenos Aires, two men tried to take away his own sisters into forced prostitution[2]. The girls

2. Cf. E. MONTES DE OCA, *Guía Negra de Buenos Aires. Marginalización en la Gran Ciudad*, Buenos Aires, Planeta, 1995, p. 77.

were not yet 12 years old. He shouted at the men and kicked them, while his sisters also shouting asked for help and struggled to free themselves from their captors. The street was full of people, yet nobody intervened. The excess of non-existence. There were hundreds of people in the street but these children are not people. This is an important clue in trying to understand our question for a *fin de siècle* liberation theology. Which gods ally with the excluded? Which God is the God of the excluded? A Disposable God? Is the crucified/tortured God also a God forced into prostitution at lunch time amongst an indifferent crowd?

Returning to Bataille, the category of excess as embodied by the excluded seems to be important from the perspective of praxis. It is from there, from the surplus of the Savage Capitalist excess or "the excess of excess" that transformation or growth can finally come. The excluded are the excess of the excess of misery and human degradation, but also the locus of the excess of God. This excess of God in their lives is manifested in the post-modern and post-colonial challenges they produce in the economy of "national meaning". In Buenos Aires, the excluded masses are referred to sometimes as "the other country". It has its own logic, its own metaphysics, its own economic theories and deconstruction of Christianity.

3. *The Hermeneutical Circle of the Excluded*

The point is that the excluded are constructing a hermeneutical circle or spiral of interpretation. They are currently developing new methodologies and tools of interpretation which come from the intersection of two dissimilar although concurrent strategies of de-hegemonization of society: post-modernism and post-colonialism. Following the methodology of Liberation Theology, which always starts with the concreteness of people's oppression as a first step towards a community-oriented, issue-based theology, our reflections on post-modernism, militant Christianity and Latin-Americans also needs to start *from* and *with* the lives of the excluded. We must search for elements which can give us hermeneutical clues to understanding how the excluded are deconstructing the subject, which Grand Narratives are *passé* and how, and which is the concept of truth leading towards the crucial issues of the Latin-American ethos: social justice and the sacred. Some clues for these theological reflections will also come from issues stemming from the process of transition to democratic government, and the effects of the Structural Adjustment Program combined with the liberal policies of the nineties.

These two theological discourses are also the subject of deconstruction amongst the excluded.

In a similar way to the post-modern discourse which announces the death of the Grand Narratives of the past, and uncovers the metaphysics of Presence in idealist discourses, Latin-American Liberation Theology has also killed and uncovered the ideological tricks of many theological narratives. For instance, the individualist discourse about God took community dimensions and features. This was an issue-based theology, with a clear option for the poor, and a rejection of the Western obsession with individual sin, Anglo-centric anthropology and empire talk about God. It challenged a theology which spoke in European languages and introduced secularized Patriarchalism into civilizations that although Patriarchal, too, had at least a different construction of sex and economy. Liberation Theology gave to the poor (a rather "blanket" and homogeneous term, one must admit, but useful in the critical times of the seventies) the status of theologians. Some of the incipient dialogic dynamics of the Gospel which were read in Jesus' own re-questioning of the questions brought to him (e.g. "and who do you say?" or, "how did you read?...".) were then taken over by the poor.

The poor became more rebellious and anti-establishment until they finally walked out on the Catholic Church at the end of the military dictatorships (when it was safe again not to be a Catholic), or by the end of the Grand Narratives of liberation theology brought about by the administrative dismantling of Base Communities by the Vatican. The poor who became evangelical eventually managed to re-construct the authoritarian patterns of past dictatorship, through heavily hierarchical, sexist church organizations. They could not manage a spiritual transition from authoritarian regimes to democracy, probably due to the fact that Christianity in Latin America had always been the representative of terror theology. Evangelism cannot be studied without also looking at the genocide it produced, or the freedom of the Gospel without the slavery of millions. Meanwhile the political, militant churches who survived dictatorships, also had a prophetic, that is. highly authoritarian structure, that of the "I have a word of God" type, which was useful during times of war, when a clear line of command was required to literally save lives, but which did not need to continue in democracy.

The point is that the excluded, by their very nature, are in confrontation with hegemonic systems, and so are liberationists; but the excluded are the ones in the unique position to surpass the colonial trimmings of Christianity in a way that churches cannot do, unless they are able to "commit suicide". In the words of Leonardo Boff, the churches in Latin America will never be able to be the church of the poor, because this will entail "class suicide".

But continuing with Bataille, we must remember that religion seems to advance upon the decomposition of the sacred. The sacred, in this case, is a trinity composed of two women and one man, that is, of a boy in the street struggling to save his sisters from rape at lunch time in Buenos Aires. Three dark, indigenous faces: a young descendent of *Viracocha*, the Inca God, and two daughters of the *Pachamama*, the Goddess (Mother) Earth. The children priestesses tortured in the light of day. Their fate symbolizes the decomposition of the Inca religion of Cosmic Reciprocity, where souls were sexed and the idea of afterlife was a productive land, where the surplus was returned to the workers. The "advance of religion" can only come from the irrecoverable past of the Ancient Religions. If as Audre Lorde has said, "the master's tools cannot dismantle the master's house", Christianity, as we know it, cannot bring liberation to Latin America.

4. *The Struggle for the Sacred*

The struggle for the sacred in Latin America is carried out in the political field of the consolidation of external sector liberalism and the destruction of lives in the realm of the domestic. The sacred is embodied by the homeless woman who crosses herself as she walks by the Cathedral while, at the same time, she keeps in her pocket a talisman of St Death. The Cathedral is the realm of public policy; St Death provides for her emotional and physical everyday needs. This is the theological discourse which comes not from the poor, but from the excluded masses. They are the ones who are announcing the death of the theology of state, sex and God in Latin America, even though they do not do it verbally. Their post-colonial and post-modern discourse is embodied in their mere presence. A presence that needs to be wiped out during the tourist seasons, or when governments feel that foreign investors are deterred by barefoot children inhaling glue in the garbage dumps. Like the errant, chaotic, prophetic communities in the Hebrew Scriptures, the excluded masses in Latin America denounce the hegemonic Argentine *theo*-social system through a "body discourse". This is a chaotic discourse deconstructing the pillars of traditional Latin-American theology: sexuality and general economics. It is in this chaos that Liberation Theology continues with particular creativity, and fierce spirituality. The excluded are talking *some* Bataille under the bridges.

II. ZOMBIELAND THEOLOGY:
POCKET GRAND NARRATIVES AND THE FRAGMENTATION OF MEANING
IN THE STREETS OF BUENOS AIRES

There is a paradox in the fact that the military dictatorships of the seventies in Latin America, while building heavily medieval discourses which sacralised the state to exceptional degrees (we could say "original degrees" in the sense that they created myths of origins for the ideology of the Fatherland), became, in the end, the very ones responsible for the breakdown of the same *Grand Narratives* in the continent. Their myths of origins and the return to colonial Christian values were in fact myths of the destruction of Christianity and the symbolism of traditional nationhood. In Argentina, those grand narratives were literally sold by the Media in portable images and phrases, easy to remember and carry into every day life. I am referring here to the "pocket" grand narratives of *Patria, Familia y Tradición* (Fatherland, Family and Roman Catholic traditions) and *Dios, Patria y Hogar* (God, the Fatherland and the Home). These were hierarchically ordered. Sometimes, between God and the Fatherland the words *El Papa* (The Pope) were inserted. Another popular pocket grand narrative was "*El Ejército es su amigo/defensor de los valores occidentales y cristianos*" (The Army is your friend and the defender of the Western and Christian values). The army's systematic violation of human rights while the economy plunged into chaos merged with a renaissance of Christian discourses supporting the dictatorship while promoting the patriarchal ideology of subordination and the master/slave dialectics. At the intersection point of master/slave the Theology of Liberation found its discourse. It was the time when language was militarized and restricted to expressions approved by Roman Catholicism and the State: using the wrong adjective or the un-accepted verbal form could mean death by proxy. It was death by association with communism. Communism meant any form of critical thinking.

As language became restricted, the spirituality of the poor became liberationist or Pentecostal. The Theologians of liberation stopped theology from talking idealism and ideology, and started to deconstruct the church as subject, with the limitations of the historical consciousness of those years (mainly the strategical limitation of living under low intensity conflicts and war). The poorest of the poor started to speak in tongues; unintelligible, therefore, uncensored. The poorest of the poor in Latin America are historically resilient and courageous. They always find a materialist response to spiritual gestures. Sometimes it looks like they accept the charismatic gifts of the Spirit but challenge the ideology present in the interpretation of texts such as the Gospels. The gifts of healing flourish amongst people without a health service. The Holy Spirit provides miraculous filling for the few teeth on the mouth of the poor. Tongues are rampant amongst the silenced.

The end of the *Grand Narratives* in Argentina as we know it today, is therefore not in large part the product of imported, foreign philosophical thought. Fragmentation has not come through an enlightened élite reading about the de-construction of the subject but it is rather the result of the praxis of fragmentation produced by ten years of the use of the National Security Doctrine on the continent. When colonial Catholic ideas were forced upon people's lives, such ideas behaved, metaphorically speaking, as living dead, as Voodoo *Zombies*, and in the end, they collapsed carrying along into their graves the meaning of life and Christianity. Although Christianity has been subjected to a Liberationist criticism in order to disentangle ideology and theology, these combined *Zombie* Grand Narratives of the Roman Catholic Church and the Military State dragged down into their graves some basic points which were not discussed in Liberation Theology: the sexual nature of Christianity and politics in the continent. At this precise intersection, the post-colonial discourse surpasses the post-modern.

1. *On the Standardization of Meaning*

"La vida no tiene sentido, no's cierto? Y a Usted que le parece, señorita?" (Life is meaningless, isn't it? What do you think, Miss?).

This was part of a conversation I had with a taxi driver in Buenos Aires, in July 1996. The taxi driver was taking me to one of the oldest Mental Hospital in Buenos Aires, a sinister place called *El Borda*, in the hot afternoon of that Argentinean winter. I felt compelled to make a joke: "I'm just going to visit it, I'm not staying there; You see, I'm not mad, yet". She answered with the courteous irony of the people of Buenos Aires: "Now, tell me señorita, who is mad? Who isn't?" She offered me a cigarette (a gesture of intimacy) and started to talk about the meaninglessness of life, so obvious in a city whose tendency is a compulsion towards a death-drive. In our dialogue, we developed the idea that in part life felt meaningless because authorities have crumbled. The younger generation did not even fear the police, their parents (the Spanish for "parents" is "fathers") or public opinion. The dialectics of decency/indecency did not rule and control women as it used to be (the pocket grand narratives of *Zombieland*: Fatherland, Family and

Church/Tradition). The taxi driver remembered how Liberation theology and the militant churches initiated the process of dismantling the structures of sacred power and divinely justified violence. I recalled that years ago, in a religious procession carrying an image of Our Lady, a priest shouted that any Argentinean who did not bow in front of the statue of the Virgin was a traitor who should be publicly executed. We got excited in our conversation and she drove the car slowly, I thought, as if to give us that little extra time to keep on talking.

Liberation Theology was still exciting to us, as it excited the Latin-American thirst for de-linking politics and divinities from the empire in the seventies. At that time, people were talking liberation under the bridges. Liberation was a common word in the mouth of people in the street, and also a censored word. That day I was going to visit *El Borda* because people under the bridges are not talking liberation anymore but transgression. The structure of socio-political, divine life in Latin America is diglotic. In Linguistics, a diglotic phenomenon is defined as such when translation is not possible (even if we accept that translation is a possibility at all) because there is no correspondence of linguistic, onto-logical experiences between the two languages. The Western colonization processes standardized meaning through a cultural and linguistic imposition, but in fact a non-correspondence of meaning always co-exists in the ideological struggle of the sign, to paraphrase Volosinov. A diglotic society is a mad society, but the positive aspect is that in the end, it manages to survive. The fact is that Latin America is built upon the ashes of decomposed civilizations; traditional cosmologies and economic systems which are still superimposed upon the Western ones, in the same way that our ancient languages co-exist with Spanish or Portuguese. This is not syncretism. Liberation is part of the diglotic scenario. In the Christian, militant Liberation Theology understanding, liberation remains within the bounds of Christianity and the Christian construction of law and order. However, in spite of the Liberationist discourse, and the fact that many priests and religious sisters joined the counter insurgency, the *guerrillas* in Latin America were not called "The Followers of the Prophet Isaiah" or "The Way of the Lord" but *Tupac Amaru*, after the indigenous leader of a defeated revolution against the *Conquistadores*. During the time of war in El Salvador, a song became very popular which announced the second coming, not of Jesus but of the *Indio Aquino*, another indigenous leader, "dressed with the light of the sun, showing the path of liberation and shouting: Long life to El Salvador!...". We do not celebrate the day that the *Conquistadores* came to bring Christianity and economic exploitation to what they called Latin

America, but we mourn it. Our Catholic priests in Guatemala are becoming Maya priests, going back to their religion. Liberation is a diglotic word. Now we are discovering that it does not carry the same meaning for Christian Liberationists as for the poor, indigenous people in Latin America. It never did.

We are talking here about the diglossia of liberation, caught up between imperial meaning, post-modern fragmentation processes and post-colonial transgressions. I was present last year when a Scottish minister from Edinburgh asked a Presbyterian minister from Guatemala, "How do you call God in your native language?" He replied, "*Llamamos a Dios, Diosa*" ("We call God, Goddess"). However, although there is a post-colonial transgressive element there, the crossing of barriers of Modernism and Colonialism comes from the urban poor, who are the excluded, the mad, the receptacles of all violence. This is why I went to visit a Mental Hospital. To talk about God with the people who could answer the question "Which gods are allying with you?" Leaving the Asylum, one of male residents gave me a poem which says that real knowledge is always knowledge of the past of our future. He was talking about *la realidad*. I told him: "Or else, we would be condemned to repeat our mistakes".

2. *The Problem of the Ex-centricity of Faith*

We have said that Carlos, the boy who named himself after a boxing star of Argentina, counted time in terms of meaningful events. "Meaningful events" are understood here in the same way as in Liberation Theology, namely, as "events of liberation". Transgression is the hermeneutical key that the excluded use in order to break everyday issues into events of liberation. Theology can subvert, but not transgress, because faith is an *ex-centric* hermeneutical key. Faith is the presupposition which is outside the text; the hermeneutical key outside the circle of interpretation. Therefore, post-colonial de-linking, counter-empire theology is not possible, unless we center faith at the core of political ideology. This is precisely what Liberation Theology did, thus unravelling theology, culture and ideology but only to return to a re-construction of faith. Faith then remained as the un-challenged hermeneutical ex-centrism. Transgression instead incorporates the issues of specific power, such as class, sex, race and historic oppression into theology. It allows us to travel between regions of cultural differences and finally to organize the praxis of a Theology of Transgression from the excluded masses in Latin America.

III. Simultaneous but Diglotic: Understanding the Theology of the Excluded from Their Prayers

1. *Worship of the Excluded*

"What would you do if you were Jesus?" "Would you stop to help the mugged homeless person or would you do as the bishop did and drive on because he could not find a parking space?" Everyday theology is made of these mundane questions, but mundane questions in post-colonial societies are deceptively simple. The diglotic nature of the coexistence between faith and religious practices can no longer be ignored. Liberation can only be manifested when people transgress those diglotic theological frontiers. Prayers and questions in the style of "if you were a deity" give important clues into popular theology. There are prayers which are said every day in Buenos Aires. These I call the simultaneous although diglotic prayers which can be exemplified by what in Spanish is called "The Our Father" and the prayer to "Lord St Death". There are prayer meetings at which these two prayers are constantly, even daily, being recited. The "Lord St Death" prayer is very simple; it says "Lord St Death, death (I wish) to my enemy". What would you hear if you were Jesus? The answer is deceptively complex.

We have said that the excluded live beyond the margins of society. They are the street children, the children of the garbage sites, the people of the lunatic asylums and the people under the bridges. However, strictly speaking, the excluded do not have spaces or geographical boundaries. They are dispersed multitudes who carry their possessions in supermarket carrier bags. The capitalist construction of the church has been developed around a metaphysics of accountancy. People come to a legal prayer place, their names are inscribed, their whereabouts organized in class and sexual categories (does this person work? How much money can she donate? Married, single or in between?). The prayer meetings are based on structures which fix space (location) and time (day and hour of the meeting), which count how many people are present and if the same person returns regularly (the numbers go up) or if she is absent (the numbers go down) from one or more meetings. Numbers, like the plastic identity cards issued by the National Police says who you are, how much you belong or do not belong to the meeting etc.

The excluded cannot participate in such structures. They do not have fixed places to live, and they move around at a pace dictated by basic needs, such as free food centers, the garbage dumps or charity lunches at churches. They can only walk; transport is denied to them, and they need to take routes which will guarantee them the maximum of "hiding" possibilities for reasons of security. Moreover, their timing is different. But theology is also structure, system. Theology is the metaphor of actions; actions are structural.

2. *Transgressor Theology*

The worship and the prayer to St Death is a rich example of a transgressor theology because:

− It dismantles *Actuality*[3] by deconstructing the falsifying of reality.
− It understands the structural nature of oppression (what Liberation Theology called "structures of sin").
− It disorganizes colonial organizations such as the structures of the church.
− It empowers people through a symbolic reversal.

Let us consider those elements in order.

a) *The Dismantling of Actuality*: The Media constructs our present as "the actual" from an ethnocentric perspective. This actuality is made and enforced in people's life. During dictatorial regimes it becomes evident; whereas in democracy, it is more subtle. However, as Derrida suggests, the important thing is to know that actuality is always actively produced. In Latin America, Christianity has collated what I would call the production of sacred actuality, a sort of "artifactuality" (actuality produced from church structures, bureaucratic, theological, ritual etc.) but in reverse, from a colonial/neo-colonialist perspective. Therefore, in the history of Christianity in Latin America there is the church-organized and church-created element of the excess of excess. This excess of excess corresponds to the *falsifying* process of sacred/political events which lie at the basis of the Latin-American societies.

Historically speaking, the dismantling of the Original Nations' calendar and festivities, linked to a particular cosmovision, or as it is called in Maya Theology, a "cosmofeeling", is an example of the primordial falsifying of reality and its replacement by Christian actuality. Gods are not foreigners to the structures of their societies. The polar sexuality, the bi-sexuality of the Maya God/ess, for instance, is related to agricultural practices and a particular division of work. The structuring of cities in

---

3. For the concept of *Actuality*, cf. J. DERRIDA, *The Dismantling of Actuality*, in *Passages* (Sept. 1995).

indigenous populations also follows the cosmofeeling order. However, the exploitation and genocide of Latin America perpetuated by the Cross and the Sword, enriched Europe. The actuality that the Christian church created amongst indigenous cultures had economic consequences, including the fact that the production of actuality tends to erase history. The excluded masses in Latin America are mainly the descendants of the survivors of the *Conquista* five centuries ago. The dark, excluded woman in Buenos Aires sits dressed in rags on the steps of the Cathedral built with her own money, the riches of her civilization. The dismantling of actuality by the excluded is different form the dismantling that Andean and Mayan theologians are doing, because the urban excluded are a heterogeneous group with only one thing in common: they do not belong. They are in diaspora. But they rescue and re-create acts of worships as St Death where the main message is that the actual peace of the country is virtual peace. Death is the only sacred reality they know, the only power which equalizes everybody; besides, religion in Latin America has never been about life.

b) *The Structural Nature of Oppression*: The excluded live in a world of enmities, of oppositions of material nature which they try to transform by spiritual means. In the prayer of St Death ("Death to my enemy"), the enemy does not necessarily need to be a person. The lack of a job, to find oneself without friends or a secure place to sleep is an enmity. The desire of death is the desire of terminating an oppressive situation by locating the roots of the conflict. It has the structural dimensions of the concept of sin in Liberation Theology but it reveals a more personal nature. It is a prayer of transformation, of a situation which must end and give way to new opportunities, and as such, it is much more favored than the "Our Father in Heaven".

c) *The Disorganization (Dismantling) of Colonial Structures*: Indigenous leaders from Central America have criticized the churches on the grounds that for over 500 years, they have been unable to incorporate any substantial, alternative, post-colonial changes into their structures. It is part of the Latin-American culture to be able to perceive structures and the metaphysics of the Sacred in mutual dependency; it is part of their cosmofeelings. The nature of the spirituality of the excluded dismantles colonial church structures by creating alternative ones. The worship of St Death is a hidden worship, because it partakes in the invisibility of the people. The statues of St Death are covered. The images a person carries with her are hidden amongst her clothes. The response to the ostentation of rituals, buildings and religious processions is a hidden, invisible worship. The main dismantling structural point is that of the embodiment of the worship. Traditionally, the image of Lord Death is carved in a tiny bone which is inserted under the skin of the worshipper. They literally become temples of the spirit by a strategy of their Materialist Christianity. It is, in fact, the Christianity of the excluded that we are talking about here, because Lord Death is a re-reading of Jesus, a mixture of Bataille and the Gospels under the bridges. By Christian Materialism we refer here to this embodiment which is the ultimate manifestation of the concreteness of the faith of the excluded. While Christianity separated souls and bodies, and at the same time, attributed the identification of the body to the considered lesser human beings (women and other races, but also the poor), the excluded have sacralised their bodies. Their faith is Latin-American faith: material, concrete, present, can be almost eaten, or drunk or carried in your body.

d) *The Reversal of Symbols*: Jesus Christ might be the Life of the World but for the excluded he is the Presence of Death, understanding death here as the equalizer, and the possibility of ending situations and starting new ones, and of undermining oppression at its very roots. Another image of Jesus worshipped by the excluded in Buenos Aires is the female Christ, who stands crucified as a woman-Jesus and carries the name of *Librada* (a name related to Freedom; to obtain freedom). This She-Christ reverses the alienating male construction of divinity of European Christianity, which is strange to Latin-American's spirituality. *Librada* was crucified by the legal powers of her time and, therefore, she helps people to escape from the police. Christ the excluded is represented by Death, invisibility and miraculous escape from the police. Her prayer is short and apparently effective: "*Librada,* help me to escape...". The gods who ally with the excluded belong to indecent pantheons, but decency is a legal discourse on sex, class and race regulations. Transgressor theologies are indecent ones, literally "unsuitable for the system", unfit and unbecoming theologies.

The best of Liberation Theology has been its capacity to be indecent; it did not fit in the church establishment, or in the model which sacralised the dictatorship in Argentina during the seventies. It produced unsuitable theological categories such as "Structures of Sin" or "Structures of Human Sacrifices" and even broke down monotheistic assumptions when it declared that we were confronted with a battle amongst gods (the gods of life and the gods of death). Classical appraisals of Liberation Theology consider some aspects such as the mistakes that have been committed in the economic analysis, the ex-centricity of faith as a non contested hermeneutical principle, however, the basic problem was that Liberationists felt impelled to work along the lines of a Systematic Theology. Perhaps this was after all, unavoidable, due to the ex-centric tensions that pervade theology, as we already have seen. But to systematize was to make categories fit in the classical theological system, to make them decent. Theology of Liberation has been and still is a subversive theology, but not a transgressive one.

Doing theology from the people, and doing it from the excluded masses in urban Latin-American cities such as Buenos Aires, is an indecent act. What is more indecent than the trans-sexuality of Jesus as presented in *Santa Librada*? Or than the prayer which calls Jesus "You, beautiful woman, who never did anything wrong but were crucified by the army?" Or than the worship of Lord Death? The real post-colonial and post-modern challenge comes from there, although we must bear in mind that in my home-country there are vast places, even whole regions, where people are still living in quasi medieval conditions.

3. *The Metaphysics of Accountancy Contested*

The post-modern challenges for the excluded are the following. First, there is the question about time. The old concept of *Concientización Popular* in Liberation Theology anticipated the deconstruction of the pseudo-reality that is actuality. Its goal was for the poor to articulate precisely the differences between actuality and the presence of the present. The whole work of Basic Communities (BCs or *comunidades de base*) was the opposite to the Derridian concept of "time that can be seen". The Metaphysics of Accountancy needs visible results, organized in the logic of capitalist success. "Time which can be seen" is manifested in work, which produces more people in the church, more money, more fame for the denomination, more buildings, more furniture etc. But the Basic Communities did not work with that logic. Some BCs worked for years with ten members; they brought disrepute to the church in the eyes of the government or the Vatican, and they were extraordinarily poor. They represented "wasted time"; for that reason when Basic Communities were introduced to the churches in Europe, they needed to be re-presented to fit with actuality: the news was spread that the BCs were expanding, in ridiculously exaggerated numbers, as high as ten thousand alone in Brazil, with hundreds of people per community, doing "visible" activities, easy to evaluate. Accountant Metaphysics. But the excluded time needs to be taken apart from the current distribution of time made by the

Media. They push time to more political limits. Let us take the example of the 30 thousand people who disappeared during the seventies in Argentina as a product of the National Security Doctrine. An amnesty has been declared for those responsible for the massacres; this amnesty covers military, civilian and church representatives. The argument used by the Media boils down to, "Let the past rest". Some people ask with irony "How many years must pass for us to be able to start again, without being haunted by the memory of the things that happened a long time ago?"

Outside the Presidential Palace, every Thursday, you can see an elderly woman amongst others, with a white scarf and a home-made placard saying, *"Con vida los llevaron; con vida los queremos"* (Alive they were when they took them away, alive we want them back). Excluded time: the disappearances are not part of the past, but of the present, because there are not meaningful events (events of justice) produced to justify that time is moving on. In fact, time has stopped in Buenos Aires. This reminds us of our dialogue with Carlos: "How many years have you been in Buenos Aires?" ("Some months... four years".). If there is no justice, there are not meaningful events produced. There are important clues here for the dismantling of actuality.

A second post-modern challenge is shown in the indifference of the excluded towards the Grand Narratives of Fatherland and Church. Their reversal of Christianity is a manifestation of their search for the referent in the religious discourses; a referent that is always material and measurable. Their answer to the present circumstances is different from that of Liberation Theologians. While the new Vatican policies dismantle Basic Communities and popular work and the economic situation in Latin America deteriorates, Liberationists look for a theological motive in the Bible. They read the Book of Job, and cry to God for the fate of the just person in the New Global Order. The excluded, however, do not read Job. Their Christianity is reversed and material, and easily deconstructed when required.

The post-colonial challenge was taken up by Liberationists. Gutiérrez was influenced by his friend, the famous indigenist writer, José María Argüedas, who wrote from the perspective of the spirituality of the Peruvian nations. Yet, theology carries with itself its own conceptual limitations. Jesus could be presented as an Aymara man, dressed in traditional clothes, *poncho* over his shoulder and a *chullo* over his head. Or as a mine worker, sharing lunch with other workers with their faces covered in coal dust. This was accepted and even inspiring after centuries of Anglo-Saxon representations of Jesus the King or, even more adequate for countries which do not have historical experiences of monarchy, Jesus the State. However, finding a Jesus of/for the excluded is a rather complex task, because it would be indecent to present Jesus as a child sniffing *Poxipol* (a brand of cheap glue) or being forced into prostitution at lunch time. Therefore we have the post-colonial reversal: Jesus-woman caught by the police; Jesus-Death, as the final word of justice. A word of caution though; the superimposition of Jesus into St Death or *Librada* is gradually fading away and will probably disappear leaving only St Death and *Librada* on their own. There are still mechanisms of legitimization projected into ancient forms of worships such as St Death. Post-colonial criticism counterbalances the ambivalence towards factuality in the post modern understanding of truth.

IV. NEGOTIATING LIBERATION FOR THE SAKE OF TRANSGRESSION

"Drink freedom... Yesterday, I dreamt about the hungry people, about the crazy ones, about the people who are in exile and in jail... Drink freedom; carry it with you: you could become corrupted, or just forgetful, but freedom will never let you down It is necessary to keep singing".

Charlie García, *Inconsciente Colectivo.*

I belong to a generation of Liberation Theologians who have been inspired by the National Rock-n-Roll Movement back home. Popular music has been and still is a theological resource in Latin America. Freedom was the objective of Liberation Theology; liberation was the path towards freedom. Freedom has never been negotiable; liberation, hopefully, yes, because paths are contextual and therefore must change according to different historical circumstances. Early on, during the beginning of the first decade of the seventies Juan Luis Segundo, an Uruguayan theologian, said that Jesus had certainly hit the head on the nail when he spoke about freedom, but that he had not had a suitable strategy of liberation. Jesus committed strategical mistakes, like Jeremiah who was a bad politician.

Any assessment of Liberation theology in the light of post-modern and post-colonial criticism needs to be done by assessing liberation, not freedom. Liberation as a hermeneutical circle in itself changes when acquiring new levels of consciousness because if it did not we would be talking of a "vicious circle" instead of an interpretative one. Currently, as I have briefly mentioned it before, such assessments are taking into consideration the lack of rigor in the economic analysis done by Liberationists, and also the fact that post-colonial criticism has been ignored.

The point that I have in mind here is that liberation as a concept in itself obeys certain masters, a certain framework of thought which in the end regulates the available strategies for freedom, even pre-emptying the notion of freedom in itself. Freedom must always come from the collective unconscious of our people: "Yesterday I dreamt about the hungry, the crazy, about the people who are in exile or in jail...". Pablo Neruda expressed it in a poem that the revolution happened in Chile only after the jails were full of dark brown eyes; the eyes of the excluded. It is exclusion which is the category which breaks with paths of liberation when they become obsolete.

1. *Heterosexuality*

What do the notion of freedom and the strategies of liberation have in common, according to Liberation Theology? That these concepts are worked out from a heterosexual perspective. I deliberately prefer to use here the concept of Heterosexuality instead of Patriarchalism, because the former is more transparent in its denunciation of dualist thinking. Patriarchalism sometimes becomes an opaque term, not clear enough to disarticulate the basic elements which precisely sustain Patriarchal faith and politics. My point is that Liberation Theology has not been able to transgress the borders of the sexual zones of politics, economics and religion in Latin America. Oppression in Latin America is not merely an economic phenomenon but it is essentially rooted in the religious and cultural heritage of our continent. That religious and cultural heritage is heterosexual. At the roots of political and economic systems in Latin America we are always confronted with the ideology of *Marianismo* (a conceptual frame based on the gender relation between Our Lady, i.e. the Virgin Mary, and God the Father and Son), which supports the objectification of women and men in our society. Macroeconomics is guided by dualistic principles of tradable and un-tradable goods. The gender-based division of labor has not suffered any major contestation in Latin America. The production of theology and the legal systems (including the Church as legal dispenser of the sacred) are masculine constructions. Terms such as "costs", "productivity", "efficiency", "God", "prayer" are ambiguous. There can be a transferring of costs from paid economy to unpaid economies all the time. Christianity could be increasing in Latin America, while Latin-Americans are getting de-spiritualised and spiritually more colonized than ever. Statistics are difficult to analyze.

Theology of Liberation did not work from an ethnocentric base where sex was comparable to destiny. However, although the praxis of Liberation

Theologians was linked to awareness-raising programs it never arrived at a gender and development approach. It never considered the epistemological implications of the critique to Heterosexuality, or the spiritual implications. Or how the belief in a particular teenager's virginity in Palestine, against the odds of advanced pregnancy, centuries ago was a determining factor for the creation of concentration camps in Argentina during the seventies. But the point is that Liberation Theology cannot *incorporate* the feminist epistemology, which I believe is at the core of any Transgressor Theology. To incorporate or to take on board some feminist concerns would finally kill Liberation Theology because it would send it back to a colonial model where master and slave coexist, in an unfair sharing, in the construction of reality but, still, the slave is given permission to exist within the boundaries of dependency. A Transgressor Theology needs to modify the path of liberation. The fact that people in the streets of Buenos Aires do not speak any more about "liberation" but about "transgression" (which prompted a friend of mine to ask me "Are they reading Bataille?") and that to be a transgressor is considered a status point shows how contested has become the field of Liberation Theology.

The Transgression Theology of the excluded has a deconstructive and constructive phase. Still social identity needs to be further fractured, to break with the identity built by actuality via the Media. Today the Media are represented by radio, cinema, and TV, which in Latin America are religious spaces of discourse. Moreover, since the xvth century the Pulpit and the confessional box have been the Media, which have re-presented reality without contestation. As part of this, there is a growing understanding of contextual values in theology as constitutive values. Theology should be determined by data from the present, and not by actuality. For instance, let us take the example of the value of human life in Latin America. Many people die in the streets of Latin-American cities every day: children get killed, their body parts are sold; women are raped; people are killed in drug abuse cases, in gang wars. Yet nobody becomes a martyr by sudden death, although people ordained into ministerial ecclesial positions seem to have always had more easy access to death and martyrdom status, not always more justified than a killing of innocents at lunch time. However, when Father Mugica was killed after presiding at Mass in a slum of Buenos Aires and Bishop Angelleli was assassinated when travelling with a suitcase containing papers related to the abuse of Human Rights perpetrated by the dictatorship in Argentina, actuality constructed theology. They were Communist, therefore, atheists, therefore, enemies of the Fatherland, the Family and the Church.

And "The Army is your friend and the defender of Western, Christian values". The pocket narratives were distributed in a hurry, and the Media changed the news after few hours, thus declaring that such deaths were not part of Actuality any longer.

2. *The Memory of the Transgressors Undermines Actuality*

The transgressor always keep the memory, the presence. If justice has not been done, the event is unfinished. Years ago, the sign-post bearing the name of the street where I lived was crossed out with paint one morning and a new name was written on it: "Father Mugica Street". The famous words of the revolutionaries such as "Romero is alive" or "Evita is alive" are dismantlers of Actuality *per excellence*. When the poor, the marginalized and the excluded get together for a political demonstration, denouncing corruption and injustice while singing "We can feel it: Evita is amongst us", one can understand how actuality is a construction, and how people contest it with passion. In the case of Evita, she exemplifies the deconstruction of post-colonialism, sexism and the church's ideology, and those are the issues which people are still trying to work with.

To conclude, let us say that the heterosexuality of Liberation Theology is the heterosexuality of Christianity. This is why a Transgressor Theology in the end, must announce the end of Christianity, or at least, its *Kenosis*, its self-emptying process. The discussion of the new paradigms of Liberation Theology, such as the cultural one, announces in a way such a *Kenosis*, although I think that the ex-centric element of faith in Christianity will not allow any genuine dialogue between Gospel, race, class, culture and sexuality. Paulo Freire spoke about the need of the teacher, at a certain point, to relinquish her authority in the class, in order to allow her students to take up their own responsibility for the teaching process. Freire used for this the metaphor of the teacher allowing the students to kill her, but not committing suicide before her time[4]. There is, after all, a question of timing and responsibilities here, and the students cannot be expected to take control over their learning processes before they are prepared for that.

Perhaps this is a useful metaphor to finish our reflections. We have seen issues of post-modern and post-colonial criticism intersecting with Liberation Theology, but, in this case, from the perspective of the excluded masses in Buenos Aires. We have considered how a theology

---

4. Cf. P. FREIRE & I. SHOR, *A Pedagogy of Liberation*, London, Macmillan, 1987, p. 37.

of transgression has been announced "under the bridges", and we arrived at the conclusion that theology of liberation cannot and will never be a theology of transgression because this is a second step, and one that must be taken independently. If Liberation Theology is being superseded, let us wait until it gets killed. It would be too soon to commit suicide, and unnecessary. But in preparation for this final *Kenosis*, the *Kenosis* of Christianity in Latin America, Liberation Theology needs to undermine any trace of systematization and of colonialism still remaining, above all, of heterosexuality. In a way, nothing has changed: we never left "Egypt", and we have never really experienced any Exodus from the lands of bondage, on the contrary, we still dream about the hungry and the crazy. And we pray with the excluded the prayer against structural oppression: "St Death, death to my enemies, the ones who reduced my people to madness, jails and hunger; and to heterosexual religion, which supported fascist governments and dictatorships dividing the world between women and men, nature and history, fallen and redeemed, Communists and Christians. May a transgressor, indecent, non-heterosexual theology guide us to the departure from the old colonial gods, including the World Bank and the Structural Adjustment Program, around which actuality theology is currently made".

A famous psychotherapist from Buenos Aires, Alfredo Moffat, who has dedicated his life to working with the excluded in our society told me one day that when you work with the marginalized, you end up becoming marginalised. This seems to me the price that theology must pay for relevance to the present, not to the actual. Theology must embody exclusion, and perhaps this is one of the meanings of the cross of Jesus which we might well consider (*if* torture can have a meaning): that the final, sacrificial *Kenosis* of Christianity is unavoidable when the symbolic system is contested, and that resurrection must be a resurrection of transgression as the only possibility of real transformation for the people who, at this moment, are "talking *some* Bataille" under the bridges of Buenos Aires.

University of Edinburgh   Marcella ALTHAUS-REID
New College, Mound Place
Edinburgh, EH1 2LX, Scotland

12

CLASH BETWEEN GLOBALIZATION
AND LOCAL CULTURES

I have been asked to evaluate the ideas put forward in the Discussion Paper of this congress. My opinions are those of an outsider and are based on my expertise in the fields of International Relations and most of all in Social and Cultural Anthropology.

When an anthropologist returns from the field, after having studied some foreign culture whose ideas and ways seem strange to his own, he is often asked: what have you learned? The anthropologist, if he is sincere, will most often reply: I have learned to understand better my own culture. If my reply to the Discussion Paper as an outsider should contain strange, or even offensive ideas to the participants and the readers of my paper, I hope that these will have the same result: a better understanding of their own ideas by those individuals and their organizations professionally engaged in the field this congress is about.

The purpose of a Discussion Paper is to put forward a vision, an analysis that stimulates further thinking, that challenges the reader to respond and forces him to muster up his knowledge and experience to do just that. This is what the Discussion Paper does. Moreover, it covers an enormous amount of space and time. The analysis goes back in time as far as the early 17th century, the dawn of modernity. It dwells on recent events and their impact, symbolized by the fall of the Berlin wall. And it opens a vision of the future: post-modernism and globalization. Globalization is the hinge between time (the future) and space (the whole planet). The commentator may call himself lucky that outer space and its future have been left out. Having but a limited space and only a short time at my disposal, I will not comment on everything in the Discussion Paper.

I. The Subject Matter

On June 7, 1494, after the mediation of Pope Alexander VI, a line was drawn over the all but accurate map of the world, and an agreement was made that the part of the world to the east belonged forever to Portugal, and to the west to Spain (Treaty of Tordecillas). The consequence of this totemistic behavior – dividing social space while at the same time freezing time is one of the characteristic features of moiety systems common among e.g. Australian aboriginals[1] – has provoked a movement in Latin America during the later 1960s and which became known as the theology of liberation.

In the 1970s, it became fashionable to speak of the North-South Divide. A conference of states was even held, if I remember, in Cancun, Mexico, to find the means to bridge that gap. The means were not found. Odd enough, some of the southernmost states in the world, Australia and New Zealand, sided with the North. Others, situated north of the equator, sided with the south. One is strangely reminded of a saying by the ancient Chinese sage Hui Shih: "I know the center of the world. It is north of Yen and south of Yueh"[2]. Yen is actually situated in the north of China and Yueh in the south. In both cases, odds and ends from the language of geography were used to fix another language, to concoct a story on a metaphorical level which – in the case of Cancun – probably meant the rich and the poor countries. The only problem was an agreement couldn't be reached as to which countries were rich and which were poor. Failing to find a diacritic, the equator was used, and at the same time not used. Space was divided in such a way that it was also divided in a different fashion. That is how myths are fabricated[3].

When this myth became obsolete, another one was created. All of a sudden there were three worlds. Of course, these were not the three worlds known since time immemorial: heaven, earth and the underworld. After all, we are moderns: we think rationally. Space was no longer divided into opposing moieties, but acquired a tryiartite structure. The division of space was no longer derived from the language of geography but from that of the Olympic games. At the Olympic games, only three athletes qualify in the end: the first (gold medal), the second (silver medal) and the third (bronze medal). By dividing space according to the performance of the countries occupying that space, there are no losers (though from the fourth place downwards, there are no medals). In the new rhetoric of the three worlds, they are not equally economically performative, but all of them win medals. But unlike at the real Olympic games, the countries constituting the first world always won the gold medals. Thus, the countries belonging to the second world did everything imaginable – including the massive use of drugs – to beat the first world in the real Olympic games. A metaphor was actually fighting in the material world to change the metonymy in the semantic world.

1. C.L. STRAUSS, *La penseé sauvage*, Paris, PUF, 1969, chapter 2.
2. F. YOULAN, *A Short History of Chinese Philosophy*, New York, Free Press, 1966, p. 86.
3. C.L. STRAUSS (n. 1), chapter 1.

The Princes of the church have recommended, in successive conferences, to analyze what in reality is a mixed bag of countries and cultures,
including Guatemala, Chile, Bangladesh, Indonesia, Sierra Leone and South
Africa. While Medellín stressed the need for socio-economic analysis,
more recent conferences and writings shift attention to cultural analysis.

For the cultural anthropologist, this is a puzzling statement. It suggests
the outlook of a feudal lord who tells his serfs: "Up to now you have
always worked in the potato fields. From now on you will take care of
the wheat, and next month you will work in the strawberry fields". This
may indeed be common in agriculture. However, is it also applicable to
human cultures?

Suppose I get this commission to study, for example, say the Inuit
(Eskimo): "You shall not study however, so the commission says, the
hunting and what they do with the catch: food, clothing, tools, housing
and so on (the material culture). You shall also disregard social culture:
groups, kinship, marriage and so forth. Just concentrate on culture.
(Meaning what? Language, songs, rituals, myths, religion?)". If that were
the task, I would have to decline the commission: how could I possibly
understand language, myths, rituals and the like (spiritual culture?) without
reference to or without studying of material and social culture? Human
culture is a connected whole, though divided perhaps in to sub-cultures.
I might distinguish between macro-, meso-, and micro- levels of culture,
but I could never disconnect material, social and spiritual culture at any
level without putting understanding as such in jeopardy. Description is not
analysis. It is perhaps possible to shift emphasis on the level of description,
like focusing attention on one figure in a picture instead of another, but
on a paradigmatic level, you cannot do so without losing sight of the picture as a whole. In practice, globalization is not an encroachment on one
aspect of local culture. It dislocates the whole of that culture.

II. MODERNITY VERSUS TRADITION

The Discussion Paper proposes a view of modernity and its advent
that is widespread and certainly not wrong. Changes in our way of ordering the universe were also brought about by great men, the Napoleons of
physics and philosophy. Other discourses are possible too, for example,
that of Michel Foucault, who stresses parallel and contemporaneous
changes in the paradigms in biology, linguistics and economics[4]. Fernand

4. M. FOUCAULT, *Les mots et les choses*, Paris, Gallimard, 1966.

Braudel points out the importance of changes in economic praxis[5]. Financial capitalism originated as betting on ships and their cargo. Galileo's famous spy-glass was used to spot incoming ships before anyone else so that one can then buy shares. Galileo only had the idea to point it to the sky one night. I sincerely wonder which practice has changed the world more. At any rate, financial capitalism has retained its horse-betting character, as witnessed by the Barings Bank and Sumitomo Company scandals. So much for rationality.

But how would, for example, a Japanese discourse on the advent of modernity sound? It would no doubt have to start with the Meiji Restoration (1868), a return to the old days when the emperor supposedly reigned supremely. The discourse would mention the return to the ancient values: the Great Learning, the Five Relations, Family, the obligation (ON) to repay the gifts (NGIRI) bestowed by successive generations of ancestors on their offsprings. In fact, none of the pillars mentioned in the European discourse have played a role in Japan's astonishingly rapid rise as a major Eastern power in the late 19th and early 20th centuries.

How would the discourse of an Arab be? Or that of a Chinese? Did not Europe borrow extensively from their science and their technology? Were they never modern?

A cross-cultural comparison might lead to the conclusion that European modernity was pushed forward by the greed, of individuals (merchant-adventurers as they were called in England) unbridled because of the weakness of the state, and legitimized by the bible's story of the conquest of the promised land. So much for the virtue of abstract thinking.

By implication, there is a hidden agenda in the discourse of modernity which in a discourse about the non-moderns, those who got no medals, the traditional societies. These societies constitue "The world on the wane", as the Anglo-American translation of "Tristes Tropiques" by Claude Lévi-Strauss aptly puts it. Of course, each traditional culture is unique, like the DNA profile of an individual. Modern societies are also unique but their DNA profiles point to various degrees of kinship. Stretching the comparison a bit, we can nevertheless point to a few basic, chemical elements in the composition of the DNA of traditional societies. There are cultures, societies, communities but not states.

Traditional culture lives off the land. It is provided for by nature itself. Space, for these cultures, is perceived as a sacred landscape. "The confrontation of the pre-Hispanic Mesoamerican cultures with their natural

5. F. BRAUDEL, *Civilisation matérielle et capitalisme (XVe-XVIIIe siècles)*, Paris, Colin, 1967.

environment (sky and earth) was a two-fold dialectical one. Truly precise observation and correct prediction of natural phenomena were intimately fused with a magical attitude and an explanation of the cosmos in mythical terms. Thus by cosmovision we understand those notions about nature and society that were combined into a coherent structural whole and were characterized precisely by this intimate fusion between the exact observation of nature, on the one hand, and myth, magic and ritual on the other"[6].

Space is at the same time a social space. It is filled with groups (bands, lineages, clans, villages, neighboring tribes) who have definite rules of communication and exchange. Marriage rules in Australian band societies are so complicated, and yet logical, that it has been very difficult (for us) to decode these. Attitudes towards each other and towards possessions are radically different, if not the opposite, from our capitalistic attitudes:

> "A Bushman will go to any lengths to avoid making other Bushmen jealous of him, and for this reason the few possessions the Bushmen have are constantly circling among members of their groups. No one cares to keep a particularly good knife too long, because he will become the object of envy... Their culture insists that they share with each other, and it has never happened that a Bushman failed to share objects, food or water with other members of his band, for without very rigid cooperation Bushmen could not survive the famines and droughts that the Kalahari offers them"[7].

Yet with these "limitations", they have created the original affluent society[8]. With their form of knowledge based on the logic of the senses, they have laid the foundations of our civilization: agriculture, cattle-breeding, pottery, weaving, conservation and preparation of food and so on[9]. They also developed ethical rules, of which the taboo on incest has spread worldwide.

When modernity intrudes in this space – it usually starts with encroachment on the land – this leads to a loss of meaning, a breakdown of social relations, and thus to cultural genocide. In some cases even – the fate of the American Indians is well known[10] – modernity has led to outright genocide. The quest for timber and all kinds of natural resources by insatiable capitalism worldwide will inevitably destroy these cultures.

---

6. J. BRODA, *The Sacred Landscape* in CARRASCO, D. (ed.), *To Change Place: Aztec Ceremonial Landscape*, Berkeley, University of California, 1991, p. 79. See also C.L. STRAUSS (n. 1), Chapter 6.

7. M. SAHLINS, *Stone Age Economics*, Chicago, Aldine, 1972, pp. 211-212.

8. *Ibid.*

9. C.L. STRAUSS (n. 1), p. 310.

10. A. DEBO, *A History of the Indians of the United States*, Oklahoma, The University of Oklahoma Press, 1970.

III. The Theology of Liberation and Marxism

Profoundly marked by his Hegelian roots, Marx believed that, in his time, the slave would finally topple his master. Capitalism had created self-conscious workers, on the one hand, and had brought them together in large factories, the very condition necessary for their organization, on the other hand. It would take only one step to expropriate the expropriators.

As for the poor, unemployed mass of slum dwellers, they were not self-conscious, and nothing could be done with them as far as the coming revolution was concerned. They constituted the "lumpenproletariat" (lump = idiot). The same was true for the large army of poor peasants and farmhands: it was impossible to organize them, for they had no cohesion, no social consciousness. They were a bag of potatoes.

The spread of capitalism around the world was a good thing. It would liberate various peoples from their false consciousness, by which earlier modes of production held them captive. In other words, this view or theory of Marx is in essence the opposite of what the theology of liberation is concerned with: the poor and downtrodden, on the one hand, and dependency theory on the other. Looking at the praxis of these theologians, an analogy with three variations of Marxism seems obvious.

a) For Lenin, as for Gutiérrez, the self-conscious working class was too small. Self-consciousness had to be brought to the masses from outside by professional revolutionaries. Why had the self-conscious workers in the highly industrialized world not (yet) made the revolution? Because they had been bribed by letting them share in the profits that capitalism made in the exploitation of the colonies. Lenin asserted this in "Imperialism: The Highest Stage of Capitalism". It was Lenin who laid the foundations for the dependency theory.

b) Guevara believed that the way towards self-consciousness could be reached by taking up arms and fighting a guerrilla war against the establishment. Armed struggle (or taking part in it one way or another) would liberate the minds of the passive campesinos, as it would liberate them from exploitation. This was, obviously, the way of Camilo Torres also.

c) For Mao Zedong, revolutionaries should not teach the masses, but on the contrary, mix with them. Above all, learn from them in a constant dialectical process. This "learn from the masses" is strangely reminiscent of the praxis advocated by Leonardo Boff.

It should be noted that none of these Marxist leaders achieved much by the methods they apparently used. If they achieved power in the end ("made the revolution"), it was for other reasons, and no one following their teachings achieved the same result. Guevara himself tried, in vain, to emulate the Cuban revolution in the Congo and in Bolivia.

I once asked a group of student leaders from various socialist countries which country was closest to communism. After some discussion, they replied – much to my surprise – that it was undoubtedly Sweden. Although this is but an anecdote, it shows an awareness that their system was still far away from reaching general welfare.

Where did that system come from? Lenin, once in power, had little idea as to how to introduce "communism" in the Soviet Union. Now, in 1917, the Germans had won the war against Russia with the help of a by centralized planning of their economy (large enterprises, mines, banks) under the direction of the WUMBA[11], led by Raathenau and Ludendorff. Lenin and his co-leaders borrowed the idea and called their central institution *Gosplan*. Stalin, finally, sold Gosplan to the world as socialism. With the fall of the Berlin Wall, this myth crumbled down too.

With the fall of the Soviet Union, there is no longer a direct or indirect threat against the worldwide spread of capitalism. Investors in foreign countries need no longer fear expropriation (rationalization). Regimes which would do so can no longer be protected by the "second world", and their products no longer have access to that market as an alternative to the capitalist market. Only internal instability, as in the case of many African countries, will prevent the spread of global capitalism in some parts of the world. In Africa, most strikingly in the Islamic world, there is a struggle for power going on between new groups (fundamentalists) and the leaders who gained power during and after the struggle for the liberation from colonialism[12]. Fundamentalists, although not always the enemy of industrialization as such, want a return to "authenticity", and offer this alternative to the people disillusioned with the economic, political and ideological systems introduced by their post-colonial leaders. It will be difficult for foreign capitalistic enterprises to intrude and invest in these parts of the globe in the foreseeable future.

IV. Globalization and the Welfare State

What Marx welcomed and Lenin loathed, the globalization of the world economy under capitalistic market conditions, is rapidly becoming a fact (turbo-capitalism) with the exception of the cases mentioned

11. Waffen und Munitions Beschaffungs Amt: Arms and Ammunition Procurement Agency.
12. E.W. Said, *Culture and Imperialism*, New York, Knopf, 1993.

above. What this means is analyzed in the Discussion Paper, and follows the analysis made by Anthony Giddens. Most of this analysis is probably true.

But Giddens is British, probably a Wasp, living in post-Thatcherite England. It is from this vantage-point that he looks towards the future: there is little difference between Tony Blair and John Major, between left and right. And the welfare state is finished.

Now the capitalist system – one does not need Marx to see this – does not only produce wealth for those participating in it but also inequality and, above all, exclusion. It is the logic of the system which is qualified by Lord Keynes somewhere as that of a crazy lover of cats who loves his cat, but the kittens of the cat more, and still more the kittens of these kittens and so on and so forth, till the end of cathood. Left to itself, not restricted and corrected by a democratic state, capitalism also produces poverty and misery for many. What made capitalism acceptable in the past and even today was precisely the welfare state, which redistributed wealth – however tentatively – at least to some extent. No one will claim that there isn't mismanagement, bureaucracy, corruption or that there is no urgent need for reform. But I do not see any alternative to the welfare state except a return to private charity that produces even more uncertainty and dependency. There is in fact some sort of alternative that is on the rise at a turbo-speed of its own: globalized crime, which in a way is a form of capitalism at its worst, as it deals in illicit commodities and services.

State-sponsored welfare has its roots neither in the left nor in the right. Bismarck was, if anything, a reactionary who needed for his wars healthy soldiers who would be cared for even better than those of Napoleon (who founded the Hôtel des Invalides, which still exists in France) before him. But as a by-product, as it were, of Bismarck's state-sponsored welfare schemes, a welfare state was created in European countries by improving and expanding the institutions created by the Iron Chancellor. It took a lot of discussions, improvisation, social struggle and the Great Depression of the 1930s – followed by the second world war – before the welfare state, as we know, it came into being. Somehow the idea was never popular in the USA, perhaps solidarity is not compatible with the Protestant work ethic. As a result, large groups of the US population live in fact in Third-World conditions. Many who have menial jobs are poor, the latter is the true Mc Donaldization of the world.

In the next century, only one-fifth of those looking for a job will produce all the commodities and services the world "needs". That means that four in five will have no income, and will starve without welfare provisions[13]. Is it really in the interest of capitalism itself to produce in the cheapest place the cheapest possible commodities (i.e. massive evasion of taxes on labor and profits) by as few workers as possible? Does not "rationalization" on the side of supply in the end, kills off the demand? Now and in the near future, Marx's theory –as expounded in the first volume of "The Capital"[14] – will be put to the test. To check this evolution, a global WUMBA or *Gosplan* – supposedly sponsored by the UN – seems both utopian and undesirable. So the state and all states that care for the welfare of their peoples still have an important role to play.

Who on earth has the organization and authority to play the international role required to check international capitalism and international institutions (like the IMF and the World Bank) in their narrow economic outlook? Does not the Roman Catholic Church gained vast experience in the struggle for justice, better wages, material conditions, and a decent life for all, in Europe and elsewhere ever since "Rerum Novarum"? Were not the Christian Democrats, together with the Social Democrats successful in the construction and defense of the welfare state?

Finally: is there no need for a socio-economic analysis, at least along these lines?

V. Towards One Global Culture?

It is fashionable to predict one global culture for the future. This may indeed happen in the long run. As Keynes used to say: "in the long run, we are all dead". Satellite television, the Internet and other means of communication may offer a global access to the same information, but there are obvious limits: the language problem and the costly infrastructure(hardware, software, and the service itself) are but two of them.

There are also cultural limits or cultural mechanisms that work against the globalization of culture. I will briefly point out some of these, each with a poignant illustration. The list is far from complete, it is just something to think about.

1. *Selective Transmission of Information to Different Cultures.*

The last Olympic games in Atlanta was a truly global event, watched by billions of viewers on TV. But in fact, no two countries saw the same games. Americans living in Europe complained that channels focused

13. M.R. SCHUMANN, *Die Globalisierungsfalle*, in *Der Spiegel* 39 (1996) p. 90.
14. K. MARX, *The Capital*, Moscow, Foreign Languages Publishing House, no date.

too much on French, German, Belgian, etc... athletes, while Europeans living in the United States complained only the performance of US athletes seemed to matter to the NBC network. In Islamic countries, most female competitions were banned from the screen. Swimming did not feature prominently in Africa for a different reason: there were no African competitors. South Africa, of course, was an exception. But Africans watched the soccer competition with great interest and Nigeria won. That same competition was given hardly any attention on American TV and also in the Far East. And in that latter part of the world, it was all Ping-Pong and judo coverage.

2. Selective Perception of the same Information in Different Cultures.

In the 1920s and 1930s, Europe and especially Germany was rocked by workers' struggles which were shown in Soviet cinema-theaters. The Russians, who still considered the German workers as the most conscious, most sophisticated, and most "kuturny" among the world proletariat, were amazed when they saw the German workers dressed in neat but heavy overcoats and wearing borsalino hats. The vanguard of the Russian proletariat, i.e., the top leadership, started to wear the same clothes and it became a kind of uniform in Eastern Europe after the events in 1945-48.

In the 1950s and after, the fashion in the West changed. No one dressed like that anymore. Only in the gangster movies about the bootlegging period and in popular TV-series like 'The Untouchables' of that period were people (the mobsters) dressed like that. Newsreels in the West showed the top leadership of the communist world dressed like Al Capone and his cronies. Here was, indeed, the empire of evil.

3. Selective Use of the same Product by Different Cultures.

There are few products with a wider global distribution than certain American soft drinks such as Coca-Cola. A colleague of mine assured me that in Africa, e.g. in Ghana, these drinks were (also) popular for their alleged contraceptive capacity. The 'logic' behind it was:

> The white man does drink a lot of soft-drinks
> The white man has few children
> Ergo: soft drinks are a good contraceptive.

4. Selective Impact of Information within the same Culture.

In October 1996 another colleague presented her Ph.D. thesis on the impact of education among Turkish immigrant women in Belgium. As

predicted women who had only low-grade education in special immigrant schools were not integrated, were dedicated followers of Islam and
lived among themselves in a Turkish network of their own. Women who
had higher education were better integrated, had Belgian friends, and
participated in Belgian activities. But, oddly enough, these better integrated women were the precisely the ones who dreamed of returning to
Turkey; while those who were not integrated wanted to stay in Belgium.
Immigration, another globalization phenomenon, seems to work against
one global culture.

5. *Selective Spread of Information within One Culture on the Macro- and Micro-Levels.*

In most Third-World countries, hard currency is hard to come by and
therefore much coveted. Sometime ago, friends of mine crossed the border into Zambia. One of their cars needed fuel so they split the money
they had changed at the customs office without any problem. The car
found a gas station in a small town several miles from the highway. When
they wanted to pay, it turned out that they had kept the local equivalent of
pennies and let the other group keep the pound notes (Kwatcha). So they
proposed to pay in US-dollars. However, no one in the small town had
ever seen US-dollars or even heard about it. My friends escaped jail only
because the fathers in a nearby missionary station had and were only to
glad to get some. Had this happened in Lusaka, people passing by would
have competed for the privilege to change the dollars.

6. *Tendency to Form sub-Groups and sub-Cultures.*

We have seen that even such small groups as Australian band societies tend to split in moieties. Although the United States seems to have
reached the stage of one, big culture, this only seems so on the surface.
As studies show[15], there is a tendency towards more divisions along
ethnic and racial lines. Religions and sects blossom. They create more
cultural boundaries around each group. Everyone seems to pick his own
tribe, as Desmond Morris argued in his TV-series, constituted by the
names and phone numbers in his agenda. Man is a gregarious animal, no
doubt, but he has a liking for small in-groups rather than for big herds
like those that the buffalo or wildebeest have.

---

15. MOYNIHAN, P. DANIEL & G. NATHAN, *Beyond the Melting Pot: The Negroes, Puerto Ricans, Italians and Irish of New York City*, Cambridge Mass., MIT Press, 1963.

VI. Towards Economic Globalization?

Now that 'socialism' (in fact: state monopole capitalism) has gone bankrupt, private capitalism and market economics do no longer have a performing competitor. In this sense, as far as one can see, the end of history has been reached. But, as Francis Fukuyama argues in his latest book[16], this is by no means the end of the story: capitalism is not the same everywhere as far as its form and structure are concerned.

Fukuyama compares development, form and structure of capitalism in a number of countries: the USA, Germany, Japan, France, Italy, Korea and China. Differences in the economic culture between those countries, and within some of them, cannot be explained by the usual materialistic economic analysis. There is another factor: social capital. Pre-industrial forms and conditions of cooperation, according to the author, seem to determine to a large extent the forms and conditions of cooperation in the capitalist system. The basic notion is trust: whom do you trust? Because it is only with those that you do trust, that you will enter into spontaneous cooperation.

Among African Americans, e.g., there is a very low degree of trust even within one family. As a result, they often fail as entrepreneurs. Even street-gangs put up a poor performance. In Mediterranean cultures – and in China – trust is centered in the family. Here we find a tendency towards the creation of family-businesses. Larger enterprises have to be state-sponsored. Only where there is a great deal of trust between individuals and a long tradition of spontaneous cooperation amongst them do we find large private enterprises: the USA, Germany, and Japan. In Japan, a high degree of loyalty even exists between different enterprises, has led to the building of networks ('keiretsu') that are difficult to penetrate. They prefer to trade with one another, even if competitors in the market offer better or cheaper commodities and services.

What Fukuyama shows is that social culture, based on tradition, is an important factor in building a capitalist economy. Global enterprises will therefore have to adapt to local cultural conditions, or else limit their expansion. In theory, as well as in practice, social culture may prevent private capitalism from taking root.

Fonteinstraat 137/35   Leo NAUWENS
B-3000, Leuven, Belgium

16. F. FUKUYAMA, *Trust*, London, Hamish Hamilton, 1995.

13

THEOLOGY AND THE POSTMODERN CONDITION
THE END OF CHRISTIAN TRUTH-CLAIMS?

Whenever one hears that we have shifted from one set of circum-stances or rules to another, one naturally wants to know where we have come and why. This leads just as naturally to an investigation of where it is we were and what it was about that time or place which made it untenable or obsolete. This sort of curiosity is certainly sharper when the shift in question is said to be a matter of "paradigms", a word which encourages us to envision side-by-side two wholly distinct characters, archetypes or, in the present case, systems of meaning and reflection. While the notion of a "shift" thus directs our curiosity to the uncertain and unsteady work of comparing and contrasting two things which are to some degree both related and distinct, the claim that it is a matter specifically of "paradigms" suggests that any apparent sameness will be somehow less important than one or more essential differences. The shift itself, one might say, has priority over any bridge built across it. This tells us in advance how to understand one part of the subtitle of G. De Schrijver's essay on the rationality of liberation theology: "From Socio-Economic Analysis to Cultural Analysis". According to the logic of paradigm shifts, liberation theology has either been forced to abandon, or given up forever, a specific form of analysis which, it turns out, has already been replaced by another. Whatever these two may seem to have in common, we must not forget that as distinct wholes they are incom-mensurable.

For the moment, let us only note the vision of history which this seems to imply – linear but discontinuous – and instead try to isolate the central question of the work. In general, the argument proceeds as follows: (1) responding to an experience of suffering attributed to exploitation by North-American and Western European economic powers, liberation theology, as developed first in Latin America, emerged from a desire for new means to inspire hope and dignity in those who suffer; (2) not finding everything necessary for this task in the traditional theology of the Church, liberation theologians turned to Marxism, an established opponent of the modern capitalism which they judged to be their real nemesis; (3) however, the rationality of Marxism itself shares with that of capitalism the same sort of universal pretensions which local, so-called "Third World" cultures and peoples had experienced as oppressive;

(4) the new synthesis of Catholic theology and Marxism thus contained significant points of agreement with the capitalism it opposed, a fact not entirely lost on the liberation theologians themselves; (5) still, this made it inevitable that the discrediting of Marxism occasioned by the fall of the Berlin Wall would also initiate a crisis in liberation theology; (6) with liberation theology therefore unclear about its own critical basis, the same worldview which emerged from the collapse of single, universal interpretive schemes has also left local, oppressed cultures vulnerable to Western capitalism, apparently the only such universal scheme impervious to that collapse. De Schrijver's worry is therefore unmistakable and, accepting the foregoing analysis, more than understandable: how or by what means can the Church still serve the poor and oppressed in today's world? In his essay, he addresses the political and economic variant of that question: how may we continue to instill hope and, where necessary, a revolutionary spirit in people suffering under regimes of injustice, whether anchored at home or, apparently more often, in the headquarters of multinational corporations (31-33; 71-80)?

It is certainly not my intention to challenge either the importance of these concerns or the instructiveness of the great wealth of information marshalled in support of them. Indeed, I would be remiss not to signal in advance the great service which De Schrijver has offered the dialogue between theology and contemporary post-Enlightenment philosophy simply by focussing it on issues confronting those who do not have the luxury of exploring either discourse. Still, I take it that the seriousness of this same gesture does not permit any hesitation in raising a number of questions. These can be arranged around two poles. I have already signalled the operative presence of a particular thesis about history. To this I add a discomfort at the important role assigned to sociology. As will become clear, these two points are closely related.

I. Vision of History

1. Context-Bound Rationality

To a significant degree, the claim that liberation theology faces a crisis of method hinges on the thesis that the Marxist principles once available to it have been essentially and permanently discredited. For De Schrijver, this is a matter of a loss in credibility in the modern, "master narratives" of which the Marxist theory of dialectical materialism is an especially vivid example. The fall of the Berlin wall will then have brought home to liberation theology what philosophers and sociologists have had to think about at least since the appearance of J.-F. Lyotard's *La condition postmoderne* more than a decade earlier, in 1979. For Lyotard and, following him, De Schrijver, our age is distinguished from modernity by the loss of a universal ground for legitimation. Here, what has been described as a paradigm shift has first to do with a change in consciousness. Statements are no longer couched in all-embracing frameworks claiming to account for all possible data, but are instead rooted only in local or even contingent contexts, with the result that rigor now demands that what one says is always already conditioned by a sense that its applicability is essentially limited. The consequences for the rationality of this new paradigm would then seem obvious. With regard to liberation theology, for instance, this would mean that, properly speaking, one's resistance to the forces of capitalism must draw not on an equally universal, rival theory of human rights and dignity, but the resources of the local tradition in which one lives and argues. Rationality, in short, appears only in specific, context-bound forms with no apriori claim over other forms rooted in other contexts. Thought through to the end, this picture of fragmented rationality abandons the familiar ideal of a 'best fit for the most data' in favor of attempts to work out the consequences of radical pluralism only within each local framework. Whereas Kant once sought the ground for legitimation in an "ultimate unity", Lyotard leads us to recognize as the postmodern condition of our knowing "ultimate heterogeneity" (39).

It bears repeating that whereas the evidence for these formulations has been gleaned from what is best referred to simply as contemporary *sensibility*, they are played out in the field of *rationality*. What is here called "postmodernity" is therefore a theory of knowledge built on a specific interpretation of what and how we experience the world around us today. In itself, of course, there is nothing particularly new about this. Just as Enlightenment thinkers took stock of their own lived situation and turned optimistically toward a social utopism to be achieved by human efforts alone, so now postmoderns respond to everyday evidence that that effort has failed with an account of experience and understanding basing itself on something other than that modern optimism. Postmodern rationality thus adds to a sensibility mistrustful of the modern spirit the additional conviction that that spirit is neither reliable nor necessary. Postmoderns do not hesitate to elevate this conviction to law: we today have at last realized that principles and values never have been and never could be universal. Be that as it may, this achievement is anything but reassuring: in contrast with the modern confidence and certitude which it leaves behind, postmodernity must be defined by a constant *lack of* confidence and certitude which, far from standing in the way of defending statements of our experience and desires, does not permit us a single moment of respite from constantly doing so. After modernity comes restlessness and insecurity. Truth and reason are essentially unstable, or better, "nomadic"[1].

The difficulty which this implies for both postmodern philosophy and, with it, post-Marxist liberation theology is readily apparent. The postmodern condition expresses the verdict of a historical shift which, paradoxically enough, puts an end to precisely the sort of claim necessary for postmodernity to be said true for all of us, both now and henceforth. This position displays both unexpected affinities with a number of the positions to which it reacts, and, beyond that, an ambivalence all its own. To begin with, one can not help noticing in the ulterior thesis of a self-grounding event – postmodernity as the general condition of a knowledge deprived of general conditions – a remarkable approach to the *causa sui* defended in very different contexts by, if not Aquinas, Descartes and Suarez. But in contrast with the certitude and purposiveness which those earlier arguments were thought to provide, it seems clear that the one thing which this postmodernity must always foreswear is a statement of fundamental aim, whether drawn from an archaic ground or directed by an overarching telos. In coming into existence strictly by disavowing the legitimacy of such a ground or telos, the postmodernity in question here has also relegated critique to a movement of negation stripped even of the right to say in advance precisely where it is going[2].

2. *Meta-Theory Gone Underground*

According to this perspective, what I have called the nomadic condition of postmodern rationality eludes every attempt to ground it in something else, leaving us to choose between either embracing what would thus seem to be the true nature of contemporary rationality or simply ignoring it. Of course, for postmoderns, this second attitude is not in fact a viable alternative. One either commits oneself to the free flow of statements, expressions and contentions or mistakenly pretends that things

1. I have taken this word from a Nietzschean defense of similar contentions by G. DELEUZE, *La pensée nomade*, in *Nietzsche aujourd'hui*, Paris, Union Générale d'Editions, 1973.
2. Cf. A. WELLMER, *Zur Dialektik von Moderne und Postmoderne*, Frankfurt, Suhrkamp, 1985, p. 57.

are otherwise. Since there is nothing to be gained from affirming this position except the alleged joy of a creativity emancipated from every commitment[3], it is more than fitting that its most enthusiastic proponents have occupied themselves at least as much with aesthetics as with traditional forms of religion, ethics and politics[4].

This free-playing aesthetic subject is only apparently close to its stated predecessor, the freely-choosing subject of modernity. Whereas, for example, Kant's analysis of individual subjectivity centers on a noumenal freedom from exterior influence in which he glimpses the possibility of making truly autonomous – or uninfluence – choices, the postmodern subject finds itself always already expelled from any and all contexts, and therefore compelled to always choose. If Kant has submitted free choice to the adoption of a definitive responsibility, certain strands of postmodernity would seem to have made the contrary move of defining responsibility according to a radically negative freedom. With this, the critical impulse of aesthetic postmodernity can be seen to consist in nothing more than evocation: the only way for a truly unconditioned freedom to awaken others to that same freedom for themselves without, however, imposing on them a definition or ideal which they *must* accept, is for those others to see the alleged joy of embracing it. One is powerless to refute the report of such emotions, but in themselves they are far from comprising anything like a viable critique of the mechanisms of oppression. For this to occur, it is necessary for those who report that joy to suppose that their listeners are capable of drawing the desired conclusions. And such discernment, in turn, requires a discourse, basic principles, and convictions which assert themselves in a way at least pretending to exceed the limits of any particular context. If, then, a sense of moral commitment and the criticism to which it gives voice in this sense continue to exceed the limits of the social or historical conditions

3. I write "alleged" with the lesson of Solzhenitsyn in mind. There is a cruel symmetry between this postmodern subject fated to always only choose and the victim of totalitarianism, deprived of anything depending on him or her alone. Though the precise reasons for this are no doubt opposed -dictators speak for all individual consciences, as the single voice of "the people"; postmoderns would have every such individual conscience speak entirely on its own – the two share a requirement that the individual abandon any personal attachment to fixed values or directives. The lessons of recent history thus make it far from clear that what some postmoderns would have us think of as 'joyful emancipation' will lead to anything but disenchantment, frustration and, in the end, malaise.

4. The most obvious example is Mark C. Taylor, but one also finds a pronounced tendency in a number of his associates to aestheticize works originally fitted to disciplines ranging from philosophy and literary theory to psychoanalysis and cultural anthropology. Given the political stakes brought out in the essay presently under consideration, the stylistic gesture seems far from innocent.

in which they occur, the definitive question of postmodernity asks not whether the truth one argues for has a universal extension, but instead how we are to understand the fact that we seem unable to do without it.

At times, De Schrijver comes close to endorsing these conclusions. "Meta-theory", he notes, "can not be dispensed with. The postmodernists simply push it underground, where it continues to function ..." (49)[5]. His sympathy with this passage is, however, only partial, as he himself immediately demonstrates by going on – only two lines further – to speak of the arrival of aesthetics in the place of ethics. Strictly speaking, there is no reconciling that sense of meta-theory with what we have already seen is the commitment by some postmoderns to a free-playing aesthetic subject, and in truth De Schrijver seems to have mentioned the former only as a means to clarify what belongs to the latter. Meta-theory, we are to see, has gone underground. This is not to say that it no longer exists, nor that it is invisible, but simply that rationality has evolved in a way which no longer admits it as a viable dimension of meaning or argumentation. In thus ruling out of play the deep structures of moral conscience and political conviction, where something non-negotiable urges itself on us, postmodernity reveals itself as explicitly and even – if there is to be any critical force in it at all – deliberately superficial[6]. Moreover, since this makes clear that the aversion to depth is also a lack of all anchors, such a postmodern condition is also through and through violent, in the sense in which anything can happen because all desires now exert themselves freely. To confine us to the surface is also to exclude any transcendental principle or authority. This is the universe of Nietzsche and perhaps Foucault, where there are only differences of powers and their constant conflict.

It is to be expected that what is presented as a theological reflection will try to distinguish this atomistic picture of humanity from the godless atomisms of both the Hobbesian "state of nature" and Nietzschean vitalism which it might otherwise seem to resemble. This move, complex and assumed, seeks at once and together new possibilities for social criticism and the rebirth of religion after the death of a God either projected from human desires or defined by human capacities. The general

---

5. De Schrijver citing D. HARVEY, *The Condition of Postmodernity. An Inquiry into the Origin of Cultural Change*, Cambridge, Blackwell, 1993, pp. 116-117 (Harvey, in turn, refers to F. JAMESON, *Postmodernism, or the Cultural Logic of Late Capitalism*, in *NLR* 146 (1984) 53-93).

6. This characterization comes from De Schrijver himself, who speaks of a "glitter on the surface" all the more insidious for obscuring our view of the power centers from which it emanates, and describes the difficulty of responding to capitalist exploitation in terms of a diminished "will to combat the enthrallment of the mirror palace".

thrust is toward a transcendence beyond the immanence of forces to which, according to De Schrijver, postmodernity confines us – but without pretending to reverse the historical process which has firmly lodged us there. The religious and social crisis of postmodernity will thus arise from an absence of the transcendence which alone can disrupt the "war of all against all" (Nietzsche) sufficiently for there to take root a critique of its violences.

II. SOCIOLOGY AS A SOURCE FOR THEOLOGIZING?

It is an unusual feature of De Schrijver's essay that it takes us to this point not only by way of the contemporary continental philosophers who have most often championed it, but also accompanied by an analysis of the capitalist "world-system" – an expression taken from Immanuel Wallerstein to summarize the way in which capitalism has acquired a global scope disregarding individual persons and communities. A benefit of this approach is its uncommonly clear demonstration that the forceful application of postmodern philosophies of radical difference – destroying every fixed and enduring principle they meet – have left many of us extremely vulnerable to exploitation by such a system. Hence the attraction of cultural analysis, and the importance of such related themes as inculturation and contextualization. Without objective principles to stand on, all that saves us from being completely devoured by the prevailing ideology is the identity which defines us at birth. De Schrijver puts his finger on this rather well: insofar as they antedate our insertion into the domain of economic exchange, cultural, ethnic, sexual and religious identity are innately resistant to capitalist exploitation. To be, for example, Nigerian, Muslim and female is to be rooted in a tradition in these many ways resistant to the identity imposed by the global marketplace.

One shortcoming of this approach, however, is that it often seems to allow sociological description to set the agenda for an analysis which then moves not to uncover the necessary conditions for that data but instead to locate it within a series of ever-widening spheres of influence and relations. The import of De Schrijver's enthusiasm for the field sociology is most evident in the nature of his brief response to John Milbank, a harsh critic of both liberation theology and, as it happens, the sociology of religion[7]. As De Schrijver reports it, Milbank is dissatisfied

---

7. J. MILBANK, *Theology and Social Theory: Beyond Secular Reason*, Oxford, Blackwell, 1995, especially pp. 245-249. Milbank attributes his inspiration for this argument to narrative theology (p. 241).

with the manner in which liberation theology first bases its social criticism on sociological reflection and only later, when necessary, appeals to theological principle. For Milbank, the field of sociology is itself thoroughly secular in a way which claims to have broken definitively with any connection to the religious narrative of Christian theology, so that what liberation theologians pretend to join as two parts of a single argument is then in fact, as he sees it, argument first from one tradition and then justification from a wholly different one. This charge, in turn, expresses a willingness to sharply isolate the Christian tradition from a rival secular tradition which leads Milbank himself to conclude that any *theology* of liberation must draw on the resources only or at least principally from the former of the two. According to Milbank, theology cannot and should not pretend to do without the meta-narrative dimension of its own Christian identity. De Schrijver is doubtful about this. Milbank's Christian tradition, he points out, would thus be a meta-narrative defined by its opposition both to each particular secular narrative and the – for Milbank – wholly secular character of the very idea of pluralism and particularity. Such a view of contemporary Christianity is at once postmodern in its willingness to admit and address the fact of that pluralism, and opposed to postmodernity in its continuing insistence on its own meta-narrativity. De Schrijver's question makes his own position unmistakable: can these claims still be maintained in a postmodern context (22)?

Plainly, the real stake of this disagreement is how theology can respond to the fall of modernity as a positive and irreversible event without simply recoiling into one or another version of sectarianism. De Schrijver and Milbank are in basic agreement that that event means quite simply that theologizing must henceforth be undertaken from a perspective informed of its own relativity. However, for Milbank this does not change the fact that truth-claims contain by necessity a universal extension. Meta-narrativity remains an indispensable – or, at any rate, *ineradicable* – part of theological rationality, even if theologians must also contend with the presence of rival, irreducible narratives. The very fact that De Schrijver questions these assertions gives the strong impression that for him the universal extension of truth-claims must not be merely qualified but in fact done away with altogether. If for Milbank the fall of modernity means that Christian theology is a *particular* tradition that nonetheless promulgates truths which are for its believers *universal* and unqualified, De Schrijver sometimes speaks of an individual – the postmodern consumer – who begins from a site outside of all such traditions, where there simply can be no universal truth-claims.

At such moments, of course, De Schrijver is certainly not speaking as a theologian, as he himself implies near the end of his essay, when he asks about the specifically theological pertinence of his analysis (74). In truth, the essay as a whole appears divided between these two perspectives – on one hand, a theological interest in concepts such as liberation, hope and redemption, while on the other hand a philosophical suspension of theological premises in order to engage the difficulties ascribed to "postmodernity". Furthermore, this division of tasks is complicated by the fact that De Schrijver's philosophy accepts, at least for the sake of argument, the critical force of a principle – radical fragmentation – which tends to neutralize the critical force of his theology. Oddly enough, then, despite the fact that it is De Schrijver who foresees a greater change in the self-understanding of theology, he might well be in greater danger of sectarianism than is Milbank: if, according to the dictates of postmodern fragmentation (itself enforced by an irreversible historical shift), theology is really detached from other, rival narratives, then its statements and arguments are meaningful only to those who are already committed to its basic principles – that is, to those who already belong to the tradition. Some philosophers might well think that this is so, but a theologian, one would expect, must begin from somewhat stronger claims.

III. THEOLOGICAL RATIONALITY ROOTED IN TRADITION

Given the fact that on De Schrijver's own account these difficulties confront theology from beyond its traditional frontiers, what is called for here is not so much a specifically theological response to them as a closer look at the philosophy which sets them forth. Recall the line of reasoning in which this has occurred: the current struggle of liberation theologians to clarify a new critical base is itself an important index of a more general crisis facing theology as a whole, as it tries to accommodate the fact that the same event which brought down the grand narrative of Marxism as a useful ally of liberation theology also discredited the grand narrative of Christianity itself. Thus, according to De Schrijver, theologians who wish to play a serious role on the postmodern scene can no more pretend to a universal account of human experience and existence than can Marxists. Whether it is a matter of the absence of an objective foundation for social criticism or a decline in the credibility of theological truth-claims, the fragmentation of cultures and traditions typifying our postmodern condition is threatening precisely to the extent that it renders every assertion and contention local and particular. Now, in its extreme form, not only would such a position strand critics and missionaries on the far side of an uncrossable distance between them and the people they wish to reach, but it would also imply the most profound difficulties for any truly postmodern debate: to argue according to the rules of the day would mean either abandoning even the pretense to a foundation for one's contentions, or remaining silent about the very principles and convictions which motivate one to speak in the first place. And yet, the simple fact that even people who acknowledge that their respective views are opposed do continue to communicate demonstrates that that fragmentation is something less than radical.

This basic discrepancy, between the fact of critical conversation and a theory of postmodernity, appears at the end of De Schrijver's analysis rather than at the beginning, which is to say as its result and not its stimulus. The fact that he never raises the issue can only be explained by what I have already pointed to as a submerged complicity between sociological description and a specific philosophy of history. In this sense, the overall argument is hermetic, shifting from each of these two strands to the other, but without apparent need of confirmation elsewhere: on one hand, the findings of several key sociologists is taken as proof that regardless of the difficulties we simply can not escape a confrontation with a radical fragmentation of cultures and systems of meaning which, more deeply, testifies to a shift in our rationality breaking from that of modernity forever; on the other hand, and at the same time, these philosophical claims are themselves brandished as the warrant for elevating sociological generalizations about contemporary sensibility to the level of theoretical *explanation*. The aporia is plain to see: what this argument by mutual confirmation seems to exclude – and not merely overlook – is an account of that basic sociological data which does more than take it over as such. The movement from phenomenon to principle must go beyond summary definition to the clarification of necessary conditions. What is still needed, it seems to me, is a proper phenomenology of the everyday experiences in question.

Concretely, this involves a rigorous description of the workings of moral and religious conscience, especially where joined to the social criticism which actively implements them in ways extending beyond the limits of the tradition and culture in which they take place[8]. To the

---

8. This turn might also explain why someone like Gustavo Gutiérrez also seems to be mired in these same difficulties. Gutiérrez, as De Schrijver tells us, seeks the consequences of the fall of modernity in an analysis of the history and philosophy of *science*, where questions of value and conviction are far from the center of reflection on shifts in

extent that postmodernists still claim to some sort of ethical involvement and critical capacity – indeed, to the extent that they offer statements with more than purely aesthetic value – they themselves imply one, albeit very problematic, candidate for such a description. For instance, the free-playing subject to whom the world of traditions and their narratives appears as so many equally possible choices would thus seem to decide among them on the instructions of a conscience not essentially committed to any one of them in particular. I have already indicated that this sort of claim is best understood as an acknowledgement that it is impossible to actually achieve the autonomy which some moderns, at least, expect to find in such an extreme freedom from commitment. Having arrived in the fields of phenomenology and ethics, we can now add grave doubts about the coherence of a subject at once without a context and somehow capable of any sort of engagement, whether religious, political or even crudely self-interested. In *stricto sensu*, action with an end in view necessarily implies roots already planted in a tradition which, by ordering the world in a particular way, both instructs us how to act in accordance with it and instills us with a sense of disturbance at events and ideas contradicting it. This contention, I am inclined to think, comes close to the intentions of Milbank: beneath the level at which traditions are indeed subject to the most personal, even eclectic syntheses, there is another level at which one's tradition continues to speak in the conscience formed by being rooted in it. It would thus seem to be the lasting insight of philosophy after modernity not that traditions no longer have us in their grasp, but that that grasp itself, while to some degree probably unbreakable, is nonetheless subject to constant reinterpretation.

In this sense, it is probably too much to speak of the end of religion as we have known it. Heightened skepticism about "master narratives" leads not to their fall as such, but to greater sensitivity to the fact that they operate at a level anterior to the rationality which, for its part, sometimes turns to analyze them. If it has been the error of modernity to pretend that things were otherwise, postmodernity would be equally mistaken to suspend the entire problematic. The fragmentation which distinguishes the rationality of today from that of yesterday does not sever us from our traditions, but exposes the proper depth at which they influence

our sense of objectivity. Still, it is striking that both Gutiérrez and, citing him, De Schrijver enter into discussion with scientific rationality in the context of analyses of what De Schrijver at least refers to as "conscientization" -the move from naive to critical consciousness (cf. DE SCHRIJVER, (22-24) and GUTIÉRREZ, *A Theology of Liberation*, Maryknoll, NY, Orbis, 1988, pp. 18-20). At such points, the remarks offered here present themselves only as an alternative approach to what is clearly a shared concern.

us. And if at this depth one such tradition is indeed wholly distinct from another, then this does not at all threaten the possibility of criticism between them; to the contrary, it makes it inevitable. If, then, the true difficulty with the cry for "liberation" lies not in formulating a basis from which to do so, but instead simply with convincing members of other traditions to first understand and then accept our criteria, De Schrijver will have been quite right to point out that ours is an age conditioned by the near-impossibility of building a consensus. Still, the status of that very observation remains far from clear. While it is certainly a powerful reminder of how easily even the pursuit of liberation can become oppressive (after all, who will define this all-important term?), there seems little cause to lament the fact itself. Might not the fact of post-modernity warn us against these very regrets? More than coincidence links this question to reflections on the weight of tradition in theological argument. The notion of a shift of paradigms for theological rationality underscores an urgent need for reflection on the most basic of alternatives: must the theologian simply carry on with apologies for a past no longer credible, or is there cause for renewed confidence in a foundation all the more plainly in hope?

Faculty of Theology, KULeuven   Jeffrey BLOECHL
Sint-Michielsstraat 6
B-3000 Leuven, Belgium

14

J.-F. LYOTARD'S CRITIQUE OF MASTER NARRATIVES
TOWARDS A POSTMODERN POLITICAL THEOLOGY

I. Theology in Search of New Recontextualization Partners

Theology, through the ages, has sought to elucidate Christian faith and praxis reflexively by relying on the critical consciousness of the age. From the outset, the Fathers of the Church made use of the philosophies of Antiquity both to show the plausibility of the Christian faith ad intra and to defend it ad extra – proclaiming the Christian faith as the true philosophy. This is also what Thomas Aquinas was doing, for instance, while he theologized starting from and recasting the patterns of thought set by Aristotle – rediscovered early in the second millennium. Time and again theologians have felt the need to reappropriate Christian faith in a reflexive way according to the contextual thinking patterns then available, and by doing this, were involved in a process of repeated recontextualization[1].

In sketching out and analyzing a number of present day patterns of reflexivity, G. De Schrijver's Discussion Paper can be situated in a new engagement in this process of theological recontextualization. In De Schrijver's assessment, the (late-)modern context has shifted towards a so-called postmodern condition. One of the most telling events in this regard is the fall of the Berlin Wall, illustrative for the loss of credibility of the Marxist, communist master narrative. As such, this shift has exerted high pressure on the established links between the liberation theologies of the seventies and the eighties, and the critical consciousness of modernity. As 'organic intellectuals', liberation theologians used Marxist social analysis to structure the context of extreme poverty and oppression that they, as Christians, lived and worked in, thereby reflecting upon and sustaining their engagement in liberating praxis. Insofar as the implosion of communism has meant the end of a viable alternative to capitalism, De Schrijver explores how this particular merger of Christian faith and modernity in Third-World theologies of liberation can survive. One of the possible solutions, according to the title of the project, is a turn

---

1. Cf. L. Boeve, *Bearing Witness to the Differend. A Model for 'Postmodern' Theologizing*, in *LS* 20 (1995) 362-379, esp. pp. 363-368; *Kan traditie veranderen? Theologie in het postmoderne tijdsgewricht*, in *Coll* 26 (1996) 365-385, esp. pp. 365-379.

to culture, and cultural analysis. Because of the vanishing of plausible models of critical social analysis, theology could seek its new recontextualization partner in the local cultures that have survived modern colonialism and imperialism. A theological reappraisal and reappropriation of this still prevalent deep cultural rootedness is judged to address the wounds of globalizing capitalism. This at least explains the significant attention that popular wisdom and popular religiosity, as well as the issue of inculturation, have received in theological circles recently. The question needs to be raised, however, whether or not the specific critical impetus of social analysis, not least towards culture, and its potential for societal praxis, is not seriously endangered. From his contextual (i.e., European) perspective, De Schrijver attempts to foster strategies to cope with the shifted context, in order to provide new opportunities for present day fides quaerens intellectum, interrelating the globalization thesis with Anthony Giddens' plea for a reflexive retrieval of traditional potentials of humanity and solidarity. In this regard, it would e.g. be appropriate to consider a rapprochement between "Christian reflexivity and the type of reflexivity Giddens deems important for coming to grips with human manufactured risks, or with the destructive side-effects of western productivism" (76).

From the late 1960s until mid 1980s, and from time to time in close connection with liberation theologies, especially those in Latin America, some theologians from the Old World were involved in a project of what one could call contextual, (West-)European theologies of liberation, commonly received as 'political theology'. This would include, to name but a few of the most prominent protagonists and their major works, Jürgen Moltmann with his *Theologie der Hoffnung* (1964)[2], Dorothee Sölle with her *Politische Theologie* (1971), Edward Schillebeeckx with parts of his second Jesus-book (1977)[3] dedicated to political theology, and Johann Baptist Metz, with his *Zur Theologie der Welt* (1968) and especially *Glaube in Geschichte und Gesellschaft* (1977)[4]. On several occasions, the latter stressed the importance of the human sciences, particularly the social sciences, for theology. In this regard, political theology was mostly inspired by the neo-Marxist *Frankfurter Schule* (including esp. W. Benjamin, Th. Adorno, M. Horkheimer, and J. Habermas) and E. Bloch. At present,

---

2. English translation: J. MOLTMANN, *Theology of Hope*, London, SCM, 1969.

3. E.T.: E. SCHILLEBEECKX, *Christ: The Experience of Jesus as Lord*, New York, Crossroad, 1989.

4. E.T.: J.-B. METZ, *Theology of the World*, New York, Herder & Herder, 1969; *Faith in History and Society: Toward a Practical Fundamental Theology*, New York, Seabury press, 1980.

the loss of the plausibility of the Marxist narrative also affected these strands of modern theology. Yet there is still more to say. In general, theologians in the First-World, both with neo-conservative and progressive tendencies, have tended to leave the social arena and have shown interest in cultural issues, particularly as these have emerged through so-called multi-cultural, postmodernist and aestheticist movements and trends. Here again, the questions implied in the subtitle of the Discussion Paper, 'From socio-economic to cultural analysis', must be confronted. Is the turn to culture, and more in particular to aesthetics, an evasion of the social problematic? Anti-modern dreams of a restoration of classical values, often phrased in a nostalgic longing for a Christian Europe (breathing by two longs, namely the orthodox and catholic churches), do not hesitate at espousing an aesthetics of harmony as a remedy for the failures of modernity. In its theological variant, this option may be dramatic in its proceedings, but ultimately results in an all-encompassing reconciliation, which is not at all attentive to what is really taking place in the historical, socio-economic level[5]. Postmodern aestheticism, on the other hand, characterized by free-wheeling playfulness and a quasi-obsessive eagerness for difference and novelty, often implies a thoroughgoing individualism; its 'life styling' (i.e. postmodernist identity construction) entails a play – 'bricolage' – where differences are interchangeable and newness is consumable, and which embraces an ever-repeating affirmation of the self as other than the others. Unsurprisingly, there is no social agenda involved[6]. Moreover, insofar as this aestheticism involves consumerism, only the happy few have access to such a life styling. On the religious field, certain forms of New Age – and the theories accompanying these – seemingly resemble this kind of aesthetic postmodernism.

In this contribution I intend to respond to the questions raised by G. De Schrijver from a Western, European context. Whether due to the lack of a plausible model of social analysis or for other reasons, must the drastic changes described lead to a paradigm shift in theology changes? Does a present-day theological recontextualization inevitably forget the societal agenda of the late modern theologies of liberation? Or might there be recontextualization partners, thinking patterns of actual critical

5. Cf. e.g. R. LUNEAU (ed.), *Le rêve de Compostelle: vers la restauration d'une Europe chretienne?*, Paris, Centurion, 1989. In this regard, it may not be surprising that theological interest in the thinking and work of H.-U. von Balthasar has had an enormous revival.

6. Cf. e.g. R. RORTY, *On the 'strong poet' in his Contingency, Irony, and Solidarity*, Cambridge, Cambridge University Press, 1989. More negative in his approach is J. BAUDRILLARD, when elaborating on our 'society of simulation', where all differentiation and difference, in the end, results in de-differentiation and indifference; see *L'échange symbolique et la mort*, Paris, Gallimard, 1984.

consciousness which would enable the construction, as it were, of a postmodern political theology?

In an attempt to grasp the critical consciousness of our time, I offer some essential elements of J.-F. Lyotard's postmodernism, in order to examine whether it can be of use for contemporary theology, especially for a theology which does not intend to overlook matters of justice and liberation in our postmodern times of plurality, aestheticism, and culturalism.

II. J.-F. LYOTARD'S CRITICAL THEORY OF THE POSTMODERN CONDITION

In the Discussion Paper, Lyotard's critical theory of the postmodern condition has perhaps not received the attention it deserves (36-39). J.-F. Lyotard was active in ultra-leftist movements until 1966 – critical of the French communist party. His philosophical career started after abandoning these political activities. Still, as a post-marxist he remained very critical towards capitalism and its offspring. When taking into account his criticism of hegemonic politics and economism, i.e. of the so-called master narratives, it must be made clear that Lyotard is not primarily making an analysis of, or even worse, a plea for, a sort of free-wheeling, playful aestheticism as an alternative to modern master narratives (globalization type I). As will be shown, there is more to Lyotard than *La condition postmoderne* (1979: about postmodern epistemology), and *Le postmoderne expliqué aux enfants* (1986: a.o. about the aesthetics of our time)[7]. An examination of his *Le différend* (1983: about language and justice), and *L'enthousiasme* (1986), as well as for instance *Tombeau de l'intellectuel et autres papiers* (1984)[8], reveals that he has developed a language pragmatics, of which his aesthetics of the sublime serves as the other side of the coin[9]. Herein Lyotard offers a critical theory of post-

7. J.-F. LYOTARD, *La condition postmoderne: Rapport sur le savoir*, Paris, Minuit, 1979 (E.T.: *The Postmodern Condition: a Report on Knowledge*, Manchester, University Press, 1984); *Le postmoderne expliqué aux enfants: Correspondance 1982-1985*, Paris, Galilée, 1986 (E.T.: *The Postmodern Explained: Correspondence 1982-1985*, Minneapolis, University of Minnesota Press, 1993).

8. ID., *Le différend*, Paris, Minuit, 1983 (E.T.: *The Differend: Phrases in Dispute*, Manchester, University Press, 1988); *L'enthousiasme. La critique kantienne de l'histoire*, Paris, Galilée, 1986; and *Tombeau de l'intellectuel et autres papiers*, Paris, Galilée, 1984.

9. For his aesthetics, see, apart from *Le postmoderne expliqué aux enfants*, especially *L'inhumain: Causeries sur le temps*, Paris, Galilée, 1988 (E.T.: *The Inhuman: Reflections on Time*, Cambridge, Polity Press, 1991), and his study of Kant's aesthetics of the sublime in *Leçons sur l'analytique du sublime*, Paris, Galilée, 1991 (E.T.: *Lessons on the Analytic of the Sublime: Kant's Critique of Judgment*, Sections 23-29, Stanford, Stanford University Press, 1994).

modernity. A brief presentation of both mutually related thinking strategies, i.e. language pragmatics and aesthetic philosophy, can bring to
light his criticism of the hegemonic capitalist narrative.

1. *Language Pragmatics*

In his language pragmatics, Lyotard begins with the apparent indis-
soluble plurality typical for our time, but does not stop there[10]. For
plurality inevitably evokes conflict. Lyotard develops this insight with reference to what happens in language, in speech, in fact in the concatenation
of phrases, one after the other. Once a phrase has happened, numerous
other phrases can be linked to it, according to the genre of discourse (what
Wittgenstein called a language game, consisting of a strategy of linking
phrases to pursue a certain goal) which regulates the linking. But although
there are many phrase candidates, only one of them can actually realize
the linking, and this according to the genre of discourse which finally
overcomes the other genres. Other phrases, fitting within the strategies
of linking in other genres of discourse, then remain unactualized[11]. This
schematical exposition makes clear that, for Lyotard, plurality never is a
static given, but a dynamic interplay of differences and otherness. This
necessarily involves conflict. Since the fact of the linking of phrases is
necessary, but the nature of the linked phrase is contingent. As already
indicated, each phrase that has happened can be followed by an indefinite number of phrases. Because of the necessity of the linking and the
concomitant contingency of the nature of the linking phrase, a struggle
for the linking occurs after every happened phrase. From a more general
perspective, this conflict can be evaluated as a conflict between genres
of discourse, because the linking of phrases is not self-regulating but
discourse-dependent[12]. In the perspective of one discourse the linking
is self-evident, and decisions are easily made because they are regulated
in order to realize the goal in the most efficient way. But in a situation
of plurality, such as ours, there are numerous discourses regulating the

---

10. For the following, I predominantly rely on Lyotard's *Le différend* (n. 8).

11. The following illustrates this: the prescriptive phrase "close the door" can be followed by "OK, I will close the door", but also, "No, it is better not to close the door
because it is too hot in here", or "No, do it yourself", or even the phrase "'close the
door' is a prescriptive phrase", and this according to the genre of discourse which is taking place – and thus the goal which is pursued in this linking of phrases. But in the end,
regardless of the many possibilities, only one phrase will be actualized.

12. Examples of genres of discourse include: teaching, story-telling, making laugh,
arguing, reasoning, etc. To teach, that is to transmit a subject-matter, the teacher does not
use phrases in an arbitrary order, but structures the teaching discourse along the specific
conditions that the transmission of a subject-matter requires.

linking, and a meta-discourse that transcends the multitude of discourses and goals, is no longer given. There is no longer a supreme, unquestioned rule of linking; in fact there is only conflict.

This conflict is what Lyotard has called a 'differend'. Based on Kant's distinction between a determinant and a reflective judgment (in his *Kritik der Urteilskraft* from 1790) Lyotard distinguishes between litigation ('litige') and differend ('différend'). In the first genre of judgment, the 'judge' has a rule at his or her disposal to resolve a conflict; in the second, this rule is not available, but must still be sought for. Litigation is the case within a certain genre of discourse: according to its strategy the conflict becomes resolved. But the plurality of discourses, in absence of a meta-discourse, installs a general condition of 'differend': there is no rule available. To do justice the 'judge' still has to seek it.

To define what is 'postmodern' in our contemporary context, the awareness of this general condition of differend is crucial. It particularly consists in the consciousness that each new phrase is really an event, the closure of an undetermined expectation. In the end, differends are usually resolved as ligitations, which means: within the framework of a specific discourse, which can never claim to be a meta-discourse. Not to forget the primordial differend – or, in other words, all those phrases which will never be actualized once one phrase realizes the linking – is precisely what Lyotard calls a postmodern attitude. As a matter of fact, the task of postmodern philosophy is to bear witness to the differend. This means two things: (1) criticizing those linking strategies which forget or exclude the differend while immediately substituting it to ligitation; and (2) looking for phrases that fit in a linking strategy, which although closing the differend, yet nevertheless evokes the aspect of undecideability which is characteristic of it – or at least: attempting to remember the forgetting of its forgetting which is inevitably implied in any linkage.

2. Aesthetics of the Sublime

As mentioned above, Lyotard develops the same pattern of thinking in his aesthetic reflections[13]. Postmodern aesthetics is an aesthetics of the sublime. In distinction from an aesthetics of beauty, which results in an

---

13. Lyotard is of the opinion that the aesthetic and the historico-political – put differently: the problematic of language – are structured analogously. See in this regard J.-F. LYOTARD, *Pérégrinations: loi, forme, événement*, Paris, Galilée, 1990, pp. 45-46; French translation of: *Peregrinations: Law, Form, Event*, New York, Columbia University Press, 1988. Perhaps better: only when Lyotard's aesthetics is presented along the lines of his theory of language can it be preserved from degenerating (cf. infra).

enjoying of reconciling sentiments of harmony, an aesthetics of the sublime cherishes the sensitivity for interruption, event, agitation, fluidity, indeterminability. Whereas an aesthetics of beauty starts from beautiful, harmonious forms and representations, an aesthetics of the sublime is concerned about what is unrepresentable, and more specifically about the paradoxical attempt to represent it nevertheless. The artistic 'avant-garde' of modernity was already striving for the sublime. Visible presentations, often abstract, formless, deviating from the 'unusual', intended to refer to what could not be directly presented, evoking interruption and ungraspability. Everything that served representation became questionable: the figurative, color, lines, frame, exposition hall, etc. "Showing that there is something we can conceive of which we can neither see nor show"[14]. It is precisely the radicalization of this program of modern avant-garde that comprises the essence of postmodernity. Yet the modern avant-garde presented the unrepresentable in the nostalgic longing for a vanished beginning or end, a foundational or anticipated presence no longer available. That which was recognizable in this longing, continued to offer some comfort and joy. The postmodern, however, no longer knows this nostalgia and is only aware of the impossible representation of the non-representable. It is "that which refuses the consolation of correct forms, refuses the consensus of taste permitting a common experience of nostalgia for the impossible, and inquires into new presentations – not to take pleasure in them, but to better produce the feeling that there is something unpresentable"[15]. Such an aesthetic experience, whose intensity depends on the extent of the variability, fluidity, agitation and evanescence of what is being presented, stands as the model for the attitude in which the postmodern person is active in the world. Just as one cannot grasp a flame and cannot fix the contours of a flowing stream, the postmodern person wants to let events happen as they do. This means taking distance from the attempts at dominating, at confining the now-moment

14. From J.-F. LYOTARD, *The Postmodern Explained* (n. 7), p. 11 ("Faire voir qu'il y a quelque chose que l'on peut concevoir et que l'on ne peut pas voir ni faire voir" [n. 7, p. 27]). Compare ID., *L'inhumain* (n. 9), p. 204.

15. J.-F. LYOTARD, "ce qui se refuse à la consolation des bonnes formes, au consensus d'un goût qui permettrait d'éprouver en commun la nostalgie de l'impossible; ce qui s'enquiert de présentations nouvelles, non pas pour en jouir, mais pour mieux faire sentir qu'il y a de l'imprésentable" [*Le postmoderne expliqué* (n. 7), pp. 32-33]. See also: W. VAN REIJEN & D. VEERMAN, *De Verlichting, het verhevene, filosofie, esthetica. Interview en uitwisseling van gedachten met Jean-François Lyotard*, in W. VAN REIJEN, *De onvoltooide rede. Modern en postmodern*, Kampen, Kok, 1987, 63-117, pp. 87-89. Or still "La 'modernité' d'aujourd'hui n'attend pas de l'aisthesis qu'elle donne à l'âme la paix du beau, mais qu'elle l'arrache de justesse au néant" [J.-F. LYOTARD, *L'inhumain* (n. 9), p. 207].

or the event, at making history, by inscribing everything into one narrative. It is letting the now-moment interrupt, and being taken by surprise. As interruptive event, it is not a product of human consciousness, but precedes it (and needs to be forgotten in striving towards a stable identity). Receptivity, 'passibilité', contemplativity, presupposes indeed a gift that is not yet mediated by 'concepts'. As in language pragmatics where philosophy is looking for the unphraseable phrase, attempting to present the interruptive event of the differend in the concatenation of phrases, in the unfolding of a discourse, contemporary aesthetics pays tribute to the unrepresentable, at the core of representation.

Analogous to postmodern aesthetics, Lyotard thinks that postmodern philosophy is called not to forget the differend and to bear witness to it. It is precisely in this sense that postmodern philosophy, or more in general postmodern narratives, are distinct from modern (and also premodern) philosophy and narratives[16]. For in Lyotard's opinion the 'modern master narratives' immediately substituted differends in their litigations by imposing their own rules of discourse, subordinating (or excluding) all other genres of discourse and narrative. In fact theirs were hegemonic mechanisms of conquering, strategies of successfully linking phrases in an irrefutable narrative. In *La condition postmoderne* two kinds of modern master narratives are mentioned: hegemonic narratives of absolute knowledge, claiming to depict accurately (and master efficiently) the world as it really is, and hegemonic narratives of emancipation, convinced in their leading humanity to its fulfillment. It has been precisely this forgetting of the differend that has made these narratives run against their limits, causing the dramas of the 19th and 20th century[17].

16. A narrative in this regard is a genre of discourse which is responsible for the general strategy of linking phrases, and in so doing copes from within its own strategy with other genres of discourse. A narrative accounts, so to speak, for the final, necessary closure of a differend and its substitution in a ligitation. In the way in which this happens, two general features can be distinguished. As I will make clear in what follows, there appear to be hegemonic, master narratives negating differends, and open narratives attempting to bear witness to them.

17. To quote Lyotard on this: "Les 'philosophies de l'histoire' qui ont inspiré le XIXe et le XXe siècles prétendent assurer les passages sur l'abîme de l'hétérogénéité ou de l'événement. Les noms qui sont ceux de 'notre histoire' opposent des contre-exemples à leur prétention. – Tout ce qui est réel est rationel, tout ce qui est rationel est réel: 'Auschwitz' réfute la doctrine spéculative. Au moins ce crime, qui est réel [...], n'est pas rationel. – Tout ce qui est prolétarien est communiste, tout ce qui est communiste est prolétarien: 'Berlin 1953, Budapest 1956, Tchécoslovaquie 1968, Pologne 1980' [...] réfutent la doctrine matérialiste historique: les travailleurs se dressent contre le Parti. – Tout ce qui est démocratique est par le peuple et pour lui, et inversement: 'Mai 1968' réfute la doctrine du libéralisme parlementaire. Le social quotidien fait échec à l'institution représentative. – Tout ce qui est libre jeu de l'offre et la demande est propice à l'enrichissement général, et inversement: les 'crises de 1911, 1929' réfutent la doctrine du libéralisme

3. *The Economic Master Narrative of Capitalism*

To illustrate the nature of hegemonic master narratives, I use Lyotard's language pragmatic analysis of the economic master narrative of capitalism which legitimated itself during the modern era as an emancipatory narrative, promising humanity a better future by the spreading of welfare. This, however, only served as a legitimating arrangement since in a closed, totalitarian economic discourse, the political question on the public good is actually not raised not even when the political discourse itself is involved in economics (in a mingled economy). For, in the end, the economic narrative can be reduced to the accumulation of capital, money, and therefore the gain of time (dominating time through money)[18]. The rules for linkage in the economic genre are clear (and show the domination of time through money): when phrase 'x' (addressor 'a' hands over referent 'c' to addressee 'b'), then phrase 'y' is presupposed ('b' gives referent 'd' to 'a'). The linkage is thus not only expected, but even presupposed from the outset: that which is intended is exchange. Phrase 'x' makes of 'b' one who stands in debt to 'a'; phrase 'y' cancels this debt. While the narrative attempts to acknowledge the event (the debt) and maintain it (reductively) by encapsulating it within the larger whole, phrase 'y' immediately attempts to erase, to undo, the event (causing debt) of phrase 'x' in the hegemonic discourse. Capitalism, therefore, establishes an all-encompassing market situation of exchange, where nothing really 'happens' any more, because events (time) are calculated and predicted, thereby thus radically weakening them as interruptive now-moments. The expectation of the phrase to come, the event, is 'erased' by the coercive logic of 'exchange'[19].

Upon further examination, it becomes apparent that modern (and contemporary) capitalism is the merger of four genres of discourse, a sort of coalition or alliance of the political, scientific, and techn(olog)ical discourses with, and under control of, the economic discourse[20]. The latter is ruled by the finality or idea of profit (the accumulation of time); the political discourse strives for the common good; the discourse of science

économique. Et la 'crise de 1974-79' réfute l'aménagement post-keynésien de cette doctrine. Les passages promis par les grandes synthèses doctrinales s'achèvent sur de sanglantes impasses. De là le chagrin des spectateurs en cette fin du XXᵉ siècle" [*Le différend* (n. 8), pp. 257-258, nr. 257].

18. Money counts as accumulated time. Compare: a laborer only has to make his time count for money. In the monetary circuit of investment, loan, and saving, time also becomes a commodity, thus banks speak of the sale of (bank) products.

19. Cf. for this J.-F. LYOTARD, *Le différend* (n. 8), pp. 248-249, 256-257, 259, resp. nrs. 240-241, 254-255, 260.

20. Cf. J.-F. LYOTARD, *Tombeau de l'intellectuel et autres papiers* (n. 8), pp. 41-56.

is guided by the idea of perfect knowledge; and the techn(olog)ical discourse attempts to reach the highest degree of performance and efficiency. In capitalism, all four of these are mutually related. Capitalism indeed includes an alliance of the economic and the political (a mixed economy), whereby states participate in the economic discourse, for example as banker, employer, employee. The technical and the scientific enter into an alliance with each other resulting in the thorough change of the nature of knowledge: the technical provides the proofs in order to declare a cognitive pronouncement valid, whereas scientific research is most often carried out in view of its possible applications. The techno-scientific alliance is finally engaged by capitalism, as an alliance between capital and state, which has grown in industries associated with the military, space travel, nuclear energy, and others – recently, for instance, the eco-industry.

But because of counter-examples, occurring especially during the 20th century, the modern master narratives have lost their plausibility. The promises of modern capitalism, for instance, were not kept: the distribution of welfare has appeared to be an illusion – the gap between rich and poor growing even greater – and, moreover, the capitalist industrial process has provoked a serious environmental crisis. As a result, the major ideologies of the 19th and 20th centuries, the diverse '-isms' (such as positivism, communism, liberalism), no longer possess the unquestioned authority to present their strategies to regulate the linkages of phrases as of necessity. Precisely their fall has made manifest the radical plurality of our context, and inspired postmodern critical consciousness of the general condition of differend.

Nevertheless, one silent master narrative has come to regulate the linking of phrases in an almost totalitarian way. Without the need for any publicly acknowledged legitimation (as was needed in the time of the master narratives), the economizing narrative presently subordinates – seemingly unnoticed – all other discourses and narratives, old and new. In this regard, the postmodern sensibility for otherness, for instance, along the lines of postmodern aesthetics of the sublime, is functionalized in a market-oriented way: the mysterious, the ungraspable, the exotic, is marketed and sold. Otherness sinks into a self-referential play of intense feelings and experiences.

In this regard, Lyotard denounces a perverse alliance between the economizing discourse and the present-day tendency towards aestheticization[21].

---

21. Cf. J.-F. LYOTARD, *Le postmoderne expliqué* (n. 7), pp. 11-34, and *L'inhumain* (n. 9), pp. 101-117, 131-139.

By this alliance, art becomes an object of consumption. In order to conceal that in a hegemonic economizing discourse nothing 'happens' any more, it subsumes the contemporary aesthetic sensitivity for experiences of interruption, and reframes its discourse. The economizing discourse 'processes' the encounter with current aestheticizing tendencies – just like the earlier encounters between science and technology – in order to revitalize and reaffirm itself. This has, however, serious consequences for the aesthetic realm. As a matter of fact, the supposed co-activity of economy and aesthetics only takes place superficially and not in mutual respect; it results in the mere insertion of aesthetic discourse into the economizing narrative, provoking the adjustment and transformation of the former into the latter. In so doing, the aesthetic sensitivity for interruptive experiences is radically damaged in a subtle (yet no less brutal) way. The event character of the experience of the sublime is ruled out. Art is bought and sold as pseudo-event, functioning within, and not interruptive to, the ongoing economic discourse[22]. Art no longer reflects the critical consciousness of our time, but becomes an image of the market. In their pleading for a free-wheeling artistic playfulness, so-called postmodern aestheticist theories in fact opt for this alliance of aestheticism and market, promoted by a silent, all-encompassing, economic master narrative[23].

It is interesting to note that the major capitalist alliance between economy and science-technology has played, and still continues to play, an important role in the settling of the postmodern variant of capitalism. The new information and communication media, and the computerization, have had especially far-reaching consequences in this respect[24]. Indeed, to begin with, computer technology detemporalizes (and delocalizes) the knowledge written down in culture's memory (which is as a synthesis of

22. Cf. also J.-F. LYOTARD, *L'inhumain* (n. 9), p. 116-117: a simultaneously artistic and commercial success is made as follows: "on reprend des formules confirmées par de précédents succès, on les déséquilibre, au moyen de combinaisons avec d'autres formules en principe incompatible, au moyen d'amalgames de citations, d'ornementations, de pastiches".

23. The advertisement industry is remarkably successful and inventive in linking the postmodern aesthetic sensibility – and the interruptive kick involved – and with the economic narrative, be it of course for the purpose of the latter. Almost all of the 'Benetton'-commercials, for example, are excellent illustrations of this: the brand name is for instance related to traces of compassion one feels with a dying aids patient (1993: picture of an aids patient), linked to traces of solidarity with the poor (1993: campaign to collect used clothing), connected to traces of moral indignation (1994: picture of a blood-stained uniform of a Croatian soldier fallen in Bosnia, accompanied by a text in which his parents give permission to use this uniform), or linked to anti-racist (and sexual) emotions (1996: picture of a black stallion covering a white mare).

24. Cf. J.-F. LYOTARD, *L'inhumain* (n. 9), pp. 57-67.

time). Elements of knowledge, always acquired in a particular 'here and now', are 'scanned' and become digitalized and converted into data which then function independent of addresser, addressee, original space and time. So knowledge-elements are extracted from their original synthesis, their traditions and local cultures, and can be abstractly taken up in new syntheses. Knowledge becomes universally readable, available, useful, usable, and operational. This not only means that the memory-function and thus the saving of time become different; the reflexive relationship with regard to the past – and the knowledge contained therein – and the creative possibilities contained therein for the present[25] are thoroughly displaced as well. The bounds of traditions disappear in a techno-scientific 'scanning' of knowledge[26]. Data can be combined in an unlimited way, new syntheses and 'surprising' discoveries can be made: "More knowledge and power, yes – but why, no"[27]. Moreover, the stringent demand for perfect performance enforces this never-ending process of 'scanning' and combining data. Techno-scientific discourse aims at recording all possible combinations in its formalized memory. All possible 'events' are thereby eliminated; what is known and predicted, no longer 'happen' or really surprises. This results not only from an anticipation, but also – and more so – from a recuperation of the future: "what comes 'after' the 'now' will have to come 'before' it"[28]. The techno-scientific foresees the happening and thus dominates time.

Taking this into account, it is clear that the encompassing alliance between capitalism and the techno-scientific is currently even more readily apparent. Scientific research, especially with its high-technological conditioning with regard to verification/falsification, demands large sums of money. Capital, as saved time, is applied in order to move forward in time. In this way the economic discourse with its techno-scientific ally, enervates the event by anticipating it beforehand. Various consequences stem from this analysis: (1) This mega-alliance in fact leads to substantial increases in research budgets. (2) It likewise entails a drastic reorganization of labor (with a depreciation of executive labor) and

---

25. I.e. tradition as a living and dynamic process of commemoration, in fact recontextualization, of the past in view of the questions and possibilities of the present (and the future).
26. "Dieu, la nature, le destin [...] sont 'balayés'. Et avec eux, le principe d'une finalité du procès de recherche et développement": L'inhumain (n. 9), p. 64.
27. J.-F. LYOTARD, The Inhuman (n. 9), p. 54 ("Savoir et pouvoir plus, oui, mais pourquoi, non" [n. 9, p. 64]).
28. Ibid, p. 65 ("ce qui arrive 'après' le 'maintenant' devra venir 'avant' lui" [n. 9, p. 77]). The present techno-scientific complex has completed the Cartesian project: 'devenir maître et possesseur de la nature'. But insofar as the person is also ranked under nature, he/she loses self-mastery. The domination is complete, but no longer human.

education, in view of the striving for performance. (3) In this regard, the major intermediary structures, as labor unions, political parties, professional organizations progressively loose their grip on the economical organization. (4) Finally, computerization pervades the daily life-world, both in its public and private dimensions, diminishing the role of the structuring patterns and frameworks of daily life.

In the end, all domains of human life and their specific discourses become reductivily integrated in one hegemonic narrative, ruled by and obedient to the market law of supply and demand. Culture thereby becomes entirely commodified. The hegemony of the allied techno-scientific, (weakened) aesthetic, and economic discourse transforms the culture into a culture-industry, wherein its event-character is stripped of the unpredictable, the surprising, the creative, the unexpected. Furthermore, other discourses and narratives are extracted from their spatio-temporal settings and fragmented into atomic elements. Cultural legacy is broken up into free 'bits', which can be combined in an unlimited way. In this way, possible events are strategically anticipated and thus become pseudo-events, 'pseudo-now-moments', 'manufactured intensity'. As mentioned, degenerated postmodern art functions in this sense; and its perversity lies in the sale of (pseudo-) events. 'Time' becomes availability, marketability, consumability, manageability.

4. *The Interruptive Event*

In this perspective, the critical potential of Lyotard's theory of postmodernity emerges. For sure, the hegemony of the economic cannot boast upon any legitimacy, since this genre of discourse is only one among many. It is precisely Lyotard's linguistic instrumentarium that can detect the insidious, not immediately observable, danger of this domination. This economic discourse, in fact, not only regulates the linkages, it anticipates them and even offers the semblance of taking events seriously, while actually producing them.

In contrast to such deception, Lyotard sets the task of bearing witness to the differend, and calls for thinkers, painters, authors, musicians to engage the conflicting heterogeneity involved in a situation of plurality, so as to unmask all pretensions of hegemony. To avoid all confusion, he calls postmodernity a matter of 'rewriting modernity' (*'Durcharbeitung'*)[29]. This does not mean a simple investigation of the past, in order to thoroughly

29. Cf. the title of one of the essays in *L'inhumain*: 'Réécrire la modernité' (n. 9, pp. 33-44). For this, Lyotard was inspired by Freud. See also: *Ibid*, pp. 64-67; W. VAN REIJEN & D. VEERMAN (n. 15), pp. 106-108.

examine the whole of modernity again and pass an independent judgment on it. Nor does it implies that the mistakes of modernity are reviewed and corrected, thus fulfilling the destiny of modernity. After all, the history of the fate of modernity would then be encapsulated once again within a hegemonic narrative, predictably at our own deception. The 'rewriting' of modernity Lyotard seeks can only be an endeavor without a regulating goal. It demands receptivity, a readiness not to judge hastily, as found in the current (postmodern) aesthetic attitude. The past in this view is not *re*presented as such, but presents itself, not as knowledge about the past, but in forms that are newly discovered. Rewriting boils down to a remembering of what one actually should not/cannot forget because it never was/can be written down: an already shattered/shattering presence of which only the interruptive event can be remembered, which in itself can never be called to mind.

III. Towards a Postmodern Political Theology?

The critical tool for analyzing the present context offered by Lyotard promises to be very interesting for a theology in search of a recontextualization partner, even if his alternative to current hegemonic narratives, as economism and estheticism, seems – from the perspective of a theology of liberation – perhaps too meager, too limited. A philosophical or artistic resistance against the organized forgetting of the differend, however praiseworthy and even effective this may be, is probably too elitist, and on the broader level of societal praxis too marginal[30]. Nevertheless, his plea for bearing witness to the differend, especially to the irreconcilability and heterogeneity which it involves, his attention to conflicts and how these are coped with, can inspire theology. It is my conviction that, like the philosopher, and the artist, the Christian can hold and live a non-hegemonical, open narrative – critical of repressing master narratives and bearing witness – which is 'doing justice' – to that which can never be captured in phrases. The end of narratives claiming universality may enable to particular narratives, such as the Christian one, to renew the opportunity of discovering within themselves their critical consciousness and liberative power, and to rephrase it. In such a project of recontextualization along the lines of an 'open narrative' Christian faith, with its

---

30. That a broader perspective perhaps is possible, Lyotard seems to suggest in *Heidegger et 'les juifs'*, Paris, Galilée, 1990 (E.T.: *Heidegger and the Jews*, University of Minnesota Press Minneapolis (Minn.), 1990), and in *Moralités postmodernes*, Paris, Galilée, 1993.

reflexive theological dimension, can regain its identity and relevance for human life, community, society and history.

On other occasions I have tried to develop a theological epistemology in which the reflexive pattern involved in the 'bearing witness to the differend' has been employed as a new way to think the dynamical relationship between transcendence and immanence, God and humanity/history/society. As an open narrative Christianity lives from the consciousness of *Deus semper major*, to whom in faith is testified, but who is never graspable, conceivable, and manageable in any human narrative. In this way an attempt has been made to construct a theology which, as 'faith seeking understanding', takes a distance from more traditional, metaphysical (onto-theo-logical) schemes to reconstruct its reflexive framework – seemingly in a postmodern era, this is the only way to proceed if one intends to (re)gain plausibility[31].

Here, however, I would like to briefly elaborate on the recontextualization of Christianity's critical consciousness on the level of politics, as is referred to in Metz's notion of 'political theology'. The field where the linking of phrases happens, is called by Lyotard the field of politics. In this perspective politics, as such, is not a genre of discourse, but the place where a plurality of discourses comes together and claims the next linkage according to the diverse strategies entailed in realizing their finalities. Each decision on this field is thereby a political one. Genres which regulate the linkages, are involved in politics, either in a hegemonic or non-hegemonic way. As a narrative, active on the field of linkages, theology is necessarily (and already) political. It must judge possibilities and make decisions. The critical consciousness of liberation theology, coined as the preferential option for the poor, must relate to this field of linkages. For each differend reveals a phrase which could not actualize itself because of the victory of another phrase (and thus discourse), and the more so where a hegemonic narrative, in particular the economical one, was active. Postmodern political theology is inevitably a theology having an acute awareness of plurality and conflict, and will stand at the side of the excluded other – in Lyotard's terminology, the side of the repressed phrase. This critical consciousness relates both *ad intra*, to its own narrative, and *ad extra*, to other discourses and narratives; both levels being mutually linked. In the conflict which appears in a differend,

---

31. For a general account of this problematic, see L. BOEVE, *Een postmoderne theologie van het 'open verhaal'*, in *OAM* 50 (1996) 210-238; *De weg, de waarheid en het leven. Religieuze traditie en waarheid in de postmoderne context*, in *Bijdragen* 58 (1997) 164-188 (with summary in English); and *Postmodernism and Negative Theology. The A/Theologie of the 'Open Narrative'*, forthcoming in *Bijdragen* 58:4 (1997).

postmodern political theology will analyze what really 'happened' in the concatenation of phrases, and criticize hegemonic pretensions of old and new master narratives. But the same critical attitude must be directed to the narrative itself, questioning whether the Christian narrative is not (in)curably hegemonic. An active praxis of commemoration and search for justice accompanies this criticism, giving shape to the witness to the differend in an appropriate way.

In this regard, the option for the poor (the excluded other) goes hand in hand with the option for the other as other. Since there is no universally acknowledged meta-narrative remaining, the other discourses – at least if one is not hegemonically subordinating them to its own narrative – remain to a certain degree inaccessible, revealing the differend between them and us. This otherness, which is revealed by differences in race, sex, social stratification, ethnic descent, culture, and so on, points to the irreducible particularity of one's own narrative and the other narratives, all of which are rooted in different particular presumptions, view points, traditions, and contexts. Respecting this otherness is then a way of bearing witness to the differend as well[32].

By recontextualizing political theology in our postmodern context with Lyotard as dialogue partner, the postmodern intuitions of Johann-Baptist Metz, appearing in his articles after 1985, can be validated reflexively, and this precisely at the stage after the fall of late modern recontextualization partners. Since 1985, Metz has more sharply criticized the modern project, which he reproached for having realized only half of the Enlightenment program, namely the scientifico-technological mastery of the world, forgetting the anamnetic basis of human rationality which points at freedom to be accomplished through solidarity. Postmodernity in his eyes then brings about a 'second analphabetism', a 'collective anamnesis', and on the religious level, a situation of 'polymythism without God'[33].

---

32. By way of illustration, we can say that in the dialogue between theologians from different contexts, for instance, this respecting the differend implies that (1) one be concious of the fact that theological positions are intrinsically and irreducibly anchored in particular contexts, and cannot be universalized as such (a generalized eurocentrism is illegitimate), nd also that (2) theologians have to be aware of this anchoring of their own and the other theological positions (Europeans cannot be blamed that they theologize from and within a European context; what needs to be criticized, however, is the uncritical eurocentric attitude they might have). In this regard, it is most unlikely that such a dialogue results in a 'meta-theology', covering the entire field of theological positions. The cause of theology is probably best served by a mutual understanding of, and respect for, the particularities of the different theological positions and contexts – assuming that all of them are attempting to bear witness to the *Deus semper maior*, encountered in the history of human liberation.

33. "Religion, gibt sich nur dionysisch, als Glücksgewinnung durch Leid- und Trauervermeidung und als Beruhigung vagabundierender Ängste, Religion als mythische Seelenverzauberung, als psychologisch-ästhetische Unschuldsvermutung für den Menschen,

At the same time, he has also put the challenges of theology's polycultural context to the fore[34]. In the light of these two foci, he has translated the dangerous memory of the Christian message both – in the face of a socially divided world – as the option for the poor, and, related to this, – in the face of a culturally-ethnically divided world – as the option for the other as being other. Concerning the option for the poor, the biblical heritage must be remembered and actualized as a ferment for a new political culture, focused on freedom and justice for all. Concerning the second option, the biblical message can serve as a starting point for a hermeneutical culture: i.e. a culture of the recognition of the otherness of the other – which contradicts the dominating tendency of the West to subdue, repress and objectify in encountering otherness[35].

The tasks of a postmodern political theology are numerous. *Ad intra*, Metz' criticism of bourgeois religion needs a recontextualization in a context where religious traditions become fragmented into items on the religious market and individuals construct their religious identity in an arbitrary way, in order to find relief, harmony, consolation, wholeness[36].

---

die alle eschatologische Unruhe im Traum von der Wiederkehr des Gleichen oder auch, religionsnäher noch, in neu aufkeimenden Seelenwanderungs- und Reinkarnationsphantasien stillgestellt hat" (from J.-B. METZ, *Religion, ja – Gott, nein*, in ID. & T.R. PETERS, *Gottespassion. Zur Ordensexistenz heute*, Freiburg, Herder, 1991, 11-62, p. 24; see also a.o. *Wohin ist Gott, wohin denn der Mensch?*, in F.X. KAUFMANN & J.-B. METZ, *Zukunftsfähigkeit. Suchbewegungen im Christentum*, Freiburg, Herder, 1987, 124-147; *Wider die zweite Unmündigkeit*, in J. RÜSEN, E. LÄMMERT & P. GLOTZ (ed.), *Die Zukunft der Aufklärung*, Frankfurt am Main, Suhrkamp, 1988, 81-87; *Anamnetische Vernunft. Anmerkungen eines Theologen zur Krise der Geisteswissenschaften*, in A. HONNETH e.a. (ed.), *Zwischenbetrachtungen. Im Prozeß der Aufklärung* (Fs. J. HABERMAS), Frankfurt am Main, Suhrkamp, 1989, 733-738; *Theologie versus Polymythie oder kleine Apologie des biblischen Monotheismus*, in O. MARQUARD (ed.), *Einheit und Vielheit. XIV. Deutscher Kongreß für Philosophie*, Hamburg, Meiner, 1990, 170-186.

34. Cf. J.-B. METZ, *In Aufbruch zu einer kulturell polyzentrischen Weltkirche*, in F.X. KAUFMANN & J.-B. METZ, *Zukunftsfähigkeit*, 93-123; *Die eine Welt als Herausforderung an das westliche Christentum*, in Una Sancta 44 (1989) 314-322; J.-B. METZ & J. MOLTMANN, *Faith and the Future. Essays on Theology, Solidarity, and Modernity* (Concilium Series), Maryknoll, NY, Orbis, 1995, pp. 30-37 (*Theology in the Modern Age, and before Its End*), 57-65 (*Unity and Diversity: Problems and Prospects for Inculturation*), and 66-71 (*1492 Through the Eyes of a European Theologian*).

35. The same two themes appear in a volume of the *Journal of Hispanic Latino Theology* 3 (1996) nr. 4. Concerning the excluded other: D.N. HOPKINS, *Postmodernity, Black Theology and the United States: Michel Foucault and James H. Cone* (Hopkins using Foucault as recontextualization partner); concerning the other as other: E. MENDIETA, *From Christendom to Polycentric Oikumenè: Modernity, Postmodernity, and Liberation Theology*.

36. The religious market segment consists of pieces from older indigenous and exogenous religious traditions, aside from a diversity of newer religious articles. Their characteristic marks include being consumable, available, manipulable, exchangeable. What I have in mind is the pluriform multiplicity of, among others, traditional religious rituals and experiences, meditation techniques, positive thinking, faith healing, natural diets, mysticism, yoga, hydropathic cures, acupuncture, astrology, Jungian psychology, biofeedback,

Ad extra, processes of globalization, especially if these are effected by an economizing logic, should be subjected to a critical examination of their hegemonic intentions. The oppression of the poor, of peoples and cultures must be made apparent and challenged. In this regard, it is worthwhile to investigate and criticize the religious features which, according to some philosophers of culture[37], the narrative of the global market takes upon itself[38]. In the end, what is at stake, is the transformation of the Christian narrative (and thus praxis) into an 'open narrative', sensitive to plurality, differences and conflicts, paying respect to the otherness which is revealed, and resisting to the hegemony of the market which oppresses other discourses and narratives.

IV. CONCLUSION

After the loss of plausibility of modern master narritives, and also of late-modern critical consciousness of neo-marxism, late-modern theology,

---

extra-sensory perception, spiritism, biological gardening, ancient mythologies, archaic nature cults, witchcraft, freemasonry, Kabbalism, herbal medicine, hypnosis, oriental miracle books, iridology, cosmic kneecap massage, graphology, reincarnation therapy, clairvoyance, telepathy, macrobiotics, ufology, and the like (for this list, see, among others, R. WOODS, *New Age Spiritualities: How are we to Talk of God?*, in *New Blackfriars* 74 (1993) 176-191, p. 177). Insofar as a religious need lives in the individual and the community – more generally described as a longing for harmony, comfort, consolation, wholeness – the market fills the void with an offer of religious and para-religious products which can satisfy this need.

37. In Flanders, e.g., this has been showed by R. LAERMANS (see for instance his *Individueel vlees. Over lichaamsbeelden* [Amsterdam, 1993], in which he analyses the religious features of contemporary body culture).

38. See also in this regard: L. BOFF, *The Market and the Religion of Commodities*, in *Concilium* 3 (1992) ix-xiii. Here Boff, following a.o. H. Assmann and F. Hinkelhammert, describes these religious features as a new form of religion, namely the religion of commodities, possessing a lot of characteristics which are proper to religion in general: the fundamental dogma of the absolute hegemony of money, reflected in a mythology spread by the media, and systematized in a scholarly theology. Advertisement function as evangelization; some commodities are perceived as sacraments. Other parallels include the temples of this religion (banks), the pilgrimages to shopping centres and Disneyworld, the priests (bankers, financiers and accountants). It owns an ethical code, focused on the norm of individual interst, and so on. "We are witnessing an immense process of idolatry, of gestures and attitudes which human beings until now reserved exclusively for the Supreme Being, the Godhead, no other creature. Now the attributes of divinity are attached to commodities. They are credited with saving powers. [...] The characteristic [of this idolatry] is to demand lives as sacrifices, and to produce frustrations in human beings". According to Boff, this religion of the commodities fullfils the religious functions in the public sphere, whereas "in the private sphere the various religions offer the 'spiritual aroma' which money does not confer" (p. xii). In my opinion, the religion of commodities invades this private sphere as well, turning the religious field into a market of religions where the religious consumer constructs his or her private religious identity (cf. supra).

such as certain forms of liberation theology and political theology (Metz), have run against their limits. Lyotard's theory of language pragmatics can offer a framework to cope with plurality and conflict reflexively, to criticize hegemonic master narratives that forget the 'differend', the conflict, otherness. In so doing, this opens new thinking patterns for a revitalization of the Christian narrative as a narrative characterized by receptivity and liberative praxis for the subordinated or excluded particular other, which is theologically speaking the instantiation of the Other, the Unrepresentable God-with-us. Through Lyotard and the proposed theory of the 'open narrative', it is possible to give shape to, what Giddens calls, the reflexive reappropriation of traditions in the context of manufactured uncertainties[39].

Faculty of Theology, KULeuven   Lieven BOEVE
Sint-Michielsstraat 6
B-3000, Leuven, Belgium

39. Most probably, J.-F. Lyotard would not be the only proponent of contemporary critical consciousness, who is available as a recontextualization partner to (western) liberation theology. Another candidate would surely be the American philosopher F. Jameson, who using a historical-materialistic vocabulary, makes an analysis of postmodernism. Jameson identifies the latter both (1) as adequate description of the contemporary cultural situation which as superstructure is linked to the economic basis of the current (third) phase of capitalism – representing on the cultural level its mode of production – and at the same time (2) as ideology of late-capitalism, an element of the superstructure, legitimating the economic basis (the end-of-ideologies as a new ideology). See his *Postmodernism, or, The Cultural Logic of Late Capitalism*, London/New York, Verso, 1991 and *Postmodernism and Consumer Society*, in H. FOSTER (ed.), *The Anti-Aesthetic: Essays on Postmodern Culture*, Port Townsend, Bay Press, 1983, 119-134.

15

POSTMODERNITY AND THE THEOLOGIES OF LIBERATION FROM THE PERSPECTIVE OF A FIRST-WORLD PASTORAL THEOLOGY

I. THE PARADOXICAL CHARACTER OF MODERNITY

Modernity has been a paradoxical phenomenon[1]. On the one hand, it means the following: (a) the globalization of information, production, and markets, (b) a uniformity of products and life-styles, and (c) a sophisticated form of suppression. This suppression is legitimized through any or a combination of the following: an ideology of rationality and the unity of the spirit, a utopia of universal progress and development, and a political or philosophical grand narrative about the reason of history and its definite fulfillment in modernity. On the other hand, modernity offers a great variety of products and information sources, makes it possible to live very different lifestyles and biographic concepts, and gives various religions, sects, world views, and value systems the chance to find their representatives.

Thus, if modernity is seen as suppressive unification, postmodernity has to be deconstructive. The latter must break open the one-dimensional rationalities, and bring forth multiple rationalities and trans-rationalities. If modernity is still seen as bewildering diversification, postmodernity has to be holistic. It must offer ways to exercise responsibility, to enable decision-making, and to pursue life-giving options.

II. POSTMODERNITY

1. Postmodernity: The Challenge of Plurality

In any case, postmodernity means the protest against and the sought-after end of a specific form of modernity. It would be too simple to banalize postmodernity as a merely bewildering and amazing plurality. Postmodernity has become a well-defined description for developments in quite different sectors such as architecture, art, literature, science, and philosophy. An excellent survey of the developments in these sectors

1. See VAN DER LOO & W. VAN REIJEN, *Paradoxen van modernisering. Een sociaalwetenschap-pelijke benadering*, Muiderberg, Coutinho, 1990.

can be found in the book of Wolfgang Welsch[2]. His point is that "post-modernity" marks the current of modernity which is its period of self-reflexivity and consciousness of plurality. So modernity becomes postmodern when it no longer tries to regard plurality as essential unity plus its merely contingent variations, or when it no longer complains about losing the sense of unifying rationality. Postmodernity seeks the challenges and chances of the heterogeneous aspects of the pulsating life.

Postmodernity is not irrational, but is interested in the different rationalities. To cite some examples: aesthetic rationality is different from the rationality of science, economic rationality from that of pedagogy, and bureaucratic rationality from that of personal relationships. And none is better than the others. So the aims of the Enlightenment will be fulfilled better by postmodernity, where modernity becomes self-reflexive about the failures of its rationality, which was linear and one-dimensional and thus unsound and dangerous.

The danger of a rationality with a universal truth-claim is the major concern of Jean-François Lyotard[3]. According to him, Auschwitz – the great catastrophe of our century – was not the consequence of a mad ideology but the logical consequence of the modern ideology. Within every form of thinking that claims universality, anything that is different, or whatever does not fit in the universal scheme, has no right to exist. And it is not even possible to present good arguments in favour of the misfit because there is no idiom to formulate them. In dealing with the misfit, every solution creates injustice as long as the solution is formed only within the prevailing universal scheme. Thus, a way of making justice must be found which does not look for a compromise or a consensus; it is crucial to develop a sense of the "differend" and to avoid a suppressive dominance of one rationality over the others.

A central philosopher and theologian in that line of thinking is Emmanuel Lévinas[4], who is cited by Lyotard and by some liberation theologians as well. For Levinas, the modern paradigm of thinking sees one subject at the centre of the world who turns all others into objects of his thinking and making of reality. In Descartes' *"cogito ergo sum"* the rational "I" is the measure of every experience, and what he does not expect to experience he will not even realize. This way of treating the world is consequently suppressive because it is only capable and willing to think

2. W. WELSCH, *Unsere Postmoderne Moderne*, Berlin, VCH Weinheim, 1993.
3. J.-F. LYOTARD, *Le Différend*, Paris, Ed. de Minuit, 1983.
4. E. LÉVINAS & N. KREWANI (eds.), *Totalität und Unendlichkeit. Versuch über die Exteriorität. (übersetzt v. W.N. Krewani)*, Freiburg, Alber, 1987.

the Same. It is necessary to undergo a paradigm shift. It is the Other who forces the I to an encounter; as long as the Other can be regarded as something, even as an enemy, he can be rejected. But if the I meets the Other face to face, the I is challenged to be responsible: the bare and weaponless face provokes a crisis in the I. The face of the Other cannot even be avoided because it is the track of the Infinite, which appears on it. To undertake responsibility for the Other means to praise the Infinite.

A more secular solution to plurality is shown by Wolfgang Welsch. He pleads for a "transversal reason"[5]. He sees Lyotard's problem as regards making the heterogeneous rationalities the basis of his concept. Welsch distinguishes two phases: in the first phase of differentiation, the heterogeneous rationalities were formed. In the second, which is occurring in our times, we are confronted with heterogeneous paradigms. Although every paradigm is incommensurably different, every one is built out of and in conflict with several others, all the paradigms use the same words but in different meanings, and all deal with the same reality but understand it within different concepts. This pluralization of paradigms asks for a transversal reason, the capacity to understand different paradigms as different and to build bridges between them wherever bridges are actually necessary. Those bridges can never be fixed for a long time because there is no super- or meta- paradigm that can guarantee them.

In this conception, both solutions of postmodernity – plurality and holism – fit together. To accept plurality, to respect the Other, and to refuse any attempt to establish meta-theories constitute one side of the coin. It can easily lead to an attitude of tolerance which strengthens the status quo, is very profitable for the rich and powerful, and is disastrous for the poor. Yet this seems to be the only way to render that sort of justice Lyotard is concerned about. The other side of the coin is equally important. Each paradigm represents a holistic vision of a good life for all, but with specific presuppositions and under certain conditions. They all take their options and have to deal with conflicts. Within a transversal reason, they can help one another form good solutions for a concrete situation. But a suppressive dominance over the others must be avoided. As they respectively have their special profiles, their advantages and disadvantages, and their strengths and blind spots, they can enrich one other only by remaining different, not by looking for a mixture or fusion. But then, they may form a network.

---

5. W.W. VERNUNFT, *Die zeitgenössische Vernunftkritik und das Konzept der transversalen Vernunft*, Frankfurt/M, Suhrkamp, 1996.

2. *Four Aspects from a Practical Point of View*

As presented above, postmodernity is marked by four aspects: self-reflexivity, complexity, alterity, and transversality. It is neither a theoretical construction nor a philosophical idea but an everyday reality. Beginning with the oil shock and the first report to the Club of Rome, then with the discussions about acid rain, the death of the forests, and the growing ozone hole, western people became more and more aware that the "glorious" and steady progress of modernity might come to a desperate end. The catastrophes of Chernobyl and Bophal brought about a profound crisis of confidence as regards technological perfection, and the latest conflicts about gene manipulation and the scandal over BSE-beef show the dangerous sides of industrial food production. Finally, the connection of Shell with the murder of the Ogoni showed that western profit is not morally innocent at all.

The fatal connections between modern industry and economy, the globalization of markets and money speculations, the increasing social and ecological problems, and the shocking misery in the southern half of the earth – the consciousness that all these factors are interlinked and are due to modernity is no longer the privilege of a marxist or christian avant-garde, but is in the minds of school pupils, homemakers, and average middle-class people. Modernity after the second world war has brought some common peace and welfare, but by the same means, it is now risking to lose all that. We cannot continue like that. This is the practical side of postmodern self-reflexivity.

A consequence of these experiences of dangerous modernity is that people lose confidence in technical, industrial, and scientific solutions. They are no longer sure that experts know what is good for them. In many instances of personal experience, they find out what they are really longing for, and they discover that expert systems, in most cases, solve only the problems that these systems have defined or even created themselves. The day-to-day problems are much more complex than the professional solutions. If for example somebody feels very tired, he finally ends up seeing the doctor, who will prescribe some drugs until the patient is able to efficiently do his job again. In fact, he will need something much more: to find out how to refuse too many demands from various social systems and groups, to resolve the conflicts within the family and the workplace, to define the sense of his personal life and then take the appropriate options, and so on. There are no modern experts for a good life.

One way to live with postmodern complexity is to deny it. This fundamentalistic temptation is found in every sector: in the simple scapegoat-mentality of the new right-wing political parties, in the traditionalistic escapism of religious groups and sects, in some holistic or romantic utopias within the new ecological and religious movements[6], and in the tiny worlds of the numerous soap operas that fill the living rooms of the tv-watching masses every day. The better consequence of complexity is the longing for orientative systems. In this field, many self-named wise guides come up everywhere, and there is a new interest in spiritual traditions. The churches and theology can benefit from this development only if they integrate the complexity of modern experience with the relevant christian traditions.

Experiencing complexity also entails the feeling that one's own wishes and expectations are different from those of many others. This is the modern chance to develop one's distinctive personality as a woman or a man. This concern is central to feminism and its critique of the patriarchal structures of our societies. Evidently, it is much easier to realize one's own demands to be different from others than to accept the Other in his or her otherness with respect to one's own presumptions and convictions. And it is even more difficult not only to be tolerant towards the Other but also to be in solidarity with the Other. This solidarity is especially demanding as regards those marginalized by the social norms such as those people who are unable or unwilling to work for ever-greater profit. This sense of alterity is perhaps the central practical challenge of postmodernity.

To practise solidarity towards the Other can even proceed from the presumption that I am rather sure of my own point of view. Thereafter, I shall evolve it more and more in confrontation with the others. In modernity, this confrontation eventually would either separate the subjects or destroy one of them. The complexity of postmodern situations and expectations, however, requires co-operative work not inspite of the differences but with the full involvement of these different qualifications and different perspectives. Thus, as the capacity to integrate incommensurable perspectives in favour of a specifically necessary solution, transversality determines the quality of life in postmodernity at all levels: personally, in community and society, and in the face of problems of injustice between the continents and the generations.

Under these circumstances, the unity of a community or an institution can no longer be guaranteed by hanging on to the same ideology or life-style. Unity will be found in the steady realization of communication, conflict, and actual participatory decision-making. Revolution and

---

6. See M. WIDL, *Christentum und Esoterik. Darstellung, Auseinandersetzung, Abgrenzung*, Graz, Wien-Köln 1995.

violence are no longer necessary and useful to transform the structures. Now, what is imperative is to make use of the dynamism of a constant paradoxical change that is going on all the time with or without our engagement. The consequence of postmodern transversality is a new balance between powerful options and humorous calmness.

III. Implications for the Church

1. *The Basis of a Postmodern Catholicism: The Second Vatican Council*

If one looks at the actual parts of the catholic church, one sees premodern, modern, and postmodern features. As regards the church's solemn, traditional, and monarchical style and content, it is premodern; as regards its legalistic, centralistic and bureaucratic structures and decisions, it is modern; as regards its great variety of religious customs, theologically reflective sectors, and autonomously deciding communities, it is postmodern. The common basis for this non-isomorphic situation is the Second Vatican Council. As Elmar Klinger has shown with much knowledge of the details[7], the prominent merit of Vatican II was threefold: first, it represented a "jump forward" or – one could say – a "paradigm shift"; second, it did not intend to formulate new dogmas but to say the old ones in a new way, or to develop the dogmatics within the pastoral questions and to develop the pastoral as a starting-point and guide for developing the dogmatics; third, it formulated a new cardinal point for all theological reasoning – the new dogma of the vocation of the human being in Jesus Christ.

Klinger also shows that latin american liberation theology is a new theology that is in continuity with Vatican II. It is a theology that is formulated from the experiences of the poor as they are addressed by the gospel and called to live in the emergent realm of God. The pastoral and the dogmatic are two sides of the same coin of evangelizing praxis and theological reflection in the midst of the communities. The liberation theologies[8], thus, produce a paradigm shift in continuity with the intentions of the council. They share in the non-uniformism of the whole church in their specific ways. The paradigm shift in the post-idealistic theologies in the first world, however, is generally not determined by this interpenetration of the pastoral and the dogmatic but by fundamental

---

7. E. KLINGER, *Armut – Eine Herausforderung Gottes. Der Glaube des Konzils und die Befreiung des Menschen*, Zürich, Echter, 1990.

8. See A. HENNELLY, *Liberation Theologies. The Global Pursuit of Justice*, Mystic, Con., Twenty-Third Publications, 1995.

theological reasoning[9]. Pastoral conclusions from the liberative praxis of latin american base communities are appropriated by first world theologians as "socio-pastoral" notions[10].

Norbert Mette and Hermann Steinkamp propose a new paradigm of christian praxis that is orientated no longer towards membership-maintenance and pastoral paternalism but towards active participation and emancipative consciousness. With personal concern about the miseries that result from the capitalistic systems, and in solidarity with the poor and the marginalized, a christian praxis has to take place which opts for the oppressed and the exploited in our society as well as worldwide. This struggle can only be fruitful within care-giving and socially active base communities. This sort of political diakonia is the deciding factor for a new evangelization that begins with the church's conversion to the poor.

2. *Postmodernity: Still a Challenge to Church and Theology*

Postmodernity is not only a fact of analysis but, more so, of prescription. It is the challenge, the chance, and the tribunal of our times. As Franz-Xavier Kaufmann points out, the modern order of differentiation made the church that particular and specialized part of society which is responsible for, and occupied with, the religious desires of people, the moral basics of their attitudes, and some symbolic expressions of the state[11]. Wolfgang Welsch has shown that, in postmodernity, paradigms are no longer segregated but interlinked while continuing to be heterogeneous. They are always perspectival, but in their perspectival characteristics, they can be universal. Paradigms become the concepts of thinking not of parts of society and their differentiated functions but of groups of people who reflexively opt for the same way. Thus, paradigms become voluntary and obligatory at the same time.

For church communities and theology, this is a great chance to imagine and produce new christian paradigms in praxis and theory. In praxis, this implies the challenge to become a model

---

9. H. KÜNG & D. TRACY (eds.), *Das neue Paradigma von Theologie. Strukturen und Dimensionen*, Zürich, Echter, 1986.

10. H. STEINKAMP, *Solidarität und Parteilichkeit. Für eine neue Praxis in Kirche und Gemeinde*, Mainz, 1994; N. METTE & H. STEINKAMP (Kreative), *Rezeption der Befreiungstheologie in der praktischen Theologie*, In R. FORNET-BETANCOURT (ed.), *Befreiungstheologie: Kritischer Rückblick und Perspektiven für die Zukunft*. Vol. 3; *Die Rezeption im deutschsprachigen Raum*, Mainz, 1997, pp. 9-25; N. METTE & H. STEINKAMP (eds.), *Anstiftung zur Solidarität. Praktische Beispiele der Sozialpastoral*, Mainz, 1997.

11. F. KAUFMANN, *Religion und Modernität. Sozialwissenschaftliche Perspektiven*, Tübingen, Mohr, 1989.

- of solidarity within the inequalities and changes of globalization and localization, and this means a new praxis of sharing and respect and new networks of communication;
- for humanizing cultures to opt for justice, peace, and a good life for all in the name of the realm of God;
- of social integration that is voluntary and liberating and which promotes the development of different personal charisms for oneself, for the community, and for God;
- of the sustainable use of natural, cultural, social, and personal resources, and this implies opposition to the following: on the one hand, the exploitation of nature, labour-power, family ties, and cultural and religious symbols, and on the other hand, the disregard and neglect of the young, the old, women, the poor, the ignorant, marginal geographical regions, and the Third-World masses in general.

In their method, the postmodern christian paradigms will be global not only in their view of interlinked developments with their risks, challenges, and chances, but also in the communication networks and solidarity structures they create between different paradigms. They will be perspectival in their experiences, local in their rootings, and optional in their responsibilities. They will be theological in their arguments in continuity with christian tradition, spiritual in their experience and expression of God's salvation and liberation in the middle of everyday life, and ecclesial in the basic functions of diakonia, koinonia, liturgia, and martyria.

3. A Postmodern "Pastoral World Theology"

In the face of Third-World liberation theologies, a paradigm of a postmodern First-World theology should not be proselytizing but complementary. On the basis of Vatican II, such a theology would be a postmodern "pastoral world theology". "World" here comprises four dimensions: the world of lay people and their vocation to reproduce and innovate day-to-day life in a reflexively christian way; the global world and its challenges for today and the future; the many perspectival worlds of living and reflecting with their contextual and pluriform praxes; the world of God's creation in which the realm of God brings forth liberation. In this conception, the basic ecclesial functions will not primarily be specializations of praxis but its dimensions based on experience and theological reflection:

The *diakonia* dimension is a response to the postmodern challenge to accept contingency without relinquishing responsibility: as struggle for physical, psychic, and social survival; as quest for consolation, support, and orientation in the context of God; as the overcoming of the modern madness of being godlike; in the efforts to enhance cultures towards legitimizing the practice of greater justice and peace in the global context. This *diakonia* dimension is developing in conformity with justice.

The *koinonia* dimension in postmodernity would be a network of binding communications with the explicit recognition that the different contexts and perspectives have equal rights for attention and participation. It builds solidarity in changing problematic situations, and aims for a unity that has to grow between different and thus complementary perspectives. It becomes possible through reconciliation.

The *liturgical* dimension arises in the postmodern longing for the event that can break up the everyday surface, which can transcend the small ego toward something incommensurably great, wonderful, and mysterious, and which can end up in prayer and rituals as commemoration, complaint, cry, thanksgiving, and praise of God. It is based on trust.

The *martyrial* dimension arises in postmodern wishes to have cause for hope despite all miseries. It shows the christian gospel as a promise that gives importance both to life and the future. It gains a footing where the gospel is confessed credibly, lived in practice, and explained reasonably. It is rooted in vocation.

Such a pastoral world theology would overcome the tensions between diakonia and community, between service of salvation and service of the earth, between ethics and pastoral needs, and between doctrine and praxis. In its method, it is perspective-transversal, and so it searches in actual situations – out of explicitly concrete perspectives and options – not only for common ways but also for incommensurably different perspectives. It would have a narrative aspect, and so it would express the concrete concerns of people and take them into account. It would be analytic in critically admitting other scientific disciplines and their points of view. It would be complementarian in seeing its own universal view as a perspectival-optional part of the whole. It would be evangelizing in making the explicit christian understanding of life dimensionally relevant in the midst of everyday praxis. It finds its scale in the realm of God, its brotherly and sisterly correction within the church, and its vocation in serving in the midst of the people.

Coesfeldweg 3   Maria WIDL
Münster, Germany

16

NEW AGE'S INTEREST IN INDIGENOUS CULTURES
THE CASE OF J. REDFIELD

The present generation of liberation theologians gives the impression of shifting the attention from the economical exploitation of the poor to the expressions of popular culture and popular religiosity that live among them and grant them an identity, despite the obvious violations of their human dignity. But also some recent New Age cult-books apparently show a learning attitude towards indigenous cultures and the way they respectfully make use of the natural resources at their disposal. In this contribution we will focus our attention on two succesful novels of the American author James Redfield, *The Celestine Prophecy* and *The Tenth Insight*[1]. We have serious doubts, however, that the elements of Indian wisdom and the signs of an ecological sensitivity in both books signify nothing more than the effort of an intelligent author to play along with the current themes of interest of his mainly European and North American readers. Redfield's most honest plea is the request for a systematic financial support of spiritual counselers, who, like himself, want to save the world with their timeless and in no way inculturated New Age message. I am afraid that the warning by I. Wallerstein (50-59)[2], that the 'culture politics' of the northern hemisphere are seldom accompanied by a real interest in ameliorating the socio-economic conditions of the indigenous groups, affects Redfield's would-be "spiritual" books as well.

I. SALES TECHNIQUES OF A SUPPLIER IN NEW AGE SPIRITUALITY

J. Redfield's 'Good News' is largely in line with what other New Age authors offer in their spiritual or pseudo-scientific publications. Their target group consists of highly educated, materialistic people from Western Europe and North America, who increasingly suffer from stress, physically and psychologically. New Age addresses the questions these people are asking about the meaning of such a life. A radical change of

1. J. REDFIELD, *The Celestine Prophecy*, London, Bantam Books, 1993; *The Tenth Insight*, London, Bantam Books, 1996.
2. See also, I. WALLERSTEIN, *Culture as the Ideological Battleground of the Modern World System*, in *TCS* 7 (1990/2-3) 31-35.

mentality, they argue, must be given highest priority. Redfield pleads for "a kind of renaissance in consciousness, not religious in nature, but spiritual"[3]. How is this to be conceived?

People should learn to derive energy from the original source of life, God or the universe. To succeed in this task they do not need the mediation of institutionalized religions, for they have the key to salvation in their own hands, undoubtedly an attractive idea to postmodern people. (In a later stage, however, people might discover that their spiritual growth takes place under the guidance of the souls of certain deceased). Since the beginning of this century quantum physics has pointed out that the universe consists of fields of energy. New Age contends that people should learn to open themselves to this energy. Contact with this energy makes them conscious of the weak spots in their character, teaches them to communicate with other people at a deeper level, makes them conscious of the amazing beauty of nature, even teaches them to understand the messages animals convey, reveals them their former incarnations, and exceptionally enables them to break through the frontiers of this reality and to establish contact with the 'celestine' world.

Redfield had the clever idea to let the protagonists of a story that keeps the readers in suspense gradually discover these insights. In *The Celestine Prophecy* they are obstructed in their search for the fragments of a Peruvian manuscript of 600 BC by a conspiration of church and state, both afraid of losing their power. In *The Tenth Insight* the suspense remains until the end, because only at the very last moment do the initiated protagonists come to the insight that a collective process of generating good energy is needed to thwart the success of high-tech research, aimed at deriving from the universe cheap energy for immediate use, at the expense of habitats for nature conservation.

The author also tries to convince the reader at the end of each book that his knowledge of the insights still ought to be further expanded, and that he therefore is willing to write another book. On the next to last page of *The Celestine Prophecy* both the hero and the reader are told that the manuscript contains a tenth insight and *The Tenth Insight*, too, ends with the hero realizing that "his journey was far from being finished". After the success of his first book Redfield in co-autorship with Carol Adrienne has edited *An Experiential Guide to 'The Celestine Prophecy'*, which contains exercises and advice for individual and collective appropriation of the revealed insights. Redfield's concern for the world's future has certainly not made him poorer.

3. *The Celestine Prophecy* (n. 1), p. 14.

His books are also appreciated by many readers who believe in reincarnation. At the end of *The Celestine Prophecy* Wil, without doubt the
most 'enlightened' character, suddenly disappears, apparently having
succeeded in overcoming the limits of temporal existence. The readers
are told that the Maya people were most probably able to make the same
journey, which would explain the sudden disappearance of their culture.
In *The Tenth Insight*, however, the theme of reincarnation is overwhelm-
ingly present. The main characters come to the insight that their encounter
is not due to coincidence. In a former incarnation they were all involved,
as victor or as victim, in the last great battle of the war of the eastern
states of America against the Indians, fought in the beginning of the
nineteenth century in the southern Appalachian mountains. This former
incarnation of the main characters has been described in detail. But Redfield furnishes as many details about the spiritual journey of the hero into
the future, a journey which started once he had reached an extremely
high spiritual level and became able to transcend the limits of space and
time. Together with him we witness a person's near death experience –
described by means of the familiar symbolism of the tunnel, the ray of
light and the life review – and we are offered a concrete picture of the
life of souls, both those who are waiting for a future incarnation and
those who are damned for eternity. A statement as: "In the past we had
to die to engage in a review of our lives; but now we can wake up earlier and eventually make death obsolete"[4], will certainly be appreciated by many people who revolt against the contingency of human
existence.

II. THE POSTMODERN REDISCOVERY OF NATURE AND
OF NEGLECTED CULTURES

Redfield is convinced that the spiritual transformation of the world
must be combined with a renewed concern for our natural environment
and a deep respect for the wisdom of premodern cultures, in his case the
Indian culture. In his books he has certainly succeeded in raising his
voice against the dominance of modern, Western culture and the world-
wide merciless depletion of natural resources. The setting of his books
are a subtropic rain forest in Peru and the Appalachian mountains, which
form a natural border between the east and west of the United States.
Both belong to the rare unspoilt wildlife reserves in the world. The vivid

---

4. *The Tenth Insight* (n. 1), p. 113.

descriptions of their natural beauty form an impressive plea to conserve them for future generations. In *The Celestine Prophecy* it is argued that through the contemplation of beautiful trees and flowers people are able to observe the fields of energy behind them. And in *The Tenth Insight* animals that accidently pass by are bearers of an important message.

In *The Celestine Prophecy*, Redfield mentions the fact that the Maya people were the first to have discovered and written down these insights, but this only serves to frame the story. No enriching interactions take place between the white seekers of wisdom and the indigenous population. In *The Tenth Insight*, however, Redfield deplores what happened in his own American history: the slaughter of the indian population by white soldiers. Confronted, in their life review, with their own role in this war, all the protagonists of the book feel guilty for not being able to rewrite this sad history. But Redfield also renders his vision of the ideal relations between the cultures in a globalized world. Respect for "local autonomy and cultural differences"[5] must become a fundamental law. "Each member of the family of nations is being recognized for this culture truth represented to the world at large"[6]. Besides his holding in esteem the value of difference, however, Redfield considers "a grassroots acknowledgment of our spiritual similarities"[7] as equally important. On the whole, thus, his plea for cultural diversity remains secondary to the value of sharing the same supra-cultural New Age belief.

III. Alliance between Cultural Openness and Economical Conservatism

Admittedly, Redfield exhibits a certain sensitivity to the worldwide discrepancy between rich and poor, for which he blames capitalism. "In every nation capitalism had failed a whole class of people, and the reason was clear: for poor people there existed no opportunity to participate in the system"[8]. The "materialism of the previous four hundred years" is also held responsible for having "pushed the mystery of life and death [i.e. all spiritual questions] far into the background"[9]. But the author is not advocating the abolition of capitalism; he rather speaks up for an

5. *Ibid.*, p. 210.
6. *Ibid.*, p. 211.
7. *Ibid.*, p. 210.
8. *Ibid.*, p. 131.
9. *Ibid.*, p. 127.

"enlightened capitalism"[10]. The development of a sound business ethics would contribute to "spiritualize"[11] capitalism. This way "a new code of ethics is being added to the equation of free enterprise"[12]. Redfield hopes that in future: (1) "we humans will voluntarily decrease our population so that we all may live in the most powerful and beautiful places on the Earth;"[13] (2) thanks to a complete automation of production processes, more and more people will be liberated from labour so that they might concentrate on the acquisition of spiritual knowledge[14]; and (3) that the mediators of these insights will be financially supported, on the basis of tithes, as this was the case in the Middle Ages when 10% of one's income went to the Church[15]. "This is how we will begin to supplement our incomes and ease out of the occupations which limit us. As more people engage in this spiritual economy we will begin a real shift into the culture of the next millenium. We will have moved through the stage of evolving into our right occupation and will be entering the stage of getting paid for evolving freely and offering our unique truth to others"[16].

Redfield is not primarily concerned about those who in this information era suffer from unemployment and poverty: the "enlightened capitalism" he promotes has everything to do with the financial recognition of himself and his spiritual companions. Did not Saint Paul boast centuries ago of being able to support himself as a tanner and of not being dependent upon the community of believers? I read in Redfields books a confirmation of Wallerstein's analysis, that the postmodern interest in local cultures often exhibits a noncommittal character, that it is not engaged in the elimination of worldwide economic injustices. Ultimately, *The Celestine Prophecy* and *The Tenth Insight* are typical products of postmodern culture. This culture is indeed sensitive to ecological problems and to the rights of cultural minorities, but would nonetheless like to see the northern hemisphere's economical advantages perpetuated.

10. *Ibid.*, p. 182 & 209.
11. *Ibid.*, p. 185.
12. *Ibid.*, p. 181.
13. *The Celestine Prophecy* (n. 1), p. 255.
14. *Ibid.*, pp. 258-259. See also *The Tenth Insight* (n. 1), p. 209: "This new business ethic would produce a grassroots deflation, initiating a systematic evolution toward an eventual full automation – and ultimately the free availability – of the basic necessities of life, liberating humans to engage in the spiritual 'tithe' economy envisioned in the Ninth Insight".
15. *Ibid.*, p. 259.
16. *Ibid.*, p. 260.

IV. "Indigenous" and "Eco-Social" Theology of Liberation
as an Alternative

Redfield, as we have stated, has situated *The Celestine Prophecy* in a Maya setting, without really listening to the spiritual message of the indigenous peoples who are nowadays the heirs to that culture. On the contrary, he seems to be a zealot of the universal, uninculturated New Age message, despite his avowed respect for indigenous cultures and the natural environment they live in. To conclude my critical presentation of Redfields' books, I simply want to refer to two recent collections of articles, which adopt a more honest attitude toward indigenous cultures and environmental problems. In each publication liberation theologians are involved.

1. *Real Learning from Maya Wisdom*

Since the 500th anniversary of the *Conquista* in 1992, one may observe a rediscovered indigenous self-awareness among the inhabitants of Abia Yala[17]; this self-awareness is reflected in many publications. There even exists a *Liga Maya Internacional*, with headquarters in Costa Rica, which is dedicated to communicating Mayan culture, values, and religion[18]. A recent collection edited by Guillermo Cook[19] provides an interesting example of the honest willingness of all contributors to learn from the age-old spiritual experience of the Maya people.

A great part of this book is descriptive. The reader is told how elements of their culture helped the Maya people to resist the imposition of both a foreign culture and religion. Their reverence for the cross, for example, can be explained by the significance the cross already possessed in their culture as a symbol of the unity of all creation. The religious leaders of the past were also able to further guarantee the cohesion of the community, because in the eyes of the invaders they only exercised a medical, not a religious function. This agelong community spirit accounts for the recent emergence of a Maya theology which bases

---

17. This term, originally meaning "land of the sun" or "ripe land", is used by indigenous leaders to refer to the Américas.

18. Their recent publications include: E. CABRERA, *La Cosmogonía Maya*, San José, Liga Maya Internacional, 1992, and D. MATUL, *Somos un solo corazón: cultura Maya contemporánea*, San José, Liga Maya Internacional, 1994.

19. G. COOK (ed.), *Crosscurrents in Indigenous Spirituality: Interface of Maya, Catholic & Protestant Worldviews*, Leiden, E.J. Brill, 1997, p. 329.

its rationale on the fact that the Judeo-Christian God revealed himself in their culture centuries before the Conquest. The Maya people can be compared in this respect with the Israelites. In both cases the revelation of God in their life was anterior to the one in the book. Many chapters also describe the content of their worldview and theology. We are informed how a deep respect for the elders and the ancestors, for the community, and for the natural environment belongs to the core of their spiritual heritage.

The reader, however, also becomes convinced that the Maya culture is not only of historical interest. It enabled the possessors of this new-discovered identity to make themselves heard, both politically and religiously. The Zapatista revolution in Chiapas, Mexico, 1994, is considered in this book as a fruit of this Maya self-consciousness[20]. The history of both the Catholic and the Protestant evangelization, however, is experienced by almost every contributor to this book as anything but liberating[21]. The same criticism applies to the plea for a new Evangelization by the Latin American Episcopal Conference, who in its documents seems to consider the local cultures as "nothing more than a 'preamble', an 'old testament' to the unique and unfailing revelation of God to the world, in the person of his son Jesus Christ"[22]. Liberation theology is regarded with much more sympathy by the authors of this book, as long as its interest in local cultures does not lead to a divorce of inculturation and liberation – an argument that could also be heard during the Leuven symposium. "Liberation is already implicit in inculturation. It is not a distant goal but a process and a permanent struggle. Inculturation is oriented toward liberating the poor and liberation can only be radical if its roots are planted in the cultural context of particular peoples". What we need is an "indigenous theology of liberation"[23].

---

20. See pp. XII, 26-29 and the entire chapter eighteen.

21. See e.g. about the Protestant presence among the Maya on p. 47: "Preaching condemned specific sins – laziness, alcoholism, sloth, witchcraft, paganism – but hoarding, low wage, exploitation and ill gotten gains were not preached against. There was no mention of social sins, much less in denunciation of what is behind the social and economic structures that oppress human beings, and the Maya people in particular".

22. *Ibid.*, p. 222, a quotation from the chapter on "The Old Face of the New Evangelization".

23. *Ibid.*, pp. 214-215, quotations from chapter twelve on "Inculturation and Indigenous Theology", which is part of a statement prepared in 1993 by Dominican missionaries. Chapter sixteen, a chapter on "Christian and Mayan spirituality" by a former Catholic priest who "has returned to the spirituality of his forefathers", also states that "the methodology of liberation theology continues to be useful" but that liberation theology has to recover from its actual state of "stagnation" and "process of involution". (*ibid.*, p. 246)

2. *Liberation Theology and Ecology*

Liberation theologians have never had a keen interest in environmental problems as such. For them the first victims of ecological agression are always the poor. "The earth is crying out and the poor are crying out". "Today, nature's most threatened creatures are not the whales or the giant pandas of China, but the poor of the world, condemned to die of hunger and disease before their time". These are quotations from Leonardo Boff's[24] and Virgil Elizondo's editorial in *Concilium* 1995 n° 5, an issue dedicated to the relations between 'Ecology and Poverty', with most of the articles written by liberation theologians. To meet the claims of the poor countries of the South, as voiced at the Rio Earth Summit of 1992, contributions are made toward the development of a "social ecology" or an "eco-social theology of liberation"[25].

The problem analysis by Julio de Santa Ana makes it clear that the present socio-economic system is responsable for both "ecological imbalance and poverty"[26]. The spirit of domination, cultivated during modernity, did not only result in a socio-economic gap between colonizers and colonized, but also came to bear heavily on nature, which, dualistically conceived of as an instrument and an object, fell prey to man's devastative power. Or, as Leonardo Boff states it: "The same logic of the ruling system, based on profit and social manipulation, that leads to the exploitation of workers, also leads to the spoilation of entire nations and eventually to the degradation of nature itself"[27]. Therefore, Boff is convinced that liberation theology, when it tackles the ecological question, has to start from social ecology, from the systems of exclusion that dominate human relations. José Ramos Regidor's plea for an "eco-social theology of liberation" has a three-fold liberation in mind, "liberation from the de-humanization and oppression of the poor", "liberation from the corruption of nature", and "liberation from discrimination against women"[28]. The *Concilium* issue does not limit itself, however, to raising protest, but also develops in one of its contributions the outlines of an

24. L. Boff's book *Ecologia, Mundialização, Espiritualidade*, São Paulo, Ática, 1993 [English translation: *Ecology and Liberation: A New Paradigm*, Maryknoll, NY, Orbis, 1995], is many times referred to in this issue. His own article is entitled *Liberation, Theology and Ecology: Alternative, Confrontation or Complementarity? Conc* 5/5 (1995) 67-77.

25. A term launched in the article by J.R. REGIDOR, *Some Premises for an Eco-Social Theology of Liberation*, *Ibid.*, 77-93.

26. J. DE SANTA ANA, *The Present Socio-Economic System as a Cause of Ecological Imbalance and Poverty*, *Ibid.*, 3-11.

27. *Ibid.*, 73.

28. *Ibid.*, 91-92.

economy that is willing to take into account the double cry of the earth and of the poor. To call a halt to the rapid depletion of non-renewable resources and other ecological disasters, the dominating "economy of unlimited growth" has to be replaced by "one of human sufficiency"[29].

From both publications we learn that to speak sensitively about nature and culture in North-, Meso- and Latin America implies a sense of responsibility for the not yet realized liberation of the majority of its inhabitants.

Faculty of Theology, KULeuven   Peter DE MEY
Sint-Michielsstraat 6
B-3000 Leuven, Belgium

---

29. B. WIELENGA, *Towards a New Paradigm of Production: From an Economy of Unlimited Growth towards One of Human Sufficiency*, *Ibid.*, 97-105.

III

"Paradigm Shift" from Various Perspectives

17

GRASSROOTS ANALYSIS
THE EMPHASIS ON CULTURE

I. Cultural Analisys and Liberation

Is it possible to do good social analysis without doing serious cultural analysis? This is the way I would phrase a very practical question that has arisen for me in many years of experience of working with popular movements for change in the United States and, over the past decade, in Africa and most specifically in Zambia.

This practical question is related directly to the important issues raised by G. De Schrijver in his Discussion Paper, "Paradigm Shift in Third-World Theologies of Liberation: From Socio-Economic Analysis to Cultural Analysis". De Schrijver traces the shift to culture in both the writings of Latin American liberation theologians and in the nuancing of the evangelization and liberation themes enunciated at the Medellin (1968), Puebla (1979) and Santo Domingo (1992) conferences.

From my own experience, I find most interesting the question De Schrijver raises at the end of his essay about the significance of the shift to culture in the activities of new social movements. He asks: Could it be that the discourse about unjust structures has been, in a sense, too abstract? Is not the cultural emphasis, especially when shouldered by the new social movements, a fresh way of tackling structural questions, a way that is more understandable to common people (80)?

Involvement with movements of what De Schrijver calls "common people" – grassroots communities – has sharpened my own appreciation of the cultural emphasis. I therefore want to focus my attention here on the role and use of cultural analysis in movements that involve local efforts for justice and peace, development, ecology, women's concerns, and religious inculturation. My intention will be to demonstrate how cultural analysis has both the potential and the reality of making a significant contribution to "liberation" in Africa.

But before moving into my "analysis of analysis" of the cultural
emphasis at the grassroots level in Africa, let me describe what I mean
by "culture". Other essays in this volume offer definitions of culture
that I certainly can agree with. But I find particularly helpful a description expressed in poetic form by a young Zambian Jesuit friend of mine.

> African culture: tell us, who are you?
> I am the pattern of values and meanings
> expressed through images and symbols.
> I am the dance, and the song, and the drum.
>
> I am the food and the manner of eating it.
> I am the dress and the way of dressing.
> I am the art in all its forms.
> I am the music.
> I am the ceremonies and the rituals.
>
> Oh, let me tell you, if I were to tell you
> everything about myself,
> you would not have enough paper and ink
> to describe me.
> For I am life, the way of life.
> And one can understand life well by living it.
>
> I want to add, though, that
> I am identity.
> A person is what he or she is because of me.
> It is I who gives meaning to life.
> Those who do not possess me are doomed.
> Faceless, a nameless shadow.
> Like a dead piece of wood floating on a river,
> tossed about aimlessly, without a destination,
> following the rhythm of waves.
>
> I am unity.
> I gather people.
> Bring them close to each other.
> Give them a sense of belonging,
> a reason to live, a reason to die.
> A common vision of the world,
> a similar destiny,
> for life cannot be lived in isolation.
>
> I am not the only culture that exists.
> There are many others, uncountable,
> like the cattle of the Ila and the Tonga people.
> I have met most of these cultures.
> For me the first meeting
> has not been very pleasant.

I was looked down upon,
nearly all my qualities spat on.

"If you want to merit the name culture",
so I was told,
"reshape, redefine, better still, abandon,
what makes you what you are,
and adopt our qualities".

I felt oppressed; it was very unfair, unjust.
I cried, but there was no one to help me.
I had no strength to fight back.
Unwillingly, I submitted.
But inside me, I kindled a flame of hope.
Someday, I said to myself,
I will be myself again.

Things are better now;
other cultures have started
slowly to recognize me.
They realize that I have something to offer.
I who was crippled have started to walk again.
My legs are still numb,
I have not been able to make great strides.
But I know that I will make them soon.
When the sun has risen,
no one can force it back to its rising place[1].

II. A Shift in My Orientation

By way of introduction, I can be very specific in indicating the explicit expression of this shift to culture in my own involvement in programs of conscientization for faith and justice in the work for social change. Two moments accounted for this orientation in the decade preceding my move to Africa.

1. Intellectual Moment

First, there was an *intellectual* moment. Here I acknowledge the insight and emphasis of my colleague for many years at the Center of Concern in Washington DC, Joe Holland. Writing in the "Preface" of the

---

1. This poem was composed during a grassroots workshop exploring culture and development. The Ila and the Tonga are two tribes in the southern part of Zambia, well-known for their prowess in cattle-rearing. The poem was first published by J.P. NTHAWIE, in the *BJCTR* (1992) 13-14.

revised and enlarged edition (1983) of the very popular book we co-authored in 1980, *Social Analysis: Linking Faith and Justice*, Holland emphasized: "It is this question of culture, and within it religion, which reveals, I believe, the most radical dimension of our social crisis"[2]. Noting that our book focused primarily on economics and politics, he stated that there was a need to search for "a deeper cultural key" to understanding both the roots and the transformation of industrial capitalism[3].

This intellectual search was not a denial that culture arises from and is shaped by the surrounding economic and political context, for culture cannot be understood except as embodied in such a context. "Culture is never an angelic spirit floating above society"[4]. On the other hand, Holland emphasized, culture is not the prisoner of its context, nor does it merely reflect economic drives and political forces and provide only an ideological justification for social structures. "Certainly culture often functions in the mode of legitimization, but it can also be the point of critique and creativity"[5].

Holland applied his cultural analysis in a variety of ways, especially developing Gibson Winter's discussion of "root metaphors" that shape civilizations[6]. Winter sees as the foundation of modern industrial civilization the "mechanistic" root metaphor, a force both in economics and politics that tends as a machine to convert people into objects and destroys both humanity and nature in its all-consuming drive that dissolves our spiritual depths. Over against this, Winter proposes an "artistic" root metaphor that sees society as a work of art, "flowing from the creativity of rooted communities in solidarity with each other". This would have implications, Holland felt, for the strategies developed to bring about social change.

In the context of social movements of Left and Right in the USA, Holland offered a critique of the Left's failure to take seriously the deep cultural symbols of the people, leaving these symbols to fall into the manipulating hands of the Right. Examples of such symbols were *flag*, *faith* and *family* (nation, religion and kinship). He felt that the Left in the United States had not adequately grasped the creative role of these collective symbols in the process of social change and had let them become

2. J. HOLLAND & P. HENRIOT, *Social Analysis: Linking Faith and Justice*, revised and enlarged edition, Maryknoll, NY, Orbis, and Washington DC: Center of Concern, 1983, p. xii.
3. *Ibid.*, p. xiii.
4. *Ibid.*
5. *Ibid.*
6. *Ibid.*, pp. xvi-xvii.

culturally conservative reinforcements of a status quo of exclusion and oppression[7].

This intellectual appreciation of the importance of paying attention to culture meant that the Center of Concern's workshops on social analysis always took seriously the cultural dimensions of situations. In the "Practical Methodology" offered in the 1983 edition of *Social Analysis*, I suggested that the following question should be asked when analyzing the important influences on a particular situation: "What are the major *cultural* structures which determine how society organizes *meaning*? E.g., religion; symbols, myths, dreams; art, music, folk-lore; lifestyle, traditions"[8]. Right from the outset, therefore, the element of cultural analysis was to be considered essential in the approaches that the Center of Concern took in promoting social analysis.

2. *Experiential Moment*

Second, there occurred an *experiential* moment that both gave impetus to the intellectual insight and also reinforced my understanding of it. This was the experience of attempting grass-root programs of social analysis in the Philippines and in Africa. In 1980, I spent a month giving a series of workshops in the Philippines, based on the first draft of the book written by Joe Holland and me. The participants in the program were mostly groups of church workers and students. Just a few weeks before I arrived, the Philippines Bishops Conference had issued an order that no more "social analysis workshops" were to be conducted under church auspices. This was certainly a challenge to the program prepared for my visit. I therefore conducted a month of "social discernment workshops". In good Jesuit fashion, I was able to work with the same topics, but under different names!

Why had there been this reaction of the Bishops of the Philippines to the approach of "social analysis"? I was told that they feared that the approach being taken in much of the work of social analysis was primarily Marxist-inspired, or at least strongly Marxist-influenced, and therefore played into the hands of communist movements. During the especially-tense times of the early years of the Marcos dictatorship, charges that social analysis programs were Marxist or communist were dangerous charges indeed. The officials of the church felt that no chances were to be taken.

---

7. J. HOLLAND, *Flag, Faith and Family: Rooting the American Left in Everyday Symbols*, Chicago, New Patriotic Alliance 1979.

8. J. HOLLAND & P. HENRIOT (n. 2), p. 99.

Having only recently arrived, I was of course not competent to judge the validity of the charges. But in many of the analytical approaches that I experienced being used in the Philippines (and elsewhere) at that time, I did find a disconcerting over-emphasis upon purely economic factors in explaining the constitution and dynamics of the local society. I recall asking a young student participating in one of my workshops about the cultural background to one problem that we were studying, something relating to family influences in politics. He dismissed the question with the sentiment that all such influences were simply economic and had no basis in popular culture. After all, culture was only a determined supra-structure and not a dynamic element on its own in shaping society. An older woman in the group smiled and commented that the student must have forgotten his up-bringing, ignored the stories and songs he would have heard at home, and swallowed too easily a foreign-imported explanation of reality. The culture of family relationships in the Philippines was too real, too strong, to be dismissed with a simple economic explanation.

Whatever the relevance of my question about culture and politics, and the ensuing discussion about economic influences, the fact was becoming clear to me that a social analysis that ignored cultural dimensions was not too helpful in explaining the Filipino reality, or, for that matter, any other social reality. Having lived for a year in Latin America in the mid-1970s, I knew the power of popular religiosity to shape perspectives and inspire actions. Moreover, I appreciated the faith of the small Christian communities and the vision of the theology of liberation. I saw that these elements in society and in the church were also present, in varying degrees, in the Philippines. I realized that only a cultural analysis could get at the underlying dynamics shaping social movements in such settings.

This experience of the necessity of cultural analysis (certainly not *replacing* socio-economic analysis, nor merely *supplementing* it, but actually *deepening* it) was reinforced during another month's tour of workshops on social analysis, this time in Africa. I came to Zambia and Zimbabwe in 1982 for programs with church workers, students, laity leadership, and members of religious congregations (many of them expatriates). What struck me – and would, of course, return to strike me more forcefully when I came back to Africa a few years later to become a full-time resident and not simply a visitor – was the fact that culture was not simply the *content* of analysis but also the *context* and the *method*. What do I mean?

As will be developed further in this essay when I review my recent work with social movements in Africa, the *content* of good social analysis must include the cultural traditions, structures, events, history, personalities, etc., of the people and their society. I experienced in Africa that these cultural elements deserve treatment on their own right, not as mere "supra-structures" based on economic foundations. But I also experienced in the workshops in Zambia and Zimbabwe in 1982 that culture was the *context* and the *method* of good analysis in the sense that the analytical framework was more than an intellectual exercise or rational explication of the reality being examined. The framework itself was influenced by song, drama, art, story-telling, religious celebration – all significant cultural elements. This meant necessarily that a cultural methodology had to be employed: artistic expression of the social reality had to be given equal weight with reasoned dissection.

III. ANALYSIS WITHIN THE PASTORAL CIRCLE

These two moments described above have influenced my own understanding of the importance of a shift to culture and shaped my practical approach to doing social analysis. While I might be reluctant to give the intellectual and experiential moments shaping my own orientation the name of a "paradigm shift", I do see the importance of what De Schrijver refers to as a "change or complementarity in method" (31). Cultural sciences are indeed as essential as socio-economic approaches in understanding the reality we confront.

1. *Approaches and Aims*

How and where one situates the task of social analysis is, of course, very relevant to our discussion here, as is the motivation for undertaking the project. I see that there can be three approaches to analysis:

Pastoral tool for use at the grass roots, for example with local development groups, justice and peace committees, student groups, small Christian communities, etc. Here the aim of the analysis is to organize a local and immediate response to some pressing social issue. For example, a group might be involved in dealing with the problems of voter apathy, or wages paid to domestic workers, or provision of services by a local council.

Academic tool for a research project carried out on a large topic, with or without the aim of any action to be taken or any response to be made. Such analysis is often carried out by professional social scientists associated with academic institutions who do "field research" through on-site visits but who do not actually live in the midst of the reality being analyzed. For example, a research team might study the transition to multi-party democracies in Africa, or the increasing growth of Islam, or the macro-economic consequences of privatization.

Organizational tool for studying major issues affecting institutions and societies at national or international levels, with the aim of providing guidelines for possible large-scale activities. United Nations' studies, government reports, and church surveys would be instances of this approach. For example, analysts might look at the global impact of neo-liberal economics, or the root causes of the rising numbers of refugees, or the process and progress of inculturation in the African context.

Although I personally have been engaged in many analysis projects utilizing the approaches of the *academic* and *organizational* tools, my primary work in recent years has been with the *pastoral* tool. That is, my engagement is with local popular movements and my focus is on moving toward some response to a pressing problem. For this reason, the social analysis I am most engaged with now has been located within the "Pastoral Circle".

2. *Moments of Interpretation*

The "Pastoral Circle" is the name given by Joe Holland and me in our book, *Social Analysis*, to describe a methodological approach that emphasizes the relationship between reflection and action. The approach relates to what authors like Paulo Freire refer to as *"praxis"* (reflection based on experience, and experience based on reflection) or liberation theologians such as Juan Luis Segundo call the "hermeneutic circle" (new questions raised to older explanations because of contact with new situations). The place of social analysis within the Circle can be seen by noting the four moments of interpretation that arise out of basic questioning a reality:

Contact: *What is happening here?* This is the moment of gathering *data* through insertion in the reality, touching it by gathering objective observations and subjective feelings.

Analysis: *Why is it happening?* This is the moment of explanation through *analysis* of the reality, probing the causes, connections and consequences of the reality. Again and again, the question "why" is asked.

Reflection: *How do we evaluate it?* This is the moment of discerning the *meaning* of the reality in light of our values, faith perspectives, community norms, etc.

Response: *How do we respond to it?* This is the moment of *action* through planning, deciding and evaluating in order to effect change in the reality.

(By way of an aside at this point, it can be seen how culture plays an important role not only in analysis but also in the other three moments of the Pastoral Circle. Thus subjective feelings are powerfully revealed in story-telling, values are uncovered through the traditional wisdom of proverbs, and customs of respect and deference influence certain styles of response.)

The reason for emphasizing that the social analysis is always set within the Pastoral Circle is to stress that it is done in vital contact with reality (not abstracted or purely academic), amidst explicit value reflections (not "value-free" or non-committal), and oriented towards action (not speculative or non-pragmatic). The analysis as a pastoral tool is not done on its own. Its location within the Pastoral Circle marks the method and the operation of the analysis that is undertaken and the result and outcome that is desired.

IV. CULTURE AND POPULAR MOVEMENTS

My own understanding of the importance in Africa of cultural analysis, particularly among some popular movements, comes from my participation in various local programs, mostly associated with development and justice and peace groups. In the examples that follow, I will note how the emphasis on culture provides the movements with deeper insights than would be available if only socio-economic analysis were relied on.

1. Culture and Development

Surely one of the most damaging consequences of the Western-inspired "developmentalism" (over-emphasis on economic growth models) propagated in the poor countries of the South has been the down-playing of culture as a major shaper of societal relationships and progress. Frequently, culture was not even seen by outsiders; it was ignored or unrecognized as a significant reality to be dealt with. The World Bank and other major Western development agencies rarely included an anthropologist on their planning teams. When acknowledged, culture was more often than not seen as a *hindrance* to economic development, as a "backward" influence that had to be overcome if true "progress" was to be achieved within a given society. Ways had to be found to go around the local cultural influences if certain externally-sponsored development projects were to be successful.

Examples of the effects of this mentality abound in the stories told about "failed" development projects. For instance, the outside development worker arrives in a village and finds the women spending hours each day around a communal water stand pipe, waiting for their turn to draw water in buckets and carry it back home. The worker (usually a man) estimates the economic inefficiencies of time lost in such activity and decides that the women need water pipes brought directly into their houses (huts) so that they will not need to gather at the village center to draw water. He leaves the village satisfied with "progress" when each house has its own tap. He returns to visit some months later, only to be disappointed to find the village unity destroyed and an alarming rise in family problems (marriage break-ups, difficulties with children, etc.). What he had failed to take into account in his *economic* analysis of water-gathering were the *cultural* advantages of providing space and time for women to share important local news, discuss mutual problems, and offer each other practical advice and commitments to help.

To counter this narrow economic focus, a development education program (DEP) approach is being used in many parts of Africa. The approach I am familiar with in Zambia uses the *Training for Transformation* manuals based upon Paulo Freire's methodology of conscientization[9]. It emphasizes participation by the local communities in identifying projects, planning and deciding, engaging in action, and evaluation. For example, the DEP team that I was part of as a field worker in the Diocese of Monze, 1989-1990, would not go into a village to do something for the people but to empower the people to do something for themselves. "Integral", "participative", "self-reliant" and "sustainable" were the key words we used to describe our approach.

I remember one workshop in a village where we asked the people to talk about the cultural traditions that they found positive (helpful) and negative (restraining) in the efforts being made to achieve the integral, participative, self-reliant and sustainable development they wanted in their area (One obvious challenge was to put all these nice English words into ciTonga, the local language!). This stimulated a lively conversation where positive elements of sharing and solidarity were recalled as central to community development, and traditions of care for widows and orphans were seen as instilling social responsibilities in the whole village. But negative elements also were noted, such as the exclusion of women and young people from decision-making processes, and the

9. Cf. A. HOPE & S. TIMMEL, *Training for Transformation: A Handbook for Community Workers*, Gweru, Zimbabwe, Mambo Press, 1995.

influence of witchcraft on the spread of fears and suspicions. The analysis that we did in that workshop enabled us to reinforce the positive elements in our training programs and try to lessen the impact of the negative elements.

Another example of cultural analysis that for me opened up new economic understandings was a look at the role of extended families. The extended family system in Africa is a significant cultural pattern that has a very large impact on development. The family should not be – and in Africa, is not – seen simply as an economic unit, a mode of production and reproduction. A whole complex set of relationships of meanings, values, expectations, norms, etc., are central to the life and activity of families. In other words, culture plays a significant role.

An example of this significance can be seen in the organization and operation of what Goran Hyden has called the "economy of affection"[10]. Looking particularly at Eastern Africa, he has explored the economic relations that arise from the extended family operating in a subsistence environment. The "economy of affection" does not of itself involve fond emotions, but "denotes a network of support, communications and interaction among structurally defined groups connected by blood, kin, community and other affinities, for example, religion"[11]. Certain economic decisions are made precisely to preserve both for individuals and for the community the "safety net" of the extended family. There are also, of course, corresponding political and social decisions, affecting who makes decisions, what levels of social interchanges take place, etc. Some decisions that go against the "logic" of the "economy of capitalism" or the "economy of socialism" are very congruent with the "economy of affection". For instance, disposition of property is neither a "private" affair (capitalistic) nor a matter of state management (socialistic). Property exchanges are viewed as good or bad in light of their impact on strengthening or weakening the extended family. Here culture and economy come very close together.

On two occasions, I found some activity very difficult to appreciate until a cultural analysis opened up the picture for me. First, the diocesan development program that I worked for ran a two-year course in carpentry for youth chosen by their local villages. At the conclusion of the course, the young carpenter would have saved enough money to purchase a set of tools with which, once back in the village, he could earn a good living. But visiting the village six months later, one was disappointed to find

10. Cf. G. HYDEN, *No Shortcuts to Progress: African Development Management in Perspective*, London, Heinemann, 1983, pp. 8-16.
11. *Ibid.*, p. 8.

the would-be carpenter sitting idle, having sold off his tools to get money for his nephew's school fees and for funeral expenses for a recently-deceased relative in the village. Within a capitalist or socialist economic structure, the young carpenter would be judged to have sacrificed his future. But within the "economy of affection", he had in fact guaranteed his future. This was so because whenever difficult times might come, as surely they would, he had maintained both in symbolic gestures and in real life the bonds of affection. Second, a young friend of mine lost his very good job because of some fraudulent actions involving small amounts of money. When I asked him why he had taken such a great risk, he answered that pressures from the extended family for assistance were simply too strong to resist if he hoped to remain in the good graces of that family[12].

2. *Culture and Environmental Concerns*

At the time of the United Nations Conference on Environment and Development (1992), the DEP focused attention on some of Zambia's serious ecological challenges such as deforestation, pollution and poaching. As part of an effort to strengthen community responses by recovering traditional sources of ecological respect, I was involved with a program of cultural analysis of attitudes toward the natural environment. In a workshop setting, we asked participants to recall stories, myths, proverbs, taboos, etc., that spoke of their relationships to nature. Many creation myths were recounted, as well as many instructions on appropriate or inappropriate attitudes and actions toward nature.

Analyzing this data, we discovered grounds for the validity, indeed the necessity, of these traditional instructions. The analytical process of continually asking "why" uncovered important reasons. Elders in the workshop were able to explain to younger members some of these reasons by reflecting on their significance in the light of current concerns about the environment. For instance:

---

12. One of the most significant efforts at utilising cultural analysis to deepen the understanding of the successes and failures of development is found in the work of T. VERHELST, *No Life Without Roots: Culture and Development*, trans. by Bob Cumming, London, Zed Books, 1990. Verhelst has organized a group of scholars from around the world, "The South-North Network Cultures and Development", that is involved in research, training, community organizing and advocacy, and publishes a bi-lingual journal three times a year, *Cultures and Development: Quid Pro Quo*. One significant collaborator in this effort, a pioneer in the effort to being cultural concerns to the forefront of development, is Dennis Goulet of the University of Notre Dame in the United States of America. See his *The Cruel Choice*, New York, Atheneum, 1971.

- Certain trees were not to be cut down since they were considered sacred. In fact, the trees grew over water sources such as springs, both marking them and sustaining them.
- The local chief would determine each year where wild fruit could be picked, because by tradition all the fruits belonged to him. This allowed for a wise pattern of crop rotation, conserving fragile plant life.
- No one was allowed to hunt for game alone but only in a designated village group, lest the spirits of the animals would attack him. Such a custom assured that all the wild animals killed did in fact benefit the whole village.
- There were cultural taboos against urinating or defecating close to huts in a village; if persons violated these taboos, evil spirits would fall upon them. Thus basic sanitary hygiene was promoted to keep the locality clean and healthy.

This process of analysis should not be viewed strictly as a "demythologizing" of culture, but rather as a recognition of the wisdom and strength of the culture. Cultural analysis, done largely through story-telling, uncovered many profound reasons for the traditional wisdom. And in a setting of use of the "Pastoral Circle", this analytical process could lead to more effective responses to meeting ecological concerns.

Another example of cultural analysis that has implications for environmental concerns is the work promoted by a network of scholars from both Third-World and First-World settings who are interested in so-called "Indigenous Knowledge" (IK). In epistemological terms, IK is contrasted with Western "scientific knowledge" in that it is knowledge based more on the belief and customs of local communities than on the empirical data gathering and logical deductions of formal scientific methodology. Especially in dealing with issues of the environment, it is important to pay attention to IK, indeed more so than in the past. Focus on culture, then, is central to IK considerations about sustainable development, agriculture, local participation, etc.

3. Culture and Women

As is true in almost any place today, the status and role of women in society (and in the church) is a critically important issue, not just for women but for men, indeed for the whole of a well-ordered society. But equality of women and men is often viewed by many in Africa – both women and men – as strictly a Western idea and not at all in line with African culture. It is certainly true that women hold a subservient role and in many circumstances are mistreated, exploited and underdeveloped. For instance, there are alarming statistics about the decline in enrollment of female children in schools. With the imposition of school fees as a result of the IMF-imposed austerity programs of structural adjustment, parents tend to see the best investment to be in boys who one day will get a job. The cultural expectation is simply that girls will "only get married".

Women by and large work much harder than men – longer hours, double jobs (outside work place and work at home). And expectations that this should be accepted as normal are deep in the culture. I commented once to a Zambian man that I was surprised and disturbed to see a largely pregnant woman walking along the road with a small baby on her back and another child clutching her right hand, carrying on her head one piece of luggage and in her left hand another, while her husband walked leisurely behind her carrying only a walking stick. I was told – with almost a straight face! – that the man was protecting his wife from any lions they might encounter. The fact that there had been no lions in this particular region for decades did not distract from the cultural imperative that men do not carry their wife's luggage in public, let alone look after children.

A particularly disturbing phenomenon present among many tribes in Zambia and elsewhere in Africa is "property grabbing" or the "stripping" inflicted upon widows after the death of their husband. The husband's family descends upon the home of the sister-in-law, and takes away everything, even basic necessities like cooking utensils or school books for the children. This is done in the name of the cultural tradition of "inheritance" whereby the widow, children and all possessions belong to the husband's family. Civil legislation now makes possible the drawing up of wills to protect the widow and children, but implementation of this protection is often extremely difficult for reasons of ignorance, expense, or fear of retaliation (witchcraft).

Local justice and peace groups in Zambia, along with development groups, have taken up the issue of women's rights. They have found that a particularly helpful approach is to do a cultural analysis looking at the deeper reasons for discrimination against women. Often the causes of this discrimination today are distortions of past efforts at protection. For example, the "looking out for the lions" explanation may in fact have been valid at one time – an instance of the orderly division of labor. More interesting and relevant is the recognition that the tradition of "inheritance" assured that the widow and children were in fact looked after by the husband's family. Care was taken that the woman was not left isolated on her own, subject to economic and social hardships. But the practice today of "stripping" – prevalent and intensified in harsh economic situations and circumstances of weakened cultural respect – does just the opposite from protection!

By asking again and again the "why" question, other insights come from cultural analysis of women's status and role in society today. These insights contribute to the promotion of greater justice for the whole of society.

4. *Culture and Church*

The issue of "inculturation" is too large for this short essay to take up, and is referred to in other essays in this volume. But this challenge for the task of evangelization by the church in Africa does indeed relate to the local use of cultural analysis that I have been discussing here. The central theme of the African Synod (1994) was inculturation[13]. An "inculturated faith" is one that is authentically Christian and genuinely African. It is a faith wherein one "feels at home" – not only in liturgical expression but also in credal symbols, theological categories, authority legitimization, instructional procedures, canonical legislation, etc.

Two analytical points seem to me to be very important in going about the process of inculturation. These points are "analytical" in the sense of going deeper into issues, their causes, connections and consequences. And both points lend themselves to discussions at grass-root levels. For at least the past twenty years, the pastoral strategy of the church in East Africa has been the building up of the Small Christian Communities (SCCs), the "church in the neighborhood"[14]. Within these SCCs, a cultural analysis of local situations can go on that facilitates both deeper understanding of the faith and more authentic inculturation of its basics.

The first point to note is the necessity of submitting to critical analysis even the most basic (1) faith expressions offered by non-African Christianity and (2) cultural expressions esteemed by Africans. This means asking again and again the "why" question. Done in a group discussion process among ordinary Christians, some very interesting observations come out. There is usually the recognition that much that we take for

13. An excellent overview of the Synod preparations, event and conclusions can be found in the essays presented in Africa Faith and Justice Network, *The African Synod: Documents, Reflections, Perspectives,* Maryknoll, NY, Orbis, 1995. This volume also contains the Apostolic Exhortation of JOHN PAUL II, *Ecclesia in Africa,* 1995.

14. Cf. R. MEJIA, *The Church in the Neighbourhood,* Nairobi, Daughters of St. Paul, 1990.

granted as being "essentials" or "the way things are done" are as a matter of fact simply an accepted cultural way of doing things in Europe or North America or Africa but unrelated to any "Gospel imperative" or essential truth of our faith.

I recall an early experience of mine in Zambia that illustrates this. I was feeling puzzled why people remained sitting during the reading of the Gospel at Mass. Why did they fail to show respect by standing, the kind of respectful gesture I had grown up with in my own country? I was told by a Zambian that in their culture, respect was shown by taking a lower place when an elder or important person was speaking. One did not show respect by standing but by sitting. I came to appreciate that the value of respect is expressed in different ways in different cultures. This is indeed a very simple lesson, but one with profound consequences in efforts to inculturate the faith.

Moreover, the analytical questioning process must also be brought to bear on elements of African Traditional Religion that need to be explained and evaluated in the light of shared community norms. For example, cultural analysis needs to examine the proverbs, myths, dreams, visions, etc., that express the religious wisdom of the people. During one workshop with community development workers, we explored the significance of traditional "rain shrine" ceremonies and the lessons that could be learned for today's experience of droughts and subsequent famine among the people.

A second point is the need to recognize that *inculturation* and *liberation* must go hand-in-hand. J.-M. Elá has frequently called attention to the fact that commitment to an inculturation that does not include genuine liberation can be only an antiquarians, an escapist fascination with folklore.

A church that seeks to say something to today's African cannot content itself with an authentically African liturgy, catechetics, and theology. The modes of expression of the faith have sense and meaning only if the church is deeply involved in the battles being waged by human beings against conditions that stifle their human liberty. The participation of the church in these battles, then, becomes the necessary condition for any liturgy, any catechesis, any theology in Africa. It is in the vital experience of the communities and of their striving for life, liberty, and justice, that any reference to Jesus and his mission – a mission of the liberation of the oppressed – will find genuine sense and meaning[15].

15. J.-M. ELA, *African Cry*, translated by Robert R. Barr, Maryknoll, NY, Orbis, 1986, p. 132.

But liberation in Africa must address not only politico-socio-economic realities that are oppressive and unjust. It must also address the cultural oppression that is the historical legacy of colonialism and the contemporary consequence of globalization. Western media pervades local settings with foreign values of individualism, consumerism, sexual license, etc. Foreign imports are often considered of greater value than local products, both in material goods and in cultural expressions. Several African scholars have spoken of "anthropological poverty" as being the most serious impoverishment experienced on the continent. This is the depersonalization of the African, a result of racist interpretations of psychology, religion and history. Cultural analysis opens up this reality and enables the church to more effectively engage in a truly liberative evangelization.

V. CONCLUSION: RELEVANCE TO AFRICAN LIBERATION THEOLOGY

To repeat again the point made at the opening of this essay, my intention here has been to demonstrate how cultural analysis has both the potential and the reality of making a significant contribution to the "liberation" of Africa today. I have tried to do this by describing how cultural analysis is utilized in many of the social movements that involve people at the local level in the process of change. Speaking from my own experience of some of these movements of justice and peace, development, ecology, women's concerns, and inculturation with the church, I believe that several conclusions can be drawn such as:

1. Cultural considerations can never be absent from any good analysis being done of the African situation. Despite the influence of the dominant neo-liberal economic environment with the consequent prominence of the "culture of the market", an environment fostered by the Structural Adjustment Programs spreading across the Continent, deep cultural realities are still in place and are influential.

2. Cultural considerations affect not only the content of good analysis in Africa but also the methodology. Socio-economic analysis relies heavily on social science methodologies of questionnaires, comparative studies, computer examinations, etc. While of course not ignoring these helps to understanding, cultural analysis also utilizes story-telling, drama, art, music, proverbs, etc., to go deeper into the realities being studied.

3. Cultural considerations are particularly relevant and important when participating in social movements that are directed toward change

at the local level. This does not mean ignoring structural issues of a more economic or political character, but supplementing analysis of these with an emphasis on culture that speaks more to people at the grass roots.

Finally, it is appropriate to leave it to theologians to draw conclusions about the implications of all this for African liberation theology. But certainly it should be obvious that in a church that takes seriously the agenda of the African Synod, grassroots analysis will necessarily put an emphasis on culture that will shape the integral evangelization task of the coming years. And central to that evangelization, of course, will be the project of liberation.

Center for Theological Reflection   Peter J. HENRIOT
Lusaka, Zambia

18

PARADIGM SHIFT?

The Discussion Paper presented by G. De Schrijver argues the claim that a paradigm shift from socio-economic analysis to cultural analysis has occurred in Third-World theologies of liberation. This shift is seen by De Schrijver as ambivalent and poses the question as to how liberation theologians should react to this new situation.

More in particular, he points to the difficulty that straightforward lines of action have been obscured, precisely because the poor are dispersed now in various cultural settings: so that we are left with only a dissipative kind of analysis (74).

Though this concern of De Schrijver's seems well-founded, based on the analysis he has presented, it seems to me that the fundamental question elaborated by the Discussion Paper really is: Can the cultural emphasis root liberation theology in the lives of the people? Or stated differently: Does it offer a fresh way of tackling structural questions of injustice, especially when shouldered by new social movements (78-79)? Here we come to the real issue that needs to be addressed, but to which the Discussion Paper fails to give a clear answer. I will begin by tackling the latter issue of cultural analysis, to then delve into the critical examination of some dominant presuppositions which threaten to vitiate the enterprise of 'recalling the religious intuitions of the people'.

I. CULTURAL ANALYSIS AND THE TRAP OF IDEOLOGICAL DISTORTION

1. *Culture as Social Construction*

In the first instance, one needs to ask whether the cultural emphases shouldered by the new social movements (of race, gender, environment) are any less abstract than the "classic" liberation theological discourse about unjust structures? This is clear when one recognizes that race is itself a category of social construction, as is "nature", and to a lesser extent gender. Consider the following quote from Manning Marable:

> "Race" is first and foremost an unequal relationship between social aggregates, characterized by dominant and subordinate forms of social interaction, and reinforced by the intricate patterns of public discourse, power, ownership and privilege within the economic, social and political institutions of society... Race only becomes "real" as a force when individuals

or groups behave toward each other in ways which reflect or perpetuate the
hegemonic ideology of subordination and the patterns of inequality in daily
life. These are, in turn, justified and explained by assumed differences in
physical and biological characteristics, or in theories of cultural deprivation
or intellectual inferiority. Thus, far from being static or fixed, race as an
oppressive concept within social relations is fluid and ever-changing. An
oppressed "racial group" changes over time, geographical space and historical conjuncture. That which is termed "black", "Hispanic" or "Oriental"
by those in power to describe one human being's "racial background" in
a particular setting can have little historical or practical meaning within
another social formation which is also racially stratified, but in a different
manner[1].

Manning makes clear that race (and I would also claim by extension,
and to lesser degrees, nature and gender) is already part of a fluid effort
to maintain social stratification. But more striking than this, because of
its incorporation into the ideological framework that maintains a certain
social stratification, like the category of class, it also does not ground
reflection arising out of it. It is just as "abstract" as the category(ies) it
replaces. Further to this, rather than grounding reflection, it imposes an
ideological framework for reflection and behavior, thus repeating and
maintaining the dominant ideology. In this light, the new theology deriving from these new social movements of race, environment and gender,
though seeming to have more "grounding" power because they stress
particularity in theory, unfortunately no more ground the human person
than the category of class did for "classical" liberation theology. The
use of these "new" categories therefore do not introduce anything new,
in the sense of a new opportunity for liberation, but reinstalls by means
of substitutive ideology, the dominant ideology. Indeed, like classic liberation theology, this new theology and these new social movements
have "constituency" problems. In other words, they have problems in terms
of whom they *really* represent.

This latter point is worth emphasizing because one of the key claims
of these "new" social movements and the theology generated by them is
that they more genuinely represent "the people". One cannot take this
lightly or purely theoretically. It is important to be concerned about the
conscientization process and the need to genuinely represent in thought
and reflection the situation and possibilities of a people. Yet, as important
as such a process is, it fails if liberation is not taking place. So the real
issue here is not one of systematization but one of veracity in representation which can aid in the process of liberation.

1. M. MARABLE, *Beyond Black and White: Transforming African-American Politics*,
London, Verso Press, 1995, p. 186.

2. *Cultural Logic of Late Capitalism*

One should also question the process of making race, or gender, or the environment the new locus for reflection and debate. Does the new cultural emphasis really present a "new" opportunity? And if it is "new", for whom? De Schrijver implicitly recognizes this problem in his Discussion Paper in his mention of the works of D. Harvey and Frederic Jameson, especially in the latter's claim that the cultural logic of late capitalism "creates a sphere of anesthetization which averts one's attention from the realities of political economy and the circumstances of global power" (49). I think this point requires more mention, analysis and exploration than is given by the Discussion Paper. If the cultural logic of late capitalism (or postmodernism) is to divert the focus of resistance by the oppressed from the machinations of the political economy to that of cultural "identity" and cultural studies, then the very shift in paradigm claimed by the Discussion Paper is an exercise in postmodern fragmentation applied to Third-World liberation theologies. This is significant in terms of the veracity of the analysis as well as the intent of the conceptuality of a "paradigm" shift. In other words, has the analysis in the Discussion Paper anything to do with what is actually going on in theology and life in the Third-World? Or is it more of a prescription than a description? I think that, here, some more attention to Frederic Jameson's analysis would be helpful.

One of the important points that Jameson stresses is that "aesthetic production today has become integrated into commodity production generally"[2]. His intent is to show the dialectical interrelationship of multinational business and postmodern culture as the "internal and superstructural expression of a wave of American military and economic domination throughout the world: in this sense, as throughout class history, the underside of culture is blood, torture, death and horror"[3]. Jameson's comments here are very pointed and real, in that, one has to be very clear as to the intent of the new social movements and the structures that patronize them, especially since the "world space of multinational capital" has as its political vocation the "invention and projection of a global cognitive mapping, on a social as well as a spatial scale"[4]. We need then to be both honest and cautious with regard to the use of these "new" social movements of race, gender and environment in understanding the plight and future of the Third-World and liberation theologies therein.

---

2. F. JAMESON, *Postmodernism, or The Cultural Logic of Late Capitalism*, in *NLR* 146 (1984) p. 56.
   3. *Ibid.*, p. 57
   4. *Ibid.*, p. 92.

Jameson's remarks seem to highlight for us that, within the gambit of postmodernism, "culture" and its associates do not further the cause of the oppressed, and rather act as life-consuming distractions from the root cause(s) of exploitation. And further to this, as the logic of late capitalism, they do not institute any real shift in paradigm, for they actually commodify the possibilities of resistance of the oppressed. This forces the exploited to continuously find and forge new ways of resistance and existence.

3. *From Global Cognitive Mapping to Deception*

If this is the case, especially with regard to the Third-World, one must question the continued drive to articulate within the limits of reason, the "impulse" to survival of any people. Is it an attempt at the further commodification of human existence? Such articulation of Third-World realities generally turn out to be prescriptive in intent and content, and serve to restore and impose a metanarrative of promise and "development" which gives rise to a "hope" for change in the direction of genuine liberation. But the history of colonization and "independence" in Third-World contexts have clearly shown that the "hope" offered by this drive to articulation of Third-World realities within the limits of reason is hollow, and ultimately betrays the exploited in the search for liberation. The deception involved is a projecting of a "hope" that is a reconception of a dominant ideology. Consider the following quote from James Newton Poling:

> A study of United States history will demonstrate that evil maintains itself through a process of debate and betrayal by those in power. In certain historical periods, communities of resistance have more successfully brought their moral claims to the public arena for debate. These times have increased hope that power could be more fairly distributed and that all people in society would have access to the resources necessary for life and creativity. In my research, I discovered such times just before and after the Revolutionary and Civil Wars. Prior to the wars, religious and political leaders debated the issues of freedom and full citizenship for African American women and men and for White women. These debates brought hope for just power arrangements. However, after both wars, debate was stifled, with structures of injustice and oppression firmly reestablished. African American men and women and White women found themselves in desperate conditions, without the protection they had hoped would come. The communities of resistance experienced this as a betrayal, especially by those who had supported their claims in the past...I have come to the conviction that such debate and betrayal is one of the ways evil maintains itself. Public debate not only creates opportunities for new moral claims to be asserted, but also enables those who have power to reconceive their interests in more effective ways. During times of transition, debate, which offers oppressed groups the hope of social change, in fact often betrays

their trust, as those with power close ranks against the groups they had promised to support[5].

Poling makes clear to us the false hope generated by the wider articulation of the will to resistance and existence of exploited peoples. And this articulation does not stop at the level of external prescription, it often incorporates an internal dimension of the legitimation of such an enterprise among the oppressed by their "leaders". I have commented on this phenomenon in the Caribbean elsewhere[6], and I continue to be amazed at the staying power of a "hope" that is based on a substitutive ideology which distorts the truth. The replication of systems of domination, the legitimation of existing authority and the distortion of truth by means of social and economic manipulation continue to be abiding traits of the attempts at articulation of the survival "habits" of a people in oppression. Interestingly enough, in far too many cases, this is also what the "new" cultural emphasis has become and remains.

In the light of my arguments thus far on the merits or lack thereof of "cultural" analysis, one can easily discern that I would consider the claim of a paradigm shift in Third-World theologies of liberation as itself partaking in the ideological distortion of liberative praxis and as prescribing a condition rather than describing it. One can understand De Schrijver's concern with the distracting power of postmodernism or late capitalism, in the sense that it is a strategy of oppression that isn't as readily clearly understood and yet is very pervasive and global in its reach. However, to understand its application in terms of a "global cognitive mapping" is to further its aims rather than to resist it, and more than this, it is to implicitly prescribe a course of action based on an analysis that is without an adequate descriptive grounding in the reality it addresses: the Third-World. It is within this context that I would like to briefly and almost bluntly answer the other major questions directly asked by the Discussion Paper.

II. Advantages of a Dissipative Analysis

1. *Common People's Dealing with Diversity*

In responding to how does one bring about the liberation of the poor when the poor are dispersed in various cultural settings, one could claim

---

5. J.N. POLING, *Deliver Us From Evil: Resisting Racial and Gender Oppression*, Minneapolis, Fortress Press, 1996, pp xv-xvi.

6. Cf. G. BOODOO, *On the Christian Presence in the Caribbean*, in P.A.B. ANTHONY (ed.), *Theology in the Caribbean Today*, vol. I, St. Lucia, W.I., Optimum Printers, 1995.

that dispersal and dissipative analysis is most problematic from a centralized perspective. That it may not be problematic in terms of "common people", needs to be seriously taken into account. In my own research on the issue[7], I have found "common people" to have absolutely no significant problems with diverse and sometimes seemingly incongruous aspects of their lives and belief systems. Indeed, the "dissipation" of their lives (pointed at in attempts at systematic analysis) sometimes seems to be their means of defying definition and thereby incorporation and assimilation. Seen from the perspective of survival in the midst of exploitation, dispersal and dissipation are thus not always "bad" things, and in some instances may be necessary to avoid identification, disruption, distortion and death. Many forms of resistance and revolution are supported by such strategies.

2. *Dissipative Analysis Only Problematic from a Hegemonic Standpoint*

One must ask then, why is dispersal and dissipation seen as negative by De Schrijver? A tentative answer to this latter question perhaps needs to be situated in the Belgian and European context. Though I am not an "official" social scientist, I will attempt an "unofficial" reading of this European context. In such a context, reflection begins from and takes for granted the social, political and economic benefits that Europe is accustomed to. The contemporary drive towards European unification is a move towards maintaining such a status. However, the current trends toward asserting cultural identity (such as the Flemish Bloc in Belgium and other "nationalistic" movements in other parts of Europe) seem to be major stumbling blocks toward unification and, by extension, towards harmonious and meaningful coexistence among European peoples. In this light, the dissipation that accompanies the assertion of "culture" in "tribal" Europe directly impacts in a negative sense the possibility of unification and the continuation of European harmony and hegemony. This postmodern condition therefore offers to the European context the possibility of a dispersal of all that Europe has enjoyed over the past few "modern" centuries.

Contrast this scenario with the colonies and former colonies of Europe, assessed not from the economic standards accustomed to by Europeans, but from the need to establish a basic level of survival and, in many cases, to institute resistance to deliberate and reflexive exploitation. Here the concern is not unification to maintain hegemony but dispersal to

---

7. Cf. G. BOODOO, *The La Divina Pastora/Suparee Ke Mai Devotions of Trinidad*, in *IRM* 327 (1993).

maintain existence. In this latter context, dispersal and dissipation are allies that allow resistance and survival. Culture, however, works in an opposing manner to that of its European counterpart, for whereas in Europe it divides, in the Third-World it "unifies" by means of *assimilation*. However, even as culture works differently in both contexts it still can be understood negatively in the Third-World, but for a very different reason, in that the resistance, or lack thereof, to "universal culture" in the Third-World is often geared towards incorporation and assimilation into the dominant society, albeit with a "difference".

My point here is to suggest that dissipative analysis only becomes significantly problematic if the overriding concern is hegemonic maintenance, and this in clear distinction from survival in the face of, and resistance to, exploitation. In this sense, the appropriation of social analysis by "classic" liberation theology has helped. It may not have answered all ills, nor itself divest the trappings of elitism, but it did offer the *procedure of questioning* in both ideological and material ways the presuppositional motivations and agencies within events and situations. Here again, is not the claim for a "paradigm" shift by the Discussion Paper more prescriptive than descriptive?

3. *Ambivalence of Christian Culture*

One may respond to this by holding that the paradigm shift in Third-World theologies can be seen in the new encounter of liberation theology with race, gender, and environment, which does make our Christian tradition more reflexive, and so constitutes a significant change. I have argued that these "new" social movements and the theology generated by them are not "new". I would rather term them substitutives to make the Christian tradition more reflexive. But is it the case that this reflexivity is "better"? Is not this type of postmodern reflexivity (59-66) itself the problem? In that it furthers the aims of exploitation and distracts the exploited from the true cause(s) of exploitation? This does not mean that we cannot give prominence to Christian culture, but it does mean that Christian culture is dubious and ambivalent, not because it is corrupted or pure, but because Christian culture is not monolithic (except in the mythic Western sense) but Catholic, so the problem here is one of internal definition (and by extension, reflexive). This is a massive problem for "identity seeking" and "identity affirming" persons, but wherein lies the problem? If my argumentative position(s) is true, then this is not an internal problem to the Third-World, but a reflexive, external necessity thrust upon it (them) with the aim of "global cognitive mapping". One can perhaps situate Afrocentrism and various other such movements in this light, in that they offer identity with the aim toward fulfilling the quest for a unified theoretical framework, no more and no less[8]. If this is the case, then we need to ask deeper questions, in terms of liberation, regarding the need for, and issuance of, identity.

Should one then relinquish formal religious structures and turn to popular religiosity? What is this turn but another search for a "grounding" or "inner centeredness" to human endeavor which is basically imperialistic in tone and outcome, and therefore another competitor in the marketplace? Another commodification of our impulses toward survival? To return to what I consider to be the central issue of the Discussion Paper, we need to attend more realistically to how liberation theology, or any theology for that matter, can be grounded in the reality of the everyday existence of all peoples. If the issue is the need to embed liberation theological reflection in the lives of common people, I would contend that what is needed is not another substitutive ideology but a solid history of religions which would ground systematic reflection in the diverse expressions (cultural, informal, social, economic, religious) of "the people".

III. Need for a History of Third-World Religiosity

This need for a history of religions, of Third-World religiosity is an important resource for genuine theological reflection on Third-World liberation theologies. This is where the Discussion Paper badly lacks some grounding. The lack of use of the history of religions of the Third-World (meager as the literature is) and even of significant Third-World theologians is an area that needs to be redressed by De Schrijver and the Center of Liberation Theology. This lack serves to raise some ominous questions regarding the intent and scope of the Discussion Paper, but it also points out where more significant work and research needs to be done in theology in the Third-World.

1. The Challenge of Recalling the Religious Intuitions of the People

In terms of the Caribbean, numerous conferences and meetings have emphasized this and attempted to kickstart the process[9]. This has been a

---

8. Cf. M. Marable (n. 1), pp. 121-125.

9. In this regard note some relatively recent international conferences on Caribbean theology and popular religiosity sponsored by the wcc (World Council of Churches), ccc (Caribbean Council of Churches), cats (Caribbean Association of Theological Schools),

concern in the Caribbean since the early and middle 1970s, when a series of conferences were held to "stimulate and present theological reflection in the Caribbean against the background of its peculiar history and experience"[10]. In general, the liberation theology espoused by the theologians in these conferences rested upon the need to "recall the religious intuitions of our people, subjecting these to scrutiny and articulating them through the symbols of faith and life", along with the cry for direction and clarity in the midst of fragmented Caribbean communities[11]. These calls for liberation in the midst of a "northward" looking Caribbean Christian church seemed to be destined to change the Caribbean church. However, on deliberately revisiting the theological and ecclesiological situation in the Caribbean in the 1990s one only seems to hear echoes of the call of the 1970s and is forced to contend with the lack of theological and ecclesiological development in the 1980s. This "lost decade" of the 1980s forces the Caribbean theologian (and I suspect many theologians in differing regions) to come to terms with this startling phenomena[12]. How is it possible for a region which seemed committed to recalling the religious intuitions of its people to have failed to do this in some lasting way, and to find itself right back where it started some 20 years ago?

I think the key to answering this is twofold. On the one hand external regional and international events made it impossible for any sustained and genuine development and on the other hand, and more to the point of this paper, there seems to be a failing in terms of the methodology of Caribbean theologians for recalling and enshrining the religious intuitions of the people of the Caribbean. On the former issue I will too briefly claim that the promise and attainment of wealth served to divert the region, and theology in the region, from addressing its long-term habitual and abiding problems: the need for the Caribbean Christian presence to confess and heal its sins of the past and present; a reorientation from a

and the Association of Caribbean Catholic Theologians. Seminar on Popular Religiosity at the Ecumenical Institute of Bossey, Geneva, Switzerland, Spring 1993; Consultation on Theological Education in the Caribbean, Union Theological Seminary, Mona, Jamaica, Winter 1993; First Inter-Faith Dialogue Conference, Georgetown, Guyana, Summer 1993; First Conference of Catholic Caribbean Theologians, Castries, St. Lucia, Winter 1994; Second Conference of Catholic Caribbean Theologians, Trinidad, Winter 1995; Third Conference of Catholic Caribbean Theologians, Trinidad, Winter 1996.

10. Cf. I. HAMID (ed.), *Out of the Depths*, St. Andrew's Theological College, San Fernando, Trinidad, Rahaman Printery, 1977. This publication is a collection of papers from conferences that were held in Guyana, 21-22 February, 1975; Antigua, 13-14 May, 1975; Trinidad, 4-5 July, 1975; Jamaica, 4-5 December, 1975.

11. *Ibid.*, p. ix.

12. Cf. G. BOODOO, *In Response to Adolfo Ham*, in H. GREGORY (ed.), *Caribbean Theology: Preparing for the Challenges Ahead*, Jamaica, UWI, Canoe Press, 1995.

preoccupation with Northern cultural aspirations to a more genuine reflection of the Caribbean reality, using Caribbean history as a resource; the liberation of the region from the shackles of mental and physical slavery. This diversion served to blind the region to the false hope generated by the newly acquired status of "independent nations" and, in some cases, by newly acquired wealth. I will not dwell on this point, though it is vitally important to pursue, but move on to what I consider of more methodological interest to our theological concerns. This is: what methodological failing in the theology of the Caribbean allowed the revisiting of the call of the 1970s without having a theological resource of the 1980s to build upon?

2. Ideological Rhetoric in the 1980s

This question deals with a history of religions methodology, and can clearly be answered by asserting that theology in the Caribbean in the 1980s was a replication and continuous substitution of the dominant ideology of the region. This was, and still is, an ideology that maintains the exploitation of masses of people in the region despite the "local" leaders of the region. In effect, the language of religion in the region is so caught in the existing web of systemic distortions that the theology from the region became ideological rhetoric and fastened religion into an ideological schema. What therefore became possible was simply, and only, substitution, or more of the same. Change never became an option, and the theology and theologians of the region became "worthless physicians" full of empty words and hollow consolation. Now this is not far off from the theology based on a type of Kantian rational framework, wherein "empty" concepts have the power to regulate life. What this type of situation creates is the illusion of activity without the benefits of real action. Praxis thereby becomes ideology and a substitution for grounding one's reflection in the lives of people.

The methodological flaw, then, is in the illusion that "independence" or the promise of self-determination, brings true freedom and choices, and that such choices arising out of our "free" status can create an ideology which will propel the region into genuine development. The falsity of such ideas of "freedom" and of the accompanying false hope generated by them have since been exposed by the very fact of the nostalgic revisiting of the theological call of the 1970s. What seems needed is a methodological disposition that would ground such theological reflection while at the same time allowing a lasting and "real" development of theological thought and living in the region.

3. *Methodological Disposition of "Being Forced"*

One of the key traits of the methodological disposition I suggest as grounding theological reflection is the fact that, at least in the Caribbean, the past, present and continuing situation of exploitation is one that is forced upon the region. This is something that has to be recognized and taken seriously by the region. Theology in the Caribbean is not done because persons like to do it. It is done because it *must be done*. Just as the region was a *forced* region, made up of international members brought together and challenged to survive, so too the theology of the region must take on this characteristic of *being forced*. This, I think, is common to all genuine liberation theology, and something that the Center for Liberation Theology at Leuven must come to terms with. The Center must present and clarify what are the realities forced upon it which impel it to urge and fight for liberation. Without such a declaration, its existence will be suspect.

As a consequence of the previous point, I further understand theology in the Caribbean, and any theology for that matter, as expressing that space of confrontation that we inhabit. In other words, if we do not and cannot find ourselves in some space of confrontation which is delimited by our very space of existence, theology will be a vacuous and empty enterprise for us.

As minor as these two points may seem, I think they are integral to theology in the Caribbean and any understanding of liberation theology in the Third-World or elsewhere. The situation of being forced and having to exist in a space of confrontation with exploitative structures is what creates and sustains the drive for liberation. Without this situation our theological reflection is not only ungrounded but also unformed, and must subsequently search for "new" ways among the social sciences and social movements. The return to the ground, to that space of confrontation that directs our desires and resistance, is what makes our theology liberative and real. It is what makes our theology, theology. If one is to prescribe a paradigm shift, let it be a shift from a theology full of "choices" to a theology that is a space of our confrontation with structures of oppression that force us to fight for liberation in the many ways that we can.

IV. Characteristics of a "Forced Theology"

In this final section, I will attempt to briefly spell out the implications of a "forced" theology arising out of our space of confrontation with structures of exploitation.

a) The first characteristic of such a theology is precisely its forced nature, whereby one does not have the luxury of "choices". The so-called availability of choices is an illusion of self-determination which is provided by, and is a concession from, the dominant political and cultural economy. As a result, such self-determination merely replicates the ideology of the dominant structure(s) and is legitimated by it. Those subject to the illusion of self-determination are thus really forced into a particular stance and are bereft of meaningful choices related to their condition of exploitation in the drive towards liberation. Having no real choices except what is handed out by the structures of exploitation clearly situates the forced individual in the position that freedom is therefore not dependent on the will, and the so-called choices made by the will. The genuine activity of the oppressed human is not the result of "reasonable choices" made or based on some exercise of one's will, nor is it the result of the development of the "character" of the individual to be informed in one's "choices". On the contrary, will and freedom are no longer issues of compatibility. Indeed, freedom is to be had irrespective of "self-determination", and by a studied destruction of illusions created by such "willing". What is at issue here is an understanding of the agency of the human which is based not on the possibility and availability of choice but on the lack thereof. Our actions are determined not by the splendid possibilities before us but by the urgency of our present condition. Our freedom and liberation from exploitation is therefore not dependent on the possibility of new and alternative structures but on our resistance to the present condition of exploitation. The future has no promise for an exploited and forced people except "more of the same".

b) In this sense, and this is the second characteristic of a forced theology, freedom is not to be understood in the light of hope but in the light of despair. It is the condition of being forced that propels the human to identify and move towards what is urgent in their existing and continuing situation. This is where many Third-World literary artists are correct in their understanding of the Third-World – the absurd rules! The condition of being forced can generate a hope which deprives one of an understanding rooted in the here and now and so gives one the illusion of "freedom" from the oppressed condition. This is best depicted in the carnivalesque, which perpetuates the illusion of freedom by means of a momentary release that captures the imagination of the oppressed in such a manner that liberation is situated within its confines. This detracts from the need for a more lasting liberative condition by suggesting that mimicry contains the dynamic for continued resistance and could thereby direct us onto the path of liberation. An example of this is "picong" (the

Trinidad term for banter between individuals related to mimicry and the cajoling of someone until they either admit defeat or are vanquished). Its intent is to exploit an already exploited person with the aim of being the victorious "survivor" who, in his victory (knowingly or not), mimics the oppressor by once more being the master of his terrain who exploits and vanquishes all who dare speak against him. As interesting as the carnivalesque and picong may be in terms of an attempt to navigate the terrain of the existence of the exploited, they only seem to replicate the dominance already existing and do not offer any lasting relatedness to the condition of the forced and exploited human. Indeed, in more recent years, this can be borne out by the observation (at least in Trinidad) that celebrations of the carnivalesque are now the domain of the dominant ideology and are being used to further the economic, political and cultural hegemony of those in power. This momentary and captivating sense of "freedom" offered by the carnivalesque is therefore an expression of the false hope that can be generated by "forced" conditions that is based solely on the mimicking of available possibilities. It can therefore only replicate the dominant ideology. The "freedom" that is gained in the light of such "hope" is exploited. It is a hope filled with hollow rhetoric, recurrent oppression, and false ideology. Can one really call this a "choice"? The illusion of self-determination and the misunderstanding that freedom can be had in the light of hope are shattered by the condition of the "forced". Any forced theology must also thus reject these claims as a valid starting-point of reflection. The only freedom that can be had is in the full recognition of the forced and despairing situation created by exploitation, which in turn propels us to confront such structures and struggle for liberation.

c) This leads to the third characteristic of a forced theology: the non-essentiality of the human condition. There is no essential condition of the human that can be appealed to in determining some prescription for the human condition. If this is the case, appeals to dignity, cultural identity and genealogy are themselves pseudo issues that take away from, and in some cases deliberately sidetrack, the movement towards liberation. These appeals are based on the misunderstanding that there is some essential human condition to which we strive and which reflexively shines forth from our "common human experience". This commonality, however, often is a veiled (and not so veiled) attempt at further manipulation and exploitation. If this is the case, what gives liberation itself some desired status? Could it not also be some false "hope" born out of the "forced" desire for some alternative? That is something that may need to be taken into consideration, as some form of "opium of the masses". But genuine liberation gets its desired and preferential status as a result of its stance of confrontation with exploitation and evil. This liberation takes on preferential status because of the belief that such liberation can only be realized with the incarnation of the kingdom of God in the face of such evil. Without the deep belief in the reality of God's kingdom as liberative and immanent, the goal and desire for liberation is itself another possible "illusion" that replicates dominance and exploitation, and possibly another rhetorical device of misdirection.

The non-essentiality of the human condition therefore forces us to strive towards the realization of a condition which allows us to be most fully human yet most fully free. Freedom, from this perspective, is the ability to maintain one's course of confrontation with empty concepts, false prophets, and the evil and exploitation they perpetuate in order to deny the realization of the kingdom of God. Isn't this the example of Job? Job shows that the one who is able to stand against, and in the face of, "worthless physicians" with their hollow promises and false understandings will be vindicated by God. Though portrayed as heretical by resisting and remaining steadfast in the face of a dominant culture, such a person turns out to be the means through which others will themselves be vindicated and saved. The lesson of Job, and of "forced" peoples everywhere, is that liberation from oppression and exploitation is to be found in the real task of realizing God's kingdom. Can any liberation theology do less?

V. Conclusion

If liberation theology is to be rooted in the lives of people, it has to take the forced character of exploitation very seriously and recognize the forced character of its own reflections. I contend, given such a "forced" reality, that freedom is not dependent on will (the illusion of self-determination), that freedom is found not in the light of hope but in the "light" of despair, and that the non-essentiality of the human condition are characteristics of such a "forced" theology. I think it is the forced character of such situating and reflecting in the space of confrontation with structures of exploitation and evil which ensures the groundedness of liberation theology and of liberation theologians. The theological task then is not one of choices and "new" possibilities but of a necessary reflection born out of our need to realize genuine freedom and liberation.

Xavier University of Louisiana   Gerald BOODOO
7325 Palmetto, Box 31a.
New Orleans, LA, 70125, USA

19

CLASH OF PARADIGMS
REPORT FROM THE CARIBBEAN

> *his people ought to use the past*
> *with the intention of opening the future*
> *as an invitation to action and a basis for hope[1].*

I. CONFRONTING THE CARIBBEAN REALITY

1. *Models of Interpretation*

The critical issue facing any student of the Caribbean, regardless of discipline, is the issue of interpretative framework. The reality of the New-World, for most of its existence, has been interpreted as an extension of the Old-World, with minor modifications. Old-World scholars have traditionally come to the New-World, seeing what they assume to be bastardizations of recognizable patterns. Accepting the Old-World idealized form as the norm, they, without hesitation, pronounce their judgment. British historian James Anthony Froude, having surveyed the New-World as a tourist traveler, concluded that "there were no people there in the true sense of the word"[2]. This imperialist interpretative framework has become the main tool through which the New-World has been mediated to the inhabitants of the Old, and to itself.

Nobel laureate Derek Walcott, commenting on an epic drama in a country village in Trinidad, says:

> The purist look on such ceremonies as grammarians look at a dialect, as cities look on provinces and empires on their colonies. Memory that yearns to join the center, a limb remembering the body from which it has been

---

1. F. FANON, *Wretched of the Earth*, Middlesex, Penguin Books, 1961, reprinted 1976, p. 187.
2. For a classic example of this, within the literary world, see J.A. FROUDE, *The English in the West Indies*, 1887. Froude's pronouncement, one hundred years ago, that in the Caribbean "there were no people in the true sense of the word" is still being reckoned with today. See, V.S. NIAPAUL, *The Middle Passage*, England, Penguin, 1975. In his chapter on Trinidad, Niapaul echoes Froude's sentiments by quoting Froude in the opening of the Chapter. Many have responded to Froude, see, for instance, E. WILLIAMS, *British Historians and the West Indies*, New York, Charles Scribners Sons, 1966; see also, J.J. THOMAS, *Froudacity*, Port-Of Spain, Beacon Books, reprinted, 1969. D. WALCOTT, *The Antilles Fragments of Epic Memory: The Nobel Lecture,* London, Faber & Faber, 1992, also responds to expose the ideology of racism inherent in this position. The volume of literature in response to Froude at least says that he struck a raw nerve.

severed... In other words, the way that the Caribbean is still looked at, ille-gitimate, rootless, mongrelized. 'No people there', to quote Froude, 'in the true sense of the word'. No people. Fragments and echoes of real people, unoriginal and broken[3].

Caribbean intellectuals, artists, and grass-root activists have exposed the poverty of this imperialist interpretative framework. For the better part of this century, they have been pushing ahead without adequate tools of analy-sis to mediate the Caribbean reality to its people. The New-World is not a bastardization of the Old. It is a whole new cultural reality. It must be taken on its terms and interpreted through its own interpretative framework[4].

Our intellectuals, artists, and activists have worked hard to clear a space for creative confrontation and dialogue with the Caribbean reality. Yet still, scholars from both New and Old-Worlds, impose an imperialist interpretative framework before the investigation of the reality. The the-ological rupture in the Caribbean was primarily about the interpretative framework.

2. Genesis of a Carribbean Theology

The paradigmatic shift in theology in the Caribbean came in 1971. Idris Hamid, principal of St. Andrews Theological College, ushered in the new tradition with his essay "In Search of New Perspectives"[5]. Comment-ing on this work, Fr. Patrick Anthony of the pastoral Center of St. Lucia says:

> Few will deny that Idris Hamid's seminal essay "In Search of New Perspec-tives" marks the beginning of a whole new era in the history of theological reflection in the Caribbean. In one stroke Idris shook the foundations of what

3. D. WALCOTT (n. 2), pp. 6-7.
4. The best example of this current today is the issue of the Caribbean family. The immorality, instability and dysfunction of the Caribbean family has been used to mystify the crude oppression and injustice by Old-World imperialists. The 1938 report of the Royal commission after an uprising in the colonies used instability of the family as the main reason for the underdevelopment. Cultural anthropologists today see this family structure as African retention from the Ashantis, or as bastardization of European norms. It has been analyzed through Marxist, colonial, classicist whether African or European, and Victorian Puritanical interpretative frameworks. J. Besson makes the point: "Rather than being passive cultural survivals from Africa or Europe, such customary tenures rep-resented dynamic Caribbean cultural creations in resistance to slavery, colonialism, the plantation system, and Euro-centric agrarian legal codes". See J. BESSON, *Land Kinship and Community in Post-Emancipation Caribbean: A regional View of the Leewards*, in K.F. OLWIG (ed.), *Small Islands, Large Questions*, Bridgetown, Frank Cass, 1995. And J. BESSON, *Land Kinship and Community in Post-Emancipation Caribbean: A regional View of the Leewards*, ID.
5. I. HAMID, *In Search of New Perspectives*, Bridgetown, Caribbean Ecumenical for Development, 1971.

was being taught in religious houses of formation throughout the region, and challenged the theological presuppositions behind Christian praxis within the churches[6].

Six theological conferences followed. The first two focusing on creative theology, were held in May 1973 in Jamaica and Trinidad, and were entitled *Troubling of the Waters*[7]. The other four, focusing on missiology, were held in Antigua, Guyana, Jamaica and Trinidad in 1975. Their title was *Out of The Depths*[8]. The theological agenda had been set; there could be no turning back.

Hamid's paper and the published work of these two conferences display a consensus concerning the tools used to analyze and interpret the Caribbean reality. For the purpose of this paper, I will confine my self to these three texts. They are the best representatives of the genesis of Caribbean Theology, and thus, their analysis will enable us to conclude whether there was a pivotal or paradigmatic shift in Caribbean Theology.

II. THREE MAJOR STEPS IN CARIBBEAN THEOLOGIZING

1. *I. Hamid's Work "In Search of New Perspectives"*

Idris Hamid's work *In Search of New Perspectives*[9] broke the tradition of theologizing from a Euro-centric perspective, and placed the Caribbean people and their experience at the center of the theological locus. As we engage with this text, we ask of it the following questions. Of what did the rupture consist? What mode of analysis did Hamid use? And What interpretative framework is employed to mediate the Caribbean reality?

Hamid uses a provocatively descriptive passage of Caribbean literature from Earl Lovelace's *While Gods are Falling*[10] as a statement before his theological text begins. In this passage Lovelace does a critique of the colonial ontology that is hierarchical and dualist. Within this ontology God is never in the concrete reality. God is always elsewhere – Heaven, the White elites, Metropolis. In this sense the text is a satire. In the face of this colonial ontological construct and the overwhelming evidence that supports it, the protagonist revolts while confessing that faith in God is difficult.

---

6. P.A.B. ANTHONY (ed.), *Editorial* in *Theology in the Caribbean Today: Perspectives*, St Lucia, Archdiocesan Pastoral Center, 1995.
7. I. HAMID (ed.), *Troubling of the Waters*, Trinidad, San Fernando, 1973.
8. I. HAMID (ed.), *Out of The Depths*, Trinidad, St Andrews's Theological College, 1977.
9. I. HAMID (n. 5).
10. E. LOVELACE, *While Gods are Falling*, London, Collins, 1965, p. 151.

This ontological suspicion comes because there is an epistemological rupture. The concrete experience of the poor black majority becomes the new epistemological ground. There is a shift from colonial rhetoric to humanism. From this ground the ideological suspicion flows, all the masses have sung that the whole colonial religious construct has nothing to do with God. "He is God of the white and rich and not of the poor black. God has left!" Although Hamid never refers to the text in his work, the reality mediated through this text is the reality that Hamid addresses. His rupture is with colonization, which for him occurs on four levels – "political, economic, cultural and religious"[11]. About the project of colonization, he says… "the theology of the church is the last bastion"[12].

In this rupture he sights four essential pillars of colonization: (1) false dichotomy between body and spirit, (2) proclaiming the spiritual needs of the soul as the really real (all that mattered) at the expense of the bodily needs, (3) an individualistic ethic that was destructive to community, and (4) a false opiate eschatology which pushed hope to the next life and negated historical engagement.

The model of analysis utilized in Hamid's text is historical-critical and uses suspicion of colonization as the driving force of the evaluative process. Thus ideological suspicion revolved around the axis of colonization and emancipation rather than the axis of social class. It is important to note that Hamid's text was written only nine years after independence in Trinidad and Tobago and Jamaica. It is also important to note that Hamid's focus is primarily on the effects of colonization in religion and culture, only secondarily is it on the political and economic realm. To investigate this further, I will highlight Hamid's position on socio-economic analysis. Then I will explore the cultural realm as the space for confrontation, dialogue, and liberation.

a) *Socio-Economic Analysis*

The first explicit mention of socio-economic analysis is half way through the text. It is seen as a sub-set of the third pillar of colonization – individualism, and it falls within the ambit of social justice. Here Hamid critiques the developmental model that measures economic growth in a way that "conceals the frustration, alienation and growing polarity between the rich and the poor. The *laissez-faire* development economics which makes the rich richer and increases poverty must be

---

11. I. HAMID (n. 5), p. 12.
12. *Ibidem*.

tempered with the claims and constraints of social justice"[13]. The epistemological ground for this claim is the priority of the community over the individual.

Going further into the analysis of the socio-economic, Hamid relies upon G. Myrdal's *An Approach to the Asian Drama*[14]. He does an ideological critique of the models of development in which the "North-Atlantic communities are held up as models and the Third-World as developing or underdeveloped". He goes on to examine the "sociology" of the development talk. (1) It is a post World-War II phenomenon connected with the "liquidation of the colonial power system and its replacement by nation states pressing for state planning to bring about economic development". (2) The second feature is the di-polar world creating the cold war. The developing nations are pawns in this war with the superpowers competing for their allegiance. He says: "In simple words the contending big powers – USA, USSR and China, have a political stake – and an economic one too – in the direction of our development. Each is trying to sell its own version of development to us and even lend us considerable aid to develop in their image. So even here there is a subtle neo-colonialism"[15].

Hamid is using historical criticism with colonization as a point of departure, thus he critiques both sides of the ideological divide as being neo-colonizers. This is important for understanding theology in the Caribbean. Our point of departure was not the economically poor; it was the ones robbed of their identity, history and culture through genocide slavery and indentureship. Thus economic theory is subjected to scrutiny.

The economic analysis is mediated through the broader interpretative framework–the rupture with colonization and the establishment of a new culture. The "long historical view" is the post-colonial view, and thus the options to be made demands a critique of all forms of imperialism. The genesis of theology taking its point of departure from the experience of Caribbean people did not use socio-economic mediation to render access to society. It suspected this mediation of a colonizing function and subjected it to scrutiny.

13. *Ibidem.*, p. 9-10.
14. G. MYRDAL, *An Approach to the Asian Drama*, New York, Random House, 1970. It is interesting that Hamid goes to Asia for this critique and not to Latin America. He quoted Gutiérrez' seminal article: *Notes for a Theology of Liberation*. See G. Gutiérrez, *Notes for a Theology of Liberation* (Lima). He must have been familiar with that position.
15. I. HAMID (n. 5), p. 12.

b) *The Cultural Realm as the Space for Confrontation, Dialogue and Liberation.*

For Hamid, the colonial is the framework of suspicion, and the cultural realm is the foundation of the ethical or the human possibility for the good. By constructing these relations thus, Hamid enters into a different mode of discourse than his Latin American counterparts. In many ways this is consistent with the intellectual movement in the Caribbean that had already experienced black governments and political independence while the imperial colonial policies and the structure of the society remained unchanged. The battleground had been the ideology of white imperial colonization that had been internalized by the black masses. An economic revolution that did not dislodge this ideology and culture would have been as ineffectual as the political revolution expressed in the independence movement.

From the genesis of Caribbean theology, the economic agenda was not central to the new way of doing theology. Furthermore, by his use of the text of Lovelace, it becomes reasonable to suggest that literature as a mode of accessing the truth of society is present in the genesis of the project. The literary artist in a short passage articulated the suspicions and new foundations that the theologian would articulate in the extended essay. I would like to propose the thesis that, at the genesis of the project in Caribbean theology it is the artist and not only the social scientist that provided the tools to mediate and analyze Caribbean reality. This thesis is strongly supported by the evidence of the tow other conferences, where works of literature and literary critiques were often used to mediate the Caribbean reality.

2. *The Two Conferences "Troubling of the Waters"*

In 1973, I. Hamid organized two conferences on creative theological reflection that were held in Jamaica and Trinidad. The proceedings of these conferences represent the second milestone in the history of Caribbean theology[16]. There were forty participants, with twenty of them contributing to the publication. These were professional theologians, economists, historians, educators and literary experts. Many were professors of the University of the West Indies. Their thinking represented the thinking within the Caribbean then.

When one reads the text of these conferences, there is no doubt of what the rupture consisted. It was a rupture with colonialism. At center stage

16. I. HAMID (n. 7).

is the exploration of "Caribbean man"[17] and "a new Antillian Culture". What is abundantly clear is that the writers, the artist and the Black power leaders are the intellectual leaders at the forefront of this movement. The key term coined for analysis is "taking a long historical view". This view is grounded on the genocide, slavery and indentureship of the peoples who now form the Caribbean. But this view goes further by analyzing the effects of colonization. It is taken for granted that colonization is an economic and political reality. The primary mode of exploration focused upon the use of religion and culture to colonize and resist colonization.

All the eleven articles and the seven responses in this volume used culture as a point of departure. Many quoted from literary artists as a way of analyzing the reality. At least three authors expressed their dependence upon the "writers' tradition" for key concepts like "Antillian culture" and "Caribbean Man". Only one of them gave priority to economics over culture. He was an expatriate Jesuit economist – Fr. Michael Campbell-Johnston, S.J. Unlike the others, he interpreted the black power movement and Walter Rodney as engaging in a rupture that was primarily economic. He says:

> ... We could bear in mind that the first task is the break with imperialism and this is more concerned with the economic structure of the region which is one in which the political force is black and the economic force is still white. So to change the color of the economic force is to break with the imperial power which controls the economic resources of the region[18].

What is amazing is that he does this while using this quotation from Mc Donald who "concludes an economic study of the region in these words":

> Yet worse than the material poverty of the region is the state of mind of its inhabitants. The effects of three hundred years of colonization and its continuation in other forms to-day have conditioned large sectors of the population to believe that there is no other way to live, that the objective of each day is to endure until the next to scrape together enough to survive[19].

Unlike the other authors who originated in the Caribbean, Campbell-Johnston uses a different interpretative framework. Economics becomes the primary sphere with culture as the superstructure. It is not as though

17. When the calypsoian Black Stalyn sang "The Caribbean Man" in 1979 it was critiqued as sexist, but In the early 1970s this was not part of the interpretative framework.

18. M. CAMPBELL-JOHNSTON, *Comment*, in HAMID (n. 7), p. 115-121 and 117-118. Campbell-Johnston quotes three authorities, Loyd Best, Dr. Omawale, and Walter Rodney. In these quotes only Loyd Best places the Economic as the primary space. Because of his interpretative framework, Campbell-Johnston uses Loyd Best and thus misinterprets the others. As we will see later Rodney placed the cultural as the primary.

19. F. MC DONALD, Quoted in ID. pp. 118-119.

the theologians were unaware of this tension. In his paper on "The De-Colonization of Theology"[20], William Watty produces material evidence of the tension and the option that the theologians made. He says:

> It is common to disparage any kind of radical theological reflection by invoking pressing problems of human destitution and need. De-colonizing theology, it is argued, will not give food to the hungry, work to the unemployed or shelter to the homeless... Experience, however, suggests that such objections derive less from a concern for the disadvantaged in society than from a fear of the likely results of such an exercise. The most vocal protagonists are invariably expatriate, and this view, interestingly enough is itself a surviving relic of colonial theology... A dog wags his tail when I throw him his bone, build him his kennel or pat his head for the stick he has retrieved. It takes a man to tell his would-be benefactor to go to hell with the bone and kennel and stick[21].

Using history and culture as an interpretative framework to mediate the reality of the Caribbean was not an accidental feature of this theology. According to Watty it was an option. His explicit comments are supported by the methodological framework of the majority of the contributors. Further more, if Watty is correct, the socio-economic mediation is viewed as a neo-colonial trick to distract Caribbean theologians from their real task – participating in the creation of the "new Antillian culture" and the formation of the "Caribbean person".

The most penetrative analysis of "Caribbean Man", among the different views held by the scholars about Caribbean history and culture, was put forward by G. Rohlehr's, "Man's Spiritual Search in the Caribbean through Literature". Rohlehr is a professor of literature at the University of the West Indies and an important figure in the interpretation of Caribbean writers.

In the introduction, Hamid notes that there is a consensus among theologians about the need for a penetrative reflection upon the Caribbean writers as the way forward for theology. This, together with Rohlehr's article and the references to the writers' conference and the frequent quotations of Caribbean literature, leads me to suggest that the theologians are dependent upon the Caribbean writers for the interpretative framework used in the analysis of the Caribbean reality. In Latin America the sociologists provided this framework for interpretation. In this sense, I am suggesting that Caribbean theology cannot be seen as a bastardization of Latin American theology. It is a creation in its own right and must be evaluated on its own grounds.

20. W. WATTY, *The De-Colonization of Theology*, in HAMID (n. 7), pp. 49-79.
21. *Ibid.*, p. 51.

3. *The 1975 Conference "Out of the Depths"*

There was a pivotal shift in the mode of analysis in the 1975 conference *Out Of The Depths*. This conference that focused on missiology was held in four venues – Antigua, Guyana, Jamaica and Trinidad. The papers presented were reworked and published[22]. Five of the fifteen authors who published, used Marxist analysis as an interpretative framework. Some of these gave a serious challenge to the tradition of theology in the English-speaking Caribbean. It is important to note that two of these, Adolfo Ham and Uxmal Livio Diaz, came from Cuba. One, P.I. Gómez, is a professional sociologist from Guyana, and the other two, W. Ramos and L.N. Rivera, are from Puerto Rico. The other ten contributors, eight coming from the English-speaking and two from the French-speaking Caribbean, used cultural analysis in different forms. The ideological divide in the region revolves around the axis of language that was ultimately determined by the colonizer. The Spanish speakers aligned themselves with the continent.

All the papers used colonialism as a point of departure, and explored the "Caribbean man" as the general theme. Up to the publication of this work, the English-speaking Caribbean had not shifted from cultural analysis. The Spanish-speaking Caribbean, however, obviously aligned with Latin America, were producing a different brand of theology. There has never been one Caribbean theology or one conceptual framework out of which the theologians worked. Our history of fragmentation, the difference in the colonizers and thus in languages, the sizes of the islands, and the racial backgrounds and cultural options of the theologians all affected the theologies produced. U.L. Diaz offers a critique of the project of a Caribbean theology. He says:

> We talk a lot in the Caribbean about the decolonization of theology, and I think that is good, but so far what I've read speaks of a negative theology set over against the one Colonialism brought us; since Theology is above all an affirmation, "Gods yes", we must go a little further and opt for a "Black Liberation Theology" in which we make explicit and tie together all the feelings of those who are racially and economically exploited in the Caribbean, and which will offer us the possibility of a liberating praxis for the people of God, from a scientific point of view[23].

From the perspective of liberation theology, Caribbean theology seems to have made no preferential option and no epistemological rupture. Without these, and here Diaz is correct, theology will remain reactionary

---

22. I. HAMID, (n. 8).
23. U.L. DIAZ, *The Role of the Third World Christians and the Churches in the Struggle Against Colonialism and Neo Colonialism*, in HAMID, (n. 8), p. 142.

and negative. From the perspective of Caribbean theology (in the English-speaking Caribbean) the issue is perceived differently. It is not that no option has been made but that this option cannot simply be imported from outside.

Terry Julien, in his paper "Christian Mission, Cultural Traditions, and Environment", counters Diaz's point. By using a quotation from William Demas, the former secretary-general of the Caribbean Community Secretariat and a prominent intellectual in the discussion of a new Caribbean society, Julien criticizes all importation of ideology. Demas says:

> All of this means that the New Caribbean Society must rest on an indigenous and not an imported ideological basis. If we are to create a distinctive society in the Caribbean, we must formulate the intellectual and moral basis of this society in the light of our own possibilities and our own aspirations. The new Caribbean man must look inwards for ideological inspiration[24].

Luis N. Rivera from Puerto Rico makes another judgement. He says:

> It is impossible to understand the Caribbean reality without analyzing the relationship between the colonial status of the islands and the oppression of the Black people. This is one of the reasons for the insufficiency of the Latin American Liberation theology with respect to the Caribbean Context. It has not developed the conceptual tools needed to study the problems of racial discrimination and the oppression of the Black people[25].

This is the dilemma of the Caribbean. Can it trust the tools of analysis and the ideological options that come from outside? If it cannot, how does it assure itself that it does not waste time and energy "reinventing the wheel"?

In this conference, the reference made to literature, art and music from the Caribbean as a viable starting-point for theology is remarkable. Terry Julian proposes that the point of departure for hermeneutics is the question "What is a cultural tradition?" He notes that the written and the folk traditions must be explored. Later on he proposes the study of Wilson Haris and Edward Braithwaite as a suitable point of departure[26]. Geoffrey B. Williams, through his use of Lonergan's transcendental method, does a critique of a classics approach to culture as promoted by both Europeanizers and/or Africanizers. By using the concept of self-appropriation, he postulates that "authentic liberation is only possible if a strong, cohesive, culture has been previously established or else liberation would merely be a descent into chaos or the vacuum in which those who have

---

24. W. DEMAS, *Change and Renewal in the Caribbean*, Barbados, CCC Publishing House, 1975, p. 19.

25. L.N. RIVERA, *Mission of the Church and the Development of a Caribbean theology of Liberation*, in I. HAMID (n. 8), p. 258.

26. Just to note some. Cf. HAMID (n. 8), pp. 22 and 26.

re-erected Europeanization, without first finding a viable alternative, find themselves[27].

Kortright Davis said: "To discern the specific trends in a people's art, literature, music, educational and political life is basically a sociological exercise"[28]. Patrick Anthony, through the work of his Folk Research Center, has made the realm of culture the epistemological foundation for the rupture in the ideology of colonialism. Anthony sees culture as a "total concept including artifacts, political and social institutions, cosmos, and habits". Anthony believes that the Caribbean is a unique cultural area unlike other homogeneous cultures. In the Caribbean, antagonisms cannot just be analyzed by class in an economic sense, since cultural option is part of the material used in the formation of these antagonistic groups. Anthony names four groups. (1) the Euro-centred elites, (2) the Euro-oriented Creole upper-class, (3) a small Creole intellectual elite, and (4) the Afro-Caribbean black population. In the case of Guyana, Suriname, and Trinidad, Anthony should have added a fifth group, (5) the Indo-Caribbean population. Here, Creole is used as a pejorative term referring to those who have assimilated the colonizers' culture for social status. This is opposed to indigenization that is rooted in resistance and survival. Through his analysis of the antagonisms in the society, Anthony has moved the dialogue further.

Through this type of analysis, the critique of ideology, rather than becoming irrelevant, becomes far more important. What is obvious here, however, is that new tools are required for such a critique. To use the realm of culture as a starting-point for theology demands of the theologian a rigorous critique of the ideology of the artists and the works being used. Not all artists and not all works of art will promote the exploration of "the Caribbean man". It is noteworthy that Anthony is dependent upon Edward Brathwaite, a renowned author, for the categories and the analysis. Also important is that Anthony does a critique of some artists, a critique that shows their irrelevance to the project at hand.

By using the realm of culture as the point of departure, theology in the Caribbean cannot become less critical, it must become more critical.

To evaluate Caribbean theology, one cannot use other theological movements and impose their categories. The only adequate base is the intellectual ferment of the sixties and seventies within the Caribbean. Was Caribbean theology faithful to this movement in search of a new society and a new "Caribbean person"? Were its tools of analysis adequate?

27. ID., p. 81.
28. K. DAVIS, *Theological Education for Mission*, in HAMID (n. 8), p. 217.

For the process of evaluation, I will look critically at two of the best-known and most-quoted sources, Frantz Fanon and Walter Rodney.

III. Evaluating the Major Steps from the Background of Two 'Classics'

1. *Frantz Fanon*

In 1961, a Caribbean psychiatrist and revolutionary, Frantz Fanon, shook the literary world with his now famous *Wretched of the Earth*. Coming out of his reflections on Algeria, this became the handbook for all "Third-World" revolutionaries in colonial countries. Fanon begins with a penetrating analysis of the social relationships in a colonized country, showing the complexity of the arrangements and hence the difficulty of analysis. He says:

> The originality of the colonial context, is that economic reality, inequality and the immense difference of ways of life, never come to mask the human realities. When you examine at close quarters the colonial context, it is evident that what parcels out the world is to begin with the fact of belonging to or not belonging to a given race, a given species. In the colonies the economic substructure is also a superstructure. The cause is the consequence; you are rich because you are white, you are white because you are rich. This is why Marxist analysis should always be slightly stretched every time we have to do with the colonial problem.
>
> Everything up to and including the very nature of pre-capitalist society, so well explained by Marx must here be thought out again. The serf is in essence different from the knight, but a reference to divine right is necessary to legitimize this statutory difference. In the colonies, the foreigner coming from another country imposed his rule by means of guns and machines... The governing race is first and foremost those who come from elsewhere, those who are unlike the original inhabitants, 'the others'[29].

In short, the categories do not fit the New-World, in quite the same way that they fit in the Old-World. Race, class, rationale for the inequalities, and superstructure-substructure – all have to be re-thought. The Old-World categories cannot be imposed. Furthermore Fanon says:

> The native is declared insensible to ethics; he represents not only the absence of values, but also the negation of values. He is... the absolute evil... At times this Manichaeism goes to its logical conclusion and dehumanizes the native, or, to speak plainly, it turns him into an animal. In fact, the terms the settler uses when he mentions the native are zoological terms[30].

29. F. FANON (n. 1), pp. 30-31.
30. ID., p. 32.

Whatever may be said about oppression in the Old-World, the ground was not primarily race or culture, nor was the humanity of the oppressed called into question[31]. The categories are fundamentally different. In the New-World, the protagonist is not only the economically oppressed, s/he is the conquered, the one stripped of humanity, of culture, of dignity. S/he is the non person, not only in an economic sense but in an existential or rather anthropological sense. The natives are the epitome of evil who must either be converted or eradicated. The rationale of the exploitation, and thus its effects, are fundamentally different.

In Fanon's penetrative reflection, the point of departure is colonization. The tools of analysis are cultural and economic, become the "substructure is the superstructure" and vice versa. His analysis of antagonistic groups in the post-colonial society is complex. Patrick Anthony comes closest to this analysis. The basic interpretative framework of this theologian is not different from that of Fanon. The critique of them that I would have is that, for the most part, they fail to use all the tools of analysis available, and so at times, they continue to mask the social reality.

The critique that the tradition would offer to Fanon would be on the role of violence. Fanon sees violence as necessary and good; this view is fundamentally against the Christian tradition. For him, violence is a way of unifying the people and of psychic purification to reclaim one's identity and equality[32]. It is on this point that the theologian and Fanon would have to part company. For while violence can never be ruled out in a situation of extreme oppression, if for no other reason than the protection of the innocent, it would remain an ontic evil in a Christian ethical framework.

2. *Walter Rodney*

In exploring the second pillar of the intellectual tradition of the West Indies – the Black Power movement – cultural analysis again emerges as the tool of choice. Walter Rodney is very clear about the epistemological rupture that is required in the Caribbean society. It is a rupture with white ideology and white imperialism[33]. For Rodney, the definition of black is very easy for the white western world has defined all non-Europeans as Black, including Indians, Chinese, Arabs, Africans, etc. As such, Black refers to those who do not have power. By conducting an analysis of power, Rodney shifts the analytical base from economics to

31. The only exception from the Old-World would be the Jews.
32. ID., p. 76.
33. W. RODNEY, *The Grounding With my Brothers*, London, Bogle-L'Overture Press, 1975, p. 16.

politics. And by making the lines of demarcation Black and White, the axis moves from social to cultural analysis. Poverty is a proof of white power and black powerlessness.

Even when speaking about the blacks who have power, Rodney does not use the Marxist term bourgeois without qualification. He chooses to explain this phenomena of black leaders co-operating with white imperialism, and thus working against the people, by calling them "Black faced, white hearted". Thus, he echoes Fanon's work *Black Skins, White Masks*[34]. Fanon had already shown that the term bourgeoisie does not fit the post-colonial middle class[35]. Fanon says:

> What creates a bourgeoisie is not the bourgeoisie spirit nor its taste or manners, nor even its aspirations. The bourgeoisie is above all the direct product of precise economic conditions...The bourgeoisie of an under-developed country is a bourgeoisie in spirit only... It is the positions that it holds in the new national administration which will give it strength and serenity... But it will always reveal itself as incapable of giving birth to an authentic bourgeois society with all the economic and industrial consequences which this entails[36].

In Rodney's analysis, it is impossible to understand the present condition of black people in the West Indies unless one first understands the historical process that led to it. Slavery that started as an economic oppression soon became racial, as the white labor was withdrawn from the fields. From this condition of black social inferiority – slavery – grew social and scientific theories defining the inferiority of the black race in essence. This scientific theory was then used to justify the social experience and to absolve the oppressor of guilt. This oppression was then internalized by the black community who handed over power to the whites. Thus the circle was completed. The superstructure has become the substructure and vice versa.

Ultimately, Rodney's point is that black power is an ideology[37]. The self-hatred that the black persons have internalized because of their color, hair texture, features, etc. has become the foundation of internal and external oppression. The ideology of black power reverses the internalized value judgments and the external social and scientific theory. Black, rather than being a curse, is now beautiful[38].

---

34. F. FANON, *Black Skins, White Masks*, London, Pluto press, 1968.
35. Cf. F. FANON (n. 1), p. 123.
36. ID., p. 143-144.
37. W. RODNEY (33), p. 21.
38. It is important to note that Rodney does not advocate black supremacy; in fact he rejects this as an "error or a deliberate falsification". ID., p. 24

The importance of black power is that it is an ideological position which analyses, mocks, and debunks the old ideology – white supremacy. The epistemological base for this rupture is not social class in the Marxist sense; rather it is a cultural option, the option to view the whole cultural world of black people as fundamentally good and positive. If the epistemological rupture is within the cultural world, then, the interpretative framework used, must be completely consistent with this new ideology, and the tools of analysis employed to mediate Caribbean reality must prove their adequacy within the realm of culture. It is not that socio-economic theory and analysis is not important, but it is certainly not the primary sphere for analysis or transformation. Rodney, like Fanon, uses a historical approach, and both depart from Marx in their tools of analysis. This departure can only be understood if one is willing to concede that the Caribbean is a new creation that cannot be understood through the old interpretative frameworks of the Old-World[39].

IV. Conclusion

This investigation into theological reflection in the Caribbean in the 1970s raises several challenges to us in theology today. For some "Third-World" contexts, the rupture to be obtained was with poverty, and so, the preferred interpretative framework was Marx's historical dialectics. For these, the tools of analysis were socio-economic. In the English-speaking Caribbean, the rupture was with colonization, and thus the interpretative framework and tools of analysis resided within the realm of culture. To speak about a paradigm shift, or even a pivotal shift from the socio-economic to culture, does violence to theology in the Caribbean. If there has been a shift in the eighties and nineties, it has been to incorporate the tools of socio-economic analysis. In our pluralistic world, the Caribbean is a microcosm of the whole. In its history, it reflects the fragmentation and thus the multiple positions possible. The way forward cannot be "either/or", it must dare to incorporate the best of both traditions.

Flat 7   Jason GORDON
13 Marloes Rd. W8 6LQ
London, UK

39. Rodney goes so far as to say that those in power would have preferred it if he were a Communist. Then they could discredit him more easily. ID., p. 61-62.

20

SEVEN INDONESIAN PERSPECTIVES ON THEOLOGY OF LIBERATION

I. SITUATING ASIAN THEOLOGIES OF LIBERATION

A simple global division of modern theologies may consider Latin America as the kernel of theology of liberation, Africa as the home for inculturation, and Asia as the center for interreligious dialogue. This division, of course, is too rough. In Africa there is a more political black theology, which inspired also the struggle against apartheid, while the 'African theology' indeed pays more attention to inculturation, to the dialogue with local cultures and religion. In modern Latin America the interreligious dialogue with the Indian religions, but also with Afro-Brazilian religions has become an important challenge[1]. Asian Christianity has developed its own style of 'liberation theologies' in the India Dalit-, and the Korean Minjung-theologies. Still, some of the characteristics which are at the base of a division in three (liberation, inculturation, dialogue) have their base in the specific conditions of Christians in those areas of the world.

As far as Asian Christian theologies are concerned, they are rather modest in their formulation of 'liberation' goals: M.M. Thomas published Christian participation in Nation-building (1960) and The Christian Response to the Asian Revolution (1966): joining rather than leading. From the very beginning of a more pronounced and specific Asian theology in the 1960s the interreligious issue has been prominent. In the Minjung-theology we clearly see, that the specific Christian character sometimes is very weak and not outspoken. Christian Minjung-theologians work together with activists, artists and cultural thinkers, who have no direct or explicit Christian background[2]. The same can be said of the Dalit-theology of India. Dalit-theology is not an exclusively Christian movement, one would rather say, that Christian Dalit-theology is not much more than one (even minor) variant within a broader Dalit movement:

1. R. VAN ROSSUM, *Latin-American Theological Journals and the Culture Debate*, in *Exchange* 24 (1997) 114-140.
2. V. KÜSTER, *Theologie im Kontext. Zugleich ein Versuch über die Minjung-Theologie*, Nettetal, Steyler Verlag, 1994; ID., *The Priesthood of Han. Reflections on a woodcut by Hong Song-Dam*, in *Exchange* 26 (1997) 159-170.

We should get rid of the notion that the gospel is an essential prerequisite for transformative action Long before Christians took the initiative in organizing popular struggles, Indian communists had done so for decades, particularly in Kerala, Andra and West Bengal. Hundreds of men and women have laid their lives in the cause of justice and only a few among them were Christians.. The majority drew inspiration from the situation of oppression itself or from other religions or ideologies. This is not to devaluate the Christian presence in India, but to see it in its proper perspective[3].

Coming to the first part of the title of G. De Schrijver's Discussion Paper *Paradigm Shift in Third World Theologies of Liberation* it may be observed that it includes a contradiction. While the plural is used for theologies of liberation, we find the singular for 'paradigm shift'. Now, one may question whether one identical or even similar paradigm shift can be found in all theologies of liberation. Also during an earlier period ("under another paradigm") a more or less outspoken Marxist socio-economic analysis was not found in all kinds of theologies of liberation.

But, especially in the case of Asia and more even East and Southeast Asia, where so many Christians and many others experienced very cruel and oppressing forms of communism, sympathy for any form of Marxism or Communism was blocked. Therefore also Christian theologians in these countries were less sensible for the 'great stories' of ideologies, which were sometimes imposed upon them as an anti-virus against communism.

More in particular, in the Indonesian context, in a country of nearly 200 million where 88% are Muslims, Christian theologians emphasize participation in development, the conditions of human rights for all, preferential option for the poor, harmony of religions, a common acceptance and integration of modern values and material technique. Although we do not discern a pronounced and specific Indonesian way of theology of liberation, perhaps its most distinctive appearance is, that in this case also some Muslim intellectuals join these ideas, some even more enthusiastic than their Christian colleagues. Therefore we will divide this paper into three parts: two Catholic interpretations of theology of liberation (Y.B. Mangunwijaya and J.B. Banawiratma), two Protestants (Th. Sumartana and Ioanes Rakhmat) and three Muslims (Nurcholis Madjid, Dawam Rahardjo and Abdurrachman Wahid).

---

3. S. KAPPEN, *Towards an Indian Theology of Liberation*, in R.S. SUGIRTHARAJAH, *Readings in Indian Christian Theology I*, Delhi, ISPCK, 1993, pp. 24-36.

II. Two Catholic Examples of Theology of Liberation

1. Y.B. Mangunwijaya

The Priest, architect and novelist, Yusuf Bilyarta Mangunwijaya, (b. 1929) was educated as a secular priest. In an area of Central Java, where the majority of priests were Jesuits, with often a double educational career: besides theology also a professional study, his bishop sent him to Germany to study architecture. After his studies abroad, he settled in several places in Central Java, where his bishop gave him ample opportunity to develop his many talents. Mangunwijaya combines aspects of the ideal 'theologian of liberation' as a social and political activist, living for a long time himself in a slum area and so preventing the transportation of its population, as a writer of popular novels, film scenario's, columns and short essays, rather than scholarly and lengthy books.

Mangunwijaya became a public figure in Indonesia since the early 1970s, writing in newspapers, designing private houses, simple churches, several 'Caves of Lourdes', places of pilgrimage, not in the grandiose style of the great buildings of Lourdes or Assisi, but rather chains of simple shelters for small groups. In this architecture of pilgrimage as well as in his churches, Mangunwijaya imitates the traditional style for places of worship in Indonesia, with a predilection for the Hindu-Balinese. Church bells are replaced by the drum, which is used in traditional Javanese mosques. Also in other respects Mangunwijaya fights the prohibitive style of the ultramontane Catholicism brought by the generations of missionaries between 1870 and 1950, with its spirit of separatism and exclusivity[4].

In spite of being a minority, Christians in Indonesia should not indulge to confessional isolationism (as is done by a number of theologians, who stress the particular values and approaches of Christian theology and religious heritage), but Christians should participate in the cultural and religious richness of the country. Therefore, in his novels, Mangunwijaya has many references to the stories of *wayang* and *ketoprak*, traditional folk plays[5]. This interest for and use of traditional cultural material is not exclusive: modern Indonesian culture and society,

---

4. On Mangunwijaya's (as always very mild!) critique on the strict, austere and often rather rigid ultramontanism of the missionaries in the early 20th century also K. STEENBRINK, *Conversion or Religious Revival? Modernist Islam and Christianity in Central Java*, in *Verbum SVD* 36 (1995) 369-388.

5. Cf. De Schrijver's comment on 'the plea to save aspects of traditional wisdom' (72).

in its response to globalization, should also acquire the true values of the realm of Greek thought and of the European Renaissance[6].

Instead, the fight for human rights should be an interreligious effort. Therefore Mangunwijaya joined the *Forum Demokrasi*, a national human rights group, with Muslims, Humanists, Hindus, rather than joining an exclusively Catholic or Christian group, which fights for the same goals. In the national ideology of the "Five Pillars", *Pancasila*, Mangunwijaya applauds not the believe in the 'One and Only Supreme Deity' as the unifying idea between the faithful of the major religions, but rather two other pillars out of the series of five: 'Just and Civilized Humanity' (*Kemanusiaan yang adil dan beradab*) and 'Social justice for all Indonesians' (*Keadilan sosial bagi seluruh rakyat Indonesia*).

> ... the essence of the European enlightenment does not lay primarily in the improvement of the physical means or the change in the external aspects of progress only, but more in *the real reverence towards the inherent value and dignity of human beings, and the effective development of those values and dignity in this world...* Human life cannot be viewed as a mere bridge or a means towards the achievement of the everlasting life; instead, it must be viewed as a purpose in itself; and so, it deserves to be developed and humanized[7].

A fine illustration of this stance is Mangunwijaya's novel *Ikan-ikan hiu* (Dutch transl. *Tussen Sultans en Admiraals*), in which he sketches the coming of Islam and Christianity in the Moluccan archipelago. One would expect a novel on Muslim-Christian relations, conflicts or encounter. In fact the novel is on the collaboration or even strategy of the rulers (sultan, admirals, traditional rulers) against the poor, the petty farmers and fishermen.

In his Novel *The Weaverbirds* (*Burung-burung Manyar*, the only novel by Mangunwijaya, translated into English)[8], the hero or central person is a Eurasian, who by coincidence chose the wrong side in the struggle for independence (1945-1949) and became a collaborator with the colonial oppressor. In all his novels, Mangunwijaya has a preference for these people of the 'wrong side': the middle layer in the palaces, results rather than architects of their own history. They are brokers for understanding between different parties. In this sense his oeuvre may be understood as a correction towards the easy division of society into rich/capitalist and poor/exploited.

---

6. Cf. Y.B. MANGUNWIJAYA, *The Realm of Greek Thought and Our Struggle, Speech delivered at the occassion of receiving the Professor Teeuw Award*, Jakarta, 15 May 1996; DE SCHRIJVER, (59-60).

7. Y.B. MANGUNWIJAYA (n. 6), p. 7.

8. Y.B. MANGUNWIJAYA, *The Weaverbirds*, transl. by Thomas M. Hunter, Jakarta, Lontar Foundation, 1991.

2. Y.B. Banawiratma

A more intellectual, academic example of the reception of the theology of liberation is found with the Jesuit professor of systematic theology, J.B. Banawiratma[9]. In many universities, all over the world, theology is often divided in separated entities: Bible Studies, Church History, Pastoral Theology, Ethics etc. If we do not consider theology as an academic and neutral affair but as an existential act of faith, within the Church and the world, as integrated within the whole person of the faithful, the separation between theological disciplines should become impossible. This central idea has deeply changed the courses of theology in the Catholic Faculty of Santa Dharma University, Yogyakarta, since the mid-1980s. The common disciplines of Bible studies, historical and dogmatic theology, practical theology and ethics were integrated through projects or programs of eight weeks, where students and professors work together, elaborating a theme, starting from experience.

There were complaints of experienced professors, who found it not always easy to work with students in this system. According to this strategy lecturers have to attend the whole process, also the instructions given by their colleagues. They have to be prepared to answer questions during many hours a week, whenever students are in need of their help. A lecturer can not give a traditional and systematic introduction of his discipline, but has to present several elements more or less as 'fast food' for students working on a special issue. But the advantages are considered more important than these inconveniences: this program generates a theology which is originating from a concrete context and directed towards an actual praxis. This process also generates a hermeneutical circle where action has prominence besides the objectivity of the Gospel and the subjectivity of personal faith. In their 1989 article Banawiratma and Jacobs reported about two projects: theology of hope and salvation. In a much longer 1993 publication by Banawiratma and Müller, the materials about poverty, development, ecology and politics have been collected from the courses of several years[10].

As to information about Third-World theology, or even theology in general, one of the interesting aspects of this publication is the fact, that this is not a kind of theology originating in the loneliness of a study or

9. See K. STEENBRINK, *Towards a Pancasila Society: The Indonesian Debate on Secularization, Liberation and Development, 1969-1989*, in *Exchange* 54 (1989) 1-28.

10. J.B. BANAWIRATMA & T. JACOBS, *Doing Theology with Local Resources*, in *EAPR* 1 (1989) 51-72; J.B. BANAWIRATMA & J. MÜLLER, *Kontextuelle Sozialtheologie. Ein indonesisches Model*, Freiburg/Basel/Wien, Herder, 1995. The last publication is a translation of their *Berteologi Sosial lintas ilmu*, Yogyakarta, Kanisius 1993.

from the general debate at an international conference, the *Sitz im Leben* of much theological material. This is the product of a seminar at a catholic theological college. It is not composed as a coherent book, neither as a collection of well-composed articles, but as a report of a collective process.

The first three chapters portray the general debate on the relation between theology and social sciences. Chapter IV and V deal with a general social analysis of Indonesia. The main part of the book are chapters VI-XII, where a socio-cultural analysis of Indonesia is the starting-point besides the doctrine of the Catholic Church, usually formulated with quotations from Vatican II. (There is perhaps no local church, where the texts of Vatican II are so often quoted as in the Indonesian). Keywords here are world, holistic theology, the Indonesian 'immunity' against secularism (VI), Kingdom of God (the final redemption versus the political idea of an ideal society (VII), personal and structural poverty (*preferential option for the poor*, VIII and IX), poverty and spirituality (X), poverty as an economic and ecological problem (XI) and the political dimension of the praxis of the Church (XII).

This book is very interesting as an Asian reception of the documents of Vatican II, brought in line with a moderate interpretation of the theologies (the plural is often stressed) of liberation, not formulated in the dogmatic style of a handbook, but in stimulating questions: "The theologies of liberation emphasize that the Church as a social institution also needs conversion and that she must scrutinize whether the ecclesiastical structures do not contradict the values of justice. Many of the faithful, included church leaders, agree that the Church is always a church of sinners: but they still have problems with the idea, that also within the Church 'structures of sin' are present. "How would you explain this attitude? What is your own opinion? Can you give some arguments for your position?"[11].

The textbook of Banawiratma and Müller stimulates the combination of social and theological analysis: the real basis for contextual theology. It has been written, however, in a very denominational style, with an abundance of references to the ceremonial language of the Vatican documents, as such not directly accessible for Protestant Christians. It may even cause more difficulties with the majority of Muslims in Indonesia. This important plea for contextuality, is not written in a contextual language. This may also be one of the characteristics of the dynamics of the Catholic Church in Indonesia. Still, a study like this shows the concrete

11. *Ibid.*, p. 131.

local impact of the more general and 'abstract' theories of the theologies of liberation[12].

III. Two Prominent Protestant Theologians of Liberation: I. Rakhmat and Th. Sumartana

1. *I. Rakhmat*

In the late 1980s a book on Latin-American theology of liberation by Protestant theologian I. Rakhmat was banned by the Indonesian government. The reasons, of course, were not open admitted, but have to be related to the constant phobia for Communism and Marxist ideology in present Indonesia. Rev. Rakhmat, professor of New Testament Studies at the Jakarta Union Theological Seminary, did not cease his publications and comments on this theology. Amidst other work, he also wrote an article on "Leonardo Boff in conflict: power and charisma", which was published in a journal with restricted circulation and therefore probably harmless[13]. As is often the case with articles on theology of liberation by Asians, this is not an effort to an academic description[14], but rather an analysis of the situation at home. Boff's sharp criticism of the ecclesiology and structure of the Roman Catholic Church is here repeated and reconsidered not in a polemic mood, a Protestant rejoicing about imperfections of the Catholics, but in the conviction that the analysis of Boff fits the Protestant churches as well as the Catholic[15]. Three models of the church are rejected: Church as City of God (*Civitas Dei*), Mother and Teacher (*Mater et Magistra*) and Sacrament of Salvation. A proper ecclesiology should start with the faith of the poor. From this paradigm several concrete conclusions related to the Indonesian situation should be taken:

> a. The bitter conflict between Boff and the Catholic hierarchy is a valuable lesson for the member churches of the Indonesian Community of Churches, who now are looking for a unified organizational model. It is possible, that the Protestant churches are now moving towards a Catholic type of church, while in the body of these churches movements towards a democratic use of power in the church are growing.

---

12. Adapted from a review by this author in *Exchange* 25 (1996) 100-102.
13. I. Rakhmat, *Leonardo Boff dalam konflik: kekuasaan dan kharisma*, in *Penuntun* 4 (1995) 295-312.
14. Cf. also the article by I. Rakhmat, *Teologi warga dan teologi teolog profesional* [Lay Theology and theology by professional theologians], in *Penuntun* I/1 (1994) 108-114.
15. Cf. L. Boff, *Church: Charism and Power. Liberation Theology and the Institutional Church*, New York: Crossroad, 1992.

b. The ecclesiology of Boff grows out of a personal involvement with the poor people of Latin America... If the Indonesian churches would show this same commitment of Boff in their context, we certainly would see a growing contextual ecclesiology...

c. Boff's emphasis on charisma, will not lead to the charismatic movements that are thriving nowadays in Indonesia, because the Basic Community, as described by him, will stay in touch with the concrete world and its problems (poverty, human rights, politics)[16].

In many other contributions Rakhmat tries to combine the interreligious and the social concern. In a contribution "The Story of Jesus' Birth in an Indonesian Islamic Context"[17] Rakhmat gives an interpretation of the Qur'anic story of Jesus' birth (Sura 19,22-33), stressing the situation of weakness, lack of power, experienced by Mary and Jesus at that occasion. Immediately after his miraculous birth, Jesus defended his mother against gossip and slander. She was about to be put in jail for adultery, but Jesus protected and liberated her by the miracle of speaking as a baby in her defense. The same *Leitmotif* is heard in the gospel of Luke, where the birth of Jesus is put against the clouds of the oppression by the Roman Emperor Augustus and his Jewish collaborator Herod. Muslims and Christians should not continue the sterile debate on metaphysical questions as the divine nature of Jesus, but celebrate this redeeming power of God:

> When this idea about the message of the Birth of Jesus in the Qur'an and the Gospel would truly and sincerely be accepted by Indonesian Muslims and Christians, their relation could produce great profit for a sincere and divine presence of humanity in this country[18].

2. *Th. Sumartana*

This same concern for a common effort for freedom, liberation, socio-economic welfare and defense of human values is found with Th. Sumartana. In his 1991 doctoral dissertation, he presents a missiological study of the encounter between colonialism, European missionaries, Islam and the autonomous indigenous developments in Indonesia, during the last century[19]. In the broad perspective of the socio-cultural history of the

16. I. RAKHMAT (n. 13), pp. 310-311.
17. I. RAKHMAT, *Het geboorteverhaal van Jezus in een islamitisch-indonesische context*, in *Wereld en zending* 25 (1996) 57-66.
18. *Ibid.*, p. 64.
19. T. SUMARTANA, *Mission at the Crossraods: Indigenous Churches, European Missionaries, Islamic Association and Socio-Religious Change in Java, 1812-1936*, Jakarta, BPK Gunung Mulia, 1993.

Dutch East Indies, Sumartana takes as the climax of the encounter not a (male) Western missionary but an Indonesian woman, Kartini. This woman, born in 1879 in a family of nobility in North Java, educated as a modern Muslim, with good knowledge of Dutch, entered into correspondence and intimate exchange with a number of Western (Dutch) women and men and developed a very personnel and modern religious attitude. She was critical towards both Islam and Christianity and finally found her mission in the organization of schools for girls:

> In the history of the nationalist movement in Indonesia, Kartini is among the first who consciously reflected on religious ideas in the context of religious pluralism. She is also among the first who in a clear manner urged cooperation between the religions as a moral force to advance society and struggle for humanitarianism and justice[20].

In 1992 Sumartana founded DIAN, *Dialog antar Iman*, a Center for Interfaith Dialogue in Yogyakarta. He carefully discarded the word religion from the name and general outline of the purpose of his foundation, because he wants to stay away from too strong, stable and self-confident institutions, which often only serve their own development. He pleads for a dynamic and engaged style of syncretism:

> In the perspective of non-exclusive theological thinking, the possibility is open to understand syncretism in another way. Syncretism must be returned to its original meaning: the political meaning. The political meaning of syncretism is nothing other than downplaying the differences that cause disturbances between groups in society...[21].

In this way Sumartana not only overcomes the incorrect antagonism between either theology of dialogue or theology of liberation, as if this were the opposition between 'Latin-American' and 'Asian' theology: in fact true theology of liberation takes the religious factor serious and true theology of dialogue is not an academic affair between some scholars of religion, but it comes to the heart of people and to the very heart of society. Sumartana in fact presents us a holistic view on reconciliation to put it in the 1997 vocabulary of the Graz' conference of the European Churches. He reminds us that conflicts between groups, be these ethnic, racial or social conflicts are multidimensional and that all aspects have to be considered in order to obtain a real and complete healing.

---

20. *Ibid.*, p. 300.
21. *Ibid.*, 340; Cf. also K. STEENBRINK, *The Rehabilitation of Indigenous Teachers. A Survey of Recent Research on the History of Christianity in Indonesia*, in *Exchange* 22 (1993) 250-263.

IV. THREE MUSLIM AUTHORS IN COMMUNICATION WITH (CHRISTIAN) THEOLOGIES OF LIBERATION

1. *N. Madjid*

During the 1960s the western academic society produced some quite interesting theological theories on the development of culture. Under the label of 'secularization' an optimistic view on the development of religion within society was at the basis of books like Harvey Cox' *The Secular City* and Arend van Leeuwen's *Christianity in World History*. According to these authors and others (after Friedrich Gogarten), secularization should be understood as one of the positive results of Christianity.

There was a fascinating Indonesian Muslim reaction on this theology of earthly realities by N. Madjid (b. 1939). As general chairman of the HMI, *Himpunan Mahasiswa Islam*, the largest Islamic Students' Movement of his country, during the period 1966-1971, Madjid launched a number of provoking ideas, that were heavily debated in the HMI, but finally accepted by a majority of its members.

The most important issue was summarized under the slogan of *secularization*. Madjid interpreted this idea along the lines of Harvey Cox in his well-known best-seller *The Secular City*. Secularization, according to Madjid, is the task of modernizing the ethical doctrines of Islam. Modern Muslims should study the Koran and formulate the basic Islamic values found therein. These should lead towards the application of these values in a modern Islamic society. Madjid did not support the idea of a political party, based on Islam as a religion or a doctrine. One of his speeches, also several times published as a pamphlet, had as its title: *Islam Yes! Partai Islam No!* The Islamic movement should not concentrate on political parties, or even the realization of an Islamic State. Politics means always corruption and compromises. The movement should rather try to formulate and to accomplish as many Islamic values in society as possible. *Rather an Islamic Society than an Islamic State*, became also one of his formulations. Anything else besides God, the eternal, and His Word, the Koran, should be considered as 'not holy': too many structures and traditions in Islam, considered as sacred, should be secularized, in its literal meaning: updated and realized into the concrete structures of the (modern) time (*saeculum*).

In a later period (the late 1980s, after he received his doctor's degree in Chicago), Madjid accepted and promoted the idea of contextualization in a sense quite close to secularization: all religious traditions, including the Islamic, have to find a modern reformulation and realization of their central ideas. Both modernization and religious harmony are major concerns for the new society of Indonesia and the great challenge for all religious leadership is to give a contribution to society in these fields[22]. Because of his western vocabulary, borrowed from Christian theologies, Nurcholis Madjid arose many criticisms, but he also got important supporters. One of these was Munawir Sjadzali, who was between 1984-1994 minister of Religious Affairs of the Indonesian Republic. The Festschrift for Sjadzali even had as its title *Contextualization of the Doctrines of Islam*[23]. The word 'liberation' sounds too revolutionary, Marxist and communist and would be impossible in the strictly controlled climate of President Suharto's New Order (since 1966), where the communist party was banned and a strong anti-Communist policy was accepted. Therefore no proper 'theology of liberation' is found in Indonesia. Still, theologies of earthly realities, close to that of the theology of liberation are found in Madjid's works from 1870 until the 1990s.

2. *D. Rahardjo and A. Wahid*

In 1983, Dawam Rahardjo, a Muslim economist and activist, organized a meeting in Jakarta to propagate the beginning of a Muslim theology of liberation. He invited two Christians: the philosopher Dr. Kees Bertens MSC and this author. The most prominent Muslim theologian was Dr. Harun Nasution, who studied in Egypt and at McGill/Montreal, where he obtained his MA and PH.D. degrees. Rahardjo explained, that there is applied sociology: a style of sociology, which looks at direct applications of sociological theories. He supposed, that theology of liberation, which he knew from Christian writers out of Latin America, could be labeled as applied theology. He hoped, that also a Muslim theology of liberation or some kind of applied Islamic theology could be developed. Harun Nasution, a specialist in Islamic philosophy, known as one of the leaders of modern and liberal Muslim thinking in Indonesia, had a rather disappointing answer. He declared that *kalam*, the Islamic dogmatical or philosophical theology, only deals with concepts and attitudes and that *fiqh*-reasoning, the study of Islamic law or *shari'a* was the proper discipline for the design of a theology of liberation. Because he

22. K. STEENBRINK, *Nurcholis Madjid and Inclusive Islamic Faith in Indonesia*, in G. SPEELMAN (ed.), *Muslims and Christians in Europe. Breaking New ground. Essays in honour of Jan Slomp*, Kampen, Kok, 1993, pp. 28-43. For a more general theory on similarity of developments within Christianity and Islam in Indonesia also: K. STEENBRINK, *Conversion or Religious Revival* (n. 4).

23. DR. SULASTOMO (ed.), *Kontekstualisasi Ajaran Islam; 70 Tahun Munawir Sjadzali. Festschrift for H. Munawir Sjadzali*, Jakarta, Paramadina, 1995.

was not a specialist in the field, he could not contribute to the proposed development of this theology.

Although this formal theology of development was not conceived then, activities in this direction continued. Rahardjo himself was for a long period the director of an Indonesian NGO, which tried to combine Islam with socio-economic development, LP3ES[24]. This organization was active in villages, but also initiated a development ideology, where not only religion was an important factor in development, but where also interreligious aspects were involved. To give just one quotation from the debates among a similar group, the Nahdlatul Ulama, one of the largest Muslim organizations of Indonesia, summarizing its general chairperson, Abdurrahman Wahid:

> When we hear the word 'theology of development', we immediately will associate it with the theology of liberation of Gustavo Gutiérrez, who from the beginning wanted to identify his theology as theology of development. After he realized that this was to tame for the repressive conditions of Latin America, he used the word theology of liberation, a terminology which is more outspoken as a movement against repression... But for countries in Asia and Africa it is much better to use the vocabulary of theology of development. This word not only displays an atmosphere of peace, but it is also in harmony with the national efforts for development. In fact, we are not obliged to employ this word, because not every religion has a message of liberation and transformation for its believers[25].

This quotation refers to an aspect of theology of Islam, where less emphasis is given to conversion and redemption, radical change, the process from original sin through liberation until the eschaton. Besides, it is also very clear, that a number of modern and revolutionary Muslims feel at home with some of the terminologies and strategies of (Christian) theology of liberation, but refrain from a too revolutionary terminology[26].

24. Lembaga Penelitian, Pendidikan dan Penerangan Ekonomi dan Sosial, Foundation for the research, training and information about socio-economic development. LP3ES received financial and moral support from several organizations in Germany and The Netherlands. It was not an exclusively muslim organizations, although the larger part of the activists were Muslim. There were several prominent Catholic theologians and social scientists in its circle.

25. A. MUN'IM DZ, *Teologi Pembangunan sebagai alternatif* [Theology of Development as an Alternative], in M.M. AMIN (ed.), *Theologi Pembangunan. Paradigma Baru Pemikiran Islam*, Yogyakarta, Nahdlatul Ulama, 1989, pp. 229-233. The conference, which produced this book was initiated and sponsored by the Nahdlatul Ulama one of the two major Muslim organizations of Indonesia, with Abdurrahman Wahid as chairperson. Some christians were invited as well.

26. For this topic also K. STEENBRINK, *Towards a Pancasila Society: the Indonesian Debate on Secularization, Liberation and Development*, in *Exchange* 54 (1989) 1-28. To mention only a few publications by Indonesian Muslims in favour of a partial partnership with theology of liberation: M.D. RAHARDJO, *Perspektif Deklarasi Mekka. Menuju Ekonomi*

The three Muslims, of course, also used very often a more strict Islamic discourse for their ideas on the relation of religious doctrine and economy. This is for their background and general audience also understandable. Nurcholis Madjid wrote in the early 1980s a doctoral dissertation on Ibnu Taimiyya under Fazlur Rahman, a modernist Pakistani Muslim, teaching at Chicago University. He often quoted Ibnu Taimiyya as a moderate classical Muslim divine who had great respect for other religions[27].

In 1987 D. Rahardjo summarized a number of his economic-theological ideas under the title of *The Perspectives of the Meccan Declaration*, referring to a conference of the Ankara/Turkey based international *Organization of the Islamic Conference*, which held in 1981 a conference on Religion, Islam and Economic Issues[28]. In this book Rahardjo focuses on economic theories (the book is full with statistics, economic indicators etc.) besides some general Islamic concepts as the prohibition of interest (*riba*) and the obligation of *zakat*, a fixed tax for the poor. In 1989 Rahardjo started a new journal *Ulumul Qur'an* (Qur'anic Sciences), where he opened the exchange with western thinkers in many social, economic and theological fields. At one moment, the journal even was named as too westernized and too open for Christian ideas. Rahardjo himself contributed a number of articles on qur'anic and economic issues.

Abdurrahman Wahid, the general chairman of the great mass organization, started in 1992 an Islamic Bank, in cooperation with some very rich Chinese Muslims of Indonesia. The basic idea behind this bank is, that a bank should take responsibility rather than mere profit in banking:

Islam, Bandung, Mizan 1987 (referring to the 'Declaration of Mecca' in January 1981, where a number of muslim economists designed a socio-economic strategy along islamic lines); ALFIAN (ed.), *Kemiskinan Struktural, Jakarta Yayasan Ilmu-ilmu Sosial: 1980* ("On structural poverty"; although the majority of the contributors were Muslim, there were also some Christian authors); M. ASY'ARIE (ed.), *Islam, Kebebesan dan perubahan social Jakarta: Sinar Harapan* ("Islam, Freedom and Social Change"; the conference was organized by an Islamic university, the book published by a Protestant publisher; the authors were equally divided amongst Protestants, Catholics and Muslims); M.D. RAHARDJO (ed.), *Sepercik pemikiran tentang Ekonomi Islam*, Yogyakarta, Ananda, 1985 ("Some Thoughts about an Islamic Economy"); A.R. HASSAN, (ed.), *Perspektif Islam dalam Pembangunan Bangsa, Yogyakarta: PLP2M* ("An Islamic Perspective on the Development of Our People").

27. N. MADJID, *Islam, Doktrin dan Peradaban. Sebuah telaah kritis tentang masalah keimanan, kemanusiaan dan kemoderenan*, Jakarta, Paramadani, 1992. Also, N. MADJID, *In Search of Islamic Roots for Modern Pluralism: the Indonesian Experiences*, in M. WOORDWARD (ed.), *Toward a New Paradigm: Recent Developments in Indonesian Islamic Thought*, Tempe, Arizona State University, 1966, pp. 89-116.

28. D. RAHARDJO (n. 26).

> Conventional banks don't feel a sense of responsibility toward their customers. The only thing they're interested in is making sure that the customer pays his debt, whether the customer is making a profit or not. As long as the debt is paid, they couldn't care less about the fate of the business. This is something an Islamic bank won't do[29].

In Egypt and Malaysia Islamic banking was in fact more a great step towards increase in crime and corruption rather than towards a good economy in favor of the poor. Also Indonesian Muslims have some doubts about the system. On very practical grounds Dawam Rahardjo has uttered his reservation about this solution:

> The administration of Islamic banking is extremely difficult. The Bank Islam has to control so much and the borrower has to be truly honest in acknowledging profit. Borrowers are inclined to underreport their reports, or not report them at all... An Islamic Bank has to supervise borrowers so directly that that creates enormous administrative costs. The result is high administrative costs and oversight procedures that are extremely complicated[30].

Notwithstanding this criticism, Rahardjo has given his support to the initiative, which he considers, besides the more traditional institutes as *zakat* and *sadaqa* (tax and alms for the poor) as an instrument of social justice and development.

Whatever may be the result of this last initiative, the very short description of the thinking of three Muslims from Indonesia, in communication with Western theologians of liberation, but also in close contact with their own Muslim community, shows, that theology of liberation is not an exclusive Christian, western affair, but exceeds the national, continental and religious boundaries[31].

V. CONCLUSION

Theologies of liberation started as one variation on the general theme of 'theologies of earthly realities'. It must be clear, that this theology never can be defined from abstract principles. In every concrete society there will be a different formulation of this style of theology. In their situ-

---

29. R.W. HEFNER, Islamizing Capitalism: On the Founding of Indonesia's First Islamic Bank', in M. WOORDWARD (n. 27), pp. 291-322, quotation from p. 306.

30. *Ibid.*, p. 310.

31. A further elaboration of the theme of dialogue between Christians and Muslims is to be found in K. STEENBRINK, *Quranic Guidelines for the Poor as a Basic for Interreligious Solidarity in Favour of the Poor*, to be published in *Mission Studies* (fortcoming) as part of the *Proceedings of the 6th Conference of the IAMS* (Buenos Aires, 9-20 April 1996).

ation as members of a social and religious minority, Christian theologians in Indonesia seek incentives, initiatives and realizations for liberation in harmony and solidarity with other political and religious powers.

Indonesian theologians did not elaborate a specific identification of their mode of modern thinking: no *dalit* or *minjung* terminologies. The most specific terminology has been taken from the interreligious and political discourse: *Pancasila*, the five-pillar ideology of the (rather authoritarian and certainly not ideal) state. This characteristic may indicate also the special style of this theology: in harmony with a national program of nation building and development rather than in opposition but certainly with critical comments; also in honest and open contact with modern representatives of other religions.

Of the seven persons presented in this short introduction, three are professors of theology (Banawiratma, Rakhmat, Madjid), four are social and political activists (Mangunwijaya, Sumartana, Wahid and Rahardjo). This seems also to be a fair division and a good basis for a contextual translation of (other) theologies of liberation. However, all seven are male, between 50 and 70 years of age and Javanese, member of the dominating majority group of Indonesians: certainly not the ideal sample of the average Indonesian person.

Institute for Missiological and   Karel STEENBRINK
   Ecumenical Research
Heidelberglaan 2
NL-23584 CS, Utrecht

21

LATIN-AMERICAN LIBERATION THEOLOGY PARADIGM SHIFT OR DEVELOPMENT-DEEPENING?

There has certainly been a paradigm shift from socio-economic to cultural analysis in the documents of the Latin-American episcopate (CELAM) from the Medellin General Conference to the Santo Domingo, as it is clearly shown in G. De Schrijver's Discussion Paper. Under the pressure from Rome, some theologians have chosen not to talk about socio-economic analysis in order to be able to keep doing a pastoral work among the poor. Others may have changed their minds because of "obedience". But a theology is neither the private property of some authors nor just "the thing theologians do". It is specified by its definition. And the classical definition of Latin-American Liberation Theology (LALT) is: a critical reflection on liberation praxis enlightened by Christian faith.

I. IN THE BEGINNING WAS CULTURE

From its first writings, LALT *did include* the analysis of the cultural dimension of social life. Let us take as a witness of this early period Gustavo Gutiérrez's *Liberation Theology. Perspectives*[1]. In this book the Peruvian theologian, besides making long developments on the history of theology and of ideas in general – which are cultural phenomena –, affirms that "to conceive history as a process of liberation of human beings (...) implies not only better living conditions, a radical change of structures, a social revolution, but much more: the continuous and always unachieved creation of a new way of being a human, a *permanent cultural revolution*"[2]. He goes on saying that "the liberation of the subcontinent goes beyond the suppression of economic, social and political dependency"[3]. And on the following page he deals with P. Freire's "pedagogy of the oppressed", which is a cultural action.

---

1. *Teología de la liberación. Perspectivas*, Lima, CEP, 1971. I give this book as an example because it is the most widely known work of LALT in its early period. But this does nos mean that I look at Gustavo Gutiérrez as the "father of LALT". Even not taking into account his later evolution, one must say that the birth of LALT was a *collective* work. Enriquse Dussel has rightly stressed this point in his short but comprehensive history of Latin American theology: *Teología de la liberación. Un panorama de su desarrollo*, México, Potrerillo Editores, 1995.
2. *Ibid.*, p. 52, emphasis original.
3. *Ibid.*, p. 121.

As a second example, one can cite – among many others – J.L. Segundo's stance at the first Escorial Congress (1972) which was perhaps the most important meeting that LALT produced in its first period. There the Uruguayan Jesuit, after having asked on pushing the critique of ideology right up to the very image of God, drew attention to the shortcomings of Marxism in the analysis of cultural realities[4].

The cultural dimension was hence present in LALT from the beginning. However, it is true that, at that early age, it stressed the socio-economic dimension. It was what Otto Maduro has called a "methodological excess": LALT stressed the point which constitutes the novelty of its *theological* method and which was also the most contentious issue because socio-economic analysis meant – beyond the theory of dependency – *class analysis*. Let us quote again Gustavo Gutiérrez: "Human brotherhood which has a ultimate foundation in our situation as God's children, is being built up in history. This history presents today conflictual characters which seem to oppose such a construction. One of those features is central: the division of humankind in oppressors and oppressed, in owners of the means of production and those who are deprived of the fruit of their work, in antagonistic social classes"[5]. (This text was later suppressed in the revised edition[6] but it still stands as a witness to LALT's original viewpoint). And class analysis has been historically linked to atheism.

However it must be pointed out that most LALT theologians did not write much on social analysis at that early stage: it was largely presupposed. Thus, one can find at that time very few theological writings dealing with it; besides Gutiérrez, Hugo Assmann[7], José Porfirio Miranda[8] and an underground – unpublished and anonymous – document: *Marxism and Christianity* must be mentioned[9]. Furthermore, while all these texts stressed that their class analysis differed from that of classical Marxism – open to religion, inspired by a democratic ethos – this difference itself was not systematically developed.

---

4. Cf. the collective work *Fe cristiana y cambio social en América Latina*, Salamanca, Sígueme, 1973, pp. 211-212 and 294-295.

5. G. GUTIÉRREZ (n. 1), p. 340

6. This text has disappeared in the 14th "revised and enlarged" edition of *Teología de la liberación* (n. 1), (Salamanca, Sígueme, 1990). Actually, the paragraph *Christian brotherhood and class struggle* (1st edition (n. 1), pp. 340-349) has been "reworked (...) in the light of new documents from the Magisterium", in the author's terms, and is entitled in the 14th edition *Faith and social conflict* (pp. 312-320).

7. Let us recall, from this early stage his: *Teología desde de la praxis de la liberación*, Salamanca, Sígueme, 1973. It is a collection of articles written between 1970 and 1972.

8. Cfr. his *Marx y la Biblia*, Salamanca, Ediciones Sígueme, 1972. English translation: *Marx and the Bible*, Maryknoll, NY, Orbis, 1974.

9. Though written in Spanish, it circulated in Brazil.

II. DEVELOPMENT AND DEEPENING

With the development of LALT from the late seventies, we have seen *both* a more explicit treatment of the cultural dimension *and a deepening* of the study of the socio-economic one. Thus we have witnessed an important production on issues where the cultural element cannot be avoided, like *popular religion* or *women's issues*[10]. Thus also – and more recently – we have seen Leonardo Boff tackling the *ecological* issue in its relationship with religious experience and critique of science, while not forgetting social analysis[11]. Moreover, Frei Betto engages in a dialogue between mystical experience, on the one hand, and quantum physics, biology and cosmology, on the other, while reaming a sharp critic in the socio-economic dimension[12].

While the analysis of cultural phenomena developed in LALT – I have only mentioned a few examples – that of the socio-economic realm gained in depth. Thus, José Porfirio Miranda in his *Marx against the Marxists*[13] made a thorough exegesis of Marx's writings in order to unearth a class analysis which rejects economic determinism and stresses the ethical element.

More recently Enrique Dussel wrote four volumes on the successive redactions of *Capital*[14]. In this important work, the Argentinean-Mexican

10. I am *not* saying that women's issues are exclusively cultural. That would amount to ignore women's exploitation at work which even today is an important socio-economic problem! I am just saying that it is *impossible* to deal with these issues without taking into account their cultural dimension In a sense, the same is true for the treatment of any issue, because of the *interrelation* between the different dimensions. But this interrelation is more evident in some issues than in others. For a global view of the first steps of Latin American women's theology cf. E. TAMEZ (ed.), *El rostro femenino de la teología*, San José, DEI, 1986.

11. Cf. L. BOFF, *Ecología -munaialização espiritualidade. A emergência de um novo paradigma,* Atica, São Paulo, 1993. And his article *Religious experience and ecology,* in *CQ* 64 (Winter 1992-1993) 16-24.

12. Cf. his books: *A obra do artista. Uma visão holística do Universo*, São Paulo, Atica, 1995[2] and *Teilhard de Charain. Sinfonía Universal*, São Paulo, Letras e Letras, 1992, as well as his article: *Socialist alternative in Latin America and in the Caribbean* in *CQ* 69 (Spring 1994) 27-30.

13. Maryknoll, NY, Orbis, 1980. The original Spanish work was published in 1978 under the title *El cristianismo de Marx*. But the English translation has the advantage of being a revised edition. I have presented this book in my articles: *Marx against the Marxists: José P. Miranda's revolutionary humanism,* in *CQ* 36 (December 1985) 3-8 and 37 (March 1986) 12-19.

14. These volumes are: *La producción teórica de Marx. Un comentario a los Grundrisse*, México, Siglo XXI, 1985; *Hacia un Marx desconocido. Un comentario de los manuscritos del 61-63,* México, Siglo XXI, 1988; *El último Marx (1863-1882) y la liberación latino-americana,* México, Siglo XXI. 1990, and *Las metáforas teológicas de Marx*, Madrid, Verbo Divino, 1993.

philosopher underlines the importance given by Marx to such issues as the peasantry, people's traditions, the nation. Thus he lays a solid foundation for a more comprehensive and flexible class analysis. He also deals with the *dependency theory*, and its crisis, and develops a relevant theoretical framework to better articulate it with class analysis[15]. Moreover, the fourth book is dedicated to what Dussel calls "Marx's implicit theology".

As can be seen, LALT has always tried to link, as closely as possible the analyses of the different dimensions – socio-economic cultural, political – which are constitutive of the one and only social life.

III. INTERPENETRATION (PERICHORESIS)

The intimate link between these different dimensions has been developed more in recent years. I once heard Leonardo Boff comparing it to Trinitarian perichoresis. Such a perichoresis is particularly clear in the works of F.J. Hinkelammert[16]. From his *Ideological weapons of death*[17] and *The mortal god: Lucifer and the beast. The legitimization of domination in Christian tradition* published in 1977 and 1978 to his most recent works like *Culture of hope and society without exclusion* (1995) or the article *The hurricane of globalization: exclusion and destruction of the environment as seen from the viewpoint of the dependency theory*[18] he develops both a sharp critique of economic structures – the market, the Soviet System – and a cultural analysis: critique of theological and philosophical tradition against the background of the *Christian utopia of bodies liberated from death*. He sees the main failure of the Soviet system at the *cultural* (and also political) level and looks for a variable alternative: the transformation of the utopia of communism adapted to the next period of world history. When delving into the roots of the

15. In *Hacia un Marx desconocido,* chapter 15. This chapter has been published in English: *Marx's economic manuscripts of 1861-63 and the "concept" of dependency* in *LAP* 65:17 (1990) 62-101.

16. I have presented Hinkelammert's work in my articles *Theology of life and economic reality* in *CQ* 56 (Winter 1990) 3-13; *Utopia, neo-liberalism and "realy existing socialism"* in *CQ* 57 (Spring 1991) 8-16 and *Latin America's external debt,* in *CQ* 61 (Spring 1992) 3-15. I have developed some main aspects of these articles in my contribution to the International Marx Congress (Paris, September, 1995), *Marxisme, Christianisme, utopie et projet viable,* published in M. LÖWY, (ed.), *Utopie. Théologie de la libération. Philosophie de l'émancipation,* Paris, PUF, 1996, pp. 9-32. The series of articles goes on in COELI's review (CQ) which has also published some articles from Hinkelammert like, for instance: *Taking stock of LALT* 76 (Winter 1995-96).

17. English translation by Orbis. All original Spanish works from Hinkelammert mentioned here have been published by DEI.

18. In *Pas* 69 (January-February 1997) 21-27.

inversion of the Christian utopia into a killer anti-utopia, Hinkelammert not only deals with medieval theology – Bernard of Clairvaux, Anselm of Canterbury – but critically engages in a debunking the *founding myths of Western civilization*. The titles of his books like *The faith of Abraham and the Western Oedipus* (1989) or *Human sacrifices and Western society* (1991) give an idea of the width of his research. In spite of a certain lack of systematization, he is not merely offering a juxtaposition of reflections because a *dialectical reason* is at work. The thinker from DEI not only tries to present "the true Marx" but also reviews his conception of a viable historical project and this without capitulating in front of neo-liberalism. This dialectical reason allow him also to sketch some very deep ideas on God, which is, after all, the Goal of any theology.

LALT is hence advocating a comprehensive all-embracing and rationally articulated analysis as the framework of any liberation theology. Or perhaps it would be better to speak of a *social philosophy* articulated with social, economic and cultural analyses

However this does not mean that all Latin American theology is following this path. This is due to the fact that *not all theology produced in Latin America is LALT*. Very early, some theologians, like J.C. Scannone, for instance, stressed the cultural dimension as a means to sidestep class analysis[19]. But Scannone is not acknowledged as a liberation theologian.

More recently, COELI and the Missio Institute of Aachen developed as a joint-venture a research project: *Evaluation and perspectives of LALT*[20]. One of the contributions to this research was the article *Indian theologies?*[21] from A. Wagua, a native-American theologian belonging to the *kuna* people (Panama). He emphasizes very strongly the importance of indigenous culture, especially religion. With an amazing "post-modern" accent he stresses the unique character of each indigenous religion, seeing a danger even in the use of the unifying expression "Indian theology". The main danger seems to be for him the Roman Catholic Church magisterium. There is no place for socio-economic analysis in this theology. But then Aiban Wagua does not pretend to be a liberation theologian. He asserts himself as a kuna theologian whose main task seems to

---

19. Cf. his book *Teología de la liberación y praxis popular*, Salamanca, Sígueme, 1976.

20. The results of this project were published in German in R. FORNET & BETANCOURT (eds.), *Befreiungstheologie: Kritischer Rückblick und Perspektiven für die Zukunft*, 3 volumes, Mainz, Matthias-Grünewald Verlag, 1997; 285+384+178 pages. Among these texts, COELI has published in English F.J. HINKELAMMERT (n. 16) and my contribution *The reception of LALT: an opportunity for Europe to re-create its roots*, CQ 77 (Summer 1995).

21. Cf. *Ibid.*, vol. II, pp. 259-276.

be the conservation of the religious heritage of his people. How this can be successful today, under a globalizing and totalitarian market, does not seem to be a key issue for him.

IV. A Danger

Since the Discussion Paper talks about "a multi-layered analysis of globalization" (73), I assume it is not advocating a shift from a kind of one-dimensional analysis of social life to another kind of one-dimensional analysis but *from a one-dimensional analysis to a comprehensive one*. Hence its title would be just thought-provoking. But I would likewise stress that we face a real *danger*. Since it is evident that socio-economic transformation is not on the agenda in the short term and since the hegemonic culture of despair exerts such a pressure on us, we risk neglecting the socio-economic dimension. And experience shows that when the hour of socio-economic transformation sounds, it is too late to think it out in depth. In 1914 Lenin said that no Marxist had understood Marx (because of their ignorance of Hegel's *Logic* which, I add, is a Trinitarian theology) but he forgot to mention that Marx needed not only to be understood but also to be corrected and completed. But then came 1917, and everybody knows what happened afterwards...

Today we are forced, at the level of action, to concentrate on actions for the survival of the poor and on cultural actions of resistance. But we cannot forget that socio-economic transformation is necessary – even if it is not a sufficient condition – in order to build a qualitatively different society. This is perhaps *the most important contribution* LALT has to offer. And post-modern slogans are not a rational proof against it.

LALT advocates a comprehensive analysis. But I am well aware that such an analysis is very difficult to make especially when confronted with the hegemonic culture of despair ("end of history", "end of great narratives", "no alternative"). It should hence be undertaken as a *collective task*. And a collective task presupposes some common basic assumptions, which I have tried to sketch in the previous paragraph.

V. Some (Sketchy) Ideas on Culture

Now, I would like to concentrate on the issue of the *different cultural settings of the poor,* which is intimately linked to that of *popular religion* – Christian or not – which, in turn, may be linked to *nature-caring* religiosity. It is certain that popular culture, all over the world, has been despised by the dominant culture. And that many an activist sincerely committed to the liberation of the poor has shared this contempt because he was a prisoner of the prejudices of the Enlightenment. The *abstract* universalism of the Enlightenment – including its left version "proletarian internationalism" – has gone bankrupt. It also seems evident to me that popular culture – including religion – could be a basic stronghold in the struggle for the dignity of the poor, provided it doesn't fall into two *traps*. A human being cannot live a dignified life without an affirmation of his/her own particular cultural identity. But there is a danger of *particularism* which plays into the hands of global capitalism which, like any domination system, follows a strategy of "divide et impera". However, this is not a fate since every culture contains elements of openness to the others. A *discernment* is hence necessary in order to build up a *concrete universalism* rooted in the different cultures of the poor.

A second trap could be a *nostalgia of the past*. Unless one holds a very pessimistic philosophy of history, according to which evil is always victorious, one has to ask the question about the elements of defeat in the defeated cultures. This is particularly clear in the conquest of America by the Europeans who, at that time, did not enjoy any significant technological superiority. The decisive factors were political and, above all, cultural (a modern against a pre-modern consciousness). The traditions which are an essential ground for the affirmation of the different peoples' identities can only stay alive and successfully resist domination, if they are retrieved in a *reflexive* way, i.e., critically interpreted in the light of the present struggles of these peoples.

This last point is related to *the attitude towards nature*. A pre-modern attitude is no longer viable in our over-populated world. We cannot do without science. But the myth of all-powerful science which will automatically solve all problems (a myth which is struggling with that of "the invisible hand" to be the main element of dominant ideology) may lead to the collective suicide of humankind. Hence we also need here a reflexive attitude in order to master science, in a similar way as we need to master the market. Nature is neither to be worshipped nor to be destroyed but to be cared as an extension of our own bodies.

Centre COELI   Adolfo ABASCAL-JAEN
Kogelstraat 31
B-1000 Brussels, Belgium

22

SOME EPISTEMOLOGICAL IMPLICATIONS OF THE SHIFT IN THIRD-WORLD THEOLOGIES OF LIBERATION

In the first part of this paper, we analyze the thesis of a shift from socio-economic to cultural analysis, from the perspective of the development of Third-World feminist liberation theologies. Third-World feminist theologies of liberation are representative of the shift that has occurred among Third-World theologians, from the use of a basically uni-dimensional to a multi-dimensional analysis of social realities. This broadening of vision, however, constitutes a radical shift in that it entails more than just adding the (philosophico-) cultural perspective to social analysis, but necessitates some recasting of the hermeneutic mediation or the context of validation of theology itself.

In the second part of this paper, we reflect further on the need to recast the hermeneutic mediation by proposing that a particular form of public discourse or community mediation, "strong transformative criticism", should be consciously adopted as an integral part of the method of doing liberation theologies, in order to enhance the reflexive process of different theological (epistemic) communities and avoid political fragmentation.

I. The Question of Mediations

1. *Increased Consciousness of the Plurality of Oppression and the Multiplication of Subjects/Cultural Perspectives*

Third-World feminist theologies of liberation, from its beginnings, have recognized the need for a more comprehensive analysis that makes use of tools for understanding socio-economic and (philosophico-) cultural realities from the perspectives of both class and gender. One can situate or understand this within the already growing consciousness among Third-World theologians, of the plurality of oppression and the multiplication of subjects/philosophico-cultural perspectives from which liberation theology can be done.

For instance, the Women's Commission of the Ecumenical Association of Third-World Theologians (EATWOT), whose initiatives have contributed a lot to fostering the development of liberation theologies from the perspective of women, was formed in the sixth international conference of EATWOT at Geneva in 1983 when the members have already converged on the need for both socio-economic and (philosophico-) cultural analysis in understanding social realities.

Since its beginnings at Dar-es Salam in 1976, EATWOT had recognized the existence and interrelation of different forms of oppression. Some groups, however, elaborated and stressed more imperialist and political domination while others focused on cultural domination. The fifth dialogue (intercontinental), held at New Delhi, India in 1981, which aimed at putting together the results of the three previous continental dialogues[1], recognized that a theology for the Third-World should consider both the socio-economic and cultural aspects of the life of a people.

> In most theological efforts today, stress is on one to the near exclusion of the other. Most of the Latin-Americans realize that their liberation theology has failed to include the cultural dimension of their people and the aspirations of marginalized groups of their continent. Some Africans, on the other hand, in stressing anthropology, traditional cultures, and religions, tend to give little consideration to the contemporary economic and political plight of their peoples. At the EATWOT Conference in 1979, it was strongly emphasized that Asian theology must focus both on Asia's poverty and Asia's religiousness. Clearly a synthesis of the religio-cultural and socio-economic elements remains a necessary task of Third-World theology in the future[2].

In the sixth international conference of EATWOT at Geneva in 1983, there was again a clamor from Asian theologians and, this time, from the women too, for the use of a more comprehensive analysis of social realities which encompass as what they consider as the main forms of oppression – racism, classism, militarism and imperialism, cultural and religious domination and sexism. EATWOT theologians affirmed that class analysis alone does not suffice to grasp the complexity of social realities.

Through the first six conferences of EATWOT, there occurred a growth in the Third-World theologians' consciousness of the plurality of oppression (class, gender, racial, and so on) and in relation to this, the multiplication of potential subjects of liberation theology as well as of perspectives from which liberation theology can be done. This became the starting-point as well of Third-World feminist liberation theologies.

---

1. The Pan-African Conference of Third-World Theologians was held in Ghana in 1977, the Asian Theological Conference in Sri Lanka in 1979 and the Latin-American conference in Brazil in 1980.

2. EATWOT, *The Irruption of the Third-World: Challenge to Theology*, in V. FABELLA & S. TORRES, *Irruption of the Third-World: Challenge to Theology. Papers from the Fifth International Conference of the Ecumenical Association of Third-World Theologians, August 17-29, 1981, New Delhi, India*, Maryknoll, NY, Orbis, 1983, p. 199.

2. Need to Recast the Classic Mediations of Liberation Theologies

This broadening of perspective does not depart from the central intuition of liberation theology as critical reflection on and from within the praxis of the poor, but deepens it. This deepening, however, does not simply involve a change in starting point, but is leading to a radicalization even of the means and the criteria used in the validation of theological assertions.

To make this point clearer, it is helpful to make use of Louis Althusser's framework of the process of knowledge production. Althusser conceives the process of theoretical practice as involving a Generality I (the object of inquiry) which is worked on by a Generality II (theory of a science and its context of validation) to produce Generality III (scientific knowledge). This framework has been adapted by Clodovis Boff in his construction of the method of a theology of liberation, as the transformation of the object of theology which is the political (a product of the *socio-analytic mediation* or Generality I) by the theory of theology (*hermeneutic mediation* or Generality II), to produce theological knowledge (Generality III). At the beginning and at the end of this process is the *practical mediation,* which deals with the direct relation between theological theory and praxis (e.g. how commitment to the poor influences the choice of topic of research, or how theological research will be put to use in the service of the poor).

In Third-World feminist theologies of liberation, the increased consciousness of the plurality of oppression and the multiple cultural perspectives from which liberation theology can be done entails a modified Generality I or starting-point. First, it involves a change from a view of the poor as a homogeneous category to one that recognizes their multiple identities based on class, race, ethnicity, sex and gender. Oppressed women assume these multiple identities. Since they occupy other social or subject positions (e.g. class or race), they are not oppressed to the same degree. The rich woman may suffer from domestic abuse but she is is not economically exploited. She also reaps from the exploitation of other women workers. The white poor woman, on the other hand, may be a victim of economic exploitation but she does not suffer the kind of racial discrimination that the black poor woman is subjected to. Secondly, the integration of different cultural perspectives necessitates not only the use of socio-analytic mediation but also of philosophical-cultural mediation to produce the object of theological inquiry. Third-World feminists are not only criticizing the patriarchal elements in their traditional culture but also appropriating indigenous cultural resources or categories to construct the object of their inquiry or even re-image or re-interpret biblical stories[3]. There seems to be a need therefore to re-introduce the philosophical mediation which has been the traditional mediation of classic theology. This time, however, the philosophical-cultural mediation must include an analysis of the local philosophical and cultural presuppositions and should not be limited to the Western philosophical tradition, as it has been in the past.

More radically, however, Third-World feminists are beginning to see as well the need for changes in the sphere of Generality II, that is, in the hermeneutic mediation itself and the means of validating a theological assertion. We shall focus on this a bit more because the hermeneutic medi-ation is the sphere of the properly theological and any recasting within this sphere signifies that a more radical change is occurring.

3. Role of Praxis within the Hermeneutic Mediation in Classic Libera-tion Theology

Clodovis Boff and Gustavo Gutiérrez represent two ways of seeing the role of praxis/cultural-contextual values in the validation of theo-logical assertions within classic liberation theology. For Clodovis Boff, praxis influences the theological process by way of the socio-analytic and the practical mediations but it does not enter *directly* the hermeneutic mediation (Generality II) which constitutes theology's context of validation or its internal regime. In the hermeneutic mediation, praxis is present only in a second moment, that is, already in theorized form as product of the socio-analytic mediation. Boff argues that no external criterion can be made to judge the validity of theological propositions: "Just as with other disciplines, theology is exempt from any wholly external criterion of truth, any jurisdictional 'tribunal' having the right to pronounce from without on the validity of its propositions. Theology is a *self-policed* practice"[4]. Boff maintains the classic theological criteriology which con-sists solely of the logical instance and the verificational instance. The logical instance sees to the internal coherence and logical consistency of theological constructs. On the other hand, theology's verificational instance, which corresponds to the criterion of empirical adequacy in

3. K. Pui-Lan, *Discovering the Bible in the Non-Biblical World*, in *Semeia* 47 (1989) 31-32; A. Brazal, *Inculturation: An Interpretative Model for Feminist Revisions of Litur-gical Praxis,* in *QL* 77 (1996) 129-131.

4. C. Boff, *Theology and Praxis: Epistemological Foundations*, trans. R. Barr, Mary-knoll, NY, Orbis, 1987, p. 199. See also P.A. Sandin-Fremaint, *Domesticating the The-ology of Liberation: A Deconstructive Reading of Clodovis Boff's Theology and Praxis*, in *Apuntes* (1987) 25-39.

other disciplines, refers to the theological proposition's conformity with the positivity or the canon of faith.

Gutiérrez, on the other hand, posits the circular relationship between orthodoxy and orthopraxis in the determination of theological truth. Gutiérrez uses the term orthopraxis to differentiate right praxis from any other praxis. Gutiérrez affirms that praxis per se cannot be used as the norm to criticize praxis. The rightness of praxis should be discerned and this is done by engaging with the sources of revelation from where the criteria for judging praxis is derived. He therefore distinguishes himself from those who would hold the primacy of praxis or would make praxis as the fundamental norm for truth[5].

Gutiérrez stresses that the *ultimate* criterion for the validation of theological knowledge comes from revealed truth as expressed in the deposit of faith and not praxis itself[6]. He, however underlines that the "deposit of faith" is not a static entity but is renewed or re-contextualized[7].

> The 'deposit of faith' is not a set of cold, warehoused truths but, on the contrary lives on in the church, where it stimulates types of behavior that are faithful to the Lord's will, calls for its proclamation, and *provides criteria for discernment* in relation to the world in which the church finds itself (Italics mine)[8].

The criteria for evaluating praxis, therefore, for Gutiérrez, can be derived from the church or the Christian community's reflection on Scripture in relation to the historical context it finds itself. Gutiérrez's hermeneutic framework clearly allows for re-contextualization of the deposit of faith in the light of liberating praxis or orthopraxis. It is, however, not clear whether or not it allows for discontinuities with the biblical tradition[9].

---

5. *Ibid.*, p. 181, n. 45.

6. G. GUTIÉRREZ, *The Truth shall Make you Free*, in *The Truth Shall Make you Free*, Maryknoll, NY, Orbis, 1986, p. 101. He quotes the document of the Peruvian bishops: "For Christians the supreme norms of truth in ethical and religious matters are to be found in revelation as interpreted by those legitimately empowered to do so. Every theology must have its basis in revelation, in the deposit of faith. With this as a foundation it is possible to reflect on anything and everything, including praxis, which always remains subordinate to revelation [Documento, no. 44]".

7. "Theology is, of course, first of all an understanding illumined by faith, and its ultimate criteria of truth are derived from the 'deposit of faith'. But our thinking as human beings is always affected by the world in which we live and by the questions that world puts to us; this means that our theological thinking must relate to the faith as lived in and by the church in the historical phase thorugh which it is passing". *Ibid.*, 114.

8. *Ibid.*, 102.

9. Elizabeth S. Fiorenza noted how the Classic liberation theologians' framework is still very much in line with the hermeneutical-contextual paradigm of biblical interpretation which stresses the meaningfulness of tradition and continuity with it. This paradigm of biblical interpretation deciphers Scripture's meaning for today through the dialogue

This latter point is important for feminist theologians who are in search of a hermeneutical model broad enough to allow them to reject the biblical texts that are oppressive to women.

4. *Deepening the Logic of (Ortho-)Praxis as Source of the Verification Principle*

Most Third-World feminist theologians appropriate either implicitly or explicitly the basic hermeneutical and epistemological standpoint of liberation theology which considers praxis/cultural-contextual values not just object of theological reflection but direct sources of the verification principle itself. They, however, are pushing further the latter's implications to its logical consequence. The increased consciousness of the multiplication of subjects of liberation theology and of cultural perspectives from which liberation theology can be done, is leading some to postulate the need for a form of community mediation as context for the validation of theological knowledge.

Linked to this is the awareness of the need to reconsider the authority of the Bible as sole source of validation for theological assertions. Elsa Tamez, a Latin-American theologian, notes that a contradiction exists when Latin-American women, on the one hand, consider the Bible the word of God, possessing the authority of divine revelation, and on the other hand, reject texts which reinforce patriarchy or machismo. Those in church positions, however, appeal to these very texts to command obedience from the women. For Tamez, it is therefore inevitable to "reformulate the principle of biblical authority, from the point of departure of our Latin-American reality"[10].

Speaking from another cultural context, Kwok Pui-Lan, a Chinese theologian, rejects both the notion of the Bible as providing the norm for interpretation itself, as well as the identification of just *one* critical principle in the Bible as the basis or norm for interpretation. From her perspective, coming from a predominantly non-Christian country, there is the danger that the biblical-theological category identified as *ultimate* norm or *the* norm will be used again against other cultures. She perceives in this probability the need for "absoluteness" and "oneness".

between the contemporary interpreter and the historical text. E.S. FIORENZA, *Toward a Feminist Biblical Hermeneutics: Biblical Interpretation and Liberation Theology*, in B. MAHAN & L. D. RICHESIN (eds.), *The Challenge of Liberation Theology: A First World Response*, Maryknoll, NY, Orbis, 1981.

10. E. TAMEZ, *Women's Rereading of the Bible*, in U. KING (ed.), *Feminist Theology from the Third-World: A Reader*, Maryknoll, NY, Orbis, 1944, p. 177.

Following Elizabeth Schüssler Fiorenza, Pui-Lan asserts that the critical principle can be derived not from the Bible alone, but determined in the community of women who reflect on the Bible and read it from the perspective of their own liberation. Each community has to come up with its own norm for interpretation, but must be accountable to the other communities. "Our truth claims must be tested in public discourse, in constant dialogue with other communities"[11]. She refers to this notion of truth as a dialogical model for truth where each one is seen as capable of contributing to the understanding of reality.

The Asian EATWOT women and the Philippine EATWOT women, on their part, have begun putting this into practice when they came up with hermeneutical principles which can guide them in their interpretation of history, Scripture, faith tradition, cultural heritage and present reality.

> The Asian Women's hermeneutical principle interpret as in accordance with God's design: whatever promotes genuine dialogue among people of different cultures, religions and ideologies; whatever fosters equality, unity, justice and peace in all personal and social relationships; whatever empowers women and other marginalized people in our cultures and societies; whatever promotes communities of men and women characterized by sharing and mutuality, joy and freedom; whatever respects and protects creation[12].

These hermeneutical principles constitute the cultural-contextual values that the community of feminist theologians in Asia have discerned as the norms to guide them in their theological reflection (e.g. choice of social theory, choice of hermeneutical model, Scriptural interpretation, and so on)[13]. The Philippine EATWOT women have also explicitly stated that these hermeneutical principles are tentative and therefore subject to changes.

To avoid misunderstanding the position of Third-World feminist theologies, it is important to make the following clarifications. For Third-World feminist theologies, the dialogue with the Christian positivity remains a *central* part of any theological inquiry. And even if not explicitly stated, epistemic values such as logical coherence and conformity with re-contextualized Christian positivity are still held as among the standards for the validation of a theological assertion, in addition to the

---

11. K. PUI-LAN, *Discovering the Bible in the Non-Biblical World*, in *Semeia* 47 (1989) 37.

12. EATWOT women, *Patriarchy in Asia and Asian Women's Hermeneutical Principle*, Quezon City, EATWOT, 1991. See also in the same publication the hermeneutical principles constructed by the Philippine EATWOT women.

13. The Asian EATWOT feminist theologians did not resolve a common understanding of what a hermeneutical principle is. For some, it is a methodology while for others, it is the norm for interpretation.

other criteria derived from the cultural-contextual values of a particular theological community.

Feminist liberation theologies, however, are in search of a coherent hermeneutical method that can allow not only for re-contextualization in continuity with the biblical traditions (as in the hermeneutical-contextual paradigm of biblical interpretation)[14] but also, in some cases, discontinuity with the tradition as when some texts which reinforce sexism have to be rejected. Some feminist liberation theologians, in this regard, see the need for integrating within the hermeneutic mediation some form of public discourse or mediation of Christian communities where theological assertions can be critiqued, modified and validated, presumably based on both epistemic and cultural-contextual values. As we shall see in the next section, a community mediation is also further necessitated within the context of the increased consciousness of the plurality of oppression and the multiplication of subject-positions and subjects of liberation theologies. This recasting can be considered a radicalization of the basic insight of classic liberation theology, that is, of (ortho)praxis as a source of the verification principle.

In our discussion above, we hope to have pointed out, albeit in broad strokes, that the consideration of different cultural perspectives in the doing of liberation theology cannot leave the Classic mediations of liberation theology, especially the hermeneutic mediation, unrecast. We would not want to enter into the debate whether one should call this a paradigm shift or not. What is more important is to realize that a change is happening which is more than just an addition of the philosophico-cultural perspective (e.g. feminist perspective) into an already established framework. Some recasting of the methodology of liberation theologies is required.

II. "STRONG TRANSFORMATIVE CRITICISM" A FORM OF COMMUNITY MEDIATION

The second part of this paper explores further the need to integrate some form of community mediation within the methodology of theologies of liberation, in relation to two questions posed by De Schrijver. The first question pertains to how one can reconcile the various attempts at reflexivity in the different theologies of liberation and prevent political fragmentation. The decentering trend in the production of theological

14. E.S. FIORENZA (n. 9).

knowledge in the neo-colonial global context demands some mechanism for preventing political fragmentation (34-36). There is the danger that each community becomes confined to its own local concerns (e.g. gender, cultural, or ecological) and is left unchallenged to broaden its horizon or to engage itself in a critique of the capitalist world system. Within feminist theological communities, there are clear attempts to integrate the different forms of oppression (class, race, culture, gender, etc.). But one cannot say this to be true of other theological communities[15].

The second question inquires whether or not the integration of other perspectives (e.g. based on race or gender) can lead to greater reflexivity in the Christian tradition (77-78). As an initial response, we can say that the encounter between different perspectives (class, gender – or culture-enlightened interpretation of the Christian tradition) can lead to a greater reflexivity in the tradition in so far as this will help reveal "hidden" assumptions/ background beliefs in a particular interpretation. When a group is homogenous, it is possible that some background assumptions become invisible to them. It is only when an individual or a group with a different set of assumptions/contextual values, is able to offer another perspective on the matter that the "hidden" assumptions of the group become apparent. For example, it was only when feminist theologians began to speak out that male theologians realized that the preferential option for the poor as a hermeneutical perspective tended to ignore women's issues.

This reflexivity, however, can be further enhanced in theologies of liberation by creating a space where different struggles/liberationist theological perspectives can be articulated. This paper proposes the process of "strong transformative criticism" as a form of public discourse or community mediation that can further enhance the various attempts at reflexivity as well as guard against political fragmentation.

1. *Intersubjective Verifiability of Knowledge*

We have critically appropriated the concept of "transformative criticism" from Helen Longino, a feminist philosopher of science. For Longino, science is a social knowledge that is constructed "not by individuals

---

15. For example African feminist theologians note how some African men legitimize the continued subordination of women in the name of culture. See M.A. ODUYOYE, *Christian Feminism and African Culture: The "Hearth" of the Matter*, in M. ELLIS & O. MADURO (eds.), *The Future of Liberation Theology: Essays in Honor of Gustavo Gutiérrez*, Maryknoll, NY, Orbis, 1989, pp. 441-449; R. JORDAN & T. MPUMLWANA, *Two Voices on Women's Oppression and Struggle in South Africa*, in *Feminist Theology from the Third-World*, pp. 165-166.

applying a method but by individuals in interaction with one another in ways that modify their observations, theories and hypotheses, and patterns of reasoning"[16]. The social nature of knowledge provides a system of checks or controls to individual subjective preferences in the very process of the production of (theological) knowledge. One such control is the requirement for knowledge to be intersubjectively verifiable. The cognitive practices of science such as observation and reasoning possess a social character. Observations and reasoning are not just the perceptions of an individual but are required to be intersubjectively verifiable. Reasoning is involved in a scientific inquiry when one establishes evidential relations, and when one evaluates a hypothesis or a theory based on these evidential relations. In both of these cases, background assumptions are involved. The basic assumptions that underly these processes are normally a function of the consensus (explicit or implicit) within a scientific community, where the individual learns the trade of becoming a scientist. The scientific community itself may not be conscious of these assumptions, but they are articulable and thus in principle public. This makes it possible to critically examine, modify, reinforce or reject them.

The tradition of intersubjective criticism, whereby a particular assertion is subjected to the examination of a scientific community, is a normal part of any scientific inquiry. This occurs through recognized venues of criticism like regular public forums such as journals and colloquiums. There is usually a set of shared standards, whether implicit or explicit, by which a particular assertion is assessed. What comes out as knowledge in this process is the product of a complicated process of absorption which involves, among others, citations by other authors, critical revisions and the integration of other points of views.

The exposure to criticism does not erase altogether the role of subjective preferences in scientific practice (whether that of the individual or the group) but it affords a mechanism for monitoring their influence in the production of knowledge: "... as long as background assumptions can be articulated and subjected to criticism from the scientific community, they can be defended, modified or abandoned in response to such criticism"[17]. With this mechanism, the acceptance of a hypothesis as (scientific) knowledge is not dependent on an individual's subjective preference. It is a function of the epistemic community's assessment.

---

16. H. LONGINO, *Multiplying Subjects and the Diffusion of Power*, in *JP* 88 (1991) 670.
17. ID., *Essential Tensions Phase Two*, in L. ANTONY & C. WITT (eds.), *A Mind of One's Own: Feminist Essays on Reason and Objectivity*, Colorado, Westview Press, 1993, p. 265.

Although background assumptions can play a role in the evidential relations, these assumptions are subject to control or check by the epistemic
community.

2. H. Longino's Strong Transformative Criticism

This process of intersubjective criticism can be strengthened to assure
not only greater reflexivity but also to provide a mechanism for different
perspectives to challenge and transform one another. We will call this
fortified version "strong transformative criticism"[18]. Strengthening the
traditional process of intersubjective criticism for the use of theologies
of liberation requires ensuring the following conditions.

First, the existence of different theological (epistemic) communities
on the local and the international level should be recognized. One can
distinguish between feminist theological communities, black theological
communities and so on. C. Boff also distinguishes liberation theologies
done on the popular, pastoral and professional levels.

Secondly, the presence of critical points of view especially from the
perspective of "others" or the marginalized should be ensured in these
theological communities. This "presence" can be further facilitated if theologians of liberation are required to lay down their background assumptions or cultural agendas, as well as acknowledge their power position, so
that the theological community can critically examine these assumptions[19].
But for theologians to become aware of their own background assumptions, especially the hidden ones, it is necessary that there already be
existing critical theories from the viewpoint of the 'others' in society.
This requirement thereby encourages the presence of critical viewpoints.
Furthermore, theologians should already consider, even while in the
process of conceptualizing their research, theories which are being
developed from the viewpoint of "others". This guarantees that critical
points of views from the perspective of "others" are assessed and integrated. Furthermore, this also assures the presentation of views of groups
in the periphery even by those who do not come from these social
locations. Sandra Harding coined the phrase "reinventing ourselves as

18. "Strong transformative criticism" integrates, for the use of theologies of liberation,
the conditions for transformative criticism as defined by Longino and Ismay Barwell's
critical evaluation of Longino's approach. See H. LONGINO, *Science as Social Knowledge*,
pp. 76-78, and I. BARWELL, *Towards a Defence of Objectivity*, in K. LENNON & M. WHIT-
FORD (eds.), *Knowing the Difference: Feminist Perspectives in Epistemology*, London,
Routledge, 1994, pp. 79-93.

19. S. HARDING, *Whose Science? Whose Knowledge?: Thinking from Women's Lives*,
Milton Keynes, Open University Press, 1991, p. 162.

others" to refer to this way of seeking knowledge that takes into account the standpoint of "others"[20].

Thirdly, shared standards for the validation of a theological assertion should be explicitated so that those who are criticized themselves accept the criteria by which their works are being assessed. These shared standards can consist of both epistemic values (e.g. empirical adequacy, coherence vis-à-vis the Christian positivity) and contextual values. These shared standards provide the individual theologians with an accountability to something else besides themselves.

Fourthly, there should be equality of intellectual authority within the theological community. This Habermasian criterion means that no set of assumptions should predominate because of the political power of its proponents. Thus, the lack of women and members of other racial or cultural groups within the scientific community, which consequently allows the white male paradigm to predominate, is a violation of this equality criterion. It protects these ideas from critical scrutiny of women and other racial groups.

3. *Basic Assumptions*

The possibility of strong transformative criticism is grounded on the assumption *not* of value-neutrality, but of the possibility that at least two or more persons can agree about the basic description of what is presented. That this is possible is based on two premises. The first premise is that people can agree on a common language to define experience and to use for reasoning. Because of this, it is possible to understand an assertion and thus accept, criticize or reject it. This latter point contrasts with some versions of postmodernism which maintain total incommensurability of language games, thus making it theoretically impossible to still criticize capitalism, sexism or racism[21]. The second premise holds that the object of experience is independent of our knowledge of it[22]. This limits what can be asserted about a certain phenomenon, and recognizes the importance of other accounts of the same experience. With theologies of liberation, it is important to uphold a modest form of empiricism, that is, to maintain to a certain degree that our theories are

20. *Ibid.*, pp. 268-295.

21. Mary Hesse demonstrated in her essay, "Theory and Observation" that, as wholists claim, there is no such thing as a theory-neutral observation language, but on the other hand, this need not lead to radical theory incommensurability or total untranslatability of different languages. M. HESSE, *Revolutions and Reconstructions in the Philosophy of Science*, Brighton, Sussex, 1980, pp. 63-110.

22. Longino recognizes the theory-ladenness of observation but unlike Thomas Kuhn distinguishes between state of affairs and observation language.

substantiated in reality[23], if these are to be the basis of political action. Postmodern accounts that tend to de-emphasize the reality out there, because of their notion of the inextricable link between theories and reality, can likewise have depoliticizing effects. Without a certain conviction that our assertions are based *in some ways* on reality, it is difficult to criticize and denounce poverty and injustices.

"Strong transformative criticism" can help not only to make our theological assertions more justifiable in the sense of having integrated different points of view and having gone through a critical screening, but also prevents our fragmentation into isolated groups with divergent interests. A theologian whose starting-point is a set of indigenous categories of a culture, should test her theories vis-à-vis the theories being developed from the perspective of the economically poor, the women and the "others" in our society. The same is expected from theologians whose starting point is class or gender perspective. We can opt to adopt this attitude not only because of the epistemological advantage of considering critical points of view but also because of a common value we presumably share as theologians of liberation – our preferential option for the poor.

III. Conclusion

The process of strong transformative criticism enhances the reflexivity of the Christian tradition by ensuring a structure whereby the different presuppositions and background beliefs that shape the interpretation of the Christian tradition can be laid down and questioned. It allows different perspectives to challenge one another, and hopefully, in providing a site for the articulation of different struggles, will lead as well to a broadened vision of liberation and to joint action against systemic oppression.

Faculty of Theology, KULeuven   Agnes Brazal
Sint-Michielsstraat 6
B-3000 Leuven, Belgium

23. There exist conventional ways of describing and measuring some experiences. For example, once the scientific community has fixed that a certain level on an instrument is equivalent to 10 units, we cannot just read it arbitrarily as 7 or 13 without the agreement of the other party and without revising other characterizations linked to the gauge. That we describe a certain experience as measuring 10 is dependent on the language a scientific community uses, the kind of instruments available and the type of data that is sought. "The reliability of such systems lies not in their ability to transparently represent the natural world as it is 'in itself' but in the fact that the gradations and changes in parameters of a system match gradations and changes in the natural world". Longino insists that in cases when our initial characterization of reality differs, we can always resort to a shared minimum level of describing the common world, that will allow us to see the variations in our inferences and experiences as this is shaped by our socio-political cultural context. Longino (n. 18), p. 222.

THE EDITOR'S POSTSCRIPT

It is obviously a somewhat risky enterprise for First-World theologians to invite colleagues from the Third-World to discuss the latters' very problems at a Symposium organized for that purpose in an academic center of the "Old-World". True, such an enterprise would decidedly be less risky, if the organizing committee prudently confined itself to just providing a platform for discussion in which renowned speakers from the South could freely take the floor and set the trend by deciding which urgent topics must be put on the agenda. The probable effect would then be a homefelt unanimity with perhaps some minor points of divergence, especially if the speakers could conscientize the participants from the North both to become attentive to the voices of the South and to refrain from prescribing the requisite strategies for making liberation projects effective. Fortunately or not, the Symposium adopted a different procedure. Of course, a platform for discussion had been provided, but this was done with the proviso that the discussion should focus on a Discussion Paper that had been prepared in advance by this author, who admittedly is more exposed to the reflections of liberation theologians than to the actual liberation struggles of the poor of the South.

This proviso turned out to be beneficial as well as inauspicious. The benefit consisted in the neat delineation of two major topics: the disputed question of the paradigm shift, and the phenomenon of globalization. The dismal effect (at least to some) came to the fore in the – foreseeable – accusation that the approach to the two topics was too western. More diplomatically, some affirmed that the Discussion Paper offered undoubtedly some interesting insights into the drastic changes that took place in the last two decades or so, but that these insights needed to be recast specifically by those who have a real experience of what it means to live at the underside of history.

Weighing the pros and cons, I am personally glad *post festum* that the Symposium had been organized the way it was, for I am convinced that it is as important – if not more important – to venture to ask some well-grounded questions (or initial questions) rather than to attempt zealously to provide the correct (and/or the generally agreed upon) answers. I formulate this in all honesty, while I realize that, even in raising questions, nobody does so from a *tabula rasa* condition. Indeed, each one's questioning is embedded in, and betrays, one's own cultural, economic, religious, and personal background. But in spite of this, raising questions is part of the communicative discourse in which the world community is engaged and to which all of us are expected to contribute.

In what follows, I am going to briefly comment on some striking reactions to my Discussion Paper, as they were voiced out in the plenary sessions of the Symposium and, later on, as they occasionally surfaced in some of the contributions to the present volume. For clarity's sake, I shall group these comments and divide them into three sections: the alleged paradigm shift, the question of globalization, and postmodernity or the consequences of modernity, as Giddens prefers to call the phenomenon.

If some readers are wondering what these (interrelated) topics have to do with theology proper, it may be recalled that being a theology of praxis Liberation Theology in its classic form makes use of three mediations: socio-economic analysis of the situation, hermeneutical application of the Word of God to the needs arising from a given state of affairs, and the believer's praxis-commitment to the cause of the downtrodden. These three approaches or mediations are intertwined, although a heavy emphasis is placed on the analysis of the situation, often undertaken with the help of elements borrowed from Marxist-social analysis. The question is, indeed, how to give an incarnated form to one's firm belief in God's yearning for the break-through of a reign of justice and peace, or to put it differently: how are we to live up, in the concrete, to the divine call to respect our fellow humans in their human dignity, especially those who are at the mercy of dehumanizing powers? This praxis-oriented theological attitude constitutes the background against which the rather specific discussions that are going to follow must be seen. Oftentimes it is only in between the lines that this theological concern, based on biblical motivations, will become perceptible. But it always will be present, even when the discussion focuses on seemingly profane matters like socio-economic analysis and its thinkable replacement (or completion) with more culture-bound approaches, such as gender, race and indigenous values. The same is true for the discussions on globalization and modernity/postmodernity. Here again the issue at stake is to what extent and under what conditions these currents are groping inner developments that are going to be beneficial, instead of being fatally detrimental, to the poor – the 'wretched of the earth', and the beloved children of God.

I. Paradigm Shift?

In the last plenary session of the Symposium, the participants proposed to add a question mark to the enunciation "Paradigm Shift in

Third World Theologies of Liberation?" The question mark is the result of a compromise. Some participants argued that replacing the classic socio-economic analysis with mere cultural analysis was out of the question, since this would imply a betrayal of the liberationist concern. Others, on the contrary, admitted that a slight yet significant (or subtle) shift in emphasis (or "axial shift") had already been taking place – socio-economic analysis being complemented with cultural analysis and vice versa – but that this focal change (or focal alternation) was not of such a nature that it could rightly be called a paradigm shift in the technical sense of the term. In this technical sense, the old paradigm, as Popper and Kuhn have made clear, is not only superseded but also invalidated by the new paradigm. Now, in matters of Liberation Theology, such an invalidation of the socio-economic paradigm is not evident at all, especially not for those who, as organic intellectuals, seriously attempt to side with the destitute of the earth, who not only economically but also culturally are deprived of their human dignity. The weak in terms of race, gender, and "respectable" cultural habits, are also the economically weak, who alas have become too often the targeted victims in the hands of their exploiters.

Some readers of my Discussion Paper may have concluded from the first section, where I review the developments from Medellin to Puebla and Santo Domingo, that I simply take the paradigm shift for granted, in the sense that the economic approach would have been invalidated by the culturalist approach. But this is apparently a misreading of my intention. In that text, which renders the essence of a longer article I wrote on this issue, I mainly called attention to the fact that, starting from Puebla and under the impulse of López Trujillo, an open confrontation was mounted against liberationists acting in the style of Medellin. As I see it, the renewed interest in culture was launched to provide a solely sacrosanct alternative to the initial liberationist analysis, which was influenced by some currents of Marxism. The covert, if not overt, aim of this alternative was to discredit the liberationist analysis – which in terms of ecclesiastical politics implied the invalidation or even the condemnation of the movement that was in favor of this analysis. I need not recall the content of the First Instruction on Liberation Theology issued by the Congregation of the Doctrine of the Faith, an instruction which solemnly 'sealed' the counter-trend that became visible in Puebla. The same counter-trend was one of the potent undercurrents in Santo Domingo, and was reinforced by the 'Romanizers' in that conference.

It comes as no surprise then that some of the key-respondents dwelt at length on this strategic sort of invalidation by asking themselves why for

God's sake had there been such a felt need, on the part of the official
church, to focus one-sidedly on (Catholic) culture, at a moment when the
economic issues in all their ramifications were far from being resolved.
One ought only to think of the world market dictating the plummeting
prices of copper, cotton, coffee, tea and so on, or of the dire 'readjustment programs' that are being enforced under the aegis of the World
Bank and the International Monetary Fund (IMF) as preconditions for
countries to become eligible to receive foreign aid, or of the back-break-
ing burden of international debt, or the ruthless practices displayed by
stateless transnational corporations (TNCs). These macro-economic realities proceed to the detriment of the poor masses in many countries of the
Two-Thirds World; they drain huge quantities of money away from the
country, thus perpetuating malnutrition, illiteracy, child labor, and other
forms of injustice. We should not forget also the complicity of the local
elite who do not hesitate to condone bribes, graft and corruption especially at the governmental level. If the church leaders are afraid of a
class struggle from below, they definitely tend to turn a blind eye to the
more global class struggle in which powerful economic institutions have
imposed, on a world scale, their ruthless rule upon the powerless, who
either are forced into a position of subjugation or are excluded. After
years of colonialism and neo-colonialism, the actual globalizing economy has turned into a sinister providence, incorporating and at the same
time excluding nations and groups of people at will, and thus conjuring
the 'end' or 'final purpose' of history, as Fukuyama has cynically named
the phenomenon.

   As for the remedies to these evils, various suggestions have been
made during the Symposium, depending on the continents the speakers
came from. Several persons referred to the "pincer movement of social
justice and inculturationt" as the most efficient strategy. Or, as one
author put it, what we need is "a multi-faceted social analysis" which
consists of a socio-economic analysis that has naturally evolved to
include socio-cultural analysis. Especially in Asia, where Christians are
the minority, there is a specific need to recover the continent's old religious roots so as to give Christianity a genuinely Asian face. Yet this
recovery, it was stated, ought to be undertaken in view of affirming –
together with non-Christian believers – the right to political self-determination. Liberation Theology in Asia is a struggle for liberation from
both cultural as well as economic domination of colonial and neo-
colonial powers. Protests against economic discrimination at the level of
world trade and world politics find their parallel in the turn towards
inculturating the faith. The same holds true, to a large extent, for African

Christians. For them, in particular, the rediscovery of their cultural identity and ancestral beliefs (to bring these to merge meaningfully with Christian motifs) is seen as a means of resisting the doom of Afropessimism. Recently, one heard representatives from the World Bank predicting that, by the year 2000, the world "would likely experience a decline in poverty, except in Africa, where things will only get worse". Poverty in cultural matters apparently goes hand in hand with resignation in the face of material poverty; although having said that, it is obvious that culture alone will not be able to solve the economic problems.

As far as Latin America is concerned, it was stressed that, ever since the beginnings of Liberation Theology, the Argentinean trend had shown a clear preference for retrieving their cultural roots – the specific *mestizaje* of pre-Columbian elements and Christian thought in early modernity. Likewise, this *mestizaje*, unlike western profit-thinking, had always been at bottom a 'pro-people' movement. It was also added that the times apparently had become ripe for allowing a cross-fertilization between socio-economic analysis, the classical tool in the continent for doing Liberation Theology, and socio-cultural analysis (and vice versa). One expression of this merger, it was stated, is the new social *imaginario*, i.e. the inventiveness among the common people to engage in a more or less organized 'parallel market', the extension of which would put some pressure on the macro-structures of economic life. (Looked at from a macro-level, however, this 'informal market' and the energies invested in it apparently constitute a mere palliative to sugar-coat the bitter pill of either a forced entry into the global market or an exclusion from it).

If we draw up the provisional balance sheet of the discussion thus far, the conclusion is that only an 'axial shift' and no a real paradigm shift has occurred. What has happened is more of a natural evolution towards the inclusion of cultural aspects into the basic analytic framework of socio-economic analysis. A testimony from a 'field-worker' in Zambia seems to confirm this evolution. When discussing, for instance, the implementation of development programs, he deplores the planners' ignorance of the way they are uprooting the extended family structure on which the African 'economy of affection' is based. At the same time, he insists on the necessity of critically examining cultural habits – through communal discernment – to determine what is good in them, and what possibly needs to be adjusted Some ingrained habits as well as the narratives and myths that support them may be beneficial to community life – such as narratives inculcating respect for nature, or those extending the blessings of peaceful coexistence after settling disputes. Other cultural justifications, however, may appear more questionable, like the subordination of women. Here, the author ironically points out that men can no longer pretend that they must have their hands free to keep the lions off their homes so much so that the work in the household and in the fields have to be done mostly by the women. In other words, a gender-bound division of labor that made sense in past circumstances can no longer be invoked to perpetuate a macho tradition.

Gender relations, it was stressed from a feminist standpoint, are constitutive of the social fabric of existence, just as class divisions are. Gender relations generate their specific types of domination that, starting with the family, run across other domains: the work situation, politics, and the cultural symbolic sphere. Women, generally speaking, have to work more for lower salaries, they are excluded more often from decision-making processes, and their work at home, including caring for the sick and child-rearing, are taken for granted or not always appreciated as they should be. As this is still the case in 'developed' countries, where, after all, a greater fairness in gender relations has been reached, how much more pertinent then is this issue for certain parts of the Two-Thirds World? Women's emancipation there (to think only of the Muslim world) often meets the resistance of an age-old cultural tradition, which – as many dare to venture – needs to be rectified.

The same is true for racism, especially when carried out on religious grounds. An example, though not discussed during the Symposium, is the Hindu caste system, where the untouchables (the Dalits, for example) are looked upon with contempt as the 'unclean'. They deserve this despicable position, it is said, because of their sins in their previous lives; therefore, in line with their *dharma*, they will have to perform all sorts of dirty jobs – the washing of clothes and corpses, the cleaning of lavatories, etc. – for the benefit of the higher castes. They have to do this in seclusion, for even a Dalit's shadow cast on a Brahmin may endanger the latter's ritual purity. Here again, and perhaps clearer than in the case of sexism, we have to do with deeply ingrained cultural habits that are now being seriously questioned. Many Dalits have converted from Hinduism to other religions – Buddhism, Islam, and Christianity – where they have developed their own Dalit Liberation Theology. One could also add the inveterate habit of reducing people, even children, to bondage and forced labor. Although all these practices evidently result in material benefits for the masters, the justifying background of the subjugation is mainly cultural.

Where have the issues of sexism and racism led us? Are they still part of the expanded socio-economic liberation paradigm, which now includes a strong interest in cultural matters? The answer is yes and no. Yes, in so far as the detection of sexism and racism requires application of ideology criticism, which Liberation circles have fostered and levelled specifically against superstructural legitimations of western capitalism and its collaborators, the local elite (and their powerful influence on the churches). No, for although the application of the liberation paradigm to the domains of gender and race does not properly change the paradigm, the application still reckons with domains for which the paradigm was not originally conceived. In other words, what was primarily an anti-capitalistic paradigm has been expanded to counteract pre-capitalistic evils – sexism and racism, which have already existed since pre-colonical times. At this juncture, the question can be asked whether or not this partially new application has entailed a certain 'diversification' in doing Liberation Theology, and what are the consequences thereof.

When studying the developments within EATWOT, one cannot but observe that, up to the beginning of the 1980s, the EATWOT conferences focused on the twin programs of socio-economic liberation and inculturation. It was only at the sixth international conference in Geneva (1983) that mention was made of various, probably interrelated but at any rate specific, aspects of oppression, namely, classism, militarism, imperialism (the old set of topics, if you like), cultural and religious domination, sexism and racism. Ecological concerns came later on the agenda. It seems that this widening of perspectives was induced not so much by a theoretical reflection on the method but by considerations on how to meet urgent needs, emergent needs owing to changing circumstances. But in retrospect, one might ask the question whether or not this and similar decisions have occasioned further 'evolutions' – unforeseen 'focal shifts', respectively – within the liberation camp. Have not these more 'specialized' forms of resistance initiated a 'dissipated' trend, as I called it in my Discussion Paper, or at least indirectly contributed to it?

While reviewing this situation, and basing herself on research done in Latin America, one of our key-respondents remarked that a growing number of 'specializations' in the realm of liberation has had the effect of making liberation theology less homogeneous than it used to be in the past two decades: "great diversity appears in relation to the constitution of a common ground from which the theological 'liberating' theory emerged". This weakening of homogeneity, she reported, has recently led to the convocation, in Latin America, of conferences with the purpose of scrutinizing the phenomenon. A conference held in Brazil in 1995 set itself the goal to study the reasons for Liberation Theology's "Paradigm Crisis"; whereas another conference, also organized in Brazil, had put on the agenda the intriguing question of "Theology and New Paradigms" (in plural). The titles of these two conferences seem to indicate that, according to some liberationists in search for renewal, the liberation paradigm was felt to be in crisis. Is it in crisis, I would ask, because it had assimilated too many items (originating from the new movements operative outside the classic liberationist base communities) or because it failed to assimilate enough of their impetus? Or, one other possibility, is not the drastic change that happened during the last seven or eight years in the world's global constellation rather responsible for the paradigm's loss of plausibility?

A seminar in Costa Rica (1996) tackled this final question. More in particular, it discussed the various tendencies in theological theory in the context of globalization, whereby no proposed encompassing method, precisely in matters of theory formation, could count on a unanimous reception, and this is in fact symptomatic of a crisis situation. The only thing that was certain is that new breath was needed in order to formulate a 'new agenda' for doing Liberation Theology. It was acknowledged that new sub-paradigms were mushrooming on the unstable ground of the liberation enterprise. Questions, too, have been raised concerning the validity and self-validation of the various (often dispersed) trends. Diversification and the awareness of a plurality of (fallible?) perspectives have made their inroads.

II. GLOBALIZATION

Although it was brought to the attention of the participants, the issue of a 'paradigm crisis' did not get the chance to be sufficiently discussed. Instead, the thesis of a possible paradigm shift came under attack, and this for two sets of reasons of which one was manifest while the other was hidden beneath the surface. On the manifest level, I already noted in the previous section the request to modify the title of my contribution as follows: "Paradigm Shift in Third World Liberation Theologies? From Socio-economic Analysis *to the Inclusion of* Cultural Analysis". This was a modification I had no difficulty in accepting because it was in line with the basic content of my Discussion Paper. As far as the covert reasons are concerned, they reared their heads in the first plenary session, which started with the secretaries of the various discussion groups reporting the findings of their members. From these reports and also from additional remarks, it became evident that the majority of the participants did resent something; some felt that they had been trapped into an invitation to applaud a European text that pretended to shed a final light on such complex matters as Third-World Theologies. Reactions could be heard like the following: "If we in our local situation want to give priority to a socio-economic analysis over cultural considerations – or even the other way round – please leave it up to us to determine which strategy is the best". "Why spend that much energy in reaching a consensus about a single model, whereas the life conditions in various places of the world are so different, impossible to capture through one single lens?" "Is not the whole discussion about paradigms and their mandatory use a typically western product?" "From where do western scholars derive the authority to dictate to the rest of the world analyses they have been concocting through mental gymnastics?"

I must admit that I felt humbled when these hidden adverse reactions eventually manifested themselves. I was only able to defend myself by explaining, first of all, that I was deeply concerned about the effects of the official church's strategy that attempts to relegate all Marxist-inspired analyses to oblivion. Not even the memory of it must survive. But will this position really prove beneficial to the uplifting of the poor? True, I had been broaching the cultural topic, but this 'shift in emphasis' (in the meantime I had accepted the validity of this term) had nothing to do with attempts at reestablishing the prestige of an officially promulgated Catholic ideology: the *Neo-Cristiandad*-idea in vogue before Liberation Theology's epistemological break. And secondly, I admitted that I did realize that my approach was as contextual as the respective approaches from the other continents; and from this local context, I had started to reflect on the world situation along the lines of situated (western) analyses that, in a post-Marxist setting though still in continuity with a Marxist ideology criticism, tried to come to grips with vital questions of the survival of humanity, especially the destitute, in the face of globalization and its culture politics.

I do not think that it was only the effect of these words which brought about a change in the mood of the discussions; this change can be gleaned from the fact that, the next day, the topic of globalization was put on the agenda. Indeed, it increasingly became evident that, to most of the discussion partners, globalization was far more than just a concept; it was acknowledged to be a forceful reality whose grasp on every locality of the globe was on the increase. The 'Fall of the Berlin Wall' (1989), which the Discussion Paper had taken as a symbol for events that drastically changed history, suddenly began to be taken seriously. Indeed, it was said that, after the end of the Cold War, we find ourselves in a situation where on a world scale there is only one center of economic power left: the 'total' or 'global' market. In this light, even the term neo-colonialism has become somewhat inappropriate since its imagery still pivots around the idea of various single nation-states or single hegemonic blocs competing to have their power expanded on a world scale. But nowadays, the very nation states, also in the Old-World, seem to have been stripped of the momentum they previously had. Globalization, as one of the contributors to the Symposium put it, is "the next phase in the capitalist revolution, which after 1989 had free reign throughout the world"; its long term agenda is "the marketization of all national economies".

The impact of this change can be seen also in Western Europe. Here, the nation-states in the post-war period succeeded for a long time in countering, through protective measures and the sealing of social pacts, the erosion of the national economies by the international flow of capital: financial prosperity went hand in hand with the existence of the welfare state, thus preventing a widening of the gap between the rich and the poor. But now, with the internationalization of capital, the World Bank and its associated institutions (in which the US and seven other rich nations have their say) are dictating which social measures governments are still allowed to take and which not. If governments fail to live up to this rule, they are threatened with exclusion from 'the benefits' of the global market. As I put it in the Discussion Paper, "Thanks to the electronic media of communication and to the dismantlement of state power, the 'total market' meets no borders that restrict the inroads of its empire. It creates at will jobs and unemployment, wealth and poverty, ordered life and crime, when and were it wishes. It acts thus as a dark providence whose decisions are not to be questioned". When the workers in a Belgian factory do not accept lower salaries, the company will transfer its enterprise to low-cost countries such as those in the former East Bloc or in the Two-Thirds World. Just as capital moves from place to place, so do companies and subsidiary companies. They do so for their own profit-enhancement, and they will not hesitate to erect 'free economic zones' (in which laborers, mostly women, have to work in conditions close to that of concentration camps) precisely in those countries of the South where governments allow them to exploit the workers, bereft of any legal protection.

Has Liberation Theology ever sufficiently responded to the globalization of the market? Apparently not or not yet fully. (i) On the one hand, a certain paralysis has been noted. A lot of common people are hardly finding comfort anymore in Liberation Theology's stock-answers that "the God who has a preferential option for the poor will empower them with resources of resistance". As long as these answers were embedded in, and could still reckon with, the enthusiasm of groups committed to social change, they certainly made sense. But the New World Order has stifled this enthusiasm. An indication thereof is, perhaps, the mushrooming of charismatic communities that, in the midst of a heartless world, wager on emotional consolation for the soul. (ii) On the other hand, we have the answer of some critics who, in the name of the victims of globalization, denounce the austerity measures that accompany readjustment programs dictated by the managers of the global market; these managers are only bent on grounding new units of production and consumption, while turning a blind eye to the fact that all this directs money and resources away from the educational and health-care needs of the masses. These critics insist on the priority of developing subsistence economies over export economies, for the latter benefits primarily the total market and its elite players. (iii) Finally, there are the new movements with rather dispersed fields of action: feminists, ecologists, indigenous movements, and human rights activists. Among them also range the many common people who, thanks to a new social *imaginario*, exert efforts in bolstering up an 'informal economy', an 'economy of affection'.

At any rate, a clear picture of concerted actors determined to combat economic globalization is not yet to be found. This brings us back to the question of paradigms. If one were to call the capitalist expansion a paradigm, then one would also have to say that, with the breakthrough of globalization, this paradigm has without doubt succeeded, indeed, in reinforcing itself. Moreover, as Hinkelammert has made clear, this strengthening has had also the effect of putting all tentative efforts of resistance into crisis. In this light, a renewed examination of what globalization is about, in order to possibly detect some weak spots in it, is in order. Some hints in this direction have been formulated during the last day of the Symposium. From the reports read in the last plenary session (and which have been recorded on tape), I was able to glean the following fragments.

1. Globalization is a complex phenomenon because of the various interrelated aspects involved in it: (a) There is, first of all, the worldwide spread of neo-liberal economies: no longer kept within national boundaries, no longer checked by separate nation-states. (b) This free market system is beset with internal contradictions (Marx) which have mainly to do with the fictitious character of money. Credit – such as a nation's debt to the World Bank or the IMF – is always 'fictitious capital'; it is a kind of money bet on production that does not yet exist. That

is why a credit-system leads to speculations about the value of the currency. Control over the rules of money-formation is, thus, a terrain of struggle which generates insecurity and uncertainty as to the 'value of value'... Part of this struggle comprises the policies to ensure that, in spite of semblance to the contrary, the money flow goes from the 'South' to the 'North' (to use these names as symbolical locations). (c) A decisive factor in winning the victory in this battle is the extent to which one gets access and control over the media of communication. The success story of globalization is unthinkable without the use of electronic media, which make quasi-instantaneous information available. This, however, creates an ambivalent situation. On the one hand, the think-tanks behind the economy try to manipulate the information channels by spreading only a selection of data meant to be made public; on the other hand, the techniques used in the information highway are such that even secret information can be obtained. (d) Fourthly, there is the enormous propaganda machine to make the sellability of commodities attractive; one might even speak of a MacDonaldization of the world: all 'nations' are expected to adopt a selfsame pattern of consumption. This attractiveness is, moreover, presented as the indubitable fact that the market can be trusted. Globalization, understood according to these four aspects, "is impacting on every society and reaching into the most remote and enclosed communities of the world".

2. Neo-liberal economy, and the 'culture' of sellability it promotes, is experienced by many as a threat, for such an economy is ruled only by principles of efficiency and by formal considerations – how to make more money? – whereas a reflection on the consequences of all this on the society at large is omitted. Social justice in the classic sense is no longer part of the vocabulary. In the struggle for economic hegemonies, there must be losers, and in the battle of all against all, the companies do not hesitate to unload the burden on the weak sectors – workers are being dismissed (think of the many jobless even in the North), or forced to accept even largely underpaid jobs. This is the underside of the glamorous spectacle of the ever growing, attractive markets for consumption. Yet when this underside, too, is going global, one may expect certain counter-movements to come off the ground. At various times, the reports from the group discussions referred to the rise of a (multi-layered) 'counter-culture', and even of a global 'international of life', and some reports added that these groups, within a world that has become a global village, already make use of the means of communication available. Because this approach is somewhat different from older types of 'internationals', I shall dwell on it a bit more at length.

3. While globalization, as described above, is primarily an economic reality, there are also other aspects to it which confirm that the 'world is becoming one'... Sophisticated means of transportation, telephone connections, radio and TV broadcasting even transmitted through satellites, as well as the information highway (faxes, E-mails, web sites on the internet, etc.) have brought about a greater internationalization of contacts and exchange of expertise. As I set out in the Discussion Paper, this aspect of a world-wide availability of contacts and flows of information through the electronic means of communication is what Giddens saw as the infrastructure not only of economic globalization, but also and more importantly, of a world-wide spread of information – two aspects that account for contemporary people's capacity to become more 'reflexive' than before the information era. Who gets more world-wide information also becomes more cautious and alert to some devastating aspects that are inherent in the steady 'progress' of the market. Getting more, and specifically more alternative, information furthers the chances for an alternative culture to prosper. For Giddens, this implies an option for the counter-culture of ecological and life-style concerns. The participants in the Symposium, in turn, made their own contribution by highlighting two further applications. First, the intensified national and international contacts made possible through the information highway are real opportunities for creating specialized networks among activists across the boundaries of nations and continents. Feminists, ecologists, people engaged in informal economies, indigenous and human rights groups, etc., will be able to enrich and strengthen their movements through a quick communication of data and reactions to them, and this on a world scale. Second, this flow of counter-cultural information will allow persons and groups to challenge the mainstream information, which is often selective if not manipulative. In a combative stance, liberationist groups should not hesitate to become 'hackers' into databases, 'epistemological terrorists' who, though excluded from the system, are infiltrating it by force. Their major assets are the alternative networks of information which, in spite of Murdoch and CNN monopolies, can hardly be kept under control.

III. CULTURE AS BATTLEGROUND: POSTMODERN INFLUENCES?

In the last plenary session, too, the question was broached as to how globalization relates to the identity of local cultures and vice versa. In this respect, it was stated that, first of all, various local contexts around the globe do not necessarily perceive the same market products in the same way. For example, Coca Cola in the US carries apparently a cultural connotation different from that of the selfsame commodity in African countries. Similarly, the sports achievements in the 1996 Olympic Games were valued differently according to the national location from where they were perceived and highlighted. From this, one may deduce that the global is being selectively received through the lens of the local, although (and this must also be added) at the same time, this lens is being transformed precisely through the impinging impact of the global. One should acknowledge, thus, the existence of a two-way influence. The global seriously comes to bear on the local, which in turn restricts, channels, and only selectively appropriates the seductive inflow of the former. Yet what will be the end-product of this dialectics is, for various reasons, unpredictable. Some opined that, because of a selective appropriation, the threat of a coercive homogenization of cultures will not be that great or imminent. Others were more cautious, and pointed out that the outcome of the story will depend on the potential of cultural resistance present in the local setting. Only on the very basis of cultural resistance can a deliberately selective appropriation of the global be effective.

What actually takes place in this dialectics of appropriation is a clash between two heterogeneous types of culture: the local culture, which in its core is religious and community-oriented, and a commodified culture propagated by the global market and its culture politics. In the first case, the religious core of a culture sets the norms for the habits and practices that have to embody what the 'good life' of the community is all about. In the second, the rules of the game are dictated by the pragmatism with which marketing techniques present their 'goods' as desirable and fashionable. For people reflecting on this disparity, it is evident that the two types of culture are hardly compatible. Hence they affirm (as was also the case in the last plenary session) that, in the various cultures, there are apparently deep-seated elements and core-values which are of a different nature, and consequently these also obey different norms from those of the global market's seductive pragmatism. These deep-seated core-values, it is believed, can in fact never be unmade or totally disrupted by the glitter of the free-market. Yet they will be seriously eroded if no resistance is undertaken at the local level, or once a considerable number of people, through a lack of alertness, have internalized the global market's mentality whole and intact. Two major reasons account for this lack of alertness. First, since the implosion of the East Bloc, no viable alternative socio-economic system has emerged, as yet, to call the capitalistic system into question. And second, the more the total market is making its inroads everywhere, the more it is ushering in a more insidious colonization (the 'colonization of the Life World' as Habermas puts it) than was ever known before.

In this respect, the question was raised whether or not cultural resistance might have the same resonance and appeal in all parts of the world. The consideration of cultural resistance is apparently a more pressing need in the Two-Thirds World than in the First World. This is the case for the simple reason that the former wants to preserve and reaffirm the non-western elements in their cultures as well as their specific ways of believing in God (in the divine, respectively). At this juncture in the Symposium, the term 'Glocalization' was brought to the participants' attention. It was said that, in the circles of liberation theologians in South Korea, Singapore, Hong Kong, and Taiwan (the Asian Tigers), there is the felt need to simultaneously analyze what is going on both at the local and the global levels, and also to examine which sorts of praxis and strategies are required to counter, both at the local and the global levels, influences that erode the quality of human life, individually and communally. It is a pity that, in the midst of the distraction that arose when some participants wanted to know more about the correct spelling of this neologism, the speaker in question was no longer given the opportunity to further explain what these strategies meant concretely. Are they inspired by a real concern for laying the foundations of a 'social market', out of – a biblical – solidarity with the weaker sectors in society? Or do they just consist of a typically Asian appropriation of capitalism, coupled with a strong revival of local religion(s) and culture(s)? The two horns of the question apparently make a difference. As one can occasionally read, some analysts wager on the fact that, precisely in some booming parts of Asia, capitalism plus religion is going to replace (or erode) socialism, secularism, and state centralism.

The question as to what new models of action are emerging from 'Glocalization' was not examined further. Instead, the session proceeded to a discussion of the possible benefits gained from, and the dangers involved in, attaching due importance to the regional, or to the particular, local context. Some portions of the discussion are worth mentioning. (a) As a matter of fact, Two-Thirds World theologies mostly understand themselves as contextualized theologies. Now, this emphasis on the local identity is to be seen as a response to the homogenization process that flows from economic and cultural globalization. Local self-esteem, national self-confidence, cultural and even racial self-respect – all these are reactions to the globalizing tendency of a 'Western culture' and all that this encompasses. (b) In the Two-Thirds World, a deliberate option for fragmentation (decentralization?) is taking place in the wake of the assertiveness with which many nations and regional ethnic groups affirm their cultural identities. This assertiveness was repressed in the colonial era, yet is now given a chance to flourish, thanks to the 'dialectics' of globalization. One of the possible outcomes of globalization is the following: in certain parts of the world, regional cultures will be pushed to go back to their roots in order to see how and under which conditions they are going to connect or reconnect to the global, from the basis of their own roots. Fragmentation dialectically relates to homogenization, for the former seeks to ward off the totalizing grip of the latter. (c) The positioning of oneself within the different fragments is not carried out in order to negate the importance of universal concerns about the well-being and the future of humanity as a whole. It rather must be seen as a method to reach out to universal values that still have to be properly defined, by consciously delving into the deep-seated core values of one's own cultural identity. The retreat into the particular constitutes, therefore, a springboard for genuine connection with the universal. (d) A danger lurking around the corner is, however, the lapse into fundamentalist assertiveness, which very easily leads to ethnic strifes (the former Yugoslavia, Rwanda, etc.). In fundamentalism, the search for genuine connection with the 'other' and the 'universal' has hopelessly been abandoned. Fragmentation, at this stage, is going to take on the form of a war of all fragments against all others. Add religious fanaticism, and the picture will be complete. Moslems destroying Hindu temples, Sikhs assailing mosques, Jews occupying Moslem sanctuaries, Christian denominations fighting each other, etc.

The term 'fragmentation' reminds one of postmodernity, and indeed, this topic was also finally deemed worthy of discussion, although in the beginning of the Symposium, it had been looked upon with suspicion as a category being imposed by the Europeans on the Two-Thirds World participants. A straightforward definition of the postmodern condition, however, was not properly given. The feeling was rather that modernity as such was in crisis not only in Europe but also everywhere else on the globe. The modern Nation-State, the achievement par excellence of the Enlightenment, has manifestly entered a process of exhaustion; its erosion is visible on many fronts. One ought only to think of the paradoxical situation that, concurrent with the cry for a European Community, a lot of separatist movements, acting on ethnic and linguistic grounds, embark on an opposite journey, determined to reach autonomy within or without the former national boundaries. Centrifugal tendencies are plain in Spain, Belgium, and the United Kingdom. Decentralization is in; examples abound such as the dismantlement of the former USSR, the split-up of Czechoslovakia, and, outside Europe, the guerrilla movements in Czechenia, Afghanistan, and Pakistan, the genocide in Rwanda, and the reshuffle of power in Zaire/Congo. It looks as if Africa's peoples are eager to redraw the boundaries dictated by the Berlin Conference.

True, from an economic standpoint, these separatist tendencies go hand in hand with the rise of the global market, which precisely defies national boundaries. Yet from the standpoint of a more encompassing analysis, it was said, one ought also to assess the phenomenon of globalization itself, as well as the various reactions it provokes, from the context of postmodernity. The global is hardly monolithic; it operates through dialectical relationships with the local. As already stressed, economic and cultural globalizations concomitantly give regional localities a chance to reaffirm their identities. Moreover, with the erosion of the modern state, the role of civil society and its various sectors becomes more prominent. From within the particular sectors, specialized counter-culture movements can freely emerge. These usually see the light of day at a regional level, then start to go global the next minute, in the sense that they feel the need to connect with international networks set up to bolster the 'international of life'. All this points not only to a greater mobility but also to a pluralization of life-styles. If pluralism is one of the characteristics of the postmodern condition, then, it was stated, postmodern tendencies are unquestionably present in Latin America, and most probably also in other parts of the Two-Thirds World. These tendencies are undeniably at work; they are spontaneously popping up even when no direct reference is made to schemes of systematic reflection to explain what is actually going on. Here perhaps lies the difference between forms of postmodernity in the Two-Thirds World and in the First-World. In the latter, there is so much talk about postmodernity, often to the point of suggesting that knowledge thereof is their locality's privilege.

IV. CONCLUSION: THE REAL SHIFT AT STAKE

A considerate contributor to this volume knew exactly how to describe the turning point that took place during the discussions in the Symposium, and I am grateful that he did so. He even had recourse to biblical imagery to evoke this turn: "The concept which the participants had rejected had become the chief cornerstone of their deliberations". At the same time, however, he apparently could not refrain from ironically mentioning in passing that the two annex theses presented in the Discussion Paper, in his view, have been invalidated. Invalidated, first, was the assertion that, in the paradigm of Liberation Theologies, a shift had taken place from economics to culture ('return to idealism' as it was called). Invalidated also was the statement that globalization is linked to postmodernity. I appreciate, of course, this stand as well as its intellectual underpinnings. Yet when looking back on the discussions I have just been reporting – relying on the tape recording of the event – a brief comment on these remarks is, I think, in place.

I acknowledge that the 'pincer movement of socio-economic and cultural analysis', as the method came to be called, constitutes a single paradigm of analysis, though at times used with varying foci of attention (the emphasis being placed now on economics, and then on cultural aspects, according to the pressing needs of the contexts under examination), but never losing sight of the fact that both dimensions are intimately interconnected. One focus must be cross-fertilized by the other. This characterization actually renders what is going on in the circles of liberation theologians and the base communities adopting their method. As far as this is concerned, no further talk about a paradigm shift is needed. Yet if the discussions in the Symposium had not moved any further, the agreement on the basic method would only have resulted in a repetition, wrapped perhaps in somewhat updated language, of what other conferences on this subject had already pointed out. No move forward, thus, and no shift from the stock-answers available.

Now, at a certain moment, the term 'shift' or 'radical change' made its appearance quite frequently, when the issue of globalization had come on the agenda. Facing up to this reality, it dawned upon the participants that the classical 'pincer movement' had to operate in domains where it was not used to act. The pair of pincers had to widen its reach considerably in order to be able to get hold of, and to come to grips with, fields of application whose existence has hardly been recognized by the promoters of the pincers... This uprooting passage to the global – a capital shift in attention, indeed, and firm steps in that direction have still to be taken – is not so much the result of internal discussions on the method, as it is forced upon by the world situation, which since the beginnings of Liberation Theologies, has drastically shifted into new directions.

As far as the planners of economic globalization are concerned, they will not rest until they attain their goal: the marketization of all national economies, not restrained or checked by social measures worked out and implemented by local governments. What this implies for the weaker sectors in society – and this on a world scale – can already be foretold.

Whoever is shown not to have the capacities to serve the system will be excluded (the many jobless), or will have to put up with the dire conditions of neo-liberalism: working more hours for less money (proliferation of sweat-shops, and labor camps in free economic zones). Many EATWOT conferences will still have to devote themselves to this subject to see which forms of social and political protest can be organized to counter this neo-liberalism gone global. In the discussions we had, the importance of the social *imaginario* has been stressed, as well as the 'international of life' and the possibility of creating bonds (also world wide) with specialized action groups through the information highway. These are only a few examples to which other actions of resistance should still be added.

Many similar conferences, too, will still have to be organized to see how globalization impacts on culture, and how cultural resistance can be organized against the marketed commodity culture – the other part of the pair of pincers. At this juncture, one cannot sidestep studies dealing with the transition from modernity to the so-called postmodernity. At any rate, elements from the 'postmodern' vocabulary came to be used when the participants discussed the importance of electronic means of communication, of furthering a growing reflexivity made possible by information, and of organizing resistance against the tyranny of the homogeneous. Expressions such as 'epistemological terrorists' or 'hackers' have a postmodern ring to them, as is also the case with 'pluralism' (insisting on the importance of a plurality of resistance groups) and 'fragmentation' (local assertiveness to underline one's specificity). At the same time, it must be stressed that such terms were used in line with the universal concern of Liberation Theologies. Fragmentation and specialization of group formation are not presented as aims in themselves; they are only methodological starting-points meant to make committed people reach out to something more than just the fragment: to the restoration of human dignity to all persons around the world – so that they genuinely may become beloved daughters and sons of God.

G. De Schrijver

INDEXES

ABBREVIATIONS

AAS	Acta Apostolicae Sedis, Rome
ABC	American Broadcasting Company
ACCT	Association of Caribbean Catholic Theologians
AETTM	Asociación Ecuménica de Téologos del Tercer Mundo
AFER	*African Ecclesial Review*, Eldoret, Kenya
AFJN	Africa Faith and Justice Network
AG	Ad Gentes
AR	Actualité Religieuse, Paris
AS	*Alternatives Sud*, Louvain-la-Neuve
BCs	Basic Communities
BETL	Bibliotheca Ephemeridum Theologicarum Lovaniensium, Leuven
BjCTR	Bulletin of the Jesuit Center for Theological Reflection, Luzaka, Zambia.
CATS	Caribbean Association of Theological Schools
CBCPh	Catholic Bishops' Conference of Philippines
CCC	Caribbean Council of Churches
CEHILA	Comisión de Estudios de Historia de la Iglesia Latinoamericana, México
CELAM	Conferencia Episcopal Latinoamericana
CEP	Centro de Estudios y Publicaciones, Lima
CESEP	Centro de Servicios y Estudios Pastorales, Sâo Paulo
CETRI	Centre Tricontinental, Louvain-la-Neuve
CLAT	Confederación Latinoamericana de Trabajadores
CNN	Cable News Network
COELI	Centre œcuménique de liaisons internationales, Brussels
COEPAL	Comisión Episcopal de Pastoral, Buenos Aires
Coll.	*Collationes*, Gent
Conc.	*Concilium*, London/Maryknoll, NY
CQ	*Coeli Quarterly*, Brussels
CS	*Current Sociology*, Den Haag
CSSH	*Comparative Studies in Society and History*, Den Haag
DC	*Documentation Catholique*, Paris
DEA	Documentos del Episcopado Argentino, Buenos Aires
DEI	Departamento Ecuménico de Investigaciones, San José, Costa Rica
DEP	Development Education Program
DIAN	Dian Antar Iman (Center for Interfaith Dialogue)
DV	Dei Verbum
EAPR	*East Asian Pastoral Review*, Manila
EATWOT	Ecumenical Association of Third-World Theologians
EF	*Estudios Feministas*, Sâo Paulo
EN	Evangelii nuntiandi
ETL	*Ephemerides Theologicae Lovanienses*, Leuven
FABC	Federation of Asian Bishops' Conferences

FD	*Foi et développement*, Paris
FW	First-World
FWO	Fonds Wetenschappelijk Onderzoek
G-7	Group of Seven
GATT	General Agreement of Tariffs and Trade
GNP	Gross National Product
GS	Gaudium et spes
GrS	*Grande Sinal*
HMI	Himpunan Mahasiswa Islam
I	*Incontri*, Rio de Janeiro
IAMS	International Association of Missiological Studies
IDS	International Development Studies
IFS	*International Fides Service,* Rome
IK	Indigenous Knowledge
IMF	International Monetary Fund
IPACS	Instituto de Políticas Alternativas para el Cono Sur, Santiago
IRM	*International Review of Missions*, London
JIT	*Journal of Inculturation Theology*
Jph	*Journal of Philosophy*, New York
KULeuven	Katholieke Universiteit Leuven
LALT	Latin American Liberation Theology
LS	*Louvain Studies*, Leuven
LT	Liberation Theology
MD	Le monde diplomatique
Med	*Medellin*, Medellin, Colombia
MEGA	Marx-Engels, Gesamtausgabe
Mercosur	Mercado Común del Sur
MEW	Marx-Engels, Werke
MIA	Missio Institute of Aachen
MT	*Modern Theology*, Oxford
N-AC	Non-Aligned Countries
NGO	Non-Governmental Organizations
NIC	New Industrialized Countries
NIEO	New International Economic Order
NIIO	New International Information Order
NLR	*New Left Review*, London
NRTh	*Nouvelle Revue Théologique*, Namur/Tournai
OAM	*Onze Alma Mater*, Leuven
OECD	Organization for Economic Cooperation and Development
OPEC	Organization of Petroleum Exporting Countries
OR	*L'Osservatore Romano*, Rome
Or	*Orientierung*, Zürich
Pas	*Pasos*, San José, Costa Rica
PCP	Plenary Council of the Philippines
Pg	*Páginas*, Lima
PNUD	Programa de las Naciones Unidas para el Desarrollo
PoT	*Political Theory,* Beverly Hills, CA
PT	*Perspectiva Teológica*, Belo Horizonte
QL	*Questions liturgiques*, Leuven

REB	*Revista Eclesiástica Brasileira*, Petrópolis
RET	*Revista de Economía y Trabajo*, Buenos Aires
RT	*Revista de Teología*, Caracas
SCCs	Small Christian Communities
SOTER	Society of Theology and Religious Sciences, Sâo Paulo
Sr	*Servir*, México DF
SRS	Sollicitudo Rei Socialis
ST	*Signo de los tiempos*, México, DF
TCS	*Theory, Culture & Society*, London
TL	Theology of Liberation
TNCS	Transnational Corporations
TW	Third-World
UN	United Nations
US	United States
USSR	Union of Soviet Socialist Republics
WB	World Bank
WCC	World Council of Churches
WTO	World Trade Organization
ZMR	*Zeitschrift für Missionswissenschaft und Religionswissenschaft*, Münster.

INDEX OF AUTHORS

INDEX OF SUBJECTS

LIST OF CONTRIBUTORS

Their current address is found at the end of their article.

ABASCAL-JAEN, Adolfo is the Executive Secretary of the *Centre Œcuménique de Liaisons Iinternationales*, Brussels.

ALTHAUS-REID, Marcella is a lecturer at the New College, the University of Edinburgh.

BLOECHL, Jeffrey is an associate Researcher at the Center for Liberation Theology, KULeuven.

BOEVE, Lieven holds a STD from the KULeuven. He is in charge of the Daily Management of the Center for Liberation Theology. He is also a Post-Doctoral Fellow FWO-V at the Faculty of Theology and an Assistant Professor of Dogmatic Theology and Religious Studies at the Faculty of Theology.

BOODOO, Gerald is a Professor of Systematic Theology at Xavier University of Louisiana, New Orleans, USA.

BRAZAL, Agnes is an Associate Researcher at the Center for Liberation Theology, KULeuven.

CASPERSZ, Paul is the founder of the *Satyodaya Centre (Dawn of Truth) for Social Research and Action* (1972). This is an inter-religious, inter-racial, inter-linguistic and inter-sex community which works for peace, founded on justice, in the plantations and villages of Sri-Lanka in the Asian region and in the world at large. Paul Caspersz continues being committed to this Center and to the promotion and defense of all its values.

DE MESA, José teaches Systematic Theology and Pastoral Issues at Maryhill School of Theology and at the East Asian Pastoral Institute, Ateneo de Manila University (Campus Quezon City, Philippines). He is also the editor-in-chief of the East Asian Pastoral Review and has been a Senior Research Fellow at KULeuven.

DE MEY, Peter is an Aspirant Researcher FWO-V at the Department of Dogmatic Theology, KULeuven.

DE SCHRIJVER, Georges is the founder and coordinator of the Center for Liberation Theology (KULeuven). Since 1974, Professor De Schrijver teaches Systematic Theology at the Theology Faculty of the Catholic University of Leuven. He is also a researcher in Liberation and Contextual Theologies as well as in Philosophical and Scientific Issues related to Theology.

ELA, Jean-Marc studied at the Universities of Strasburg (Strasburg, France) and *La Sorbonne* (Paris, France). From 1971-1985, he worked as a missionary to the

Kirdi of North Cameroon. He taught sociology at the Univeristy of Yaounde and, afterwards, he has also been guest Professor in *Lumen Vitae* (Brussels, Belgium) and at the Catholic University of Louvain (UCL). At present, he teaches Theology and Sociology at the Univerity of Laval (Québec, Canada).

GONZÁLEZ, Dennis teaches systematic theology at Maryhill School of Theology in Manila, Philippines.

GORDON, Jason is a Doctoral Student, London, UK.

HENRIOT, Peter J. has been trained as a political scientist with special interest in the political economy of development. He has worked in Zambia since 1989 and is currently the director of the Jesuit Centre for Theological Reflection in Lusaka.

IRARRAZAVAL, Diego is the Director to the Aymara Institute (Puno, Perú) and an active member to the EATWOT. He also teaches at the Regional Seminary and does research on Latin-American Cultures and Religions. Among others, he is the author of *Rito y Pensar Cristiano*.

KEE, Alistair is a Professor of Religious Studies at the University of Edinburgh.

MAGESA, Laurenti is a former Lecturer and Head of the Depatment of Religious Studies at the Catholic University of Eastern Africa, Nairobi. He is the author of numerous articles on African Theology, the co-author of *African Christian Marriage* and some other books as well as the author of *Liberation Theology in Africa*. At present, he works as a Parish priest.

NAUWENS, Leo is a Freelance Researcher and Writer.

ROSADO NUÑEZ, María José is a sociologist. She holds a doctoral degree from the École des Études en Sciences Sociales in Paris. She has worked with and studied Base Communities in several parts of Brazil. She is the vice-president to the Institute for Religious Studies (ISER). In addition to numerous articles, she has written *Vida Religiosa nos Meios Populares* (Petrópolis, Brazil).

SCANNONE, Juan Carlos is the Rector of the Theological and Philosophical Faculties of San Miguel (Buenos Aires, Argentina). He has been guest professor at the Universities of Frankfurt, Salzburg, Münich and, at the present, at the Gregorian University of Rome. Among others, Scannone is the author of these publications: *Sein und Inkarnation; Teología de la Liberación y Praxis Popular; Teología de la Liberación y Doctrina Social de la Iglesia; Evangelización, Cultura y Teología: Nuevo Punto de Partida en la Filosofía Latinoamericana.*

STEENBRINK, Karel is a Senior Lecturer at the Interuniversity Institute for Missiological and Ecumenical Research (IIMO).

WIDL, Maria is a Post-Doctoral Researcher to the Austrian Program for Advanced Research and Technology, Austria.

BIBLIOTHECA EPHEMERIDUM THEOLOGICARUM LOVANIENSIUM

SERIES I

* = Out of print

*1. Miscellanea dogmatica in honorem Eximii Domini J. Bittremieux, 1947.

*2-3. Miscellanea moralia in honorem Eximii Domini A. Janssen, 1948.

*4. G. PHILIPS, La grâce des justes de l'Ancien Testament, 1948.

*5. G. PHILIPS, De ratione instituendi tractatum de gratia nostrae sanctificationis, 1953.

6-7. Recueil Lucien Cerfaux. Études d'exégèse et d'histoire religieuse, 1954. 504 et 577 p. FB 1000 par tome. Cf. infra, nᵒˢ 18 et 71 (t. III).

8. G. THILS, Histoire doctrinale du mouvement œcuménique, 1955. Nouvelle édition, 1963. 338 p. FB 135.

*9. Études sur l'Immaculée Conception, 1955.

*10. J.A. O'DONOHOE, Tridentine Seminary Legislation, 1957.

*11. G. THILS, Orientations de la théologie, 1958.

*12-13. J. COPPENS, A. DESCAMPS, É. MASSAUX (ed.), Sacra Pagina. Miscellanea Biblica Congressus Internationalis Catholici de Re Biblica, 1959.

*14. Adrien VI, le premier Pape de la contre-réforme, 1959.

*15. F. CLAEYS BOUUAERT, Les déclarations et serments imposés par la loi civile aux membres du clergé belge sous le Directoire (1795-1801), 1960.

*16. G. THILS, La «Théologie œcuménique». Notion-Formes-Démarches, 1960.

17. G. THILS, Primauté pontificale et prérogatives épiscopales. «Potestas ordinaria» au Concile du Vatican, 1961. 103 p. FB 50.

*18. Recueil Lucien Cerfaux, t. III, 1962. Cf. infra, n° 71.

*19. Foi et réflexion philosophique. Mélanges F. Grégoire, 1961.

*20. Mélanges G. Ryckmans, 1963.

21. G. THILS, L'infaillibilité du peuple chrétien «in credendo», 1963. 67 p. FB 50.

*22. J. FÉRIN & L. JANSSENS, Progestogènes et morale conjugale, 1963.

*23. Collectanea Moralia in honorem Eximii Domini A. Janssen, 1964.

24. H. CAZELLES (ed.), De Mari à Qumrân. L'Ancien Testament. Son milieu. Ses écrits. Ses relectures juives (Hommage J. Coppens, I), 1969. 158*-370 p. FB 900.

*25. I. DE LA POTTERIE (ed.), De Jésus aux évangiles. Tradition et rédaction dans les évangiles synoptiques (Hommage J. Coppens, II), 1967.

26. G. THILS & R.E. BROWN (ed.), Exégèse et théologie (Hommage J. Coppens, III), 1968. 328 p. FB 700.

27. J. COPPENS (ed.), Ecclesia a Spiritu sancto edocta. Hommage à Mgr G. Philips, 1970. 640 p. FB 1000.

28. J. COPPENS (ed.), Sacerdoce et célibat. Études historiques et théologiques, 1971. 740 p. FB 700.

29. M. DIDIER (ed.), *L'évangile selon Matthieu. Rédaction et théologie,* 1972. 432 p. FB 1000.

*30. J. KEMPENEERS, *Le Cardinal van Roey en son temps,* 1971.

SERIES II

31. F. NEIRYNCK, *Duality in Mark. Contributions to the Study of the Markan Redaction,* 1972. Revised edition with Supplementary Notes, 1988. 252 p. FB 1200.

32. F. NEIRYNCK (ed.), *L'évangile de Luc. Problèmes littéraires et théologiques,* 1973. *L'évangile de Luc – The Gospel of Luke.* Revised and enlarged edition, 1989. X-590 p. FB 2200.

33. C. BREKELMANS (ed.), *Questions disputées d'Ancien Testament. Méthode et théologie,* 1974. *Continuing Questions in Old Testament Method and Theology.* Revised and enlarged edition by M. VERVENNE, 1989. 245 p. FB 1200.

34. M. SABBE (ed.), *L'évangile selon Marc. Tradition et rédaction,* 1974. Nouvelle édition augmentée, 1988. 601 p. FB 2400.

35. B. WILLAERT (ed.), *Philosophie de la religion – Godsdienstfilosofie. Miscellanea Albert Dondeyne,* 1974. Nouvelle édition, 1987. 458 p. FB 1600.

36. G. PHILIPS, *L'union personnelle avec le Dieu vivant. Essai sur l'origine et le sens de la grâce créée,* 1974. Édition révisée, 1989. 299 p. FB 1000.

37. F. NEIRYNCK, in collaboration with T. HANSEN and F. VAN SEGBROECK, *The Minor Agreements of Matthew and Luke against Mark with a Cumulative List,* 1974. 330 p. FB 900.

38. J. COPPENS, *Le messianisme et sa relève prophétique. Les anticipations vétérotestamentaires. Leur accomplissement en Jésus,* 1974. Édition révisée, 1989. XIII-265 p. FB 1000.

39. D. SENIOR, *The Passion Narrative according to Matthew. A Redactional Study,* 1975. New impression, 1982. 440 p. FB 1000.

40. J. DUPONT (ed.), *Jésus aux origines de la christologie,* 1975. Nouvelle édition augmentée, 1989. 458 p. FB 1500.

41. J. COPPENS (ed.), *La notion biblique de Dieu,* 1976. Réimpression, 1985. 519 p. FB 1600.

42. J. LINDEMANS & H. DEMEESTER (ed.), *Liber Amicorum Monseigneur W. Onclin,* 1976. XXII-396 p. FB 1000.

43. R.E. HOECKMAN (ed.), *Pluralisme et œcuménisme en recherches théologiques. Mélanges offerts au R.P. Dockx, O.P.,* 1976. 316 p. FB 1000.

44. M. DE JONGE (ed.), *L'évangile de Jean. Sources, rédaction, théologie,* 1977. Réimpression, 1987. 416 p. FB 1500.

45. E.J.M. VAN EIJL (ed.), *Facultas S. Theologiae Lovaniensis 1432-1797. Bijdragen tot haar geschiedenis. Contributions to its History. Contributions à son histoire,* 1977. 570 p. FB 1700.

46. M. DELCOR (ed.), *Qumrân. Sa piété, sa théologie et son milieu,* 1978. 432 p. FB 1700.

47. M. CAUDRON (ed.), *Faith and Society. Foi et société. Geloof en maatschappij. Acta Congressus Internationalis Theologici Lovaniensis 1976,* 1978. 304 p. FB 1150.

48. J. KREMER (ed.), *Les Actes des Apôtres. Traditions, rédaction, théologie*, 1979. 590 p. FB 1700.
49. F. NEIRYNCK, avec la collaboration de J. DELOBEL, T. SNOY, G. VAN BELLE, F. VAN SEGBROECK, *Jean et les Synoptiques. Examen critique de l'exégèse de M.-É. Boismard*, 1979. XII-428 p. FB 1000.
50. J. COPPENS, *La relève apocalyptique du messianisme royal. I. La royauté – Le règne – Le royaume de Dieu. Cadre de la relève apocalyptique*, 1979. 325 p. FB 1000.
51. M. GILBERT (ed.), *La Sagesse de l'Ancien Testament*, 1979. Nouvelle édition mise à jour, 1990. 455 p. FB 1500.
52. B. DEHANDSCHUTTER, *Martyrium Polycarpi. Een literair-kritische studie*, 1979. 296 p. FB 1000.
53. J. LAMBRECHT (ed.), *L'Apocalypse johannique et l'Apocalyptique dans le Nouveau Testament*, 1980. 458 p. FB 1400.
54. P.-M. BOGAERT (ed.), *Le livre de Jérémie. Le prophète et son milieu. Les oracles et leur transmission*, 1981. *Nouvelle édition mise à jour*, 1997. 448 p. FB 1800.
55. J. COPPENS, *La relève apocalyptique du messianisme royal. III. Le Fils de l'homme néotestamentaire*. Édition posthume par F. NEIRYNCK, 1981. XIV-192 p. FB 800.
56. J. VAN BAVEL & M. SCHRAMA (ed.), *Jansénius et le Jansénisme dans les Pays-Bas. Mélanges Lucien Ceyssens*, 1982. 247 p. FB 1000.
57. J.H. WALGRAVE, *Selected Writings – Thematische geschriften. Thomas Aquinas, J.H. Newman, Theologia Fundamentalis*. Edited by G. DE SCHRIJVER & J.J. KELLY, 1982. XLIII-425 p. FB 1000.
58. F. NEIRYNCK & F. VAN SEGBROECK, avec la collaboration de E. MANNING, *Ephemerides Theologicae Lovanienses 1924-1981. Tables générales. (Bibliotheca Ephemeridum Theologicarum Lovaniensium 1947-1981)*, 1982. 400 p. FB 1600.
59. J. DELOBEL (ed.), *Logia. Les paroles de Jésus – The Sayings of Jesus. Mémorial Joseph Coppens*, 1982. 647 p. FB 2000.
60. F. NEIRYNCK, *Evangelica. Gospel Studies – Études d'évangile. Collected Essays*. Edited by F. VAN SEGBROECK, 1982. XIX-1036 p. FB 2000.
61. J. COPPENS, *La relève apocalyptique du messianisme royal. II. Le Fils d'homme vétéro- et intertestamentaire*. Édition posthume par J. LUST, 1983. XVII-272 p. FB 1000.
62. J.J. KELLY, *Baron Friedrich von Hügel's Philosophy of Religion*, 1983. 232 p. FB 1500.
63. G. DE SCHRIJVER, *Le merveilleux accord de l'homme et de Dieu. Étude de l'analogie de l'être chez Hans Urs von Balthasar*, 1983. 344 p. FB 1500.
64. J. GROOTAERS & J.A. SELLING, *The 1980 Synod of Bishops: «On the Role of the Family». An Exposition of the Event and an Analysis of its Texts*. Preface by Prof. emeritus L. JANSSENS, 1983. 375 p. FB 1500.
65. F. NEIRYNCK & F. VAN SEGBROECK, *New Testament Vocabulary. A Companion Volume to the Concordance*, 1984. XVI-494 p. FB 2000.
66. R.F. COLLINS, *Studies on the First Letter to the Thessalonians*, 1984. XI-415 p. FB 1500.
67. A. PLUMMER, *Conversations with Dr. Döllinger 1870-1890*. Edited with Introduction and Notes by R. BOUDENS, with the collaboration of L. KENIS, 1985. LIV-360 p. FB 1800.

68. N. LOHFINK (ed.), *Das Deuteronomium. Entstehung, Gestalt und Botschaft / Deuteronomy: Origin, Form and Message*, 1985. XI-382 p. FB 2000.

69. P.F. FRANSEN, *Hermeneutics of the Councils and Other Studies*. Collected by H.E. MERTENS & F. DE GRAEVE, 1985. 543 p. FB 1800.

70. J. DUPONT, *Études sur les Évangiles synoptiques*. Présentées par F. NEIRYNCK, 1985. 2 tomes, XXI-IX-1210 p. FB 2800.

71. *Recueil Lucien Cerfaux*, t. III, 1962. Nouvelle édition revue et complétée, 1985. LXXX-458 p. FB 1600.

72. J. GROOTAERS, *Primauté et collégialité. Le dossier de Gérard Philips sur la Nota Explicativa Praevia (Lumen gentium, Chap. III)*. Présenté avec introduction historique, annotations et annexes. Préface de G. THILS, 1986. 222 p. FB 1000.

73. A. VANHOYE (ed.), *L'apôtre Paul. Personnalité, style et conception du ministère*, 1986. XIII-470 p. FB 2600.

74. J. LUST (ed.), *Ezekiel and His Book. Textual and Literary Criticism and their Interrelation*, 1986. X-387 p. FB 2700.

75. É. MASSAUX, *Influence de l'Évangile de saint Matthieu sur la littérature chrétienne avant saint Irénée*. Réimpression anastatique présentée par F. NEIRYNCK. *Supplément: Bibliographie 1950-1985*, par B. DEHAND-SCHUTTER, 1986. XXVII-850 p. FB 2500.

76. L. CEYSSENS & J.A.G. TANS, *Autour de l'Unigenitus. Recherches sur la genèse de la Constitution*, 1987. XXVI-845 p. FB 2500.

77. A. DESCAMPS, *Jésus et l'Église. Études d'exégèse et de théologie*. Préface de Mgr A. HOUSSIAU, 1987. XLV-641 p. FB 2500.

78. J. DUPLACY, *Études de critique textuelle du Nouveau Testament*. Présentées par J. DELOBEL, 1987. XXVII-431 p. FB 1800.

79. E.J.M. VAN EIJL (ed.), *L'image de C. Jansénius jusqu'à la fin du XVIIIe siècle*, 1987. 258 p. FB 1250.

80. E. BRITO, *La Création selon Schelling. Universum*, 1987. XXXV-646 p. FB 2980.

81. J. VERMEYLEN (ed.), *The Book of Isaiah – Le livre d'Isaïe. Les oracles et leurs relectures. Unité et complexité de l'ouvrage*, 1989. X-472 p. FB 2700.

82. G. VAN BELLE, *Johannine Bibliography 1966-1985. A Cumulative Bibliography on the Fourth Gospel*, 1988. XVII-563 p. FB 2700.

83. J.A. SELLING (ed.), *Personalist Morals. Essays in Honor of Professor Louis Janssens*, 1988. VIII-344 p. FB 1200.

84. M.-É. BOISMARD, *Moïse ou Jésus. Essai de christologie johannique*, 1988. XVI-241 p. FB 1000.

84A. M.-É. BOISMARD, *Moses or Jesus: An Essay in Johannine Christology*. Translated by B.T. VIVIANO, 1993, XVI-144 p. FB 1000.

85. J.A. DICK, *The Malines Conversations Revisited*, 1989. 278 p. FB 1500.

86. J.-M. SEVRIN (ed.), *The New Testament in Early Christianity – La réception des écrits néotestamentaires dans le christianisme primitif*, 1989. XVI-406 p. FB 2500.

87. R.F. COLLINS (ed.), *The Thessalonian Correspondence*, 1990. XV-546 p. FB 3000.

88. F. VAN SEGBROECK, *The Gospel of Luke. A Cumulative Bibliography 1973-1988*, 1989. 241 p. FB 1200.

89. G. THILS, *Primauté et infaillibilité du Pontife Romain à Vatican I et autres études d'ecclésiologie*, 1989. XI-422 p. FB 1850.

90. A. VERGOTE, *Explorations de l'espace théologique. Études de théologie et de philosophie de la religion*, 1990. XVI-709 p. FB 2000.

91. J.C. DE MOOR, *The Rise of Yahwism: The Roots of Israelite Monotheism*, 1990. *Revised and Enlarged Edition*, 1997. XV-445 p. FB 1400.

92. B. BRUNING, M. LAMBERIGTS & J. VAN HOUTEM (eds.), *Collectanea Augustiniana. Mélanges T.J. van Bavel*, 1990. 2 tomes, XXXVIII-VIII-1074 p. FB 3000.

93. A. DE HALLEUX, *Patrologie et œcuménisme. Recueil d'études*, 1990. XVI-887 p. FB 3000.

94. C. BREKELMANS & J. LUST (eds.), *Pentateuchal and Deuteronomistic Studies: Papers Read at the XIIIth IOSOT Congress Leuven 1989*, 1990. 307 p. FB 1500.

95. D.L. DUNGAN (ed.), *The Interrelations of the Gospels. A Symposium Led by M.-É. Boismard – W.R. Farmer – F. Neirynck, Jerusalem 1984*, 1990. XXXI-672 p. FB 3000.

96. G.D. KILPATRICK, *The Principles and Practice of New Testament Textual Criticism. Collected Essays*. Edited by J.K. ELLIOTT, 1990. XXXVIII-489 p. FB 3000.

97. G. ALBERIGO (ed.), *Christian Unity. The Council of Ferrara-Florence: 1438/39 – 1989*, 1991. X-681 p. FB 3000.

98. M. SABBE, *Studia Neotestamentica. Collected Essays*, 1991. XVI-573 p. FB 2000.

99. F. NEIRYNCK, *Evangelica II: 1982-1991. Collected Essays*. Edited by F. VAN SEGBROECK, 1991. XIX-874 p. FB 2800.

100. F. VAN SEGBROECK, C.M. TUCKETT, G. VAN BELLE & J. VERHEYDEN (eds.), *The Four Gospels 1992. Festschrift Frans Neirynck*, 1992. 3 volumes, XVII-X-X-2668 p. FB 5000.

SERIES III

101. A. DENAUX (ed.), *John and the Synoptics*, 1992. XXII-696 p. FB 3000.

102. F. NEIRYNCK, J. VERHEYDEN, F. VAN SEGBROECK, G. VAN OYEN & R. CORSTJENS, *The Gospel of Mark. A Cumulative Bibliography: 1950-1990*, 1992. XII-717 p. FB 2700.

103. M. SIMON, *Un catéchisme universel pour l'Église catholique. Du Concile de Trente à nos jours*, 1992. XIV-461 p. FB 2200.

104. L. CEYSSENS, *Le sort de la bulle Unigenitus. Recueil d'études offert à Lucien Ceyssens à l'occasion de son 90e anniversaire*. Présenté par M. LAMBERIGTS, 1992. XXVI-641 p. FB 2000.

105. R.J. DALY (ed.), *Origeniana Quinta. Papers of the 5th International Origen Congress, Boston College, 14-18 August 1989*, 1992. XVII-635 p. FB 2700.

106. A.S. VAN DER WOUDE (ed.), *The Book of Daniel in the Light of New Findings*, 1993. XVIII-574 p. FB 3000.

107. J. FAMERÉE, *L'ecclésiologie d'Yves Congar avant Vatican II: Histoire et Église. Analyse et reprise critique*, 1992. 497 p. FB 2600.

108. C. BEGG, *Josephus' Account of the Early Divided Monarchy (AJ 8, 212-420). Rewriting the Bible*, 1993. IX-377 p. FB 2400.

109. J. BULCKENS & H. LOMBAERTS (eds.), *L'enseignement de la religion catholique à l'école secondaire. Enjeux pour la nouvelle Europe*, 1993. XII-264 p. FB 1250.

110. C. FOCANT (ed.), *The Synoptic Gospels. Source Criticism and the New Literary Criticism*, 1993. XXXIX-670 p. FB 3000.

111. M. LAMBERIGTS (ed.), avec la collaboration de L. KENIS, *L'augustinisme à l'ancienne Faculté de théologie de Louvain*, 1994. VII-455 p. FB 2400.

112. R. BIERINGER & J. LAMBRECHT, *Studies on 2 Corinthians*, 1994. XX-632 p. FB 3000.

113. E. BRITO, *La pneumatologie de Schleiermacher*, 1994. XII-649 p. FB 3000.

114. W.A.M. BEUKEN (ed.), *The Book of Job*, 1994. X-462 p. FB 2400.

115. J. LAMBRECHT, *Pauline Studies: Collected Essays*, 1994. XIV-465 p. FB 2500.

116. G. VAN BELLE, *The Signs Source in the Fourth Gospel: Historical Survey and Critical Evaluation of the Semeia Hypothesis*, 1994. XIV-503 p. FB 2500.

117. M. LAMBERIGTS & P. VAN DEUN (eds.), *Martyrium in Multidisciplinary Perspective. Memorial L. Reekmans*, 1995. X-435 p. FB 3000.

118. G. DORIVAL & A. LE BOULLUEC (eds.), *Origeniana Sexta. Origène et la Bible/Origen and the Bible. Actes du Colloquium Origenianum Sextum, Chantilly, 30 août – 3 septembre 1993*, 1995. XII-865 p. FB 3900.

119. É. GAZIAUX, *Morale de la foi et morale autonome. Confrontation entre P. Delhaye et J. Fuchs*, 1995. XXII-545 p. FB 2700.

120. T.A. SALZMAN, *Deontology and Teleology: An Investigation of the Normative Debate in Roman Catholic Moral Theology*, 1995. XVII-555 p. FB 2700.

121. G.R. EVANS & M. GOURGUES (eds.), *Communion et Réunion. Mélanges Jean-Marie Roger Tillard*, 1995. XI-431 p. FB 2400.

122. H.T. FLEDDERMANN, *Mark and Q: A Study of the Overlap Texts*. With an *Assessment* by F. NEIRYNCK, 1995. XI-307 p. FB 1800.

123. R. BOUDENS, *Two Cardinals: John Henry Newman, Désiré-Joseph Mercier*. Edited by L. GEVERS with the collaboration of B. DOYLE, 1995. 362 p. FB 1800.

124. A. THOMASSET, *Paul Ricœur. Une poétique de la morale. Aux fondements d'une éthique herméneutique et narrative dans une perspective chrétienne*, 1996. XVI-706 p. FB 3000.

125. R. BIERINGER (ed.), *The Corinthian Correspondence*, 1996. XXVII-793 p. FB 2400.

126. M. VERVENNE (ed.), *Studies in the Book of Exodus: Redaction – Reception – Interpretation*, 1996. XI-660 p. FB 2400.

127. A. VANNESTE, *Nature et grâce dans la théologie occidentale. Dialogue avec H. de Lubac*, 1996. 312 p. FB 1800.

128. A. CURTIS & T. RÖMER (eds.), *The Book of Jeremiah and its Reception – Le livre de Jérémie et sa réception*, 1997. 332 p. FB 2400.

129. E. LANNE, *Tradition et Communion des Églises. Recueil d'études*, 1997. XXV-703 p. FB 3000.

130. A. DENAUX & J.A. DICK (eds.), *From Malines to ARCIC. The Malines Conversations Commemorated*, 1997. IX-317 p. FB 1800.
131. C.M. TUCKETT (ed.), *The Scriptures in the Gospels*, 1997. XXIV-721 p. FB 2400.
132. J. VAN RUITEN & M. VERVENNE (eds.), *Studies in the Book of Isaiah. Festschrift Willem A.M. Beuken*, 1997. XX-540 p. FB 3000.
133. M. VERVENNE & J. LUST (eds.), *Deuteronomy and Deuteronomic Literature. Festschrift C.H.W. Brekelmans*, 1997. XI-637 p. FB 3000.

PRINTED ON PERMANENT PAPER • IMPRIME SUR PAPIER PERMANENT • GEDRUKT OP DUURZAAM PAPIER - ISO 9706

ORIENTALISTE, KLEIN DALENSTRAAT 42, B-3020 HERENT